The History
and
Practice of Magic

Partial Contents: At the Gates of the Supernatural; The Mysteries of the Pyramids; Ancient Oracles, the Sibyls and the Fates; Magic from the Beginning of the Christian Era to the End of the Middle Ages; Supernatural Sciences and Curiosities; General Theory of the Horoscope; General Keys of Astrology. Numerous charts and diagrams. Rare Rituals are included. This Massive Work on Magic should be in every Magician's Library.

Paul Christian
(A/K/A JEAN BAPTISTE)

ISBN 1-56459-471-8

Kessinger Publishing's Rare Reprints
Thousands of Scarce and Hard-to-Find Books!

We kindly invite you to view our extensive catalog list at:
http://www.kessinger.net

THE HISTORY AND PRACTICE OF MAGIC
VOLUME I

EDITOR'S NOTE

THE method followed in this rendering of a work of some quarter-million words into English has been in the main straightforward translation, the first five books having been translated by James Kirkup and the two latter books, Six and Seven, by Julian Shaw. The taste however of French writing of 1870 is not that of the average English reader today, and certain small omissions, mostly of expressions which the modern reader might regard as exaggerated and sentimental, are indicated by the use of *points de suspension* . . . Any substantial omission or substitution is indicated in a footnote and the reason given.

Footnotes in the French original are given without alteration. Footnotes added by the present editor and his collaborators, to the number of 140, are distinguished by *Ed.* at the end of each.

Material additional to the text is marked by italic headings, as well as by signatory initials at the end of each article. In two cases, however, added material could not thus be distinguished since it was required as almost line-by-line interpretation, i.e. in the commentary upon the medieval herbalist remedies (p. 335) and in the interpretations of the meanings of dreams as given by S. Nicephorus of Constantinople (p. 377). Here a difference of type was adopted, with explanatory notes.

As well as the historical and other editing by the general editor, substantial editorial additions have been made by those mentioned on the title page who have contributed to this work in the following ways: Mr. Lewis Spence has provided material for much of the editing of the chapters on Celtic and fairy lore; Margery Lawrence has written an incorporated article on spiritualism; Dr. Charles R. Cammell has permitted quotation from his articles in the *Atlantis Quarterly* on the Faust legend; Mr. Mir Bashir, in addition to a section on Chirology or Cheiromancy, has contributed extensively to the interpretations of the dream material which goes under the name of S. Nicephorus of Constantinople; Julian Shaw, besides writing an article on *Astrology 1952*, has acted as general consultant on astrological matters; Mr. Edward Whybrow has provided the bulk of the modern glosses on the old herbal remedies and Mr. Gerald Yorke has made editorial suggestions generally as well as editing the more narrowly magical part of the work in detail.

In addition to these title-page names, the help of the librarians of the Paris Bibliothèque Nationale and of the Arsenal library, of members of the staff of the British Museum, of Mr. John Hargrave (on Paracelsus), of the editor of *Astrology* for kind permission to reproduce the three twentieth century horoscopes used in Julian Shaw's article and of Messrs. Hodder & Stoughton and the executor of the author for permission to reproduce part of E. Lucas Bridges' *The Uttermost Part of the Earth*, must be thankfully acknowledged.

To all these willing collaborators, without whom this English edition would have lacked certain distinctive and indeed essential elements, the general editor wishes to express his gratitude and appreciation for help enabling him to complete a laborious task in a comparatively brief period.

R.N.

PAUL CHRISTIAN: A MEMOIR

JEAN BAPTISTE or Christian Pitois, commonly known as Paul Christian but also as Dom Marie-Bernard and Charles Moreau, was born in the Vosges district of France at Remiremont on 15 May 1811. His christian names appear in the civil register of Remiremont as Jean Baptiste. It was intended by his family that he should become a priest, and he had a religious upbringing with the little Paris community of the *Clercs de la Chapelle Royale*. As a youth he went for a time in 1828 to a Trappist abbey to test his vocation; he had been much influenced by his devotional reading, especially by the *Legend of the Fathers in the Desert*, and there had been a family bereavement. Either he or the Trappists decided that his vocation was not genuine and he left after a short stay; but its influence remained with him for life. Here it was that he had assumed the name Marie-Bernard, and when later he came to write his *Heroes of Christianity* it was to a fictitious monk of this name that he attributed it, though he eventually had to admit his own authorship in the last volume. His son too bore the names Paul Marie Bernard.

What the young man did, in the formative years from 17 to 26, is obscure. The articles on Christian in *La Lumière* refer to his fighting in Spain and to his leading a native rising in Dominica, then French, for the abolition of slavery, and these adventures presumably occurred then. He does not appear upon the literary scene until he had become the close friend of Charles Nodier, curator of the Paris Arsenal Library, through whom, as he narrates in the opening pages of the *History of Magic*, his interest in the occult was aroused. With him he published as his first work a joint series of three volumes, *Historic Paris: Walks in the Streets of Paris*, 1837-1840. Henceforth the pen of Paul Christian, as he now began usually to style himself, was rarely idle; he became a prolific journalist, editor and translator as well as author. He was a nephew of the publisher and bookseller Pitois-Levrault who soon published his nephew's translation of the popular stories of Schmid, 1839, when his *Studies of the Paris Revolution* also appeared. And in the same year came a decisive event in his life when he was appointed Librarian at the Ministry of Public Education.

In that year the Minister, the Comte de Salvandy, took an important step in rehabilitating the educational and literary life of France, severely disorganised during the troubles of fifty years by recalling for redistribution all available spare and uncatalogued books. For this purpose he ordered the accumulation at the Ministry in Paris of the many duplicate books from the libraries in the provinces and of the books from the monasteries which had been seized when they were suppressed in 1790. Young Pitois was given the arduous task of sorting, after which the bulk of them was sent out again chiefly to new libraries. A job which even to a bibliophile might have seemed largely a wearisome piece of routine work was to him delightful because, as he says, of 'the interesting discoveries I made daily'. He and Nodier pored over the books on super-natural, magical and philosophic subjects, and the story of their joint adventures in discovery forms the framework of the introductory section of the *History of Magic*. It was these months that laid the foundation of Christian the occultist. In this congenial security and encouraged by friends, his real capacities began to expand. A bent towards historic studies led to the appearance of his two-volume *History of the French Clergy* in 1840; and his wide interests as a man of letters were shown in such writings as an introduction to a volume of Helvetius and a memoir on Ernest Hoffman. He began to contribute to learned and general journals.

This peaceful literary life was pleasingly interrupted by the acceptance of a private secretaryship to Marshall Bugeaud, 1843—1844, during his campaigns in Algeria and Morocco, where Pitois was wounded. Returning to France in 1845 he put his experience to good use in his *Memoir of Marshall Bugeaud the Administrator in Algeria and Morocco*, published the same year, and in his *Account of the French Conquest and Rule in Morocco*, 1846.

Journalistic activities on a considerable scale seem to have followed, and led in 1851—1852 to his becoming editor-in-chief of the *Moniteur du Soir*. That this had not entirely absorbed his energies became apparent when next year, 1853, his substantial *History of the Terror* appeared. 'Marie-Bernard's' account of the Cistercians came out with Christian's avowed introduction and notes in 1853, and from then until 1857 were published the eight volumes of his massive *Heroes of Christianity*, mentioned above. His translation of MacPherson's *Ossian* appeared in 1858; and in 1860 devotional works, *Marriage: the Angel of Wehrda* and the *Flowers of Heaven*, were the precursors of a considerable little series of such manuals. His talent for story-telling had been apparent in many of his books, and in 1863 the thrilling *Red Man of the Tuileries* had a considerable vogue; so already had his *Stories of the Marvellous from All Times and Lands* [1844], whilst the favour of the court was apparent in the title of the *Stories of French Valour Told to the Prince Imperial*. He again turned to journalism in 1865—1866, directing the *Moniteur Catholique*. A comparative lull in Pitois' activities occurred for four years, at the end of which appeared in 1870 the present work, the full title of which ran: *Histoire de la Magie, du Monde Surnaturel et de la Fatalité à travers les Temps et les Peuples*.

It will be seen from the above brief resumé of some of the main products of a busy life that it was with a very full equipment of knowledge and with the practised pen of the successful journalist and author that Christian had undertaken his *magnum opus*. He had been steadily reading all the works on occultism that he could find since 1839 and he was now 59; he was an established historian, a writer of historical romances and the translator of the most 'romantic' of Celtic poets, whose equivocal status in England did not detract from his vogue abroad. His reputation as a writer of Catholic devotional works and the favour he enjoyed with the régime and with the Imperial household in particular certainly qualified his approach to his material in some ways. Whilst a mild anti-clerical strain and a strong anti-Masonic bias are apparent, careful genuflexions are made to Christianity throughout the work. More important, Christian would not include full particulars of black magic or its rituals; his book would contain strange and authentic matters, but nothing that might involve proscription or even loss of favour in a Catholic empire. The word *magie* has in fact a different connotation from the corresponding English word; it may be considered as the equivalent of 'the mysteries' as the phrase is used by writers on the classical period, and these would not necessarily contain any 'black' elements.

From 1815 onwards nineteenth century France was influenced by occultism in many ways. During this period, as Enid Starkie has remarked 'occult theories were, amongst certain writers, the same common coin that Freudian and Marxist theory is today amongst many who have never read a line from these two thinkers'. In England one may recall the Brownings' and Bulwer Lytton's interest in the occult. Across the channel, originating perhaps in the normal desire to compensate for lack of achievement in the real world by dreams of success in another, the lively intellects of defeated France seem to have indulged in supernatural speculations in reaction against the rationalists of the Revolution period. Paris became and has remained a happy hunting ground for astrologers, chiromants, fortune tellers *et hoc genus omne*, genuine and spurious, To the present day astrology, which to Christian was such a large part of *la Magie*, has a more serious following and is more scientifically studied than in any other western country. In particular, the literature of the period bears in many directions the mark of this widespread prepossession. In 1840 Le Boys' new translation of Swedenborg's works was published and strongly influenced Baudelaire, whilst Joseph le Maistre's and Lavater's well-known works on magic further shaped his thoughts. Illuminist doctrine, as Viatte shows,[1] formed a large element in the thought of Le Maistre and of Christian's life-long friend Charles Nodier. A great deal of Victor Hugo's philosophy was based on the Qabala of which good French versions existed.[2] The Parnassians were very much *au fait* with Buddhism and eventually quite as much with Burnouf's translations of the *Bhagavad Gita, Purana, Rig Veda* and other Indian sacred texts. Gerard de Nerval appears to have had a considerable acquaintance with alchemy. The most striking example however of magic in the stricter sense having provided the very crucible of a poet's genius is Arthur Rimbaud. At Charleville, a local official, Charles Bretagne, had interested him in and lent him occult and philosophical works. There may be a link with the Saint-Martin group—Louis de Saint-Martin [1743-1803] had been a prominent society intellectual, peripatetic in his life, a group of whose followers were at Lyon; he was known as 'The Unknown Philosopher' and his doctrines were redolent of Herschel's astronomy, of Pasquales, Swedenborg and Jacob Boehme. Again, from Baudelaire Rimbaud obviously derived interests stemming

1 Viatte *Les Sources Occultes due Romantisme.*
2 Dennis Saurat. *Le Religion de Victor Hugo.*

from Swedenborg and Lavater. Still, he seems to have had no other definite sources of knowledge than those provided by books easily available to him; he drew from Eliphas Levi and Pierre Leroux the symbolism that is the essence of *Les Illuminations, Un Saison en Enfer* and *Le Bateau Ivre*, whilst the famous 'sonnet of the vowels' has something magical in its transposition of the senses—part of that 'systematic derangement of all the senses' which was to qualify him as a *voyant*. 'He dreamed', says Peter Quennell, 'of the supreme power which the magicians . . . had promised to their adepts, and hoped to transform the language . . . ' Moreover he was prepared actually to practise the magic whose symbolism he exploited, though whether he actually did more than dabble lightly is doubtful; he probably knew a good deal more about it than T. S. Eliot knew of the Tarot when he wrote the *Waste Land*, but it was essentially a similar process of finding a wineskin into which to pour new wine—the wineskin suffering somewhat by the combination.[3]

The *History of Magic* was at once received as a standard work in this period which, as we have seen, was filled with occult interests. Christian's preoccupation with intuitive divination by means of the letters that spell out a name or question, which he called the Prenestine Fates, both reflected and intensified the taste of the time. The work became widely known abroad and Madame Blavatsky referred to it in 1888 in the *Secret Doctrine*.[4]

The book's career suffered the same check as did the rest of French life from the Franco-Prussian War which began the year of its publication. Christian was in Paris during it and witnessed the siege of Paris and the régime of the Commune. Once again he turned his experiences to good account in his last published work, the *History of the War with Prussia and of the Two Sieges of Paris, 1870-71*, published 1872-3.

[3] Enid M. Starkie, *Arthur Rimbaud*; also P. Debray, *Rimbaud: le Magicien Désabusé*; A. E. Waite *Louis Claude de Saint-Martin, the Unknown Philosopher*; Peter Quennell's introduction to the English translation of Verlaine *Confessions of a Poet*, 1950.

[4] 'The "army of the voice" is a term closely connected with Sound and Speech, as the effect and corollary of the cause—Divine Thought. As beautifully expressed by Paul Christian . . . the word spoken by as well as the name of every individual largely determines his future fate.'—Commentary on Stanza IV of the *Book of Dzyan* in the *Secret Doctrine*, Book I, p. 93 [first edition].

His energies would seem to have flagged with the decline in his health after this, for no later published works are traceable and he died at Lyons 12 July 1877, at 66.

There does remain, however, according to a Dorbon catalogue, an unpublished work of more than 10,000 lines, of considerable importance to occult students.

Dated from February to June 1871, it is an epistolary course in what is called 'onomantic astrology', the letters being addressed to a pupil of his, Jacques Charrot. They form, it appears, a very detailed and complete series of instructions, in the course of which occur vivid allusions to the stirring contemporary events which he illustrated by horoscopes and comments on various personages such as Eliphas Levi [M. Constant] whom he disliked and Edmond the palmist. He speaks of his own life, complains of very poor health, and states his intention of starting a Faculty of Occult Sciences. He makes moreover certain corrections to the *History of Magic*.

Christian's journalistic activities and collaborations are detailed, together with other particulars, in an uncompleted series of articles in *La Lumière* 1893-94, a monthly review for which his son was then writing on occult subjects. Other sources for his life are scattered and unsatisfactory. Material for the foregoing notes has been drawn mainly from his own prefaces, the review *Polybiblion* and a notice in the *Bibliotheca Esoterica* of the publishing house of Dorbon, with the kind assistance of the Service de Documentation of the Bibliothèque Nationale.

R.N.

ANALYSED CONTENTS

VOLUME I

EDITOR'S NOTE

PAUL CHRISTIAN: *A memoir*

ANALYSED CONTENTS

LIST OF DIAGRAMS AND TABLES

BOOK ONE

AT THE GATES OF THE SUPERNATURAL

BOOK III

THE ANCIENT ORACLES, THE SIBYLS AND THE FATES

BOOK FOUR

MAGIC FROM THE BEGINNING OF THE CHRISTIAN ERA TO THE END OF THE MIDDLE AGES

VOLUME II

BOOK FIVE

SUPERNATURAL SCIENCES AND CURIOSITIES

BOOK SIX

GENERAL THEORY OF THE HOROSCOPE

BOOK SEVEN

THE GENERAL KEYS OF ASTROLOGY

LIST OF DIAGRAMS AND TABLES

VOLUME I

VOLUME II

BOOK ONE

BOOK ONE

I

I COMPLETED in 1839, with Charles Nodier of the French Academy, a book of reminiscences on the antiquities of Paris,[1] that throne of so many great men, scene of such proud history, which to-day is slowly, stone by stone, crumbling away beneath the pick and hammer of the demolition gangs and of which there will soon be left behind no more than a legend.

Profound thinker and remarkable antiquary, Charles Nodier not only had a love of books, but also elevated his regard for them to the position of a religion. For the Church is the house of God, the library is the temple of the human spirit, the tabernacle of the written and printed word. Whatever the position of man in society, it is only by means of the qualities instilled in him by books that he can be of service to it, give service to it, and maintain his position in it.

Books are the first instructors, and often the final friends. The workman who can read may raise himself to the level of the greatest citizen. The man of wealth and leisure enriches his life by covering monumental editions with bindings of gold, and kings themselves are contributors to the book that will perpetuate their memory.

'Ah!' Nodier used to say to me, 'let us be guardians of this cult of the spirit throughout this earthly life, whose future rises time and time again out of a foundation of ruins! Let us love ancient books, those immortal guardians

---

[1] Paris Historique, 3 vols., 8vo., with 202 plates, 1839.—Nodier was curator of the library of the Arsenal, Paris.—*Ed.*

of the epochs of great faith, of profound science and proud passions! Let us adore them, to give to our beings strength on the threshold of uncharted times.'

One evening, in Nodier's house at Sully, we were talking about that wild woman from Italy who, though a pope's niece, was the hell-cat of France. And we read the following passage from the *Memoirs* of that time: 'On the 24 August 1572 noblemen and archers, together with all manner of people, were plundering the houses and killing their inhabitants, Paris seemed like a city overrun by conquering invaders. Dismembered bodies were tossed from the windows, the doorways were piled with heaps of dead and dying, the streets filled with corpses that were being dragged away into the Seine. Hatred, blood and death hung with such horror over the city that their Majesties, who were the authors of it all, were unable, in the palace of the Louvre, to keep the terror from their hearts . . .'[2]

This date marked the Massacre of St. Bartholomew.

These sorry majesties were Catherine de' Medici, widow of Henri II, and Charles IX his son.

—Well, what else could she have done, this poor woman, who at the death of her husband had five young children to look after, and found her position menaced by two families, the Bourbons and the Guises, who were both contemplating an attack upon the throne? . . . Was it not natural that she should have played such a strange rôle, partly to deceive her enemies and partly to preserve the lives of her children, whose successive reigns were the result of the wise conduct of such a clear-sighted woman?—This is the judgment passed on Catherine by Henri IV, if we are to believe the *Memoirs* of Claude Groulard, president of the Parlement of Normandy . . .'[3]

---

[2] The *Memoirs* from which I quote are by Gaspard de Saulx-Tavannes. Marshall of France—a courtier and an accomplice.

[3] No English word conveys the meaning of *Parlement*. There were 13 of these bodies, headed by that of Paris. Primarily, they were law-courts without appeal from their decisions; but they furthermore 'registered' the royal

Yet is it possible that this king of France and of Navarre, of whom Voltaire, master of paradox, said that he was
the conqueror and the father of his people—is it possible
that he could have judged in so sanctimonious a fashion the
bloody queen of the XVI century?

And yet, why not? Under the fatherly rule of Henri IV
the prisons were crammed with wretched people imprisoned
as a result of the salt tax : as many as 120 dead bodies were
carried away at a time. His Majesty, say the *Registers of the
Parlement of Rouen,* was implored to have pity on his
people. But, knowing that this tax was a source of immense
wealth, the king decreed that it should be kept in force, and
made a joke of all the rest . . . 'My counsellors,' Henri would
say, 'are responsible for so many more taxes . . . !' A pretty
confession, indeed. If you cannot believe in such crudity,
read the *Journal* of Pierre de l'Estoile; it is the ordinary
Paris citizen's view of the last of the Valois and the first of
the Bourbons.

Whatever may be the truth, after Matins on the day
following the massacre, when the intoxication of slaughter
was dissipated, Catherine, 'this clear-sighted woman,' was
vainly begging hell and heaven for a little respite from the
haunting memory of her transgression. Pursued in the
shadowy solitudes of the Tuileries by the ghosts of her
victims, she surrounded herself with magicians and covered
her garments with talismans; yet she was unable to exorcise
the horror that to her murderous eyes seemed to sully the
world for her.

A celebrated Italian astrologer, Luc Gauric, Bishop of
Civita-Ducale, consulted by the queen, sent Catherine the
following enigma : *St. Germain shall see you die.* The
oracular obscurity of the message gave it added prestige.

Immediately, says Mézeray, Catherine was seen avoiding all places, all churches called by this baleful name. She

edicts, that is, the king's governmental decrees were not valid until this
was done. They had however no final power to refuse registration. They also
devised local administrative regulations.—*Ed.*

no longer went to St. Germain en Laye, and because her palace was in the parish of St. Germain l'Auxerrois, she even left it for a mansion which was part of her property near St. Eustache. There she had built, in the form of a Doric column, a small observatory whence on clear nights she would watch the stars and seek for their fateful signs. Come Ruggieri, her close friend and confidant, and Auger Ferrier, her doctor, used to keep her company and protect her from the terrors of her remorse.

This Ruggieri was a Florentine priest, renowned for his great skill in the arts of composing love-philtres and of casting spells by which he could cause the gradual or instantaneous death of an enemy. Catherine had had him brought from Italy as an entertainment for the court, and also as a person who might be useful to her. In order to keep a hold on him, she had given him the rich Abbey of St. Mahé, in Brittany. In 1574, foiled in the La Mole and Coconas plot, he only escaped punishment through the intercessions of the benefactress whom he was betraying. Condemned to hard labour for life, he took his secrets to prison with him; but the needs of the Queen Mother procured his release and pardon. Later he was accused by Henri IV of having made a wax image of the King in which he stuck thirteen needles every day, pronouncing magic words to which were attributed evil powers. Ruggieri declared to the President of Thou, who was called upon to interrogate him, that he had saved the future king's life on the Eve of St. Bartholomew by swearing to Catherine that she had nothing to fear from the prince. 'How then,' he cried, 'could I desire to harm the man who owes his life to me?' Henri apparently remembered what he had done; he ordered Ruggieri's release, and bestowed a pension on him with the title of historiographer. It was Ravaillac's dagger that was to be the instrument of fate: had Ruggieri foreseen it?

Auger Ferrier, like all the doctors of antiquity, believed in the influence of the stars. He could calculate, on a table, showing the phases of the moon, sometimes a fatal crisis, sometimes a convalescence. The effect used to follow so swiftly on the doctor's prognostics that it was his reputation as a magician rather than as a doctor that brought him fame. This success persuaded him to take up a profounder study of the horoscope. He showed himself such an adept at it that Toulouse, his native town, became too small a place for his talents. When he was taken to Rome by Cardinal Bertrand, he astonished the Medici Pope Pius IV [1559-1565] and, on his return to France, letters of introduction from the Pope assured him of a warm welcome from Catherine, who made him her official doctor and her unofficial prophet. Faithful to his benefactress, he never left her until his death in 1589, some months before her own.

When Catherine had withdrawn into the obscurity of Valois, from which was to emerge the Dominican Jacques Clément, the Hotel de la Reine, as it was called, was acquired by Charles de Bourbon, Comte de Soissons, and kept its new name until 1763, when it was demolished to make room for the Cornmarket. Catherine's observatory column is all that is left, a mute and material witness to the terrors of that wicked woman.

II

THESE are the facts of history; but, as Nodier remarked to me, 'how few readers to-day would learn without a shrug of the shoulders what was the outcome of the prediction made to Catherine by the master Luc Gauric? Nevertheless, it appears that the priest who was present at the deathbed of the aged queen was called Nicolas de St. Germain, Bishop of Nazareth. Catherine, when she heard his name, imagined she saw the figure of Death rise behind him and this final terror killed her.'

'Coming from you,' I said to my friend, 'the anecdote is not without value; but might it not be one of those little tales made up after the event, just as certain words are attributed, after their death, to famous men?'

'It is not impossible, and I willingly leave you my St. Germain for what it is worth. But, as we are on the subject of singular happenings, here is one which seems to carry the stamp of truth.'

And at these words Nodier took out carefully from a glass case in which he kept the rarest specimens of his collection a small 24mo volume of about a hundred vellum pages, bound in burnished ivory with gold corners and clasp delicately engraved with Catherine's and Henri II's monogram, a C and an H interlaced beneath the royal crown.

'I am ready to wager,' he pursued, 'that what I am holding is the breviary that Catherine used in her observatory. It must have passed through many hands before reaching me; it is a fragment of the wreckage left behind by the revolutions. The letters engraved on the binding prove beyond doubt that this copy belonged to Catherine.'

Not without a certain tremor, but concealing my emotion as best I could, I opened Catherine's little book while Nodier, in the enthusiastic tones of the successful bibliophile, pointed out the date 1563 and the name of the publishers, Jean de Tournes, of Lyons, the celebrated printer to the royal household.

The title was: *Iugements Astronomiques sur les Nativités*, by Auger Ferrier, Physician to the Queen. Above this title were the arms of Jean de Tournes, an escutcheon surrounded by a serpent with its tail in its mouth, with motto: *Quod tibi fieri non vis, alteri ne feceris* (do not to another what you do not wish done to yourself).

The author addressed himself to *That Most Illustrious and Virtuous Princess, Catherine Queen of France*. 'Knowing the pleasure you take in reading all works concerning the lofty science of the Stars, I have been emboldened to write and dedicate to you the present *Traicté des Iugements Astronomiques* ... which shows the good and evil consequences which befall humanity in the guise of *natural causes*, through the influence of the Stars. The which I beg of you to look favourably upon, having regard to the good will of the person who destines all his meditations, studies and works to the service of Your Majesty.'⁴

In this way, by this public declaration, the Queen Mother was known to be an adept, an avowed protector of the occult sciences. She had an official manual of divination, prepared for herself by a man in her employment who was doubtless well versed in these strange matters. But why was Ferrier's work printed? Why were the Louvre and the City allowed to scrutinise the secret practices of a queen so famed for her dissimulation? Precautions had been taken, said Nodier, and they were very simple. Ferrier's black-book was incomprehensible without a certain key which the author did not allow to be made public. It was sufficient, in those days, to be mysterious in order to impose, even on great intellects, a sort of respect mixed with superstition.

This Catherine well knew. The *Traicté des Iugements Astronomiques* revived the enigma of the Sphinx, and there was no Oedipus to solve it. Gentleman and fine ladies, the clergy, the leaders of finance and military affairs, attracted by the unknown would probably consult this popular physician on the state of their love affars or their wounded ambitions. Ferrier would have to talk sufficiently to show his superiority, and keep a discreet silence which would flatter his prestige; it was, I suppose, his great gift to know how to discourage confidences in order to make them flow more readily. Catherine used him like a fish-hook to catch her enemies in the troubled waters of their dangerous confessions. Perhaps her magic arts were no more that this; though this should not be taken as a disparagement of the real occult sciences.

'Do you really believe in them?' I cried.

'I believe,' continued Nodier, 'that it is impossible to

---

⁴ A copy exists in the Bibliothèque Nationale of this very rare book. Not so luxuriant as Nodier's copy, it is bound in oak boards.

deny or affirm things which do not fit in with the little rules
of our little minds. The occult sciences have their roots too
far in the past, and they have aroused too much interest
throughout the history of humanity, for them to be devoid
of meaning. They have only interested me as a bibliophile;
their memory is kept alive in rare editions, illuminated
manuscripts and curious woodcuts in my collection and
elsewhere. But here is a pathway to be explored, leading
back into the darkness of time. Madness may be at the end,
or maybe the supreme wisdom; it is a dangerous way, but
triumph would not be without its reward. As for myself,
I imagine that, if man can recapture in the mirror of
memory the fugitive images of the past, he may well be
able, either through some evolution in his being, or through
the resurrection of a forgotten science, to create or re-dis-
cover some means to illuminate the future, the other face of
the eternal Janus. What do you think?' And Nodier smiled
as he held out his hand.

It was impossible to reply.

III

IN THIS same year 1839 Comte de Salvandy, Minister of
Public Education, caused to be brought to Paris some
thousands of the old books which, since 1790, date of the
suppression of the monasteries, had existed in duplicate in
nearly all the provincial libraries, piled up because of the
Revolution. Charged with putting these literary treasures
in order—treasures which the wise minister intended should
form the basis of new libraries—I devoted myself to this
work with a fervour justified by the interesting discoveries
which I made daily.

The first, and without doubt the most precious, was the
Apotelesmatique of Ptolemy de Peluse, with comments and
additions by Junctin de Florence, Doctor of Theology

and Almoner of François de Valois, youngest brother of Henri III.

Ptolemy, living in the early days of the Christian era, was one of the last doctors of the celebrated Alexandrian Schools. His work, written in Greek and divided into four, explains the whole doctrine of Egyptian Magic according to the Hermetic tradition and the famous sanctuaries of Thebes and Memphis, of which the origins are long lost.

Junctin his commentator adds page by page, with immense erudition, notes from all the doctrinal concordances which he has been able to glean in researches into Chaldaean astrology, the Hebrew Qabalah and the Arab, Greek and Latin sacred speculations. He does more: he puts the complicated mechanism of this encyclopaedia of occult sciences into action, and, in order to demonstrate the power of his strange views, he multiplies examples of horoscopes. He finds his subjects everywhere, among emperors, popes, kings, cardinals, bishops, celebrated warriors, notable citizens of the principal towns of France, Germany and Italy. The ancient rules are given on one side, their modern applications on the other. Follow, from one example to another, this preacher of Christian doctrine, this master of sacred and orthodox theology [*sacrae theologiae doctor*], who is suddenly transfigured into a hierophant of Isis and talks to us of a world buried under fifty centuries of time; and if you are not persuaded by these proofs of superhuman learning, you will at least be compelled to admit their marvellous scholarship.[5]

The copy I had before me, in two folio volumes dated 1581, had been the property of Morin de Villefranche, royal professor of mathematics at the Collège de France and astrol-

---

[5] Κλαυδίου Πτολεμαίου Πηλουσίου, τῶν Ἀστρολόγων πρώτου, ἢ μαθηματιχῆς ἢ ποτελεσματιχῆς Τετραβίβλιον.— *Speculum Astrologiae*, universam mathematicam Scientiam, in certas classes digestant, complectens: auctore *Francisco Junctino* sacræ Theologiæ doctore. 2 vol. in fol. Lugduni, 1581 [Paris, Bibliothèque de St Geneviève (Library), V, 143].

oger to Anne of Austria, wife of Louis XIII; for it was he who was called, says Voltaire, to the bedside of that queen in order to draw up at the exact moment of birth the horoscope of the child who was to be Louis XIV. There is another copy at the Saint-Geneviève Library in Paris, part of a bequest of sixteen thousand volumes made to the Canons of the Order of Saint Geneviève by the Cardinal Maurice Letellier, Archbishop of Rheims, who died in 1710. This very learned prelate, a great lover of rare books, doubtless venerated the ancient magi as precursors of the Apostles; and his friends of the Order of Saint Geneviève must have taken part with him in the secret cult of primitive religion, since the books of occult science which he bequeathed to them are in many places underlined and annotated either by himself or by them.

Junctin's edition is dedicated to Marghard, Bishop of Spire and Counsellor of the Holy Roman Empire. It was printed by the prerogative of the Emperor Rudolf II. This is a double proof of the great esteem in which its author was held, of his eminence as a scholar and of the admiration accorded to his work by the throne and the pontificate. He was also probably much sought after by Catherine; maybe he owed the favour of the title of almoner to the Crown Prince, François de Valois, Comte d'Alençon, later Duc d'Anjou, who died of debauchery at the age of thirty. But neither the tragic history nor the scandalous chronicles of the time show that Marghard was involved in the corruption of that court. He lived and died in solitude, in love with his own inner world peopled with the chaste visions that surround genius between earth and heaven.

My second discovery was the *Traité des Mathématiques Célestes*, written by Julius Firmicus Maternus, a Sicilian priest who flourished in the IVth century A.D., towards the time of the Emperor Julian (the Apostate). This work, divided into eight books, is actually a practical manual of Astrology, drawn up according to the doctrine of Ptolemy de Peluse, and recommended again and again, in Junctin's

Commentaires, as a first-class authority on occult matters. The edition of this manuscript had been printed at Basle in Switzerland by a certain Nicolas Pruckner of Strasbourg and dedicated to Edward VI of England.'

Later, by similar good fortune, I chanced upon a little duodecimo volume covered with very dilapidated parchment. It was all that was left of the *Curiosités Inouïes sur l'Art Talismanique des Persans, l'Astrologie des Patriarches, et le Moyen de Lire dans l'Alphabet des Etoiles les Révolutions des Empires*. As we must never judge a thing by its outward form, do not think that I had made an unfortunate mistake. The author was worth a hundred others, for he was Jacques Gaffarel, who had one of those magnicent heads that seem to be sculpted in Corinthian bronze and lighted by a reflection of the sun of Greece. An indefatigable traveller in Europe and Asia, he had indeed sucked the honey of knowledge: a doctor of canon law, prior of St. Gilles, Abbot of Sigonce, Protonotary Apostolic, and above all, librarian to Cardinal Richelieu, that determined prelate who was in power from 1624 until his death 1642. This iron-willed man knew how to choose his servants. What had attracted him towards Gaffarel and the occult world was the consciousness of his own power and the need to increase it constantly. None better than the interpreter of the *Mystères de la Divine Kabale*, brought from the East,' could have satisfied the great instinct for absolute power which, among his colossal enterprises and his murderous enemies, sustained Richelieu on the serene heights of his unbreakable will.

But I am wrong. In the despotic minister's private council there was another man, less well-grounded perhaps

---

' Julii Firmici Materni junioris, Siculi, viri clari, ad Mavortium Lollianum *Matheseos Libri* VIII, 1 vol. folio, *Basileæ*, 1551 [Bibliothèque Impériale, V, 184].

' *Abdita divinæ Kabbalæ Mysteria*, contra sophistarum logomachiam defensa, auctore Jac. *Gaffarel*, Juris canonici doctore. 2-vol. 12mo, Amstelodami, 1676 [Paris, St. Geneviève Library, V. 676-7].

in theory than Gaffarel but more audacious in practice. I
have already mentioned Morin de Villefranche. At first he
was only a physician without patients but not without
intrigues. Dreaming of gold mines in some remote corner of
Hungary, he had been prospecting for them too long at the
expense of Claude Dormi, Bishop of Boulogne, and Dormi,
discouraged, had refused further aid when Morin met in a
German inn a certain Scotsman called Davidson who was
seeking his fortune in another way and equally unsuccess-
fully. These two spirits in distress had an electrical effect
upon one another. 'Let us pool our misfortunes,' the Scotsman proposed, 'and if you will teach me the arts of healing,
I shall give you in exchange the key of the prophets.' This
key was Astrology. The strange bargain was accepted and
faithfully carried out.

On his return to Paris, Morin raised money by the sale
of horoscopes which gradually found their way from the
antechamber to the boudoir. Chance, which is providence to
those who know how to grasp it, suddenly opened up to him
the prospect of unexpected fame. Louis XIII had fallen ill
at Lyon, and two inferior fortune-tellers put into public
circulation a prediction of the king's immediate death. This
impertinence should have been enough to prove their
stupidity. Now, either because Morin was really more
skilled in the occult arts, or whether it was because he had a
subtler intuition of where his best interests lay, he sent to
the queen-mother, Marie de' Medici, a horoscope which said
exactly the opposite, stating the certainty of the immediate
recovery of the king and its date. Events proved him right,
and his rivals were imprisoned for life. From that day forward Morin became the fashion. Soon great noblemen and
prelates, including Marshall de Montmorency and Cardinal
de la Rochefoucauld, were among his best clients. Descartes
himself considered it no insult to philosophy to consult him.
These illustrious people, who were assuredly not gossips,
yet talked about him so much both at court and in town that

Richelieu could not help paying some attention to what was said.

French politics was at that time dominated by the ambitions of Gustavus Adolphus, King of Sweden [1611-1632], and by the military power of Walstein, generalissimo of the house of Austria. Morin predicted for both a violent death and the year in which it would happen, which was not long to be awaited: Gustave was killed in 1632, at the battle of Lutzen, and Walstein was stabbed in 1634 by order of the Emperor, who suspected him of having designs on the crown of Bohemia. Richelieu, already impressed, hesitated no longer: Morin had become necessary to him. It is said that one day about 1642 the young Cinq-Mars, master of the horse and favourite of the king, came laughing to the first minister with his horoscope in his hand. 'Can you believe it, Monseigneur,' he cried, 'this madman Morin claims, according to this scrap of paper, that my head will be cut off?'

Richelieu never laughed and never forgot. A few months later the wild Cinq-Mars and his friend de Thou, son of the famous president, were trapped in a puerile and dangerous conspiracy with Spain. It cost each of them his head, and the Cardinal, who was on the point of death, bequeathed the master in Magic to his successor Mazarin [in power 1643 with brief intermissions until his death 1661] as a precious instrument of government. Morin lived on until 1656, a pensioner of the court and of the minister, held in great affection by some, feared by others but making his power felt by all with whom he came in contact. Before his death, the Queen of Poland, Maria de Gonzaga, whose physician the Scotsman Davidson had become, had accepted the dedication of the works of the last French astrologer and had them printed at her own expense.[3]

---

[3] Astrologia Gallica, principiis et rationibus propriis stabilita, operâ et studio *Joan. Bapt. Morini*, doctoris medici, et Parisiis regii Mathematum professoris. 1 vol. in fol. Hagæ-Comitis. 1661 [Paris, St. Geneviève (Library), V, 144].

IV

WHEN we see through the eyes of history Cardinal Richelieu descending to such unusual studies, admitting their adepts into his private life, always so jealously guarded; when we see that inflexible spirit, of whom Balzac or Sully said that 'God had set no limits to his power,' pause, in spite of its cold logic and immense pride, in front of the spectre of Fatality, I believe that the occult sciences, too much despised in our own times, are equal to the loftiness of mind shown by such a disciple. But let us go further: for Richelieu is not the only patron they can claim.

Let us open, for example, the Prefaces of St. Jerome [*circa* 340-420], placed by order of Popes Sixtus V [1585-1590] and Clement VIII [1592-1605] as introduction to the Bible. 'Pythagoras and Plato,' says St. Jerome, 'those masters of the genius of Greece, visited as pilgrims seeking after knowledge and as humble disciples the sacerdotal college of the soothsayers at Memphis [Memphiticos vates], preferring to be initiated with respect to the ancient doctrines of that distant land, rather than impose on their country the yoke of their own ideas. The Magus Apollonius of Tyana visited India in order to sit before the golden throne of the famed Hiarchas, who instructed a select audience in the arcana of nature and the movement of the skies. He returned by way of Babylon, Chaldea, Assyria, Phoenicia, Arabia and Egypt, whence he reached Ethiopia, where the Gymnosophists showed him the famous *Table of the Sun*. And the more he learned at these sources, the better he became,' adds St. Jerome. 'I shall not speak,' he says later, 'of the philosophers, the astronomers, the astrologers, whose wisdom, so useful to mankind, is confirmed by dogma, explained by method, and verified by experience. I now pass to inferior arts.'[*]

---

[*] 'Taceo de philosophis, astronomis, astrologis, quorum scientia mortalibus uti lissima est, et in tres partes scinditur. το δόγμα τὴνμεθοδον, τὴν ἐμπειρίαν. Ad minores artes veniam,' etc. [S. HYERONOMI, Prologus galeatus, in Bibl. saer.].

It is easy to see that St. Jerome does not lightly give a place to astrology among the higher sciences, distinguishing it from astronomy, its mere instrument. And if Pope Sixtus V, creator of the Vatican library and restorer of the Egyptian monuments transported to Rome by the Caesars, was not afraid to preface the Bible with these passages from the works of wise St. Jerome, it is perhaps a silent homage rendered to the erudite Junctin, who had predicted, on a system of calculation by hermetic circles, the accessions of Popes Julius II, Leo X, Clement VII, Paul III, Julius III, Paul IV and Pius V.

Let me add that Ptolemy de Peluse, Ferrier, Junctin, Gaffarel and Morin were not the only ones whose works persuaded me to take up the thread that leads through the labyrinth of the occult sciences.

Let me cite these from ancient times: Manetho, high priest of the sun; the philosophers Plotinus, Iamblichus, Porphyry, Proclus and Artimidorus.

From the Christian era: on the one side, the rabbis of Judaea; on the other, popes, princes, bishops, doctors.

Among the popes: Leo III, Sylvester II, Honorius III, Urban V.

Among the princes: Alphonse X of Spain; Charles V of France; Rudolf II the German Emperor.

Among the prelates: St. Dionysius the Areopagite, Bishop of Athens; St. Caesarius, Bishop of Arles; St. Malachy, Archbishop of Armagh; Synesius, Bishop of Ptolemais; Nicephorus, Patriarch of Constantinople; Albert the Great, the Dominican master of the Holy Palace; Jean de Muller or Regiomontanus, Bishop of Ratisbon; Leopold, Duke of Austria and Bishop of Freysing; Cardinal d'Ailly, Chancellor af the University of France; the Cardinals Cusa and Cajetan; Giovanni Ingegneri, Bishop of Capo d'Istria; Bernard de Mirandole, Bishop of Caserta; Udalric de Fronsperg, Bishop of Trent and many more.

There should also be named: the Dominicans Savonarola and Campanella; the Franciscans Raymond Lulle and

Roger Bacon; the Benedictine Trithemius; Joachim of Celico, the Cistercian Abbot of Corazzo; the Jesuits Athanasius Kircher, Guillaume Postel, Torreblanca de Villalpanda; Marsilius Ficinus, Canon of Florence; Pierre Bungo, Canon of Bergamo; Pedro Cirvello, Canon of Salamanca; Jérôme Cardan, physician to Cardinal St. Charles Borromeo; Adrian Sicler, physician to Camille de Neufville, Archbishop of Lyon and numerous others.

Indeed the church had not forgotten its heritage from the ancient world. Abbot Lebeuf, in his learned *Dissertations* on the ecclesiastical history of Paris, reports that the College of Maître-Gervais, founded in 1370 by Charles V, had as its aim to teach astrology considered in its relationships with medicine, and that Pope Urban V, at the king's request, confirmed by papal bull the privileges of this institution . . .

The occult sciences were protected by the Church; they were cultivated in the silence of the cloisters, in the theologian's study. Without being confused by them, their doctrines were ranked with the monuments of the Church's own labours; they were considered as a distant tradition of the revelations of God to former men—revelations of the hidden forces that control by fixed laws the economy of the universe. 'All knowledge,' said the Church, 'comes from God; therefore all knowledge is theological and divine.' The most rigid Christian faith has never stigmatised or condemned any but sinister or wretched charlatans, sorcerers, necromancers, distillers of secret poisons, spell-binders or amulet-vendors, who claimed protection from the profaned name of Magic for their absurd and often criminal industry.

V

THE WORD MAGIC is derived from the Chaldaean word *Maghdim,* which means wisdom with the addition of the general sense that we give to the term *philosophy.*[10] The

Magi, or the adepts of Magic—we may even call them the priests of the wisdom of antiquity—were philosophers dedicated to the study of the universe, that sphere whose centre, they said, is everywhere, whose circumference has no bounds, and at the heart of which are united without being confounded—or are separate, without being lost from sight—the *physical*, the *intellectual* and the *divine* worlds: the triple face of all knowledge, the triple base of all analysis, the triple stem of all synthesis.

The physical world is composed of material, mineral, vegetable, animal and fluid kingdoms; of their separate existences, of their affinities and of their contrasts, of their perpetual minglings and transformations, and of the organic laws that maintain the essential unity of substances in the infinite variety of its products.

The intellectual world manifests itself through the spirit of man. Our innate faculties develop and extend through sensation, knowledge, judgment, will. Sensation is the affirmation of life; knowledge distinguishes the forms of that life; judgment compares them; will acts upon them, and suffers or links their reactions.

The divine world, which embraces both these worlds, is the eternal source of all life, on the physical and on the intellectual plane, both of which are governed by supreme knowledge and absolute wisdom.

But the Magi refrained from attempts to explain God. They called Him the Ineffable, and they had inscribed, on the pediments of their temples, this sentence which has survived them: *I am all that is, all that has been, all that shall be; and none may lift my veil.*

They tried however to make the divine presence felt by saying: that God communicates himself to us through the perception of truth, through the consciousness of good and through the creative will. That He is therefore *Truth*,

---

[19] Webster: From Greek *Magos*, Old Persian *Magu*. Skeat: Persian *Mugh* = fire-worshipper. Found at Behistan in Egyptian cuneiform characters.—*Ed.*

Justice, Harmony, and unfolds in the three dimensions which we can imagine but not measure : infinite height, breadth and depth. He is beyond all reality *Perfection*—beyond all reason *Providence*—beyond all justice *Love*—beyond all intellect *Light*—beyond all knowledge *Mystery.* He is *Because He Is,* and nothing can *be,* except in Him and for Him.

Thus the famous words of St. Paul 'in Him we live, move and have our being,' were anticipated by three thousand years.

The Magi recognised that apart from the divine immutability, everything else changes, is transformed, advances and improves. Could a perfect providence do less than display its works as a perpetual progress stretching to infinity through time and space, the product of the continual development of beings and worlds? This idea of progress is the aspiration of humanity towards a *relative* ideal of perfection, happiness and holiness, whose *absolute* reality increases with every man who believes he is approaching it. Every free and moral being brings to each station of this eternal pilgrimage the fortuitous significance of his merits or his faults. Expiation, as well as recompense, awaits him; God punishes but does not avenge. The supreme father does not desire a single creature that has issued from his breast to curse him for ever.

If, on the contrary, the being who has been initiated by death into a new cycle of progress is found worthy of the ranks of the elect, he can become a messiah, a teacher of sacred laws to those on a lower plane. Later, ascending to more sublime virtues, if he should arrive at that unutterable number of perfections that illuminate the sphere of the men-gods, the Ineffable will hold in reserve for him treasures of the highest glory—of resplendent knowledge—of powers still more marvellous ranged beyond all conception along the indescribable ways to even more divine exaltations.

*   *   *

Has this theory of the Magi a basis in some positive revelation, or is it but a mirage of oriental musings? We can establish its existence, but its precise origin escapes us. There were Magi in India, Persia, Chaldea, Egypt; but which were the oldest? and among the oldest, who was the originator of their primitive dogma? We have only scattered fragments from the history of vanished civilisations, fragments altered by the passage of time. Nevertheless, what still remains of the *Vedas*, the most ancient holy books of India, of the books of *Zend*, the theology of the Persians, and of the writings of *Thoth* or of *Manetho* of Egypt, seems to prove that the peoples who lived in the remotest times already professed the doctrine of the unity of God and believed in the migration of the human soul to the stars. We read there that this immortal soul, on leaving its terrestrial body, goes to inhabit, in order to submit to other tests, the worlds of recompense and expiation to which his works belong. Among our ancestors the Celtic Gauls, who came from Asia, the Druidic priesthood had transmitted the same beliefs to the West. The oral traditions that have come down to us in default of more reliable documents are of great value; but in the course of the centuries they have become disfigured, like those corroded medallions whose age archeologists try to ascertain. . .

We have considered the general idea the Magi had of the supreme Divinity and of its influence upon humanity. I do not pass judgment on it: I merely define it as it appears to me, in its radiant simplicity, far above the sterile conflict of metaphysical discussion. I must admit that this theosophy does not seem to me unreasonable.

Let us transport ourselves, in thought, to the top of a mountain, at the hour when the fragrance of summer rising from the distant plains, their valleys and woods, mounts slowly with the last murmurings of nature into the immensity of the darkening skies. The sun has disappeared in a river of jewels, whose final brilliance dies away on the horizon. For the captive heart which guesses nothing of what may lie beyond daily joys and miseries, it is night. The slave of wretched poverty or ignoble labour, of unsuccessful genius or powerless pride, of crushed ambition or wounded greatness, asks nothing more of nature's pity than a little sleep before taking up the yoke again. Such is the destiny of the multitude.

But for the being magnetised by a higher life, as the shadows rise from the depths and cover the mountain tops the dawn of the Infinite breaks and shines. Those myriads of stars, living jewels in the crown of God, do they not appear to spread, in ever-widening circles, into the ethereal depths of an endless, fathomless ocean? If now, from the banks of Time, we plunged into the waters of that unknown life—if we were able to follow its course through the centuries with the speed of light: after having traversed this immensity, and seeing one vastness merge endlessly with another, nascent creations following those that perish, the abysses of the past and future flowing into one another— would anyone still believe that the author of these wonders, He from whom we receive an insatiable desire to know all, can hold in store for us as an eternal proof of His omnipotence only the endless night of the tomb?

This daring protest of the human soul against the possibility of annihilation can be expressed in two words: *Mountain Theology*. Which of us has not at some time or other felt that, as we rise above the dwelling-place of our passions and our miseries, the magnetism of solitary heights instils in us something of their unchangeable purity? We are there, as Rousseau says, serious without melancholy, peaceful without indolence, happy to be and to think. And as our eyes perceive fresh aspects of infinity, we feel the reflection in our consciousness of an even brighter radiance from the divine majesty; it somehow reaches us through all its works and makes us participants in its grandeur. The ultimate physical altitude of being touches the threshold of that supernatural world, the poetry of our dreams and the future reality of our hopes. It is the Mount Sinai of intelligence, the Mount Tabor of contemplation, the Calvary where faith redeems the blasphemies of the atheist.[11]

It is therefore natural that mountains, hills, and high places in general should have been the first altars of the most ancient of religions, the first schools of transcendental ideas. The Magi of India who, following a tradition adopted by many Fathers of the Christian Church, were descended from the race of Seth, the son of Adam, give us proof of this. Proud inheritors of the revelations of Genesis, they had carried with them to the furthest eastern regions a mysterious tradition which foretold a new star shining in the heavens when the Redeemer promised to the sire of mankind should appear on earth. Isolated from the corruption which had overrun the world after the Flood, they passed their lives from generation to generation waiting for the miracle promised by their ancestors. Twelve of them were chosen to keep a ceaseless watch over the sky and to seek in the stars the warning sign of universal redemption. Their functions, handed down from father to son, formed the ritual of a priesthood which awaited the fulfilment of the oracle whose shrine they guarded. Established at the foot of an eminence named, no one knows why, the Mountain of Victory, they always had three observers at the summit. Each year, after the harvests, these three Magi were relieved from their posts by three others. Their time was spent in prayer and study of the celestial fields; the inhabitants of the lower region looked after their material needs, so that nothing might trouble them at their saintly task.

---

[11] There is general agreement amongst scholars that the supreme deities of the pre-Christian religions, at least in Western Europe, did inhabit the heights. To Mercury was dedicated the Puy de Dôme, Paris; Ludgate Hill is very probably named from Lugh, Gaelic god of light, possibly also of creation. By papal direction and policy the heathen dedications, including those of such heights, were adapted to suitable surrogates within the Christian scheme, St. Michael being found particularly useful as a replacement for the local god. Hence the number of dedications of churches to St. Michael, which was further encouraged by the miraculous vision of St. Michael in a later century.—*Ed*.

Who can tell what solitary labours, what mysterious visions and wonderful illuminations they may have had? Who would dare state that, beyond our physical world, they did not have some revelation of the supernatural world that presses on us from all sides? Perhaps they guessed that all those stars that float like islands in the ocean of eternity are peopled by civilisations superior or inferior to our own and that they contain progressive series of thinking beings, from the lowest intelligences, barely distinguishable from the matter that gave them birth, to the divine powers to whom it is permitted to contemplate the Creator in all his glory and to comprehend the sublimity of all his works . . .

This idea was that of the best philosophers of antiquity. It reappears today from the pen of a penetrating and bold astronomer whose thesis, brilliantly sustained, makes many converts at this very time. 'In mathematics,' he writes, 'there is a theory called the "theory of limits". It demonstrates that there are heights to which we may strive, unceasingly, without ever reaching them; we may approach them but never attain to them. The man who is initiated into the nature of numbers and who ponders over this theory, in order to examine its inner meaning and to apply it to the whole universe, will see suddenly rise before him an amphitheatre with endless tiers. This amphitheatre is the hierarchy of worlds. The lower limit, the beginning, will be lost in the depths; the upper limit, absolute perfection, will be equally inaccessible. Between these two limits beings arise in infinite progression. If we place our earth in the lower tiers of this immense amphitheatre, you will understand at once our imperfections and our miseries in the presence of the wisdom of the Creator. If our earth were the only inhabited world in the past, the present and the future: if it were the only nature, the only sojourn of life, the only manifestation of creative power, it would be incompatible with the eternal splendour to have formed a world so miserable, so imperfect. He who believes in the existence of a single world is inevitably led to this conclusion: that the divine hypostases, eternally inactive until the day of the creation of our earth, have only manifested the flow of their infinite power to create a grain of animated dust.

'But,' concludes the author I have cited, 'if we consider the stars as stations in the sky and as the future mansions of our immortal life, from the heights of the eternal summits to which our contemplation has led us, the vanity of earthly things appears to us in its true light. The Creator in His great majesty is magnified to us in proportion as our conceptions are developed and raised. We see all the beings of the universe linked together by the law of unity and of solidarity, both in material and spiritual things; it is one of the first laws of nature. Then we feel that nothing is unfamiliar in the world, that a universal kinship unites us to all creatures. No, the universe is not a useless spectacle of deceptive appearances; and when these distant stars shine forth with marvellous brightness and our dreams follow them to the infinite depths, other humanities, our sisters, pass before us.'[12]

These maybe were the visions that enraptured Indian Magi on the Mount of Victory during the centuries of waiting that separated them from the Man-God; and when at last the promised star appeared on the horizon of their observatory they must have recognised it by signs that left no doubt in their minds. According to a belief recorded by Ephraim of Syria, a child's gentle face appeared on a cross of light at the centre of the mysterious star. Let us not be too hasty, incredulous or sceptical in condemning as apocryphal this singular detail. The cross was for the Magi a symbol of the infinite in its aspects of height, breadth and depth. They said that this figure was the signature of God, and, whether they really did distinguish it in the heavens at the moment of the star's appearance, or whether it was only their manner of expressing the mystery of this new

[12] Camille Flammarion, *les Mondes imaginaires et les Mondes réels*, a critical review of human theories, ancient and modern about the inhabitants of the stars, 1 vol. 12mo (Paris 1868).

era, we may consider it as one of the supreme hieroglyphics of the philosophic and religious doctrine of the earliest times.

'When they arrived at Bethlehem,' says Ephraim the Syrian, 'they had no fear of having come to the wrong place. The occult knowledge which had brought them there must have clothed in glorious light that place of poverty; and beyond terestrial forms they saw for a moment the splendours of the Word Incarnate. They brought to the cradle of the Child-God three symbolic gifts: incense, offered to His divinity; myrrh, a perfume that is used for preserving the body, as an honour to His imperishable humanity; and gold, sign of the royal wonder of His future. And then,' continues Ephraim, 'the following conversation took place between the Virgin Mary and these ambassadors from the east.

' "Why do you do these things, noble strangers?" she said to them. "What hand has led you from the palaces of the dawn to this wretched abode? Why do you place these costly gifts at the feet of an unknown Child, the poorest and youngest in all Israel?"

' "May blessings rain upon you," they replied, "O Virgin who has given birth to this Child; for we see in Him the King of the future."

' "Alas," replied the divine Mother, "what King ever had as His cradle an armful of straw left by the camel-drivers of Syria? Where are His throne and crown? Tell me by what signs you recognise His greatness."

'And the Magi replied: "We are sure that this Child's soul has descended from heaven. In this tiny body dwells the soul of the Son of the Ancient of Days. He wished to be born poor and with the weakness of the newly-born, because He comes here among us to comfort the poor and free the oppressed. But one day all the kings of the earth will bend the knee to Him and confess His divinity."

' "My lords," went on Mary, "tell me who reveals these things to you? Have the angels of the Almighty appeared to you on the distant mountains from which the sun begins its course?"

'"Blessed Mother," replied the holy pilgrims, "we saw shining in the skies a star never before seen by human eye, and we heard a voice that filled our souls with joy. We obeyed that voice, and the star has led us on the road we had to travel: the signs given by the Eternal are never wrong."

'"Ah," said the Virgin, "be careful not to repeat those words in this unhappy land! Jerusalem has lost its liberty; wicked Herod, who governs us, has heard of a King who has just been born, and he would use the sword to cut down this frail plant before it has flowered!"

'"Have no fear, O gracious Mother," replied the messengers from the east with superhuman majesty; "this Herod shall perish at the hand of God, and your Son, rising above all earthly palaces, shall found an empire in eternity in which all kings to come shall be no more than servants."

'"Then may blessings rain upon you also," said the Virgin, with a celestial smile, "for I see that God has favoured you by making you the equals of the prophets. May the same star take you safely back to the lands where your virtues flourish. Go and spread the joyous news on the most distant shores. Tell the world that the divine dew has watered the seed of the fruits of eternal life. May the peace of Heaven rest upon you and remain with you; when the days of your glory are ended, this King of the future, whose cradle you stand beside, will come to waken you in your tombs." '[13]

VI

INDIA, which the rest of the world took so long to discover, and which had until recent excavations no history before

[13] Other traditions tell that the Apostle Thomas met these Magi forty years later and baptised them: that later the Empress Helena caused their bones to be collected and brought to Byzantium, and that these witnesses of the Nativity now rest in Cologne Cathedral.—*Ed.*

Alexander's expeditions, preserved in the secret schools of its Magi a primitive theology of great purity. The *Shasta-Bad*, the oldest of its sacred books, begins thus: 'God is one, creator of all things, the sphere of the universe, without beginning, without end. God governs everything by providence and by unalterable laws. Seek not for the essence and the nature of the Eternal which is one, indivisible, ineffable: your seeking would be vain and sinful. It is enough that, day by day, night by night, you should adore his power, his wisdom, his goodness, in all his works.

'When God alone existed and no other being existed with him, He conceived the plan of creating the universe. He first of all created Time, then Water, then the Earth; then, from a mingling of the five elements, Earth, Water, Fire, Air and Light, he made the various beings and gave them the earth for their home. He made the globe that we inhabit in an oval (like an egg). Then, in the fulness of time, he desired to communicate his being and his splendour to beings capable of feeling. These beings were still non-existent: the Eternal willed it, and they were.'

But this doctrine was too abstract to be suitable for the intelligence of the ordinary man. He needs visible symbols, and these wooden, metal or stone images soon become the prototypes of a fantastic legend which is seized upon by superstition to give it greater power.[14]

In Indian theology, the ineffable God received the name of Parabaravasta, and the priests endowed him with a wife called Parachatti, by whom he had three sons, Brahma, Vishnu and Siva. He gave to the first the power to create, to the second the power to preserve, and to the third the right to destroy. Brahma created man and woman from mud, and placed them in the *Chorcam*,[15] a delightful

[14] The marvellous has a great place in Christianity. The most interesting I have collected in my work called *Heroes of Christianity Throughout the Ages*.

[15] The Hindi word for heaven is *swarg.—Ed.*

garden where they were to live and multiply in a world of pure happiness, under the protection of Vishnu.[16]

This happiness lasted for several centuries; but Siva, the god of destruction, jealous of the work of Brahma, resolved one day to destroy it in a flood. Brahma could not entirely prevent his brother from carrying out his plan, but he had the power ceaselessly to re-create what Siva destroyed, and Vishnu was able to preserve something of his condemned creation. So Brahma made known to Sattiavarti, the holiest of all men, that there was to be a universal flood and advised him to construct a boat in which he was to take refuge with his family and with two of every kind of animal and vegetable seed. The flood came. When the waters covered the face of the earth, the vessel needed a pilot to avoid the reefs formed by mountain-tops; so Vishnu changed himself into a fish and guided the ship over the ocean of the flood. The three sons of Parabrahman, having thus exercised their several powers, then agreed to share between themselves the government of the universe, and it is since that time that life and death, good and evil, creation, destruction and rebirth follow each other on the road of time.

Another Indian belief places next to the creation of Brahma, Vishnu and Siva that of deities inferior to these three sons of the supreme God, but issued, like them, from the divine substance. These deities bear names which

[16] That Brahma, Vishnu and Siva, forming the Trimurthi, are aspects of Parameshwara, and that in the cult of any one of them is contained the worship also of the other two, is one of the basic conceptions of Hindu theological thought. This has many differing developments; the Aryan and the Tamil are two of the main groups of conceptions contributing to it. The whole Buddhist tradition is, again, entirely separate. One of the accounts of the Hindu pantheon better known to the west is that of the followers of Vishnu, the Vaishnuvite. This represents the endless serpent of the potential, Ananta, who floats in the undifferentiated waters and coils about the creator god Vishnu, as separating off from itself a ring-serpent of time, Sesha, whilst a bud comes from the side of the recumbent Vishnu and floating up to the surface opens as the thousand-petalled lotos. At its centre is the four-faced Brahma, from whom issue the detailed particulars of creation; four rivers flow from his four sides

express the innumerable attributes of divine perfection of which each one is a personification; but the supreme God gave them liberty to be faithful or unfaithful to him. Soon they divided into two camps; the one, jealous of the pre-eminence of the elder sons of the eternal Father, revolts against him under the leadership of their chief Moizazor. The other remains obedient, fights the rebels, drives them from the sky and throws them into Omdura, the Indian hell. It was then that men were created, that they might by the exercise of virtue take the places lost by the erring deities, or share their punishment if they imitated their disloyalty to the supreme gods.

These legends from the *Shasta-Bad* appear to be anterior to the ancient Hebrew accounts of the fall of the angels, the creation of man in the earthly paradise and the flood. Does that mean that the Jewish elements in our faith came from Indian sources at a time so far distant that the human memory has forgotten it? This is a problem, the key to which seems to be forever lost.[17] Whatever origin this part of our faith may have, there has been found in the oldest Indian theology references to the Trinity [*Trimurti*]; for although the idolatrous multitudes worshipped Brahma,

(cp. the rivers in Genesis). The floating petals represent the lands of the world, conceived as four main areas and centred on India; the stamens are the great mountains of the central *massif*. The Vishnu worshipper exalts the god Vishnu to be the creator, preserver and dispenser, in fact containing all the Trimurthi or aspects of the supreme being Parameshwara. Brahma is the plan and material carrying-out of creation—and, in another aspect, spirit. Siva is a later force. From a vast pillar or *lingam* (male sexual organ or its symbol) that thrusts apart heaven and earth, Siva appears from a womb-shaped rent. Siva has attached to himself a mass of functions, but fundamentally he appears to be sex in all its forms, as diverse as asceticism, the guardianship of animals, war and protective affection. He is god of the rhythm of life, both its waxing and waning, both in cosmic creation and in the individual life. He is infinitely more than the mere destructive principle to which he has often been reduced in brief western accounts.—*Ed*

[17] Since Christian's time the Biblical creation stories have been traced back to cognate origins in Babylonia and Sumeria; but still no scholar of note appears to have done any serious work on the problem of the relationship between these and other middle-eastern elements in religious traditions and the distant origins of Indian beliefs.—*Ed*.

Vishnu and Siva as three separate gods, learned priests agreed that these three names merely signified three attributes of the supreme God;[18] that this God is called Brahma when he is considered as a creator exercising his omnipotence, Vishnu when he is worshipped for his charity and goodness, and Siva when he brings his justice to bear on the crimes of man. The same theology professes that Vishnu appeared on earth in several incarnations as the saviour of mankind. Baptism is still practised in India by immersion in the sacred rivers, and equally with Christianity the Indian faiths too attribute to it the power of cleansing the soul of guilt and sin. Each year the sacrifice of a lamb is accompanied by a prayer: 'When shall the Redeemer appear who takes away the sins of the world?' This sacrifice, called *ekiam,* recalls the Hebrew paschal lamb. It is so significant and solemn a ceremony that the priests, who have taken a vow to abstain from all flesh, are released at this period from their vow, and have to consume their part of the sacrifice. There is also an offering of rice which is distributed among the congregation in the temple and which is called *Prasadam* [divine grace], a word similar to the Greek word εὐχαριστία, thanksgiving, which we translate as Eucharist. There is another resemblance [there are many more that we could cite] in confession, part of the Indian ceremony: the faithful who make the annual sacrifice of the lamb have first to make a public confession of the most humiliating sins, just as was practised by the Christians in the days of the primitive Church.

These resemblances are strange but correct.[19] We shall not discuss them here; let us not endeavour to find out if the Indian dogmas could have been known to the Egyptian Magi, from whom Moses probably borrowed some of the

[18] See note 16, p. 29.—*Ed.*

[19] These are to be found in the *Memoirs of the English Society of Calcutta*; in a letter to the learned Huet, Bishop of Avranches, from the Jesuit P. Bouchet; and in the corroborative notes added by Chateaubriand to *The Genius of Christianity*.

features of Genesis concerning the flood and the Garden of Eden;[20] nor whether the creation of the first Christian rites was taken, with the elements of the new cult, from the same source. The dignity of Christianity is not here in question, and if it were, we should be forced to accept its obvious superiority.

The Christian tradition, considered apart from the obscure metaphysics of Plato on the triune essence and from the Mosaic legend of the temptation [obviously Indian],[21] shows us the first human pair created by one God in a state of innocence and perfection that made them rulers over all things on earth. Their primitive destiny, which was in their own hands, was to elevate them and all their posterity to a state of pure and endless bliss through the immortal progress of their intelligence in the knowledge of divine wonders. One condition had to be observed —obedience, the filial virtue, an act of gratitude and love towards their heavenly Father, an act that must be free; it would have had no merit otherwise, for it is through his freedom that man is the image of God.

The biblical Adam [*Adimo* in Indian], led astray by pride, abused this sacred liberty. Instead of sitting at the feet of his Creator, like an obedient child who hopes, waits and receives everything from the wisdom of the father, according to his needs and his rights, he ventured to cross

[20] The discovery of the city of the 'heretic' Pharaoh Aakhuenaten or Akhnaten at Tel-el-Amarna, with his monotheistic religion and hymn to the sun-disk the Aten, so similar to certain of David's alleged psalms, now sheds a flood of suggestive light upon the origin of the Hebrew religion. See Arthur Weigall's *Akhnaten*. Akhnaten's reign was perhaps during the 1450—1400 B.C. period. His original name was Nefertsheperurauaenra Aten meri Amenhetep IV, which he changed to symbolise his break with the Theban priesthood and gods.—*Ed.*

[21] In the *Chorcam*, declare the Indian sages, is a marvellous tree which gives immortality. The demigods were able to send to sleep the giant serpent guarding it and tasted the forbidden fruit in order to gain the privileges of the superior gods. On his awakening, the serpent became so furious that he emitted venom which poisoned the Chorcam. The demigods were about to die, but a good spirit Chiren pitied their misery and taking human form swallowed the monster's poison, thus saving the miscreants.—See note 15, p. 28.—*Ed.*

the threshold of the mysteries to which all approach had been forbidden him under pain of death. The result of his disobedience was made clear to him: he defied the warning, and this fault was punished by all our sorrows. God could not prevent the abuse of the liberty with which he had crowned the faculties of man. His absolute justice imposed the punishment for the crime: but at the same time His infinite goodness promised a Saviour for those who would repent. This is the tradition which, in various mythical forms, opens the history of humanity. 'The knot of our condition,' Pascal says, 'twists and turns in that abyss, so that man is more inconceivable without this mystery than the mystery is inconceivable without man. It is not possible that an absurd fable should have become the tradition of the universe.'

When Adam descended into the regions of suffering and stopped to measure with his eye the distance covered on the road of expiation, he looked around him terrified. A great storm was following him. The creatures who had obeyed him now fled his approach; only the woman, his companion, remained at his side in tears. The thorns of malediction lay across the field of life; the flowers hung on their stalks, the leaves turned yellow on the trees and foretold their death, and the earth on which they were scattered was the first bed of pain where the first sinful man was sorry for the loss of God. Of the life of happiness there now only remained a memory, a dream. Of all the wonders of his being, only one was left, the power to lift his eyes to the heavens and cry to God at each hour of peril: a perpetual act of faith which suffering teaches us, a melancholy recollection of the lost land, an involuntary homage that the ungodly himself pays to heaven, in every language, when the lightning strikes at his feet.

God had withdrawn his visible presence from the world; the stars spread across his face a veil of darkened flame. But, while evil was opening up the sepulchre of the world, the promise of grace had resounded through the centuries. Behind the tears shed by the first woman on the first-born of her sorrows Adam saw a smile and gave blessings to the Eternal, for Eve's smile foretold the coming of Mary, and the Virgin Birth which was to be the sign of the new alliance of man with God.

In order to ascend again to the divine mountain-tops, humanity had to descend to the depths of the abyss before climbing through one test after another the opposite slope. Soon the race of Adam opened the doors of crime by the hand of his first-born, and the first murderer, armed by envy, reddened the earth with innocent blood. God marked with a sign the forehead of the fratricide, condemning him to the abhorrence of all peoples and ages. He made him a wanderer on the face of the earth, so that the memory of his forfeit was left by his remorse in every land. Cain became the ancestor of vices that were to be the undoing of primitive humanity.

As iniquity gained ground after the death of Adam, on all the habited earth there was, after sixteen centuries, only one family without spot or stain worthy of the Creator's clemency. The extent of evil, overflowing on all sides, destroyed the moral equilibrium and then overthrew the balance of nature. The great inundation fell from the heavens and rose from the depths of the sea to drown the perverted race of men. In vain did humanity seek refuge in the high places of the world: there was everywhere destruction. The ocean pursued mankind to the highest peaks and, lifting still higher its funereal immensity, allowed only the frail vessel with its virtuous family to sail the stormy solitudes.

This is the second tradition in our cosmic history.[22]

---

[22] Recent work on the approach and final disintegration of a former moon or moons of the earth, possibly within the period when early men were already upon earth, may revise former ideas on the incredibility or merely local character of this world flood. See *Built Before the Flood* by H. S. Bellamy. In brief, the theory, backed up by the competent mathematical and physical calculations of the Viennese astronomer, Hoerbiger, alleges that several moons have been captured by the earth from amongst smaller

VII

BEFORE this catastrophe, a man it was said could live as long as ten centuries. But afterwards Death, armed with every weapon of destruction, came soon and without warning; it no longer counted for anything among the fresh generations who arose and followed the path of evil. A single murder had opened the first tomb, in the east; and war took murder to the uttermost parts of the earth. As soon as man breathed the smoke of battle, he made an art out of destruction and sought in it a means of self-glorification. But a darkness of the spirit descended on the fury of his passions. In practising violence, he claimed to find his model and excuse in the animals now grown wild and savage as himself.

As at the time of the deluge, again a single family remained to typify patriarchal life. Its head, Abraham, a simple shepherd, left Chaldea on divine inspiration to become the father of a new race, the ancestor of the Man-God who, in the fulness of time, was to change the face of the earth, and the signal of whose coming the Magi awaited on the Mount of Victory, century after century.

But around the tiny sanctuary of the Magi the cult of materialism had invaded the furthest provinces and lands. The pseudo-sacred legends of Brahma, Vishnu and Siva had taken on the most monstrous forms that the disordered minds of a brutish people could devise. Just as, under the rays of a torrid sun, from far and wide through

---

planets, that each has slowly circled into the earth causing at a near approach immense tides and finally a girdle-tide sweeping round the equatorial region at a great height, thereby denuding the further northern and southern hemispheres of water. The satellite speeding up its centripetal course would by the ordinary laws of physics disintegrate at a certain distance from the earth and rain down upon it in colossal fragments from a westerly direction. The theory would explain many otherwise seemingly inexplicable phenomena, but it is not accepted as yet in 'official' astronomical circles, although the gradual approach of the present moon to the earth is an established fact. A further explanation of traditions is essayed in *Worlds in Collision* by I. Velikovsky.—*Ed.*

an immense system of roots and branches the sap is brought
which in temperate climates hardly keeps alive the few
puny trees, even so the exuberant fecundity of the eastern
plains inspired in Indian idolators the colossal personifica-
tions of the forces that destroy, in their eternal struggle with
the forces that create. This is the source of the fanatical
adoration of evil as incarnated in Kali, the goddess of murder and wife of Siva, whose sacred sect of stranglers under
the name of Thuggs persists to this day.[23] Another ferocious
mode of religiosity called *satee* still sends widows to the
pyre, enriching with their possessions the insatiable avarice
of the priestly caste.

The Thuggs, the secret priests of Kali, have formed
since time immemorial an association with widespread rami-
fications, with its own so-called sacred laws, its occult signs of
recognition. It long defied attempts at repression. The
traveller, who had good reason to fear, commonly joined
a caravan, which however was often composed of the very
thuggs he hoped to avoid. Whenever the authorities succeeded in apprehending a few of these fanatics they accepted
punishment without trying to deny guilt. One of their
leaders, called Durga, fell into the hands of the English
about twenty years ago and was accused of murdering a
trader who was travelling to the province of Oudh; he himself gave the details of the ambush that he had prepared with
imperturbable sang-froid. 'Our brothers,' he said to the
judges, 'had learned that the traveller was to leave with an
escort of fifty men. We simply formed a band three times
as large and went to wait for him in one of the jungles
which he would have to pass through and in which there
was a statue of the goddess Kali. As we are forbidden by
our priests to enter into armed combat, because our sacrifices are only acceptable to Kali if the victims are overtaken
by sudden death, we gave a welcome to the travellers and
offered to accompany them, and thus give each other pro-

[23] See note 16, p. 29. Kali is one of several mates of Siva.—*Ed.*

tection from all danger. They accepted without suspicion; it only remained for us to choose a suitable moment. Two of us went with each traveller, ostensibly for conversation and to render many of the small services which make a long journey pleasant.

'After we had been together three days, we were firm friends; there was no time to be lost. I persuaded them to strike camp two hours before dawn to avoid travelling during the heat of the day. We left at the proposed time, each traveller walking between two Thuggs. It was not completely dark: there was a starlit twilight when I gave the sign to our brothers. Immediately, one of the two Thuggs who accompanied the victim threw a lassoo round his neck while the other seized him by the legs and overturned him. This movement was carried out in each group with the swiftness of lightning. We dragged the bodies into a neighbouring river-bed, then left them. One man escaped us; but the goddess Kali is watching him, his fate will overtake him sooner or later. As for myself, I was once a pearl at the bottom of the ocean; today I am a prisoner. The poor pearl is taken: it will be pierced and hung on a string, and it will float unhappily between heaven and earth. That is the wish of the great goddess Kali, who will punish me for not offering up to her the number of bodies that was her due. Oh black goddess! thy promises are never empty ones, thou whose name is *Koun-Kali* [man-eater], thou who ceaselessly drinkest the blood of demons and of mortal men!'

Similarly the river Thugg insinuated himself into the traveller's favour and invited him to board a boat whose captain and crew were members of the association. At a pre-arranged signal, he was strangled and thrown overboard. Many Indian families used to lead this life of homicidal adventure, which did not have robbery as its prime motive but sheer fanaticism.

A still more horrible crime and a cowardly one was the induced suicide of widows after the death of their husbands. The hypocritical greed of priests always managed to acquire the whole or part of the inheritance by imposing, in the name of heaven, on the woman's moral helplessness. 'Offer yourself for suttee,' the Brahmins of her village or town would tell her, 'and you will deliver your husband from hell; you will open for him the gates of immortal happiness. You will purify your father's and your mother's family. If you refuse to sacrifice yourself for the ones you love so well, you will be overwhelmed by disgrace in this world and endless torture in the next. Your body will be re-born in the shape of a filthy animal and in all its future transmigrations you will be born into shame and cursing.'

Such is not the language of the religion of Brahma; in no passage in the sacred books of India is this immolation prescribed or recommended. The priestly cast invented it for personal gain, and until quite recently it was well supported by custom. What could a poor widow do, overwhelmed by the exhortations of the priests and of heirs eager to share her belongings? If she refused the fatal honour the mob often became the servant of her executioners. For the building of her pedestal of martyrdom a site was chosen beside the nearest river or stream. . . Four tall beams planted in the earth form the corners of a square. They support four thick planks firmly held by mortices. Between these beams is built a pile of logs in such a manner as to leave an empty space in the centre which is filled with chips of dry wood and resin. Around and above this pile are heaped branches that will burn easily and brightly. The roof of this funeral temple is made of planks covered with turf. The dead man's body is placed on the pile of wood and the widow lies down beside him. The crowd gathers round to prevent any chance of her escape; if she tries, the priests force her back into the flames with bamboo poles.

Thevenot, a French traveller, one day saw one of these wretched victims brought with great pomp to the funeral pyre. Her face was calm; her very weak intelligence did not allow her to imagine the atrocious sufferings she was about to endure. Some Christians who had been attracted by this sacrifice approached her and asked her if she was dying of her own wish. 'Yes,' she replied, with a sort of pride that amazed them. The songs of the Brahmins burst forth with convulsive enthusiasm, bringing their conversation to an end. The procession went three times round the pyre, after which the widow climbed slowly, but without hesitation, the steps that led to the summit of her tomb. A Brahmin then went up to her and handed her a flaming torch, so that she might set fire herself to the four corners of the pyre.

At first she looked with a calm eye on the flames that darted among the dry boughs, but when the heat grew more intense and she felt the first attacks of pain, she tried to leap out of the circle of flame. At once the Brahmins brought down the roof on her head; but the energy of despair lent her superhuman strength, and, leaping out of the flames, she ran towards the river. The Brahmins ran after her. In spite of the efforts of the Christians, who were outnumbered, they brought her back to the pyre that was now well alight and looked like an enormous furnace. A short struggle took place between the unfortunate woman and her executioners; the crowd screamed and yelled; the Christians still made attempts to save her, at the risk of perishing themselves, when finally three sturdy Brahmins, lifting her from the earth to which she clung, flung her into the middle of the flames. She still struggled for a minute, uttering piercing shrieks, until the Brahmins pulled away the burning beams. . .[24]

After such revolting scenes we can no longer interest ourselves in the spectacle of the lesser Indian superstitions. Let us leave the Fakir crouched in his cave under a blazing sun, or lying on a bed of nails; let us turn aside in disgust from those madmen who bury themselves alive or who seek their murderous idols under the chariots of Siva and Kali.[25]

[24] A very similar example here follows.—*Ed.*

[25] In south India the Juggernaut, the huge car under which fanatics used to cast themselves, is the ceremonial vehicle in the festival of Kali.—*Ed.*

Let us abandon to their own obscurity fables that are as absurd as they are cruel. The important thing to observe is that one still meets in India practitioners, inheritors of the doctrines of Magic [the ancient wisdom] who, in sacred schools, teach their disciples that the real idols are only mis-understood figures veiling the hierarchy of the forces of nature, forces governed by a supreme Being who is the sole author of all things.

VIII

IF we go on to Persia, which for a long time held a prominent place in the history of the ancient east, the Magi still appear to us as distant patriarchs of a world lost in the mists of time.

The cult of the Sun or of Fire, considered under the name of Mithra as the principle of universal life, forms here the basis of a primitive mythology which disappeared before the invasions of the Muslims or Musselmans,[26] but not without leaving traces of its contemplative spirit. The Quran could not, at one fell swoop, destroy the ancient national religion, the daughter of the centuries; the old myths of Hurmuzd [often spelt in the west as Ormuzd], genius of Good, and Ahriman, genius of Evil, both fathers of an innumerable army of angels or lesser ministers, amal-gamated with the mixture of Judaism and Christianity from which Muhammad allegedly derived his religious system.

God, say the modern Persian theologians, first created the sun and the moon to illuminate space while he was making the earth. When his labours were ended, he ordered the angel Gabriel to rub the face of the moon with his wing, and that dead star shone by reflection from the sun. God created 180 sources of fire in the east, and the same

[26] *Muslim* = one who believes in the conceptions of the Islamic religion and follows them almost to the point of ritual technicalities in the life-pattern and conduct of his prophet Muhammad. *Musselman* = one who is recognised as a follower of the Islamic faith in a general sense.—*Ed.*

number in the west. The sun during its course passes through all these sources, each one protected by a celestial spirit.

Above the firmament God hung a great ocean, not a drop of which falls on the earth. The orbs of the Sun and the Moon, of Saturn, Jupiter, Mars, Venus and Mercury, swim in this celestial sea piloted by guardian angels: and when light passes away, it is because a black angel has spread its wings between the sky and the earth. And it shall be so until the number of the elect predestined by God shall be complete. Then the angel of judgment will sound his trumpet and all the dead will rise from their graves to receive the reward or the punishment due to them for their days on earth.

From earth to heaven an invisible bridge is thrown, over which all the dead must pass. When they are crossing this bridge, which is finer than a hair, their actions will be weighed by the angel Istafil, guardian of the Book of Fates. God is merciful to those whom he chooses. The rejected fall into a bottomless pit, and the elect see opening before them a garden of delights set in the seventh heaven, above the throne of God. In it there grows the tree of happiness, which offers boughs laden with fruit for the pleasure of the faithful. This tree is so immense that the swiftest horseman could not ride out of its shadows in a hundred years. The rivers of the sacred garden spring from its roots; their waters, whiter than milk, more fragrant than amber, gives complete forgetfulness of all pain. Each one of the elect receives in this paradise a separate home; there he is surrounded by seventy-two wives created from the purest musk and endowed with eternal virginity. Young boys more radiant than the dawn present him every day with three hundred golden dishes, each containing a different food, for the appetite of the blessed guests of the All-High is increased a hundredfold and everything they eat is dissolved in a perfume that scents the air of paradise. But these are merely the vulgar rewards offered to the humblest

of the elect. As for the delights reserved for those who enjoy
God's favours to an even higher degree, they are, say the
learned doctors, beyond all powers of description; the most
ineffable is to contemplate, face to face, in perpetual ecstasy
the supreme beauty of the Divine.

In contrast to this sensual theory is the wisdom of the
Sufis, who claim to preserve in its integrity the ancient
doctrine of the Magi. Despising the voluptuous Muslims,
they practise an abstinence whose excessive severity is
rewarded by hallucination. Their name Sufi means *clothed
in wool* and symbolises their renunciation of even the most
innocent satisfactions of material life. Many of them say
they are privileged to communicate intimately with God.

According to their theology, the supreme Creator flows
like a river through all his works. The emanations of his
divine essence, like the rays of the sun, are continually being
shed and re-absorbed. It is towards this re-absorption in
God, the immaterial principle of our whole being, that all
our efforts should be directed. The universal life that makes
nature fruitful is not the work of God, but simply a part
of his being that infuses everything. Re-absorption therefore constitutes the annihilation of human personality in
the divine source. The supreme bliss for the Sufis consists
in a total insensibility that neither the splendours of creation nor the wonders of the intellectual sphere can any
longer move; and this apotheosis of self-abasement is reached
in four stages.

The first is called *humanity*. To this class belong those
disciples who practise rigorously, in a spirit of simple obedience, the precepts and rites of the cult to which they belong
by birth and nationality. The Sufis consider this mechanical
obedience as the guiding-rein that holds mankind on the
path of law and order.

The second stage is called *the way of perfection*. The
adept, having given proof of blind obedience, is authorised
to cut himself off from all exterior forms, in order to practise the adoration of God 'in spirit and in truth'. And this

cannot be achieved, say the masters of the art, without much virtue and courage. In order to merit the permission to renounce all exterior practices in the cult, the disciple must have arrived, through sheer devotion, at the knowledge of the nature of the Divine.

The third stage is one of communication through *contemplative intuition,* which is a knowledge equal to that possessed by the angels; each disciple thereby becomes perfect in communion with his Creator. Unfortunately, in this doctrine the Sufis who claim such close union with the Divine have not even been able to reach a state of harmony among themselves. Some, called the Inspired, hold that God descends into their privileged soul, a favour that they refuse their dissident brethren; and these dissidents, called Unitarians, uphold on the contrary that God is one with every soul. They compare God with fire, and our souls with embers, so that, by virtue of the ubiquity of the flame-God, every ember-soul takes fire at its contact and becomes flame in its turn.[27]

A large number of Sufis teach that the universe is un-created and therefore indestructible. Some claim to have the power to raise the dead. A life of solitude, mortified by asceticism, predisposes them to ecstasy, the precursor of that moral annihilation in which they set their sad conception of eternal bliss.

Apart from the Sufis we find another remnant, also much debased, of the ancient astrology that flourished under the Magi. The traveller Chardin tells us that the King of Persia, Shah Abbas, spent every year a sum equivalent to four millions in our money on his court astrologers. More recently, in 1800 Sir John Malcolm, British Ambassador at Teheran, met two royal magicians on his arrival in the city who were charged with the task of noting the precise second of his entry through the city gates. One of them took his horse's bridle to regulate its pace; the other held a watch.

[27] The fourth stage consists in living in a state of eternity whilst still in the flesh.—*Ed.*

And so the English diplomat's entry took place, it was said, under good auspices. . .

A few years later Malcolm, recalled to England, decided to consult one of these wise men on the good or evil fortune that might accompany his return. The horoscope predicted a violent storm, which the traveller would survive only to fall into bondage on the inhospitable coast of Africa. 'I should be indeed unhappy were I so weak as to believe you,' said Malcolm to the seer, 'for such a prediction would make a wretched torture of my crossing, which will last several months. And if your oracle is lying, as I sincerely hope it is, I shall not hesitate to send your king proof of my safe arrival, to disillusion him of his foolish confidence in you.'

The wise man shrugged his shoulders at this little threat and these, according to Malcolm, are the words he used to justify his art: 'If you are saved from the fate I have predicted, it will be because, during the crossing, a salutary fear of the judgment of God will have raised up your soul on the wings of prayer to the throne of his divine providence. The prophet Jesus, seated with some of his disciples at the gates of Jerusalem, saw a woodcutter pass by who came out of the city singing on his way to work, Jesus said: "There is a man who would not sing if he knew that he would be dead this evening." The evening came; Jesus was still seated in the same place and the woodcutter, who had not heard his words, came back the same way, his axe over his shoulder, singing as before. The disciples murmured among themselves against the prophet's words, and were about to desert him. Jesus, divining their thoughts, said to them gently: "That man was about to die; but he encountered in the forest a poor starving man to whom he gave half his bread. As a reward for this good deed God spared his life. Go up to this man and open the bundle of wood he is carrying on his back." The disciples obeyed, and a serpent was found hidden in the bundle: thus was the divine word of Jesus verified. So go in peace, man of the

Setting Sun, and never again call false the signs written in the heavens by the hand of the Eternal.'

Malcolm neglects to tell us whether he profited from this strange lesson; but we must record it here and recognise that the adepts of the high art of Magic, among whom are numbered ancient and modern astrologers, only consider those men bound by fate who turn from God and deliver themselves up to the course of events.

Fatalism, on the other hand, is the fundamental point of the Muslim religion, whose very name, Islam, signifies *obedience to God,* not in the sense of filial obedience to his providence, but in blind, necessary, absolute resignation to inevitable destiny. A Turk, an Arab, a Persian, struck down by some misfortune, seeks what consolation he can in the words: *It was written.*[28] However, as such passiveness in the human spirit instinctively shocks the least enlightened minds, superstition, in default of philosophy, attempts to make its own protest. Thus one meets in Persia, as in India, Turkey and Africa, many people who cover themselves with amulets, some attached to the arms, between the elbow and the shoulder, some hung round the neck or round the waist. Some of these charms are engraved on stones and encased in small golden, silver or copper boxes, according to the wealth of their possessors. They are hung from the necks of valuable horses to protect them from accidents; over thresholds, to keep out thieves; at the entrances to bazaars, to attract customers. There are itinerant dervishes who make a living by soliciting persons celebrated for their saintliness and begging them to write and sign a short prayer on a long strip of paper. When they have acquired in this way forty or fifty prayer texts with

[28] According to its exponents, Islam is not a fatalistic religion for fatalism would entirely abstract the virtue from moral choice and freewill. It believes in good and evil, and that each individual is responsible for his or her own actions, which are rewarded in accordance with deserts. *Kismet =* the share or quota of good and evil allotted to each during life, of which he or she can make much or little. There is no basic disunity over these concepts of Islam amongst the Sufi adepts.—*Ed.*

their authentic signatures, it is easy for them to earn quite
a lucrative income by reciting this chaplet of prayers. They
also have charms against snake-bites and scorpions, and
especially against the influence of the evil eye, which is a
kind of spell that the Persians fear above all. They also
consider it unlucky for a mother to praise a child's beauty
in its own presence; it is unlucky to congratulate a man
on his riches or his successes; and each time a woman shows
herself in the streets, on re-entering the house she must
perform certain purifying rites which are intended to
neutralise the effect of dangerous glances which may have
fallen upon her.

IX

I have touched only briefly on India and Persia in
my search for the fugitive traces of the Magi. In the first
of these countries they appear only in the vague form of
a legendary tradition, and in the second as a sacerdotal
revolution in which the priests tried to seize power after
the death of King Cambyses 521 B.C. [by the Behistan
inscription]. This attempt had only a brief success and was
overcome by the massacre of the Magi; it has left in the
annals of history only a date, written in blood and called
the *Magophony* [522 B.C.].

If we go on to Chaldea, Nineveh and ancient Babylon, conquered by the Persians in 539 B.C., we find the Magi
taking a more prominent position in the social state and
exercising more definite powers over science and art. But
in its institutions, monuments and customs Chaldea, which
was the cradle of Assyrian domination, is in so many ways
like Egypt and exhibits such resemblances of philosophic
and religious doctrine, that, in order to avoid repetitions,
we must concentrate all our attention on Egypt.

It is in Egypt that we must look for the illumination
that Asia still withholds. Let us not forget that Egypt gave
the world, in her renowned schools at Alexandria, the most

fruitful and extensive university ever known to the human mind. Under the reign of Ptolemy Philadelphus [285-247 B.C.] Alexandria became a second Athens. All the distinguished scholars of Europe, Africa and the Orient seem to have been drawn to it. We know that in the seventh century A.D. the library at Alexandria, the *Mother of Books,* was burned to the ground by the Arabs;[29] but copyists had fortunately preserved the writings of the most illustrious thinkers, and to these obscure clerks we owe the precious traditions that are links in the great philosophic chain.

Many people regard as fables the accounts in the ancients of the great number of Egyptian towns. Their wealth seems no less incredible. There was not one which was not filled with wonderful temples and splendid palaces, in whose immense galleries were displayed sculpture and painting which the Greeks took as models. Thebes especially outshone in grandeur and luxury all the cities of the ancient world. Its hundred gates have been sung by Homer, and in lyrical exaggeration it was said that ten thousand warriors could simultaneously pass through each gate. The Greeks and Romans celebrated it as one of the wonders of the world, yet they only saw its ruins.

Fayyûm, a sort of appendix to the Nile Valley, was as intensively developed as the Delta. There it was that, probably sometime between 2200 and 2000 B.C., the Pharaoh Enmaātra Amenemhat III constructed Lake Moeris or El-Fayyûm, whose sixty square leagues receive the surplus waters from the river in years of excessive flooding. In the centre of the lake rose two pyramids 600 feet high, 200 feet being beneath water. The statues of Amenemhat and his wife stood on their tops. These gigantic works were yet

[29]   The temple-museum of the Serapeum, filled with art treasures, was destroyed by a fanatical Christian, Theophilus, Patriarch of Alexandria; the separate Serapeum library, supposed to have held some 300,000 books, was burnt by 'Amr ibn el-Asi in 641 A.D. at the order of Khalif 'Omar. The story is that the manuscripts sufficed to heat the city's public baths for six months.—*Ed.*

merely tombs for their authors. On the lake shore stood
another wonder called the Labyrinth, of the same period.
It was a chain of twelve courts in regular formation repre-
seting the twelve signs of the Zodiac. Each court had thirty
rooms, a number equal to the degrees of each sign. This
edifice, crowded with mysterious and sacred images, was
built over subterranean rooms no less magnificent awaiting
the mummies of future dynasties.[30]

Is it not an admirable spectacle to see every year at
the summer solstice a great river suddenly change colour,
take on that sanguine tint of which the Bible speaks and
increase in volume until the autumn equinox, when its
waters overflow their banks; then, for a similar period,
gradually return to its former level? The ancient Egyptians
thought it was a miracle and adored the Nile as a god, Hāpi.
But the Magi ascribed to a more reliable providence the
regulating source of this annual fertilisation; they knew
that the torrential rains that fall on southern Abyssinia
begin always in the month of March and flow slowly down
towards the Nile. The river therefore took three months
to overflow in the month of June and three months to return
to its original level. But for the people it was thought better
that they should believe in a miraculous event and give
thanks to Heaven.

[31]Sixty years ago the only information we had about
Egypt was from sketches of the ruins made at random by a
few travellers in the military posts set up during a short
and fruitless occupation. To-day, thanks to the progress in
archaeology, we are able to peep through the curtain that
shrouded the pharaonic mysteries. The deciphering of hiero

[30] According to Herodotus, the labyrinth had twelve enclosed courts, with fifteen
hundred rooms above and the same number below ground. He describes the
upper ones as 'surpassing all human works'. Each court was colonnaded. See
Herod. Book II, 148.—Ed.

[31] For general account of Egyptian history, customs and traditions, the best
book still seems to be Sir E. Wallis Budge's 'Dwellers on the Nile', in its
revised and enlarged form 1926. Christian's narrative, embodying the knowledge of his day, has been only amended on points of fact and names.—Ed.

glyphs has shed additional light on the information given us by Herodotus, Diodorus Siculus, Plutarch, Iamblicus, Appollonius of Tyana and other ancient writers, and tell us decisively that the first inhabitants of Egypt made up a sacred republic, all of whose powers, institutions, sciences and arts were in the hands of the governing priesthood. The Magi formed the nation's highest class; the warriors were in the second class; and the people, the masses of labourers, merchants and workmen, were grouped below these. The revolution that established royal power was military in nature; it seized material power, but could make no progress without spiritual guidance, and all spiritual guidance was in the hands of the priests. There was therefore a natural compromise between the Pharaohs and the Magi which gave the latter authority over the triple domain of legislation, public administration, and speculative and practical sciences. The monarchy took over the government of Egypt exactly as it had been organised by the Magi: it was made to last for a length of time unequalled by any other empire.

This constitution of Egypt was as monumental as its architecture. It was based on religion; its three floors were property, education and work, and its roof the equality of all before the law. The priesthood, in the topmost social rank, shared the possession of considerable sources of revenue. The temples collected taxes, in wheat or in money, on all cultivated lands, and in kind on all vineyards and pasture land. There was also a personal and property tax. The dead themselves, installed in their immense subterranean necropoli, guarded by priests, paid, through their families or heirs, an annual levy. Royalty in its turn made a previous deduction from all ecclesiastical sources of revenue, and amassed enormous wealth.

The Magi, a body sacred by virtue of the hierarchy of its functions, intermarried; their sons and daughters never married into the other classes and this was a means of preserving the *esprit de corps* which was the source of priestly influence and power. The young girls, until the time of their marriage, were educated in the temples and consecrated to the service of the Divinity. The sons studied from childhood to maturity. Geography, natural history, physics, chemistry, mechanics, medicine, surgery, music, drawing, architecture, painting, sculpture, law, moral philosophy, vulgar and sacred astronomy, religious rites, the mysteries of hieratic symbolism—these were all parts of the chain of general knowledge that they had to acquire. Thereafter they specialised in one or another branch of these studies, according to the special aptitudes they might display. All found a career, thanks to the wide diversity of professions which were so specialised that, for example, each doctor had to devote himself to one particular malady, each judge to one specific point of jurisprudence, in order to excel in practice as well as in theory.

The laws stated that this people, above all other peoples, was the one which had preserved in its greatest splendour the primitive wisdom of humanity. The Egyptians, a grave and serious nation, have had the distinction of being referred to as the most grateful among men; they were of course the most sociable. He who, when able to save the life of a fellow creature, renounced his duty, either through cowardice or indifference, was considered to be as guilty as a murderer. In cases where a man was powerless against the use of violence, he had at least to denounce the aggressor, and there were punishments for the witness who remained silent.

A man convicted of calumny suffered the same punishment as that with which he had intended to visit the innocent man. Criminal assault upon a woman was punished with mutilation. The death sentence was imposed for perjury and murder; and parents who killed their child were compelled to hold its body in their arms for three days and nights.

Women in pregnancy, accused of a crime, were not put to judgment before their delivery, so that the child, if the mother were condemned, would not be dishonoured and might enter life during the presumed innocence of his mother.

A debtor could only discharge his debts with his own goods, never by offering his person for imprisonment. One was allowed to borrow with one's father's mummy as security; but in cases of non-payment, the borrower and his children were refused the honour of a religious sepulchre.

Each year one had to state one's place of abode and one's means of subsistence to a magistrate; the death penalty was imposed on the citizen or the stranger who could not account for his income or for his profession.

Marriages could be dissolved by law, because it was held that to force two people to live together who no longer love each other is to try to unite a dead body with a live one. The law did not recognise any child as illegitimate, for all creatures are equal in the sight of their Creator.

No citizen was allowed to be a useless burden to the state; the law assigned each family to its proper class and to its rank within that class, and this position was unchanged from father to son. No one could hold more than one office or profession, nor change it without proving his ability for the new one; but all manner of being useful to society was equally honoured, and no one could without criminal consequences despise men whose work, whatever it might be, contributed to the public good. By this means, all the sciences and all the arts were allowed to attain their full perfection.

These laws were lessons to the childhood and youth of all classes. It was a consolation when one died to bequeath one's good name to the estimation of one's contemporaries because, of all earthly goods, it is the only one that death cannot take from us. But it was not allowed to praise all the dead equally and to write panegyrics indiscriminately on tombs; the backing of public opinion was needed if such honour were to be done to their memory.

The Pharaohs themselves were not exempt from this posthumous justice; their reigns were judged by the tri-

bunal of posterity, and, if condemned, the mortal remains
of a sovereign were not accorded the solemnity of a state
funeral. This custom of judging the reign of a dead king
made the rulers of the state remember that they only held
their power by the grace of God and that, if their majesty
put them above other men in their life-time, death levelled
them.

During far the greatest period of its recorded history,
the political administration of most of Egypt was divided
between three sacred cities, Thebes, Memphis and Heliopolis. Their three great sacerdotal colleges flourished, with
Thebes in supreme command. Each college sent ten judges
to the tribunal at Thebes, the oldest becoming president.
Ten books contained the code of laws and each judge
studied one; thus three judges in the tribunal of thirty
knew the same book thoroughly, each belonging to a different college. Cases were presented in writing; prosecution,
defence, witnesses on both sides argued pen in hand. No
words were allowed, lest the judges might be swayed by
eloquence. Notes passed from hand to hand in a religious
silence; convictions were recorded by a secret ballot; then
the President consulted the book of laws to pronounce
sentence.

In matters of small importance, plaintiffs could have
their cases dealt with by the Magus of their district or village; he was the equivalent of our justice of the peace; and
as every judgment was a religious act, performed before a
statue of Seti, a form of Isis (c.p. Sanskrit *satya*, 'supreme
truth'), appeals to the supreme tribunal were only granted
in exceptional circumstances.

By means of settlements in Greece and Asia, Egypt
promoted civilisation. The great law-givers and philosophers
of antiquity all admitted that they went to Egypt to learn
wisdom. Peace, that majestic quality of all great states, was
held in honour there because peace, the companion of justice, is also the nurse of genius. When Egypt had her first
war-like Pharaoh, in the XIXth Dynasty, she said good-

bye to the traditions that had laid the foundations of her greatness. When she conscripted soldiers for ends other than those of defence, she taught her neighbours to measure her strength and to estimate the extent of her armaments. At first, Egypt owed her great victories, taking her even to the Ganges, to the fame which preceded her. Conquering races who fight without being drawn to war by any necessity in their nature only teach other races how to conquer them. Sooner or later they fall, conquered in their turn, with their trophies, among the ruins that they tried to build up again: that will always be what human glory comes to. The glory that was Egypt was to disappear under the heel of the Persians, as the Persians, in their turn, disappeared before the Greeks, who then themselves fell to Rome; and Rome, finally, fell to the barbarian hordes, bringing a new world with them on the waves of their irresistible ocean.

X

IT is to the Egyptians that we owe our method of dividing the year according to the apparent progress of the sun and the moon into months and weeks that make up a total of 365 days.[32] It is to them, too, that we owe the first alphabet representing sounds by graphic signs. These ideas have become universal among all civilised peoples. The temples of the Magi had on their roofs observatories consecrated to astronomical studies.[33] These Magi when studying the skies must have built up for themselves a traditional theogony. It originated from their lawgiver Hermes-Thoth. The books

[32] Until their contacts with the Greeks the Egyptian calendar was seriously at fault, and was reformed only in the time of Ptolemy III, 247-222 B.C.—*Ed.*

[33] Egyptians were not systematic sky-students like the Babylonians, but rather star observers who believed in their influence upon people and events. The Zodiac was not theirs but was introduced to them by the Greeks, who appear to have imported it from Chaldea—which in turn had learnt it from Sumeria-Babylonia, the system at each migration changing considerably.—*Ed.*

written by this Hermes were very numerous, and each one was devoted to a science or an art. They were destroyed in the Egyptian revolutions except for a few fragments of two treatises, one of which is called *Pymander* [divine thought], and the other *Asclepios,* from the name of a disciple for whom he had written it. However deplorable we may find the loss of such precious original documents, the little that has survived suffices to prove that the most ancient civilisation in Egypt was founded on lofty spiritual heights.

The *Pymander*[34] considers God to be omnipotence balanced by eternally active intelligence and by absolute wisdom. The *Asclepios* has as its object God in His relationships with the universe and with man.

'None of our thoughts,' says Hermes-Thoth to his disciple, 'could apprehend the nature of God, nor any language define it. What is incorporeal, invisible, without form, cannot be grasped by our senses; what is eternal cannot be measured by the short rule of time : God is therefore ineffable. He is the absolute truth, the absolute power; and the unchangeable absolute cannot be comprehended on this earth.

'God can, it is true, communicate to a few of the elect the faculty of raising themselves above natural things in order to perceive some of the radiance of his supreme perfection; but these elect are unable to find words to translate into ordinary speech the immaterial vision that has made them tremble with delight. They may be able to explain to humanity the secondary causes of the creations that pass before our eyes like the images of universal life : but the first cause remains shrouded in mystery, and we shall only begin to understand it when we have passed through death.

'This death is for many men a dreadful phantom; and yet it is no more than our deliverance from the bonds of matter. The body is merely a garment of the inferiority

---

[34] Ποιμανδρες. English spelling Pymander or Pimandir; both are incorrect, but we adopt the more usual.—*Ed.*

that prevents us from rising in the worlds of progress; it is a chrysalis that opens when we are ripe for a larger and higher life. Look at the flower that charms our eyes and makes us drowse with its perfumes: it was born from a seed fallen in the earth. Even so when our body returns to this earth from which it was taken, the spirit that it held captive is breathed out like a perfume into the heavens; for the spirit was contained in the body, just as the perfume was in the seed.'

In the *Pymander*, Hermes is represented beneath the veils of solitude and night, suffering the agonies of a troubled slumber. He seems to feel his soul wandering in an endless circle, and that his thought is unable to rise in prayer towards the author of all things. At the height of this moral anguish, he suddenly sees glimmering and becoming brighter in the darkness a figure that, as it grows more and more radiant, takes on the proportions of a colossal and perfectly beautiful man. This apparition looks at him with great kindness: 'Thou sufferest, O son of earth,' it says to him, 'and I come to give thee strength, for thou lovest justice and thou seekest after truth. I am *Pymander*, the thought of the All-Powerful: make a wish, and it shall be granted thee.'

'Lord,' replies Hermes-Thoth, 'give me a ray of thy divine knowledge.'

'Thou hast chosen well,' says Pymander. 'Mayst thy wish be granted.'

Immediately Hermes, rapt in ecstasy, is surrounded by a spectacle that no human tongue could describe. All forms, all the beauties that might be dreamed by an ardent imagination, appear around him in a sphere of light that completely surrounds him, whose revolutions, from west to east, produce, accompanied by the harmonies of the most enchanting music ever heard, a succession of changing pictures, each more marvellous and more splendid than the last.

While Hermes is giving himself up to the charms of this contemplation, the light dies slowly, the visions fade away gradually into chaotic darkness, and this darkness, becoming more and more intense, with deeper and deeper shadows, fills him with an ungovernable terror. And out of this shadow comes a discordant noise, like bursts of thunder, and a voice, louder and deeper than thunder, crashes through this fantastic tempest. Here we must translate Hermes, recording as faithfully as possible the text of the sacred *Pymander*:

'It seemed to me,' he says, 'that this great voice was the voice of the vanished Light, and from it came the Word of God. This Word seemed to be borne on a current of celestial water whose coolness I could feel, and from it rose a clear, pure flame that dissolved into the air.

'This air, subtle as the spirit itself, floats between the water and the fire, and in the waves of this current of air our earth was held in equilibrium, like a mass of some unshaped substance that awaits the creator's hand.

'And God's Word shook this world; and the more it shook, the brighter the great Light shone again, and the innumerable manifestations of the wondrous Form appeared again, one after the other.

'And it seemed to me that I could see all these things in the mirror of my thoughts. And then the divine voice of Pymander was heard again, speaking kindly and softly: "Thought is God the father; the Word is his son; they are indissolubly united in eternity, and their union is Life.

' "Thought and the Word create the acts of the All-Powerful.

' "From the All-Powerful come seven Spirits who move in seven circles; and in these circles are all the beings that compose the universe; and the action of the seven Spirits in their circles is called Fate, and these circles themselves are enclosed in the divine Thought that permeates them eternally.

' "God has committed to the seven Spirits the governing of the elements and the creation of their combined products. But He created man in His own image, and, pleased with this image, has given him power over terrestrial nature.

' "Now man, having seen his father in the figure of the supreme Creator, at one time conceived the ambition of making himself equal to His omnipotence, and desired to penetrate the circles whose government had not been given him. Troubling in this way the divine harmony, he made himself guilty, and his punishment was to become the slave of his body. Though he is immortal in his soul, which is the image of God, he made himself mortal by a love of changing and perishable things.

' "But he was given liberty to raise himself again, as far as he could, to his original heights by cutting himself off from the servitude of the body and reconquering his immortality.

' "God desires therefore that every man should learn to know himself for what he is, and to distinguish his superior and invisible being from the visible form, which is only the shell. When he has recognised the duality of his creation, he no longer allows himself to be seduced by the charm of impermanent things; his thought has no other aim but to seek and pursue, across the infinite, the absolute beauty whose contemplation is the sovereign good promised to his rehabilitated mind.

' "The man who triumphs over sensual temptations increases his mental faculties; God gives him his measure of light in proportion to his merits, and progressively allows him to penetrate the most profound mysteries of nature.

' "That man, on the contrary, who succumbs to the temptations of the flesh falls gradually under the power of the fatal laws that govern the elements, and condemns himself to perpetual ignorance, which is the death of the spirit.

' "Happy is the son of earth who has kept pure the image of God and has not defaced it or darkened it with the veil of ignoble concupiscence. When the hour comes for him to leave this world, his body is indeed given up to the realm of matter; but his spirit, freed from the shell that

time has worn away, rises into the seven concentric circles
that envelop the terrestrial system.

' "In the circle of the *Moon*, he recognises his immortality; in *Mercury*, he feels his insensibility; in *Venus*, he
clothes himself again in innocence; in the *Sun*, he is given
the strength to bear without difficulty the rays of the divine
splendour; in *Mars*, he learns humility; in *Jupiter*, he takes
possession of the treasures of an intelligence made divine,
and in *Saturn*, he sees the truth of all things in its unchangeable beauty.

' "Beyond the circles lies the *Infinity of Worlds*, that
goes with him in his pilgrimage from heaven to heaven
towards the supreme God whom he approaches ceaselessly,
an eternal asymptote, without ever attaining him." '[35]

These were the words of Pymander, and the divine
vision then was swallowed up again in its ethereal sanctuary.
But it had illuminated the soul of Hermes-Thoth and had
made him, in a way, a messiah whose task it was to preach
to men of the great mystery of the soul's vocation.

Let us note at once in this fragment of the *Pymander*
the concept of a single, invisible, ineffable, omnipotent,
infinite God, and seven Spirits, messengers of His will and
agents of His providence: this is the foundation of all
Astrology, that is to say, the highest of all the occult sciences.

Here we find, then, the existence of superior spirits,
intermediaries between God and man, affirmed as a dogma
three thousand years before the birth of Christ; and dogmas
cannot be argued with. In any case, if we were to refute this
one we should be opposing ourselves to Christian theology
itself, which has given its sanction to angelic intervention in
all the great scenes in the Bible, the Gospel, the Acts of the
Apostles and the Apocalypse. From the cherubim with the
sword of flame who guard the threshold of the lost paradise,
to the angels with the seven trumpets and seven cups who
were seen by the prophet of Patmos in his vision of the end

---

[35] Ἑρμοῦ τοῦ Τρισμεγίστου Ποίμανδρες, seu *Mercurii Trismegisti Liber de
Potestate et Sapientiá Dei* [Venetiis; folio 1481].

of the world, the angelic universe is continuously mingled with the religious history of mankind. The Magi believed in this mission of the angels and they studied its character and extent in the examination of the stars. This study was their supreme wisdom; it was, under the name of Astrology, the gate to the supernatural world, and under the name Horoscope was the key to the mysteries of the future. The Zodiac was the book in which they claimed to read the plans of the divine wisdom and the signs foretelling the course of fate.

Everyone knows that the Zodiac is a celestial zone cutting the earth's equator at two equinoctial points. The sun's path is in the middle, at an equal distance from the two edges of this zone, which can be imagined as two concentric circles, in which the planets, or 'wandering stars,' perform their revolutions.

The Magi divided the Zodiac into twelve equal parts, each one originally occupied by a constellation, after which it is still named, that is, by groups of fixed stars called *Signs*. These twelve signs are the *Ram* [Aries], the *Bull* [Taurus], the *Twins* [Gemini], the *Crab* [Cancer] the *Lion* [Leo], the *Virgin* [Virgo], the *Scales* [Libra], the *Scorpion* [Scorpio], the *Archer* [Sagittarius], the *Goat* [Capricornus], the *Watercarrier* [Aquarius], and the *Fishes* [Pisces]. These signs each take as their number the one which marks their hierarchic order, beginning with the *Ram*, the first sign, and finishing with the *Fishes*, the twelfth sign.

The planets that circulate in the Zodiac are: *Saturn, Jupiter, Mars*, the *Sun, Venus, Mercury*, and the *Moon*. Their angelic spirits distribute their influences in seven concentric circles whose composition I shall describe when I deal with the theory of the horoscope.[36]

---

[36] See Books VI and VII of this work.
It will be noticed that Christian knows nothing of the three outer planets: *Uranus*, discovered in 1781, *Neptune* in 1846 and *Pluto* in 1930. The discovery of *Uranus* heralded great revolutionary changes, a break-through of the time-honoured wall of *Saturn*. The discovery of *Neptune* was the prelude to a stirring of the social conscience and to the long-over-due humanitarian

By a second and more mysterious operation the Magi divided the zodiacal zone into twelve spaces or *solar Houses*. Each of these Houses contains one of the twelve signs and receives the aspects of the planets, which are infinitely variable according to the time of birth which serves as a basis for the Horoscope. These aspects indicate the planetary influences.

The Horoscope is therefore a figurative table of the signs and aspects whose mysterious combinations, explained by a general traditional doctrine, allow us to foretell, from the moment of birth, the good and evil that will befall the new-born child.

The figure given here is more or less the planisphere of the sky of destiny. It shows us the circular zone of the Zodiac divided into its twelve equal parts, or Houses, each of which contains a sign and its corresponding number, from the Ram which is I, to the Fishes which are XII.

This zone is subdivided by a cross whose upper point, corresponding to the number X, marks the middle of the sky, the Zenith. The lower point, corresponding to the number IV, marks the bottom of the sky, the hypogeum or Nadir.

measures introduced in the 19th century. The discovery of *Pluto* preceded the great Depression and the show-down of the nineteen-thirties which led to World-war II.—*Uranus* as Awakener in world-movements becomes the reformer in good maps, the crank in weak ones. *Neptune's* high inspiration of brotherhood—'the sons of men are one and I am one with them'— becomes delusion in maps where the constructive aspects are weak, and high ecstacy is then translated into a craving for drugs, for sensation at all costs. Many divergent views are held about *Pluto*. The fact that it is a small body is significant, for we no longer equate magnitude with potency. In fact, *Pluto* has been compared to the seed, the grain of mustard seed of the Gospels. Such a concept easily leads to related ideas which are to-day seeking entrance into men's minds: the minimum dose in medicine; the discovery of hidden powers below the threshold of the conscious mind, even as the seed stirs in the darkness of the earth; the vast potentialities for the whose world revealed by the splitting of the atom . . . The three outer planets should first be studied in connection with world events, and influences which should be available to all mankind, irrespective of race or national boundaries. All their gifts may be misused; to take examples, radio may be prostituted to propaganda purposes, the cinema to distorted views of life and atomic energy to total destruction; but we have not yet seen, and few have the constructive imagination to grasp, the full implications of the wonderful future which may await mankind.—*Ed.*

The horizontal arms of the cross mark, on the left the east, corresponding to the number I, and on the right the west, corresponding to the number VII.

The numbers I to XII indicate the successive order of the Houses as well as of the Signs, starting with the first House at the cardinal point of the east, and the rest follow in an anti-clockwise direction. The fourth is at the bottom

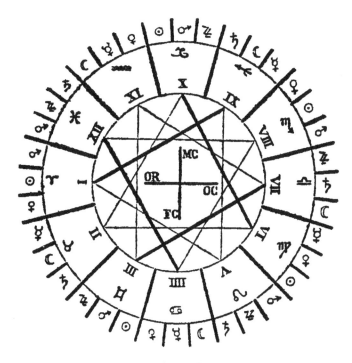

Scheme of the Horoscope

of the sky which corresponds to our north or Septentrion; the seventh is in the west; the tenth is in the middle of the sky, that is to say at the culminating point of the horoscope, which corresponds to the meridian or south. The other houses extend, according to the order of the signs, downwards through the east, from left to right, to the fourth House, and then upwards from left to right, to the eighth House; from which we proceed from right to left until we reach the point from which we started, the first House.

The numbering of the *Houses* is the same in all horoscopes; the first House is always in the *east;* the following ones occupy therefore invariably the afore-mentioned positions around the zodiacal zone. But the *Signs* change their position according to the date of birth: for example, the *Ram,* though still the first sign of the Zodiac, would be in the *west,* in House VII, for the horoscope of a person born under the sign of the *Scales.* The second House in this horoscope would therefore contain the *Scorpion;* the third *Sagittarius,* and, completing the circle, *Virgo* would occupy the twelfth House.

The Arcana of House I, the cardinal point of the east, contain the chances of long life, the mystery of the physical temperament and of intellectual and moral aptitudes.

House II receives the Arcana of material goods, of mineral wealth, of profit due to work, industry or play.

In House III are found all things that concern the relationships between brothers, sisters, and near relatives; other relatives and short voyages.

The fourth House, at the bottom of the sky, contains whatever relates to father and mother, to ancestors, patrimony, unknown or hidden things, and landed property.

House V belongs to the prediction of good fortune, to the lighter side of life and to the procreation of children.

House VI includes the prognosis of more or less serious ailments; more or less serious troubles which a person, according to his position, may meet with in his relations with those in lower positions than himself, with subjects, servants or neighbours.

House VII, the cardinal point of the west, embraces alliances in general and marriage in particular. It also gives, by the analogy of contraries, whatever concerns disputes, trials, bad feeling, and war.

In House VIII the reply is found to questions concerning natural or violent death, prospects of inheritance or unforeseen legacies.

House IX deals with religious questions, and with long or distant journeys on land and sea.

House X, the culminating point of the horoscope, is the House of ascending or declining fortune. There we can study the chances of honours, dignities, promotion and security, and those of decline and fall.

All that concerns friendship, good will, favour or support is grouped under House XI.

Finally, persecutions, proscriptions, captivity, exile, and great disasters of all kinds, hidden enemies and their activities, more or less formidable, can be foretold by an examination of House XII.

According to the special predictions allotted to them, the twelve houses are divided into angular, succedent and cadent Houses, of which the strongest is the angular, the weakest the cadent.

The first House is *angular,* and generally fortunate. The second is *succedent,* that is to say, it is entered on leaving the preceding House and following the order of the signs. It is generally fortunate. The third is *cadent.* The fourth is *angular* and moderately fortunate; the fifth is *succedent* and is a lucky House; the sixth is *cadent* and deals with illness and difficulty; the seventh is *angular* and fortunate; the eighth is *succedent* and unfortunate; the ninth is *cadent* and moderately fortunate; the tenth is *angular* and generallly fortunate; the eleventh is called the House of friends and is moderately fortunate; the twelfth is *cadent* and unfortunate. We shall see in the art of foretelling the future how the astral influences are modified according to the character of each House.

It is difficult to understand, at first, why the Houses are so arranged; and one wonders why the chances of death, for example, are placed in the domain of the eighth House instead of being, more naturally [or so it would seem] in the twelfth and final House. Let us look again at the diagram given here and this peculiarity disappears.

The twelve Houses have their fixed positions. The

diagram gives us a star with twelve points formed by four equilateral and concentric triangles whose apexes correspond to the Houses and to the numbers I, IV, VII and X, that is to say, to the four cardinal points indicated by the central cross.

These triangles have as their object the *Triplicities*, that is, the general and successive triple phases of life.

For the Magi, as well as for ourselves, human life had its four cardinal points: infancy, youth, maturity, and old age. They explained the principal characters of these periods by the triangles of the horoscope.

Man, they said [and by man they meant both sexes], at first lives in himself, that is, he feeds himself, develops physically, like all other organized beings, according to the laws proper to his kind. His complexion, his temperament, the future faculties whose germ is born with him, are naturally determined by the astrological signs which belong to the first House, the east of life and apex of the first triangle.

As the child grows in physical strength, his moral being begins to manifest itself; his parents early in life give him a first idea of God according to his age, for this idea corresponds with his simple curiosity. Since all that exists in nature comes from God, and returns to Him as to its principal and natural end, our journey across the expanse of physical, intellectual and moral life corresponds, by analogy, to future changes in terrestrial situation. Religion and travel are therefore perfectly expressed by the ninth House, placed at the second point of the first triangle.

After having built up his physical and moral being by food which fortifies his constitution and education which develops his faculties, man's general destiny is to transmit life to posterity, fulfilling the word of God: 'grow and multiply.' This new condition brings us to the fifth House, to which correspond the Arcana of procreation and which is marked by the third point of the first triangle.

When he has reached the complete fulfilment of his

aptitudes, the man must seek his destined place and rank. He will be fortunate or unfortunate, powerful or weak, or continue in his original state, according to the workings of occult laws which reveal the astral influences, laws which may to a certain extent modify the acquirements by education, the workings of his will and perseverance in activities. This phase of social development is seen in the signs relating to the tenth House, the apex of the second equilateral triangle.

The sixth House, on the second corner of this triangle, contains those predictions which will tell whether his future will place him above or below his fellows, and whether he will have to fight against the power of others, or against the weaknesses of his own nature.

Degrees of material good, whether wealth, moderate comfort or future poverty, can then be measured by the Arcana of the second house, the third angle of the second triangle.

This general forecast is completed by examining the person's private relationships. The first is created by the affectionate attraction of the sexes, which has marriage as its social aim. The others consist in alliances for purely material ends, and, by the analogy of contraries, they also include disputes, discords and open enmity. These are the property of the Arcana of the seventh House, at the apex of the third triangle.

Apart from the new family grouping created by marriage, and the sympathies and hostilities that may surround it, life's closest ties are between a man and his brothers, sisters or near relatives. This kind of relationship is the property of the third House, the second angle of the third triangle. And as this House faces the ninth, it gives notification of small changes of abode, short journeys and affairs that do not reach far beyond the social group.

After the ties of consanguinity, the expansive faculties of man demand friends; in the preservation or the pursuit of security he may need protectors; his uncertain or impoverished position may lead him to seek the benefits that more fortunate people can confer. Will he find sympathy or indifference? Will his friends be devoted and faithful? Will their support be powerful or merely illusory? House XI, third angle of the third triangle, will give the replies.

Finally, however promising the general aspect of a person's fate may seem, every life contains its portion of inevitable trials which have to be endured—pain, vicissitudes, hindrances, struggles, bitter deceptions and even reversals of the greatest good fortune. In the first place, man is influenced by good and evil, either physically or morally inherited from father, mother or other sources that govern his temperament. This primitive condition is often the determining cause of his whole future. There are also hidden things whose discovery may bring about the most unexpected events, either good or evil. The nadir of the heavens, downward apex of the last triangle of the triplicities, is the more or less impenetrable dwelling place of the secrets guarded by the fourth House, which is that of the close of life, amongst other meanings.

The abysses of misfortune into which any destiny may fall lie in the twelfth House, second angle of the last triangle, and Death, which puts an end to everything here below, raises its scythe in the eighth House, last angle of the four Triplicities that we have examined.

XII

This is the plan irradiated by the evolutions of the luminous thrones that carry through the ether the seven Spirits revealed to Hermes-Thoth. How can the influences of these sources of light determine the actions that take place on earth? How is it that they act in a certain way on one person, in another way on another? That, it must be admitted, is a mystery to which the key has not yet been rediscovered. We must limit ourselves to the experiments allowed by the ancient traditions whose remnants are left to us. I have already said that I do not dogmatise: I relate and explain.

One might object that, if such a system must be accepted, and if its reality could be demonstrated, man, bereft of intellect and morality, would be no more than a cog in the wheels of the universe. But the secret initiates in the art of Magic did not believe in a blind fate: they professed a doctrine more closely connected with the dignity of human stature, created, as they knew, in the image of God. They admitted, and with reason, the inevitable chain of effects and causes in the circle of life's general laws; but they also believed in the eternal Wisdom whose counsels, hidden to us, arrange the accidents of every existence in a series of tests destined to educate the human intelligence and will. These tests, they said, are like spurs on the path traced by the twelve solar houses of the hermetic Zodiac; and they can be seen more or less clearly, according to the will of God, through the science of numbers and hierograms, or sacred letters, which are combined on the symbolic order attributed to each of the seven travelling ministers of changeless Providence.

These seven Spirits of the Egyptian theogony are the seven *Devas* of ancient India—the seven *Amschaspands* of Persia—the seven *great Angels* of Chaldea—the seven of the ten *Sephiroth* of the Hebrew Qabala—the seven Archangels who, in the Christian Apocalypse, are seen by St. John before the throne of the Ancient of Days. What is the meaning of these different denominations, according to their country and language, since the principle is everywhere the same, from all time?

Dionysius the pseudo-Areopagite has written a book on the hierarchy of the celestial spirits which reconciles the Christian idea with the traditions of Hermes. He enumerates in ascending progression the *Angels, Archangels, Principalities, Virtues, Powers, Dominations, Thrones, Cherubim* and *Seraphim*, which are, below God, at the summit of the sacred ladder.

In the hermetic hierarchy, the earth is at the centre of ten circles of light which are also the crowns of the divine Essence.

The first circle, crown of the *Supreme Power,* contains the *Seraphim,* which extend over the infinity of the heavens, beyond the fixed stars, the veil behind which God conceals himself from mortal sight.

The second circle, crown of *eternally active Intelligence,* contains the *Cherubim,* guardians of the fixed stars, on which are engraved the archetypal ideas that precede natural forms.

The third circle, crown of *absolute Wisdom,* contains the *Thrones,* an order of spirits whose head is Rempha, the genius of Time, who travels on the planet Saturn and brings back the dead to the arms of God.

The fourth circle, crown of *infinite Love,* contains the *Dominations,* an order of spirits whose head is *Pi-Zeus,* who travels on the planet Jupiter, and presides over the government of beings composed of spirit and matter.

The fifth circle, crown of *absolute Justice,* contains the *Powers,* an order of spirits whose head is *Ertosi,* who travels on the planet Mars and presides over the punishment of the guilty.

The sixth circle, crown of *supreme Beauty,* contains the *Virtues,* an order of spirits whose head is *Pi-Rhé,* who travels on the Sun and presides over general combinations of matter.

The seventh circle, crown of the *divine Reign,* contains the *Principalities,* an order of spirits whose head is *Suroth,* who travels on the planet Venus and presides over the harmonies of vegetable nature.

The eighth circle, crown of *Eternity,* contains the *Archangels,* an order of spirits whose head is *Pi-Hermes* or *Thoth,* who travels on the planet Mercury and presides over the generation of animals.

The ninth circle, crown of *universal Fecundity,* contains the *Angels,* an order of spirits whose head is Pi-Ioh, who travels on the Moon and presides over the waxing and waning and the renewing of human beings.

The tenth circle, crown of *Humanity*, image of God, contains the tribunal of human conscience and the altars dedicated by religion to the supreme Being.

In ancient Chaldea, the fatherland of Abraham, the genius of Saturn is called *Oriphiel*; of Jupiter, *Zachariel*; of Mars, *Samael*; of the Sun, *Michael*; of Venus, *Anael*; of Mercury, *Raphael*; and of the Moon, *Gabriel*. Among these we can recognize our archangel Michael, leader of the faithful angels who plunged Satan and the unfaithful angels into Hell, a tradition from the religious beliefs of Persia; we also recognize Raphael, guide of the youthful Tobias, and Gabriel, angel of the Annunciation.

According to Dionysius, who had doubtless studied the doctrine of the Magi to adapt it to the Christian form, the angels or genii of the supraterrestrial spheres have the task of protecting humanity, working for its betterment and its ascent towards higher worlds. Those who preside over the first House of the horoscope have as their mission to keep misfortune from us and to favour us with good fortune. The masters of the second House of the horoscope minimise the temptations that may beset us. Those of the third assist us against invisible enemies. Those of the fourth offer to the Eternal our prayers and our good works. Those of the fifth open up the ways of sanctity to us. Those of the sixth inspire and illuminate us. Those of the seventh reveal to us, in dreams or visions, secrets the understanding of which enlarges our whole being. Those of the eighth turn us away from sin that kills the moral life. Those of the ninth inspire us to seek in God the sovereign good. Those of the tenth console us in our afflictions and raise us up when we have fallen. Those of the eleventh lessen our difficulties when our strength fails. Those of the twelfth House awaken in us conscience and remorse when we have done wrong.

This theory, much more complicated than the dogma of the guardian angels, surrounds us with help and guidance from birth to death. How is it that under such auspices and in spite of such powerful help and guidance, human societies should be so full of vices, crimes, miseries and catastrophes? It is so, reply the Magi, because the will is free to do good or evil. The man who seeks after Truth and who looks for Justice is upheld by the celestial Powers. He who abandons himself to material instincts or who despises the divine precepts, suffers the inevitable consequence of his determinations and his acts; thus he himself creates the fatality that becomes his punishment.

'The Seraphim,' says Dionysius, 'contemplate in God the supreme goodness; the Cherubim, absolute truth; the Thrones, justice. Through the Seraphim, God inspires us with the love of all perfect things; through the Cherubim, He communicates to us religious and moral truth; through the Thrones, He brings His justice to bear upon us. The Dominions govern the functions that the Angels fulfil towards us. The Principalities watch over the leaders of the peoples. The Powers stop the efforts of demons who would overthrow the world. Through the Dominions the majesty of God is manifested; through the Principalities, His reign; through the Powers, His tutelary providence. The Virtues perform the miracles of creation; the Archangels are the messengers bearing divine decrees, and the Angels follow us, invisible but ever-present, till the end of our earthly days.

'We must,' says the same author, 'put ourselves in communion with the Angels through our obedience; with the Archangels, through our zeal in studying the divine law; with the Virtues, through our compassion for all suffering beings; with the Powers, through our resistance to temptation; with the Principalities, through our humility; with the Dominions, through our power over ourselves; with the Thrones through our justice; with the Cherubim through the elevation of our soul in the conception of the divine Wisdom, and finally with the Seraphim through our universal charity.'[37]

Thus the existence and the role of the celestial Genii, imagined or revealed by Magic, have modified themselves to the Christian point of view and Astrology was allowed by the theologians of the new dogma in so far as it did not oppose in any way the doctrine of free will. Origen, the famous Christian writer of the third century, wrote: 'Just as the power of the human will is not rendered useless because God's foreknowledge sees the acts that will be ours in the future, even so the celestial signs by which we may be initiated into the foretelling of that future are not a declaration of a loss of free will. The occult influences demonstrate a tendency, but do not submit us to blind fate. The sky is like an open book in which are written the signs of past, present and future which God embraces with a single glance. It is the book of universal life according to which we shall be judged, because it presents the series of tests which composes the circle of each individual existence, and because the evidence of the Angels will add to it the account of our liberty.'

Three thousand years before Origen, Hermes-Thoth, the legendary founder of Magism, said: 'Fortunate is he who knows how to read the Signs of the Times, for that man shall escape many misfortunes, or at least be prepared to withstand the blow.' Astrology is therefore not a science of fatalism; one might even say with St. Jerome that it is a Treaty of Providence extremely useful to mankind.

This doctrine of the celestial influences needed affirmation. Manu among the Indians, Hermes among the Egyptians, Zoroaster among the Persians, Confucius among the Chinese, Numa among the Romans, did not hesitate to make it known that they enjoyed the privilege of conversation with the Divinity, or with supernatural beings elected

[37] S. Dionysii Areopagitæ *Opera Omnia* [De cœlesti Hierarchiâ], 1 vol., folio *Lutet Par*, [1544]. St. Geneviève Library, CC 7 and 8.

to the government of the universe. Moses, who had been instructed by the sacerdotal colleges of Egypt, obtained from them the marvels with which he filled the books of Genesis and Exodus. Muhammad in his turn borrowed from Christian and Judaic traditions the idea of his relationships with the angel Gabriel. These famous legislators were believed and taken at their word because their brilliant imaginations dominated the epochs in which they lived. Were they really inspired by celestial powers? In the present state of our knowledge it is impossible either to affirm or to deny it. The thinkers of all time, sensualists or *Epicureans*, idealists or Platonists, sceptics and mystics, still fall into these four camps, and no human authority has yet been able to unite them.[35]

Sensualism belongs to the Greek schools of Thales and Epicurus and to the Latin school of Lucretius, who was its greatest exponent.

Pythagoras, Socrates and Plato are the fathers of the first *idealist* schools.

Scepticism is represented by Pyrrho, the Sophists and the Cynics, notably Diogenes.

Much later was born the *mysticism* of the Egyptian school at Alexandria which under the name Neoplatonism was largely taken over by Christian philosophy; it fused the doctrines and dogmas of Egypt, Phoenicia, Assyria and Persia with the psychological ideas of Plato. The school of Alexandria re-established as the summit of human concepts a single God, free from polytheist idolatry and dominating a hierarchy of supernatural intelligences and powers that are no more than workers in the perpetual creation of which God remains the eternal and ineffable architect.

It is of this doctrine, restored and purified, that Ptolemy de Péluse, Porphyry, Plotinus, Proclus, Iamblicus,

---

[35] Bertrand Russell's recent great *History of Philosophy* gives the fullest account of early as well as of later philosophy; but for readers who want a simplified account, G. H. Lewes' *Biographical History of Philosophy* is still very useful. C. E. M. Joad has also written an *Outline.—Ed.*

Maximus of Ephesus, Edesius, Chrysanthus, Olympiodorus, Firmicus Maternus and others were the expounders; a doctrine that has always run parallel to Christianity and the most interesting commentaries on which we owe to the clergy themselves, the princes of the Church and the doctors of Catholic theology.

XIII

I HAVE insisted from the beginning of this work that the study of Magic is by no means incompatible with reason, is not hostile to religious beliefs and is something entirely apart from the abuses which have been perpetrated in its name by ignorance, fanaticism and superstition. I shall add here, in its favour, some more modern views.

The Jesuit Father Athanasius Kircher, 'a man unusual and perhaps unique for the extent of his knowledge' [*Encyclopédie Théologique*], has left us, in his immense works on Egypt and China, an *Ecstatic Voyage* among the mystical inhabitants of the planetary worlds.[39] A Jesuit who leaves for a trip to the moon accompanied by the genius Cosmiel, visiting on his way the planets Venus, Mercury, the Sun, Mars, Jupiter and Saturn—does all this not seem to take us beyond the bounds of orthodoxy? Nevertheless his book was very well received, was printed at Rome under the auspices of Pope Alexander VII and spread throughout Europe as a new Apocalypse and a glory without parallel to the Society of Jesus.

In five hundred pages Kircher expatiates on the

[39] *Iter Exstaticum, in quo Mundi opificium exponitur ad veritatem*: 1 vol. quarto [Romæ 1656].—The three most important works of this Jesuit are the *Œdipus Egyptiacus*, or history of the sacred mysteries of Egypt from its monuments, 4 vols. folio [Romæ 1653]: *China Illustrata*, 1 vol. folio [Amstelod., 1652 and 1667] and *Mundus Subterraneus, in quo universae Naturae majestas et divitiae demonstrantur*, 2 vol. folio [Amstelod., 1668]. Kircher, who died in 1680, held the Chair of Mathematics in the Roman College at Rome. The celebrated naturalist Buffon has used his nature classification without acknowledging his indebtedness.

marvels of oriental supernaturalism, the study of which was
one of the consuming passions of his life. The Moon appears
to him deserted like a reef in the ocean of the ether; but
Venus makes up for it. This is a magnificent island whose
vegetable life is spread out like sparkling flowers under the
rays of the sun. The air is perfumed by the scents of musk
and amber. The traveller meets there a group of young
angels of indescribable beauty, who dance and sing divine
praises while strewing space with lilies, roses, hyacinths and
narcissi. The Genius Cosmiel tells him that these wonderful
beings pour over the earth the influences of love and abund-
ant perfumes. The good Jesuit wants to stay for ever in
such charming company, but his guide draws him away
from this temptation and carries him off to the mountains
of Mercury, from which he gazes upon plains of quicksilver
scattered with golden trees hung with bunches of precious
stones. The inhabitants of this third planet are graver spirits
than those on Venus, and their task is to measure out to
human beings their intelligent faculties. But the neighbouring Sun soon attracts Kircher's attention. The star of day is
peopled by angels of fire who swim in seas of light around a
volcano from which pour myriads of meteors that dissolve
in starry dust, each atom of which is a germ of universal
life. The light is too bright for mortal eyes, if the protecting
Genius were not there to spread his wings like a veil over
this blazing space. This St. Paul of the Society of Jesus
would have been devoured like a straw in this great crucible
of nature at work. But wise Cosmiel, pursuing his upward
flight, soars with him towards the sphere of Mars, through
whose red mists they fly without stopping and come to rest
on the Elysian shores of Jupiter, which are inhabited by the
guardian angels of all the virtues. The voyage ends in the
contemplation of Saturn, whose sinister Genii administer
divine justice to the wicked and suffering to the righteous.
Beyond this seventh zone rises the Empyrean, the land of
the predestined, to which the entry is only given to immacu-

late souls or to those who have regained their original purity through penitence.

This work of Kircher deserves to be read by the timid who fear to do justice to their Christian consciences by reading my researches on Magic and Astrology. It is interesting, in considering the history of Christianity, to see the Jesuits supporting, in the middle of the XVIIth century, the ancient doctrine of planetary influences on which Astrology is founded, and admitting, consequently, the glimpses of destiny offered by apotelesmatic calculation. In any case, we cannot deny the value of Astrology unless we deny at the same time the prophecies which fill the Bible.

La Bruyère, a friend of Bossuet who obtained his appointment as a tutor of history to the son of Louis XIV, and whom one would never suspect of not being a good Catholic, felt himself obliged to treat Magic with extreme reserve. 'The theory is very obscure; its principles are vague, uncertain and somewhat visionary. However, there are undeniable facts, confirmed by serious men who were witnesses. To admit all these facts, or deny them, seems to be equally inconvenient, and I daresay that in this matter, as in all extraordinary matters that stand outside the general rules, there is something to be said both for the freethinkers and for the superstitious.'[40]

Still closer to our times, Joseph de Maistre, the pro-Papal writer, gave the opinion in 1820, in his *Soirées de Saint-Pétersbourg,* that comets are the harbingers of divine justice, and that 'divination by Astrology is by no means an absolutely chimerical science.'

I have just cited three names, Kircher, La Bruyère and Joseph de Maistre to convince those believers who are held captive in the chains of dogmas originating nineteen centuries ago. But our own epoch has seen the rise of a great army of free-thinkers who submit God Himself and His mysteries to the tribunal of their proud reasoning.

[40] Alfred Maury, of the Institute. *Magic and Astrology* [Paris 1867].

To these adversaries of the supernatural I shall oppose the arguments of Balzac, a great adept in occult sciences.[41]

This address to the free-thinkers of the XIXth century may seem strange to more than one reader. It needs to be re-read and meditated in the complete work from which I have taken it.[42]

For those who knew him—and I had that happiness—Honoré de Balzac's faith did not die with him, and the *Seven Spiritual Worlds* whose mystery is unfolded in the ancient books have by no means withdrawn their Arcana from the contemplation of thinkers. The Zodiac explained by the ancient Magi still holds open for them the gates of the supernatural world, through which pass and repass ceaselessly the seven messengers of eternal Providence, whose task is to distribute to every living thing the plan of its career and the programme of its tests.

I say test, mark you, and not fatality; the mind can react to the shocks of matter and sometimes avoid them or even neutralise them; but there are also destinies so extraordinary that we must recognise in them the actions of a power superior to all the efforts of our intelligence and our will. The Magi knew this; the prevision of future things raised them to the heights of the free moral arbiter. They taught their disciples not to live like machines without wills, but to bless, long before they happened, the benefits of divine grace if the future was revealed under favourable signs. In receiving both good and evil as from God, they were contemplating his providential justice, so high above

---

[41] 10 pages follow from *Séraphita* which we do not print as it can easily be found in Balzac's collected works. The main theme of the passage is that we must distinguish between physical science and spiritual science; that no two things are identical, so that it is only an abstraction to say that two and two make four. He discusses Newton, pointing out that his laws were not absolute and that he died in despair. From Number he passes to Light and Colour, to Electricity and to sympathetic attraction.—*Ed.*

[42] H. de Balzac, *Etudes philosophiques* [Séraphita] Tome XXXVIII des Œuvres complètes. [*Edit.* Michel Levy, Paris 1868].

our petty human conceptions. They made, in all humility, some merit for themselves in religious obedience, whilst other men, fallen into the darkness of polytheism and superstition, degraded themselves in the invocation of deaf gods, fetishes made by their own vile hands, in the image of their blindness and their vice.

To obey and to adore does not mean living like a machine: it means practising the true, unchangeable religion that lies behind changing dogmas. Jesus said: 'Whosoever will come after Me, let him deny himself, and take up his cross, and follow Me.' Now to take up one's cross is to resign oneself; all morality is summed up in patience. True greatness lies in submission and sacrifice: without this Divine Law there is no Truth and consequently no salvation. God carves, according to His good pleasure, the cross for each of us; but at times He ameliorates the sorrowful way for those who accept it with obedience.

Although this law is hard for some and terrible for others, it is none the less holy in its mystery, since it is seen to be superior to our feeble intelligence and fallible justice. If man is sometimes brought by predestination to a heart-rending trial: if he cannot flee from the invisible sword whose unmoving point awaits his end, he may still realise that he was happier than others or that he meets his end with more gentleness. In his heart he can pardon the friend who betrayed him, the enemy who struck him. While dying, he can bless the hand of God which purifies him in the crucible of Destiny. Lastly, he can die joyfully for the safety of his country or for the triumph of truth and justice; that is his inalienable privilege—he becomes one of the elect before the Giver of all Good.

While pursuing our studies, let us keep before us this consoling thought that the Arcana, like dreams, like presentiments which sometime come to us, affirm more

positively than our doubts that there is a real affinity between our normal existence and the unseen world. They
are significant warnings which God grants us. They are
guides that are often severe but always kindly, causing us to
see that suffering is a path and that the earth is not the end
of our journey.

BOOK TWO

BOOK TWO

THE MYSTERIES OF THE PYRAMIDS

I

IF the beginnings of the great religious institutions of Egypt are as obscure as those of the nation which owes its greatness to them, its monuments leave us in no doubt that theocracy was its first form of government.

We have already seen that from far distant times the Egyptian priest was also the scientist uniting in himself the two most noble missions given to man: the worship of God and the development of intelligence. Supreme power was in the hands of the High Priest or Hierophant ['he who utters the Sacred Word']; and his authoritative orders were passed on, in the name of God, by subordinate priests throughout the whole country. The centre of the national life was in Upper Egypt, around the sacred city of Thebes. As the population increased in numbers it spread out over Middle Egypt, reaching the Delta when the raising of the ground level by the Nile's constant mud deposit filled up the marshes of the region.

The political division of the people into three classes, priests, warriors and working populace, goes far back into dimly-lit ages. The intermediate class, the warriors, supported by the others for the common defence, lived in insolent idleness. They wearied of priestly government and, since they were armed, their revolt under the leadership of Menes[1] speedily replaced the golden tiara of the pontiff

[1] Thus Manetho; he may mean either Narmer or Aha, since each took Men as a name. There had been independent kingdoms in Upper and Lower Egypt perhaps since 4500 B.C.; their union from which is dated the Egyptian

by the iron crown of a soldier-king. Menes is the creator of Egyptian royalty; he is described as such in the list of dynasties drawn up by the priest Manetho and on the monumental inscriptions of antique ruins. But the royal power could not be absolute, for it lacked the knowledge of science which cannot be obtained by revolution. The priestly caste, while no longer possessing executive power, could not be deprived of its directing influence upon a people eminently religious, which owed its early institutions, its morals, its laws, its arts to its theocratic government. Thebes lost none of its prestige and the Pharaoh Menes was obliged to found a separate capital in which he fortified himself, thereby confessing that his usurpation had no other sanction than physical force. The new capital was called Memphis. To-day it has disappeared from the face of the earth; the mounds between Cairo and Sakkarah give not the faintest indication of its site; the Nile and the sands have buried all, while at Thebes the appearance of the ruins reveals something of the greatest display of monumental grandeur which has ever appeared in history.

Immediately facing Cairo, on the plateau of Gizeh, a spur from the Libyan mountain chain, the left bank of the Nile yet carries three monuments which have defied both time and man: the Pyramids.

These three monuments with square bases, a little unequal in size, form by their positions a triangle with faces looking towards the north, the west and the east. The largest, situated at the northern angle and towards the Delta, symbolises the force of nature; the second, a short distance from the first, is the symbol of movement; and the last, built to the south-east of the second, symbolises time. South of the third, on a line running from east to west,

First Dynasty is somewhere between 3500-3350 B.C. Both these kings' tombs have been found and show an advanced degree of culture. Christian's account follows Manetho, who wrote his history in the third century B.C. for Ptolemy II [Philadelphus].—*Ed.*

three more pyramids of smaller size rise up; near them many large stones are piled, leading one to suppose that they are the ruins of a seventh pyramid. It is permissible to suppose that the Egyptians wished to suggest by seven flamelike points the seven planetary worlds whose Rulers govern the universe as revealed by Hermes.[2]

The origin of these monuments has no established chronology. Herodotus, the great Greek historian, claims that the Great Pyramid was built by the Pharaoh Cheops; Diodorus Siculus attributes it to Chemmis; Georges le Syncellus to Souphis; others ascribe its foundation to Thoth

---

[2] According to the *Encyclopædia Britannica* [11th edn.] to Hermes, or Thoth-Hermes, or Hermes Trismegistus ['thrice-greatest'], the Scribe of the Gods in the Egyptian pantheon, were attributed in Greek times the books of Egyptian wisdom generally known as 'hermetic'. Clement of Alexandria reckons 42 of them; they formed, he says, the sole authority for any knowledge of Egyptian religion. He states that they were divided into 6 groups: [1] 10 books concerning laws, deities and priestly education, matters under the authority of the 'prophet' [2] 10 books of ritual concerning the treatment and decoration of the statues of gods, various prayers and hymns and processions and other matters in the charge of the official responsible for them, the *stolistes* [3] 10 books called 'hieroglyphics', in charge of the 'hierogram-matist', containing information about topography, geography and the plan of the universe [4] 2 books of the 'charter', with songs and a description of the life of Pharaoh and his household [5] 4 books given to astrology and astronomy, in charge of a 'horoscopus' [6] 6 books on medicine in charge of the Bearer of the Pastor or 'Pastophore'.—Forty-two was the number of assessors of the dead in the court of Osiris; it was also the normal total number of the nomes or administrative divisions, 22 in Upper and 20 in Lower Egypt.—In the 3rd century A.D. and later numerous writings purporting to provide a system of occult philosophy which was to rival the rising influence of Christianity and which was mostly drawn from Neoplatonic and Q'abalistic sources, with contributions from the type of Judaism developed by Philo of Alexandria and his followers, were circulated under the name of 'Hermes'. A few remain, the best-known being *Poimandres* or *Pymander,* 15 chapters dealing with cosmology and treating illumination as the principle of deliverance for man [chief edition, Paris 1854]. Other fragments have been collected by Patricius, *Nova de Universis Philosophia* [1593]. Later, Hermes was connected with alchemy. Hermes was linked in such writings with Anubis the jackal or dog-headed weigher of the *ka* of the dead, and with Horus the sky-god, as well as with Thoth. Paracelsus used the term 'Hermetic healing'. In medieval times there purported to be a 'Hermetic freemasonry'. See G. R. S. Meade *Thrice Greatest Hermes* [1907].—*Ed.*

or Hermes.[3] The same obscurity wraps the origin of the others. The Jewish historian Josephus states, without adducing proof, that all the Pyramids were the work of the Hebrews during their captivity in Egypt; and I read somewhere that 365,000 workers were employed over 78 years at this gigantic task. Doubtless this problem will never be solved, any more than others about which archaeologists vainly dream.

The rock which forms the pedestal of the Pyramids presents an absolutely arid surface, raised about 100 feet above the great waters of the Nile, and forms a granite mass of which the base has not yet been found even by fathoming to a depth of 200 feet the hollow shaft which is found in the largest Pyramid. This Pyramid's base is about 755 feet long [originally probably 775]. The mass of the monument has a volume of some 85,000,000 cubic feet; that is to say stones enough to build a wall 6 foot high which would extend for 1,000 miles and which could encircle France. Above the first course, surrounded by a trench hollowed out of the rock, 202 more courses may be counted laid successively, forming a slope of many tiers. The sum of these tiers gives the vertical height, 451 feet; but it is recognised that in its present state two courses at least have been destroyed at the top, so that the original height must have been about 481 feet: that is, the height of the tower of Strasbourg, or more than twice that of the towers of Notre Dame in Paris.

This Pyramid is orientated with extraordinary precision: each of its angles faces one of the four cardinal points. One concludes from this that for thousands of years the position of the terrestrial axis has not appreciably

---

[3] The attribution of the Great Pyramid to the second Pharaoh of the Fourth Dynasty, Chufu or 'Cheops', rests now on a firm foundation: his cartouche or official name in hieroglyphs was found written on the stones within it. Modern chronology, less positive than formerly, assigns the building to somewhere between 3100—2965 B.C. The second of the great trio of pyramids was the work of Cha-f-ra or 'Chephren', Chufu's successor, and the third by Men-kau-Ra or 'Mycerinus'.—*Ed*.

varied; and the Great Pyramid is the only monument which, by its antiquity, can give grounds for such an observation.

The actual entrance is found in the north-eastern face on the level of the fifteenth course, at about 45 feet in elevation above the base. Formerly it was concealed by a stone slab which could be moved from right to left to give access to an inclined passage, at the end of which appeared a landing skirting the opening of the well-shaft of which I have spoken already and which communicated with tunnels in which, without doubt, pure air circulated by means of ventilators skilfully constructed. From this landing one ascended again by another passage, leading to two sepulchral chambers, placed one above the other; each of these when opened contained a granite sarcophagus devoid of inscription. Now as all obelisks, all temple ruins and all tombs in ancient Egypt are normally covered in hieroglyphs, the bare surfaces within the Great Pyramid mark it as belonging to a previous era, a mysterious witness to remote antiquity. It has been stated that with all our science it would now be a difficult problem to construct in a mass of rock like the Pyramids chambers and inner corridors which, in spite of the millions of pounds weighing on them, preserve after some fifty centuries the whole of their original regularity and have not given way at any point.

The Sphinx, crouching a little distance away from the foot of the Great Pyramid, is carved out of the granite plateau itself; there is no break between its base and the original rock. Its height, about 75 feet, gives some idea of the enormous labour it must have entailed to free it of unwanted stone and to level the base. Its total length is 150 feet; its height from breast to chin is 50 feet and from the chin to the top of the head 25 feet: the circumference of the head, taken round the temples, is 80 feet, the face being 14 feet wide and the head 30 feet long. The layers of granite from which it has been carved divide its face into horizontal bands in a curious way; its mouth is formed partly by the space between two of the layers of stone. A

hole several feet deep has been drilled in the head: this
was probably used for the placing of ornaments, such as
the priestly tiara or the royal crown.[4]

This carved rock, reddish in colour, has a tremendous
effect as it stands overlooking the desert sands. It is a phantom that seems keenly attentive; one would almost say that
it listens and looks. Its great ear seems to hear all the sounds
of the past; its eyes, turned towards the east, seem to look
towards the future; its gaze has a depth and fixity that fasci-
nates the spectator. In this figure, half statue and half mountain, can be seen a peculiar majesty, a great serenity and
even a certain gentleness.

Greek mythology, inspired by travellers' tales, said that
the Sphinx was a monster half man, half beast, whose curious
fantasy it was to ask terrified travellers a riddle that they had
to solve under pain of being eaten alive. Oedipus took up
the challenge. The Sphinx asked him which was the animal
that walked on four feet at sunrise, on two feet at noon,
and on three feet at sunset? The hero replied without hesitation: 'It is a man. . .' The Sphinx, which apparently had
never before encountered such intelligence, was overcome
with amazement and Oedipus, taking advantage of its surprise, killed it.

This rather childish fable distorts the magnificent
Egyptian symbolism which was unknown to Greek philosophy until Plato was initiated by the Magi of Memphis
into the mysteries of Hermes-Thoth. The Sphinx, the
original of which stands in front of the Great Pyramid, was
reproduced on the thresholds of all the temples. It forms
a key to the occult. Here is a description of its various parts
and their symbolic meanings.

---

[4] It now seems certain that the Sphinx dates from some period considerably
prior to Chufu or Cheops who is recorded as having repaired it. The Sphinx
was regarded as the image of Ra-Harmachis, a God who appeared in vision
to Tchutimes [Thothmes] IV [18th Dynasty, *circa* 1600-1350 B.C.] before
he became Pharaoh, and promised him the double crown if he would dig
his image out of the sand. Harmachis, more properly Her or Hru-em-aakhut,
was 'Horus in the horizon', that is the rising sun of morning. The Egyptian
name for the Sphinx itself seems to have been Hu.—*Ed*.

The Sphinx, the Greek etymology of which [Σφίγγω] expresses the idea of embracing or tightly holding, is composed of four parts taken from four symbols. These are the head of a *Woman*, the body of a *Bull*, the paws of a *Lion* and the wings of an *Eagle*. This fantastic combination is divested of monstrosity as soon as the meaning of the symbols is understood.

The *woman's head* personifies human intelligence, which has to consider the aim of its aspirations, its means of attaining them, the obstacles to be avoided and the barriers to be broken.

The *bull's body* means that man, armed with science, goaded by a tireless will and bearing the yoke of each trial with ox-like patience, must slowly travel by his own road towards success or failure.

The *lion's paws* mean that, in order to attain the aim set by his intelligence, man must not only desire he must also venture; it is not enough merely to work, it is necessary sometimes also to fight and to make a place for oneself by force.

The *eagle's wings,* folded over the Sphinx's powerful mass, mean that man must hide his plans beneath a thick veil until the moment comes to act with a resolution that if need be reaches the heights of audacity.

The Hierophant used to tell the novice: 'Learn to see clearly, to desire judiciously, to attempt everything your conscience allows; learn to keep your plans secret; and if, on the following day, your perseverance results only in the continuation of the preceding day's efforts, go on—go on until your end is achieved. The seven Spirits of the Rose-Cross, guardians of the sacred key that shuts the door of the past and opens that of the future, will lay on your forehead the crown of the Masters of Time.'

The Sphinx was therefore neither an idol nor the devouring monster imagined by Greek fables: it was the symbol of the incalculable strength that can be used by the human will when directed by the highest intelligence.

It is the Alpha and Omega, the first and the last word of the great initiation.

Initiation, the crown of knowledge, was not granted to all, even among members of the Egyptian priestly class. In the sacred colleges there was a hierarchy of aptitudes and functions, a scale of scientific grades, each of which had a test that had to be passed. Each test gave the measure of the degree of intelligence and moral strength possessed by the aspiring initiate. He who failed in one of these tests was never allowed a second chance. If he were the son of a Magus, he remained at the point beyond which he had been unable to pass; a position was conferred upon him in the temples in accordance with his natural aptitude, but progress to higher positions was barred to him.

If the new member were a foreigner, he had at first to submit to a detailed inquiry into his antecedents; and if the result was favourable, the assembly of the college authorised or refused, by secret vote, his admission to the tests. In case of admission, the first test was sufficiently gruelling to make him turn back unless he had a very strong character, and then he was allowed to retire of his own free will. But if the first symbols of occult knowledge had been revealed and explained to him, and if he failed to pass one of the following tests, an inflexible law condemned him to death: he never again saw the light of day.

Thales, Pythagoras, Plato and Eudoxus were the most famous Greeks to pass successfully through all the phases of initiation. Pythagoras had as his master the arch-prophet Sonchis. Plato, according to Proclus, was taught for thirteen years by the Magi Patheneitb, Ochoaps, Sechtnouphis and Etymon of Sebennithis. And so the famous doctrine which has kept the name *platonic* and which has had such a great influence on the philosophical development of Christian ideas came originally from the sanctuaries of Memphis, the town of Menes, and from Heliopolis, the town of the Sun.

Iamblicus, who lived in the first half of the fourth century A.D., has left us a treatise on the Egyptian mysteries,[s] in which are related the principal scenes of the initiation tests. This very curious relic of antiquity deserves our attention for a space.

II

THE Sphinx of Giseh, says Iamblicus, served as an entrance to the sacred vaults in which the Magi held their tests. This entrance, frequently blocked, can still be traced between the forelegs. In former times it was closed by a bronze door whose secret spring was known only to the Magi. In the body of the Sphinx were constructed corridors that communicated with the subterranean portions of the Great Pyramid; these corridors were so skilfully arranged that anyone who undertook the journey from the Sphinx to the Great Pyramid without a guide was inevitably brought back through their mysterious network to the point whence he had started.

The two initiates who came first in seniority, with the rank of Thesmothetes or guardians of the rites, were given the task of introducing at night the postulant who had been admitted to the tests. The latter had to give himself over entirely to the discretion of his conductors; he had to follow their advice as if it were an order and refrain from asking questions. Let us suppose that the drama of these subterranean tests is about to take place; let us follow it step by step.

The postulant, his eyes bandaged, is led to the foot of

---

[s] Iamblichi de mysteriis Ægyptiorum: [folio, Oxonii, 1678]. 'ΙΑΜΒΛΙΧΟΥ, Περὶ Μυστηρίων Λογος: It is Proclus [412-485] who appears to attribute to Iamblichus this celebrated On the [Egyptian] Mysteries, although this is actually more probably by the philosopher's disciples. Very little remains of the numerous works with which the ancients credited him. In general, he further elaborated the classifications of Neoplatonism and developed wholesale the method of mythical interpretation. Julian the Apostate regarded him as superior to Plato.—Ed.

the Sphinx. The bronze door opens and closes silently at the touch of a hand that has pressed the spring releasing the interior mechanism. One of the Thesmothetes takes a lamp and walks in front to light the way; the second leads the postulant by the hand down a spiral staircase of twenty-two steps. At the bottom a second bronze door is opened giving access to a circular room. The door's interior is covered with granite matching the walls, so that it is impossible to discern. Now the tests begin. The two Thesmothetes suddenly stop the postulant and make him believe that he is on the brink of a precipice: one more step and he will fall to the bottom. 'This abyss,' they tell him, 'surrounds the Temple of the Mysteries and protects it against the temerity and curiosity of the profane. We have arrived a little too soon; our brethren have not yet lowered the drawbridge by which the initiates communicate with the sacred place. Let us wait for their arrival; but if you value your life, do not move, cross your hands on your breast and do not take off your bandage until the signal.'

The postulant knows that henceforward he is no longer his own master; his must be a passive obedience without which he will not be able to survive perils testing his soul's strength and his self-control. He submits; but, however strong he is, he still has feelings; his whole being trembles on the threshold of the unknown.

Whilst he is steeling himself the Thesmothetes take from an altar two robes of white linen, a gold and a silver belt and two masks, one of a lion's head, the other of a bull's. The robe is the emblem of the Mage's purity; the gold is consecrated to the sun, the silver to the moon; the lion's head symbolises the zodiacal sign which astrological language calls the throne of the genius of the sun; the bull's head symbolises the sign in which the genius of the moon exercises its most powerful influence. The Thesmothetes are therefore the representatives of the two Egyptian genii Pi-Rhé and Pi-Ioh who respectively govern the evolutions of the sun and the moon, the planets to which Magism attributed the most direct influence on the creation, the dissolution and the renewal of earthly beings. This symbolism meant also that the study of the laws of nature is the first step towards the highest illumination. But the meaning of the material signs was not revealed to the postulant until his tests were passed.

As soon as the Thesmothetes have put on their masks, a trapdoor opens with a deafening roar in the ground; from it a mechanical spectre half-rises brandishing a scythe and cries: 'Woe to him who comes to disturb the peace of the dead.' At the same time the postulant's bandage, torn off by one of the Thesmothetes, brings him face to face with the three monstrous figures. If, in spite of the horror of this surprise, he has courage enough not to faint before the sweeping scythe whose blade brushes his head seven times in a rapid swinging motion, the spectre vanishes, the trapdoor closes again, the Thesmothetes take off their masks and congratulate him on his courage. 'You felt,' they tell him, 'the chill of murderous steel and you did not recoil; you looked at the horror of horrors and your eyes defied it: well done. In your own country you could be a hero, admired by all and dedicated to the homage of posterity. But amongst us there is a virtue higher than manly courage, and that is the voluntary humility which triumphs over the vanity of pride. Are you capable of such a victory over yourself?'

The postulant, reassured by the kindness of his guides, thinks the physical test is over and offers himself for the moral tests. 'Very well,' he is told, 'will you crawl flat on the ground right to the innermost sanctuary where our brethren await you to give you knowledge and power in exchange for humility?'

The postulant accepts again. 'Then take this lamp,' say the initiators, 'it is the image of God's face that follows us when we walk hidden from the sight of men. Go without fear; you have only yourself to be afraid of in the test of solitude.'

While he receives from one of the Thesmothetes the
lamp that is to light his way, the other touches a hidden
spring in the wall which makes an iron plaque slide to one
side: behind it opens a corridor in the form of an arcade,
but so low and narrow that it was impossible to crawl
through it on hands and knees. 'Let this path,' the Thesmothetes would say, 'be for you the image of the tomb in which
all men must find their rest in the evening of life, yet only
to awake freed from the darkness of material things in the
eternal dawn of the life of the spirit. You have vanquished
the spectre of death: go, triumph over the horrors of the
tomb.'

If the postulant seemed to hestitate the Themosthetes
had neither to reproach him for his weakness nor to
encourage him to carry on with the test. They waited a few
minutes in silence with their right hands extended towards
the opening; if he could not bring himself to do it, his eyes
were covered again and he was led out of the sacred place.
The law of Magism did not allow him to attempt the test
again; his weakness had been judged. If he willingly submitted, the Thesmothetes gave him the kiss of peace and
wished him God-speed. As soon as he had disappeared in
the granite tube, the bronze plaque fell back in place
behind the postulant with a terrible clang and a far-off voice
cried: 'Here perish all the fools who coveted knowledge and
power!'

This phrase, which, by a remarkable acoustic effect,
was repeated by seven distinctly-spaced echoes, attacks the
postulant's reason. 'Do the Magi condemn to death all
foreigners who wish to penetrate their mysteries? But in
that case, why did they not strike me down with the scythe?
Why bury me alive? Why give me the lamp?' Indecision
mingles with his terror, as if to make him appreciate to the
full the menace of a prolonged death-agony. Nevertheless
he goes on and on, and notices with increasing anxiety that
the tunnel penetrates deeper and deeper into the earth.

Where will it end? What would he do if the little lamp went out?

He crawls one and on. Suddenly, the tunnel seems to grow larger; the roof rises, but the ground, still sloping downwards, stops at the edge of a vast crater constructed in the form of an inverted cone, the walls of which are covered with a smooth cement. An iron ladder leads down into bottomless darkness. In front of him lies the unknown, behind him the forbidden way of retreat; between these two threatening extremes is a torturing inertia with the prospect of death: it is enough to send the most stoical philosopher mad. But reason prevails with a final piece of advice, which is to go on, step by step, to the limits of the possible.

The iron ladder has seventy-eight rungs. When he arrives at the lowest the postulant realises, with fresh terror, that the cone terminates in a gaping pit which draws him on. Shaking with terror he climbs back a few rungs, he examines carefully the narrow space lit by the feeble rays of the lamp. On his left he sees a crevice that he had not noticed during the descent; this crevice is wide enough to admit a man. Clinging to the ladder with one hand, carrying the lamp in the other, he discovers that there are steps inside: it is probably a way out, but where does it lead? its first step is surely a place of safety, a resting-place? Hope and faith revive; without being able to guess how, he instinctively feels that he will soon find his release; he reproaches himself with having doubted the Magi, and remembers their warning: 'Go without fear; you have only yourself to be afraid of in the test of solitude.'

After a few moments of calming reflection he rises and enters this crevice. The stairway turns in a spiral. At the twenty-second step is a bronze grating through which the postulant can see a long gallery lined each side by cariatides in the form of sculpted sphinxes: there are twenty-four. Between them the wall is covered with frescoes representing mysterious personages and symbols. These twenty-two pairs of pictures face each other, lit by eleven bronze tripods arranged in a line running down the middle of the gallery. Each tripod carries a crystal sphinx in which burns an amianthus wick in incense-laden oil.

A Magus, who here bears the name of *Pastophore* ['guardian of the sacred symbols'],[*] comes to open the grating to the postulant. 'Son of Earth,' he says smiling, 'be welcome. You have escaped the pit by discovering the path of wisdom. Few aspirants to the Mysteries have triumphed over this test; the others have all perished. Since the great Isis is your protector, she will lead you I hope safe and sound to the sanctuary where virtue receives its crown. I must not hide from you that other perils lie in store; but I am allowed to encourage you by explaining these symbols, the understanding of which creates for the heart of man an invulnerable armour. Come with me and contemplate these sacred images; listen carefully to my words, and, if you can mind them in your memory, the kings of the world will be less powerful than you when you return to earth.'

Thereupon, passing in front of each of the twenty-two paintings in the gallery, the postulant received from the Pastophore the information which follows.

III

THE Science of Will, the principle of all wisdom and source of all power, is contained in twenty-two *Arcana* or symbolic hieroglyphs, each of whose attributes conceals a certain meaning and which, taken as a whole, compose an absolute doctrine memorised by its correspondence with the Letters of the sacred language and with the Numbers that are connected with these Letters. Each letter and each Number, contemplated by the eye or uttered by the mouth, expresses a reality of the *divine world*, the *intellectual world* and the

---

[*] See note 2 of this Book. p. 89.—*Ed.*

physical world [Book I, p. 19]. Each arcanum, made visible or tangible by one of these paintings, is the formula of a law of human activity in its relationship with spiritual and material forces whose combination produces the phenomena of life.

✱ ARCANUM I

[Letter *Athoïm* (A)—Number 1]

THE MAGUS: *Will*

A—1 expresses in the *divine world* the absolute Being who contains and from whom flows the infinity of all possible things: in the *intellectual world,* Unity, the principle and synthesis of numbers; the Will, principle of action: in the *physical world,* Man, the highest of all living creatures, called upon to raise himself, by a perpetual expansion of his faculties, into the concentric spheres of the Absolute.

Arcanum 1 is represented by the Magus, the type of the perfect man, in full possession of his physical and moral faculties. He is represented standing upright, in the attitude of will proceeding to action. He wears a white robe, image of purity. His belt is a serpent biting its tail: the symbol of eternity. His forehead is enclosed in a fillet of gold, signifying light; this expresses the continuum in which all created things revolve. The Magus holds in his right hand a golden sceptre, image of command, raised towards the heavens in a gesture of aspiration towards knowledge, wisdom and power; the index finger of the left hand points to the ground, signifying that the mission of the perfect man is to reign over the material world. This double gesture means that human will ought to be the earthly reflection of the divine will, promoting good and preventing evil.

Before the Magus on a cubic stone are placed a goblet, a sword and a shekel—a golden coin in whose centre a cross is engraved. The goblet signifies the mixture of passions contributing to happiness or misfortune, according to whether we are their masters or their slaves. The sword symbolises labour, the striving that overcomes obstacles and the tests that pain makes us undergo. The shekel is the image of aspirations fulfilled, works accomplished, the apex of power attained by perseverance and will-power. The cross, seal of the infinite with which the shekel is engraved, announces the future ascent of that power into the spheres of the future.

✻ ARCANUM II

[Letter *Beïnthin* (B)—Number 2]

THE DOOR OF THE OCCULT SANCTUARY: *Knowledge*

B—2 expresses, in the *divine world*, the consciousness of the absolute Being who embraces the three periods of all manifestations: the past, the present and the future. In the *intellectual world*, the Binary, reflection of Unity; Knowledge, perception of visible and invisible things: in the *physical world*, Woman, the matrix of Man, who joins herself with him in a similar destiny.

Arcanum 2 is represented by a woman seated on the threshold of the temple of Isis, between two columns. The column on her right is red; this signifies purity of spirit. The column on her left is black, and represents the night of chaos, the impure spirit's captivity in the bonds of material things. The woman is crowned by a tiara surmounted by a crescent moon covered by a veil whose folds fall over her face. She wears on her breast the solar cross and carries on her knees an open book which she half-covers with her cloak. This symbolic figure personifies occult science waiting for the initiate on the threshold of the sanctuary of Isis to communicate to him nature's secrets. The solar cross [analogous with the Indian *Lingam*][1] signi-

---

[1] The Lingam was the symbol of the union of the sexes. No thought of shame was connected with contemplation of the reproductive organs in the religious systems of antiquity; the monuments of Mithra, of Persian inspiration, are proof of this. The corruption of morals made it necessary later to relegate these smybols to the secret sanctuaries of initiation, but morals were not improved thereby.

fies the fecundation of matter by spirit; it expresses also, as the seal of the infinite, the fact that knowledge proceeds from God, and is, like its Source, without bounds. The veil enveloping the tiara and falling over the face means that truth hides itself from the sight of profane curiosity. The book half-hidden by the cloak signifies that the mysteries reveal themselves only in solitude to the wise man who wraps himself in the cloak of silent meditation. . .

If Arcanum 2 appears in your horoscope, knock resolutely on the door of the future and it will be opened unto you; but study long and carefully the path you are to tread. Turn your face towards the sun of Justice and the knowledge of what is true shall be given unto you. Speak to no one of your purpose, so that it may not be given over to the contradiction of men.

✱ ARCANUM III

[Letter *Gomor* (G)—Number 3]

Isis-Urania: *Action*

G—3 expresses, in the *divine world,* the supreme Power balanced by the eternally active Mind and by absolute Wisdom: in the *intellectual world,* the universal fecundity of the supreme Being: in the *physical world,* Nature in labour, the germination of the acts that are to spring from the Will.

Arcanum III is represented by a woman seated at the centre of a blazing sun; she is crowned by twelve stars and her feet rest on the moon. She is the personification of universal fecundity. The sun is the emblem of creative strength; the crown of stars symbolises, by the number 12, the houses or stations through which the sun travels year after year. This woman, celestial Isis or Nature, carries a sceptre surmounted by a globe: it is the sign of her perpetual activity over things born and unborn. On her other hand she bears an eagle, symbol of the heights to which spirit may soar. The moon beneath her feet signifies the weakness of matter and its domination by the Spirit.

Remember, son of Earth, that to affirm what is true and to desire what is just is half-way towards creating those things; to deny them is to condemn oneself to destruction. If Arcanum III manifests itself among the signs of your horoscope, you may hope for success in your enterprises, provided that you know how to unite productive activity with the rectitude of spirit that makes your labours bear fruit.

✱ ARCANUM IV

[Letter *Dinaïn* (D)—Number 4]

THE CUBIC STONE: *Realisation*

D—4 expresses, in the *divine world,* the perpetual and hierarchical realisation of the virtues contained in the absolute Being: in the *intellectual world,* the realisation of the ideas of the contingent Being by the quadruple effort of the spirit: Affirmation, Negation, Discussion, Solution: in the *physical world,* the realisation of the actions directed by the knowledge of Truth, the love of Justice, the strength of the Will and the work of the Organs.

Arcanum IV is represented by a man wearing a helmet surmounted by a crown. He is seated on a cubical stone. His right hand holds a sceptre and his right leg is bent and rests on the other in the form of a cross. The cubical stone, image of the perfect solid, signifies the accomplishment of human labours. The crowned helmet is the emblem of the strength that conquers power. This dominating figure holds the sceptre of Isis, and the stone which serves him as a throne signifies conquered matter. The cross described by the position of his limbs symbolises the four elements and the expansion of human power in every direction.

Remember, Son of Earth, that nothing can resist a firm will, which has as its support the knowledge of the true and the just. The struggle to realise these things is more than a right, it is a duty. The man who triumphs in this struggle does no more than accomplish his mission here on earth; he who succumbs in his devotion to the cause acquires immortality. If Arcanum IV appears in your horoscope, it signifies that the realisation of your hopes depends on a being more powerful than yourself: seek and find him, and he will be your support.

★ ARCANUM V

[Letter *Eni* (E)—Number 5]

THE MASTER OF THE ARCANA: *Occult Inspiration*

E—5 expresses, in the *divine world*, the universal Law, regulating the infinite manifestations of the Being in the unity of substance: in the *intellectual world*, Religion, the relationship of the Absolute to the relative Being, the Infinite to the Finite: in the *physical world*, inspiration; the test of man by liberty of action in the closed circle of the universal law.

Arcanum V is represented by the image of the Hierophant (Master of the Sacred Mysteries). This prince of occult doctrine is seated between the two columns of the sanctuary. He is leaning on a cross with three horizontals and describes with the index finger of his right hand the sign of silence on his breast. At his feet two men have prostrated themselves, one clothed in red, the other in black. The Hierophant represents the Genius of good intentions and the spirit of conscience; his gesture invites to meditation, to listen to the voice of the heavens in the silence of the passions and of the instincts of the flesh. The column on his right symbolises the divine law; the one on the left signifies freedom to obey or disobey. The triple cross is the emblem of God pervading the three worlds in order to produce in them all the manifestations of life. The two men, one red, the other black, represent the genii of Light and of Darkness, both of whom obey the Master of the Arcana.

Remember, son of Earth, that before saying a man is

happy or unhappy you must know to what use he puts his will, for all men create their lives in the image of their works. The genius of Good is on your right, Evil on your left: their voices can only be heard by your conscience. Meditate, and it will tell you what they say.

✱ ARCANUM VI

[Letter *Ur* (U, V)—Number 6]

THE TWO ROADS: *The Ordeal*

U, V—6 expresses in the *divine world* the knowledge of Good and Evil: in the *intellectual world*, the balance of Necessity and Liberty: in the *physical world*, the antagonism of natural forces, the chain of cause and effect.

Arcanum VI is represented by a man standing motionless at a crossroads. His eyes are fixed upon the earth, his arms crossed on his breast. Two women, one on his right, one on his left, stand each with a hand on his shoulder, pointing out to him one of the two roads. The woman on his right has a fillet of gold around her forehead: she personifies virtue. The one on the left is crowned with vineleaves and represents the temptations of vice. Above and behind this group the genius of Justice, borne on a nimbus of blazing light, is drawing his bow and directs the arrow of punishment at Vice. The whole scene expresses the struggle between the passions and conscience.

Remember, son of Earth, that for the ordinary man vice has a greater attraction than virtue. If Arcanum VI appears in your horoscope, take care to keep your resolutions. Obstacles bar the road to happiness; contrary influences hover around you; your will vacillates between opposing sides. In all things indecision is more fatal than the wrong choice. Advance or retreat, but never hesitate; remember that a chain of flowers is more difficult to break than a chain of iron.

✱ ARCANUM VII

[Letter *Zaïn* (Z)—Number 7]

THE CHARIOT OF OSIRIS: *Victory*

Z—7 expresses in the *divine world* the Septenary, the domination of Spirit over Nature: in the *intellectual world*, the Priesthood and the Empire: in the *physical world*, the submission of the elements and the forces of matter to the Intelligence and to the labours of Man.

Arcanum VII is represented by a war-chariot, square in shape, surmounted by a starred baldaquin upheld by four columns. In this chariot an armed conqueror advances carrying a sceptre and a sword in his hands. He is crowned with a fillet of gold ornamented at five points by three pentagrammes or golden stars. The square chariot symbolises the work accomplished by the will which has overcome all obstacles. The four columns supporting the starry canopy represent the four elements conquered by the Master of the sceptre and the sword. On the square representing the front of the chariot is drawn a sphere upheld by two outstretched wings, sign of the limitless exaltation of human power in the infinity of space and time. The crown of gold on the conqueror's head signifies the possession of intellectual illumination which gives light to all the arcana of Chance. The three stars which decorate it at five points symbolise Power balanced by Mind and Wisdom. Three squares are engraved on the breast-plate: they signify rectitude of Judgment, Will and Action which gives the Power of which the breast-plate is the emblem. The lifted sword is the sign of victory. The sceptre, crowned by a triangle, symbol of the Spirit, by a square, symbol of Matter, and by a circle, symbol of Eternity, signifies the perpetual domination of the Mind over the forces of Nature. Two sphinxes, one white, the other black, are harnessed to the chariot. The former symbolises Good, the latter Evil—the one conquered, the other vanquished—both having become the servants of the Magus who has triumphed over his ordeals.

Remember, son of the Earth, that the empire of the world belongs to those who possess a sovereign Mind, that is to say, the light which illuminates the mysteries of life. By overcoming your obstacles you will overthrow your enemies, and all your wishes shall be realised, if you go towards the future with courage reinforced by the consciousness of doing right.

✱ ARCANUM VIII
[Letter *Heletha* (H)—Number 8]
THEMIS: *Equilibrium*

H—8 expresses in the *divine world* absolute Justice: in the *intellectual world* Attraction and Repulsion: in the *physical world* the relative, fallible and narrow Justice which is man's.

Arcanum VIII is represented by a woman seated on a throne wearing a crown armed with spear-points: she holds in her right hand an upward-pointing sword and in the left a pair of scales. It is the ancient symbol of Justice weighing in the balance the deeds of men, and as a counter-weight opposing evil with the sword of expiation. Justice, which proceeds from God, is the stabilising reaction which restores order, equilibrium between right and duty. The sword is here a sign of protection for the righteous and of warning for the sinful. The eyes of Justice are covered with a bandage to show that she weighs and strikes without taking into account the conventional differences established by men.

Remember, son of Earth, that to be victorious and to overcome your obstacles is only a part of the human task. If you would wish to accomplish it entirely, you must establish a balance between the forces you set in motion. Every action produces its reaction, and the Will must foresee the onslaught of contrary forces in time to lessen or check it. All future things hang in the balance between Good and Evil. The Mind that cannot find equilibrium resembles a sun in eclipse.

✱ ARCANUM IX

[Letter *Théla* (TH)—Number 9]

THE VEILED LAMP: *Prudence*

TH—9 expresses in the *divine world* absolute Wisdom: in the *intellectual world* Prudence, the governor of the Will: in the *physical world* circumspection, guide to Action.

Arcanum 9 is represented by an old man who walks leaning on a stick and holding in front of him a lighted lantern half-hidden by his cloak. This old man personifies experience acquired in the labours of life. The lighted lantern signifies the light of the mind which should illuminate the past, the present and the future. The cloak that half conceals it signifies discretion. The stick symbolises the support given by prudence to the man who does not reveal his purpose.

Remember, son of Earth, that Prudence is the armour of the Wise. Circumspection allows him to avoid reefs or pitfalls and to be forewarned of treachery. Take it for your guide in all your actions, even in the smallest things. Nothing lacks importance: a pebble may overturn the chariot in which the master of the world is riding. Remember that if Speech is silver, Silence is golden.

✱ ARCANUM X

[Letter *Ioïthi* (I. J. Y)—Number 10]

THE SPHINX: *Fortune*

I, J, Y—10 expresses in the *divine world* the active principle that animates all beings: in the *intellectual world* ruling Authority: in the *physical world* good or evil Fortune.

Arcanum X is represented by a wheel suspended by its axle between two columns. On the right Hermanubis, the Spirit of God, strives to climb to the top of the wheel. On the left Typhon, the Spirit of Evil, is cast down. The Sphinx, balanced on the top of this wheel, holds a sword in its lion's paws. It personifies Destiny ever ready to strike left or right; according to the direction in which it turns the wheel the humblest rises and the highest is cast down.

Remember, son of Earth, that ability depends on the will; if your will is to be accomplished, you must be daring; and to dare successfully you must be able to keep silence until the moment comes for action. To possess Knowledge and Power, the will must be patient; to remain on the heights of life—if you succeed in attaining them—you must first have learned to plumb with steady gaze vast depths.

✱ ARCANUM XI

[Letter *Caïtha* (C, K)—Number 20]

THE TAMED LION: *Strength*

C, K—20 expresses in the *divine world* the Principle of all strength, spiritual or material: in the *intellectual world* moral Force: in the *physical world* organic Force.

Arcanum XI is represented by the image of a young girl who with her bare hands is closing, without effort, the jaws of a lion. It is the emblem of that strength which is communicated by faith in oneself and by innocency of life.

Remember, son of Earth, that deeds necessitate faith in your ability to accomplish them. Proceed with faith: all obstacles are phantoms. In order to become strong, silence must be imposed on the weaknesses of the heart; your duty must be studied, for it is the rule of righteousness. Practise justice as if you loved it.

✱ ARCANUM XII

[Letter *Luzain* (L)—Number 30]

THE SACRIFICE: *Violent Death*

L—30 expresses in the *divine world* the revelation of the Law: in the *intellectual world* the teaching of Duty: in the *physical world* Sacrifice.

Arcanum XII is represented by a man hung by one foot from a gallows which rests on two trees each of which has six branches cut from the trunk. The hands of this man are tied behind his back, and the bend of his arms forms the base of an inverted triangle the summit of which is his head. It is the sign of violent death encountered by tragic accident or in expiation of some crime, and accepted in a spirit of heroic devotion to Truth and Justice. The twelve lopped branches signify the extinction of life, the destruction of the twelve houses of the Horoscope. The inverted triangle symbolises catastrophe.

Remember, son of Earth, that devotion is a divine law from which none may have dispensation; but expect nothing, only ingratitude, from men. Let your heart be always ready to tender its account to the Eternal; for if Arcanum XII appears in your horoscope, violent death will lie in wait for you on your path through life. But if the world makes an attempt upon your earthly life, do not die without accepting with resignation the will of God and without pardoning your enemies; for whoever does not forgive shall be condemned, beyond this life, to an eternal solitude.

✱ ARCANUM XIII

[Letter *Mataloth* (M)—Number 40]

THE SCYTHE: *Transformation*

M—40 expresses in the *divine world* the perpetual movement of creation, destruction and renewal: in the *intellectual world* the ascent of the Spirit into the divine spheres: in the *physical world* death, that is, the transformation of human nature on reaching the end of its organic period.

Arcanum XIII is represented by a skeleton scything heads in a meadow; out of the ground on all sides appear men's hands and feet as the scythe pursues its deadly task. It is the emblem of destruction and perpetual rebirth of all forms of Being in the domain of Time.

Remember, son of Earth, that earthly things last only a brief space, and that the highest are cut down like the grass in the fields. The dissolution of your visible organs will come sooner than you expect; but do not fear death, for death is only birth into another life. The universe ceaselessly reabsorbs all that is her own and has not been spiritualised. But the freeing of material instincts by the voluntary adherence of the soul to the laws of universal movement constitutes in us the creation of a second man, the celestial man, and is the beginning of our immortality.

✳ ARCANUM XIV

[Letter *Naïn* (N)—Number 50]

THE SOLAR SPIRIT: *Initiative*

N—50 expresses in the *divine world* the perpetual movement of life: in the *intellectual world* the combination of the ideas that create morality: in the *physical world* the combination of the forces of Nature.

Arcanum XIV is represented by the Spirit of the Sun holding two urns and pouring from the one into the other the vital sap of life. It is the symbol of the combinations which are ceaselessly produced in all parts of Nature.

Son of Earth, take stock of your strength, not in order to retreat before the works of your hand but in order to wear away obstacles, as water falling drop by drop wears away the hardest stone.

✳ ARCANUM XV

[Letter *Xirön* (X)—Number 60]

TYPHON: *Fate*

X—60 expresses in the *divine world* predestination: in the *intellectual world* Mystery: in the *physical world* the Unforeseen, Fatality.

Arcanum XV is represented by Typhon, the spirit of

catastrophes, who rises out of a flaming abyss and brandishes a torch above the heads of two men chained at his feet. It is the image of Fatality which bursts into certain lives like the eruption of a volcano, and overwhelms great as well as small, strong and weak, the cleverest and the least perceptive, in its equal disaster.

Whoever you may be, son of Earth, contemplate the ancient oaks that defy the lightning, but which the lightning strikes after having avoided them for more than a century. Cease to believe in your wisdom and your strength, if God has not granted that you may receive the key to the mysteries that make a prisoner of Fate.

✱ ARCANUM XVI

[Letter *Olélath* (O)—Number 70]

The Lightning-Struck Tower: *Ruin*

O—70 expresses in the divine world the punishment of pride: in the *intellectual world* the downfall of the Spirit that attempts to discover the mystery of God: in the *physical world* reversals of fortune.

Arcanum XVI is represented by a tower struck by lightning. A crowned and an uncrowned man are thrown down from its heights with the ruins of the battlements. It is the symbol of material forces that can crush great and small alike. It is also the emblem of rivalries which only end in ruin for all concerned; of frustrated plans, of hopes that fade away, of abortive enterprises, ruined ambitions and catastrophic deaths.

Remember, son of Earth, that the ordeals of misfortune, accepted with resignation to the supreme Will of the All-Powerful, are the steps in a predestined progress for which you will be eternally rewarded. Suffering is working in order to free yourself from the bonds of material things; it is the putting-on of robes of Immortality.

✳ ARCANUM XVII

[Letter *Pilôn* (F, P)—Number 80]

THE STAR OF THE MAGI: *Hope*

F,, P—80 expresses in the *divine world* Immortality: in the *intellectual world* the Inner Light that illuminates the Spirit: in the *physical world* Hope.

Arcanum XVII is represented by a blazing star with eight rays surrounded by seven other stars hovering over a naked girl who pours over the barren earth the waters of universal Life that flow from two goblets, one gold, the other silver. Beside her, a butterfly is alighting on a rose. This girl is the emblem of Hope which scatters its dew upon our saddest days. She is naked, in order to signify that Hope remains with us when we have been bereft of everything. Above this figure the blazing, eight-pointed star symbolises the apocalypse of Destinies enclosed by seven seals which are the seven planets, represented by the seven other stars. The butterfly is the sign of resurrection beyond the grave.

Remember, son of Earth, that Hope is the sister of Faith. Abandon your passions and your errors and study the mysteries of true Knowledge, and their key shall be given unto you. Then shall a ray of the divine Light shine from the occult Sanctuary to dispel the darkness of the future and show you the path to happiness. Whatever happens in your life, never break the flowers of Hope, and you will gather the fruits of Faith.

✳ ARCANUM XVIII

[Letter *Tsadi* (TS)—Number 90]

TWILIGHT: *Deceptions*

TS—90 expresses in the *divine world* the abysses of the Infinite: in the *intellectual world* the darkness that cloaks the Spirit when it submits itself to the power of the instincts: in the *physical world*, deceptions and hidden enemies.

Arcanum XVIII is represented by a field that a half-clouded moon illuminates with a vague twilight. A tower stands on each side of a path that disappears into a barren landscape. In front of one of these two towers a dog is crouching: in front of the other, a dog is baying at the moon: between them is a crab. These towers symbolise the false security which does not foresee hidden perils.

Remember, son of Earth, that whosoever dares to confront the unknown faces death. The hostile spirits, symbolised by one dog, wait in ambush; the servile spirits, symbolised by the other, conceal their treacheries with base flattery; and the idle spirits, symbolised by the crab, will pass by without the slightest concern for disaster. Observe, listen—and learn to keep your own counsel.

✳ ARCANUM XIX

[Letter *Quitolath* (Q)—Number 100]

THE BLAZING LIGHT: *Earthly Happiness*

Q—100 expresses in the *divine world* the supreme Heaven: in the *intellectual world* sacred Truth: in the *physical world* peaceful Happiness.

Arcanum XIX is represented by a radiant sun shining on two small children, images of innocence, who hold each other's hands in the midst of a circle of flowers. It is the symbol of happiness promised by the simple life and by moderation in all one's desires.

Remember, son of Earth, that the light of the Mysteries flows dangerously in the service of the Will. It illuminates those who know how to use it; it strikes down those who are ignorant of its power or who abuse it.

✳ ARCANUM XX

[Letter *Rasith* (R)—Number 200]

THE AWAKENING OF THE DEAD: *Renewal*

R—200 represents the passage from life on earth to the life of the future. A Spirit is blowing a trumpet over a half-open tomb. A man, a woman and a child, a collective symbol of the human trinity, are shown rising from this tomb. It is a sign of the change which is the end of all things, of Good as well as of Evil.

Remember, son of Earth, that fortune is variable, even when it appears most unshakeable. The ascent of the soul is the fruit of its successive ordeals. Hope in the time of suffering, but beware of prosperity. Do not fall asleep in laziness or forgetfulness. At a moment unknown to you the wheel of fortune will turn: you will be raised or cast down by the Sphinx.

✱ ARCANUM O

[Letter *Sichen* (S)—Number 300]

THE CROCODILE: *Expiation*

S—300 represents the punishment following every error. You can see here a blind man carrying a full beggar's wallet about to collide with a broken obelisk, on which a crocodile is waiting with open jaws. This blind man is the symbol of he who makes himself the slave of material things. His wallet is packed with his errors and his faults. The broken obelisk represents the ruin of his works; the crocodile is the emblem of fate and the inevitable Expiation.

✱ ARCANUM XXI

[Letter *Thoth* (T)—Number 400]

THE CROWN OF THE MAGI: *The Reward*

THIS, the supreme Arcanum of Magism, is represented by a garland of golden roses surrounding a star and placed in a circle around which are set at equal distances the heads of a man, a bull, a lion and an eagle. This is the sign with which the Magus decorates himself when he has reached the highest degree of initiation and has thus acquired a power limited only by his own intelligence and wisdom.

Remember, son of Earth, that the empire of the World

belongs to the empire of Light, which is the throne reserved by God for sanctified Will. Happiness for the Magus is the fruit of the knowledge of Good and Evil; but God only allows it to be plucked by the man sufficiently master of himself to approach it without covetousness.

By joining together the 22 meanings inherent in these symbols the whole may be resumed in the following terms as the synthesis of Magism:

Human Will [I], illuminated by Knowledge [II] and manifested by Action [III,] creates Realisation [IV] of a

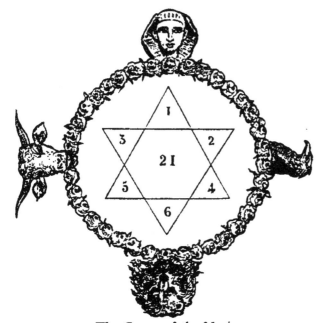

The Crown of the Magi

power that it can use rightly or wrongly; according to its good or evil Inspiration [V], in the circle described for it by the laws of universal order. After having overcome the Ordeal [VI], which is imposed on it by divine Wisdom, it enters, after its Victory [VII], into possession of the work it has created and, retaining its Equilibrium [VIII] on the axis of Prudence [IX], it dominates the fluctuations of Fortune [X]. Man's Strength [XI], sanctified by Sacrifice [XII], which is the voluntary offering of himself on the altar of dedication and expiation, triumphs over Death; and his divine Transformation [XIII] raising him above and beyond the tomb into the tranquil regions of an infinite progress, opposes the reality of an immortal Initiative [XIV] to the eternal falsehood of Fatality [XV]. The course of Time is measured by its ruins; but, beyond each Ruin [XVI], we see the re-appearance of the dawn of Hope [XVII] or the Twi-light of Disappointments [XVIII]. Man aspires ceaselessly to whatever is beyond him, and the sun of Happiness [XIX] rises for him only behind the tomb, after the Renewal [XX] of his being by the death that opens for him a higher sphere of will, intelligence and action. All will that lets itself be governed by bodily instincts is an abdication of liberty and condemns itself to the Expiation [O] of its error or its mis-take. On the other hand, all will that unites itself to God in order to demonstrate Truth and operate Justice enters, after this life, into participation with the divine Omnipo-tence over beings and things, the eternal Reward [XXI] of enfranchised spirits.

IV

THE Pastophore has by now led the postulant to the end of the gallery of the Arcana and opens a door giving access to another long narrow vault, at the end of which roars a blazing furnace.

At this the postulant trembles. 'Where am I going now?' he wonders half-aloud. 'It's an inescapable fate—it's death!'

'Son of Earth,' says the Pastophore, 'death itself frightens the imperfect only. If you are afraid, what are you doing here? Look at me; once I too passed through those flames as if they were a garden of roses.'

Encouraged by the Magus' kindly smile, the postu-lant reassured steps forward while behind him the door is closed on the gallery of the Arcana. Reflection reminds him that the teaching he has just received would be useless to a man about to die. He does not know how this new ordeal will end; but had he foreseen how the others would end? And as he approaches the barrier of fire, his confidence increases, the danger diminishes in his eyes. The furnace is nothing more than an optical illusion created by small piles of resinous wood arranged on iron grills between which is traced a path. He goes eagerly forward, for he thinks he has come through the ordeal; but suddenly the unforeseen happens. In front of him the vaulted passageway ends abruptly at a stagnant pool, whose broad still surface covers unknown depths. Behind him a cascade of oil falls from the opened ceiling and leaps into flame: the furnace is a real furnace now.

Penned between this curtain of flame and the sheet of water which may conceal a trap, he has to judge the lesser danger. He enters the dark water and walks carefully down a slippery slope. With each step the water level seems to rise—it reaches his chest—goes higher—his shoulders: one more step and the water will close over his head. But the light from the furnace shows him that he has reached the middle of the lake. Further on the slope beings to rise again, and at the water's edge on the opposite bank a flight of steps leads to a platform surrounded on three sides by a lofty arcade. On the wall at the end is a brass doorway that seems divided into two by a narrow twisted column sculptured with a lion's jaws which hold a large metal ring.

This door is closed. The postulant, soaked to the skin and shivering, with difficulty mounts the stairs. On reaching the platform he is surprised to find himself walking on a floor of hollow-sounding metal. He stops outside the door to get his bearings. Beyond the water the reflection from the furnace dims and then is extinguished. Darkness reigns again under these unknown vaults, the silence is filled with dread: how can he go forward, how retreat?

But listen—mysterious words are heard in that empty gloom: 'If you stop,' says this voice, 'you will perish. Behind you is death; before you, salvation.'

One can imagine the anxiety of the poor postulant.

Driven by terror, trembling in the darkness, he feels round the sculptures on the brazen doorway, trying to discover the secret mechanism that will make it open. The ring he saw just now in the lion's jaws, representing a serpent with its tail in its mouth—could it be a sort of knocker to be lifted and let fall on the sonorous metal of door? He has barely seized it in his hands when by a mechanical trick the metal floor collapses under him and he is left suspended over a gaping pit.

This ordeal had the appearance of great danger, for the postulant might lose his grip; but the Magi foresaw the possibility. The depths over which the metal floor opened were divided by several lengths of cloth stretched horizontally one above the other; this simple precaution was enough to lessen any fall, and besides, several Pastophores were hidden there ready to catch the postulant in their arms. But if he did not fall, the metal floor was immediately raised again and screwed back in its original position. When the postulant felt his feet touch ground again, the brazen door opened before him. The leader of an escort of twelve *Neocores* [guardians of the sanctuary] bandaged his eyes and led him by torchlight along the final galleries leading from the Sphinx to the Great Pyramid. At regular intervals they had to pass through secret doors which the officers of the temple opened only after having received a password and a recognition sign.

The College of the Magi awaited the future initiate in a crypt hollowed out in the centre of the pyramid.

On the polished walls of this crypt symbolic paintings represented the 48 Spirits of the year, the 7 Spirits of the planets and the 360 Spirits of the days. It was an illustrated Bible whose pictures, separated by strips of gold, contained all the traditions that Magism had received from Hermes-Thoth, the great revealer. All the sacerdotal knowledge was inscribed above each painting; but this writing could be read only by initiates, to whom the Hierophant confided the key to a mysterious alphabet which they were sworn to keep secret. The same formidable oath covered all adepts, from the Zealot [title of the first grade] to the Rose-Cross [ninth grade] who received the seal of the supreme initiation.

At the four corners of the crypt stood four bronze statues on triangular columns. The first represented a man, the second a bull, the third a lion, and the fourth an eagle —the symbolic divisions of the Sphinx. On the head of each was a receptable shaped like a crown whence a light shone. Seven three-armed lamps, suspended from the vaulted ceiling at the points of a golden rosette with seven rays, completed the illumination.

The Hierophant, clothed in purple, on his forehead a circlet of gold decorated with seven stars, occupied a silver throne set up on a platform in the centre of the assembly; the other Magi, in white albs, wearing circlets of plain gold, were arranged in a triple semicircle on both sides of the master, but on a lower level.

Behind the throne, under a purple canopy, appeared a colossal statue of Isis, personification of Nature, composed of an alloy of lead, tin, iron, gold, copper, quicksilver and silver, each sacred to one of the planets.

Isis wore a triangular diadem of silver with an aigrette of twelve rays and on her breast a golden rose, representing the universe, at the centre of a cross of the same metal indicating by the direction of the four extremities the four cardinal points of the earth and the avenues of the infinite : height, breadth, depth. The two arms were stretched out a little in front of the body; their distance from one another formed the base of an equilateral triangle whose summit was the top of the forehead. The hands were open, each projecting earthwards five rays of gold. These ten rays and the twelve in the aigrette represented the 22 Arcana.

In front of the Hierophant at the centre of the crypt was a great silver table, circular in shape, on which was engraved the diagram of the horoscope which has already been presented to the reader [Book I, page 61]. This table was supported by twelve cariatides, each of which represented one of the signs of the Zodiac. The same signs were also engraved in monograms on a large hoop of gold fitted into a groove made round the table. This circle, divided into twelve parts and set in motion by gears, could be turned to bring to the east the sign which corresponded to the exact time of anyone's birth. In the centre of the table was a pivot to which were attached seven movable pointers, each made of the metal sacred to the planetary spirit represented. When the zodiacal perimeter was fixed, the planet designated by each pointer was directed to the spot determined by magical calculations. The east and the west of this uranographical planisphere were marked by two bronze plinths carrying two wax tablets on which the Magus could inscribe the results of his observation.

This formed the supreme test of initiation. The member to be elected received from the Hierophant a horoscope which he had to work out and explain in front of the whole assembly; and he had to do this without the slightest error, under pain of having his admission to the rank of Magus of the Rose-cross postponed indefinitely.

But let us return to our postulant, whose tribulations have not yet reached an end. Brought in like a man saved from shipwreck, he is set before the Magi at the entrance to the crypt and the twelve Néocores are drawn up on each side. Two of them hold his arms and compel him to stand still.

'Son of Earth,' the Hierophant says to him, 'the men of your country believed you to be learned and wise, and you felt within yourself even greater pride than was deserved by their admiration. One day you heard that we possess a store of supernatural knowledge, and you knew no rest until you received permission to enter among us. Here you are, wretched, captive, given up of your own accord to the power of an unknown society whose secrets you coveted and which, as a first punishment for your audacity, has imprisoned you in the bowels of the earth. You had heard of our ordeals; but, as our mysteries are well guarded, you imagined, in your pettiness, that postulants were submitted only to rudimentary trials, capable at most of astonishing vulgar minds, and that you would soon see the apotheosis of your easily-tested courage. You never dreamed that we, masters of life and death, could give such a cruel lie to that presumption. I have only to give the sign and you will be plunged alive into subterranean depths to eat the bread of remorse and drink the waters of anguish until the end of your days. But our clemency deigns to show itself greater than your sincerity; all it will ask of you, even if you wish to be restored to liberty, will be your solemn oath that you will never reveal to anyone the least detail of what you have seen and heard this night. Will you give this oath?'

The postulant, prompted by one of the Néocores, replies: 'I will.'

The Hierophant then gives orders to the Néocores to make him kneel at the foot of the altar. Then he recites in a loud voice, and makes the postulant repeat phrase for phrase, the following formula: 'In the presence of the seven Spirits who execute the will of the ineffable Being, eternal and infinite, I . . ., son of . . . , born . . . , swear to be forever silent, never to speak of what I have seen and heard or of what I shall see and shall hear, in this sanctuary of the priests of the divine Wisdom. If ever I betray my oath I shall deserve to have my throat cut, my tongue and heart torn out and to be buried in the sand of the ocean, that the waves of it may carry me away into an eternity of oblivion.'

'We are the witnesses of your oath,' goes on the Hierophant, 'and if ever you become guilty of perjury, an invisible vengeance will follow you in all your ways. It will reach you wherever you may be, even on the highest of thrones, yes, and it will make you suffer the fate that you yourself have just pronounced. From this hour forward you are counted among the number of the disciples of Wisdom, and you will bear, among us, the title of Zealot until, by some great act of obedience and self-abnegation, you have deserved to be raised to a higher rank.'

While these last words are being spoken two Néocores, each bearing a goblet, come and place themselves silently on each side of the altar; a third takes his place behind the postulant, in order presently to untie the bandage over his eyes. A little further back four Melanophores [funeral officers] spread out a great black veil.

'All the Magi,' continues the Hierophant, 'owe me absolute submission. Swear to me a similar obedience.'

The postulant swears a second oath.

'Beware,' cries the Hierophant. 'If you have sworn only with your lips, know that we can read into your heart; and falsehood, in our world, is punished by death!'

A tempestuous roaring, produced by a hidden apparatus, sounds menacingly in the pyramid depths; explosions of burning naphtha imitate peals of thunder; the seven lamps hung from the vaulting are suddenly extinguished and the crypt is only lighted by tremulous fires.

During this artificial storm the postulant's bandage, loosened by the third Néocore, falls to his feet. He sees in that fantastic light all the Magi standing over him and pointing their swords at his breast: a terrible spectacle.

'These swords,' goes on the Hierophant, 'symbolise human justice; but this is often fallible or slow, and the fear it inspires does not stop man's audacity. We want heaven itself to guarantee the faith of the new initiates. You have sworn me absolute obedience: you must test it by an ordeal from which only the All-Powerful can save you—if he judges you worthy of life.'

At this the Magi lower their swords and the Néocores with the two goblets approach the postulant.

'You see these goblets?' continues the Hierophant. 'The contents of the one are harmless: in the other there is a violent poison. I command you to seize, without reflection, one of them and empty it at a single draught.'

If the dismayed postulant refuses, a fresh roll of thunder announces that the initiation is not to be; the four funeral officers throw a black veil over him, roll him up in it and carry him away.

The man who thus refuses to sacrifice the life now forsworn by a double oath is forever disgraced. Could he be allowed to return to his fellow-citizens and say: 'I wanted to be initiated into the mysteries of those renowned Magi before whom all Egypt bows as if they were gods; but they are only rogues and madmen, and no one is allowed into their society unless he luckily survive the risk of poisoning himself. Such an ordeal revolted me; they drove me away with the utmost scorn. But I revenge myself by denouncing them as monsters to the whole of the civilised world'?

No; retreat or revolt on the part of a sworn postulant would no longer allow him a liberty which he would only abuse. Yet the Magi do not put him to death. He is imprisoned for seven moons in a cellar in the Pyramid with a lamp, and some bread and water brought to him each day by two silent visitors. By his side was placed a book of maxims containing the duties of man towards the supreme Being, towards his fellow-creatures, and towards himself. The perusal of this book, written by Hermes-Thoth to be used as an elementary catechism by the initiate, offered the captive some elements of consolation. He could learn from it the possibility of rising from his fall. After the seven moons had passed, the two goblets were again presented to him. This time he accepted the ordeal, even if he did so only reluctantly. The magic law was satisfied; nevertheless the liberated initiate remained a mere Zealot, he could never aspire to higher rank. If he again refused, the captivity was continued another seven moons, followed by a fresh offer of the goblets, and so on until obedience or natural death terminated his existence.

When the ordeal of the two goblets had been courageously faced in the presence of the college, which is what happened at Plato's initiation, the Hierophant hastened to acquaint the postulant with the lack of danger, and say that

both goblets contained pure wine with a little myrrh to add
a slight bitterness.

V

After such prolonged tension rest became indispensable; but even this contained, unknown to the initiate, a
final ordeal, the only one really to endanger life. The
Neocores led him into a room next to the sanctuary ornamented with all the luxury of a royal bedroom. Servants
took off his soaking garments, massaged him with perfumed
attars [essential oils], clothed him in a robe of fine white
linen and brought to him a table laden with exquisite dishes
and wine. During this meal an invisible orchestra intoxicated his imagination and made him fall into amorous
visions. The folds of a green tapestry of myrtle-boughs
[colour and plant dedicated to Venus] were slowly drawn at
the end of the room to reveal a gallery where, in a soft light,
groups of young girls were dancing, joined to one another
by garlands of roses. These were the daughters of the Magi,
brought up in the sanctuary and consecrated to Isis until
the day when they received a husband. They were masked
so that the initiate would not recognise them later if he
were successful in his ordeal; but all they wore was a short
tunic spangled with golden bees, a gauze scarf and a few
flowers.

Scarcely had he crossed the gallery threshold than two
of the seemingly abandoned dancers captured him in a
rosy chain. All the others disappeared like startled doves.
The light, suddenly dimmed, gave no more than a misty
twilight in which the two temptresses continued their wild
dance, each in turn shaking the chain to provoke the initiate
into a choice. If by the slightest sign of weakness the imprudent man dared profane the purity of the mysteries, a
Néocore who had glided unnoticed behind him struck him
dead. If he remained motionless, or broke the chain of roses,
a sign from the Néocore sent the two women away and a

procession of the Magi congratulated their new brother for having triumphed over the attack on his virtue.

'Worthy Zealot,' the Hierophant said, 'Magic is composed of two elements, knowledge and strength. Without knowledge, no strength can be complete; without some sort of strength, no one can rise in the slightest degree in the world of knowledge. Learn how to suffer, that you may become impassive; learn how to die, that you may become immortal; learn how to restrain yourself, that you may be worthy of obtaining your desire: these are the first three secrets of the new life into which we have initiated you by ordeal. Every Magus is called to become the priest of Truth, that is, the confidant of its mysteries and the possessor of its strength. But few realise this lofty destiny completely. Learn therefore always to dominate your senses in order to preserve the liberty of your soul: that is the prologue to our sacred studies. The intuition of God will be its crowning reward. In our brotherhood high intelligences attain to *prophecy* and *theurgy*. The first revives the past, penetrates the reasons of the present and unveils the future. The second power creates works similar to those of God by the progressive discovery of the secrets of universal life. You may attain to the dignity of *prophet* and *theurgist* after seven years' silent solitary work and after passing examinations in all branches of knowledge accessible to man. Go on as you have begun and may great Isis be your support and helper. But remember, whether you decide to live among us in life-long fellowship, devoting yourself to the pleasures of study and the duties of the positions which, if you show yourself worthy, may one day be entrusted to you; or whether you prefer to return to your native land to teach Truth and Justice to your countrymen, remember the oath you have sworn. And that it may never be effaced from your memory, come with me and observe, before your return, the punishment we reserve for perjurors.'

The procession of Magi thereupon re-entered the sanctuary. Each member of the sacred college took his place

again in the semicircle; the Hierophant armed himself with
the sword and sceptre from the altar and, raising his arms
till they formed with his body the sign of the cross, cried
amid the general silence: 'Brethren, what hour is it?'

'The hour of Justice,' replied all the Magi with one
voice.

A gong echoing prolongedly beneath the earth was
struck seven times, slowly.

'Since it is the hour of Justice,' went on the Hierophant, 'let Justice be done!'

At the foot of the altar a brazen trapdoor was now
lowered over a pit whence came the noise of rattling chains
and struggle, followed by the roars of a beast and the
cry of a human voice in dreadful agony, then . . . nothing: only the cold stillness of a sepulchre. 'Thus do perjurors meet their end,' said the Magi.

'Justice is done,' goes on the Hierophant, turning to the
neophyte. 'Come, observe its handiwork.'

The twelve Néocores surround them; six go before, six
behind; all descend, one by one, the narrow pit opening.
And there, in the pallid lamplight, the neophyte discerns
a sphinx tearing at a human body lying before it. He
staggers and almost faints; but the Néocores support him,
and when they have revived him the vision is gone. Let us
here hasten to say that it was but a pretended murder by a
mechanical sphinx on an artificial victim. It was the last
act of the drama of initiation and was followed by a
religious banquet.

Plato lived for thirteen years among the Magi of Memphis and of the city of the Sun. Many centuries before Plato
the child Moses, saved from the Nile waters by Thermuthis,
daughter of the Pharaoh Amenophis,[a] was also brought up

---

[a] 'Pharaoh's daughter' and the Pharaoh of the period himself are really un-
identified. He may be Tehutimes ['Thothmes'] II, when the 'Pharaoh's
daughter' becomes the masterful Queen-Pharaoh Maetkara Hatshepsut; these
are of the earlier 18th Dynasty. Amenhetep or 'Amenophis' is the name of four

by the Magi and derived from the secret teachings the religious, political and social ideas which were the basis of the laws of the Hebrews after their flight from Egypt. This Biblical story is too widely known to repeat. Sufficient that the laws and rites of Magism for the most part passed into the theocratic constitution of which Moses was the founder. Surprisingly, the dogma of the soul's immortality does not figure in Mosaic law; neither does the idea of rewards and punishments awaiting the soul on the threshold of the future life. This dogma was held in the highest esteem by the Magi as one of the most sacred teachings of moral philosophy. When they carried their doctrine, arts and sciences into Greece and Asia, the Egyptians did not forget this concept of divine justice. The fable of Minos, Iacchus and Rhadamantus, the judges of death, is magical in origin; the Tartary of the peoples of antiquity, known by various names, is reminiscent of the Egyptian *Amentis,* which means hell or the lower region through which, according to Mystic theology, all souls must pass on leaving earth to enter new existence.

At the entrance to the judgment-hall of Amentis was a guardian monster named *Oms,* the hound of Typhon. This was a compound between crocodile, hippopotamus and dog. whence the Greeks derived their Cerberus or dog with three heads. The soul having left the body arrives in this lower region conducted by two spirits; one called Justice, the other Truth. It is received by a third spirit, Themis, daughter of the Sun [the Persephone of the Greeks—Latin form Proserpine]—who presides over thirty-two judges.' These have various animal heads, each type symbolising a

---

Pharaohs to the second of whom the Exodus has been attributed, perhaps about 1448 B.C. The fourth holder of the name rejected it in favour of Aakhuenaten and was the famous 'heretic' Pharaoh [see note p. 32]. Earlier opinion considered the building and warlike Pharaoh Rameses II of the 19th Dynasty [1321-1205 B.C.] to be the Pharaoh of the Exodus.—*Ed.*

' According to Hesiod, Themis [law or order: Greek word *to establish*] was one of the twelve primordial Titans, children of Uranus and Gaia, and sister to a sun-god, Hyperion.—*Ed.*

virtue or a vice in which he or she is examiner. In the midst is a pair of scales in which are separately weighed good and evil actions represented by weights given by Thoth, alleged first legislator of Egypt. The supreme Being, represented by Osiris, welcomes the pure souls into spheres of happiness détermined by their types of merit, and sends guilty souls to purify themselves in a sphere of expiation.

This idea, so simple, so profoundly religious, expressed by symbols borrowed from nature, was debased in the course of time by ignorant commentaries from popularisers who did not possess the key to Magism. They made the world believe that Egyptians worshipped animals. Hermes-Thoth himself had foreseen this, for he wrote somewhere, in the *Pymander* or the *Asclepios,* these sadly prophetic words: 'O Egypt, a time shall come when, instead of a pure religion and an intelligent cult, you shall have nothing left but ridiculous fables that posterity will find incredible; and there shall be nothing left to you but words graven upon stone, dumb and almost undecipherable monuments to your ancient piety.'

The sons of the Magi began their studies from their fifteenth year; the complete course lasted twenty-one years. This included all sciences. First lessons were in the natural history and distribution of plants, minerals and men. Then drawing, so that they might learn to depict memorable objects; then mathematics, physics, chemistry, medicine, surgery, sculpture, architecture, music and mechanics. From these applied sciences the teaching passed to the study of general world history and of foreign languages and institutions. It culminated in the religious sciences, divided into vulgar and sacred astronomy, horoscopy, symbolic writing, philosophy, rituals, prophecy and theurgy. Each year examinations increased in difficulty with the instruction. The sons of the Magi were given no physical ordeal, for education itself constituted their initiation; and bound to the priesthood by family and birth, brought up in its traditions among sacred ceremonies, they were able easily to learn the

meaning and understand the spirit of Magism. Needless to
impose discretion as part of a fearful dogma; it was in them
a racial virtue, of which they showed themselves proud and
worthy very early; it was the crown of knowledge, the
guarantee of the world's respect. The Order of the Magi
has engraved its name on history as the sole society whose
monumental works still reveal to us the existence of arts
practised to the maximum perfection in a civilisation with
which not India, China, Assyria nor Persia achieved anything comparable.

We have seen that the foreigner, after having survived
the physical ordeals of the postulant, at once received the
title of Zealot. If he wished to attain a higher rank, he had
to study for twelve years with the Magi, submit to an austere
régime and a rigorous solitude. As he advanced in knowledge, he was admitted to the second grade with the title of
Theoricus; in the third grade, he became a *Practicus*; in
the fourth, *Philosopher*; in the fifth, *Minor Adept*; in the
sixth, *Major Adept*; in the seventh, *Enfranchised Adept*; in
the eighth, *Master of the Temple*; and in the ninth, *Magus
of the Rose-Cross*. But this final grade, having complete
knowledge, was only for those with almost miraculous
memories, for it had to embrace hieratic sciences whose
religious law forbade the giving or receiving of written
communications. The Magus had to be a living encyclopædia, all the divisions and chapters of which appeared as
on a single page immediately on being called to mind.
Astrology alone opened up countless Arcana to which it was
necessary to know how to apply one of the seven keys of
the symbolism revealed by Hermes. The Magi of the ninth
degree alone were invested with the right to govern the
state and to judge. When overthrown by the warrior class
their power did not abate; from the depths of sanctuaries
the Magi continued dominating by the prestige of supernatural arts, and warrior kings dared not undertake anything
without consulting the kings of the occult sciences. Their
spiritual power, exempt from the political anxieties, in-

creased as it became more enfolded in the serene contemplation of time, more and more apart from life's fugitive
ambitions, until it imposed its oracles on the world from
afar.

VI

It requires hard work to study with success these strange
relics of a sovereign science, a *royal art* as it was called in
the Middle Ages, which in our own time is no more than
a memory ignorantly belittled and condemned. Where are
the concentrated, silent, solitary spirits that still preserve
some of its traditions? They exist, doubtless; but their
books, whether in manuscript or print, mostly incomplete,
are difficult to read. One feels that it was most reluctantly
that they wrote down the doctrine which sages of old
allowed only to be communicated by word of mouth. Moreover, these singular works were not addressed to the public;
their sole object was to help the memory of the ageing
teacher, or to assist the stumbling steps of some disciple.
Bursts of illumination to the practised soul, twilight to the
researcher, a limitless darkness to the ordinary man, these
books are the last of the oracles. But where are the priests
or sibyls who knew how to make them speak? What has become of those strange doctrinaires to whom the science of
the *cross*, the *triangle* and the *square*, the triple key to the
seven mobile circles, composed each of 22 letters linked
with 22 numbers and 78 symbols, was sufficient to evoke at
the cradle of a new-born babe the angelic influences on its
future life, its good or evil fortune and its death? This
knowledge and this power—double columns upholding the
occult sanctuary of Isis—were they completely destroyed in
the cataclysms of the ancient world?
One cosmopolitan association replies: 'I am the heir
of the Magi, the living, immortal, indissoluble link with
the ancient traditions of the east! I am the source of the

present or future progress of Humanity: my name is Free-masonry.'

Let us examine the origin and value of this curious title and ambitious claim.

[19]About 1646 Elias Ashmole was studying in a library at Oxford. Weary of seeking the philosopher's stone and the elixir of life, Ashmole could think of nothing better than to resuscitate, as he said, the supernatural doctrine of the ancient Magi whose mysteries he had discovered, and of which he would be the new Hierophant. A certain philan-thropic colonel called Mainwaring gave him entry to a lodge of building-workers which met at Warrington under the title of Freemasons. Societies of this nature, founded with a view to purely material interests among people of the same trade, were then fairly widespread, and, in search of security, patrons received the honoray title of Freemason Accepted. In this quality Colonel Mainwaring introduced and obtained entry for Elias Ashmole.

The practical masons of Warrington were hard-headed men who understood very little about the theories of in-tellectual masonry presented by their new member. He described to them in vain the vaporous magnificencies of a universal temple of which they could be builders and priests; those good old masons merely shrugged their shoulders and went back to the work which kept them and their families. But Elias Ashmole was not discouraged; the title of Freemason Accepted gave him the right to enter other Lodges, and soon he went to London to make another, he hoped more successful, attempt.

It was the period of the English Revolution; Charles I, dethroned since 20 January 1647, languished awaiting his

---

[19] The following account of Masonic matters is allowed to stand, somewhat shortened, but no attempt has been made to edit it. Christian was not a Mason; of several matters he seems to give muddled accounts and his attitude to Masonry is frankly biased. He appears to have given an English aspect, from the English origins that he traced, to French material. For a fuller account of these English origins, see Dudley Wright, *England's Masonic Pioneers.—Ed.*

fate in prison, whence he went on 9 February 1649 to lay his head on the executioner's block. The Stuart partisans tried to rally by covering themselves with the name of Free-masons, which put Cromwell's secret police off the scent. Ashmole was to find among them the exalted minds he needed to realise his dreams of an occult society. But the royalists wanted to cloak themselves in a mystery with the principle of vengeance as basis. Ashmole sensed that he would have to play a part and put his zeal to the service of this baser passion. Renouncing therefore the philosophic, religious and purely speculative sides of the doctrine of the Magi, he contented himself with proposing the kind of ordeals of which I have just given an outline, reducing them to a mere phantasmagoria devoid of the prestige imparted by the majestic pomp and grandiose setting of the ancient priesthood.

To justify a claim to the title Freemason, under which the conspirators vowed to the avenging of Charles' death concealed themselves, the initiation was divided into three degrees: Apprentice, Companion and Master.

The Apprentice was only admitted after a detailed secret examination of character, antecedents, means of support, friends and habitual companions. After the tests he was made to pronounce the oath prescribed by the Egyptian mysteries, and in order to engrave more deeply on his mind the idea of the death that would be the traitor's lot, he learned a *sign of recognition* and a *touch*.

To give the sign, he had to stand and, first, put his right hand flat beneath his throat, the four fingers joined, the thumb at right angles, the left arm hanging; second, withdraw the right hand horizontally towards the right shoulder, making the gesture of cutting one's throat, then let the hand fall.

To communicate the *touch*, the Apprentice had to take the right hand of the brother to whom he wished to make himself known, strike with the thumb three times against the first phalanx of the index finger, then press this phalanx lightly with the thumb-nail. These three taps were a call to which the other member had to reply by pronouncing the word BOAZ which is Hebrew for fortitude. Apart from this, the Apprentice received no confidences; he was simply asked to deserve *illumination* by conduct and silence.

The degree of Companion, accorded after a more or less lengthy delay, according to the Adept's qualities, was only a reward and encouragement; the promised light was still withheld. He was given a new *sign* and a new *touch*.

The sign was: first, put the right hand on the heart, fingers curved as if about to seize something; at the same time raise the open left hand, palm outwards, elbow close to side; second, withdraw right hand to right side, let fall and at the same time lower left arm and hand.

To give the touch, he had to take the other member's right hand, strike with the thumb five times on the first phalanx of the middle finger, then place the thumb between that phalanx and that of the ring finger, in this position pronouncing the password *Shibboleth*, Hebrew for an ear of corn. The other brother must reply *Jachin* [*wisdom*].[11]

The setting for the third degree revealed at last the secret of the Master Masons. The reception room was draped in black ornamented by skulls, white tears and cross-bones. On two columns, erected each side the doorway, stood a funeral urn, whence leaned an acacia branch, symbol of future life. Nine tall candles grouped in threes burned at the cardinal compass points. A veiled sun rose behind the president's seat. In the middle of the room on a coffin covered with a shroud was placed a third acacia branch; at the coffin's head was a set-square, at the foot a pair of compasses.

The member-elect could only be admitted by unanimous vote, and after having given unequivocal proofs of discretion and courage. While being prepared in a neigh-

[11] Boaz and Jachin were the names of the left and right-hand pillars respectively of the Temple of Solomon.—*Ed.*

boring room for the final ceremony of initiation, Elias
Ashmole, president and director of this little comedy, recalled to the assembly this legend.

A certain Hiram, supposed architect of the temple built
by King Solomon, had divided his workmen into appren-
tices, companions and masters; and, to avoid trickery when
the latter presented themselves for payment, each had to
whisper into an expert's ear a secret word which varied
according to degree and the architect's decision. Now it
happened that fifteen companions, seeing the temple nearly
finished and dissatisfied at not having reached Master's
degree as recompense for their services, plotted to obtain,
even if by murdering Hiram, the password of the higher
degree. As their plan could only be accomplished by an
ambush, twelve companions had time to think over and
repent of their folly; but the three others [whom Elias
Ashmole called *Jubelas, Jubelos* and *Jubelum*] persisted,
and arranged to lie in wait one evening behind the doors of
the temple when, the rest of the workmen having departed,
Hiram came to inspect their day's work. When the
architect was leaving the south door, the first companion
demanded to be told the secret of the masters. When Hiram
refused, he struck him in the throat with a blow from an
iron ruler. Hiram, wounded, had the strength to run to
the west door, but the second companion was waiting there
and struck him full in the chest with a set-square. The
unfortunate man then tried to drag himself to the east
door, but found there the third companion, who killed him
by a blow on the forehead with his mallet.

After this useless crime the three murderers effaced the
bloodstains, secretly carried away the body of their victim
and buried it far from Jerusalem. Hiram having disappeared, Solomon ordered a search to be made, unsuccess-
fully. The twelve companions then suspected the truth and
confessed to the king. Solomon charged them to pursue the
murderers with the promise to raise them to Masters if
they discovered the body. They divided into four groups of

three each and departed immediately, to north, south, west and east.

The first stopped at a cave mouth to rest. They heard a mournful voice from its depths which said: 'If only my throat had been cut and my tongue torn out! If only I had been buried in the sands of the sea, instead of being an accomplice in Hiram's death!' Another voice replied: 'If only I, too, had had my heart torn out, instead of shedding innocent blood!' And a third voice added: 'If only my body had been sawn in half, rather than commit that crime, for it is I who struck the hardest blow!' In this way the murderers of Hiram were discovered. Brought back to Jerusalem, they asked to be punished by death and Solomon ordered them to suffer the torture that each had described in his remorse: Jubelas had his throat cut, Jubelos had his heart torn out and Jubelum was sawn in two.

Solomon then ordered nine masters to depart and find Hiram's body. They went by instinct towards Mount Lebanon and one day reached a small mound, the earth of which, freshly dug, seemed to carry as a sign an acacia branch. Digging in this mound, they soon found a body and recognised the unfortunate leader of the temple workmen. They carried him back to Jerusalem where Solomon honoured his memory with splendid funeral processions.

This fable, invented by Elias Ashmole, was in part re-enacted in the ceremony in which the Companion passed to the rank of Master. A member lay in the coffin, his head blood-daubed, to represent Hiram's body, that is, the Charles I whose assassins had to be punished. The new Master then became fully aware of the aims of the royalist society of Freemasons, a childish conspiracy, without power or money, which never dared look Cromwell in the face and was only too happy to escape his spies. The Master-Mason, disillusioned, retained to console him a *sign* and a *touch* superior to those of the Companion and the Apprentice. To make the sign, he had to bring his open right hand in front of him, fingers stretched and joined, the thumb at right angles touching his left side; then he had to raise both hands to the heavens, fingers stretched but not joined, saying: *Adonaï* [Lord], and then let his hands fall to show his surprise and horror at the sight. The touch was made by first approaching a brother, right foot against left foot, knees touching; second, each was to put his left hand on the right shoulder of the other and to take the other's right hand, linking middle fingers in a gesture of intimate union. There was also a *sign of help* in war or peril: the two hands were joined and raised above the head, palm outwards, and the following words pronounced: 'Help, children of the Widow!' This ridiculous call to England, widowed by her decapitated king, would merely have aroused jeers from the London mob.

Ashmole was by no means the last to sense the imprudence of his political follies. He was careful enough to retreat in good time and with minimum fuss from such a perilous circle. In 1680, feeling secure once more after the military coup which set the Stuarts again on the throne, he finished his career a dreamer of dreams as he had begun it, and the legend of Hiram seeming to him a work of art worthy of a wise posterity, he made him the symbolic representative of the pseudo-magical initiation which has kept his memory alive. Hiram has become the Sun, the Egyptian Osiris, the symbol of the struggle against the spirit of Evil, represented by Winter, over whom he triumphs every year on his return at the vernal equinox. To Freemasons the sun is 'the father of nature, the sole author of all things, the great architect of the universe[11A] . . . To the true Mason, Divinity and Nature are the same things; the Masonic triangle signifies the *Great All*; it is what we call God, the Hebrew's name Jahweh; it is the Soul of Nature.'[12] At the general masonic convention held in Paris 1865 a member

[11A] *Formulaire maçonnique* by F. ·. Tessier, Sovereign Grand-inspector-General of the Scottish Rite. 1 vol. octavo, pp. 57 and 65.

[12] *L'orateur Maçonnique* p. 270 Discourse for Reception into the Grade of Master. 1 vol. octavo [Paris 1823].

of the Council of the Order said on 6 June: 'They are wrong who define Masonry as a society of moralists. The ideas of the existence of God and the immortality of the soul do not come into question. There are some minds that reject them; that is because they cannot be proved by actual evidence.' Another Mason [a self-styled Rose-Cross], a *Venerable* of the *Free Knights of St. Andrew* of Bordeaux, cried: 'I demand the spreading of the belief in God and the immortality of the soul because of the respect I have for liberty of conscience.' Another orator, a *Venerable* of the *Persevering Friends* of Périgueux, replied: 'Take care. If we suppress this item in our constitution, the report will be spread abroad, and then, I ask, what will be our position before the world and even before our own families? And when we go to other lands, they will reject us, will look upon us as poor men, and they will be right.' This reply excited a violent outburst which was calmed by the *Venerable* of the *French elected Scottish* lodge of Bordeaux, on his proposing this middle course: 'To question the principle of God's existence is, to my mind, an error. We cannot prove the existence of God nor the immortality of the soul; but we would do well to avoid these difficult matters, and admit, for the sake of tolerance, the existence of God and the soul.'[13] This motion was carried by the assembly.

VII

I SHOULD have refrained from entering into these details if Freemasonry did not claim to possess the sacred inheritance of ancient Hermetism.[14] Reduced to bare facts, this society, born of the empty fantasies of Elias Ashmole, goes

---

[13] *Bulletins du Grand-Orient de France*, official journal of Freemasonry, 1865, number 4, meeting of 6 June.

[14] French Masonry is based on the English principle, as Christian correctly indicates. There is no real evidence of continuity with the Egyptian rites, and few responsible writers today claim it.—*Ed.*

no further back than 1646. It was only in 1725 that it was brought to Paris and installed at the wine-shop of a certain Hure, Rue des Boucheries St. Germain, by the Englishman Derwentwater who, on his return to his native land some years later, was condemned to death as a conspirator.

The passion of the French for any sort of novelty made the wine-merchant's fortune; soon he had many rivals. From 1729 to 1732 other gatherings of the same nature flourished at the houses of the traitors Le Breton and Landelle, neighbours of the fortunate M. Hure; then, as several noblemen deigned to include Masons in their fine assemblies, a certain Duc d'Antin was pleased to accept the title of Grand Master. After him it was the turn of Louis de Bourbon, Comte de Clermont, and in 1743, thanks to these high-sounding names, the society also had branches in the principal provincial cities. But next year the Chambre de Police du Châtelet claimed the right to intervene in the supervision of masonic meetings, and after a certain enquiry a fine of 3,000 livres was made the penalty for any person who allowed his premises to be used for meetings. The Comte de Clermont judged it prudent not to risk name and reputation in this way; he ceased to appear in mystical assemblies and bequeathed his dignified position to a dancing-master Lacorne who rendered him, it was said, unmentionable services: 'all men of good breeding and decency thereupon handed in their resignations.'[15]

Masonry did not die out, for those whom it amused, apart from gentlemen like Lacorne, attempted to hold their meetings elsewhere, and, through their intermediary the Duc de Montmorency-Luxembourg, they succeeded in obtaining the patronage of Philip of Orleans, 1771. This protection from one so close to the throne was the real foundation of French Freemasonry. Interrupted 1792 by the catastrophes of the Revolution, it was quietly restored under the Directory, strengthened under the Empire and

[15] *Orthodoxie Maçonnique*, by F. ∴ Ragon, Vénérable des Trinosophes Paris 1853. 8vo, p. 46.

up to our own time has not ceased to carry a certain weight in the political see-saw.

The association is divided today into the French and Scots rites and the rites of Misraïm and of Memphis, divided into nearly 500 Lodges under the control of a central committee, the Grand Orient. There is nothing oriental about it except the name. The true Masons only recognise three symbolic grades: Apprentice, Companion and Master. But clever speculators have been able to make profit out of man's self-esteem by selling at a high price cordons and decorations which, even in more enlightened days, attract crowds of buyers convinced of their value. The humble Apprentice and the modest Companion, reduced to an apron of white leather with bib raised or lowered, envy the *grand cordon bleu* that passes from the right shoulder to the left hip of the Master. He in turn covets the higher grades where every honour has a tariff, proceeds dedicated to the social chest. These outbursts of vanity are given strange titles which allow some of their happy possessors to dress like princes.[16]

It would be a strange delusion if anyone attempted to find among these ambitious titles and decorations the slightest trace of rational system or symbolism. It has long been recognised that this phantasmagoria was in fact due to the collaboration of the dancing-master Lacorne and a few Jews. In a book whose author is today an authority on Masonry,[17] this Lacorne is termed the 'low agent of the secret pleasures of Louis de Bourbon, Comte de Clermont'; as for the Jews, they were pawnbrokers who naturally, in this affair, made a nice profit from selling whatever jewelry and decorations were required. Legends of such ineptitude that beside them the tale of Hiram would pass as a masterpiece were manufactured by them and attached to

[16] Descriptions of titles and decorations in the French rite and of the thirty-three grades in the Scottish rite follow. Since 1870 these are easily obtainable, e.g. in Loth, *Emblems of the Thirty-Three Degrees.—Ed.*

[17] *Le Tuileur Général*, Manual for the Initiate, by Ragon, founder of the Trinosophes: Paris, 1853 octavo, p. 103.

each grade, under the profaned title of initiation. In 1797
'other adventurers,' as the book describes them, claimed to
be under the patronage of the King of Prussia. Helped by
their impudent lie, they succeeded in giving the dignities
and decorations of the so-called High Masonry an importance which still exists. I shall not attempt further to describe
this silly charlatanism. Sufficient to say that whoever wishes
to form a separate Masonic sect is certain to attract a flock
of Panurge's sheep. Statistics covering this bizarre association show that there are 75 Masonries properly so-called, 52
rites, 34 Orders, 26 androgynous masonries and more than
1,400 grades. After the French and Scots rites, which today
have the greatest number of adherents, the only others existing now in France are the rite of Misraïm and the rite of
Memphis, two pseudo-Egyptian caricatures. The rite of
Misraïm is composed of 90 grades dating from 1814; the rite
of Memphis has 92 grades dating from 1839. The former was
no more than a brazen trafficking organised by two Jewish
merchants who claimed to have received in Naples an Egyptian initiation; but their profound ignorance did not allow
them to think out a single ordeal or test which might pertain
to this rite. The latter was invented by an illiterate man of
letters who was unable to make it pay, although he offered to
confer upon the public the actual decoration of the Golden
Fleece of which the kings of Europe until then had considered themselves the sole proprietors. This so-called Prince
of the Magi of the Memphis Sanctuary, this Grand-Hiero-
phant of Light, Sublime Interpreter of the Hieroglyhs, this
Supreme Sage of the Pyramids, lived to see his rite given the
epithet 'monstrous' by the author of *Masonic Orthodoxy*,
and if I remember rightly, the Grand Orient recently forbade him to ascend his tripod.[18]

---

[18] This man, who died recently, called himself Marconis de Neigre. He was an
     inoffensive dreamer after the style of Elias Ashmole. He left several works
     such as *Sanctuaire de Memphis*, *Rameau d'or d'Eleusis*, etc. But we look
     in vain for a vestige of science of any kind in this latest system of Freemasonry.

VIII

NEVERTHELESS, if Freemasonry has never, as a science, deserved thoughtful attention, it would be unjust not to recognise that since the middle of the 18th century the toleration it enjoyed favoured in France the intercourse of energetic minds who were looking for a rallying-point for the conquest of political liberty. These intellects, far ahead of their time, by no means despised the childishness of masonic symbolism: it was a safe cloak under which they could hide. Skilfully multiplying the number of banquets at which the king's health was drunk, they were no less skilful in setting up under these manifestations more intimate circles in which, solemnised by the masonic oath, a more serious initiation was being prepared. Hiram, transfigured, became for them the emblem of despotism; the secret password which the three companions had failed to obtain was: Liberty, Equality, Fraternity—the triple device of the French Revolution. Hiram's murder was no longer looked upon as a crime; it symbolised the supreme effort needed.

Each new initiate was chosen from among members of lodges whom close observation picked out as men of action with pliable minds. After having made him write and sign a confession of his past life under the pretext of admitting him to a higher grade, a register was opened in his presence where all his past actions were inscribed. His confessions were compared with these mysterious notes: honesty alone was the sign of good faith: the smallest falsehood debarred him from continued membership. If considered worthy of admission, he learned that a host of unknown agents, termed *Frères Insinuants*, controlled hour by hour the conduct of every member of the Order and that the slightest suspicion of treachery would be rewarded by death. He was then led blindfold and gagged into a secret place where, his bandage removed, he found himself surrounded by masked men wearing white robes and red scarves and pointing drawn swords at him. Before his eyes on a table covered with a black veil and patterned with red tears a gold cup shone between a crown and a sword. At the end of this table were his robe and scarf, the costume worn by other members.

The masked president then said to him: 'Behold these symbols of the passions, of pride, of slavery. If you desire wealth, symbolised by the gold, or power, symbolised by the crown, we can give you either one or other; but you will only be their slave; if you are worthy the name of man, you will prefer Equality, which the sword confers.'

The adept's reply was dictated by the awe-inspiring atmosphere of this scene: he reached out his hand towards the sword. Then a scarlet curtain opened, beyond which was an altar bearing a cross on which was nailed a dead body, pierced through the heart. 'Kneel!' went on the president. 'Swear, at the foot of this cross which shows you how traitors perish, swear everlasting hatred to thrones and to the usurpers of the earth!'

The adept's oath, written on parchment with blood drawn from a small incision in his left arm, was then thrown on a brazier by the president with this comminatory phrase: 'If you belie your faith, may your heart be burned thus and may your ashes be strewn on the dust of the road that free men tread.'

This audacious misrepresentation of the Masonic initiation fascinated the petty natures who were wanted as instruments of war. These auxiliary troops of the army of unconquerable thought were full of enthusiasm at forming the arms of a lever whose fulcrum, they were told, was becoming bigger every day. From the beginning of the reign of Louis XVI the secret society possessed in the banks of London, Amsterdam, Genoa and Venice a fortune amassed by members' subscriptions. These gifts, apparently philanthropic, were not mere sources of benevolence where distress was linked with conspiracy; they were also, and chiefly, instruments of widespread propaganda. Strange travellers appeared in many kingdoms, living in unheard-of luxury, speculating on curiosity in order to obtain an entrance everywhere. Giuseppe Balsamo, better known under the name of Count Cagliostro,[19] travelling from Germany to Strasbourg, had persuaded Cardinal de Rohan that he possessed the secret of manufacturing gold. The Duke of Luxembourg and the celebrated naturalist Ramond regarded him as a worker of miracles. In 1781 he appeared in Paris, where he was already famous and was soon the only man sought out by fashion, for he gave something to everyone, like a messiah scattering the treasures of earth and high heaven. An incomparable trickster, sowing brilliant superstitions in the midst of worldly frivolity, proclaimed Father of the Poor by the beneficiaries of his bottomless purse and given the illustrious title of Divine by the enraptured ladies of the best society, this son of a Palermo shopkeeper reigned more royally than the King of France.

Decorated with the title of *Athersatha,* or Prince of Wise Men according to his interpretation [actually *'Hathir Sākta'* (Sanskrit), one operating a deity's power], Cagliostro had erected, in the Rue de la Sourdière, a sort of Temple of Isis of which he made himself high priest. There he gave private lectures to audiences enthralled by his personality, his descriptions of the Golden Age and the imminent return of that myth of universal happiness. His eloquence was moving and familiar in tone, but always delivered with that fine feeling for courtesy which is the special gift of the Italian; and it seemed especially to affect feminine susceptibility. He was listened to with rapt attention as he described fantastic voyages in the enchanted lands of oriental magic. A pilgrim among the ruins of Babylon

---

[19] 'Alessandro Cagliostro', 1743-1795, educated at the Caltagirone monastery in Sicily, expelled for misconduct. Forgeries were chiefly responsible for his flight thence. He wandered in many lands picking up miscellaneous lore, first appearing as Count Cagliostro to the Grand Master of the Knights of Malta where he studied alchemy with him and obtained access through him to Roman and Neapolitan society. With his equally unprincipled wife, Lorenza Feliciani, he travelled Europe, and the rest of his career is adequately told in Christian's text.—*Ed.*

and Ninevah, Palmyra and Thebes, he had, he claimed, encountered men whose wonderful knowledge had enabled them to enjoy perpetual youth. These masters of time who had seen so many things rise and perish and who were able to penetrate all the secrets of life from a blade of grass to a star, only showed themselves from time to time to God's elect when the moment came to teach the world the law of a new evolution in the ascending spiral of progress. Cagliostro therefore set himself up as one of God's elect; he affirmed this personal privilege in a tone of calm conviction, as a fact that no one could doubt or find in the least surprising.

He did not expect to be asked for proofs of his mission; small miracles were nothing to him; he promised greater ones to be performed by his own disciples as soon as they believed in him. Faith cannot be ordered or imposed, as he knew, and he disdained to solicit it among men; but he also knew that in France women are the queens of public opinion, and it was by their unreserved admiration, their irresistible power that he meant to succeed in conquering the dictatorship of a new world.

Creator of an *Egyptian rite* imitated from the formulae of ancient Magism, which revealed on his part a knowledgeable research into the doctrines debased by Elias Ashmole, he declared in 1785 that, by the example of the priestesses of Isis, women could be admitted to participation in the mysteries. To make certain of the protection of the court, he was able to obtain, through the representations of the Duc de Luxembourg, the patronage of the Princess de Lamballe, bosom friend of Queen Marie Antoinette, who was pleased to accept the title of Grande-Maîtresse d'Honneur. The decoration of this title consisted in a sky-blue scarf trimmed with silver fringes, worn from right to left and fixed to the right shoulder by a white rosette and three golden tassels. From the knot of the scarf was suspended a golden circle enclosing a sceptre, a hand of justice and an antique crown. The Grand Mistress, clothed in white, was supposed to sit on a gold and white throne raised on seven steps beneath a silver-starred canopy. The *Athersatha* had the taste to give himself a much lower throne. The design of the sanctuary and models of the mystic jewelry were presented at Versailles and declared perfectly charming. Marie Antoinette, gracious and intoxicated by flattery, still did not know what bitter tears a queen can shed. She not only insisted that her friend should accept the title, but also that she should attend meetings regularly, for the assemblies in the Rue de la Sourdiere would doubtless provide some entertaining tales to enliven the majestic boredom of the Trianon gardens.

Madame de Lamballe was received into the dignity of Grand Mistress of Honour on 20 March 1785. It was a brilliant solemnisation, arranged by Cagliostro with oriental splendour and luxury. The highest born noblemen were present, for the founder of the Egyptian rite did not want to let slip through his fingers such a precious opportunity of impressing everyone by the fascination of the pomp of Isis. For this occasion the vast house he lived in in the Rue St. Claude was transformed into an earthly paradise. The Princesse de Lamballe appeared as a radiant divinity. The temple glittered with gold, was decked with purple and flowers. After the symbolic ceremony, in which there was no trace of any mystery that might alarm the gracious queen of the occasion, a banquet presided over by Cagliostro was attended by all the guests.

The masonic lodges in Paris viewed jealously the favour with which the celebrated foreigner was greeted. They set to work to call together a general assembly or *Convent* of the principal dignitaries of Freemasonry, in order to discuss and solve certain problems organically concerned with their existence. The programme of questions contained the following items:

1. What is the essential nature of the masonic science? 2. What origin and what date are reasonably attributable to it? 3. What societies or what individuals can be proved

to have formerly possessed it, and what bodies did it successively pass through in arriving at its present form?
4. What societies or what individuals can be said to be
now the true depositories of this knowledge? 5. Has it been
preserved by oral or written tradition? 6. Has masonic
science any connection with the sciences known under the
name of occult sciences? 7. With which of these secret
sciences has it connections, and what are they? 8. What kind
of advantages ought one to expect from masonic science?
9. Which would be the best of the present regimes or rites
to follow? 10. What is the origin and true meaning of the
symbols, rites and secret language taught to Freemasons?

It is enough to read these questions to see that Masonry,
imported into France by Englishmen 69 years before, had
no scientific basis, that its so-called mysteries were hocus-
pocus. The gentlemen, magistrates and men of letters who
had been received into its bosom hoping to learn supernatural things no longer wished to be the dupes of their
own credulity. Several eminent men, both French and
foreign, resident in Paris, had put forward a proposal for
an enquiry. Among the Frenchmen were MM. Du Trousset
d'Héricourt and Duval d'Eprémesnil, Presidents in the
Parlement of Paris; de Pontcarré, President of the Parlement of Rouen; de Beyerlé, councillor in the Parlement of
Paris; de Paul, Lieutenant-General of the Seneschalship of
Marseilles; le Duc d'Havre, le Duc de Luxembourg, le Duc
de la Rochefoucauld, from Paris; Bacon de la Chevalerie
and the Vicomte de Virieu, Marshals; Marquises, magistrates and many more. Among foreign Freemasons in the
front rank were Strogonoff, the Russian Ambassador, the
Marquis de Gages, Chamberlain to the German Emperor,
Baron de Stahl, Swiss Ambassador, Baron de l'Isle, Dutch
Consul, Baron de Corberon, Minister of the Prince de Deux-
Ponts and others.

These serious-minded men, who had thought to find
in Freemasonry an academy of the higher sciences, desired
illumination on the chaos of absurdities which the masonic

lodges decorated with the imposing title of Mysteries. They consulted the learned orientalist Court de Gébelin,[20] and as the almost miraculous renown of Cagliostro was at that time drawing everyone's attention, they asked the Sicilian to attend a conference at which Court de Gébelin would speak for them.

IX

CAGLIOSTRO accepted this invitation to an interview with a picked audience. He presented himself on 10 May 1785.[21] From the very beginning of the conference his great simplicity and perfect courtesy attracted the sympathies of the whole assembly. Court de Gébelin, who as an oriental specialist was asked to speak first, was enchanted to recognise in Cagliostro a traveller with wide knowledge of the traditions of Greece, Egypt, Arabia and Persia. But when it became a question of discussing the points which were to form the basis of the assembly's enquiry, the Sicilian's expansiveness was suddenly damped like a faulty firework; he became cold, reserved, almost inattentive, answering only in vague terms and circumlocutions which avoided the subject under discussion. Pressed by Court de Gébelin, by the Duc de Rochefoucauld and by Savatte kindly to explain himself without reserve before an assembly which professed for him the utmost confidence and admiration, after a few moments of silent meditation he stood up to speak.

'Gentlemen,' he said, 'in accepting the invitation with which you have honoured me, I did not foresee as clearly as I do now the seriousness of such an interview. If I am not mistaken, you believe that Freemasonry should possess the key to the occult sciences, and, not having been able to discover this key at your lodge meetings, you came here in

---

[20] Antoine Court de Gébelin, 1725-1784. His main work, *Plan General . . . du Monde Primatif*, was published 1772.—*Ed.*

[21] The date of this conference seems uncertain, since Court de Gébelin died in 1784. See A. E. Waite *The Secret Tradition in Freemasonry.—Ed.*

the hope that I would be able to cast some light on your researches. Well, gentlemen, honesty compels me to tell you that you can learn nothing from Freemasonry. The so-called mystery of Hiram is no more than a grotesque absurdity, and the title of Great Architect of the Universe which you give to God is only a name invented by an Englishman lacking entirely in common sense. You yourselves feel that the supreme Being cannot be defined by such wretched anthropomorphism. The immense variety of the manifestations of Life at the centre of the Universal Order reveals to our consciousness a First Absolute Cause which you are seeking to define in spite of the inadequacy of the human language. Gentlemen, you need seek no longer for the symbolic expression of the divine idea: it was created 60 centuries ago by the Magi of Egypt. Hermes-Thoth fixed the two terms. The first is the *Rose,* because this flower is spherical in shape, symbol of the most perfect unity, and because its perfume is a revelation of life. This rose was placed at the centre of a *Cross,* a figure expressing the point at which are united the apices of two right angles whose lines may be produced in our imaginations to infinity, in the triple directions of height, breadth and depth. The material of this symbol was gold, which in occult science signifies light and purity; and in his wisdom Hermes called it the Rose-Cross, that is, Sphere of the Infinite. Between the branches of the cross he wrote the letters I N R I, each of which expresses a mystery.

'I [*Ioïthi* in the sacred language] symbolises the active creative principle and the manifestation of divine power that fertilises matter.

'N [*Naïn*] symbolises passive matter, the mold of all forms.

'R [*Rasïth*] symbolises the union of these two principles and the perpetual transformation of created things.

'I [*Ioïthi*] symbolises again the divine creative principle and signifies that the creative strength which emanates from it ceaselessly returns to it and springs from it everlastingly.

The Symbol of the Rose-Cross.

'The ancient Magi wore the Rose-Cross hung from the neck on a golden chain; but so as not to reveal to the profane the sacred word INRI they replaced these four letters by the four figures which are brought together in the Sphinx: Man, Bull, Lion and Eagle.

'Compare with this simple explanation of the Rose-Cross of the ancients, the pitiful farce used at your rituals which makes your so-called initiates say in explanation of the word INRI: "I come from Judea, I have passed through Nazareth led by Raphael; I am of the tribe of Juda." Gentlemen, how could such stupid nonsense be accepted by intelligent Frenchmen? If you wish to revive among you the majesty of the doctrines which illuminated the ancient world and rekindle on the heights of human intelligence the beacon of divine radiance, you must first of all destroy the legend of Hiram and your meaningless rituals. You must give up these comic decorations and these titles of Sublime Princes and Sovereign Commanders; four planks under a few feet of earth will show if you are any more worthy than the lowest beggar.'

The assembly was stirred by this pronouncement of Cagliostro's. 'But is it enough,' cried Court de Gébelin, 'to destroy everything in order to prove one's superiority? If Freemasonry is only phantasmagoria, by what signs can you prove to us that the light which is refused to us shines from the mysteries to which you hold the key? If you are the inheritor of the ancient Magic, give us a proof, a single proof, of its power—if you are the genius of the Past, what have you to say for the Future?'

'I reveal it,' replied Cagliostro coldly, 'and if you will give me the masonic oath, or better, if you will swear your-selves to secrecy on your word of honour, I will prove what I claim.'

'We swear secrecy,' everyone cried, and all hands were raised to confirm the oath.

'Gentlemen,' continued the Sicilian with a magnetic look, 'when a child is born, something has already preceded its entry into life. That something is its *Name*. The name completes its birth, for, before naming, a king's child and a peasant's are no more than small pieces of organised matter, just as the corpse of the most powerful ruler in the world, shorn of the brilliance of funeral pomps, has nothing to distinguish it from the remains of the lowest slave.

'In modern society are three sorts of names: the family, the Christian and the surnames. The family name is the common impress of race which is handed down, transmitted from one being to another. The Christian name is the sign that characterises the person and distinguishes the sex. The surname is a secondary qualification, applied to any indi-vidual in a family in particular cases. The family name is imposed by civil requirements; the Christian name is chosen by the affectionate intentions of father and mother. The surname is an accidental title, sometimes used only in one lifetime, sometimes hereditary. There is finally the social title, such as prince, count, duke. Now I can read in the ensemble of these personal designations the most outstanding features of any destiny; the more numerous these designations are, the more clearly does the oracle within them speak.

The Alphabet of the Magi

'Do not smile, gentlemen. My conviction in this respect cannot falter, for it is based on fairly numerous experiments and on proofs too striking to be ignored. Yes, each one of us is named in the heavens at the same time as on earth, that is, predestined, bound, by the occult laws of increate Wisdom, to a series of more or less fatal ordeals before he has even made the first step towards his unknown future. Do not tell me that such certainty, if it existed, would be the certainty of despair. . . All your protests will not prevent Predestination from being a fact and the Name a sign to be feared. The highest wisdom of the ancients believed in this mysterious connection of the name and the being who holds it as if it were a divine or infernal talisman that could either illuminate his passage through life or destroy it in flames. The Magi of Egypt confided this secret to Pythagoras, who transmitted it to the Greeks. In the sacred alphabet of Magism each letter is linked to a number; each number corresponds with an Arcanum: each Arcanum is the sign of an occult power. The 22 letters of which the keyboard of the language is composed form all the names which, according to the agreement or disagreement of the secret forces symbolised by the letters, destine the man so named to the vicissitudes which we define by the vulgar terms of *luck* and *misfortune.*

'But what relationship, you will ask, can possibly exist between mute letters and abstract numbers and the tangible things of life? Well, gentlemen, is it necessary for you to know the impenetrable secret of the mystery of generation before you will consent to think, walk, will and act? God illuminates us by means compatible with wisdom, and He always prefers the most simple. Here it is the Word, the work of God, which is the instrument of prophetic revelation.

'One experiment will serve to make me better understood.

Est-il possible à l'esprit humain de chercher et de découvrir les secrets de l'avenir, dans l'énoncé littéral de l'événement qui vient de s'accomplir, ou dans la définition d'une personne par les noms, titres et actes qui constituent son individualité?

'Is it possible for the human mind to seek and discover the secrets of the future in a literal statement of the event which has just taken place, or in the definition of a person by the names, titles and deeds which constitute his individuality?'

'You see only, gentlemen, the obvious or material sense of this question. But, while you ponder, the higher Magic has already read a second meaning which gives the true answer. Here is the art of unravelling this occult meaning. Remember the invariable RULE.

'The text is made up of 203 letters, to which must be added a progression of numbers ascending from 1 to 203, as follows:

E1 S2 T3 I4 L5 P6 and so on.

'All these letters, with their numbers, are placed in a circle, so that the eye may take them all in at a glance. The alphabet of the Magi, which I place before you, fixes the value of the letters. Note that the French language has no double consonants like Th or Ts; we therefore can ignore these for our present purpose. But note also that the letters U and V, the letters I J and Y, the letters F and P, the letters K and Q, are marked in this alphabet by the same sign; consequently they can be taken one for the other according to the needs of our deciphering. If, for example, there are three U's and one V in the visible text, and if we need two U's and two V's to express the occult text, the third U will do for the necessary second V. If there are three P's and no F, and if the occult text demands two F's, two of the P's are transformed into F's, and vice versa. All the other letters retain their absolute value.

'With this rule kept in mind, we must let our eyes wander slowly round the circle in a vague contemplation of new groups that the letters may form. Gradually a few words appear: we remove from the circle the letters of which they are composed and note them down, with their corresponding figures. Then we continue the circular contemplation until new words complete the new meaning and exhaust the circle. This operation is accomplished more or less quickly according to the intuitive faculties of the mind —some will be less practised than others. It often happens that the first words we find have no rational meaning or are contradictory. As soon as this is perceived, the letters must be brought back into the circle and the study begun afresh. But as we become more and more familiar with this sort of work the difficulty disappears and, by a mysterious instinct, the mind rejects words created by chance and attracts those born in the light of a second examination.

'Proceeding in this manner, we are able to extricate from the question that occupies our thoughts the following sibylline reply, the *metathesis* or transposition of the letters in the original text, forming as follows the assembly of elements composing the occult meaning:

"LE 5 13—VERBE 47 52 57 11 16—HUMAIN 22 23 24 25 26 27—EST 29 53 59—UN 102 107—REFLET 120 130 131 154 155 3—DE 177 185—LA 200 14—LUMIERE 15 46 116 119 142 145 150—ETERNELLE 165 168 172 19 67 75 81 88 90—ECLAIRANT 92 113 118 124 132 153 169 182 187—ICI 105 114 136—TOUTE 202 7 122 135 144—VIE 195 196 203—LE 12 32—SAGE 54 64 183 1—INITIE 4 72 82 83 103 106—SAIT 111 112 134 161—LIRE 51 68 69 80—ET 58 84—RETROUVER 86 96 108 37 158 198 104 98 50—DANS 139 152 157 160—LES 63 66 67—MOTS 97 77 21 126—ENOCES 167 186 188 190 30 36 60—LE 64 85—PRONOSTIC 117 164 139 192 45 146 163 176 34—NON 78 115 125—LOINTAIN 127 137 162 95 100 128 178 99—DES 109 110 156—DESTINS 193 38 166 171 181 133 173—QUI 174 175 191—DOIVENT 197 121 194 65 94 138 180—S'ACCOMPLIR 8 71 79 170 147 159 6 91 201 33—DANS 40 87 141 179—CHAQUE 44 31 199 101 140 41—SPHERE 2 18 35 43 48 55—DES 61 62 9—INDIVIDUS 10 148 28 49 93 20 42 184 17."

'*Le Verbe humain est un reflet de la lumière eternelle, éclairant ici toute vie. Le Sage initié sait lire et retrouver, dans les mots enonces, le pronostic non lointain des destins qui doivent s'accomplir dans chaque sphere des individus.* "The human Word is a reflection of eternal light, illuminating all life here below. The wise initiate can read and recover, in the words pronounced, a prognostic not far removed from the destinies which must be fulfilled in each individual sphere."

'Thus the Sage, the initiate, not only reads our fate as it is written in the stars; he also finds indications of these very destinies in the simple words announcing a fact or which characterise a human individuality. This is the meaning contained in the Mosaic Genesis, a work Egyptian in inspiration, where God makes all living beings pass before the first man, so that he might give each a suitable *name*; for to name is to define.

'Returning to the elements of the occult text, you will see that there remain in the circle 10 letters, namely: T39 C56 D70 D89 N76 D123 D129 P143 N149 and P51. These letters are mute, that is, no word can be made out of them. To extract a meaning from them we must use the procedure of the Sibyls who prophesied in the ancient Roman temples of Fortuna, at Preneste or Antium, and in some way make a prophetic phrase, a human Word, spring from each initial. It will come to us after a few moments of meditation, and, in order to imitate the ancient oracles as closely as possible, I shall think in Latin, and express myself in the following terms:

Tacentes Casus Denuntiat Nomen;
Decreta Dei Per Numeros Præfantur

which means: "The Name announces the events that still remain in the silence of the future, and divine decrees are predicted by Numbers." Names and Numbers: these are the foundations of, and the keys to, the sanctuary of the Oracles.

'Certainly nothing is simpler and more innocent than this little operation; a child could perform it. The minds of the ancient Magi demanded of these combinations of the human word, in appearance the results of chance, sometimes philosophic replies, sometimes revelations of the future. I have promised you proofs, and I can give you many: grant me, gentlemen, your closest attention.'

X

AFTER a few minutes' silence in which one sensed the rising curiosity of his hearers, Cagliostro went on as follows:

'It is from the history of France that I shall take my proofs, so that the study of them may interest you all the more. We are told by your historian Mézeray, if I remember rightly, that an Italian astrologer had predicted to Catherine de' Medici that "St. Germain would see her die." That queen immediately began to hold in horror that saint's annual festival and fled from all places bearing his name: her fear was useless and her precautions vain, for the oracle was of the kind that does not reveal its true meaning until after the event. At her death, this prediction was recalled when it was learned that the dying queen's confessor was called St. Germain, Bishop of Nazareth. This, briefly, is what Mézeray tells us; but what the historian could not explain was related in the works of Luc Gauric, Bishop of Civita-Ducale, author of the prediction. Catherine de' Medici, the Queen-mother, had become regent in December 1560 on the accession of Charles IX her son, who at that time was scarcely ten years old. This ambitious woman, egotistical and wicked in all she did, wrote to Luc Gauric, a very famous astrologer of those days, to question him on her future prospects of power. Luc Gauric replied with his pronouncement on the regency that had just begun: *Catherine de' Médicis, roine-mère, devient régente de France, pour son fils Charles Neuf, au mois de décembre mil cinq cent soixante.* "Catherine de' Medici, Queen-Mother, becomes Regent of France for her son Charles the Ninth in December 1560."

'In the 16th century *reine* was written roine. The sibylline operation is exactly the same as in the former example. You all understood it, gentlemen, and you can read for yourselves, as easily as Luc Gauric did, the new meaning, thus: *St. Germain admis voit fin de la reine-mère, en lit, couche funèbre, exténuée en ce monde-ci par flèches de sinistre remords.* "St. Germain, admitted, sees the end of the Queen-Mother, her bed a funeral couch, weakened in this world by arrows of sinister remorse."

'Bishop Gauric naively admits that he could not understand the meaning of the word St. Germain and he was careful not to tell Catherine of the judgment on her life contained in the oracle's final words. He contented himself with announcing that St. Germain would see her die in her bed. The most sinister remorse that was to torture and bring to an end the life of this criminal woman began on the Eve of St. Bartholomew. Bishop Nicholas de St. Germain witnessed Catherine's terror but not her repentance, for she died in the convulsions of a hideous despair.

'In the fatidic circle there remained 4 mute letters, C O D Q, which became, as in the previous example, the initials of the following words: *"Cruore Oblisa, Defecit Queritans"*, which means: "The blood with which she is gorged stifles her in a final groan." Her murderous soul cast itself into eternity accompanied by the echoes of her own infamous curses.

'Would you like to hear the oracles formulated by Ruggieri [d. 1615] on the last of the Valois and the first Bourbon? Let us go back to the accession of Henri III 1574 and ask the fatidic circle the following simple question: *Henri de Valois, duc d'Anjou, roi de Pologne, puis de France, sera-t-il heureux jusqu' à la fin de sa vie, et léguera-t-il le trône à son fils?* "Henri de Valois, Duc d'Anjou, King of Poland, then of France, will he be happy to the end of his days, and will he leave the throne to his son?"

'The reply enclosed in these 105 letters announces in the following terms the end of a race and a tragic death: *Ce royal Valois, fin de sa souche defaillie, qui n'est heureux et n'aura fils, perira egorgé devant le soldat, non loin de Paris.* "This royal Valois, the last of an extinct race, who is not happy, will have no son, will die with his throat cut in front of the soldier, not far from Paris.''

'There remain 5 mute letters, D U J U U, signifying: *Decidit Ululans; Junctim Ullus Umbratur,* which means: "He falls with a loud cry; but he is avenged presently, before being wrapped in the shadow of death." We know that Henri III was stabbed in his camp on the heights of St. Cloud on 1 August 1589 by the Dominican monk Jacques Clément, whom guards massacred in the king's tent immediately afterwards.

'Let us go on to Henri IV, who was to fall beneath Ravaillac's knife on 14 May 1610, and let us ask the same question: *Henri IV [de Bourbon, duc de Vendosme], roi de France et de Navarre, sera-t-il heureux jusqu' à la fin de sa vie, et léguera-t-il le trône à son fils?* Before ascending the throne, Henri IV bore the title of duc de Vendosme in right of his father Antoine de Bourbon, Duc de Vendosme and King of Navarre. Here Ruggieri's oracle is no less lugubrious: *Roi brave, qu'étendra décédé sous fer un exécrable meutre, il doit léguer le vain trône à son fils aîné, qui, alors, aura neuf ans de vie.* "A fine king, laid low in death by the blade in dastardly murder, will bequeath the useless throne to his eldest son who will then be nine years old."

'5 mute letters remain, H T D D H, signifying: *Harpe Trucidatus, Demissus Decidit Hians,* which means: "Struck dead by a knife, he falls, and the supreme cry is extinguished on his open lips." We know that he died from a knife-blow without regaining consciousness.

'Louis XIII who succeeded was indeed only nine years old when his father died. The expression *Vain Trône* seems to have a double meaning; it signified that royalty does not preserve us from catastrophe, also that the son of Henri IV would have the merest pretence of a reign. This latter meaning was verified by the despotism that was to be exercised on the weak-minded Louis XIII by the ambition of Cardinal Richelieu, his minister.

'But let us hasten, gentlemen, to confront the future and to question it by the same means. Do not be afraid to take as your subject your king, Louis XVI, and the unfolding of his destiny. This prince succeeds after a reign which did nothing to increase public respect. He is reproached, if I am not mistaken, with allowing himself to be governed by a greedy circle of advisers who, after exhausting his favours and purse, will not be his courtiers at the end. However, gentlemen, let us ask without prejudice, if you please, of the oracle this simple question: *Louis, seizième du nom, roi de France et de Navarre [Auguste, duc de Berri], sera-t-il heureux jusqu' à la fin de sa vie, et leguera-t-il le trône a son fils?* "Louis, sixteenth of that name, King of France and Navarre, will he be happy to the end of his days, and will be bequeath the throne to his son?"

'I add to Louis, the royal name, those of Auguste, Duc de Berri, because he received them at his birth and because they complete the definition of his individuality. This text is composed of 116 letters. Now still operating on a circle, we shall find that the reply is enclosed in the question itself: *Que Louis XVI, roi fictif, abattu du trône ruiné de ses aieux, se garde d'aller mourir sur l'échafaud, vers sa trente-neuvième année d'âge.* "Let Louis XVI, supposed king, cast down from the ruined throne of his ancestors, beware of dying on the scaffold towards the 39th year of his life."

'There remain in the circle 6 mute letters, L O I J L L, meaning: *Latescit Omen Infaustum: Jactura, Luctus, Lethum,* signifying: "The direful oracle is expressed in three terms: Fall, Affliction, Violent Death." Here we actually see Louis XVI cast down from the crumbling throne left him by Louis XV. The threat of violent death will be in the 39th year of his life. Now he was born in 1754, on the 23 August; 1793 would be therefore the fatal date announced by the oracle.

'But you will say that is only an isolated case. No matter gentlemen, we can go further. Let us consider the simple statement of the present reign in these terms: *Louis Seize* [*Auguste, duc de Berri*], *roi de France*. Nothing unusual about that; no fatidic manifestation in these princely denominations which might decorate a medal. But by the operation with which you are now all familiar, we read in these 38 letters: *Louis, Roi*: . . . *SEIZE decidera funeste augure*. "Louis, King: . . . SIXTEEN will decide the fatal augury."

'There remain 4 mute letters, D C B R, whose Roman interpretation by the initials, signifies: *Damnatur Capite, Belli Reus,* which means: "He is condemned to lose his head, for being guilty of war."

'Now does this mean a foreign or a civil war? I do not know; but it seems to me that the king will be accused of having incited an armed conflict and that this will be one of the most serious causes of his downfall. As for the number XVI, which announces his dynastic rank, it corresponds to Arcanum XVI in the crypt of the Pyramids, which is symbolised by the image of a lightning-struck tower. The reign of Louis is therefore struck by a fatal augury indicated by XVI, whose occult meaning announces the conflict of material forces, crumbling powers and overwhelming catastrophes [see *page* 107].

'Let us make a second examination of the same 38 letters. It yields: *Gis, roi SEIZE* . . . *livre à funeste bourreau*. "Lie low, SIXTEENTH King . . . delivered to a fatal executioner." The executor of the augury is clear. You see appear beside him again that curious number, symbol of the lightning-struck tower; with gloomy prosopopœia the oracle addresses the king himself: "*Gis*—lie stretched out, *Roi seizieme du nom*—King sixteenth of that name—in the bloody grave where your executioner has laid you." '

'But, Sir, what you have just told us is damnable,' cried a few voices.

'Yes,' went on Cagliostro, 'but what will you say one day, if it is true? Gentlemen, Freemasons, free-thinkers do not always think freely! If you have objections to make, go back to the legend of Hiram. I can say no more.'

The greater part of those present were completely under his spell. The Sicilian's strange speech had the exciting taste of forbidden fruit. The interrupters themselves begged him to continue and he went on triumphantly: 'I invent nothing. I foresee the future in flashes of sibylline illumination. I can hear not far away the tolling bell, and the cannon vomiting the wrath of the streets on besieged palaces. Whither have they come, these unknown roaring crowds who had no to-morrow, and now seize the future in their hands? How is it that in one hour so much power can crumble to nothing, so much wealth, such splendours vaunting themselves eternal? An entire people, maddened and sweating under the ignominy of an inflexible yoke— outside, Europe in arms—inside, famine inciting the mob to pillage—murder become a national occupation: what a spectacle! and what a lesson!—This, gentlemen, is the result that follows regicide; believe me, there will be regicide!

'Look at these 6 mute letters, which I forgot to interpret to you: D C D E D C: why have they detached themselves from the text? It is because they mean: *Damnatur Capite—Damnatur Exilio—Damnatur Capite*, that is: "He is condemned to death—to banishment—and again to death." Opinions are divided: some demand death, others pity—it is in the balance. But fate casts another weight on the side of murder, which is victorious.'

'Unhappy France, unhappy king, if you are a true prophet,' murmured a few horrified voices.

'You may add *unhappy queen*,' continued Cagliostro,

'for the queen will follow the king; look, gentlemen, I put the question in these terms: *Marie-Antoinette-Joséphine-Jeanne de Lorraine, archiduchesse d'Autriche, reine de France.* These 75 letters give the following oracle: *Malheureuse en France—riche sans trône, ni or—ridée—à ration—enchaînée et décapitée.* "Unfortunate in France—rich without throne or money—wrinkled—put on a meagre diet—imprisoned—and beheaded."

'Yes, gentlemen, Marie Antoinette was born with all the gifts of nature and fortune; but her happiness passes. Destiny desires her one day to be "unfortunate, unhappy in France". I see her a queen without throne or money, cast down from the heights into the anguish of poverty. She shall be wrinkled before her time through grief. She shall be reduced to a meagre ration, which adds to extreme distress a foreboding of captivity. She shall be imprisoned, and will eventually be beheaded.

'There remain 6 mute letters J H D I I D, signifying: *Jacturæ Horrifera Dies Imminet, Ineluctabile Damnum,* which means: "The day of her fall hovers over her—a day filled with horror and inevitable disaster." I wish I were mistaken, gentlemen, for I too am seized with horror before such a prediction. Well, let us cast into chaos again these 75 letters, conjuring the sovereign master of destinies to derive some different meaning. In spite of yourselves and myself, this defiance of the ancient god *Fatum* is taken up by him in this very unexpected form: *Reine de France, et si jeune encore, je mourrai par hache—la tête tranchée dans nid de son.* "Queen of France, and still so young, I shall die by the axe—my head severed into a nest of bran." Do you not seem to hear Marie Antoinette's plaintive voice prophesying her fate? and what is the meaning of *"nid de son"* [nest of bran] into which her severed head will fall? My personal opinion is that this cowardly murder of a woman will be carried out by means of an apparatus frequently employed in Florence whose mechanism makes the victim's head fall into a basket filled with bran to absorb the blood. The word *nest* used here instead of basket is a repulsive irony.

'There remain four mute letters, I I I H, signifying: *Inermis Immolor—Inexpiabilis Hostia!* which means: "I am immolated, unarmed—inexpiable victim." Unarmed, do you hear? It is by no means a queen falling in the defence of her crown but a woman cold-bloodedly murdered; God alone knows what misfortunes will arm themselves to avenge her.'

XI

CAGLIOSTRO stopped, contemplating his audience with an inscrutable gaze. He seemed then the incarnate spirit of that fearful fate in whose name he had just prophesied.

Court de Gebelin the learned orientalist was no less stupefied than the rest of the audience. 'M. le Comte,' he said, 'you have just prophesied unbelievable catastrophes with unexampled daring. The benefits of the most laudable of revolutions are as nothing, if paid for at such a price! But as a man of good will, if convinced you are right can you not think of some means of warning the victims? For if God is pleased to let us see into the future, doubtless it is to remind us that He is its sovereign and that our prayers may influence Him. The King is a devout man, and Madame de Lamballe, the queen's friend, is Grand Mistress of Honour in your Egyptian temple. Have you confided these fatidic observations to her?'

'No, Sir,' replied Cagliostro, 'she would never believe me and I should be committing uselessly a dangerous imprudence. Women, as we know from the ancient sibyls, sometimes become prophetic instruments; then their secret power is a support to natural weakness. But apart from this rarity, they are not made for sharing with men the weight of such serious studies. The Magi allowed them to decorate the festivals of their religion, but not to enter into the higher mysteries. Moreover, how could I be so cruel as to reply to Madame de Lamballe, if her curiosity was aroused to ask me about her own fate: "You will be massacred"?'

·   'But this is madness!' cried the Duc de la Rochefoucauld.

'No,' went on Cagliostro calmly; 'it is merely, as before, predestination. I define in the following terms the personality of Madame de Lamballe: *Marie-Thérèse-Louise de Savoie-Carignan, Princesse de Lamballe*. Arranging these letters in a circle, we read: *Belle—grande—malheureuse —isolée—et massacrée à Paris*. "Beautiful, great, unhappy, alone and massacred at Paris." Yes, Madame de Lamballe is one of the most beautiful women at the French court; great, because of the dignity which attaches to the service of the queen, also by her own virtues. Yet her destiny must be fulfilled: she will be unhappy. Suddenly cut off from all affection and support, she will find herself one day alone, in deep distress; and, as if it were not enough not to have a confidant, she will suffer a terrible death, massacred at Paris, in the revolutionary torment in which the King and Queen will also perish.

'There remain 8 mute letters: D O I I N I N C, meaning: *Domum Obitûs Intrat Infaustis Nuptiis, Infandâ Nece Claudit,* which means: "She enters the house of Death through unfortunate marriage and a frightful murder imprisons her there." For her, France is that house of death, whence she will not be allowed to escape. She has taken possession of it by marriage; there, unknowingly, she awaits the fatal hour. This idea of massacre, applied to a defenceless woman, revolts our delicacy of feeling and provokes disbelief. How and by whom can she be massacred? Let us attempt to clarify the oracle by a fresh transposition of the original statement, and we read again: *Mais ici—rebelle— roide—et massacrée; la—sauvée de la prison*. "But here—a rebel—rigid—and massacred—there—saved from prison."

'Here, gentlemen, we have two scenes. *There*, at one

point, Madame de Lamballe will be *saved from prison*. Her catastrophe begins, then, by imprisonment. But *here*, at another point, outside prison, the unfortunate princess will meet with danger: she will *rebel*, that is she will be revolted; she will be *rigid*, that is, with the contraction of nervous disgust and terror and *massacred* without pity by the witnesses of the horror which she is not able to conceal. Connecting these predictions with those concerning Marie Antoinette, her queen and friend, we can foretell that Madame de Lamballe's catastrophe will be manifested in the overthrow of royal power.

'There remain 5 mute letters: H E G N N, which a Latin Sibyl would translate thus: *Hinc Erepta Gemens, Nefarie Necatur,* which means: "Taken moaning from there, she is murdered by evil-doers."

'But see, I believe we can make out yet another illuminating fact: the place where she will die appears in half-darkness—but it could be expressed by: *Gênée—reprise —on la massacre—au coin—de la rue des Ballets.* "Thwarted, recaptured, she is massacred at the corner of the Rue des Ballets." Is there, in Paris, a street bearing that name?'

'Of course,' replied Court de Gébelin. 'The Rue des Ballets starts from the Hôtel de la Force and at the other end it turns into the Rue St. Antoine.'

'Well,' went on Cagliostro, 'that street may be the murder scene. Madame de Laballe, released either by escaping or by the intervention of friends—but, as I said, thwarted, impeded by some obstacle or tragic encounter—will be recaptured by fate. Leaving her peaceful native land to come and live in such a tempest, passing like a shooting star through the splendours of Versailles only to finish by dying wretchedly at the corner of some filthy street, what a fate![22]

22 Madame de Lamballe was the widow of the son of the Duc de Penthièvre, She was arrested with the royal family after the happenings of 10 August 1792 and was first imprisoned in the Temple, then in the Force. It is said that her father-in-law by paying a large sum of money arranged for Manuel,

'There are 6 mute letters M I H E I I, whose meaning is in Latin: *Mors Irruens Hic Extremas Instruit Insidias,* that is: "Leaping death has prepared there its final ambush."

'I shall stop here, gentlemen, unafraid of having talked too much; for you are gentlemen and would not dishonour yourselves by betraying me. You asked for some proof of the superiority of the Egyptian initiation over Anglo-French Freemasonry: truth is on my side, illusion on yours; history will prove it.'

'In 1793?' cried Court de Gébelin. 'That is the year assigned by you for the last act of the royal tragedy. But, M. le Comte, if you can give the date of that crisis, you also ought to be able to date its first act?'

'Yes,' replied Cagliostro. 'If I am not mistaken, France is divided into three groups: clergy, nobility, and people. The first two are in possession of land and public positions; the people alone is therefore interested in starting a revolution. As for its origin, the horoscope of the birth of Louis XVI, which I regret I cannot lay before you now, appears to place it in 1789. In effect, on this chart the position of the sun presages a future uprising of armed enemies against the king. Now according to the cyclic Table of Time[23] the years 1774 [accession] to 1793 [death] belong to the 8th cycle of Saturn, composed of 36 years [1765-1800]; in the course of this cycle the spirit of the Sun joins the

attorney of the Paris Commune, to order her release. One of the butchers named Truchon was charged to escort her. But at the sight of the heaped corpses, their blood streaming down the street, Madame de Lamballe could not repress a cry of horror. However, Truchon succeeded in leading her, pale and fainting. She was passing the last house of the Rue des Ballets when she found herself face to face with four men whose names have been recorded: Grison, Charlot, Mamin and Rodi. The first struck her a blow which caused her to fall; the others cut her in pieces; then her head, cut off by the wigmaker Charlot and for a long time exhibited in the streets, was finally thrown on a heap of rubbish in a corner.

[23] The horoscope of Louis XVI drawn by Cagliostro no longer exists. But I have tried to reconstruct it according to the hermetic rules and my work is confirmed by the indications given here by the celebrated Sicilian [p. 495]. This study will be found in Book VI. Consult, in particular, Chapter 1 of that Book for information about the Cyclic Table of Time [p. 463 seq.].

spirit of Saturn to govern the years 1768, 1775, 1782, 1789 and 1796. The presumed fatal date for the king being 1793, I foresee that the revolutionary uprising foretold by the Sun will begin in 1789, the nearest solar year to 1793, the Saturnine year.

'This reason, gentlemen, seems obscure to you, for you do not know the mysteries of the horoscope; but be so kind as to accept it for a moment with me and let us ask the sibylline circle what occult meaning could be linked with this astronomical account of a future yet four years ahead: *Révolution faite en mil sept cent quatre-vingt-neuf, par le Tiers-Etat contre Louis seize, roi de France?* "Will there be a revolution of the people in 1789 against Louis XVI, King of France?" From these 84 letters can be drawn a prognostic of a murderous republic: *La Démocratic sanglante tue Roi et Reine prisonniers en tour et étouffe leur fils en captivité.* "Bloody democracy kills the King and Queen imprisoned in the tower and suffocates their captive son."

'Five mute letters remain, V C Q T Z, signifying: *Vastatio, Cruor, Querelœ, Terror Zonatim,* which means: "A circle of devastation, blood, groans and terror."

'Of the two sons of Louis XVI, it is the second who is predestined to conclude his family's series of funeral processions. The first, *Louis-Joseph-Xavier-François, Dauphin de France,* carries from his birth the presage of a premature end: *Rachis exilera en fosse Dauphin franc:* "Spinal disease will make the grave the exile of the French Dauphin." The part of the body ['PAXIΣ] indicates the seat of the infirmity. This prince will die of a rachitic spinal affection.

'The 8 mute letters, O I J O V U P D, signify: *Obit Infans, Jacet Oriente Vitâ, Ultimœ Pacis Donum,* or: "Gift of a peace that touches its end, he dies still a child, lying down, at the dawn of his life." Born in 1781, he will not go far. His successor in the quality of Dauphin will be *Louis-Charles, Duc de Normandie, Dauphin de France,* whose premature death is also announced: *Déchu de palais, mourra duc, en l'enfance, hors nid;* that is, "deprived of his palace he will die in childhood, in darkness" [like the night-bird called *duc*] "away from his nest and the arms of his family". The two mute letters D I complete the oracle: *Defecit Inclusus*—"he dies imprisoned, captive."

.'If now I ask of fate how your stormy democracy will end, I read in the words *Revolution française* the following reply: *Un Corse voté la finira*: "an elected Corsican will end it". I conclude from this that after the royal catastrophe a man from the island of Corsica, elected by French suffrage, will take up again under a new title the power fallen from the hands of Louis XVI. What does it matter now, gentle-men, whether you believe or not? The future is with God; but man, God's image, can see the future's image. Do as I have done; the method is easy and, as I have done, you will see.'

When he had spoken these words, a tall silver-haired old man rose slowly in the mid-auditorium. It was Jacques Cazotte, a man of letters less well-known for his *Amorous Devil,* a forgotten book, than for his daughter's courage; she rescued him from murderers in September 1792. The austere exaltation of his face, as Lamartine writes, gave him the majestic look of a prophet; he sometimes had a prophet's eloquence and rapture. An ecstatic, he saw the approaching Revolution as an ordeal by fire through which France had to pass in order to win the crown of martyrdom. At present he was trembling at Cagliostro's words.

'One last word, sir, please,' he cried, holding out his hands in an attitude of prayer. 'Cannot your learned art predict the name of this Corsican, predestined to the throne of the Bourbons?'

'Ah, sir,' replied Cagliostro, bowing to him, 'you have just made a prophecy yourself; my reply is entirely con-tained in the 112 letters composing the 27 words you have just pronounced. Allow me to find by simple transposition the name and destiny of the unknown person who has aroused your curiosity:[24] *Le Corse héroique se nommera Napoléon Bonaparte, sera élu sur le trône des victoires, puis ruiné bientôt par un très-dur destin.* "The heroic Corsican will be called Napoléon Bonaparte, will be elected to the throne of victory, then soon ruined by a most unfortunate destiny."

'Eight mute letters remain, D V T I U T I D, signifying: *Dux Victor Thronis Imperat; Ulterius, Tristem Insulam Demetat*; "a victorious general, he dominates thrones; finally he paces the circle of a melancholy island." '

XII

GREATLY surprised were the dignitaries representing Freemasonry. Without believing in these oracles which they thought impossible, they contemplated thunderstruck the strange person standing before them. Court de Gébelin, passionately interested in the occult, who has left the above account in his manuscript *Memoirs*, declared himself strongly in favour of a masonic alliance with the Sicilian Magus. But the noblemen who formed the greater part of the audience were afraid of compromising themselves with such a strange prophet who at the very least could be accused

---

[24] At the time of the prediction Bonaparte was still only a student at the military school. He left it on 17 September 1785 as lieutenant of an artillery regiment which garrisoned Vienne in Dauphiny. Cagliostro's power of rapid and luminous intuition seems to pass, eagle-swift, from one to the other of the two outstanding features of the Napoleonic epic: the one of glory, the other of misfortune. Extract the 27 italicised words in the question put by Cazotte, attach to the succession of the letters the numbers 1 to 112 and the oracle is formulated by the transpositions which follow: LE 15 29—CORSE 67 70 71 72 73—HEROIQUE 87 88 89 99 7 84 85 92—SE 97 4—NOMMERA 6 11 64 10 42 54 94—NAPOLEON 104 22 43 50 60 61 63 82—BONAPARTE 98 103 2 30 53 3 58 80 83—SERA 105 8 9 38—ELU 44 48 51—SUR 52 100 101—LE 21 55—TRONE 91 93 17 39 159—DES 65 66 79—VICTOIRES 16 23 69 12 26 34 75 76 13—PUIS 20 45 47 19—RUINE 28 1 14 41 68—BIENTOT 102 57 78 49 24 110 17—PAR 74 106 5—UN 27 62—TRES 32 31 96 33—DUR 56 18 109—DESTIN 77 112 35 40 86 111. The 8 mute letters carry the following numbers:— D3 V37 T46 181 U84 T85 I90 D95. Put all these numbers back in their order of succession and Cazotte's question will re-appear.

of dangerous temerity. The Duc de la Rochefoucauld himself, although an almost fanatical supporter of Cagliostro, believing him to possess the secret of manufacturing gold, prudently put himself at the head of the opposition. In any case Cagliostro would not have accepted the alliance save on condition of being given the title Grand Master of all the Rites and of being invested with absolute power for reformation. The conference was not continued. The programme of the ten famous questions was abandoned owing to lack of evidence.

Freemasonry lost claim to be scientific, but this repute was soon replaced by the terrorists' red cap. In effect, when the States General of 1789 met at Versailles and the king appeared, Mirabeau, a member of the Lodge called *La Candeur*, turned to the colleagues beside him and, pointing out Louis XVI, pronounced these words: 'There is the victim!' The first call to arms was given by Camille Desmoulins, member of the Lodge called *Les Neuf Sœurs*; Doctor Guillotin, inventor of the machine that bears his name, and Danton belonged to the same Lodge.

The secret of the predictions which I have just related was ill guarded. Cardinal de Rohan, whose way of life was less well-ordered than a churchman's should be, spent his time poking into thorny intrigues which to his stupidity seemed harmless until he was scratched. Under the pretext of consulting him about studies in alchemy he went to see Cagliostro and said: 'I happened to hear the other day in the King's antechamber an ardent discussion between two gentlemen concerning Fate. In my quality of bishop I was careful not to join in for fear of making a *faux pas*, for my theology is very limited and the gentlemen had the taste not to ask for my opinion. The supporters of fatalism seemed to be the stronger and I couldn't help hearing them say now and again: "You'd better ask M. de Cagliostro." I must confess I would give half the philosopher's stone, if I possessed it, to whoever could tell my fate. What do *you* think about it?'

THE MYSTERIES OF THE PYRAMIDS

'Monseigneur,' replied Cagliostro, 'if that is all your Eminence desires I should be glad to satisfy you at once, without any charge beyond the continuance of your favour.'

'And how would you do it?'

'Would you kindly give me as sole basis for my reply your full sur- and Christian names and birth date, as they appear in the Court Almanack? The more there are, the better I shall be able to work out your fate.'

'Why sir, that would be a miracle!'

'No, it would be quite ordinary. If Monseigneur will be so kind; I put myself at his disposal and await his instructions.'

'Here they are, then: Louis René Edouard, Prince de Rohan-Guémenée, né le sept septembre mil sept cent trente-quatre.'

A few moments sufficed the Sicilian to write the prophetic metathesis: *Haut posé, mené entre trône et collier de reine, qu'il se gare nettement d'imprudentes aventures.* 'Highly-placed, led between the throne and the queen's necklace, let him beware of imprudent adventures.'

'What does it mean?' cried Mgr. de Rohan.

'The advice, Monseigneur, is very obscure. One part of the oracle is fulfilled, the Roman purple has set you in the highest Church position, and that privilege of fortune has led you near the throne. As for the queen's necklace mixed up with imprudent adventures, I seek vainly its meaning in the seven mute letters P G P B S P C, which conclude the oracle by a strange threat that I cannot venture to show you.'

'Yes, yes! You must show it to me sir; it may be of some advantage.'

'Very well then; I read: *Prælibans Gaudia, Pœnam Bibens, Subit Portam Carceris,* which means: "In the cup of a premature happiness he drinks the bitter dregs of punishment behind the bolts of a prison." '

'It does not make sense.'

'Of course not, Monseigneur. So I should like to see if there is any more reasonable meaning in your titles. Would you deign to dictate them to me?'

'Louis René Edouard, Prince de Rohan-Guémenée, Cardinal Evêque de Strasbourg, Grand Aumonier de France——'

'That will be quite sufficient for the moment, Monseigneur; I can already see a little more clearly—15 words, 83 letters.—There are dark patches in your sky, I regret to say; but as you know I can neither lie nor flatter. The text you have given me is at once transfigured; read for yourself.'

The Cardinal took the paper and read as follows: *Que ce Rohan se garde de grand ennui d'or, advenu au roi, et de prison fermée à cause d'un collier mangé.* 'Let Rohan beware of great trouble concerning gold, caused by the king, and of prison bars, the result of a necklace being eaten.'

'Difficulties concerning gold, and a necklace being eaten —what riddles are these?'

'Well Monseigneur, oracles nearly always express themselves in innuendoes. In any case, we have here a very material fact which will be revealed. It will be a question you may be sure of *gold* and a *necklace*. Let us suppose that Your Eminence found himself involved in some vulgar pecuniary matter which would arouse the king's displeasure and that you went to prison because of a necklace which does not, apparently, belong to the Order of the Holy Ghost, of which you are the Commander. The oracle said a queen's necklace. How can it be eaten, and by whom? It is a mystery on which, as a well-bred man, I must keep silence.'

'You are an insolent lunatic, a wretched charlatan whom I hope never to see again!' shouted the Cardinal.

Mgr. de Rohan was too optimistic. They were soon to meet again, in the Bastille.

The oracle had left three mute letters, B R R, signifying: *Bifariam Rapti Reus,* which means: 'accused of two kinds of larceny.'

On 15 August following, Mgr. de Rohan was arrested in his pontifical robes at Versailles by the King's order, charged with having received from M. Bohmer, jeweller to the Crown, on the forged signature of Marie Antoinette, a necklace valued at sixteen hundred thousand francs. He declared in his defence that a Comtesse de la Motte, claiming descent from the Valois whom he had believed to be attached to the royal suite, had brought him the note with the order to go in the Queen's name to purchase the necklace. He had considered himself honoured to carry out such a gracious command. The necklace had been handed to Madame de la Motte at Versailles by the Cardinal himself. Madame de la Motte was then immediately arrested; she defended herself by calumnies against Queen and Cardinal. Louis XVI ordered an inquiry by the magistrates of the *Parlement.* The inquiry found that Madame de la Motte had destroyed the identity of the necklace by unstringing it and that her husband had fled to England to sell, here and there, various portions of its jewelry, spending the proceeds on hectic orgies in London. This, then, was the 'necklace being eaten.' Marie Antoinette had been justified in the eyes of the King, the Cardinal was acquitted and Madame de la Motte, branded by the executioner, was condemned to life imprisonment.

The oracle had been fulfilled; but at the cost of an unforgettable scandal. The people had seen a Cardinal first accused of being swindled by Hebrew jewellers, then suspected, on the word of an intriguing woman, of wanting to buy possession of the Queen of France with a present of 1,600,000 francs. The people had seen the Queen's name dragged into a criminal trial where her majesty was completely extinguished. Royalty, deprived of the people's respect after having been cross-questioned in court, had taken the first step towards its Calvary.

Cagliostro was also arrested on 22 August 1785 and

taken to the Bastille as supposed accomplice of the Cardinal. His preventive detention lasted nine months, although the judicial enquiry could not bring a charge against him. Finally before the Parlement of Paris he proved that his connections with the Cardinal were concerned purely with the study of alchemy. Laughed at by the judges when he claimed he could manufacture gold, he was about to begin an exposition of the art but was ordered to be silent, and, on 31 May 1786 was acquitted as an inoffensive day-dreamer. On the following day, the Marquis de Launay, Governor of the Bastille, announced to him that by the king's command the warrant by which he was a state prisoner was changed to a banishment order and that he was free only to choose the frontier beyond which he was to be escorted.

'I was expecting without any anxiety at all the decision of the *Parlement*,' replied Cagliostro, 'for I had nothing to reproach myself with concerning the King of France. But I regret the decision which jealous minds have persuaded His Majesty to make. My presence in Paris, far from being a danger, might have offered me a chance of showing my devotion to that good-natured prince. Obedient to the will which desires my banishment, I wish to cross to England. If that will should change and desire my return, I shall obey Louis XVI's slightest wish, as though I were his subject.'

On leaving his cell in the tower called 'La Liberté,' Cagliostro, smiling, commented to the Marquis de Launay on the fact that the tower's name, strange in a State prison, had been of happy augury.

'In that case,' replied the Governor, 'you might have spared yourself the trouble of inscribing on my wall with a nail, in capital letters, a sort of monumental copy of your entry in the prison register.'

'Indeed, sir,' replied Cagliostro, 'a wretched prisoner has to do something with his time and his person in such a hermitage. I have at any rate written nothing vulgar or false. After all, the unfortunate creature who will succeed me here will only see in this inscription a proof of resignation to the will of God. This example may make patience easier for him; you will do well to let the writing remain.'

'Indeed, I see no reason why it should not,' answered M. de Launay; 'besides, you are a fairly well-known character and one would naturally want something to remember you by.'

This is the inscription scratched by Cagliostro on the wall of his cell: *En dix-sept cent quatre-vingt-sinq, le vingt-deux août, Giuseppe Balsamo de Palerme a été enfermé dans la Bastille à Paris par le roi de France, Louis seize.*

'On 22 August 1785 Giuseppe Balsamo of Palermo was imprisoned in the Bastille in Paris by the King of France, Louis XVI.'

Certainly the Governor could have seen nothing vulgar in this pastime of his strange prisoner. Giuseppe Balsamo was the Sicilian's real name, but he rarely used it; Europe and Asia had known him under many others. According to his changing fortunes, he had been known alternately as Lischio, Phœnix, Belmonte, Pellegrini, Harad, Melissa and finally as Comte de Cagliostro, to put him on an equal footing with the French nobility. By signing *Giuseppe Balsamo* on the walls of the Bastille he wrote his last prophecy, for this is what an initiate might read: *Paix, peuple ami!—En dix-sept cent quatre-vingt-neuf, la Bastille assiégée, le quatorze juillet, sera renversé par toi, de fond en comble, dans Paris.* 'Peace, friends!—in 1789 the besieged Bastille, on the 14 July, shall be destroyed by you, from top to bottom, in Paris.'

Six mute letters remaining, C G M A D A, to Cagliostro would signify: *Carceris Gramen Metietur Arcem, Domitor Arcis,* meaning: 'Grass will conquer the citadel and take the measure of the prison walls.'

Cagliostro's predictions had not been sown in idle minds. A few of his audience made a practice of thus consulting the occult meaning of human speech. This mystery spread into some society circles and it is perhaps not unreasonable to suppose that these strange studies were the cause in 1789 of the prudent emigration of more than one great nobleman threatened by the auguries. Unfortunately prophets, who know so well how to read the destinies of others, hardly ever seem to know how to take advantage of·these warnings. Cagliostro is a remarkable proof of this. England did not prove at all hospitable. London's Freemasons, shocked by his desire for domination, set traps for him from which he could only escape by emigrating. Their calumnies caused the subsidies to be cut off which he received from all the great Lodges of Europe and made him an outlaw from the association. He took refuge in Switzerland, in Piedmont, then at Genoa and Verona, without finding anywhere a safe hiding-place. Finally he was imprudent enough to visit Rome where his fate was awaiting him. Arrested by the Inquisition on 27 December 1789, he was condemned to perpetual imprisonment. He died in 1795, forgotten, perhaps poisoned, in the dungeons of the Castle of St. Angelo.   .

BOOK THREE

BOOK THREE

THE ANCIENT ORACLES, THE SIBYLS AND THE FATES

I

WE have seen in the theology of the Magi the belief in an ineffable, infinite God governing the universe by a hierachy of providential ministers whose task it was to carry out the general and unalterable laws of absolute Wisdom.

These co-operators or, to use a more familiar expression, these Angels, guardians of the divine creation, appear to us invested, according to the hermetic doctrine, with special powers corresponding to their functions in the universal economy. Each one is a mind, a will, a force acting in its allotted circle.

Egyptian cosmogony teaches us also that these ethereal beings, intermediaries between God and humanity, form innumerable legions each member of which has his own task to perform, while together they work as one in the maintenance of universal order.

Of these legions there are seven which govern the portion of the astral system of which our earth is the centre. Each occupies one of the seven orbits in which the Moon, Mercury, Venus, the Sun, Mars, Jupiter and Saturn accomplish their planetary evolutions.[1]

These planets are considered as thrones or centres of influence of the seven superior spirits or Archangels, each one of which is in command of one of the angelic legions.

This hierarchy of the supernatural world is mentioned by Iamblichus in his *Treatise on the Egyptian Mysteries*. The angels or divine messengers, servants of eternal Provi-

---

[1] See Book I, p. 59 for the influences of the three 'new' planets.—*Ed.*

dence, are spirits more perfect in essence than men. They help us, yet without restricting our will, which is always free to choose between good and evil. They work out the plan of the various ordeals to which every human being is submitted during earthly life; they give an account of our actions to God and lead our souls after death into the region of rewards or expiations.

Among the Greeks with their brilliant imagination, heaven came down to the summit of Mount Olympus; their gods ascended no higher than the clouds.[2] But the wonderful thing about Egyptian magic is that it penetrates so far, from one heavenly body to another, from universe to universe, out into the emptiness of space . . . In vain do telescopes explore every corner of the sky, in vain they pursue the comet to beyond the confines of our astral system, for the comet finally escapes them; but it does not escape the Archangel round whose unknown pole it revolves who in the fulness of time will bring it back by mysterious paths into the radiance of our own sun.

Christianity has inherited these tutelary powers whose images unite grandeur with gentleness: the Angels of solitude, of morning, of night, of silence that precedes night, of the mystery that follows it; Angels of the seas, of tempests, of time, of death—all have their own poetry. The Angel of holy love belongs to the virgins, the Angel of harmonies dowers them with graces. The upright man is blessed by the Angel of virtue; the unfortunate man is received by the Angel of hope who tells him of comfort and peace beyond the tomb.

Blind Fate is not admitted in earlier religion. Man is predestined to a certain series of ordeals; but these have as object the exercise of intelligence, will and all physical and moral faculties. Evil is by no means imposed upon man as a condition of being. Courage, faith in oneself, perse-

---

[2] See *The Greeks and Their Gods* by W. K. C. Guthrie for a new authoritative account of Olympus and those who inhabited its upper air or *aither.—Ed.*

vering effort, and the invocation of God are in the long struggle the means of gaining him a victory over evil and himself. If man did not have to fight and conquer, he would be neither an intelligent nor a moral being; he would learn nothing and do nothing but be a mere machine and the world would lack glorious history. Now the great men who appear on earth, the great things which are being ceaselessly accomplished, the progress of science, the marvels of art, the masterpieces of philosophy, are all obvious demonstrations of God's triple manifestation in our being through mind, reason and will. 'Fatality,' says Hermes, 'is the chain of cause and effect in the order established by supreme Reason. But will is the direction of the forces of the mind in order to reconcile the liberty of the individual with the necessity of things. Action, born of the union of mind and will, makes fate itself work for the fulfilment of the good or evil desires of the man who knows what he wants and wants what he knows.'

Given this, I consider it useless to discuss the ancient doctrine of the supernatural world as personified by the angels. They are introduced into Genesis by Moses, who was educated in the school of the Egyptian Magi. They recur in thousands of contexts in our sacred books. When Jesus was arrested by the priests of the synagogue, Peter went to his defence, but the Man-God restrained him by these words: 'Thinkest thou that I cannot now pray to my Father and he shall presently give me more than twelve legions of angels?' [Matt. xxvi, 53.] This is an undeniable confirmation from the Christian viewpoint of the existence of angelic legions to which God commits the government of the universe; if Jesus was able to express himself thus, the doctrine of the Magi is sufficiently justified. The Gospel also reveals the existence of devils or spirits of darkness, who strive to make man fall into sin by disobedience to the divine laws. Satan, the Christian devil, is the same being, under another name, as the Egyptian Typhon, the Persian Ahriman and the Indian Siva or Shiva.

And so we have perpetuated, in the religious tradition of humanity, the concept of an eternal conflict between the spirits of darkness who work ceaselessly for our downfall and the spirits of light, whose sole aim is to save us. Just as an angel is the representative of each virtue, so a devil is attached to every vice. Good and evil, two poles of human will, are balanced by Providence which preserves order; and the total weight of evil can never be greater than that of good.

In this case, says the learned astronomer M. Camille Flammarion, common sense is our judge. In all ages and among all peoples man has distinguished just from unjust. Man has everywhere and at all times understood the ideas of duty, virtue and self-sacrifice . . .

This spiritual elevation was preserved in all its purity in the sanctuaries of Egyptian Magism. The initiates, possessing the key to the sacred symbols, did not worship these material representations of their spiritual thoughts. But the people, uneducated and able only to grasp visible forms, could not help falling into a superstitious contemplation of them. This was the origin of 'idolatry'.

Greece had received from Egypt its material civilisation; she also received its popular errors. The Egyptian statue ceased to be the mysterious allegory of some attribute of a single ineffable God; it was taken for God Himself by the ignorant populace, and the collection of theological emblems became thus the granite or bronze pantheon around which the mob bowed down in worship. Magic, supreme science of the great nature mysteries, the revelation of its elementary forces, a stronghold ceaselessly strengthened and enriched by human discoveries, changed at the same time as religious dogma; it was brought down to the level of a suspicious activity in the hands of priests.

It would, I fear, be offensive to the good taste and intelligence of my reader if I were to present him with the tedious details of the magic practised in the ancient world under the profane title of divinatory sciences by fanatics and frauds. History should concern itself only with the great deeds which have dominated the customs and the spirit of nations and whose memory has been transmitted to us under the auspices of an impartial criticism. Among these things we must include the Oracles, the Sibyls, the Fates and Astrology.

II

THE Oracles were prophetic revelations, sometimes spontaneous, sometimes accorded during consultations which could only be made in a few privileged places, after the performance of ceremonies in honour of the local celestial power. The sanctuary dedicated to this power was itself given the name Oracle, which means place of invocation, place of the sacred Word. It was under this name that the most renowned were known: the Greek temples at Delphi in Phocis, at Dodona in Epirus, at Lebadea in Bœotia and at Tænarus in Laconia. No satisfactory explanation has ever been given for the physical phenomena whose manifestations, exploited by priests, favoured these localities: the wonder of the art disappeared two thousand years ago. The most notable men of antiquity consulted them at least once in their lives, which qualifies them for inclusion in the world's annals.

Delphi, surrounded on three sides by precipices, stood at the foot of two spurs which terminate the Mount Parnassus *massif* southwards. The temple of Apollo dominated the higher part of this town. Surrounded by a vast enclosure, it possessed treasures of great value, the accumulated offerings of all the Greek peoples and those of neighbouring nations. On the temple pediment was the inscription: 'Let no man approach this place except his hands be pure.' At the end of this building was a magnificent statute of Apollo in gold, and behind this statue was the entrance to the crypt in which the god pronounced his oracles. This cave, says Plutarch, had been discovered by accident. Some goats who had been grazing amongst the rocks had approached a cavity from which rose intoxicating gases; these had suddenly caused the goats to be seized with convulsive movements. The shepherds and inhabitants of the neighbourhood experienced the same sensations; they could be heard uttering in a sort of delirium strange words obscure in meaning. When the priests were consulted they decided that they must recognise by these signs the presence of a god who desired to communicate his wisdom through the medium of human speech. Apollo, god of eloquence, became their treasurer and repaid them in great wealth for the fame which the priests had brought him.

A virgin, bearing the sacred name of the Pythia, descended once a month into the cavern and sat upon a tripod to give tongue to the prophetic hallucinations produced by the subterranean emanations. Her head was crowned with laurel, her forehead was bound with a fillet of white wool. Sometimes in her trances she wrestled with the sacred pythons reared by the priests in honour of Apollo's victory over the serpent Python. There was at first only one Pythia at Delphi; later there were as many as three when the oracle was more frequented. At first they were chosen from among the most lovely daughters of the town's first families; but when one of them disappeared with a handsome Thessalian who had won her heart the priests, who were severely compromised by this scandal, thenceforth only attached to their temple prophetesses fifty years old and from the obscurest families. They were perpetually enclosed and took it in turn to mount the tripod. The oracle could never be consulted by the poorer classes; it only replied to questions asked by cities, princes or foreigners of high rank. The celebrated philosopher Apollonius of Tyana recounts thus a visit he once paid to the Pythia, accompanied by his disciple Damis.

'After purification by washing in holy water, we made an offering to the god of a bull and a goat. That this sacrifice might be agreeable to the god it was necessary for the bull to eat without hesitation the barley-flour presented to him; and after cold water had been thrown over the goat, its limbs had to be seen to shake for a few moments. The good-will of these animals having proved the purity of our intentions, we entered the temple, our heads crowned with laurels, holding in our hands a laurel bough decorated with a band of white wool. These are the symbols with which consultants must approach. We were shown into a cell where, say the priests, at a moment neither pre-arranged nor foreseen by themselves, one suddenly smells a wonderfully sweet perfume. A little while after one of them came to find and take us into the hidden sanctuary whose walls are decorated with the rich offerings that attest the truth of the oracles and the gratitude of those consultants who have been favoured by fate. At first we had difficulty in seeing anything; the burning incense and other perfumes filled the place with dense smoke. Behind the statue of the god is the crypt, into which one descends by a gradual slope; but the servants of the temple keep the consultants far enough away from the Pythia to make their presence unnoticeable.

'The Pythia, much fatigued, refused to answer our questions. The priests around overwhelmed her now with prayers, now with threats. Finally giving way, she placed herself on the tripod, after having drunk the water that runs through the sanctuary, said to have magic properties. Hardly had the woman sat down before we saw her chest swell, her face flush and pale; all her limbs were seized with nervous trembling; but she uttered nothing but broken cries and long-drawn moans. Gradually her convulsions became more and more violent, her eyes sparkled with fire, she foamed at the mouth and her hair stood on end. Unable either to resist the overpowering fumes or to leave the tripod on which the priests held her firmly seated, she tore off her fillet and between the most terrifying howls pronounced a few words which the priests hastened to note down. They immediately put them in correct order and handed us the message in writing. I had asked whether my name would be handed down to posterity; my disciple, without having consulted me on the subject, had asked the very same question. The reply was that my memory would pass into future ages, but would owe its perpetuation to the calumnies that would be attached to my name. I tore up the paper as I was leaving the temple; that is what all consultants do whose pride had not been satisfied.'[1]

Apollonius was well versed in the occult sciences of ancient Egypt. The Delphic oracle seemed to him unworthy of praise because it had not said anything flattering: and yet the Pythia, or the priests whose task it was to interpret her language, had not been mistaken, for the philosopher of Tyana, after having been venerated in his lifetime as almost the equal of a demi-god, was thereafter treated very badly by the fathers of the Christian church . . .

A rival to Delphi was the oracle at Dodona, situated at the foot of Mount Tomaros, at the southernmost extremity of Epirus. The town, consecrated to the worship of Zeus, had possessed its oracle from time immemorial: as at Delphi, visitors flocked thither with rich offerings. The temple was tended by prophetesses no less venerated than those at Delphi, though they led a less strenuous existence. There was no question of hallucinations or convulsive frenzies. The oracle had its sanctuary in a forest of ancient oaks watered by fresh streams from the mountainside.

Tradition singled out the sacred tree, standing in the middle of a clearing, which made the predictions. According to this tradition, two black doves dedicated to Isis flew away one day from the city of Thebes in Egypt and, winging their way in different directions, eventually arrived the one in Libya, the other at Dodona. The latter, having perched on an oak at whose foot were resting some rude inhabitants of Epirus, distinctly uttered the following words in their

---

[1] From a great crack in the floor of the cave still rise the mephitic vapours which apparently were the physical basis for the psychic powers possessed by the Pythias whose tripod straddled this geologic fault. Practically all the eminent ancient Greeks, including Plato, were initiates of Delphi.—*Ed.*

own language : 'This is a place beloved by the gods : here they will reveal the future to worthy men.' The other dove made exactly the same pronouncement in Libya and both were considered messengers from heaven by those who witnessed their miracles. Absurd as this story may seem, it is based on fact. Egyptian traditions tell of two Theban priestesses who, divinely guided, once undertook a great journey in order to preach the knowledge of God as far as their strength would carry them. The first went west and stopped in Libya, the second went north and arrived in Epirus. Both fulfilled their religious calling by civilising the men who welcomed them. If one remembers that in the language of the ancient dwellers in Epirus the same word stands for *dove* and for *old woman,* one has the key to the sanctuary of Dodona.

At the foot of the prophetic oak was a mysterious spring which dried up suddenly whenever the sun reached its zenith and began to flow again towards the hour of midnight. The prophetess whose task it was to consult the oracle would go, followed by the scribes of the temple, to the foot of the oak on which tradition said the dove had perched. She listened attentively either to the soft murmur of the leaves swayed by a gentle breeze or to the moaning of boughs tossed by the storm. Sometimes she also derived her prognostications from the whisper of the spring which flowed out of the earth near the sacred tree. Skilfully seizing the various gradations and nuances of sound, she would explain them according to the rules contained in a ritual of great antiquity. She used the same method in interpreting the echoing sound of seven copper bowls suspended from the inner walls of the sanctuary and hung so closely together that if one were struck it set all the others in movement too. The scribes of the temple rapidly wrote down the indications she dictated, and as all the phenomena of the trembling of the branches and the vibrations of the sound were noted in the ritual, with their commentary on the opposite page, it was sufficient to refer to the ritual in order to find the answers. It was a purely sylvan oracle whose fascination was that which is attached to the most ordinary objects when the soul, preoccupied by questioning or passion, lends to all around it the fantasy of a fortunate or a fatal omen.

The third great oracle of the Greeks, bearing the name of Trophonius, was in Bœotia, on the slopes of a mountain from which springs the small river called Hercynos, which forms in its course numberless cascades near the town of Lebadea. Trophonius was an architect who, with his brother Agamedos, had built the temple of Delphi. Certain traditions say that they made an underground secret passage by which they entered that sacred edifice at night and stole the rich offerings left there by day. Agamedos having been caught in a trap set for thieves, Trophonius cut off his head so that he would not be recognised and later himself perished in a landslide. Other legends claim that the two brothers, having completed the temple, begged Apollo to reward them, to which the god replied that they would receive their reward in seven days. At the end of this time they fell asleep and died. Moreover, the motives are unknown which made Trophonius the recipient of divine honours. His cult was perhaps one of those local adorations of which nearly all religions give us examples, without being able to assign any certain or at least reasonable origin to them. The architect of Apollo rivalled the god himself. It was in a way an imitation of the Delphic oracle, but the Bœotians were not particular about that, and its success proved they were right.[*]

The cavern inhabited by the oracle had been well chosen by the priests in order to give visitors a terrifying shock. One went down to a certain depth by means of a ladder; then one had to crawl, feet foremost, down a long and narrow hole, at the bottom of which one felt oneself carried away with terrifying speed to the depths. If one

[*] W. K. C. Guthrie in *op. cit.* has a full account of a visit to this oracle.—*Ed.*

tried to climb back, one was thrown down again headlong, with the same force and speed. The honey-cakes which one had to hold in each hand under pain of death, did not allow one to touch the springs which worked the ascent or descent. One only undertook this dreadful pilgrimage at night, after long preparations and a rigorous examination. Pausanias tells us that a Theban named Tersidas who had come to consult the oracle had at first been shut up for three days and nights in a chapel dedicated to Fortuna where he had had to submit to an almost unbroken fast. When the time came for him to be admitted to the sanctuary he was made to drink water drawn from two springs, one called Lethe ['sleep'], the other Mnemosyne ['memory']; the first cup effaced all memory of the past, the second disposed the mind to remember everything of what he was about to see and hear. Next he had to put on a linen alb and was led by torchlight to the ladder which led down to the cavern. He did not come out until morning, pale and helpless, held up by priests, his eyes, dull and glazed, recognising no one. After having collected a few broken words regarded as the oracle's reply, his conductors led him back into the chapel of Fortuna. There he gradually recovered the use of his senses; but his mind held only confused traces of his sojourn in the cave and traces of the terrible shock he had sustained. Most visitants retained for the rest of their lives the mark of an ineffaceable sadness.

Plutarch has transmitted to us the story of a certain Timarcus as told by himself: 'I had come,' says Timarcus, 'to ask the oracle of Trophonius what one should think of the *daimonion* or familiar spirit by which Socrates believed himself to be inspired. At first I found nothing but darkness and silence in the cavern. I remained a long time lying on the ground, unknowing whether I slept or waked. After long and anxious prayers I heard distant music; then the darkness surrounding me seemed to disperse gradually into a mysterious wavering light. I could make out on my right different-coloured islands that floated, revolving, on the surface of a lake of fire. On my left appeared a blazing pit similar to a volcanic crater, on the edge of which hovered small stars or rather will-o'-the-wisps, some almost without light, others almost brilliant, but half-veiled by a floating mist. And from the depths of this pit rose confused noises, among which I thought I could make out human groans.

'While I was contemplating this vision, a deep voice called me by name and said: "The radiant isles that float on the lake of fire are the sacred regions inhabited by pure souls. Each obeys a god, and man cannot enter there unless he has cast off the bonds of flesh. The will-o'-the-wisps you see hovering on the brink of the pit are souls just departed this life; they are divided into three orders. Those that death has surprised when enslaved by material bonds and the senses, arrive here almost extinguished; the spark of the divine fire which they have profaned separates itself from them and lets them fall into the eternal night of Chaos. Those who have divided their lives between good and evil appear to you as if veiled by a more or less dense mist from which they must free themselves by plunging into the burning pit. Those who have kept their original purity amid the ordeals of their first existence are clothed in divine radiance by crossing the lake of fire, source of eternal life, and go on to find among the luminous islands of the blest the dwelling-place inhabited by the virtue whose most perfect image they have realised. The soul of Socrates was one of these; always superior to his mortal body, his soul had become worthy of entering into communion with the invisible worlds, and his familiar spirit, a deputy sent from them, taught him a wisdom that men did not appreciate and therefore killed. You cannot yet understand this mystery; in three months it will be revealed to you."

'Then,' goes on Plutarch, 'the unknown voice stopped speaking. Timarcus immediately fell into a deep swoon, and when he recovered he found that he had been carried outside the temple of Trophonius. The memory of what he had seen and heard absorbed his whole being in a silent dream : at the time indicated by the oracle he died, babbling of luminous islands and lakes of fire and holding out his hands towards the image of Socrates which he said was coming towards him.'

III

THE Sibyls shared with the Oracles the veneration of the Greeks, who were followed shortly by the Romans and the peoples of antiquity classed under the general name of Barbarians. The Sibyls were women who revealed themselves as possessed by a divine spirit whose organ they became. The Oracles remained attached to their places of origin; the Sibyls often went to other countries and led a wandering life among various nations. The term Sibyl seems to be derived from the Chaldean *Kibel* [tradition, communication of God's word]. Some Hellenists give as its etymology the words Σιο, a contraction of Ζηντέω [I consult] and Βουλή [will], because these prophetesses consulted the will of the gods in order to reply to the questions that were asked them.[5] This divinatory hallucination was considered by the ancients as a privilege accorded to perpetual virginity. St. Jerome includes it in this sense in the number of incontestable truths; and in the philosophical wars waged against polytheism sibylline predictions were often invoked by the doctors of the church in favour of the new faith. In any case the fatidic power attributed to Sibyls has been no more and no less authenticated than that of a host of Christian visionaries including Catherine of Siena, Theresa of Avila, Catherine Emmerich de Dulmen and Marie Alacoque. These mysteries of human nature, now accepted and now denied by men of great intelligence, will doubtless always remain impenetrable. In the face of these supernatural facts, modern science has shown itself so

---

* The more usual version is that Σιο-βολλα was the Doric form of θεοῦ βουλή the will of God.—*Ed.*

narrow-minded that the only thing it knows, if it were to tell the truth, is its own profound ignorance.

The famous Sibyls were ten in number. It is believed that the oldest was called Sambeth, daughter of the patriarch Noah. The first Christians attributed to her the power of making predictions in verse or in rhythmic phrases concerning the origin, the succession and the course of empires from the time of the deluge to the coming of the Messiah, on which subject she is said to have gone into great detail, conforming in each point to the Hebrew prophecies. We have no means of verifying this claim. The only indication we have—and it is not enough—is in the line *Teste David cum Sibyllâ* which, in the well-known funerary prose of the *Dies Iræ*, invokes as proofs of the last Judgment and the destruction of the world by fire the Psalms of David and the verses of the Sibyl.

The second of these inspired women is cited by Pausanias under the name of the Lesbian Sibyl; he gives her the name of Elissa and claims she was the issue of Zeus and the nymph Lamia, daughter of Neptune.

The third, called Artemis, daughter of Apollo, was a great traveller. Greek traditions place her birth a hundred years before the Trojan War and give her successive habitations as Delphi, Sicily, Rhodes, Samos, Erithræa and Claros.

The fourth, called the Thessalian, was named Manto, daughter of Tiresias, the celebrated soothsayer of Thebes in Bœotia, sung by Homer.

There were further the Phrygian Sibyl named Sarbis; the Tiburtine Cassandra; the Colophonian Lampusa, daughter of the soothsayer Calchas who followed the Greeks to the siege of Troy; Phyto, the Samian Sibyl; also the Hellespontine and Cumæan Sibyls. The former, known by the name of Amalthea, lived in the time of King Crœsus; the latter was called Hierophila, and, according to Dionysius Halicarnassus or Diodorus Siculus, she was the most famous because of an adventure which history has duly recorded.

During the 3rd century in Rome, at the close of the

reign of Tarquinius Superbus, whose memory remained to all Romans a symbol of tyranny, a tall, unknown woman clothed in the Grecian costume one evening entered Rome by the Capana gate and walked slowly towards the palace. Struck by the majesty of her bearing, the crowd stood aside to let her pass and silently followed her with their eyes, with a respectful curiosity. They thought she was a foreign companion of those priestesses of Fire who, under the name of Vestal Virgins, guarded in the Capitol the Roman Palladium and the image of the sacred she-wolf who was said to have been the nurse of Romulus.

Led before Tarquinius, with whom she asked for a private audience, this woman refused to give her name. She simply said that she was a Greek, vowed since childhood to a life-long virginity which the gods had honoured with the gift of prophecy, and that she had come from Cumæ in order to announce to the King of Rome the fate of his race, which was on the brink of fatal happenings.

Tarquinius Superbus was an unbeliever to the point of impiety; but even he became curious. 'Reveal your secrets to me,' said Tarquinius. 'If they are worthy of my attention, my gratitude shall equal your knowledge.'

'King of the Romans,' replied the Cumæan Sibyl, 'I once inhabited the island of Erithræa, where I was renowned for my beauty. Not finding any man worthy of my love, I had consecrated my virginity to chaste Diana, when one day Apollo descended from the skies into my secret retreat and offered me his love. Faithful to my vow I repulsed the seductions of the most beautiful of the Immortals. "Then ask of me," said the god of day, "whatever you desire, and I shall give it you." I took up a handful of sand and wished that my life might be prolonged for as many years as my hand held grains. "Your wish is granted," cried the god, "and may the old age of centuries avenge me for your disdain." At that very moment by a cruel trick my hair tourned white and my face was covered with wrinkles. Overwhelmed with despair I left the island for ever and hid my wretched life in Italy, in the profoundest solitude. That was long ago. I no longer know how old I am. Generations pass before me like shadows; I alone do not change. While everything around me falls into the past, my spirit lives endlessly in the future. From time to time I write at the dictation of an invisible spirit who sends me to carry his revelations to whomsoever he chooses. Your turn has come now, King of the Romans. Like all the mortals I have visited, you will read my writings and not believe me; and therefore it is that the evils which threaten you will become inevitable.'

With these words the Cumæan Sibyl presented him with a fresh roll of papyrus covered with Greek verses and with hieroglyphics. 'Tarquinius,' she went on, 'all the destiny of Rome is contained in that scroll. Give me three hundred pieces of gold, and they will give you wisdom.'

Tarquinius laughed and had the Sibyl sent away. 'Poor mad creature,' he murmured.

She covered her face with her veil and withdrew silently, without complaint. But next day she re-appeared at the palace doors while the King was holding a public audience. 'Sir,' she cried, 'last night I burned three of my sacred books. I offer you the six that remain; buy them, if you are wise, at the same price as I asked before, for all your royal treasures are not worth a single line of those written in my books.'

Tarqinius had her driven out by the guards, forbidding her in threatening tones to appear again.

She came back the next day; this time she wore a wreath of verbena—not a very strong defence, but sufficient to protect her from outrage, for priestesses wearing this were considered by popular opinion inviolable. She was carrying a small tripod of beaten brass in which coals and scented woods were burning. The palace guards were paralysed by these religious signs. She placed the tripod before the King, and drawing herself up to her full height: 'Tarquinius,' she said in a grave voice, 'the Spirit that brings me back here is more powerful than your proud disdain. I have burned three more of my books, chosen at random like the others. As you despise the advice given by heaven, destroy for yourself the last three in the flames of this tripod. Their loss or preservation will change nothing in your fate.'

And she held out to the King of Rome, who was trembling at the fixity of her stare, the last three books.

The witnesses of this scene were stupefied. Tarquinius was for a long time silent and confused. Then regaining his calm he said, as if trying to confound the Sibyl: 'Woman, if you are as you claim an envoy of some god, and inspired by heaven, why do you ask for gold in exchange for predictions whose value cannot be ascertained before their fulfilment? Do the gods sell their revelations?'

'No,' replied the Sibyl, 'but I need the money for alms for a certain king, whom I see among the Etruscans. . .'

Tarquinius, unable to understand this strange reply or to obtain further enlightenment, at once called the priests whose task it was to consult oracles. They tried in vain to extract the meaning of the begging king from the mute Sibyl. To regain some of the favour lost by their powerlessness, they attempted to obtain flattering phrases for the King by asking the question: 'Tell us O inspired virgin, when will the power of Rome reach its peak?'

They expected her to indicate the current epoch.

The Sibyl raising her eyes to the heavens crossed her hands over her breasts and slowly answered: 'When *the son of the Lamb* is seen to pasture with *the son of the she-wolf* on the grass of the seven hills, Rome shall be the sheepfold of the nations.'

This second enigma was no less obscure than the first. 'If you do not understand,' added the Sibyl, 'the ignorant shall be your masters. Blessed are the simple, the unlettered, for they shall see the times that I foretell, and the wise shall then be as blind men.'

Overcome by terror at this phlegmatic woman who spoke to them in an unknown language, the priests advised

Tarquinius to buy at any price the three manuscripts still not thrown into the flames. The Sibyl received the three hundred pieces of gold, lowered her veil, left the palace without speaking and left Rome that very day. Her oracles were studied carefully by the College of Pontiffs; but the gaps created by the destruction of six rolls had so confused them that it was impossible to piece together their contents. The fragments that remained announced nothing but disasters. The Pontiffs were forbidden under pain of death to communicate any of their contents to the public. The scrolls were locked up in an iron chest and buried beneath the statue of Apollo. Soon the revolution broke out which banished the last Tarquinius from the Roman throne. He took refuge in the small town of Cære in Etruria where he found an obscure asylum in the oblivion of the tomb. The Roman priests then remembered the Cumæan Sibyl and the prediction of the King begging. Its predictions considered proved, the authority of the Sibylline texts now became immense. Later during the great dangers that threatened the republic the senate ordered by a solemn decree that these books should be consulted; and, if we are to believe the historians, Rome more than once owed her salvation to the illumination that the College of Pontiffs claimed to discover in them.

Several centuries later about 50 B.C. all the religions of the known world trembled in expectation of a great and mysterious event. Travellers from Gaul and Asia brought every day from those distant limits of the known civilised earth traditions of an imminent future event. The Roman priesthood, studying afresh the Cumæan oracles, found some confirmation of these rumours. The great Cicero himself, an enemy of superstition, wrote in his *Treaty of Divination* about this foreboding which had seized the minds of all and defied even his own reason. A colony of trading Hebrews established in Rome had added their national prophecies to the rest and, so it is said, the language and calculations of Daniel and Isaiah coincided with the Sibyl's secular texts and with the hymns that the Roman legions had heard chanted by the Druidesses of Britain on the borders of the northern sea. All these voices based on tradition announced that a new king was about to rise in the east, to proceed to conquer the world and to give back to all nations of the earth, reunited under his power, the Golden Age of the earliest times.

But who would be this supreme king? Was he still unborn? From which race would he arise, by what sign would one foretell his coming? The oracles were silent on this point, and this favoured the growth of all sorts of illusions. Rome was full of astrologers come from distant lands to seek their fortunes. These soothsayers worked by star-gazing, the calculation of letters and numbers and by magical incantations whose detail it would be impossible fully to describe. Not one of them could solve the general problem.

A single man was at that time the focus for all eyes: Julius Cæsar*, master of Rome and of the empire by audacious strokes of good fortune, the Cæsar to whom Rome in one day gave more honours than had been received in centuries by famous men. This fortunate soldier, intoxicated by his fame and seeing nothing beyond it, was amazed at the conception of someone who should rise higher than he. He laughed at the auguries and prognostics which claimed miracles in every small happening and had too much faith in himself to stop at the sight of a crow or an owl or the appetite of a chicken, or the peculiar quiverings of a sacrificial ox's entrails. But he shared to a certain extent Rome's veneration for the Sibylline books. Uniting in his temporal empire the titles of Sovereign Pontiff and demigod—for his bronze statue stood in the Capitol bearing the name Jupiter-Julius—he believed that the apogee of Roman power was the time of his own exaltation. While from India, Gaul, Egypt, Greece and Judæa rose prophetic voices proclaiming

* Many of the then current prophecies later held to refer to the advent of Jesus Christ were in fact applied at the time to Julius Caesar.—*Ed.*

the same revelation, was it not natural that an all-powerful man, amongst a people everywhere victorious, should seek in his own destiny the crown of all ambition? Could the amazed world hesitate to recognise in him the destined conqueror of a century already filled with wonders? Did he not hold in his hand the keys to that future?

·The Roman people seemed to him clearly indicated by the term *Sons of the she-wolf.* As for the *Sons of the Lamb* also mentioned, did they not represent conquered nations herded like sheep in the fold of Roman domination? The enlarging of this fold by the rights of citizenship by the conferring of which Cæsar had gratified whole peoples, the splendours of vast wars and trophies, the disarmed nations whence he had shaped his victorious soldiers from Germany to Asia and from Gaul to Syria—his daring, promptitude and an unparalleled good luck—the career of this genius who in ten campaigns had enlarged the Roman camp to strands which to an earlier Rome did not exist—the irresistible will that in five years' civil war had shaken all the Mediterranean: could such prodigious preliminaries be less than the dawn of an era of domination for the soldier who had vanquished Rome herself? True, the prophets of Judæa seemed to promise their own land the honour of bearing this divine king; but was not Judæa the servant of Cæsar? They had seen her dragged in triumph by Pompey, and Cæsar had overthrown Pompey. What more did he need, this man of destiny, to bring the world to his feet? Only to work a final miracle: make war on Asia, plunge his sword into the depths of the India that had halted Alexander, to return by the Caucasus and Scythia to Germania and Gaul, to ride his steed through the waves lapping the edge of each bay in that River of Oceanus, the fabulous limit of the world described by Homer. Then he would return to Rome laden with the dust of all those shores, wet with the spray of all those coasts. Was that not sufficient to complete in super-human majesty the type of the supreme master whose appearance the universe was now awaiting?

This was Cæsar's dream; but not what the oracles meant. Magic itself had taken every care to undeceive him: 'Beware the Ides of March,' the astrologer Spurinna had told him on the very day when twenty-three daggers awaited him in the senate. The despised occult science could do no more to save the hero's life and he delivered himself to fate at the foretold hour.

Octavius, who assumed the style of Augustus, the avenger and the inheritor of Cæsar's fortune, believed in his turn that the destinies foretold by the oracles were to be fulfilled in his own person. He had recognised and struck down all his adversaries at the right time. To consecrate his good fortune he had erected a Temple of Peace and had consulted the Delphic oracle on its duration. The oracle replied: *This peace will last until a virgin gives birth to a child and yet remains a virgin.* Accepting this as a promise of eternal peace, the new master of the world had inscribed on the entablature of the building a dedication to everlasting peace [Templum Pacis Æternæ]. Now at the time when the Judaic prophecies were heralding the actual nativity of Christ this splendid monument collapsed inexplicably on its foundations.

The historians tell us that the Roman senate, flatterers of fame, had come to offer the Emperor the title *God of the Nations.* Augustus' pride could desire nothing greater; a servile humanity wished to raise altars to him.[1] But before accepting supreme homage he consulted the

---

[1]   To treat this as a mere story of personal pride is scarcely fair to the essentially practical Augustus, who was no Alexander indulging in unbalanced dreams. The man who carefully refrained from upsetting the ancient Roman constitution and took for himself merely the modest title of *princeps* or 'chief-amongst-equals' was driven only by a realistic appraisement of the lack of any strong bond between the peoples of his empire to conclude that a cult of the figure in whom inevitably Rome's power was incarnated was the only means whereby they could be forged into any whole. Even so, it was always the *genius* or indwelling spirit of the current emperor, which might be held to be merely a personification of the divine destiny of Rome, to which homage was made obligatory. Some 300 years of relative political stability, unparalleled in the history of the western world, proved his political sense. —*Ed.*

Tiburian Sibyl, to whom he submitted all his plans and
who until then had not failed of the most favourable
auguries. This prophetess lived nearby on the Palatine
Mount, in a temple whose doors were opened only to the
Emperor. He went at midnight and asked her if there
should ever be born a prince greater than himself. The Sibyl
was examining ancient holy books for her reply, when suddenly above the Roman countryside appeared a meteor
whose radiance filled the solitary hall with light.

'Look!' said the Sibyl. 'Do you see in that circle of
burning gold a young woman holding a little child in her
arms? That is the sign of the future that an unknown god
reveals to you. At this time one world is ending and another
world begins:[*] kneel and worship, for that child whose
image you see in the heavens has just come upon earth.
He is the King of future centuries, the true God of the
Nations.—I see he is of lowly birth and belongs to a small
and distant race. His divinity is hidden from the weakness
of men; and when he finally speaks and makes himself
known, men will persecute him as an impostor. He will
work miracles of goodness, but he will be accused of making
pacts with evil spirits; to him will be returned evil for good,
and after suffering terrible atrocities he will be put to death.
But I see him later a victor over death, rising from the tomb
where his murderers believed him imprisoned. I see him
hovering over all nations and reuniting them at his feet
like lost sheep. Adored on earth and glorified in the heavens,
he shall hold eternity in his hand; he shall divide the elect
from the damned. Those who believed in him when he
walked among them under the veil of humanity shall be his
eternal and blessed subjects. Those who only recognise him
when the thunder roars will become humble too late; he
shall say to them: "I do not know you." '

[*] The Precession of the Equinoxes was well-known to the ancients. That the
2160 or 2164 year-period dominated by Aries the Ram was then ending and
that the Great Day of Pisces the Fishes was just beginning was in fact the
astrological basis of all these expectations of a saviour.—*Ed.*

While the Sibyl spoke the mystic meteor divided into three stars which separated into the form of a triangle and gradually disappeared into the depths of the sky.

The same traditions say that Augustus went next day to the senate and told his vision. The patricians ordered the account to be placed in the state archives, later discovered by the Emperor Constantine. I would not affirm the authenticity of this story, although the learned Muratori has catalogued it in his *Antiquities*. The first Christians were with some justice accused of fabricating the predictions which they attributed to the Sibyls and then of using them as defences against polytheism. St. Jerome, St. Justin, Lactantius, Clement of Alexandria and Origen all pronounce themselves in favour of its authenticity however.

V

I HAVE mentioned the Druidesses of Brittany. These priestesses of our Gallic ancestors may be considered as the last Sibyls of the ancient world. The history of Magic owes to them a national tradition contemporary with Cæsar.

As far back as we can trace the Gauls are found in process of detaching themselves from the Asiatic race called indiscriminately Scythians. Driven either by war or a barrenness of soil from the Black Sea and Caspian regions, they reached the Scandinavian forests and found themselves wandering under a daily colder and more mournful sky. Repelled, they wandered westwards to the country and peninsular which we know by their name, translated later by the Romans as Gallia. To their vanished speech a few proper names, Latinised in Cæsar's commentaries or deciphered from stones, are the sole guides. This race worshipped *Tarann*, the power of the thunderbolt; it invoked our sun under the name of Bel; and Teutatês presided over the domestic hearth.

Seven centuries B.C., a fresh immigration·from Asia,

known as the Cymri [the Cimmerians of the Greeks, the Cimbri of the Romans] and following the same path as the Gauls mingled with them and brought a new cult, Druidism, whose spirit and doctrines seem to have emanated from oriental religions. Learned men have searched for the etymology of this word. Some think it came from the Celtic substantive *deru* which meant *oak* and have concluded that Druidism was a cult offered to this king of the forests. The ancient heroic legends seem to confirm their supposition, for they tell of how Hu-Ar-Bras [Hu or Hesus the Strong], chief of the Cymri, seized the great forests in the north and east of Gaul; how after his death his followers made him a god of war and, in honour of his memory, hung the arms of their conquered enemies from the branches of ancient oaks which were thereby sanctified. Another interpretation holds that the word is composed of two Gallic words *de* or *di* and *rouidd*, which can be translated as Doctrine of God. Mystery surrounds the rites of this religion. A mixture of pantheism and metempsychosis borrowed from Indian notions, it taught the eternity of the universe; it offered to believers a future life in which warriors would find everything that had made them happy here below. Faith in this resurrection was so eagerly accepted by the Gauls that at funerals they would throw on the blazing pyres letters written to the inhabitants of the eternal land; sometimes even mutual debts were stipulated as payable in this paradise. One can imagine with what disdain of death this dogma must have inspired naturally belligerent races.

The Gallic peoples had the savage but chaste customs that characterise the infancy of society. The cult of the oak formed a kind of mysterious transition between the impure materialism of Greek and Roman idolatries and the cult of the spirit revived by Christianity. The druidic priesthood, a jealous guardian of the first-fruits of ancient knowledge, taught a small number of chosen disciples the principles of astronomy, medicine, magic and moral philosophy. To the masses it preached the future life under material forms that merely conformed with their instinctive needs. Holding a general sway by the people's ignorant terror of supernatural things, it conferred the benefits of political union.

Its hierachy was composed of three degrees. The *Ovates*, guardians of the sacred rites, practised the divinatory art—the function of the Greek and Roman Augurs and Haruspices. The *Bards*, religious poets and warriors, sang the praises of the gods, the mysteries of nature and the national heroes. Finally, Druids properly named formed the superior caste in a supreme pontifical college gathered around the sombre majesty of the religious Arcana, with the official right to instruct, pass judgment and declare war or peace. Whether writing was unknown to them, or whether they considered that their power required mystery, the fact seems to be that no part of their teaching was vulgarised by being written down. Schools hidden in remotest solitudes were the depositories of living traditions which elder members of the priesthood repeated to their followers in a novitiate that lasted twenty years. A supreme head, elective but absolute, governed the Druids: he was at the same time temporal king of all the Gallic peoples. His omnipotence upheld his great prestige for a long time, even after the conquest of the country by the Romans; it was only overthrown by the violent fusion of many nationalities.

In the light of this theocracy we must consider these famous women magicians who uttered their oracles on the shores of the Armorican sea. Their principal centre was in the Island of Sayne, at the eastern end of Cape Finisterre. They were called Druidesses because they were the daughters of Druids. Hardy, dedicated to the perpetual youth of an inviolable virginity as soon as the wreath of verbena touched their foreheads, in their blond adolescence they became, by the superstitions of their race, supernatural beings. To them was attributed the power of making themselves invisible, they could command the elements and take on whatever outward form they liked. When they appeared at the national festivals all bowed their heads at the sight of their majesty and innocence; when in their prophetic exaltation they waved oaken branches in time to war hymns, warriors took it as a sign of victory.

A general assembly of Druids took place each spring and took the form of a court of justice, held in a sacred forest of the Carnutes, now the region of Chartres. In the midst of the aged oaks was a vast heath scattered with high stones marking the tombs of heroes whose memory was not allowed to perish. Before proceeding to political deliberations the awe-inspiring members of the priesthood performed a solemn rite in the cutting of the mistletoe, which grows on oaks that have reached their 30th year, and which popular superstition claimed to have divine virtues favouring the cure of all sorts of ills.* The mistletoe was cut with a golden sickle; its sprigs were gathered in a white veil and distributed to the heads of families. At home they reverently placed them in vases filled with spring water which was held to have curative properties. In peace time this festival was followed by the sacrifice of two white bulls. But in time of danger it is said that the offering of animals was not enough; the gods demanded men. Either prisoners of war or criminals condemned to death were used. Thus the Gallic races raised execution to the rank of a religious institution and were the only ancient people we know who sanctified the executioner.

In the forest shadows colossal figures woven from osiers into human shape were filled with these victims of the gods. *Eubages,* the priests of the sacrifice, bore them on their shoulders, chanting mournful hymns, to the summit of an enormous bonfire on which each tribal clan had thrown its faggot. Then the people withdrew, and when night had fallen the priests set fire to the holocaust. They studied the shrieks and the crackling of the flames for

---

* By modern anthropological accounts, the mistletoe represented, in fact was, the external soul of the oak, and was also its exposed or fatal aspect. The slaying of Baldur and his burial in a treetrunk is an allegory of the killing of the oak by the parasitic mistletoe—Baldur is slain by a mistletoe arrow.—*Ed.*

auguries. If justice had no criminal to deliver up, the cult of the Teutates insisted on the sacrifice of an old man. If no volunteer were forthcoming, one was chosen by marking the forehead of a man in the crowd. Over a table of hollowed stone a virgin of the island of Sayne slit his throat with a sacred knife and the blood was collected in an iron basin where the rising vapour was attentively studied for signs. . .

In his struggle against the Romans Vercingetorix, the opponent to whom Caesar pays tribute as the noblest and toughest of his foes, was greatly encouraged by the Druidesses of Sayne. He went there to consult the oracles on the fate of the town of Alesia, a stronghold which he hoped to make the throne or the tomb of Gallic independence. The Druids of the sacred rock honoured him fully. The nine virgins who guarded the fatidic sanctuary went down to the western beach to perform the rites that evoke Tarann. While on a granite altar burned perfumes dedicated to this spirit of the tempests, one of them led Vercingetorix to a small boat. She stood upright at the prow, chanting incomprehensibly; it seemed that through the potent incantation the boat was launched. Suddenly the sky changed and became the colour of lead; a violent gale lashed the sea and lightning, striking three times on the left of the hero of the Arverne mountains, broke the top of a lighthouse built on the island cliffs. 'Tarunn has replied,' said the Druidess: 'Alesia shall be struck even as that lighthouse. Son of the Gauls, remember our ancestors' war-cry: "Woe to the conquered!"' Once more only will you wield your two-bladed axe in the battle of the heroes, and the sun will go down in blood. The eagles with golden claws shall eat the brains of the Gauls, and the virgins of the land of oaks will be left alone to weep for the dead.'

Still however Vercingetorix believed in a god who would save his heroic race. When hope was lost, he offered himself to Cæsar in order that the remainder of his armed companions might be spared. The legions were standing round Cæsar, seated on the throne of military justice, when

Vercingetorix arrived alone and threw his sword and helmet at the Roman's feet. He then proudly awaited his fate.

Cæsar insulted his misfortune by putting his great adversary in chains and sent him to Rome. He dragged him behind his triumphal procession and then delivered him to the executioner. But perhaps the axe which ended the agony of Vercingetorix was used to forge the daggers soon to fall on his murderer.

VI

GREEK magic was easily accepted in Rome. The imperial city did not merely content itself with legal divination practised in public or with private sacrifices by inspection of the entrails of victims. As conquests increased, Rome welcomed all sorts of superstition as well as all beliefs. The disciples of the Egyptian and Persian Magi were drawn to it by the prospects of favour and fortune. Each patrician family had its astrologer. The birth of a child and the marriage of a daughter were always occasions for consultations. This reached even the Emperor's palace. Livia, wife of Augustus, who was with child by Tiberius, had been foretold the birth of a son by the mathematician Scribonius, who had dared to add that the child would one day be emperor. The event justified the horoscope. Poppæa, wife of Nero, surrounded herself with strange magicians; one of these, Ptolemy, an Egyptian, revealed to Otho, proconsul of Spain, his future as emperor, and, in effect, Otho did succeed the aged Galba.

Unfortunately for themselves, the true disciples of the hermetic art made poor courtiers; some were imprudent enough to presage catastrophes and were treated like state criminals for their pains. They were not called before tribunals, for fear of scandal, but they were made to disappear into the secret dungeons of the palace, or died beneath the daggers of servants. Soon the magical art itself had to be banned as though it were treason. Augustus himself, in spite of his experience with the Tiburian Sibyl and the astrologer Theogenus, who promised him the happiest of reigns, one day ordered more than two thousand books on magic to be burned in Rome. He did not doubt the value of the science, since he continued to use it; but he feared lest his subjects might find in it some means of overthrowing him. Tiberius banished whoever was convicted of practising this art. Nero, poisoner and matricide, did not want his enemies to be able to divine by the Egyptian Arcana the punishment which the gods were meditating for his atrocities. Vitellius, who succeeded Otho, thought he could assure his safety by decreeing the general banishment of magicians from Rome. They replied by placarding at all the crossroads a notice announcing his imminent death; and he perished in a wretched, cowardly way before the end of the year.

In following reigns, the same prohibitions were repeated against most classes of soothsayers and interpreters of dreams. But rigorous measures could not suppress the practice of various divinatory arts cultivated by high society, nor the witchcraft that obsessed the poorer classes of Roman society.

The origin of witchcraft was very ancient; it began in Thessaly, a country as celebrated for its witches and wizards as for its Vale of Tempe or its Thermopylæ. The Thessalian women who dedicated themselves to the profession of this spurious magic possessed, says Plato, the power to stop the sun in its course, to bring upon the earth the spirits of evil, to raise or calm tempests, to bring the dead back to life or kill the living. Anacharsis in his travels was curious to see them at close quarters. 'I had myself conducted,' he says, 'in secret, to some of these witches, whose sordid poverty equalled their ignorance. They prided themselves on having secret remedies against snake-bites and on being able to concoct spells which would kill bees, flocks and herds, or would deprive of children those newly-married couples who refused them an offering. I saw some kneading waxen figures; they heaped curses upon them, stuck needles in their hearts, and then exposed them in different parts of the town to gratify their hatred. Public superstition was so great that people who saw themselves modelled in this way believed themselves destined to die, and often this terror shortened their lives. I surprised one of these old women turning a spinning-wheel with great rapidity and uttering mysterious words. Her aim was to recall young Polyclete who had abandoned Salamis, one of the most distinguished women of the town. In order to learn the outcome of this adventure, I made a present to the witch. A few days later, she said to me: "Salamis does not wish to wait for the working of my first spells; she will come tonight to try more powerful ones. I shall hide you in a corner, from which you will be able to see and hear everything."

'I arrived promptly at my rendezvous. The witch was preparing her mysteries. All around her were laurel boughs and aromatic plants; some brass plates engraved with unknown letters; tufts of lambs' wool dyed purple; nails from a gibbet, still bearing traces of human flesh; skulls half-eaten by wild beasts; fragments of fingers, noses and ears torn from corpses; entrails of victims stolen from temples; flasks in which was stored the blood of men who had died a violent death; a waxen figure of the goddess Hecate, painted white, black and red and holding a whip, a lamp and a sword entwined by a serpent; several vases, some full of water from sacred fountains, others of milk and mountain honey. There were also some of Polyclete's hairs and a piece of his cloak. While I was looking at this chaotic mass of stuff a light step announced the arrival of Salamis, and the witch made haste to hide me. The beautiful Thessalian entered, burning with rage and love. The ceremonies began.

'The witch first of all made several libations with water, milk and honey over the entrails. Then she took Polyclete's hairs, plaited and tied them in various ways, and, having mixed them with certain herbs, threw them on a burning dish. That was the moment when Polyclete, subjugated by an invincible power, should have presented himself and fallen at Salamis' feet. After waiting in vain for this to happen, Salamis, doubtless initiated in some of the precepts of the magical art, cried out: "I will take my own revenge! Goddess of night, lend me a favourable light; and you, infernal spirits, aid me as you aided the fury of Medea! I cast this salt into the fire: may the bones of Polyclete burn thus! May his heart melt like this wax I throw into the brazier! Let us grind this lizard in a mortar, mix flour with it and the juice of these poisonous herbs; and you will go tonight and bury beneath the threshold of his house this fearsome composition. If he still resists, we shall employ secrets that bring death!"

'I do not know', goes on Anacharsis, 'what the result of these enchantments was, but they seemed to me of a very doubtful worth. Salamis went away, a little calmer, and I did not bother to prolong my stay in the town to await what was a most improbable result. Another sorceress had flattered herself, after the payment of a sum of money, that she could show me an evocation of the dead in a cemetery near her home. She dug a grave, into which she spilled the blood of a black lamb; then she began to recite, in a barbarous tongue, formulae and imprecations which produced more noise than anything else. Her howls were doubtless heard and attracted a few of the night-watchmen, for on leaving the cemetery she was arrested and thrown into prison. Fortunately I was too well-known for the judges to think of troubling me, but they gave me to understand next day that I would be well advised to continue on my travels, and to take my curiosity with me. I learned that, while tolerant, the people held witches in horror and regarded them as the cause of all evils. The law did not formally forbid sorcery, but it often attacked witches as the authors or accomplices of secret crimes among which poisoning played a great part. And it is stated that these wretched creatures had to pay the most dreadful forfeits.'

The raising of the dead was particularly practised on

the promontory of Tænarus, in Laconia. This eminence
was crowned by a sacred wood dedicated to Neptune, god
of the sea. The god's temple served as entry to an immense
cavern which the priests claimed to be one of the mouths
of Hell. It was through this hole, they said, that Orpheus
had been given permission to bring his finally-lost Eurydice.
The cave of Tænarus was the place whither magicians from
every city came to appease the spirits that tortured the living. They were offered expiatory sacrifices, especially when
one was guilty towards them of some injustice or crime.
A certain Callondas, the murderer of the poet Archilochus,
was obliged to go to Tænarus to obtain his pardon. Pausanias, a Greek general, having killed his mistress Cleonice,
was everywhere pursued by this woman's ghost. The wise
men he consulted led him to Tænarus; the shade of
Cleonice, when it was evoked, told him that he would find
'peace in Lacedæmon'. He went there, was judged and condemned to death. Convinced nevertheless that the oracle
given by Cleonice was a promise of safety, he took refuge
in a small temple which enjoyed the right of asylum; but as
no one brought him food, he died there of starvation, and
in this way indeed found 'peace'. Later, as his ghost disturbed the temple by its moanings, it was in its turn conjured by the priests of Tænarus and silenced by their
funerary rites.

These communications of the living with the dead were
obtained in polytheistic religions through the sacrifice of
animals. A square grave was dug in which first three libations had to be poured, one of milk and honey, the second
of pure wine, the third of water drawn from a sacred fountain. Then a layer of the purest wheat flour was put down
and at last a black ram was slaughtered; its blood, flowing
from the wound in the throat, had to mingle with the libations. The remainder of the ceremony consisted of votive
prayers which promised the dead a thanksgiving sacrifice
in return for their good will. Homer in the Odyssey retraces
for us in this way the evocation of the soothsayer Tiresias,

which was obtained by Ulysses after fulfilling rites indicated by the witch Circe. The soul of Tiresias appears, drinks a little of the blood spilt over the grave and reveals to the King of Ithaca the perils which await him on land and sea, until the favour of the gods allows him to see his home again. A host of other dead people crowd round the grave, and each of them talks to Ulysses after being allowed to taste the victim's blood. This fantastic scene has a striking effect in Homer's poem; but it would be childish to believe that it could happen in reality.

The science of poisoning was the most authentic part of ancient witchcraft and its traditions go back as far as the Homeric Circe. The sorcerers and sorceresses who from Thessaly had spread over the whole of the Graeco-Roman world, had raised to a very fine art this truly infernal science. At Rome in the time of the Emperor Claudius there was a certain Locusta who had been imprisoned in the dungeons for numerous poisonings. Agrippina, wife of Claudius, offered her life and freedom in exchange for the recipe for a secret poison which, without killing immediately and without leaving any visible traces, would hasten the death of the Emperor. Locusta was worthy of such royal confidence; she surpassed herself in the art of disguising a murder. Agrippina was ungrateful towards her accomplice; but Nero paid her debt at the price of Britannicus' death. Locusta had invented an essence so subtle that a dog on which Nero made the test before applying it to his brother was struck down as if by lightning. She obtained her liberty, considerable property, and Nero even assigned to her a retinue of imperial slaves as disciples, in order that a genius so useful to princes [as the crowned monster said] might not be irremediably lost.

Magic, let us make haste to say, never had anything in common with the rogues who usurped its name in order to exploit the passions or the crimes of powerful men. When Nero after the murder of his mother sought in a holiday in Greece forgetfulness of his crime, he was received with sinister coldness. The oracle of Apollo at Delphi, which from time immemorial no famous man passed by without consulting, cursed him to his face through the audacious voice of its Pythia: 'Go back, matricide!' she shouted at him. 'Your presence outrages the god you come to seek. . . The number 73 marks the hour of your punishment.'

· Nero was only 30 years of age and he thought the Pythia was threatening him with a catastrophe after another 73 years of life. The hope of so long a career flattered him; but the remorse aroused by the oracle's reproach brought on a fit of madness. The ministers of the temple expiated in horrible tortures the Pythia's imprudent words. Their hands and feet were cut off and the Pythia was buried alive with these mutilated bodies in the fatidic grotto whose door was then walled up. As for the number 73, it was noticed after Nero's death that this number represented the age of Galba, his successor. The incident at Delphi had made him look upon oracles with disfavour; all he could see in their priests were plotters, and maybe he was not mistaken. He turned aside from the direct route to Athens, because he would have had to pass the temple of the Avenging Furies and the one of Ceres at Eleusis, two seats of higher Magic where the art of divination was celebrated. He was afraid to see there the appearance, at the Hierophant's voice, of the melancholy procession of the victims of his reign. The superstitions of a cowardly soul peopled his dreams with menacing spectres. First he would see himself devoured by legions of ants; then he thought he had been transported to the theatre at Pompeii and the statues of the fourteen nations of the Empire, descending from their pedestals, enclosed him in an inescapable circle. There stood on the Mount Palatine a wood of laurels planted by Augustus where each new emperor at his accession added a fresh plant. It was observed at the deaths of Augustus, Tiberius, Caligula and Claudius that the tree which each had planted died also. A few days after the tragic fall of Nero the whole wood died; a thunderbolt struck off the heads of all the imperial statues, and broke the sceptre held by the statue of Augustus. These facts are attested as presages by the historian Suetonius; they had the whole of Rome for witnesses and formed the historic epitaph of the Caesarean dynasty, whose last representative found only a cave for final resting-place and a slave's mattress for a funeral couch.

VII

DURING the first century of the Christian era, which begins under Augustus and ends with Domitian, the town of Tyana, in Cappadocia, gave to the world a travelling Magus of whom I have already spoken. He was Apollonius. Born of a family renowned for its ancient ancestry and for the public offices which its members had held, Apollonius had been brought up in the Platonic schools from which, as we have seen, the doctrine of hermetic theosophy had emanated. His naturally contemplative spirit had inclined him from an early age to transcendental studies, and as he possessed a fairly large fortune, he gave himself up to them entirely. After having travelled through India, Persia and Egypt and being initiated, in each country, into the mysteries of the Sages whom he met in the sanctuaries, he desired to go to Rome, ruled in 63 A.D. by Nero, to see as he said the face of a tyrant.

As he was approaching the city accompanied by 72 disciples, among whom a Ninivite named Damis had already won his tenderest affection and confidence, he saw coming out of the wood of Aricia one of his compatriots named Philolaüs, whom he knew to be a wise man but lacking in courage. 'Unlucky man,' Philolaüs said to him, 'you are doomed! How can you venture to come to Rome with a train of disciples and wearing the mantle of a philosopher? Do you not know that Nero has banned all friends of wisdom and knowledge, and that your costume will betray you to the guards at the gates?'

'What does Nero do with his time?' asked Apollonius calmly.

'He likes to drive chariots at the circus, to play on the flute and to cut the throats of men whose existence is a mute criticism of his own.'

'Very well,' went on Apollonius, 'the contemplation of a prince who casts away honour is the highest lesson philosophers can study. Let those who are afraid to follow me any further look after their own safety; I shall not condemn their weakness, but I will not shelter my own cowardice behind it. The true sage recoils only before the threats of heaven.'

Sixty disciples abandoned him and fled with Philolaüs; but the 12 others who were faithful swore to share the fate of the master they admired. The guards at the gates did not arrest the travellers and, after having walked around Rome quite openly, Apollonius left peacefully with his little procession. 'We have given proof of our courage,' he said, 'but one must not provoke fools any more than gods. Let us go back to the Greeks and Egypt; we shall be better placed there to view the future. Revolutions are like colossal statues: they should be contemplated from a distance.' This last remark, which he did not explain, was considered after the event as a prophecy of Nero's downfall.

There are also attributed to him very precise prophecies concerning the reigns of Galba, Otho, Vitellius, Vespasian, Titus and Domitian. He was at Ephesus and was speaking in public on the very day when in Rome Domitian fell with seven dagger wounds in his body. Suddenly he lowered his voice and leaned to one side, like a man listening; then he walked three or four steps, and made a gesture of command, saying: 'Strike! Strike! the gods command it!' The astonished audience thought he had been attacked by feverish delirium when, rising to his full height, he told them in a thunderous voice: 'Ephesians, it is done. At the moment in which I now speak to you the tyrant has fallen and I see Rome on its feet, acclaiming its liberty!' A few days later the news of the murder reached Ephesus, and the time indicated by Apollonius was exactly that announced by the travellers who had come from Rome. This fact is verified in the Roman history by Dion Cassius.

Ammianus Marcellinus [d. 304] ranked the philosopher of Tyana with Pythagoras, Socrates and Numa Pompilius among the number of privileged men who lived assisted by a familiar Spirit. The Emperor Alexander Severus [146—211 A.D.] placed him with Orpheus, Abraham and Jesus Christ. The Empress Julia Domna, second wife of Septimus Severus, had ordered the rhetor Flavius Philostratus, teacher of eloquence at Rome, to write the life of this singular individual after the memoirs left by the Ninivite Damis his favourite disciple. This biography recounts many miracles and predictions of which the priests of the oracles had shown themselves jealous, because Apollonius gave them freely and without incorporating any bloody sacrifice or superstitious rites. Thus it came about that Apollonius, who had come on a visit to the Athenians wishing to take part in the mysteries of the temple of Eleusis, was told by the Hierophant that he would never admit a man who despised the religious ceremonies. This affront did not perturb the Tyanean thaumaturge who simply replied: 'You might have reproached me with something much worse—that I, a true initiate of Egyptian Magism, the only source of occult knowledge, had come to bow down before your arrogant ignorance.' The witnesses of this remark felt that Apollonius, whose renown was great, might harm the sacerdotal industry of Eleusis by decrying it on his travels and they pressed the Hierophant to apologise; but Apollonius disdained to listen to their excuses and pleadings.

This is how he sums up his doctrine. 'I studied in my long journeyings the wisdom of all countries. All the philosophic sects appeared before me, wearing the ornaments each had created for itself, and I retired into the solitude and dignity of my being to consider my choice. All seemed to me beautiful in their own ways, and of a superhuman appearance; some insinuated themselves into my reason with seductive graces and attempted to capture me with marvellous promises. One announced to me that, cradled and rocked in its dreams, I should see descend upon me the swarming pleasures of a voluptuous life; another did not pride itself on sparing me the sorrows of life but it offered, as the end of these trials, a perpetual blissful quietude. Yet another offered me a soul in perfect equilibrium between good and evil; and still another encouraged me to venture everything in order to find happiness. All agreed in binding me to earth by what they called the legitimate satisfactions of the material half of my being.

'Only one of these forms of wisdom, the Egyptian, kept itself aloof, silent and reserved. It appeared last of all, when it saw that its companions had not succeeded in capturing me. "Young man", it said to me, "I am the daughter of the past and the mother of the future; I am the queen of the spirits and God's reflection on earth and in all the worlds. To be admitted into my empire you must renounce the vanities of earth, sensual delicacies and the pride of life. I forbid love to my disciples as a dangerous madness of the soul, and I command their silence so that they may always feel themselves in the presence of God. I abhor bloody sacrifices that suppose in the Supreme Being the ferocity of a tyrant, and I teach filial prayers which are, with the offering of incense, the only cult worthy of the Father of all things. If you have the courage to follow me to the heights where Truth abides I shall make a new man of you; I shall give you new eyes which shall be opened upon the infinite world of immortal essences. You shall measure all time with a single glance; you shall embrace all beings as one, in a single thought; the divine powers shall reveal their secrets to you and the forces of nature shall obey you." In this manner was I addressed by the wisdom of Egypt, the great Magic of the sons of God: I followed it, and it has kept its promises to me.'

Apollonius of Tyana left this earthly scene in the year 96 of our era, shortly after Domitian. By a curious fate worthy of his life his death was a mystery. His disciples spread the report that he had been raised to the heavens by planetary spirits without passing through the tomb, and this found many supporters. The envious claimed that on the contrary he had thrown himself into some abyss in imitation of Empedocles, to make people believe he was a divinity. His fellow townsmen settled the question by dedicating to him a temple to the cost of which the Emperor Caracalla contributed, and which Apollonius honoured, it is said, with numerous appearances.

His prophecies on the imperial destinies of his time from Nero [d. 68 A.D.] to Nerva [reigning from 96] had done much to make him famous. In those short 28 years seven emperors had succeeded to the tragic imperial purple : Galba was massacred by a military conspiracy, Otho was stabbed by his own hand after a defeat, Vitellius had his throat cut by the mob and Domitian was assassinated by his wife's servants. Among these murders only Vespasian and Titus seem to have been spared. Apollonius had announced to his disciples the fate of this one and that. Domitian had him cast into prison as a dangerous character and fixed the day for judging him. The accusation was twofold : Apollonius had spoken imprudently in the presence of a public informer of the imminent elevation of the senator Nerva to the throne of Domitian, who was to be struck down by the avenging gods. It certainly was a capital crime; nevertheless the Magus made his stand with disturbing self-possession.

'Prince,' he said, 'what support shall I ask for in my defence? I shall invoke the memory of your father Vespasian, who visited me in Egypt before he became emperor. It is I [why should I not confess it?] who prophesied to him his future greatness: you are therefore under a natural obligation to me, following him on the throne. I used no enchantments to excite him to attempt the conquest of the

empire; I never flattered myself in his presence with statements that I could alter the course of the sun at my pleasure
nor change the progress of human events. I did not even
desire him to bend his eyes upon the mysterious Tables
on which the disciples of Isis are able, with great difficulty,
to study the signs of the horoscope. I found it suffcient to
consult, as you yourself, prince, might do at any time,
the venerated fates of the Prenestine Fortune. Need I tell
you that this system of divination was in former times
taught to the Etruscans by Egyptian travellers, and that
Servius Tullius, 6th King of Rome, set up in its honour,
in the town of Preneste, a sanctuary whose fame is greater
than that of Delphi? I wrote down the three names of
Vespasian [Titus Flavius Vespasianus] letter by letter on
cubes made of laurel wood. After having thrown the cubes
pell-mell into an urn of silver, the metal sacred to Isis, I asked
your father to take them out at random one by one and
to arrange them on the table between us. Here is the order
in which they appeared:

PSFSELANTAASUTIVSVUIUIS

'Then, raising my voice in secret prayer to the spirit
hidden under the name of the Prenestine Fortune, I wrote
at its dictàtion this imperial oracle:

Prænestinæ Sacris Fortunæ Sortibus Electum
Lente Ascendit Nomen Tuum Ad Alta;
Sed, Undique Tandem Insignis,
Victor Sine Victoria,
Urbis Imperium, Unus Imperator, Suscipies.

'That is to say: "Thy name, chosen by the sacred
fates of the Prenestine Fortune, ascends slowly towards the
heights of the future; but at last, become everywhere celebrated, a vanquisher without conquests, thou shalt receive,
as sole emperor, the empire of the City [Rome]."

'Now you know, prince, that the initials of these words
of prophecy replaced in their natural order, reconstruct

exactly the three names of your father: *TITUS FLAVIUS VESPASIANUS.* Did I not speak the truth? Did not all this happen to Vespasian?

'Give ear no longer, O prince, to vile spies who accuse me of conspiring against you, with or without Nerva. Nerva is a wise man. If it is true that we have innocently talked of destiny, if I have cited, which I may well have done, one or two princes as my examples, I said that the divine will is irresistible. . . If that is conspiracy, examine yourself the fates of Preneste and you will be guilty of conspiring against yourself! But it would be better, prince, if you spent your time gaining the favour of heaven by showing clemency and justice; for each head you cut off, each patrimony you confiscate, each exile to whom you become an enemy adds a formidable risk to your fate. Condemn me now if it is your caprice, but know that my destiny is not made to perish at your hands.'

Domitian had never before heard such language; pale, frozen to his seat, he seemed numbed by that fixed gaze. The philosopher from Tyana slowly left the Pretorium; unhindered he left Rome the same day, unpursued. Taking refuge with the Greeks he was greeted as one returned from the dead, for it was the first time that the imperial tiger had let a victim escape. It is said that Domitian did consult the Prenestine fates and that, horrified by their threats, he called the astrologer Ascletarion who confirmed his fears. 'And you,' the Emperor said to him, 'do you know how your end will come?'

'I shall be eaten by dogs,' replied Ascletarion.

'To prove to you the foolishness of your predictions,' went on the Emperor, 'I shall have your head cut off and your body burned to ashes and thrown into the Tiber.'

This order was immediately carried out; but when the flames reached the victim's body a storm came on accompanied by torrents of rain which put out the pyre and dispersed the executioners. When these returned to finish their task, they found the remains of the unfortunate man being devoured by a pack of wandering dogs.

VIII

THE Fates of Preneste have survived the destruction of the Temple of Fortune. It was through research with them that at the end of the 18th century the true form of *Onomatomantia* [Greek 'Ονοματομαντια: divination by names] was practised. It was founded on the symbolic doctrine already mentioned which assigned to each verbal or written emission of the sacred alphabet a correspondence with the things of life. The *Name* being considered, among all peoples, as the sign which distinguishes and defines human beings, Magic claimed to find in its variable and transposed forms an occult revelation of the good or evil which was to be manifested in the career of the individual so distinguished.

The example offered by Apollonius of Tyana on the subject of Vespasian, and the celebrated formula S P Q R, *Senatus Populusque Romanus*, in which form the name of the senate and the Roman people was attached to public documents and written on standards, remind us of the Greek and Latin custom of making inscriptions composed of the initial letters of various words.

When the individual appellation only gave a small number of letters, the magician exercised his intuition on the relationships that might exist between these letters by taking them as the initials of a meaning to be discovered. He informed himself of the social group to which his consultant belonged, or allowed himself to be asked a clear and concise question the terms of which, divided into component letters, formed when mingled with the letters of the name a fairly numerous 'pool' of letters, so that the first idea that came into his head could bring without great difficulty a host of others in its train. If the *metatheses*, or transpositions of letters furnished by the question, could create applicable words, this meaning was regarded as an oracle, and, *mirabile dictu,* this oracle, which at first might seem extravagant, sooner or later nearly always proved wonderfully accurate.

Finally, this type of divination extended its range in proportion to the number of actual events incorporated in the statement. For example, by adding to the consultant's name a list of his outstanding actions or achievements, the dignities of his past or present condition, the degrees of good or evil fortune that characterised his present existence, a new text appeared and extended the anticipated account of his destiny. Naturally I do not wish to support or to condemn this doctrine, which was resuscitated on the eve of the 1789 Revolution by Cagliostro,[10] and which caused even the powerful mind of Napoléon to hesitate more than once. In these cases examples are worth more than theories; and in addition to certain unknown traditions with which I have already been furnished, I shall give a few others closer to us in time over which believers and sceptics may fight to their hearts' content.

There lived in Paris about 1790-1805 an old man whom his neighbours believed to be either a sorcerer or a madman. This patriarch of the profession which popular naïvete still calls *fortune-telling,* lived in the Rue du Puits de l'Ermite [Street of the Hermit's Well] in the Faubourg St. Marceau. His divinatory tripod was mounted in a dilapidated garret of one of those tumbled-down houses which could reveal so much if stones had tongues. This prophet or harmless madman was called Pierre Le Clerc or more familiarly Father Pierre by neighbours. His story is not long. He was one of those learned Benedictines who carried in their heads the whole encylopaedia of the ancient world. Driven from his monastery in 1790 by the suppression of religious orders, the poor scholar slowly found his way to

10 See Book II, p. 139 *seq.—Ed.*

Paris where he sought a humble asylum. Only poverty and the Terror greeted his threescore and ten years. The republic had no need of priests, scholars or old men; it sent its children to look for bread and shoes on the battlefields, proclaimed the cult of the Fortune of War and each day consecrated a hecatomb to it. The old monk knew about these critical times; he had directed on the comet of the revolution the ancient hermetic astrolabe and knew he could promise historic immortality to all the young heroes who were going to die for their country's salvation. In spite of his dangerous quality of priest, which was obvious to all and which moreover he did not attempt to conceal, the hired assassins of the Terror had spared him because of his occasional little patriotic predictions concerning our armies which were justified by their victories. He had made a certain reputation in this field and received many notable visitors, including Philippe d'Orléans, Charlotte Corday, Maximilien Robespierre and General Bonaparte.

The need to seek some form of diversion for his unhappy thoughts, a little curiosity and maybe a mysterious compulsion had brought the Duc d'Orleans to the old man's garret. Pierre at once recognised him and made a great effort to dissuade him from the consultation. 'Sir,' he told him brusquely, 'for a long while I have read nothing but violent deaths in the book of fate. We live in murderous times; spare me the sorrow of having to add a cross to the long obituary of my predictions.'

'What does one more cross matter, if I accept?' replied the duke. 'Give me a lesson in your much-praised art and, so that I may the better understand, take myself as your subject.'

'I have already done what you ask,' countered the old Benedictine, 'and I am afraid I have made no mistake. That is why, sir, I wished to remain silent.'

'Well, let's wager that you have made a mistake and verify it together.'

'Did not Monseigneur at his birth receive the title of Duc de Montpensier?'

'Yes, with the names Louis-Philippe-Joseph, I am the Duc de Montpensier; but I became Duc d'Orleans by right of seniority.'

'Monseigneur also publicly accepted and bears the name of Egalité.'

'I have to; it's my only defence.'

'Therefore, Monseigneur, assembling the signs of your past and present individuality we have: *Louis-Philippe-Joseph, Duc de Montpensier ... Duc d'Orleans ... Egalité ... Député à la Convention Nationale de la République Française ..*.'

Pierre Le Clerc then explained to the prince the method of divination by the Fates, then he added in a trembling voice: 'See for yourself sir, since it is your will; for this is the design of Destiny:[11] "The scaffold which he voted for the tottering throne will soon become his own: God ordains his 'egality' through execution".'

Philippe d'Orléans trembled and paled. He seemed to see the ghost of Louis XVI holding out his arms to him.

"There remains in the circle six mute letters, P J P P P A,' went on Pierre Le Clerc. 'They mean: *Pari Jure, Proscripto Principi Proscriptus Æquatur*, which being translated means: "By the law of retaliation, the proscription makes him equal to the prince he proscribed." Ah sir, the name *Egalité* and the National Convention have brought you ill luck. But God by allowing our meeting has perhaps resolved to save you: you still have time—flee.'

'No my friend, I am staying. A Duc d'Orléans does not run away from danger: men may kill me, but God shall be my judge.'

Two months later, fate knocked at the door of his palace by the hand of the Committee for Public Safety, and

---

[11] To verify this sibylline experience and the following ones, the rule explained by Cagliostro should be referred to. [See Book II p. 148 *seq.*].

after the agony of the dungeons it cast him on 6 November 1793 into the blood-stained arms of the executioner.

The visit of Charlotte Corday d'Armont had more dramatic consequences. This young woman whom one would call heroic if it were possible to applaud a murder punishing villainy, arrived in Paris on 11 July 1793 with the firm resolve to kill Marat in order to avenge that monster's victims. She stayed at a small hotel in the Rue des Vieux Augustins, at the sign of the 'Providence.' The next day passed in studying how to carry out her project without fail. Returning in the evening, overcome by excitement and weariness but by no means discouraged, she noticed stuck in the side of a mirror the printed card of Pierre Le Clerc. The poor man must have had to distribute his cards here and there in public places, thus appealing for clients to bring in enough money for his daily bread. Charlotte smiled sadly at the idea of consulting a fortune-teller when she knew she must almost certainly die very soon. On 13 July, the fatal date she had chosen for her interview with Marat, she knocked early at the seer's door. 'Sir,' she said, lowering her eyes in case her expression should betray her thoughts, 'a lady who is a friend of mine must request help of the most serious nature from a very powerful member of the Convention. As I am myself very interested in the result of this proceeding, would it be possible for me to obtain somehow, without giving you forbidden explanations, some prospect of the luck, fortunate, happy or otherwise, which awaits us?'

At the sight of this beautiful young woman, whose trembling showed some interior struggle, Pierre Le Clerc thought it was merely a question of some little love affair. 'Mademoiselle,' he replied, 'no young woman has ever left my humble study without taking with her a smile from Providence. I wish to know nothing of your secrets, yet I shall tell you the whole truth. Sit down at that little table, far enough away from me to prevent me from seeing what you write. Take this pack of plain cards; write on each one of the letters making up the surname and Christian names of the person whose future you wish to consult. Add to these in the same way a clear and truthful statement of the desire or will of that person, and conclude with the names of the powerful man you spoke about, followed by his rank. If you have to make use of dates and numbers, do not use figures, but write them out in full. Next you will shuffle the cards until all trace of the names and the meaning of the written words has disappeared. Your secret will be well hidden in that chaos whence I shall evoke a reply, and you shall take the cards away with you after the operation.'

Charlotte wrote rapidly the following words, while Pierre Le Clerc turned his head away so as not to embarrass his client: *Le treize juillet mil sept cent nonente-trois, Charlotte de Corday d'Armont vent tenter de tuer, à Paris, d'un coup de couteau, Jean-Paul Marat, député à la Convention Nationale de la République française*: 'On the thirteenth of July seventeen hundred and ninety three, Charlotte de Corday d'Armont wishes to attempt to kill, in Paris, by a blow from a knife, Jean-Paul Marat, deputy of the National Convention of the French Republic.'

The old Benedictine took up the shuffled mass of these 164 letters on cards, arranged them in several concentric circles and ran a contemplative eye over them. Gradually his face brightened; he took from the circles and slipped rapidly into his right hand letters he chose here and there until there were only six left, L Z C R A A. This operation took ten minutes; Charlotte watched uncomprehendingly. Suddenly Pierre Le Clerc shuffled the cards again to obliterate the reply he had received and threw the cards down with a gesture of discouragement. 'Mademoiselle,'' he said to Charlotte, 'are you quite sure you made no error in your writing?'

'None,' replied Charlotte.

'Very well,' went on the seer. 'All I can tell you is that prudence is necessary. Tell your friend not to go to this powerful man: it would be quite a useless proceeding.'

'Why sir?'

'I give you an example of prudence by remaining silent!'

Indeed Pierre Le Clerc could not tell an unknown woman the sinister reply that the Fates had given him. Here it is: *Ce coup tuant, planté en ta poitrine, doit te tuer, à Paris, au bain, livide Marat. L'échafaud conventionel est le piédestal d'où cette martyre, couronnée de la vertu antique, doit planer sur le monde*: 'This mortal blow, struck at your breast, is to kill you in Paris in your bath, pale Marat. The scaffold of the Convention is the pedestal from which that woman martyr, crowned with the virtue of the ancients, must take her flight over the world.'

The six mute letters L Z C R A A signified: *Lividi Zona Cruoris Rubefacit Amplexantem Aquam*, meaning: 'A circle of livid blood reddens the water which embraces the dead body.' This fatidic image is connected with the bath in which Marat was murdered.

Pierre Le Clerc thought he was the plaything of a caprice of the spirits who inspired the oracles; whereas Charlotte as she went away regretted the childish urge which had brought her to this fortune-teller as a profanation. But on the evening of that day the first half of the oracle had been fulfilled and Pierre Le Clerc, who had not forgotten the reply of the Fates, was able to reconstruct letter by letter the names of Mlle. de Corday, Marat and the announcement of the avenging knife.

The words uttered by fate were no less decisive when Robespierre was tempted in his turn to consult the future. He talked for a long time with the old man about the ancient mysteries and only submitted to a divination after making sure of his high purpose. His personality was stated in the following terms: *Maximilien-Marie-Isidore Robespierre, député à la Convention nationale de la République française.*

Here is the oracle's reply: *Républicain rare . . . inflexible . . . il ira mourir décapité, au nom de la nation, par vote de ses ennemis*: 'Republican of rare quality, inflexible, he shall die beheaded in the name of the nation by the vote of his enemies.'

There remained six mute letters A I E E O Q, signifying: *Ab Iniquis Eversus, Extortus Odio Quiritum,* which means: 'Overthrown by the league of the wicked, tortured by the hate of the bourgeois.' This was verified in 1794 by a fact which shows to what lengths political fury can go. Gravely wounded, whether by his own hand or by an assassin's, at the time of his arrest, Robespierre was dragged bleeding into a house near the Convention where the colleagues who used to tremble before him came one after another to insult him as he lay dying. . .

I mentioned Bonaparte. In 1795 as a general deprived of work by the jealousy of the War Committee he was vegetating in Paris, discouraged and hard-pressed for money, without the slightest notion of the rôle assigned to him. Chance, that god of those who have nothing to do, led him one day to Pierre Le Clerc, with the sole object of killing time. The seer was occupied with a horoscope. A glance at the circles, triangles and calculations interested Bonaparte and made him wish to see such calculations used on his own destiny. The request for his date of birth seemed to him quite natural but as soon as he was invited to give his names, rank and profession in order to give the grounds for this key to his future, he considered the questioner had gone too far and put a sudden end to the séance.

'You are perhaps wrong to draw back,' Pierre Le Clerc told him quietly, 'for my art is much more powerful than you would imagine. Moreover there exists a prophecy made by a certain Count Cagliostro ten years ago on the French Revolution, which then had not begun. This prophecy announces that a *Corsican* will be *voted,* that is, elected by the people, who *will end it,* probably by dictatorship. It would be a splendid future for you, since you are Corsican and in any case, if you really are singled out by fate, you can only gain by knowing it.'

But Bonaparte thought he was in the presence of an old charlatan wanting money. He threw a small coin on the table and left.

Four years later on 8 November 1799, the eve of the famous day which has retained the name of 18 Brumaire, the general who had been stripped by the Convention had become under the Directory the favourite of that fortune whose interpreter he had disdained. Covered with laurels from Italy and Egypt, he only had to venture to have everything at his feet: and he was about to venture. The plan was mapped out, success calculated, danger foreseen. In quiet contemplation in his lonely room he suddenly had a vague recollection of the old man in the Rue du Puits de l'Ermite and it seemed to him that Cagliostro's prophecy: 'French Revolution—an elected Corsican will end it,' rang in his ears with the sound of a distant bell . . .

He decided to see him again. It was evening. Pierre Le Clerc did not recognise him. Nothing was changed in his humble abode; there was if anything greater squalor, a sign of the rarity of clients. 'Sir,' Bonaparte said to him, slipping into his hand a gold coin with which the old man made a sign of the cross to bless the Providence by which he thought he had been forgotten, 'could you answer a very urgent question?'

'With the horoscope, no,' replied the old man, 'for one needs long preparation in its calculations; but provided the question is complete and unequivocal, yes, by the sibylline Fates.'

Bonaparte quickly wrote his question on 119 cards, shuffled and handed them to Pierre Le Clerc who arranged them in the usual circles. The question unknown to him was in the following terms: *Que deviendra le Corse Napoléon Bonaparte, général, par suite du coup d'Etat risqué par lui, à Paris, le dix-huit brumaire mil sept cent nonante neuf?* 'What will become of the Corsican Napoleon Bonaparte, general, after the coup d'état made by him in Paris on 18 Brumaire 1799?'

We can see here that Bonaparte had not forgotten the *elected Corsican* mentioned by Cagliostro. *Nonante,* used instead of quatre-vingt-dix [90], was then a current expression.

'Indeed sir,' said Pierre Le Clerc after a few minutes' thought, 'whatever the question may be, whoever the man, this is what I read: *En mil-huit-cent-quatre il montera sur le trône à pique; puis, coupé en dix et un, sera renversé par la canonade du soldat d'Angleterre.* "In 1804, he will ascend the throne of pikes; then, cut into ten and one, will be overthrown by the cannons of the English soldier." '

The word throne and the date 1804 must have excited Bonaparte; but his expression remained impenetrable and it was in a tone of perfect indifference that he asked what the two riddles could mean.

'The oracles,' replied Pierre Le Clerc, 'often have a side which does not come to light until after the event. However I perceive in the image *a throne of pikes* a sort of military shield, representing a great power surrounded by Cæsarian banners. The other enigma is a number marking a cut in continuity, a lapse of time: *ten* and *one* make *eleven,* and 11 added to 1804 fixes in 1815 the dangerous appearance of the *English soldier.* But that is only supposition. Moreover, of the 119 letters contained in your question, 13 have remained mute: B O P P I A I B I P A U F. These however can also speak: *Bis Oriens, Populi Princeps, In Altum Incedit. Bis Incedit: Per Anglos Ultima Fata.* Which means: "He rises twice, prince of the people, and soars in the heights. Twice he falls: his final disaster will come from the English." '

Bonaparte was inwardly shaken, but he resolved to try a sort of counter-proof. 'Sir,' he said to Pierre Le Clerc, 'allow me a second and shorter experiment.' He wrote on 69 cards letters forming: *Joséphine-Marie-Rose de Tascher de la Pagerie, femme du général Napoléon Bonaparte.*

After a long silence, the old man replied: *Trop âgée,*

le diadème impérial, porte en son second mariage, ne fera pas le bonheur. 'Too old, the imperial diadem worn in her second marriage will not bring her happiness.'

'Enough, enough!' cried Napoléon. 'Your word-play carries a dead weight of idiocy heavier than the Pyramids!'

And sweeping the cards from the table he stormed out of the room.

We who have read the question before the answer came, cannot so easily dismiss the oracle; sibylline intuition could not have made a better job of the metatheses. There remained 3 mute letters H E A, signifying: *Herois Extinctus Amor,* which means: 'Love dies out in the hero's heart.'

This was correct. Born in 1763, married in 1779 to the Comte de Beauharnais, Joséphine saw her husband perish on the scaffold. Becoming Bonaparte's wife in 1796 at the age of 33, she was 41 when she was crowned empress. *Too old* according to the usual laws of nature to give a son who would inherit the empire, she was the victim of political calculation. The high rank to which she was raised brought her no happiness; the imperial diadem did not prevent her from dying in unhappy isolation on 29 May 1814, of that incurable disease, a broken heart.[12]

IX

WE READ both in the *Memoirs* of Madame Ducrest on the Empress Joséphine and in the *Mémorial de Sainte-Hélène* a strange anecdote which is regarded as authentic. Mademoiselle de Tascher de la Pagerie was born in Martinique. Shortly before she came to France for her first marriage an old negress who lived on her family's estate made her the following prediction: 'You are going to marry, but that

---

[12] This story and the following ones were told me, thirty years ago, by an old man named Jean Roibin, formerly a bookseller of the Convention, who had known Pierre Le Clerc and who possessed some further pages of *Mémoires* written by this strange individual.

marriage will not be happy; you will become a widow, and then—you will be queen.' It is well-known that the coloured peoples of Africa have their witch-doctors as the Greeks had their Sibyls. This prophecy by a negress has therefore nothing surprising about it. We may well ask what form her powers took, but these records do not say.

If we submit the names *Josephine-Marie-Rose de Tascher de la Pagerie* to the methods of sibylline examination, we read in these 38 letters: *A l'âge de rose, Joséphine sera impératrice.* 'At the age of the rose, Josephine shall be empress.'

What does the expression 'age of the rose' mean? The rose symbolised perfection for the Egyptians, and for the Greeks beauty. According to the language of the flowers the rosebud signifies a young girl who has not yet ripened. The rose, an open flower, represents the splendour of woman in all the fulness of her charms. The expression therefore means 'when Josephine is a woman'; and as the opened rose only preserves its loveliness a short while, the age of the rose also signifies the moment when the full sun of youth begins to decline.

There remain 3 mute letters H D E, signifying: *Honores—Divortium—Eclipsis,* that is 'divorce', placed between the 'honours' of the throne and the 'eclipse' of that magical happiness in the gloomy sadness of the Château de Malmaison which was indeed for Joséphine the house of evil.

The great conqueror of Europe was anxious at times about the number *cut by ten and one,* and about the phantom in hiding behind the problem of the sibylline fates. With the advent of the Empire Pierre Le Clerc was generously rewarded for the first part of his prediction. Housed since 1804 in the outbuildings of the Château de St. Cloud, he had reached his 79th year and was ordered to be given every comfort by a master who was certain of being obeyed. His old age seemed a belated spring under these showers of kindness. Napoléon had made him swear never to reveal to anyone what their original relationship had been; to his servants he passed him off as an old and valuable orientalist attached to the Egyptian Institute and, in that court which was as well-disciplined as a barracks, no one dared to doubt his word. But soon the events which shook Europe in 1805 separated for good the benefactor and his protégé. While the Emperor was ascending the supreme heights of fortune, Pierre Le Clerc was secretly drawing up the account of the future. Feeling death grow near, he wanted to repay his debt of gratitude to Napoléon by bequeathing to him the final judgments of destiny.

This testament, sealed in three envelopes, was to have been sent with the state despatches; but doubtless it was put into unreliable hands which confiscated it as a piece of impertinent fooling that must at all costs be kept from His Majesty. By a curious stroke of luck—if such a thing as luck exists—I discovered this strange document in 1839 at a book-sale held after the death of an alienist. It was bound up with half-a-dozen brochures on different varieties of mental affliction. Here is the most interesting part: 'Sire, over-whelmed by your generosity I must tell you the truth, or at least what seems to me to be the truth. When on 8 November 1799 you visited, unknown to me, my humble abode, you placed before the Fates the following question: *Que deviendra le Corse Napoléon Bonaparte, général, par suite du coup d'Etat risqué par lui à Paris, le dix-huit brumaire mil sept cent nonante-neuf?* 'What will become of the Corsican Napoléon Bonaparte, general, after the coup d'etat ventured by him in Paris on 18 Brumaire 1799?'

'Your Majesty has not forgotten the reply given by the fates and the first half of the oracle has been fulfilled. The other half which foretold misfortune has still to come: will that too be fulfilled? We read in the *Hundred Aphorisms* of the occult science, drawn up by the learned Hermes-Thoth and recalled by Ptolemy in his *Tetrabiblion*, that every man to whom with God's permission the mysteries of future time are revealed may uphold Good and triumph over Evil by the wise direction of his mind and will. Your Majesty's genius has shown itself until now to be apparently of superhuman strength. But have you reckoned with another power which, though invisible, is even more to be feared? Are you prepared to sustain the blows of fate?

'The oracle which communicated with you in 1799 described the minister of fate as an English soldier, that is, a symbol of armed war. Now, the immense fame and honour which have been yours since the battle of Austerlitz inclined me to think that my intuition had been wrong. Unfortunately, Sire, on submitting the same question to a fresh examination, I see this new reply take shape: *Napoléon empereur, vaincu en Europe, abattu, exilé, captif des Anglais par trop dur destin, ira mourir dans Sainte-Hélène, île de l'Océan.* "The Emperor Napoléon, conquered in Europe, beaten, exiled, captured by the English by too hard a fate, will go to die at St. Helena, an ocean island."

'There remain 10 mute letters Q U B R P T Q U U T, which signify: *Quatefacit Umbra Britannicam Rupem Primipotentis Tanti; Quassat Ululans Ultima Terræ,* which means: "The shadow of the man who was so great and the strongest of all makes the British rock tremble: his groans will shake the ends of the earth." This image announces that you will reign for ever in the memory of man; but I see in you the Prometheus of modern times, if you disregard the warnings of heaven.

'I then wrote in simple terms the statement of your departure for that campaign in the East which earned for you the name of miracle-worker: *Napoléon Bonaparte, général en chef de la République française, sort de Toulon, le dix neuf mai mil sept cent nonante-huit, sur une flotte, avec trente-six mille soldats, pour aller conquérir l'Egypte.* "Napoléon Bonaparte, commander-in-chief of the French Republic, leaves Toulon on 19 May 1798 with a fleet and 36,000 troops to go to the conquest of Egypt."

'And this is what the spirit of the fates replied: *La gloire conquise devant les Pyramides fera couronner le haut*

*chef Bonaparte. Son étoile brille d'un pur éclat, mais pâlit
tôt. Elle flotte, perdue en exile, sur un orageux océan, et
s'éteint.* "The fame won before the Pyramids will crown the
great leader Bonaparte. His star shines with a pure radiance,
but soon sets. It floats lost in exile upon a stormy ocean and
is extinguished."

'There remain 9 mute letters P Q N F M N N N L,
signifying: *Prœlia Quœrens, Nactus Fati Marmor, Nefastae
Navis Numina Lacessit,* meaning: "Seeking incessant quarrels, he encounters the unmoving sea of fate and provokes
the threatening oracle with a tragic vessel."

'This, Sire, is what the auguries say. I beg of you, take
heed. Now let us examine the following: *Napoléon Bonaparte, empereur des Français et roi d'Italie.* "Napoléon
Bonaparte, Emperor of the French and King of Italy."

'Here is the solution:

'*A bas par OOO, détrôné, et captif en mer, il périra dans
une île.*"Overthrown by OOO, dethroned and a captive at
sea, he will die on an island."

"The letter O [*Olélath* in Egyptian],[13] corresponds to
Arcanum XVI of the hermetic doctrine, the symbol of
which is a lightning-struck tower, emblem of downfall, ruin
and final powerlessness. Repeated here three times, it would
seem to foretell three reversals of fortune, precursors of
the catastrophe. I repeat, an island may be fatal to you;
would its name be St. Helena? The future will tell.

'I am sending Your Majesty two hermetic figures. The
one will recall to you the horoscope of your birth, set up
under the reign of *Suroth,* the spirit of the planet Venus,
and under the 23rd degree of influence of *Momphtha,*
spirit of the constellation of the Lion, corresponding to
15 August 1769. The other horoscope is that of the fate
which will threaten you in 1815, and which I have revealed
to you by a study of the stars. You now know the art of
deciphering the occult language of these symbols. It only

---

[13] See, the symbolism of the 22 Arcana, explained in Book II p.95 *seq.*

remains for me to beg of Your Majesty not to despise this
warning, if there is still time to profit by it.[14]

'May God grant, Sire, that I am really just an old fool

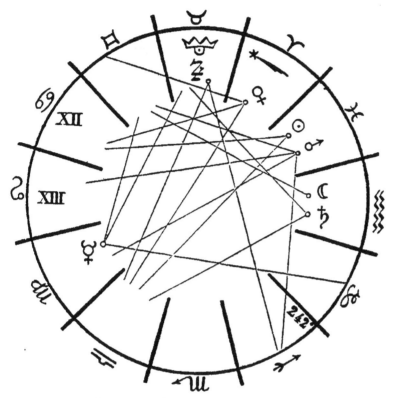

Horoscope of Napoléon: birth, 1769.

on whom you will have pity; but should your anger crush
me, I shall never regret having listened only to the voice
of my conscience in serving you.'

The last prediction made by Pierre Le Clerc was by
no means wrong. The three reversals of fortune which preceded the dethronement of the great captain were the Rus-

[14] It has been stated frequently—but authorities are not given—that Napoléon
falsified his birth certificate, giving the date of his brother's birth as his own,
since he himself was born a British citizen and he wished as a French one
to go to the Academy at Brienne. Since Corsica became French in January
1768, presumably he gave a younger brother's date or used his certificate,
not his elder one's as has been alleged.—*Ed.*

sian disaster, the first invasion of France and Waterloo. The
captive at sea recalls the treachery of England towards the
heroic guest aboard H.M.S. Bellerophon.

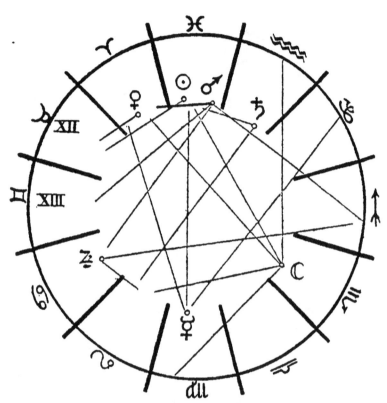

Horoscope of Napoléon: exile, 1815.

Pierre Le Clerc died at St. Cloud at the beginning
of 1807. His flame of life was extinguished gently. His last
word was prayer for the Emperor whose bread he had eaten.

I could easily add to this curious study a host of other
examples gleaned from history which would seem to prove
that the more a person is in evidence in the drama of public
life, the more the characteristic signs of his individuality
and of the rôle to which he is predestined become sibylline,
that is, indicating the course of the future. The generating
law of these mysterious manifestations escapes us and, unable to explain their origin, we declare them absurd. So be it

then; giving ourselves rein, let us risk, if the reader pleases, a few further absurdities in the same vein. Three notable events show the action of Fate on the last Bourbons of the elder branch: the assassination of the Duc de Berri, the posthumous birth of the Duc de Bordeaux and the Revolution which overthrew Charles X.

The individuality of the Duc de Berri is stated in these words: *Charles-Ferdinand d'Artois, Duc de Berri, son of Monsieur, Comte d'Artois, brother of Louis XVIII, King of France and of Navarre.*

From this statement the following prediction emerges: 'The said Berri will be murdered one evening with cold steel in his side. It will be near the exit of a theatre . . .'

The individuality of the Duc de Bordeaux is stated in these terms: *Henri-Charles-Ferdinand-Marie-Dieudonné d'Artois Duc de Bordeaux* . . . Here is the arcanum hidden in the simple announcement: 'Exiled from a shattered throne, he will never have the crown of France . . .'

Here is the statement of the event which dethroned Charles X from which we shall seek a prediction. *Revolution made by the bourgeoisie of Paris the 27th July, 1830, against Charles X, King of France and of Navarre.* From these 111 letters the following oracle appears; it was possible to obtain it from the first signs of the insurrection. 'The French King Charles, defeated, exiled. Louis-Philippe of Orleans will become King. The new reign will also be shattered.'[15]

XII

THE historical memoirs of Suetonius, who was the contemporary historian of 12 reigns, are full of anecdotes of all the forms adopted by Magic to foretell the justice of heaven to the oppressed.

[15] Only the preceding three shortened 'absurdities' are here given, and accordingly this book continues at Chapter 12. Christian did not err in calling this material absurdities: revelations extracted from sayings by

One day Julius Caesar cried out in the Forum: 'Remember, citizens, that I am descended from Ancus Martius, one of your ancient kings, and that my ancestress Julia was the daughter of Venus. You will find therefore in my family both the majesty of kings who build great nations and the sanctity of gods who make great leaders.' Shortly before his tragic death some of the veterans to whom he had given lands in Campania discovered when digging foundations a brazen sword on which was a prophetic inscription in Greek which said that at the time when it was unearthed an illustrious descendant of the race of Julia would be murdered by his friends, but that Rome's misfortunes would avenge his death.

A hundred days before the death of Augustus lightning struck his statue in the Field of Mars and obliterated the letter C in the name Caesar. The astrologer Thrasyllus, who was later the confidant of Tiberius, told him that in a hundred days he would be elevated to the rank of god, because the letter C signified 100 in Latin arithmetic and because the word AEsar in Etruscan signified 'god'. Augustus was under no illusion as to the true meaning of this flattery; from then on he had a presentiment of his approaching end

the Duc de Berri, the Duc de Bordeaux. Charles X, Louis XVIII, Louis Philippe and others. Christian's general reflections however at the beginning of Chapter 11 are more worthy and run as follows: 'Are these sibylline experiences providential warnings, or should we consider them as simple games of chance? Superficial minds which go with the stream attach no value to them; but I know serious, enlightened men, highly placed in the world, who practise these strange arts in secret and who confess in confidence that we are surrounded by unfathomable mysteries. It is childish to say that such predictions could only be made after the event. Thousands of examples are immediately available to prove the contrary and, despite the protests or disdain of freethinkers, it remains none the less true that the fate of a man can be foretold almost always by a simple statement of his individuality, of the social level of his birth, of the act which he wishes to accomplish or of the important event which has just altered his position in life. And what is particularly striking—I think I have already said so—is that the more a person increases in stature and the more he holds the destiny of history in the making, the more clearly his own destiny will be indicated by the simple phrase which defines his present condition or by the question which poses a fact, the consequences of which are still hidden.'—Ed.

and the half-explained augury of Thrasyllus was soon fulfilled by the onset of a mortal illness.

Tiberius was said to have had a thorough knowledge of divination. His villa at Capri was full of astrologers and theurges whom he had brought to him at great expense from distant lands. Among them were charlatans and rogues who exploited his appalling passions and were the accomplices of nearly all his crimes.[16]

Caligula received from the astrologer Sylla the advice that he should beware of plots hatched by his enemies, and the Oracle of Antium even revealed the name of Cassius, one of the Emperor's future murderers. Caligula accordingly had Cassius Longinus, proconsul of Asia, killed and quite forgot that the leader of his own guards was called Cassius Chærea; he in fact struck the first blow.

The history of Rome is full of belief in the occult arts. Astrologers often gave false predictions, 'but', as the grave Tacitus says, 'must the value of magical science be denied because it is often made use of by impostors or ignorant men?' We may add that true mages often paid with their heads for some imprudent revelation of an emperor's destiny, and a number of notable citizens who, from curiosity or ambition, had consulted astrology or the fates, found themselves accused of treason. But these persecutions, far from bringing Magic into disrepute, consecrated it anew and the more dangerous its practice became, the more its mysteries increased their hold on the ancient world. 'The emperors,' says Alfred Maury, 'never ceased to believe in astrological divination, but they wanted to keep it to themselves. They wanted to know the future, but they also wanted

[16] Tiberius has been heavily maligned. A more likely reading of events is that, tired of the incessant intrigue and scandal-mongering of Rome, he organised his rule from more pleasant and private surroundings. That his apparent retirement was joyfully interpreted in Rome as abandonment to the extremities of vice probably disturbed him little. Administrative records show that the Empire was carefully governed. Similar but more justified scandal-mongering over Nero is apt to obscure the fact that for the majority of his reign the administration was both careful and vigorous.—*Ed*.

their subjects to be kept in ignorance of it. Nero would not allow anyone to study philosophy, saying that this occupation was a vain and frivolous thing and a mere pretext for fortune-telling. It would have been dangerous, indeed, if people could read in the stars the fate reserved for their princes. Many who bowed the knee because they thought the time of their deliverance was far would have been prouder, and trusted in better times to come, had they known of the revolution that was being prepared. Moreover, one's curiosity might be stimulated to ascertain when and how the emperor would die; indiscreet questions, the reply to which was conspiracy or assassination. It was of this that such heads of the state as Tiberius, Caligula, Nero, Vitellius, Domitian, Commodus, Heliogabalus and Valerian constantly went in fear.' But it was useless for them to keep on banishing, imprisoning and torturing people, for astrology survived the astrologers who had their throats cut and the sibylline fates of Preneste or Antium were not disproved.

BOOK FOUR

BOOK FOUR

MAGIC FROM THE BEGINNING OF THE CHRISTIAN ERA TO THE
END OF THE MIDDLE AGES

I

SINCE the time when Augustus had ascended the bloody steps to his throne [27 B.C.] until the advent of Constantine the Great [reigned 323—337 A.D.], all the emperors had mingled the horror of personal crimes with the public misdeeds that were part of the imperial tyranny. In that society humiliated by its rulers and made rotten by vice, a desire for health and sanity nevertheless made itself felt in the false resignation of despair. Among patricians of noble mind and also among the lowest classes of that society could be found instinctive aspirations towards unknown hopes, a preparation of the soul. People were still Stoically courageous in dying, but they began to revolt against the idea of the complete annihilation of life after death. A new idea, Christianity, which came into being under the reign of Tiberius, slowly began to filter, a mysterious radiance, into the blood-red darkness of a disintegrating society. By doing away with the bonds of matter and freeing the fetters from the imprisoned spirit, this idea taught people to despise tyrants and roused their consciences; and it gave meaning to the sufferings of all men by opening out to them horizons of a future life in which justice would be meted out to those crowned vampires, their tyrannical rulers. It was a humble consolation, but adapted itself to all kinds of misfortune, and went on developing as Rome became more and more wretched. When the spade digs ground filled with ancient remains, it opens the tombs of many generations. This has analogies in the moral order.

In ransacking a world based on secular corruption, the pioneers of the future had to embrace the pestilence which was at its heart.

By ordering the procuring of stone from the nearest source for a new Rome, Nero [34—68 A.D.] had unwittingly created in those immense quarried galleries a subterranean camp alike for the Jews and for the legions of banished men who were to plant in the old ruins the standard of the freed races. These gloomy Catacombs did not then inspire the fugitives with the cold horror of the grave. They sheltered there to encourage each other to further sacrifices. These Magi of a new faith brought back to the world the ancient symbol of the Cross; it was essential that this sign should rise higher and higher until it could be seen by all the earth.

Nearly all the great cities of the empire were built, like Rome, on catacombs. And everywhere these subterranean vaults became the meeting places of an immense secret society which slowly enveloped all the foundations of the past, then tore them down at a single blow when it raised against Rome in the voice of Tertullian [*floruit circa* 155— 222 A.D.] this triumphal battle-cry: 'We are of today, but you are still eight centuries behind. Open your eyes! We are taking everything that once belonged to you, your cities, your towns, your fortresses, your colonies, your municipia [self-governing cities],—all we leave you are your temples! . . . Whenever you have been able to lay your hands upon us, we have perished day by day in unmentionable torture. If we wish to avenge ourselves, what reprisals we could take, we who are worn out neither by physical debauchery nor spiritual slavery!'

This violent apostrophe was addressed to Rome and to the Emperor Septimus Severus at the beginning of the third century A.D. The Empire replied by redoubling its tortures and inventing horrors which are beyond all belief. In the fourth century, condemned people were suspended, without distinction of age or sex, over a fire whose heat, skilfully modulated, made the skin swell up until it split. The human fat which then fell on the fire produced a light, penetrating flame which slowly roasted the flesh and stripped it from the bones. From time to time, to make the agony as long as possible, great jars of icy water were thrown over the victims in order to slow down the process of combustion and to bring back to the deadened senses all the agonies of pain. The executioners then armed themselves with burning brands which they plunged into the smoking wounds, and the histories of the time recount that so skilful were they that they were able to sustain the essential workings of life in a body for a whole day.

Only three provinces, Gaul, Spain and Britain, governed by Constantius Chlorus, or the Pale, adopted as son by the Emperor Maximian in 293, took no part in the great attempt to exterminate the Christians in 303. The innumerable fugitives from Italy and the East found a refuge there under a power which respected justice and peace. When this prince died in 306 at Eboracum [York], his son, Constantine, succeeded him. The unity of the empire was disrupted; he shared with Maximian and his son Maxentius the government of the West: Galerius, Licinius and Maximinius Daia shared the East. These six emperors disagreed: Maxentius, ruler of Italy, desired Gaul; and, in memory of Constantine Chlorus, the Christians took up arms in favour of his son, whose clever political programme promised them that their liberty to worship as they pleased would be respected if he succeeded, with their help, in conquering Italy. Maxentius was beaten. Constantine, master of Rome in 312, and still supported by the Christians, finally, in 324, reunited under his sole domination the whole of the Roman world.

Faithful to his promise to the Christian population because to them he owed his empire and needed their support for its continuance, this prince whom the old historical tradition calls the first Christian Emperor protected the new

faith by the Edict of Milan 313[1], but did not himself renounce the cult of his ancestors. On 11 May 330, seven
years before his death, proceeding to the inaugural ceremonies of the new capital at Byzantium which he had
created and called Constantinople, he had his triumphal
statue drawn in a chariot, carrying in its hand an image
of the goddess Fortuna, although the inaugural ceremonies
were performed by Christian officials. It was partly because
he thought it best to leave Rome to the pagans and the
older religions that he had transferred the seat of the empire
to the east, to the new city he had dedicated to the Virgin
Mary; but partly also because he had become disliked in
Italy after he had put to death his wife Fausta, his son
Crispus Caesar, his father-in-law Maximian, his brother-in-
law Licinius and a child of eleven, son of this same Licinius.
Stricken, like Nero, by unavailing remorse, he had asked
the philosopher Sopater, grand master of occult science,
if there were magical rites powerful enough to rid his
dreams of the ghosts of his assassinated family. 'Magic',
replied Sopater, 'condemns the parricide to the infernal
spirits.' The Christian priests were more indulgent; they
promised him God's forgiveness in exchange for certain services which he was to render to Christianity. Constantine
thereupon revived the old imperial edicts which threatened
with death those who exercised the Magic of which he was
so afraid. The bishops, whom he kept around him as a sort
of protective guard against the terrors of conscience, persuaded him that the gods of Greece and Rome were the
infernal spirits with which Sopater had threatened him.
They represented the temples as laboratories in which his
enemies could hatch mysterious plots with the powers of
evil, and the temples too were put under a ban.

This violent measure dealt a heavy blow at polytheism,

---

[1] Numerous critics of today have confirmed that no Edict emanated from Milan
in 313. There was, however, a Rescript of Licinius published in the eastern
empire in agreement with Constantine and emphasising the policy decided
upon between them at Milan.—*Ed.*

but did not destroy it. Sacrifices were prohibited, but the temples remained. They were not even closed in some places, notably in Rome, where the ancient majesty of the Senate still authorized the continuance of the national ceremonies. Avowed polytheists were still in possession of the highest posts and honours. Innumerable citizens had been led, by expediency, to the practice of Christianity; but in their hearts they had not renounced the traditions of their ancestors. The power of polytheism had doubtless suffered an immense defeat; but it was still supported by a rearguard of the highest order: the majority of literary men, scholars and philosophers provided a bulwark with their schools and their books. Vanquished on the battlefield of fact, they retreated into the arsenal of theory, and their defence was brilliant.

It was true, they said, that the polytheism practised by the public could never form a system compatible with logic and reason. But the apparent absurdity of its conceits was enough to show that it ought to be carried further, that the crude outer covering of symbols had to be penetrated and their hidden meaning more generally revealed. The mystery had truth at its centre; it had been veiled from time immemorial to make it more respected by those who sought its meaning, and more difficult of access to those unworthy of possessing it. 'Moreover', they went on, 'we profess to recognise one supreme God, the source and principle of all beings. All other gods are in part the personification of His attributes and in part lesser ministers of whom He is the father and king. We look upon the universe as a picture of which this great God is at once the subject and the painter; therefore, in honouring creation and its creatures we are doing homage to the Creator. Nature is filled with spirits. These subordinate intelligences preside over the stars, the elements, kingdoms, cities—a host of particular localities; over the sciences, the arts, the virtues—each one according to the position or function which the universal Master has deigned to give him. The souls of just men are admitted after death amongst the number of these intelligences with the name of *heroes* or *demigods*: is it not right that they should be honoured as the lieutenants of that supreme Majesty and the distributors of His benefits? As for the worship of statues representing these privileged beings, it is not mere stone or bronze which is worshipped: we allow these superstitions to continue among the less educated people, for they, being spirits bound by material fetters, need tangible emblems as a kind of intermediary and vehicle of the homage which we address directly to the divine beings. This cult is therefore only apparently materialistic. The gods accept it, as the emperors kindly accept the honours which we offer to their images, although we can easily do without them. Rome's century-long prosperity and its predominance over all other nations are manifest proofs of the purity of our intentions and the sacred nature of our teaching.'

This allegorical defence of polytheism was nothing new. For a long time philosophers, and especially the disciples of Plato, shocked by the use of a theology unworthy both of God and man, had been trying to recall the fables of Olympus to the spiritual values of the Magi. But the Christians replied: 'If you want to convince us, begin by suppressing the history of your so-called spirits. A religion which has not as its aim the betterment of men stands self-condemned; your Saturn, your Jupiter, your Mars, your Venus, your Mercury are all guilty of crimes or shameful vices and you merely imitate them. Let us disregard your systems which deal with the generating principle of things; tell us if the people, who in their ignorance are helpless when confronted with these learned spiritual speculations, have ever seen or ever will see in the emblems of mythology anything but the justification of the most abandoned passions? Oh, how nice to surround knowledge with a tissue of fables that sanctify all the vices! It would be just as wise to give poison to a sick man because, with the aid of science, certain useful drugs can be extracted from that poison!'

This is how the two parties argued in the conflict over doctrine. The moral victory was undoubtedly gained by the supporters of the Gospel, but the philosophers still held a position in the highest society difficult to assail. The fame of those who taught in the schools of Athens had spread to every corner of the Empire. There were arguments for and against them even in the remotest provinces. Constantine died in 337 surrounded by these verbal quarrels. St. Eusebius of Nicomedia sprinkled him with the holy water of baptism just before he died; this ceremony, which the dying emperor had perhaps not desired, was published far and wide as the official consecration of Christianity.

The Empire was divided between his three sons, Constantine II, Constans and Constantius. The first two made war upon each other and both were killed. Constantius received their inheritances [353—361 A.D.]. His childhood had been spent in study with the bishops. As soon as he ascended the throne he prohibited at their instigation, under pain of death, the performance of public or private polytheistic ceremonies. But he was soon forced to recognise that unless he wanted to precipitate a revolution in the empire he would have to compromise in the West, and above all in Rome, with the ancient national religion. His will was thwarted by the very excess of its violence. The masters of the old dogmas, who had thought their last days had come, breathed again. The size of their audiences had, it is true, gradually diminished, but they took pride even in these losses, for, they said, the number of true sages, of really enlightened spirits, would always of necessity be very small, whilst the great mass of men, lost in spiritual darkness, could only abandon one error in order to give themselves to another.

If these old masters had been Christians, they would have been lost in the host of the new believers; as philosophers they remained isolated, but not defeated, among the

ruins of the old world, the last torches lighting what were
once the grandeurs of Greece and Rome. Their works would
survive them, just as in the ruins of empires now covered
by the sands of the ancient east we find here the skeleton
of what was once a famous city, broken columns, fallen
cornices, sphinxes motionless as the desert silences: and
there a few pyramids, outlasting the very gaze of time.

II

PLATO'S spiritual doctrine, borrowed from memories of his
initiation at the hands of the Magi, had suffered, like most
other things, from the disintegrating effects of political
revolutions; it had fallen from its heights into the chaos
of a crowd of rival sects. But the masters of occult knowledge, leaving the bickerings of the schools to vulgar
wranglers, took refuge in the mysterious regions of Theurgy,
to which only an infinitely small number of picked disciples was ever admitted. Theurgy was the art of establish-
ing contact by the practice of secret rites with the invisible
powers which bridge the distances between God and man.
Plato, following the example of the Magi, had peopled
the universe with lesser spirits, ministers of Providence and
executors of God's decrees. His successors, called Neoplatonists, studied the means of evoking these spirits, of
gaining their favour by special sacrifices, either in order
to gain knowledge of the future, or in order to raise themselves under their protection to the state of intuition of
the supreme Being. The most learned polytheists believed
fervently in the efficaciousness of this occult knowledge, and
were not afraid to say so openly. St. John Chrysostom
[circa 346—407 A.D.] even accused the Christians of his day
of being for the greater part affiliated to theurgical societies.
Recourse to divinatory arts, to charms and magic drugs
had become so usual that in his writings this father of the
Church seems tempted to glorify as a sort of martyrdom the

constancy of sick people who refused to look for means of alleviating their sufferings to these occult practices. Christian mothers tied talismans round their children's necks and young women obtained philtres to make their husbands love them. This tendency towards the supernatural and the marvellous could be observed even in the highest intelligences, especially since the Emperor had decreed death to all who could be accused of the practice of magic. The need for secrecy in the performance of these forbidden rites, the danger of discovery and immediate death, increased their attraction and made the fortunes of theurgists.

Among these the venerable Edesius of Pergamos [d. 355][2] enjoyed an immense reputation, but laden with years and riches, he was no longer accessible except to very rare visitors, chosen with extreme care, with whom he was pleased to talk about magic, though he never consented, either from weariness or prudence, to give them any fresh proofs of his art.

At that time there lived also, unknown and solitary, on the borders of Asia, an orphan descended from the reigning family. A delicate relic escaped from the fury of a military plot whose cause has not been discovered, but which had succeeded in massacring around the tomb of Constantine I the sons and grandsons of the second wife of Constantius Chlorus, this child was called Julian [born 331 A.D.]. The Emperor Constantius had had him brought up far from the court, deprived him of his patrimony and limited his education to the material practice of a narrow and servile Christianity, fearing that an education suitable for a prince might arouse in him sooner or later the ambition to rule. Eusebius, Bishop of Nicomedia, whose task it was to guide his pupil's inclinations towards the priesthood, had admitted him, it is said, to minor orders as reader of the sacred scriptures. His plan was to prepare him in the distant future for some remote bishopric in which he

---

[2]   Edesius was a follower of Iamblichus. For these and other neoplatonists, see T. Whittaker *Neoplatonists.—Ed.*

would forget all traces of his imperial origin. When the
direction of his mind seemed safely established, Constantius'
anxieties diminished, and his miserly conscience restored to
Julian a portion of his heritage. Julian, accustomed to the
habits of an almost ascetic existence, yet conscious of his
superior calling, desired nothing better than to be allowed
to study; and his solitary meditations raised him gradually
to heights which had hitherto been concealed from him.
As soon as he came into possession of his little income,
instead of wasting it on frivolous pleasures he adopted the
mantle of the Greek philosophers, began attending their
schools, and soon felt the stirrings of an eager curiosity
for those secret teachings which a few chosen disciples, with
the aid of money, were able to obtain. Glad to be able to
pay for this knowledge, he came from Macellum in Cappadocia, where he had been brought up with his brother in
lonely seclusion, to Pergamos, where he sat at the feet of
Edesius. His innocent eagerness to learn everything made
the old philosopher smile, but nevertheless he prudently
refused to initiate a disciple descended from the imperial
race which had been the cause of his persecution. He gave
his age as an excuse, and transferred Julian to the hands
of his two disciples, Eusebius and Chrysanthus.[1]

Julian however still went on visiting the master in
secret. Chrysanthus was a passionate admirer of Theurgy;
but Eusebius seemed to despise it. The latter ended all his
lessons with this invariable phrase, which he accompanied
with a learned gesture: 'These are what I call the palpable
verities, worthy of understanding by any well-organised
brain. As for the wonders with which certain miracle-
workers like to wrap their doctrines, I recommend wise men
to distrust them; nothing is closer to error than the credulity
of weak minds confronted with natural happenings of which

[1] Eusebius of Myndus; dates unknown. Fragments collected by Stobaeus in
his *Sermones* may be his. Chrysanthus, dates also unknown. His worldly
prudence as told here resulted in his remaining high priest of Lydia until
his death.—*Ed.*

they do not know the cause.' Julian, surprised at hearing the same conclusion every day, drew Chrysanthus on one side and said: 'If you love truth, explain to me these words which Eusebius is always repeating. Are they not an indirect criticism of the doctrine pronounced by the great master Edesius concerning the invisible powers?'

'When the master has spoken', replied Chrysanthus, 'it is to him alone that you must bring your objections.'

Julian did so. Eusebius smiled. 'If you knew Maximus', he told him, 'you would have understood me immediately, for it is to him that I refer. Maximus is undoubtedly one of the oldest and most brilliant pupils of the learned master Edesius; but, like all men who become exalted, he tends to lose his way at times, and I fancy he is not a little mad. Here is an example. Not long ago, after a scientific discussion among friends, we entered a temple of Hecate. After having bowed to the goddess, Maximus made us sit down. "You are about to see", he told us, "whether or not I am an ordinary man." And, taking from a golden box seven grains of incense, he burned them on the altar, pronouncing unknown words. At once the statue of Hecate seemed to give a shout of laughter. We were a little afraid, I can tell you, and although I am accustomed to finding out the natural cause of every phenomenon, I could not help giving a shiver of apprehension. But Maximus, delighted with his success, would not let us go. "Do you think my knowledge is so limited?" he asked. "Watch! The torch carried by the goddess will be lighted without my touching it." And indeed, no sooner had he finished speaking than we were the witnesses of this second wonder. My companions were enraptured; but I reserved my opinion: when I see something that my reason cannot explain I say that my eyes are deceiving me. *Reason*—that is the real guide, the one who never deceives us.'

'Then I shall leave you to her mercies!' cried Julian. 'Maximus, the man of *fact,* is more useful to me than the man of *theory*. I am going to find without delay this master who does not waste time in idle argument but practises what he preaches.'

Maximus, the neoplatonist of Ephesus,[4] was almost as old as Edesius. This ancient's great height, skilfully draped in the folds of his toga, commanded that instinctive respect which is due to the mightiest natures. His voice was penetrating, his eyes piercing, his whole personality fascinating. According to him, all he had received from Edesius was the first key to the universe and its mysteries; a more exalted form of revelation, obtained only after the performance of the most formidable rites, had gradually opened for him the door of the sanctuary where the Divine Artist fashions his works eternally. He gave himself out to be a revealer; but whence came this privilege of second sight? 'The dead have appeared to me', he used to say. 'These spirits, delivered from the bonds of matter, enter into communion with chaste men who have vanquished their sensual natures by fasting, solitude and long hours of study. They give the knowledge of heaven as the prize for the renunciation of the things of this earth; but to obtain that illumination of the soul, the aspirant must have passed difficult tests which are rendered useless if he shows the slightest weakening of purpose. All are called to receive the divine afflatus; but few succeed in following to its very end the hard path of theurgical initiation.'

Julian attempted it. Maximus seemed to him to be greater than all humanity. Unable to understand him completely, he admired him as one of those superior beings who from time to time pass through this earthly life, concealing from us the radiance of their celestial origin. Charmed by his friendly talk and fascinated by the magic in his eyes, he gave himself up to him without reserve and absorbed his teachings with the avidity of a young man who for the first time is present at the banquet of the occult

---

[4]   Usually called of Smyrna. After Julian's death he was imprisoned and then put to death by Valens.—*Ed.*

sciences. Proud of his disciple, Maximus was aware of the hopes which his future aroused among members of the Christian party. After making Julian swear never to betray his master, he decided to open to him the door of the mysteries whose rites were condemned by imperial law.

At the time fixed for this initiation Julian was led at night out of the city of Ephesus into the subterranean vaults of a ruined temple. Maximus, assisted by a few chosen adepts who filled the rôles of assistants to the priestly conjuror of the spirits of the dead, advised the neophyte to remain unmoved, no matter what the nature of the visions which were about to appear to him.

The ceremonies began. Incense burned inside the magic circle; only the words of the sacred ritual, slowly pronounced by Maximus, could be heard beneath the silent vault. Julian in a fever of impatience awaited in fear and trembling the beginning of the wonderful events promised him. Suddenly a hollow rumbling rose from the shaken earth and phosphorescent ghosts appeared in clouds of perfumed smoke.

Julian, seized with terror, recoiled, involuntarily making the sign of the cross.

The vision disappeared. Maximus had not noticed the young prince's dismay nor the sign he had made. Absorbed, he redoubled his conjurations. The spectres appeared again; but as at first, they disappeared when Julian protected his frightened body by crossing himself.

'I cannot understand it', cried Maximus. 'My familiar spirits are silent and fly from me: and yet there are no profane persons among us.'

'Master', replied Julian, 'I am perhaps the cause of their silence and their flight. I confess that I was afraid, and in my fear I made the sign of the cross. The Christian God is therefore stronger than your spirits, since He can frighten them away without showing himself.'

'Ah!' replied Maximus, 'I should have foreseen this! Your childhood prejudices have closed the path of illumination to you. Go then, return to Nicomedia and serve the priests of the god Christ; renounce the knowledge which is too strong for your feeble will.'

'No', cried Julian, 'I will not renounce it! Pardon my weakness, Maximus, and I will renounce Christ. At all costs, open the gates of the future for me.'

Whether Maximus, as the philosopher Libanius recounts, caused the magical revelations to speak to Julian, or whether, suddenly switching from the rôle of hierophant to that of confidant of the most celebrated members of the polytheistic sect, he made Julian see a vision of the glorious imperial future that would be his if he swore to overthrow Christianity and mount the imperial throne, the young prince gave himself up entirely to wild dreams. Raised by this adventure to the summit of an occult sect which had supporters everywhere only waiting for a leader to rally them, he looked upon himself from that moment as an instrument chosen by heaven to restore the religion of ancient Rome. He was advised to be silent and patient if he wished to be worthy of the spirits and their protective power.

A short while after, he was raised to the rank of Caesar and provided with a wife by the Emperor [355], then sent into Gaul at the head of a Roman army. Whenever a prince of the imperial family went to take possession of his command it was the custom to suspend crowns of laurel in the streets of the towns through which he passed. In the first small town he entered in Gaul one of these crowns fell and wreathed his head; this was considered a fortunate omen. Passing through Vienne on the Rhône he encountered an old woman who greeted him as if he were already emperor and favoured of the gods. Julian stored the memory of these auguries in his heart, but his impassive countenance betrayed none of his thoughts; he did not forget the advice given him by Maximus of Ephesus. His campaign was victorious; he won a great victory over the Alananni in 357, and proceeded to reorganise the government of Gaul for some years, with intermittent successful campaigns. He was resting in Paris after the hardships of war when the Emperor Constantius, jealous of his successes and uneasy at the powerful position he had made for himself, suddenly ordered him to send his best troops back to Italy.

The legionaries greeted this command with defiance; many of them had married women from among the Gauls and had come to consider Gaul as their second home. They rose up and proclaimed Julian as their emperor [361].

It was revolution. At first Julian did not dare to believe his good fortune. He shut himself up in the Palace of the Baths, his mind in a whirl. Night came, and still the soldiers called for him. Their deputies came and shouted, every minute of the night: 'Long live Julian *Augustus*!' but still he could not make up his mind.

Worn out by indecision he had recourse to the rites which his master in magic had taught him. Scarcely had he accomplished the performance of the occult formulae than he fell into that half-sleep which is neither rest nor movement but which seems to free the soul into fantastic regions. As he later described it, he seemed to see beside him a young man of incredible beauty holding in his arms a cornucopia. This apparition resembled a statue on the Roman Capitol representing the Spirit of the Empire. 'Julian', said this mysterious apparition, 'I have followed you since the day you were born, presiding over your destiny. Without ever having seen me you have heard me speaking to you in your dreams of the future, and your weakness of spirit has often alienated me. Today, if you refuse the Empire, my protective mission is at an end; if you accept it I shall be your guide until the end, which is in the hands of the supreme God; and you will see me once again, when your life is about to end.'

Whatever the explanation of this vision, Julian was awakened from his dream by the noise of troops breaking down the barriers round the palace. The impatient army wanted him, dead or alive: a thousand strong arms carried him off, surrounded by flaming torches amid a forest of lances; a buckler was used as the awning. He was given a diadem, improvised as spontaneously as was his own tumultuous election: a soldier's chain circled the forehead of the new Augustus, and the purple of the imperial flags floated from his shoulders. It was to be nearly fifteen centuries before Paris witnessed the proclamation of another emperor within its walls.

III

BELIEF in the apparition of supernatural beings was held in high esteem among the most enlightened Greeks and Romans. Maybe this is not sufficient reason for its acceptance, but at the same time it must persuade us not to reject it as utterly absurd. We hardly need to recall the nymph Egeria who dictated the first Roman laws to King Numa— an early poetic tradition; the familiar spirit of Socrates, the *daimon* in which this celebrated philosopher's disciples all believed; or all the other accounts of supernatural visions which have come down to us through the ages. Reflecting upon these manifestations we may observe that every religious cult known to humanity is more or less based on communications, real or imaginary, with the supernatural world. The Middle Ages possess the greatest number of these popular accounts, because that period seized, and transformed for its own ends, the entire occult heritage of the ancient world. I have space to deal with only two of these examples, the first taken from polytheistic dogma and derived from the life of Apollonius of Tyana,[5] the second

---

[5] Born rather before the Christian era; a Neo-Pythagorean. The numerous books and articles on him include Philostratus' *Life* and one of J. A. Froude's *Short Studies*. He made a lifelong study of comparative religions, travelling considerably to add to his store of knowledge of them. Apparently outliving St. Paul, and belonging to the same region, it is therefore extremely odd that he never mentions Christianity at all, nor do early Christian writers appear aware of him.—*Ed.*

from the Christian faith, reported on the reliable authority of James of Voraggio [b. *circa* 1230], a monk in the Order of Preaching Friars and Archbishop of Genoa [1292] who is the most voluminous author of XIIIth century historical anecdotes.

Philostratus 'the Athenian' [b. *circa* 172 A.D.] tells us that during the visit of Apollonius to Corinth there was among his favourite disciples a certain Menippus who came from Lycia. This young man possessed a mind of great distinction and also was of remarkable physical beauty. His fellow-students soon began to spread the rumour that he was abandoning science for the art of love and that he was to be seen at certain hours in the company of a woman who was quite unknown in Corinth but who appeared to be very wealthy. According to Menippus, his beloved was a young Phoenician woman who was very fond of travelling. Indeed, he soon announced to his master his forthcoming marriage and begged him to honour the nuptial feast with his presence.

Apollonius on hearing this news gave an involuntary shudder and, as he possessed the faculty of second sight, he asked Menippus if he were quite sure of his future wife's love and fortune. 'If I may believe the evidence of my own eyes', replied the young man, 'the acquaintance of someone so rich, so lovable and so loving is the most precious gift the gods could have given me.' Apollonius shook his head and replied calmly: 'If that is so, I must not fail to bring you a wedding-present.'

On the appointed day just when the guests were about to pass into the banqueting-hall Apollonius, who arrived late because he wished to be certain of the presence of all the company, the majority of whom were his disciples, suddenly appeared carrying in his hand a golden wand on which were engraved mysterious signs. His entry was greeted by a murmur of satisfaction and Menippus came forward to present his young wife. But the latter had barely set eyes on the theurgist and encountered his fixed, cold gaze than she began to tremble as if stricken with terror. 'Does this fine house and these splendid furnishings belong to you or to your wife?' asked Apollonius.' The young man replied: 'Master, everything you see belongs to my wife; the only things that belong to me are the clothes on my back.' Apollonius answered: 'Very well, they must suffice you, for your wealth is only an illusion and your wife a ghost.'

Then, pointing his golden wand at the woman's forehead, he added in a voice like thunder: 'Demon, leave this borrowed form, and return to what you really are!'

To the general stupefaction, the woman uttered a hoarse cry, her rosy cheeks dissolved like vapour and left nothing beneath the wreath of flowers and the bridal veil but a bleached skull and a rattling skeleton which fell to the ground in a heap, while a sort of phantom, apparently half woman, half adder, crawled hastily away into the garden and disappeared.

When the witnesses of this scene had recovered a little from their horror the house and everything it contained had vanished like a dream; to their amazement they found themselves in a wild and deserted place. Apollonius, erect and impassive, appeared to them like a god. 'You see the use of secret knowledge', he said to them. 'Not one of you would have suspected that this so-called woman was an *Empusa,* one of those demons that haunt sepulchres and who sometimes clothe themselves in very impressive forms in order to deceive the living. Without my fortunate arrival, this Empusa would have consummated her marriage by sucking the blood of Menippus while he slept.'⁶

The *Empusa* of Apollonius became the *incubi* and *succubae* of Christian demonology. Satan himself was not averse from disguising himself as a daughter of Eve the better to tempt, not only philosophers, but also the most devout servants of God. James of Voraggio tells us that there was once a bishop—his name, country and period

⁶ Keats' poem *Lamia* is based on an Italian version of this story.—*Ed.*

could not be told for fear of the scandal it might cause to descendants of his pastoral flock—who, like St. Augustine, had made it a rule to speak to women only in the presence of witnesses, even in cases of absolute necessity, so afraid was he, even at his advanced age, of the magic in a woman's eye. In vain the Devil whispered to him that God in his divine wisdom would not make unnatural laws, that the celibacy of priests has no scriptural authority [for St. Peter himself, the first Pope, had been married]; the brave bishop stuck to his principles: he had vowed celibacy under the protective tutelage of the apostle St. Andrew.

Now it happened that one evening just before dinner a young and very beautiful woman, her rich attire covered by a long veil, came knocking at the door of the episcopal palace and most urgently solicited a private interview with the bishop. She said that she had something of the greatest importance to tell him which could brook no delay. The bishop, informed of this unexpected visit, asked his almoner to inquire her name and business. But she refused to answer. 'If the bishop refuses to see me', she said, 'I can do nothing, for he is the master, and I shall go away: but his refusal will weigh like a curse upon his head.'

The almoner was much intrigued, for the young woman was not merely beautiful, her language and her bearing indicated a high-born personage, and the interests of the Church might suffer if she were refused. This last consideration weakened the bishop's resolve. 'Perhaps you are right', he said to the almoner, 'and if it is God's will that has sent me this person I should, as one of His servants, be committing an error by refusing to admit her. Will you therefore bring her before me—and may St. Andrew,' he added in a whisper, 'watch over my eyes!'

As soon as the young woman entered she threw herself weeping on her knees before the bishop. Since he was as charitable as his visitor was fair, the sight of such distress moved him deeply. 'There there, my child', he said, with paternal tenderness, 'calm yourself, and tell me what it is that is troubling you so.'

'Father', replied the strange lady, 'you see before you a young and helpless woman threatened by the very worst misfortunes. My family is one of the most respected in this town by virtue of birth and fortune. My mother brought me up to love God, and I had resolved to devote myself to a life of religious meditation; but God called her away from me at the very time when her presence and pious encouragement were most necessary. Now, in the interests of ambition, my father wants me to marry a man whose lack of piety is the scandal of the whole town. This dreadful ceremony is to take place tomorrow: in my utter despair I ran away and have come to seek protection beneath your roof.'

The bishop, who admired this evident fervour and distinction of birth combined in such a lovely woman, could not shut his heart in the face of such dire distress. 'Do not worry, my child', he said to her with great kindness, and without consulting St. Andrew. 'You can have confidence in me. Did anyone see you come in?'

'No one', replied the young woman, 'saw me leave my father's house and no one saw me come in here, for at this time of night the streets are almost empty.'

'Good', said the bishop. 'You are therefore safe with us here, at least for the time being, under the protection of my priests and myself. It is not usual, of course, for a young woman to pass the night under a bishop's roof, but the motive of your coming is my excuse in the eyes of God. Tomorrow I shall choose a convent for you where you will find safe refuge and repose.'

'No no, reverend Father', cried the lovely stranger, casting on him a glance full of strange fascination. 'No, I cannot stay here. The slightest indiscretion on the part of your servants might compromise you in the eyes of the world. Your pity for my misfortune must not become a pretext for calumny.'

'Come, come', replied the bishop, smiling, 'evil be to him who evil thinks! The world knows me well enough and long enough not to accuse me without reason. In offering you hospitality, I am committing no imprudence; God sees us and watches over us. Will you kindly accompany me into the refectory? for I am dining with my vicars and it would not be charitable to keep them waiting.'

The young woman took her seat at the table facing the bishop. The holy man of God, forgetting to eat and drink, allowed himself to fall into a silent contemplation of this seductive creature, who also abstained from touching the food that was placed before her. In his secret heart the bishop felt sorely tempted, so much so that he said to himself: 'If in my weakness I succumb to temptation, God alone will know my secret, and in His infinite pity will forgive me for having loved a little too much the most beautiful of his works.' And he thought of choosing some convent far away from the town where he could hide his protegée and visit her without fear of being discovered.

As though his wavering virtue were about to commit, in all its vileness, a sin by intention, three violent knocks were heard at the outer door. A servant took a torch and went to see who it was. He soon came back, announcing that a strange man, dressed as a traveller, was asking to be let in immediately.

'If it is a poor man', said the bishop, 'give him the best we have in the kitchen, and enough money to pay for his lodging in a nearby hostelry. I shall receive his visit tomorrow.'

Again there were three knocks at the door, so furious that they made the whole house shake. The servant ran to the door to beg of the importunate visitor to behave with more respect to a bishop's palace. He returned, saying: 'My lord, the stranger is not a poor man; he speaks with great elegance and declares that if he is not received kindly, he will force his way in as swift as lightning.'

The vicars seemed very worried and the young woman

grew pale. 'My child', said the bishop, 'the man who presents himself so threateningly at my door can only be your father, or else the suitor whom you have refused in order to devote yourself to God. Whatever happens, I have promised to protect you; but in truth, I hardly know what to do.'

With redoubled violence, the blows again shook the episcopal household.

'It is neither my father nor my fiancé making such a noise', the young woman said, 'for they would have made known who they were and asked for me by name. But whoever this stranger may be, get someone to ask him this question. If he replies in a ridiculous manner, it will prove that he is a mere madman, and your servants will only have to lay hands on him and lead him to a place where he cannot do harm.'

'Very well', replied the bishop, 'what shall the question be?'

'Ask him *what is the most wonderful thing that God created in a little space?*'

The stranger, to whom the servant went and asked the question, replied:

'It is the infinite diversity of faces, for, among so many men who have lived since the beginning of the world and who will live until the centuries of time are done, there have never been two whose features were exactly alike; and on the smallest face God has placed the most precious organs of the senses. Go and tell the lord bishop that I am not mad as he thinks and that I beg of him to let me enter without delay.'

The bishop was about to give the order to let him in, when the young woman stopped him. 'Venerable Father', she said, 'allow me to ask him a second question, for the reply to the first may have been a stroke of luck. Have him asked *what part of the earth is higher than the heavens?*'

The stranger replied to the servant: 'It is that which is in the sky where, since his divine ascension, the body of

Our Lord Jesus Christ still dwells. Our flesh was made of earth: the Saviour's body, which was made of our flesh, comes therefore from the earth, and so it is certain that where that beloved body dwells, the earth is higher than the Heavens. Moreover, you may tell my lord bishop that the correctness of my replies is not due to luck, and that he must hurry and let me in *so that I may tell him something he does not know.*'

When this reply was brought to the pontiff, the young woman grew even paler and seemed to be suffering great pain.

'What is the matter?' the vicars asked her, astounded at this scene. 'Who is this stranger who knows what we are talking about and whose replies to your questions so upset you?'

'I do not know him', said the young woman in a trembling voice. 'But if my lord bishop would care to have him asked *what is the distance between Earth and Heaven?* his reply will tell us who he is.'

The servant soon brought the stranger's third reply: 'Ask the person who thought of the question, and tell her to reply to it herself, for she herself has measured an even greater distance—that between Heaven and Hell. Moreover, tell the lord bishop that it is no woman whom he entertains at his table, but the Devil!'

At these words, the bishop conscience-stricken trembled all over and fell on his knees, covering himself with the sign of the cross. At this sacred sign the woman vanished like smoke, leaving behind her a strong smell of sulphur. 'Run', cried the bishop, 'bring me the saint sent from heaven to break this infernal spell: whether he be angel or mortal man, let him receive our thanks and offer them to our Eternal God!'

The stranger had disappeared. But the following night the apostle St. Andrew appeared to the bishop in a dream and revealed to him how, with God's permission, he had saved him from the toils of Satan.

The *Golden Legend* of James of Voraggio and the *Lives of the Saints* of Surius of Lubeck [1522—1578] the Carthusian monk are full of these supernatural tales which all more or less resemble each other. The visions of Marguerite Alacoque [1647—1690], who was recently canonised,[1] and the doubtful appearance of Nôtre-Dame de la Salette which a few years ago was a subject of much controversy,[2] are sufficient proof that every era needs a seasoning of the marvellous. If we doubt the theurgical wonders performed by the Emperor Julian, and those, no less renowned, of Apollonius of Tyana, we are led inevitably to a negation of all modern phenomena which reason and science are unable to explain. If we suppress the element of the marvellous, the supernatural, that is *the permanent relationship between the visible world and the unseen,* we are following a course at the end of which all religions fall one after the other into the same abyss. . . Let us certainly seek for truth in a rational manner; but in the place of the gods we overthrow let us not call forth the spectral vacancy of nothingness.

IV

JULIAN believed in the supernatural world, in the divine unity, in the immortality of the human soul. The writings which he has left us inspire us with the wish to breathe the air of that ancient wisdom that pervades them of which a few philosophers in his day still observed the traditional rites. His school companions, such as Basil and Gregory Nazianus [*circa* 329—389], who later became bishops and saints, insulted his memory by calling him the Apostate. But how could Julian have admitted the divinity of Christ

[1]   M. Alacoque beatified by Pope Pius IX. She was bidden in her mystical ecstacy to establish the festival of the Sacred Heart, first celebrated in Paray 1685, spread later by the Jesuits from 1690 onwards.—*Ed.*

[2]   Appearance of the B.V.M. in the diocese of Grenoble to Maximin Giraud and Mélanie Matthieu, 19 Sep. 1846; devotion authorised in 1852.—*Ed.*

at a time when the bishops themselves were unable to come to any agreement on His nature? in a century when, according to the confessions of the heads of the Church [*vide* Gregory Nazianus], the clergy themselves belied the morality of the Gospel by the licentiousness of their own lives?

As soon as he heard the news of the military revolution which proclaimed this new emperor, Constantius gathered together a number of troops in the East. But Julian, swiftly crossing Italy by forced marches, landed among the Greeks, to whom he was well-known. His proclamations announced the re-establishment of the ancient splendours of Hellenic ritual. As a guarantee that he would keep his word he publicly abjured Christianity. In the sacred city of Eleusis the Hierophant of Ceres lowered him to the bottom of a pit covered by a slab of stone pierced with a hole through which the blood of a bull was poured over him, the usual ceremony for effacing the holy water of baptism. Then a sacrifice was offered to the goddess Fortuna. The augurs noticed on the victim's entrails the mark of a cross contained in a circle. This disconcerted all who were present, for they thought it was a sign of Christ's future triumph, the circle, in Magic, being the symbol of Eternity. But the priest of Ceres Eleusina at once gave another interpretation. 'The circle', he said, 'surrounds the cross; therefore the power of Christianity is surrounded on all sides, and its final hour is at hand.'

This belief was strengthened when almost at the same time the news arrived of the death of Constantius. Now uncontested head of the Empire, Julian re-opened the ancient temples, adopted the title of Pontifex Maximus or supreme priest held by the earlier emperors, and passed many laws in favour of the revived national religion. Maximus and Chrysanthus, the two friends of his obscure younger days, were not forgotten; both were living at Sardis and he wrote to them personally, asking them to come and stay with him.

Maximus at first was not at all anxious to end his days in the splendour of a palace. Eunapius, who has left us an account of his life,[*] tells how he and Chrysanthus used theurgical rites to find out if they should accept this imperial offer. The results were threatening. Chrysanthus declined; Maximus decided to go. When he heard of the former's refusal Julian smiled at his weakness and in compensation made him governor of the temples in the province of Lydia. Maximus, defying auguries, made his way to Constantinople with all the pride of a successful parvenu. The city magistrates and most prominent men mingled with the crowds who came to do homage to this imperial favourite as he passed through their streets. From Sardis to Constantinople his journey was a triumphal procession. Julian's own palace was given to him for a home; the Emperor never stirred without having him at his side. Both of them passed whole nights together, consulting the Fates on all questions concerning the Empire. Maximus, intoxicated by the extent of his power, forgot his philosophic humility and became haughty and disdainful, making many secret enemies. The future showed that his friend Chrysanthus had been the wiser. At the end of Julian's reign, which was brief, Maximus was thrown into a state prison; he was accused of robbing the imperial treasury of immense sums of money. He long remained prisoner, his gaolers treating him most cruelly, and when they were tired of keeping him he was executed. Thus the auguries were fulfilled.

In 362, Julian, confident in the protection of his tutelary spirit, had decided to wage war in Asia on the Parthians, the only people who for the last four centuries had offered an unconquerable resistance to the Romans. He felt that this long expedition would be the crowning point in his career.

He arrived in the town of Antioch at the end of July,

---

[*] Born 347 at Sardis, studying under Chrysanthus, later living mainly in Athens. His *Lives of the Sophists* is the only source for his period's Neoplatonism.—*Ed.*

in the midst of the melancholy festivals celebrated by the townspeople in honour of Adonis. This was a fateful omen, according to occult doctrine; Julian could have avoided it, but at that moment his military plans occupied his thoughts so much, and Maximus flattered him so persistently, that he believed himself to be beyond the reach of all misfortune. At the gates of Antioch was a sacred wood called Daphne, where for many centuries a famous oracle of Apollo had attracted the most wealthy visitors. This sanctuary had been abolished by Constantius; Julian wished, by offering up nocturnal sacrifices, to bring back the oracle.

The Christians, who never forgave him for having abandoned their religion, accused him after his departure of having performed monstrous rites in which he had sacrificed little children. He was also accused of having committed secret atrocities with the aid of Maximus in the temple of the Moon at Carrhae in Mesopotamia. He had had the doors of this temple walled up, and left guards to await his return. He did not come back; but the temple was opened by Jovian, his successor, and scandal had it that they found the body of a woman hanging by her hair, her arms outstretched, disembowelled. In justice to the memory of Julian, it is sufficient to counter this dreadful accusation by applying the noble recorded words of this prince. A governor of the province of Narbonne in Gaul had been accused of having pillaged his district. This officer simply denied everything, and his calm disconcerted his enemies. Delphidius, the celebrated advocate from Bordeaux, who spoke for the plaintiffs, tried to make up for the lack of proofs by shouting: 'Caesar, if judgment were based always on denials, what guilty man would ever be condemned?' Julian replied: 'If condemnation were based always on mere accusations, who would ever be innocent?'

The war against the Parthians was not a successful one. The enemy retreated before the Romans, but destroyed everything in their path. Courage and endurance could do nothing against an adversary that could not be reached and a countryside devastated by fire. On the night of the 25—26 July 363, the exhausted legions lay down on the plain and asked Julian for food when he did not even have a crust of bread for himself. The unhappy Emperor, shut in his tent, listened with aching heart to the complaints of his starving companions; he implored the gods to afford him at least the consolation of a hero's death.

While he was meditating on his sad fate the Spirit of the Empire seemed to emerge suddenly from the floor and stood at his side as it had done in his palace in Paris on the eve of his election to the purple robes. It was the same face, but pale, and as if ravaged by tears. As on the first occasion, this fateful spectre was carrying a horn of plenty; but this time it was wearing a long black veil and bowed to Julian without speaking. Then, pointing to the ground with a sinister gesture, it turned its head away and left the imperial tent, gliding like a wraith at a funeral.

Julian, more frightened by the silence than by the apparition, rushed after it. Throwing aside the curtains of his tent he saw a red star fall out of the dark blue of the night sky on his left leaving a wake of light; it went out before reaching the horizon.

Overcome by this double vision, he wakened the chief of the Pretorian Guard, told him of his uneasiness, and asked to have sent to him the Tuscan soothsayers who were following the army with the Sibylline Books. The texts were obscure but sinister; the soothsayers declared that, according to the rules of their art, it was necessary to abstain from all activity during the seven days following the appearance of a meteor.

'Fools!' cried Julian, 'do you want us all to be slain if the enemy attacks us at dawn?'

Back in the solitude of his tent, he fell once more a prey to the dire presentiments which obsessed his brain. The glory of which he had dreamed was vanishing, his great plans were falling through : the future seemed no more than a sepulchre which would be desecrated by the barbarians.

Well, at least let that future be no longer delayed. Let one thing be left to him, the splendour of his final hour! Posterity had always been kind to princes who died with glory and dignity. Chief of the Pretorian guard, let the trumpets sound . . . The army rises and surrounds its leader's tent. The appearance of Julian, now reduced to the poverty of the meanest soldier, awakens a last cry of 'Long live the Emperor!'—a touching witness to fidelity in misfortune. Soon the enemy appeared, the battle began; despair urged on the Romans to victory. But the young emperor fell, mortally wounded.

He did not go down to the tomb alone. With his body the ancient gods laid themselves to rest.

His last hours were heroic. Laid on a mattress surrounded by his soldiers and wise men, he left them with these few words: 'Friends, I feel already how much stronger the soul is than the body. I hope I have preserved without spot or stain that power which I received from God and which emanates from Heaven. I thank God for taking me from this world at the height of a glorious career. I shall refrain from appointing my successor, fearing that I might not choose the worthiest for this high position. As a man of honour, I wish that the Republic may find after my death a sincere and faithful leader.'

Those around him burst into tears. Julian went on: 'Why weep for a soul which is about to be re-united with the spirits of the stars?' And it was with this act of religious faith that he died in the arms of Maximus and Priscus, the last two masters of ancient Magic.

V

THIS prince who died so young [he was scarcely thirty-three] was the last representative of the ancient mysteries. He perished as it were on the threshold of his reign and in the springtime of a great future. The imperial army, in

despair at his loss and starving in a land which the enemy
ravaged as it retreated, no longer thought of advancing,
and their withdrawal was a disaster. One of the officers of
the Imperial Guard, named Jovian, tumultuously elected
emperor [363] to lead back to Europe the wretched sur-
vivors of a sterile victory, was not equal even to this dismal
task. After having signed a shameful treaty with the Persians, he lost on the desert roads the majority of his
exhausted soldiers who were accompanying the late
emperor's body and begging for their bread. Jovian died
also on the last stage of the journey. His successor [364] was
an unlettered soldier named Valentinian. The latter chose
as his colleague his brother Valens [eastern emperor 364—
378], to whom he granted the provinces of Asia, Egypt and
Greece, keeping for himself Italy, Gaul, Spain and Africa.

Both were Christians, and both dipped their hands in
blood. The two capitals, Milan and Constantinople, were
the scenes of their murderous fury. Valentinian had as pets
two she-bears whose names, *Innocent* and *Golden Spangle*,
have come down to us in history; he fed them on human
flesh. Imagine how many sacrifices it required to keep these
beasts fed! The slightest crime was punished by death: if
the accused man asked for trial before a judge, it was to the
Judge of the Dead that he was delivered. The debtor paid
for his debts with his head. A workman who had made a
mistake in the fitting of an imperial garment, a palace servant who on a hunting trip had let the dogs loose too soon
—these were decapitated or thrown to the flames at a sign
from Valentinian. This raving maniac died in 375 in a fit
of madness.

Valens, his brother, a hypocritical and sly character,
kept the empire of the east under control by a widespread
network of spies. Pale and sinister-looking, he had the shifty
eyes which denote a crafty mind. Power had enlarged his
pretensions without strengthening his will. A moral eunuch,
he parodied despotic virility and succeeded only in producing still-born schemes. To please him one had only to invent

some little plot which he took pleasure in stamping out with much unnecessary noise.

One day a few philosophers and courtiers had met in a country house to make secret experiments in occult science under the direction of a theurgical master named Palladius,[10] highly praised in the chronicles of Ammonius Marcellinus, Sozomenius and Zosimus. They met to ask the Qabalistic arcana about the fate of Valens and about his successors in the next election, for he had no offspring.

Palladius set up a triangular tripod constructed after the model of the one at Delphi, surrounded by branches of laurel gathered in a sacred wood. After having scented it according to the usual rites of the Hellenic mysteries, he placed on this tripod a large basin made of the seven metals which regulate the planets: lead, tin, iron, copper, mercury, silver and gold. Around the edge of this basin were engraved the letters of the Greek alphabet. Then, wearing a wreath of verbena on his brows and his hands covered with a winding-sheet stolen from the grave of a dead baby, Palladius suspended over the basin on a linen thread a golden ring engraved with mysterious signs. According to the above-mentioned historians, while the theurgist was reciting in a loud voice the conjurations which evoke the seven plane-tary spirits the tripod was seen to tremble and the ring began to sway from side to side, striking now one, now another of the letters on the side of the basin. Those present made a note of the letters as Palladius spelt them out and from them made the answers to questions they had previously asked. This was one of the ancient methods of questioning the fates.

To the first question the oracle replied that all those present would pay for their imprudent curiosity with their lives. The second reply announced that the Emperor Valens would end his life by a violent disaster. The third question asked the name of his successor; the ring, still swaying, had

[10] Possibly Rutilius Taurus Aemilianus Palladius, an inferior poet of agricul-ture in the fourth century.—*Ed.*

already struck the letters Θ...E...O...Δ [Theod . . .] when
the silence demanded by Palladius was broken by a courtier
who cried the name: 'Theodore!' The man so named held
under Valens an office similar to that which we call private
secretary. He was a simple honest citizen, without ambition
or enemies, who had no idea that other people might be
interested in him.

The assembled company departed without carrying the
experiment any further. Like all free-thinkers they laughed
at auguries: only Palladius felt afraid of what the morrow
might bring. And with reason; for, betrayed by an unknown
informer, the unfortunate theurgist was seized by the Pretorian Guard, put in irons and dragged before the prefect
Modestus. His house had been entered and the instruments
of his fatal art taken as evidence; there was no means of
defence against these silent but damaging witnesses. Put to
the torture, he confessed everything he was required to and
named his accomplices in a crime which the Prefect of
the Palace wished to work up to the proportions of
attempted assassination in order to gain favour with the
emperor. Valens was merciless. The innocent Theodore was
also tortured and put to death. A new law [373] proclaimed
the extermination without trial of all philosophers, magi,
soothsayers, prognosticators of dreams and other occultists.

This sentence was carried out with terrible speed; the
packed prisons overflowed with heaps of heads chopped off
by the public executioners. Every town in the Empire was
lit by the sinister light of huge pyres of the victims of secret
informers. There were no trials, no witnesses, no judges:
it was sufficient to have an enemy to be arrested, to pass
before the imperial commissioners, to be judged guilty and
condemned without appeal. The terror grew to such proportions in a few days that in the whole of Europe no one dared
to show himself wearing a Greek mantle without running
the risk of being taken for a philosopher and being arrested.

The intoxicating fumes of so many murders went to
Valens' head. Wishing to wipe out superstition, he absorbed

it himself at every pore and thought he could see his fatal successor everywhere he went. Forgetting that no tyrant has ever killed his successor, he imagined he could overcome his fears by sacrificing all people of any standing whose name began with the letters ΘΕΟΔ.   An inquisition seized all who were named Theodatus, Theodore, Theodosius. Even in their madness Caligula and Nero had never thought of condemning a man to death because of his name; this Christian Herod was repeating the massacre of the innocents.

Nevertheless, the words of the oracle were fulfilled to the letter. Valens perished in a defeat by the Goths; and he had as his successor one Theodosius, who had remained undiscovered by the satellites of the emperor in a remote part of Spain.

When Theodosius came to power in 369 he remembered how dangerous the professors of Magi could be. His first step was to confirm the proscriptive measures taken against them by Valens. A law of 25 May 385, threatens death to anyone having the temerity to practise, even in the greatest secrecy and with the most harmless intentions, any of the mysterious rites for foretelling the future. The closing of all the well-known places where oracles had been known to exist was rigorously enforced. Another law of 9 May 391 renews this persecution, and provides that if a father is accused of magical practices his children's patrimony shall be confiscated, as well as he himself suffering death. On 8 November 392 new laws were passed to encourage the zealous persecution of magicians by the provincial governors, threatening with enormous fines those who did not carry out their duty with the utmost severity . . . Theodosius did not treat lightly those found guilty of high treason. It was he who had the entire population of the town of Thessalonica massacred by imperial troops in order to expiate the bad behaviour of a few unknown rowdies who had insulted his statue.

The last remains of the now-forbidden polytheism and the adepts in the occult arts had found refuge in the remote

country districts far from cities, in market towns, villages
and hamlets which were free from official supervision. This
was the origin of the word *pagani*—pagans or people of the
small country towns [Latin *pagus*], which denoted the last
worshippers of the ancient gods. Theodosius II did not
scruple to trace them to their obscure retreats; in 426 he
ordered a search to be made for the remotest sanctuaries.
But as the adepts became fewer their occult influence grew
stronger; and it is the secret societies which have handed
down from century to century the religious traditions of
magic.

On the other hand, polytheistic rites were mingled with
the Christian ceremonies. The people on whom a new culture was being imposed by fear consoled themselves by
transferring under new names the religious customs which
had formed a part of the ancient observances. Processions
replaced the Hellenic ritual marches [θεορία]. 'Italy,
and above all southern Italy', says M. Alfred Maury, 'still
preserves a thousand and one traces of paganism in its
religious devotions. The popular cult of the Madonna at
Naples certainly comes from that of Vesta and Ceres. The
modern Romans give the old temple of Vesta the name of
the Church of the Madonna of the Sun [fire virgin]. The
famous procession of the Madonna del' Arco, in which the
pilgrims come back dancing the tarantella, wearing on their
foreheads ivy-leaves and flowers, and shaking *thyrsi* decorated with nuts and chaplets, in which the worshippers, in
riotous abandon, are borne along on chariots decked with
foliage—is a remnant of the rustic festivities which celebrated in times gone by the goddess Ceres queen of the
corn and Bacchus the god of wine, her husband.'

Lamps burn in every Neapolitan hut and cottage before
the image of the Virgin which has taken the place of the
ancient household gods; these revered images are handed
down from father to son and are looked upon as protectors
of the family. Prayers are offered up to them on all sorts
of occasions; their tutelary influence is put even before that

of God and they are covered with a veil every time that a dishonest or guilty action is being considered, for fear that it might incur their wrath.

In France, the *Pardons* of Brittany, the *Ducasses* and *Kermesses* of the northern provinces, still preserve a pagan quality also. In them we find customs which have their origin long before the rise of Christianity: as in the pagan festivals, processions always form the main part of the proceedings and generally an image is carried in the place of the ancient idol.

In Sicily, the Virgin has taken possession of all the sanctuaries of Ceres and Venus, and the pagan rites practised in honour of these goddesses were partly transferred to the religious ceremonies in honour of the Mother of Christ.

In Greece, the Virgin opens the doors of the morning; St. Nicholas calms tempests; St. George protects the labourer; St. Demetrius looks after shepherds; St. Elias, worshipped in the mountains, has been substituted for the Sun, once held in adoration in mountainous regions. In Italy, St. Antony has taken the place of Neptunus Equester, the god of circus races; he has become the patron saint of the horse. A host of apocryphal saints have inherited both the name of an ancient divinity and the corresponding religious rites. The Aidoneus [Adonis] of Epirus has become St. Donatus; the goddess Pelina, St. Pelino; the goddess Fortuna, of the common good or happiness, has become St. Felicity. The worship of St. Roch appears to have its origin in the legend of the cult of Æsculapius. The son of Theseus, Hippolytus, has become a martyr. The star Margarita Coronae has given us St. Marguerite. St. Michael has replaced Mercury.[11]

[11] Also he has replaced Zeus or the corresponding chief god on innumerable hill sites throughout Europe, e.g. the Puy de Dôme, Paris. The famous Apparition of St. Michael occurred in the 5th century to the Bishop of Siponto following which the famous monastery on Mount Gargamo was built [Capitanate district, near Naples]. In the 11th century the fortress-

The processions led by priests and augurs for the prosperity of the vineyards and plantations and for the welfare of the people were consecrated in the new form of the Rogations. Holy water has replaced the lustral bowl; the talisman has become the Agnus Dei. The Hebrew names of God and of the angels, together with those of Abraham and Solomon, were substituted for those of the Greek and oriental deities who figured on the phylacteries and talismans. The Fates were no longer invoked as at Preneste: instead, the Bible was consulted at random and prognostications discovered in the meaning of the first words at the top of a page.

The Oracles had been silenced by order of the emperors, but relics of the saints and martyrs prophesied in their place; instead of giving to the priest of the Oracle the note containing the request that was to be addressed to the gods, it was placed on the saint's tomb.

Formerly, at St. Regulus' Well,[12] in Wales, invalids who came to consult the saint made offerings of a cock, in the case of a man, or a hen, in the case of a woman. These birds were placed in a basket and carried round the well, then taken to the graveyard. The sick person then went into the church and laid himself under the communion table with a Bible beneath his head. He lay there until daybreak; then, having made an offering of six pence, he went home, leaving the fowl in the church. If it died, it was considered to have caught the consultant's disease and the latter's recovery was then believed to be certain.

The *obolus*, the coin offered to Charon, the ferryman of the dead, is still in use in some parts of the Jura, where a coin is placed under the deceased person's head. Elsewhere, pennies are placed on the eyes of the dead.

The sacred fountains of antiquity have not disappeared

church off the Cornish coast was built, corresponding to Mont St. Michel in France. See Sigebert's *Chronicles* and the German monk Charles Stengelius' *S. Michaelis principatus Apparitiones*, etc., 1629.—*Ed.*

[12]   S. Regulus or Rievl of Senlis, *circa* 250 A.D.—*Ed.*

but have merely changed their names: a great number exist in Brittany. At Sainte-Eugénie, Côtes-du-Nord, pins were thrown in as offerings by those who wished to cast spells on their enemies.

Even the custom of saying 'God bless you!' when someone sneezes is a relic of pagan cults.

The consecration of the Yule Log is an extension of the idea found in the ancient myths that a person's or a family's good fortune can be assured by keeping a brand from it. Nearly all the ceremonies which, in the Germanic and Scandinavian countries, are observed at this season, have their origin in the festival of the winter solstice and in the belief that the gods at this time would appear to mortals. Similarly, the Midsummer or St. John's Fires are connected with the ancient festival of the summer solstice which persisted in its Christian form with a host of other natural festivals. The last-named festival appears to derive from ceremonies observed at the *Palilia* or festivals of Pales, goddess of the flocks, at which shepherds would light bonfires. These fires were supposed to put demons to flight and it was believed in the Middle Ages that whoever found a four-leaf clover on Midsummer Night could command the spirits that guard hidden treasure. Volumes could be and have been written on these transfigurations of the ancient ritual which so enriched the clergy.[12]

VI

THE prolonged death-throes of the Roman Empire to the time when the last wave of invading barbarians succeeded in overwhelming it do not rightly belong to my subject. But the mingling of barbarians with the ancient world does, since it added fresh beliefs to the pantheon of supernatural beings. The religion of the Norsemen was as wild and fierce

[12] A most readable popular one is the late Arthur Weigall's *The Paganism in our Christianity.—Ed.*

as themselves; they had a paradise which they called Valhalla, last home of the brave, for bravery was to them the
greatest virtue.

Valhalla has five hundred and forty doors; through
each one of these doors eight hundred dead warriors may
pass, valiant skeletons who amuse themselves by breaking
each other's bones and who return to Valhalla to carouse
together. There are twelve warrior goddesses called Val-
kyries who each day descend to the earth on horseback
in order to select those who are to die in the next battle. The
earth is separated from the sky by a bridge of three colours;
cowards cannot cross it. These conceptions of violence,
attributed by earth to heaven, could not be influenced by
Christian propaganda. But between the Rhine, the Danube
and the Vistula there were many races known by the general
name of Germans [*gher* or *wehr-Mann*, men of war is
one derivation, but authoritative dictionaries will go no
further than to say that Lat. *germanus* is probably of Celtic
origin, and indicates a possible link with the other root
meaning of 'fully akin', whence English 'germane'], who
had been made more susceptible to Christian influence
because of their long contact with Greek and Roman populations. The immortal Tacitus has described them to us
with great eloquence.[14] The barbarians were morally
superior to the Romans on account of the respect and the
sort of cult which they had for woman.

Without temples or cities, these Germans, like the
Gauls, held religious assemblies in the depths of the forests,
but, in contrast to Druidic custom, they abhorred human
sacrifices. The silent awe inspired by wild nature, that vague
fear in the soul which peoples the shadows underneath the
great dome of the forest trees, the splendid furnaces of

[14] Tacitus' *Germania*, a eulogy of the noble Germanic races, generally considered to have been intended as an implied comment upon the degeneracy
of Italy with which his Germans in their simple virtues are so obviously
intended to form a contrast. The following description is drawn from this
source, which remains our fullest literary account.—*Ed.*

dawn, the soft dreamings of twilight about the openings of caves and rocks, over precipices and chasms—all this created for the Germans many a magic sanctuary which had nature herself for an altar and for incense the poetry of pure meditation.

These great images, made divine by the dreaming imagination which is fostered by a life under the open heavens, inspired beliefs whose mystical reflection endured through the centuries, right up to the legends engendered by the Christian Middle Ages. The fairy priestesses of ancient Germania are eternally enshrined in the fables whose memory still casts an enchantment over solemn conversations held round German firesides on winter evenings. Flowers of silence and solitude, the fairies reigned over the minds of their time in a double majesty both of grace and of mystery. Having become estranged from the things of this life, they passed their days in perpetual retirement. Ceaselessly occupied by meditation over nature, invisible as their gods and venerated like them, they heard oracles in the rumbling of distant waterfalls; they sought the voice of the spirits in the melancholy complaining of the evening winds, in the echo of that creative harmony which rises from the earth at certain hours of the night and which makes us believe we can hear the seed piercing the furrow, the sap rising in trunks, the leaves unfurling and bursting through the bark of branches and the flowers of the field leaning towards each other to whisper tales of divine wonder.

The poems of Ossian,[15] of which I made a translation in 1842[16], are full of curious details about the beliefs of the old

[15] Until recently *Fingal, an Ancient Epic . . . composed by Ossian, son of Fingal* [1761] was treated generally, as by Dr. Johnson at the time, as practically entirely the work of its alleged discoverer and translator James Macpherson [1736-1796]. More recent scholarship however is inclined to be kinder to Macpherson and to consider that he really did find a substantial amount of Gaelic poetry, even if he did combine much of it together and rewrite it in his own style. 'Ossian' is the Irish Oisin, son of Finn, a legendary 3rd century hero.—*Ed.*

[16] Published Paris, 1858.—*Ed.*

mountain-dwellers of Scotland, who were called Gaels.
Like the Germans, they had no temples, no religious
ceremonies. God seemed to them too high and too far away
to bother with man or to listen to his prayers. But the
regions of the air were to them the infinite reaches of
immortality, the kingdom of heroic souls. When this life
was ended those who had shown courage and virtue were
admitted to palaces in the air which were more or less
wonderful according to the merit of the spirits who came to
receive their reward. The wicked and cowardly were condemned to wander for eternity on the winds and in the
tempests. Neither angels nor spirits appeared in this
fantastic world, but the souls dwelt in permanent and
affectionate relationship with the inhabitants of earth; they
were interested in all events, happy or sorrowful, and there
is perhaps no other country where the belief in ghosts has
exercised such a vast influence. The Gaels of the Middle
Ages, wandering on wild heath and barren rocks, were often
obliged to sleep surrounded by howling winds and the roar
of torrents. Troubled by the warring elements they
imagined they could hear voices of the dead. They claimed
to be able to recognize the difference between evil and good
spirits. The latter were active during the day, in green and
solitary valleys; the former only showed themselves at night,
in gloomy places and in stormy weather. Ghosts also were
easily recognised; death did not alter the beauty of the
women and their presence inspired no feeling of terror. The
men still retained the appearance of vigorous manhood and
seemed to be covered by diaphanous armour, light as the
ghost itself. Each mountain-dweller had a tutelary spirit
which followed him from the day of his birth. When his end
was drawing near the protecting spirit, borrowing his shape
and his voice, appeared in the place where he was to die and
at intervals uttered plaintive cries. If it was a nobleman, a
chieftain, a renowned hero, the souls of the Bards came and
wailed for three nights over the dwelling that death was to
visit.

The Highlanders of Scotland still believe that a ghost is heard crying at the place where a murder is about to be committed[17]. The ghost arrives, mounted on a falling star, and goes three times round the place where the blow will be struck, then departs in the direction that will be taken by the funeral procession and disappears at the very spot where the dead person will be buried. Old legends attribute the greater part of natural phenomena to spirits. If an echo was heard among rocks, it was the spirit of the mountain repeating what it had heard. If the wind causes a few vague harmonies to be heard—today we still call this sound an aeolian harp—it was the voice of the ghosts predicting the death of a chieftain. If some unfortunate man died of grief, it was because the ghosts of his ancestors had come to seek him and carry off his soul.

This belief in spirits, linked with extremely materialistic customs, gave an opening to Christianity; but the latter necessarily became barbaric to accommodate itself to the imaginations it wished to conquer. So it borrowed from ancient Greek myths, from descriptions by Virgil and Ovid, the outline of a Hell. The fable of the Titans gave it the fallen angels who were changed into monstrous demons to become the eternal ministers of God's vengeance. As for the idea of a temporal Purgatory, it was taken from the accounts of the mysterious journeys made by the ancient Initiates into the kingdom of the dead. With young and violent peoples, the element of the marvellous was the only means of prediction which could command an attentive audience; nevertheless this resulted only in superstition. Disfiguring the religion of mercy, pity and love which Christ had brought to the earth, the priests and monks of the Middle Ages abolished from the Lord's Prayer that touching and

[17] This is popularly known as a banshee, although this word *beansidhe* is strictly speaking a fairy woman, corresponding to the *sidhe* or male fairy, the traditions about these beings seeming now to be more plentiful in Eire than Scotland. See Lewis Spence *The Fairy Tradition in Britain* and other works.—*Ed.*

sublime phrase: 'Our Father which art in Heaven.' Representing the Creator as the destroyer of his own works, they were preparing for the horrors of the Inquisition, the massacres and the fanaticism, the scourge of the religious wars which were unknown to antiquity and the lack of religious faith evident in the fixed habit of so many great minds today.

VII

From the mountains of Scotland we come to the hills of Ireland, the Emerald Isle, where, under the name of St. Patrick's Purgatory, originated what we may call demoniacal theology.

St Patrick, commonly called the Apostle of Ireland, died in the fifth century A.D. leaving behind him a reputation for great virtue and miraculous powers. The marvellous legend of his Purgatory does not appear to have been written before the twelfth century and I shall give its principle outlines here because it contains many of the popular beliefs of olden times concerning the torments which an ignorant and brutal clergy attributed to God's invention for the punishment of evil-doers. St. Patrick, so the hagiographers tell us, finding it impossible to convince the newly-converted Christians of the terrible reality of eternal torment, had prayed to the Lord to provide a miraculous manifestation which would triumph over the incredulity of his flock. God appeared to him one morning, according to the Abbé Migne's *Encyclopédie Théologique,* and led him to a small island situated on Lough Derg formed by the river about six miles from Donegal. On this island He showed him the entrance to a cave and said: 'Whoever confesses his past sins and will enter this place with good heart and firm faith, will see here the punishments which are to be the lot of the wicked and the rewards which will be given to the righteous after this life, and will come out having gained complete remission of all his sins. But whoever enters merely to satisfy his curiosity will be condemned to stay there until the Day of Judgment.' On the next day St. Patrick called together all the people of the district to tell them of this miracle, which soon began to be talked of far and wide. There were, it is said, some pious people who attempted the proposed pilgrimage and who came back with tales from the other world. There were also imprudent and inquisitive people who never came back, so the legend says, and this is what the rough faith of the Irish peasantry believed for a long time without question. Later the Inquisition examined this belief and affixed to it the seal of its approbation.

A monastery of Augustinians was established in the twelfth century near St. Patrick's Cave. The prior examined all postulants, for not everyone was allowed to attempt the test of this living Purgatory. No one gained entrance to the monastery without bringing letters of recommendation from his bishop.

First the monks put every possible obstacle in the postulant's path and tried to dissuade him by frightful warnings from his project. If he were courageous enough to persist in it, he was shut up for seven days in a narrow cell, where he undertook a rigorous fast. On the eighth day, towards evening, he was led into another cell built in the form of a vertical coffin, in which he passed the night without being able to move hand or foot, alone with his thoughts. If not overcome by physical exhaustion, he was by this time ripe for hallucination, and everything was ready on the ninth day for his solemn, public introduction into the sanctuary of God's judgment.

From early morning all the priests of the neighbourhood and a great crowd of curious sightseers had filled the convent church. The pilgrim received the sacrament after which the prayers for the dead were said for him; then he was led in solemn procession to the mouth of the cave, closed by a door to which the prior held the key. This door, so low that it could only be entered on hands and knees, was constructed in a rock which was concealed on three sides by a high-walled enclosure. After having given the pilgrim his final blessing, the prior led him into the cave, locked the door again carefully, and the procession went back to the church chanting penitential psalms. The monks and priests spent the next twenty-four hours in prayer, and then the procession returned in the same order to the cave, followed, as on the previous day, by a large crowd.

The prior opened the door and if the pilgrim appeared —which did not always happen—he was found to be in a state bordering on madness. He was carried off in triumph as if he were a saint come back to life, and was given every attention to bring him back to normality. The account of the visions he had seen was listened to as if it were some divine lesson and became a legend, of which copies, hawked through the whole Christian world by itinerant monks, brought in great sums of money for the monastery. If no one appeared when the door was opened, there was great consternation among the sightseers; the prior took the event as a text for a sermon on the impenetrable wonders of divine wisdom and the religious awe which surrounded the mysteries of the sacred island did not allow anyone to make indiscreet inquiries. Prayers were said for the dead man and that was all.

There still exist several old accounts of journeys made to St. Patrick's Purgatory. The most notable is that of an adventurer named Louis Ennius, a native of Ireland who had emigrated to Toulouse and from there had ridden on horseback through the world, doing everything and anything except good. Having squandered all he possessed and finding himself sought after by the law for many very dubious exploits, he had finally felt the need to imitate the devil who, according to the popular saying, turns monk in his old age. Converted in a Catholic church by a chance meeting with an eloquent preacher, he was thinking of ending his days in some lonely hermitage, when he heard of St. Patrick's Purgatory and of the wonderful blessedness promised to successful pilgrims on this sacred journey. The narrator took pains not to minimise the perils; but Louis Ennius had been a mercenary and a swordsman, and the profession of criminal rapacity had endowed him with no mean courage. Our adventurer resolved, partly through devotion, partly through temperament, to add to the experiences of an exciting life this dangerous excursion into the supernatural world. It was moreover a way to rehabilitate himself in the eyes of his countrymen and to expiate, according to the ideas of the time, his past crimes and follies. Let him speak for himself[18] :

"When the cave door was locked behind me, I found myself at first in total darkness, through which I groped my way with outstretched hands, guiding myself by feeling the rocky walls. I advanced in this way for about half an hour, fearing more than any enemy some sudden pit in which those of my predecessors who had never re-appeared must have been dashed to their death. After several hundred steps in a sort of labyrinth, the ground suddenly seemed to give way beneath my feet. This sensation gave me a sort of vertigo; stumbling like a drunken man, I was finally obliged to sit down, and, my eyes not seeing the faintest glimmer of light, I decided that it was useless to move from that position, and that I only had to wait, for better or for worse, until the twenty-four hours were up. I was worried nevertheless by a strange idea. I wondered whether the St. Patrick's Purgatory were not a mere fable of which I had been made the victim, and whether, guilty as I was of many an ill deed against the Church, its ministers had not drawn me into this trap intending to keep me there for the rest of my days; unless I was meant to perish through sheer exhaustion? This sinister feeling gave me a cold sweat accompanied by a con-

---

[18] Patrick's Purgatory was an immense source of profit to the Lough Derg monks in the later middle ages. It may be surmised that they saw to it that visitors did not leave without satisfyingly horrifying experiences. It will be noted that much of the following phenomena could be produced by mundane arts and the general *mise-en-scène* appears to owe much to Dante's *Inferno* or its immediate conceptual forerunners.—*Ed.*

traction of the heart rather like sea-sickness. I fell into a kind of swoon which lasted I know not how long and from which I was roused by a terrible clap of thunder. The commotion was so violent that part of the cave fell down on my head. When I had recovered a little from this happening, I found myself at the entrance to a ruined cloister, whose broken arcades rose up like stony phantoms in a reddish light similar to that cast by the flames of a distant conflagration. The air I breathed seemed to smell faintly of sulphur.

'I got up out of the rubble where I was sitting and advanced a few steps, trying to get my bearings, when I saw coming towards me out of this ruined cloister twelve old men dressed in white robes with a cross embroidered on the front. This group of venerable men stood in a circle around me, and one who seemed to be their leader addressed me in the following manner: "Thanks be to God who has given thee the courage to enter this dreadful place where thou shalt expiate the sins of thy lifetime! Gather all thy courage up for the tests which are to come, for scarce shall we have left thee alone when the demons, instruments of divine justice, will begin to assail thee from all sides. But if thou trustest in thy faith their efforts shall not harm thee. Each time thou feelest thy heart fail within thee, pronounce the almighty name of thy saviour Jesus: He will give thee back thy strength and will bring thee forth victorious."

'After this speech, the twelve old men embraced and blessed me, then vanished like ghosts. Left alone, I recommended my soul to God according to the counsels they had given me, and I went and sat down in a corner formed by two arcades, so that I might see everything that went on in the cloister and not be attacked from behind.

'Hardly had I taken up this position than frightful howls were heard, and from all sides terrible monsters rose up out of the earth; they seemed to be under the command of a black man whose head and feet were those of a goat, beating his enormous bat's wings exactly as one sees Satan depicted by painters. These hellish monsters leapt all round me as if they wished to throw themselves upon me and devour me. But Satan, for I suppose that it was he himself, stopped their caperings by hitting them with a flaming rod. "Salute our friend Ennius," he told them, leaping from one to the other, "and let us congratulate him on having come to visit us while he was still alive. He has done some fine things on earth, wishing no doubt to obtain a place of honour among the damned. But his hour is not yet come; he must return to earth and recruit fresh souls for us. I shall receive his adoring homage as his sovereign lord and I shall send him away blessed with every gift I can give him, so that he may end his days happily in every possible variation of vice and crime."

'As I remained rooted to the spot, motionless and speechless but inwardly shaking with terror, the prince of the demons became angry: "Master Ennius," he cried, "has forgotten his manners: give him a lesson in good breeding!" At these words, striking the earth with his wand of fire, Satan caused a large circular brazier to appear in the centre of the cloister. Four demons, armed with long hooks, seized my clothes and, having first knocked me down and tied my hands and feet, raised me up above this brazier. But just as they were about to throw me in, I shouted Jesus, and the spell was broken.

'Then I felt myself carried as if by a great wind across freezing clouds of fog into an immense and gloomy plain, black as a burnt-out forest. It seemed to me as if I were flying at some considerable height over this desolate plain, and thus I was able to contemplate the most terrible of scenes. A host of men and women of every condition peopled this plain. All these wretches were being submitted to all kinds of torture, the form varying according to the crimes they had committed during their lifetimes. Some were chained face-downwards to the earth, their bodies studded with huge red-hot iron nails which demons were driving in with hammers. Others were being eaten away by lizards or serpents. Some were surrounded by groups of demons who chopped off pieces of their victims' flesh with flaming swords; some were writhing in rivers of boiling oil and melted lead. Others were plunged into great baths of icy snow, and when they tried to get out, they were thrust back by demons with long sharp skewers. In the centre of the plain was an immense wheel to which the wretched sinners were tied by their feet, their heads hanging down over a pool of blazing sulphur; and when the demons turned this wheel, which was furnished with sharp spikes and razor-like knives, the unfortunate prisoners felt their skin being torn to shreds. And all these horrible wounds were healed at once, so that they might be constantly re-inflicted. A little further on, I saw a very high building, over which hung thick and evil-smelling vapours; I felt myself borne upwards to look inside, and I saw, in the middle of the building, a vast reservoir filled with boiling filth, in which millions of tortured men and women were struggling, and whenever they tried to escape, the demons standing all around shot blazing arrows at them. Further on I saw a great pit like the mouth of a volcano; the damned were hurled up on fountains of flaming lava to a great height, from which they would drop like stones, only to be constantly thrown up again. The demons, who were rushing about in every direction, kept bumping into me and trying to drag me away with the rest of the damned; but heedful of the warning I had received I countered each attack with the sacred name of Jesus, and they were obliged to fly away uttering shrieks of anger.

'I noticed that on the plain of torment there was a region where could be heard none of the blasphemies uttered by the damned. The torments were the same, but the groans and shrieks of pain were broken at times by moments of quiet, in which the chanting of penitential psalms could be heard giving comfort to the souls of the damned. I realised that this was Purgatory; but in this region, where pardon is not impossible, it seemed to me that the demons were even more savage: the thought of seeing purified souls escaping from their hands made them endlessly inventive and they seemed always to be thinking up fresh tortures. As I was meditating on this spectacle Satan came and dragged me to a wide river of boiling mud which was crossed by a bridge so narrow that it seemed impossible to reach the other side without falling into the river, which was swarming with open-jawed monsters. I saw a long procession of souls passing over this bridge, and most of them were seized by the monsters of the river. Satan wanted me to pass over also, and as a legion of demons had cut off my retreat, I felt myself this time to be in great danger; but the blessed name of Jesus carried me over to the other side of the bridge, as if I had been borne up by some elastic and invisible force. The infernal spirits could follow me no further.

'As soon as I reached the other bank the landscape miraculously changed. I found myself at the entrance to a beautiful valley all brilliantly carpeted by marvellous flowers, with here and there delightful shady nooks. After a pause in which I recovered a little from the horrors I had lived through, I made my way along a path bordered with rose bushes which, after having meandered beneath overhanging boughs peopled with singing birds, led me to a vast clearing in the middle of which stood a palace made entirely of shining gold. As I approached it the door opened, and a long procession of men, women and children in white robes passed before me chanting hymns of joy. After them came kings, bishops and popes, each bearing the insignia of his temporal state. The procession described a large circle, over which hovered immense choirs of angels bearing harps of gold and filling the air with celestial harmonies. As they passed by me one of the bishops, whose name, Patrick, was engraved on a golden triangle hung about his neck, took my hand and made me join the procession. "My son," he said to me as we marched along, "I am well pleased with the courage and perseverance thou hast shown on this pilgrimage. By now thou wilt have understood the mysteries of divine justice which are taught on earth by the ministers of God. Thou hast beheld the punishments inflicted on sinful men; thou beholdest now the happiness and blissful peace that all our saints enjoy. When thou returnest to the living, thou shalt give witness of all these things, that men of good will may find profit in what thou hast seen. Those who shall believe thee shall do penitence for their sins in order that God in his clemency may spare them the sufferings of Purgatory. Those who believe thee not shall suffer the consequences of their unbelief; but let thyself beware and imitate them not in their dangerous ways, for the sufferings thou hast seen are not empty enchantments."

'At this moment we were approaching the door of the house of gold, which the greater part of the procession had already entered after having described the great circle I mentioned. St. Patrick made me kneel down to receive the benediction from the bishops and popes who came at the end of the procession. When the last had passed before us he raised me up and, embracing me with a father's tenderness, he added: "This celestial house, inhabited by the grace of God, may receive no earthly visitant. Learn to become worthy of entering it one day, and I shall come myself to receive thy soul and escort it hither. So depart in peace, my son, and follow the path by which thou didst come. Thou shalt witness the same scenes, but as thou hast been sanctified by the vision of paradise the demons will no longer have the power to insult and threaten thee. They will fly away at thine approach and thou shalt reach the opening to the cave without further trials. Go then, and do not stop anywhere on thy way back, for fear thou dost overstep the time at which the holy men await thee: for if they opened the door without seeing thee they would believe thee lost for ever. They would return, overcome with regret, to their monastery; there would be nothing left for you to do but to die of starvation in the darkness of the cave and then, as thou art far from having merited the entire remission of thy sins, the demons of Purgatory would seize thy soul and I should be powerless to help thee."

'I sadly obeyed the bishop's order. It seemed very hard to me to have to return to the earth after having seen the abode of the blessed so near. Nevertheless I went away with strengthened faith and the hope that sooner or later under the auspices of divine mercy I might be able to return once more. I went back over the mysterious bridge and the infernal plain, joyfully aware that the demons were flying away from me as I approached, as good St. Patrick had told me they would. I reached the ruined cloister and found the twelve old men still there, who congratulated me on the successful outcome of my journey, then entered the gloomy vault which led to the threshold of the cave. I dragged myself with difficulty over the ruins, crawling on hands and feet as before. While I was struggling along, a fresh clap of thunder burst overhead, and the cave was again so violently shaken that I was breathless with terror. I fell down in a swoon, and when I had regained possession of my faculties I found myself in the enclosure which lies outside the cave, surrounded by the priests who had found me stretched fainting beside the doorway and who gave me the greatest care and consideration.'

Such, very much curtailed, is the revelation of Louis Ennius; I have cut out interminable repetitions and mystical self-communings and will only add that the adventurous pilgrim's spirit was so overwhelmed by what he had seen that he would not leave the Augustinian monastery, where he died a few years later in saintly seclusion.

What are we to make of this legend? It would be blasphemy to believe in the reality of the infernal scenes which Ennius had claimed to see. It is reasonable to suppose that, before allowing him to enter the sacred cave, the monks had given him some drug which had the virtue of producing a long and vivid hallucination which seized his brain a few moments after the door was shut behind him. Weakened by fasting for nine days and influenced by the mournful thoughts which the monks had instilled in him, he was naturally predisposed to seeing in his dreams a chaotic succession of demoniacal scenes, the account of which, when published and attested as true, and obviously embellished by those who heard it, must have had a dramatic effect on the ignorant imaginations which received it when backed up by endless fanatical discourses from priests and preachers. It was out of similar stories that the selling of indulgences arose and became a wholesale and retail business, seizing the poor man's mite and the rich man's fortune and filling the money bags of the greedy adventurers who travelled the whole known world selling heaven to the credulous.

VIII

CHRISTIANITY, it must be said, is not responsible for these aberrations. The primitive Church was content to practise virtue as a sacred duty in the hope of emulating the works of the saints. Its immortality lies in those hearts which lift themselves up to God by simple and hidden ways. It is undemonstrative, but does good by stealth and has no need of terrifying legends or revolting untruths to prop up its faith. It must nevertheless be recognised that clerical literature has had better sources of inspiration. The marvellous as an instrument of vengeance is blasphemy towards God; but the marvellous, used as an instrument of mercy, resembles the tales of the good fairies and their deeds in that they may not much elevate the mind but do at least respect the innocence of the heart.

Such is the tale of the Rhenish Count Berthold.

In a manor-house perched like an eagle's nest on the ridge of a moutain, separated by deep ravines from the abbey Nôtre Dame des Eremites, a gathering of sportsmen of noble birth seated at the table of the lord of the manor drank deeply of Rhenish wine in large German goblets.

Night fell in mist and storm. Vivid flashes of lightning were seen through the leaded windows of the festal hall; the wind roared and rumblings of thunder announced a convulsion of nature.

The host, a pious man, fell silent; he felt that the majesty of the Almighty was to be heard in this great voice of the tormented elements. But his convivial guests became more riotous and to each threat of the tempest they opposed the clink of their foaming goblets.

Suddenly the door opened. The servants led in a poor traveller, under vow to make the pilgrimage to Nôtre Dame des Eremites barefoot in order to obtain from Heaven, in that place consecrated by numerous miracles, the healing of his son, stricken by a mortal malady.

In the midst of the vices of existence in feudal days one virtue from an older age balanced the violence of manners, namely hospitality, charitable and discreet. The host rose and conducted his new guest to the corner of the vast hearth where oaken logs burned; then, filling with his own hand the goblet of the newcomer, he presented it to him. When the pilgrim was comforted by the warmth and the wine, his place was ready at the lower end of the table and the servants placed before him what a touching custom called 'God's portion', that is to say, the portion reserved for the poor traveller. This duty fulfilled, the huntsmen paid no more attention to the unknown visitor and fell again to drinking and to noisy discussions, the impiety of which knew no limits. The host vainly begged them to be more moderate so as not to provoke the divine anger and the lightning flash. They laughed at his reproaches and looked sideways at the devout stranger to see what impression their daring blasphemies were making. But the stranger was silent and his face as unmoved as marble.

However, the storm died away, the skies calmed and between the clouds the moon shone like a pale ship. 'Let us go!' cried the convivial guests.

'Stay,' said the host. 'This is the hour when the spirits of night traverse the world to sow harm; and after having offended God all the evening by the intemperance of your tongues you will be liable to some unfortunate encounter in the mountain. Wait under my roof until dawn.'

'Stay indeed!' cried Berthold, a Rhenish count, the wildest of the fools who would have risked their souls for a jest. 'Wait till dawn for fear of mountain spirits? that is the attitude of a serf! Even if the Devil crossed my path in person I should no more fall back before him than before God!'

'Are you so sure, sir knight?' murmured the pilgrim, crossing himself as though to keep away the malediction provoked by the blasphemy.

'I will answer for it with my head,' cried Berthold. 'On a question of courage my friends here can tell if I boast. And as a proof, most saintly man of God,' he added, draining a last cup, 'I drink to the health of Satan. I offer him a thousand thanks if he will be so gallant as to escort me this night.'

'Alas, valiant lord,' replied the pilgrim, 'I shall pray for you through the night. You will need such ministration.'

'Many thanks! but you would be better employed sleeping,' replied the Rhenish Count. 'I trust more in my good dagger than in the paternosters of a whole monastery.' And some minutes later they heard him pass the drawbridge of the manor on his great charger.

The hour was late, the silence profound, the solitude absolute. The full moon appeared from time to time from behind heavy clouds which rolled to the horizon, then darkness came again. Berthold, preoccupied in sustaining the hesitating step of his mount in the crumbling paths, thought no more of the pilgrim's warning. Each time the horse stumbled a heavy oath escaped his lips.

The direction he took descended suddenly between walls of rocks, into a tortuous gorge over which old bare trees crossed their dried branches like the bones of the dead.

No one is nearer to superstition than a braggart. Count Berthold suddenly shivered at finding himself alone, this man of iron who met lances on the battlefield without fear. But in battle the enemy is seen; here the shades were filled with invisible touches—the enemy was hidden in the traveller's conscience. Berthold sought to reassure himself; he was ashamed of his fears. 'Certainly the Devil must be laughing,' he cried, 'if there be a Devil, and if he saw my face, he would use me as a lantern!'

At once a green light appeared out of the double rock-wall as if through crystal; two monstrous hands appeared before the head of his horse. Cold sweat beaded itself on Berthold's forehead, but his heart did not fail.

'*Bergmaennlein* [mountain spirits],' he cried, drawing his long sword. 'Miserable mountain hands! Go away, rubbish from hell! go and frighten the cowherds on the Alps!' And riding his horse at full speed, he forced the passage as if he were going through a fog.

The hands dissolved into mist. But suddenly behind the Rhenish Count was heard the frenzied galloping of two horses. He turned his head and saw two knights completely armed who hastened towards him.

Their armour was black, black were their coursers. In the hollow of their lowered visors their eyes shone like carbuncles; hung by a chain from the right arm of each was an iron club with sharp points and will-o'-the-wisps flamed like plumes from their helmets.

They came up with Berthold at lightning speed. At each side of his horse they seized the reins and, without saying a word, they drew him in their furious course from ravine to ravine and from mountain to mountain.

Sparks flew from hooves; hardly was a vista seen than it was passed. Berthold did not know that by magic his phantom guides were drawing him towards unknown heights.

Thus they reached the region of eternal snows; and then their ride began again with new fury towards an enormous trench where a torrent of melted snow cascaded down. From the abyss raucous voices howled: 'Give us the blasphemer!'

'Here he is, we have him!' replied the black knights.

Then Berthold's hair stood on end; his heart, so strong heretofore, was conquered. He understood that he had fallen into the power of nocturnal prowlers from that hell he had so often defied. No human succour could save him, and to whom in heaven could he turn, he who had laughed at everything?

And the voices from the abyss continued to rise, the black knights made the same reply, the three horses on the edge of the pit still reared. Another step and all would be finished.

'My God!' cried Berthold, 'I am lost!'

It was perhaps the first time in his life that this feudal unbeliever had raised his soul to God in a prayer. It was but a cry of terror; yet it was counted to him as an act of faith.

At this Name the black knights halted and reeled. The threatening clouds opened and a blue light in which thousands of golden stars stood out spread to the confines of space, revealing to Berthold the gulf. At the same time a mysterious bell sent silvery notes into the air. Berthold looked beyond the precipice and saw in the distance the white statue of the Virgin which surmounted the church of Nôtre Dame des Eremites. Around him the echoes of the solitary place repeated the infernal clamours which died away little by little amongst the mountain crags. At his feet he saw the two black knights on their horses now changed into two monstrous hippogriffs crawling towards

the abyss from which came sulphurous lights; then all disappeared and he found himself alone, in the shadows, on
the icy plateau.

But in the distance the statue of the Virgin remained
mysteriously illuminated and from it came a beam of light
tracing with celestial clarity a line from one rock to another,
from monastery to the summit whither the powers of darkness had carried the Rhenish Count. The descent bristled
with dangers, but the miracle which still shone from the
summit of the abbey drew Berthold gently on.

He made a vow to consecrate himself to the Virgin
if she accomplished his deliverance and then, without cal-
culating risks which would have halted prudence, he let
himself slide from rock to rock, holding on with feet or
hands as it pleased Providence to guide his instinct, but
never losing from view the sacred light which served him
as a fixed star.

Daybreak found him on the threshold of the monastery.
He told the monks his strange adventure; they in their turn
told him how they had heard the church bell sound during
the night, although no hand had touched it. All marvelled
at the goodness of God and Berthold, faithful to his vow,
never again desired to return to the world.

I know another story still more simple and touching
about a French knight who, after having fought for long
in the Crusades against the Saracens returned disabled to
finish his days in his own country. On his estate he found
that the people he had loved were no more; God had taken
all from him, as from Job. The poor knight repressed every
complaint from his wounded heart; no one saw him shed a
tear, for great sorrows are mute and incommunicable. Life
in the world no longer meant anything to him, but he felt
that God remained. After giving all his wealth to the poor
he renounced his heavy armour at the gate of a cloister.
At that time rank and learning seldom walked in company; the sons of heroes, like their fathers, hardly knew how

to write their names. Therefore the good monks wished to instruct their new brother so that he could sit in his choir-stall and sing with them in the sacred tongue the psalms of the penitent life. So first he had to be taught to read. An old monk charged himself with this duty, but after a year's effort he only arrived at teaching his pupil how to put together the two first words of the *Ave Maria*. After having repeated them several times, the good knight would wrap himself in silent meditation from which nothing could rouse him for hours.

He died shortly after making his vows and was buried, according to custom, in the garden within the cloisters. The very next day, a lily of surpassing whiteness opened out over his grave. On each flower of this Virgin's plant could be read in letters scintillating like flames the two words *Ave Maria* which were all the warrior's learning. The monks, contemplating this marvel, repented that they had sometimes criticised his ignorance. 'Truly he was a saint,' they said to one another. 'He has been in the midst of us like a perfume from heaven and we did not know it.'

Then the prior of the monastery caused the grave to be opened with care, so that he might look once more on the face of the elect who had returned to God. With wonder they saw that the root of the lily came from the mouth of the knight who had so many times repeated the angel's salutation.

The Virgin Mary was the fairy queen of the Catholic Middle Ages. The incomprehensible mystery of her virginal motherhood formed the second page of the legend about the earthly paradise that starts with the Mosaic account. A spirit of darkness, Lucifer or Satan, had risen from Hell to send us into exile in this vale of tears; an angel of light, Gabriel, descended from the heavens bringing the news of God's gracious pardon. The infernal spirit had spoken to Eve, who ceased to be pure; the celestial spirit speaks to Mary, who remains virgin. The tyranny of the devil over mankind had begun with Eve and found its consummation in Adam; our deliverance began with Mary and was consummated in Jesus.

A new angel therefore, a new Eve and a new Adam became the poetic figures of the new cult. There was also a new Tree, the cross, whose fruit, the food of immortality, was to cure the evil caused by the forbidden fruit. 'Behold,' says St. Thomas Aquinas, the great mystical Doctor, 'behold Mary elevated to a kind of dignity whose quality is infinite; and in that divine act which raises a humble daughter of Adam above all creation we may glimpse the farthest bounds of the mystery of all-powerful God. Mary has become a golden bridge uniting divine grandeur and man's nothingness: she is the bridge needed to cross the abyss between the Word and humanity. Pity and justice have been joined in an endless kiss of peace; the throne of their alliance was in Mary's breast; and from that Virgin's heart immortal harmony ascended from Earth to Heaven and found its resting place in God, its eternal principle.'

Such were the beautiful dreams that were born in the silence of the cloisters. Are they not like the preface to some Paradise Regained? Unfortunately, after eighteen centuries of evangelism history still refuses to accord the final seal of fact to these supernatural aspirations.[19]

Voltaire wrote on 8 March 1754 to the Duchess of Saxe-Gotha: 'History is nothing more nor less than a vast panorama of weaknesses, faults, crimes, misfortunes, among which we may find a few virtues and a few successes, as one might come upon a fertile valley in a long chain of rocks and precipices.'

---

[19] This supernatural fact was nevertheless officially decreed as a dogma obligatory upon all Catholics of the Roman obedience by the bull *Munificissimus Deus* of Pope Pius XII 1950. The Assumption of the Blessed Virgin Mary had already been in effect taught as a fact rather than a pious opinion for several centuries, this being mainly promoted by the Jesuit order. Any collection of XVIIth and XVIIIth century religious pictures will illustrate the general nature of the belief; the subject is a favourite one.—*Ed.*

A century has passed since those lines were written, and they are still true. They are the words of a fatalist, and in spite of the alleged progress of enlightenment, the reply has still not been found.

.

IX

MAGIC after the fall of the Roman Empire lost all public support. Driven from a barbarian world in arms, history, philosophy, the sciences and the arts took refuge in a few monasteries which providence seemed to have preserved as arks of the future in the general flood of disaster and destruction. Priests are the first and last savants of societies which are just beginning and civilisations which are about to die. It is to the Christian clergy that we are indebted for having exhumed the scientific and literary relics of antiquity, and the few books which have handed down to us the almost incomprehensible traditions of the past. In the reign of Charlemagne [conquers Lombardy and Rome 774: coronation as emperor by the Pope 800: d. 814] there was an attempt to revive the powers of the human spirit. An English monk, Alcuin, brought over and protected by this prince who was far in advance of his times, had been able to set up schools of theology, history, astronomy, grammar, medicine and law. While the great soldier was rebuilding the Roman Empire, the great monk was trying to rebuild a Christian Athens. Both deserved to succeed, both made these tasks their life-work. However, Charlemagne's work was to end with his death, and Alcuin's was unable to flourish among the new ruins which were to surround his end[20]. . .

About the beginning of the year 1000 a terrible famine struck the whole of Europe. Then pestilence added fresh

[20] A brief and unsatisfactory historical account of the medieval period here follows. Textbooks on it are now easily available, such as the brief H. W. C. Davis' *Medieval Europe* [Home University Library] or the full-scale *Cambridge Medieval History*.—Ed.

horrors. It almost seemed as if some avenging angel was riding over the earth on the white horse of the Apocalypse and that his fiery legions were casting their burning brands over a third of the human race. The earth, which had drunk in the blood of invasions and murders, seemed sated . . .

The chronicles of the latter tenth and early eleventh centuries are filled with strange tales of the complete overthrow of both the natural and moral orders of life. Wise men could find no explanation for them. According to ancient traditions, the heavens were an illuminated book in which were depicted in letters of fire the symbols of earthly fate. The appearance of a comet was considered dangerous to all regions lighted by its nocturnal rays; it foretold the downfall of princes, bloody battles, epidemics, famines, floods and disastrous conflagrations. Now in the year 1000 an immense comet had been in the heavens for three months, coming from the west; it burned so brilliantly, says the monk Glaber, that it extinguished the light of all the other stars; then it would disappear at cockcrow, to return the following night. At several points a rain of large stones had fallen so heavily that they had formed great piles in the fields. At other places the stones marking the boundaries of fields had been hauled out of the ground by an unknown power and found again far from their original position. A colossal crucifix placed in the church of the Abbey of Pucelles had wept tears of blood. What was even more extraordinary, a wolf which had found its way into the cathedral at Orleans had seized the bell-rope in its paws and teeth, as if to sound an alarm, and a few days later a terrible disturbance had devastated the city.

Nearly the whole of Europe was at this time witnessing similar curious happenings. Here and there were earthquakes, again, volcanic eruptions; in other places dreadful conflagrations whose origins were unknown. Rome was practically reduced to ashes and Naples was almost wiped out by a sea of molten fire from Vesuvius.

When the violence of these natural disturbances had abated, there remained a formidable witness in the Devil himself, enthroned in history by a reign of universal terror. Christianity was obliged to follow in the wake of the human spirit in this divagation, if only to prevent Satan from replacing God completely. The survival of the world after the mysterious fatalities of the year 1000 had so violently shaken the people's religious sense that they were now quite prepared to share their altars between the god of Evil and the god of Righteousness.[21] The Church sought to compromise too with this popular movement; inside, temples were consecrated to God: outside, they were covered by a profusion of monstrous figures which we can still see on the walls of old basilicas. The medieval priest knew very well the advantages to be gained from the work of popular sculptors. He accepted, as a powerful auxiliary influence over ignorant minds, the fantastic army of painted and carved monsters which laid siege to sacred places. He took care to include among them angels and saints, and from this barbarian mythology were born legends and witchcraft.

X

THE great period of the Crusades, which filled the whole of the twelfth century, brought to Europe the narrative genius of the oriental races which told, far more attractively than was the manner of the rather monotonous mysticism of Christian legends, of the marvellous deeds and adventures of chivalry, all mixed up with fairies, giants and miracles. Among these innumerable tales, one of the most

[21] The more usual interpretation of the wave of Gothic building in the XIth century which forms the fine flower of medieval craftsmanship is that it began at any rate as a spontaneous thankoffering by the people to God for having spared the world from its threatened destruction. Passages from the Apocalypse and elsewhere had been generally interpreted to mean that the world was to end in the year 1000 and the Last Judgment and the general resurrection were to follow.—Ed.

popular is the story of the enchanter Merlin and the beautiful fairy Vivien.[22]

There are various versions of Merlin's death. Some legends say he died of extreme old age, for magicians are no more immortal than other men; some pretend that he was carried off by the Devil. But in Brittany, popular belief has it that he is still alive, that he is still living beside the beautiful Vivien and that he has the appearance of a handsome young man, thanks to the elixir of life whose secret he alone possesses. It is also claimed that the forest of Brocéliande still exists in Finistère; but it is only visible to those who believe in Magic.

The art of restoring lost youth has been the object of long researches by hosts of dreamers, before and after Merlin. The ancients had their fountain of youth; the Middle Ages had its elixir of gold. At the beginning of the XIVth century Arnaud de Villeneuve, doctor to Pope Clement V, invented the following recipe, which should be used, he advised, every seven years.

'On the first day of the operation,' says Master Arnaud, 'a plaster made of one ounce of saffron, half an ounce of red roses, two of sandalwood [which is also red], a measure of aloe wood[23] and a similar quantity of fine amber, should

[22] Here follows the well-known story of Merlin and Vivien—too easily available to us to be given place here. Christian illustrates, at considerable length but with his usual narrative art, the gradual enslavement of the wizard. Before he imparts to Vivien the fatal secret which gives her complete power over him, he is able to respond to an appeal for help from King Arthur, an appeal which is not borne by a visible messenger but by the spirits under Merlin's control. He leaves Broceliande to hasten to the King's aid; here the author gives a diverting account of the exploits of Gargantua, whose parents were created by the wizard's magic arts.
'That is a sample of Merlin's magical knowledge', comments Paul Christian, 'or rather', he adds, 'of the literary imagination of the XIIth century. It belongs to the grotesque: here is the sentimental.' He then recounts how Merlin, his work for the King successfully accomplished, returns in haste to Vivien who, at the price of the final secret, consents to marry him. When King Arthur appeals again for help, Merlin is unable to leave the forest.—*Ed.*

[23] Probably the resinous oil of aloes is intended. The biblical spices were mostly tree-gums—myrrh, cassia and cinnamon are all Jewish purification oils from India or Arabia.—*Ed.*

be placed on the heart during sleep. These elements should be ground into fine powder, mixed with half a pound of purified white wax and worked up with a sufficient quantity of oil of roses. On wakening, this plaster should be taken off and kept in a leaden box until it is time to use it again.

'Next, the patient must live for some time on fowls prepared in a certain way: for sanguine temperaments, sixteen days; for phlegmatics, twenty-five days; for melancholics or phlegmatic temperaments, thirty days. He must obtain as many fowls as are indicated by his natural appetite; they must be kept in a large, airy yard with clear water but no grass, or any other kind of food, because they must be given only the kind of food that I am about to describe.

'This is to be made of as many vipers as there are fowls. These reptiles must be whipped in a tub until their heads and tails fall off; then, having skinned them, they must be soaked in vinegar and rubbed with coarse salt shaken on to a piece of rough material. After having been cut into small pieces, they must be thrown into a large pot with half a pound of rosemary, fennel, calamint and spignel, all in equal quantities, to which is added half a pound of cummin. The pot should be two-thirds filled with pure water and must be brought gently to the boil until the vipers are completely cooked.

'Then a quantity of wheat, finely-sifted and sufficient to feed the fowls for the number of days indicated by the experimenter's temperament, must be slowly poured in. The wheat must be cooked until the essence of the reptiles has soaked into it; care must be taken to keep the pot covered, the better to preserve their quality, and the pot must be placed on a tripod so that it receives an equable and gentle heat until the mixture thickens. If need be, a little more water may be added, to prevent the mixture from burning. A preserve of citron, borage and rosemary and a pound of very fine-sifted sugar must finally be incorporated in the preparation, which must then be poured into a new, airtight jar. It must be taken every morning before breakfast and in the evenings before going to bed: quantity—half a spoonful. And the great efficacity of this rare restorative will,' says Arnaud de Villeneuve, 'soon make itself felt, for it can restore to youth the most decripit old age.'

XI

ANOTHER physician, Theophrastus Paracelsus,[24] revived in the XVIth century the ancient doctrine of *Talismans,* which he claimed to be able to use successfully in the treatment of illnesses and accidents. This medical doctrine, derived from the Qabala, or secret tradition of the Jewish rabbis, was said to be borrowed from the ancient occult sciences of Chaldea and Egypt. The talisman [*tsilmenaia*] signifies an image, a figure, and was engraved in the form of an emblem or symbol on metals consecrated to the genii of the seven planets. This magical task had to be carried out at a fixed time of a certain day, with the firm intention of attracting to the talisman the beneficent influence of the genius which was invoked, whether for health or any other protective measures. We owe to the celebrated Paracelsus the explanation of these secrets whose efficiency is recognised by many serious thinkers, in the same way as that of the Agnus Dei, so-called miraculous medals, and objects which have touched saintly relics. Now the genii of the Orient being the original types of the Christian angels, that is to say, representing the intermediary powers acting between God and man, it is possible that the invocation of one or the other may not be entirely pointless. Dogmas vary from one century to another and rites are modified; but belief in God, in the soul of the world and in the sovereign power of nature is always the same: it is to God, invisible to our eyes but visible to our consciousness, that we address our prayers, whatever the form they take. Talismans belong to the domain of faith and are amenable to free discussion:

[24] For more general treatment of Paracelsus, ref. Book V, p. 397, *et seq.* Paracelsus was born in 1493, near Zurich.—*Ed.*

I shall confine myself therefore to their description, and neither denigrate them nor plead their cause.[25]

I The *Talisman of Saturn* is a preservative against danger of death through apoplexy, cancer, decaying of the bones, consumption, dropsy, paralysis, phthisis; against the danger of being buried alive while in a state of coma; against the danger of violent death through secret plotting, poison or ambush.

This talisman preserves women from the mortal perils which accompany or sometimes follow childbirth.

If in time of war the leader of an army hides the talisman of Saturn in a place which is in danger of falling into the enemy's hands, that enemy will be unable to cross the limits set up by the presence of the talisman and will then retreat, either discouraged or overcome by a resolute counter-attack.

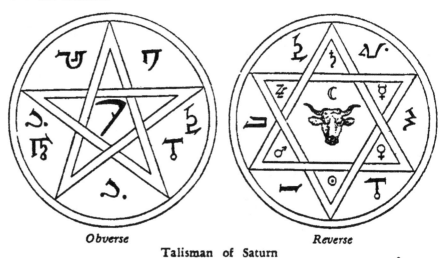

Obverse   *Reverse*

Talisman of Saturn

In order to make the talisman of Saturn, a plaque of very pure lead must be obtained, cut in the form of a circle about the size of an ordinary medal, and the two faces polished smoothly.

[25] The more usual of these talismans are described with illustrations in Book I, chapter XVIII of the *Clavicula Salmonis* as edited by S. Liddell May, 1889. —*Ed.*

On the first face is engraved with a diamond-pointed burin the image of a scythe, enclosed in a pentagram or a star with five points.

On the other side is engraved a bull's head enclosed in a six-pointed star, and surrounded by letters composing the name *Rempha*, the planetary genius of Saturn according to the alphabet of the Magi. [See Book II, p. 147.]

The person who is to wear this talisman must engrave it himself, without witnesses of the deed and without having communicated his intention to anyone.

He must choose for the commencement and termination of the task a Saturday, *Dies Saturni*, the day consecrated to Saturn, when the evolution of the Moon is passing through the first ten degrees of *Taurus* or *Capricorn*, in a favourable aspect with Saturn, according to the theory of the horoscope which is set out further on.[26]

To find out if there is a favourable aspect between the Moon and Saturn the interested person should cast his own horoscope on the nearest Saturday containing the lunar evolution just mentioned; and if Saturn is in a favourable aspect, that is, *trine* or *sextile* with the Moon, that day will be favourable for working on the talisman. If, on the contrary, Saturn and the Moon are found to be in *square* or in *opposition*, each following Saturday must be tried until a favourable aspect is met with.

It is the table of Epacts which gives us the beginning of each lunar evolution [see Book VI]. On the 1st day the Moon is in conjunction with the centre of the Ram; on the 2nd she passes through the first 15 degrees of Taurus, and on the 22nd day the first 10 degrees of Capricorn. If therefore the 2nd or 22nd day of the Moon correspond to a Sunday, and if Saturn is in a favourable aspect, one or other of these days is suitable for working on the talisman.

Having found a Saturday, it is still necessary to find

---

[26] This talismanic theory presupposes some knowledge of astrology and employs many of its terms. The needful explanations will be found in Books VI and VII.—*Ed.*

the hours which are governed by the genius of Saturn : these are indicated for the whole week in the following table, beginning at noon to one o'clock in the afternoon, the hours here given in the continental manner as 12.00—13.00, etc.

Day	SUN.	MON.	TUES.	WED.	THURS.	FRI.	SAT.
Governing Planet	SUN ☉	MOON ☽	MARS ♂	MERCURY ☿	JUPITER ♃	VENUS ♀	SATURN ♄
Hours							
12.00—13.00	☉	☽	♂	☿	♃	♀	♄
13.00—14.00	♀	♄	☉	☽	♂	☿	♃
14.00—15.00	☿	♃	♀	♄	☉	☽	♂
15.00—16.00	☽	♂	☿	♃	♀	♄	☉
16.00—17.00	♄	☉	☽	♂	☿	♃	♀
17.00—18.00	♃	♀	♄	☉	☽	♂	☿
18.00—19.00	♂	☿	♃	♀	♄	☉	☽
19.00—20.00	☉	☽	♂	☿	♃	♀	♄
20.00—21.00	♀	♄	☉	☽	♂	☿	♃
21.00—22.00	☿	♃	♀	♄	☉	☽	♂
22.00—23.00	☽	♂	☿	♃	♀	♄	☉
23.00—24.00	♄	☉	☽	♂	☿	♃	♀
24.00— 1.00	♃	♀	♄	☉	☽	♂	☿
1.00— 2.00	♂	☿	♃	♀	♄	☉	☽
2.00— 3.00	☉	☽	♂	☿	♃	♀	♄
3.00— 4.00	♀	♄	☉	☽	♂	☿	♃
4.00— 5.00	☿	♃	♀	♄	☉	☽	♂
5.00— 6.00	☽	♂	☿	♃	♀	♄	☉
6.00— 7.00	♄	☉	☽	♂	☿	♃	♀
7.00— 8.00	♃	♀	♄	☉	☽	♂	☿
8.00— 9.00	♂	☿	♃	♀	♄	☉	☽
9.00—10.00	☉	☽	♂	☿	♃	♀	♄
10.00—11.00	♀	♄	☉	☽	♂	☿	♃
11.00—12.00	☿	♃	♀	♄	☉	☽	♂

According to this table, the hours of Saturday which are the most favourable for the making of a talisman of Saturn are from midday to 1 o'clock; from 7—8 p.m.; from 2—3 o'clock after midnight; and from 9—10 a.m. of the following morning, reckoning the day as beginning and ending at midday. The work of engraving, interrupted during intermediate hours, ought therefore to be resumed during the hours influenced by the genius of Saturn. It is completed by the magical consecration of the talisman.

This consecration consists in exposing the talisman to the fumes of a scent composed of alum, assa-foetida, scammony and sulphur, which are burned with cyprus, ash and stalks of black hellebore lighted in an earthenware chafing-dish which has never been used for any other purpose and which has to be ground to dust and buried secretly in an unfrequented spot after the operation. The talisman is then placed in a black silk sachet which is hung on the breast by bands of the same material interwoven and tied in the form of a cross.

II   The *Talisman of Jupiter* brings to those who wear it the good-will and sympathy of everyone. It drives away all cares, is favourable to honest enterprises and increases well-being according to social standing.

It gives protection against unforeseen accidents and the perils of violent death presaged by Saturn in the natal horoscope.

It gives protection from death caused by diseases of the liver, inflamation of the lungs, malignant tumours, or that cruel affection of the spinal marrow called *tabes dorsalis*.

In order to make the talisman of Jupiter a plaque of very pure tin must be obtained, cut in the form of a circle about the size of an ordinary medal, and the two faces polished smoothly.

On the first face is engraved with a diamond-pointed burin the image of a crown with four points at the centre of a pentagram, or five-pointed star.

On the other side is engraved the image of an eagle's head at the centre of a six-pointed star, surrounded by letters composing the name *Pi-Zeus*, the planetary genius of Jupiter, according to the alphabet of the Magi [see Book II, p. 147].

A Thursday [*Jovis Dies*] must be chosen for the commencement and termination of this work, when the evolution of the Moon is passing through the first ten degrees of the Libra and is found in a favourable aspect, that is to say, sextile or trine with Saturn and Jupiter, according to the theory of the horoscope outlined further on [Book VI].

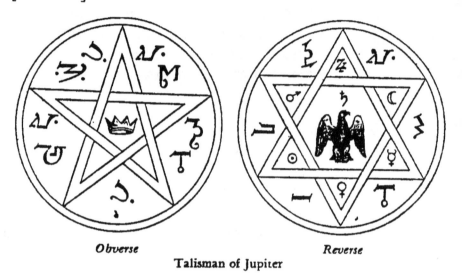

Obverse   *Reverse*

Talisman of Jupiter

In order to find out if this aspect is favourable or otherwise the horoscope must be set up on the first Thursday containing the above-mentioned lunar evolution. If the aspect of the Moon with Saturn and Jupiter is unfavourable, each following Thursday must be tried until a good aspect is met with.

The beginning of each lunar evolution can be found by reference to the table of Epacts [given in Book VI]. On its 15th day it passes through the first ten degrees of the Scales; if therefore the day corresponds to a Thursday and if Saturn and Jupiter have a favourable aspect, the time is suitable for the creation of a talisman.

Consulting the table of hours given above, we find that the hours of Thursday governed by the genius of Jupiter are: from mid-day to 1 o'clock; from 7—8 p.m.;

from 2—3 a.m.; and from 9—10 a.m. the following morning.

The consecration of the talisman consists in exposing it to the fumes of a scent composed of frankincense, ambergris, balsam, cardamon, saffron and mace [the inner bark of the nutmeg tree], all of which are burned with oak, poplar, fig and pomegrate branches in an earthenware vessel which must afterwards be destroyed, as above. The talisman is then placed in a sachet of sky-blue silk [*in cyaneo serico*] and hung on the breast by bands of the same material interwoven and tied in the form of a cross.

III   The *Talisman of Mars* is a preservative against the attacks of dangerous enemies. Its influence keeps at bay the danger of death in battle or argument. It preserves the wearer from death by St. Anthony's fire, malignant ulcers or epidemic. It neutralises the danger of violent death by torture presaged in a birthday horoscope.

If this talisman is hidden in a citadel by the commander defending it, no attack from outside will succeed.

In order to make the talisman of Mars a plaque of very pure iron must be obtained, cut in the form of a circle about the size of an ordinary medal, and polished smoothly on both sides.

On the first side is engraved with a diamond-pointed burin the image of swords enclosed in a pentagram.

On the other side is engraved the image of a lion's head at the centre of a six-pointed star and surrounded by letters composing the name *Ertosi*, the planetary genius of Mars, according to the alphabet of the Magi [see Book II, p. 147].

A Tuesday must be chosen for the work, the day consecrated to Mars [*Martis Dies*], when the evolution of the Moon is passing through the first ten degrees of the Ram or Sagittarius and is found in favourable aspect with Saturn and Mars.

In order to find out if this aspect is favourable, the horoscope must be set up on the nearest Tuesday containing the lunar evolution with Saturn and Mars in favourable aspect.

The beginning of each lunar evolution can be found from the table of Epacts. On its 30th day it passes through the first ten degrees of the Ram and on its 19th day the first ten degrees of Sagittarius. If therefore one of these days corresponds with a Tuesday, and if Saturn and Mars are

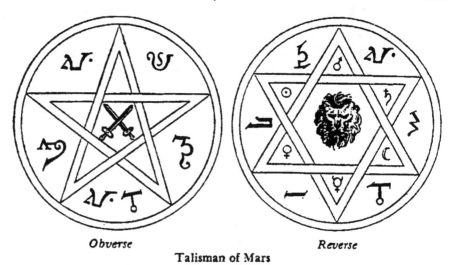

Obverse   *Reverse*

Talisman of Mars

in a favourable aspect with the Moon, the time is suitable for the creation of the talisman.

Consulting the table of hours given above, we find that the hours of Tuesday governed by the planetary genius of Mars are from mid-day to 1 o'clock; from 7—8 p.m.; from 2—3 a.m., and from 9—10 a.m. the following morning.

The consecration of the talisman consists in exposing it to the fumes of a scent composed of desiccated absinth and rue. The talisman is then placed in a red silk sachet, hung on the breast as described above.

IV The *Talisman of the Sun* brings to those who wear it the good-will and the favour of those in high positions. It preserves the wearer from death by syncope, heart disease, aneurism, epidemic and conflagration.

To make the talisman of the Sun a plaque of very pure gold must be obtained.

On the first side is engraved the image of a circle enclosed in a pentagram.

On the second side is engraved a human head enclosed in a six-pointed star and surrounded by letters composing the name *Pi-Rhé*, the planetary genius of the Sun.

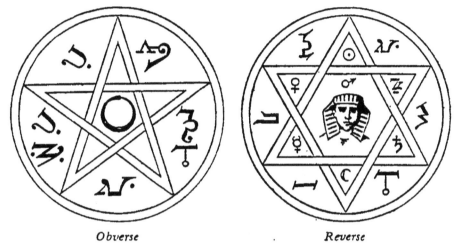

Obverse   *Reverse*

Talisman of the Sun

A Sunday must be chosen for the operation [*Solis Dies*], day consecrated to the Sun, when the evolution of the Moon is passing through the first 10 degrees of the Lion and is found in favourable aspect with Saturn and the Sun.

In order to find out if this aspect is favourable, the horoscope must be set up on the nearest Sunday containing the lunar evolution with a favourable aspect of the Moon with Saturn and the Sun.

Consulting the table of Epacts [p. 483], we find that the lunar evolution in its 10th day passes through the first 10 degrees of the Lion; if therefore this day corresponds to a Sunday, and if the Moon, Saturn and the Sun are in a favourable aspect, the time is suitable for the creation of the talisman.

Consulting the table of hours, we find that the hours

of Sunday governed by the Sun are: from mid-day to
1 o'clock; from 7—8 p.m.; from 2—3 a.m., and from
9—10 a.m. the following morning.

The consecration of the talisman consists in exposing it
to the fumes of a scent composed of cinnamon, frank
incense, saffron and red sandalwood, which is burned with
laurel and dried heliotrope stalks in an earthenware vessel.
The talisman is then placed in a sachet of pale yellow silk
[*in sindone luteâ*], hung on the breast.

V   The *Talisman of Venus* preserves harmony and
affection between man and wife. It keeps away those who
may offend by envy and hate. It preserves women from the
terrible illness cancer. It protects men and women from
violent death by poisoning, criminal or accidental. It
neutralises the dangerous presages given by the genius of
Mars in a natal horoscope. If it is possible to make a sworn
enemy drink a liquid in which the talisman of Venus has
been dipped, that enemy's hatred is transformed into
affection and devotion for life.

To make the talisman of Venus, a plaque of very pure
copper is required.

On the first side is engraved the image of the letter G,
enclosed in a pentagram.

On the second side is engraved a dove at the centre
of a six-pointed star surrounded by letters composing the
name of *Suroth*, the planetary genius of Venus.

A Friday must be chosen, day consecrated to Venus
[*Veneris Dies*], when the evolution of the Moon is passing
through the first 10 degress of the Bull or the Virgin and is
found in favourable aspect with Saturn and Venus.

To find out whether or not this aspect is favourable,
the horoscope must be set up on the nearest Friday containing the lunar evolution with the Moon in favourable
aspect with Saturn and Venus.

Consulting the table of Epacts, we find that the lunar evolution begins in its 2nd day to pass through the first 10 degrees of the Bull, and on its 13th day through the first 10 degrees of the Virgin. If therefore this day is a Friday, and if the Moon, Saturn and Venus are in favourable aspect, the time is suitable for the creation of the talisman.

Consulting the table of hours, we find that the hours of

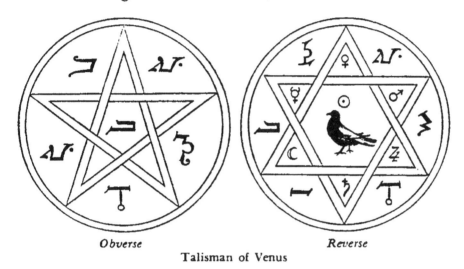

Obverse　　　　　　　　　　　*Reverse*

Talisman of Venus

Friday governed by Venus are from mid-day to 1 o'clock; from 7—8 p.m.; from 2—3 a.m. and from 9—10 a.m. the following morning.

The consecration of the talisman consists in exposing the talisman to the fumes of a scent composed of violets and roses burned with olive wood in an earthenware vessel. The talisman is then placed in a sachet of either green or pink silk and hung on the breast.

VI　The *Talisman of Mercury* is the protector of all kinds of commerce and industry. If it is buried in the ground underneath a shop or place of business, it attracts clients and prosperity.

It preserves all who wear it from attacks of epilepsy or madness.

It protects from death by murder or poison. It guards

against treason. If it is placed beneath the head during sleep,
it produces prophetic dreams.

To make the talisman of Mercury, a plaque composed
of an alloy of silver, tin and mercury is necessary.

On the first side is engraved the image of a winged
caduceus with two serpents enlaced, at the centre of a
pentagram.

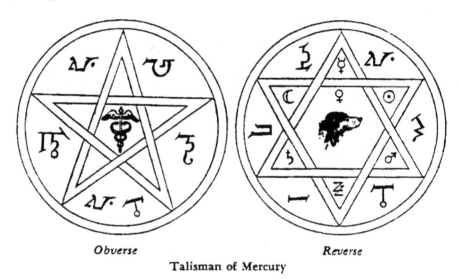

Obverse   *Reverse*

Talisman of Mercury

On the other side is engraved a dog's head, enclosed
in a six-pointed star surrounded by letters composing the
name *Pi-Hermes*, the planetary genius of Mercury.

A Wednesday must be chosen, day consecrated to
Mercury [*Mercurii Dies*], when the evolution of the Moon
is passing through the first 10 degrees of Gemini or
Scorpion and is found in favourable aspect with Saturn and
Mercury.

To find out if this aspect is a favourable one, the horoscope must be set up on the nearest Wednesday containing the lunar evolution with a favourable aspect of the
Moon with Saturn and Mercury.

Consulting the table of Epacts we find that the beginning of the lunar evolution passes on its 4th day through

the first 10 degrees of Gemini and on its 17th day through the first 10 degrees of Scorpio. If therefore one of these days is a Wednesday, and if the Moon is in a good aspect with Saturn and Mercury the time is favourable for the creation of the talisman.

Consulting the table of hours, we find that the hours of Wednesday governed by Mercury are: from mid-day to 1 o'clock; from 7—8 p.m.; from 2—3 a.m.; and from 9—10 a.m. the following morning.

The consecration consists of exposing the talisman to the fumes of a scent composed of benzoin, mace and storax which is burned with the dried stalks of lilies, narcissi, fumitory and marjoram in an earthenware vessel. The talisman is placed in a sachet of purple silk which is hung on the breast.

VII   The *Talisman of the Moon* protects travellers and persons dwelling in a foreign land. It preserves the wearer from death by shipwreck, or from epilepsy, dropsy, apoplexy and madness. It also keeps at bay the perils of violent death presaged by the saturnine aspects of the horoscope.

To make the talisman of the Moon, a plaque of very pure silver must be obtained.

On the first side is engraved the image of a crescent, enclosed in a pentagram.

On the other side is engraved a goblet enclosed in a six-pointed star and surrounded by letters composing the name *Pi-Ioh*, the planetary genius of the Moon.

A Monday must be chosen, day consecrated to the Moon [*Lunae Dies*], when the lunar evolution is passing through the first 10 degrees of the Virgin or Capricorn, and is found in favourable aspect with Saturn.

To find out if this aspect is favourable, the horoscope must be set up on the nearest Monday containing the lunar

evolution and with the Moon and Saturn in favourable
aspect.

Consulting the table of Epacts, the lunar evolution
begins to pass on its 13th day through the first 10 degrees
of the Virgin, and on its 22nd day through the first
10 degrees of Capricorn. If therefore one of these days is
a Monday and if the Moon is in a favourable aspect with
Saturn, the time is suitable for the creation of the talisman.

Consulting the table of hours, we find that the hours

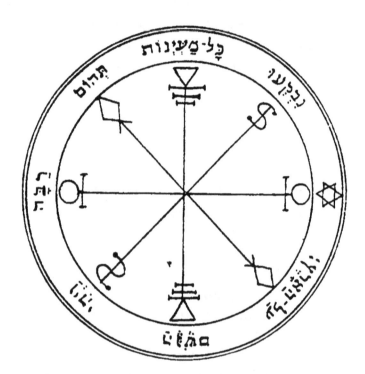

The above version of the Sixth and Last Pentacle of the Moon is not in the
text of Christian's book, whose instructions it does not follow, but is an alterna-
tive version taken from S. L. M. Mathers *The Key of Solomon the King*. It is
composed of mystical characters of the Moon, such as the geomantic sigil and
is surrounded by a versicle (Genesis viii, 11, 12): 'All the fountains of the
Great Deep were broken up . . . and the rain was upon the earth.' In the
original text the pentacle is thus described: 'This is wonderfully good, and
serveth excellently to excite and cause heavy rains, if it be engraved upon a
plate of silver; and if it be placed under water, as long as it remaineth there,
there will be rain. It should be engraved, drawn, or written in the day and
hour of the Moon.'

of Monday governed by the Moon are: from mid-day to
1 o'clock; from 7—8 p.m.; from 2—3 a.m.; and from
9—10 a.m. of the following morning.

The consecration consists in exposing the talisman to
the fumes of a scent composed of white sandalwood, cam-
phor, aloes, amber and pounded cucumber seeds, which is
burned with dried stalks of artemisia, selenotrope and
ranunculus in an earthenware vessel. The talisman is then
placed in a sachet of white silk and hung on the breast.

These are the principal Talismans whose traditions
have been preserved for us by the most ancient monuments
of the highest magical art and by the most reliable archæ-
ologists in this type of research. These talismans are recommended under the name of *Teraphim* by the Hebrew
Qabalists of the Middle Ages,[27] who replace the names of
the planetary Genii of Egypt by those of: *Oriphiel*
[Rempha], *Zachariel* [Pi-Zeus], *Samaël* [Ertosi], *Michaël*
[Pi-Rhé], *Anaël* [Suroth], *Raphaël* [Pi-Hermes] and
Gabriel [Pi-Ioh]. These Qabalists add another seven talismans to which they attribute the power of conjuring the
influence of seven demons who, according to their doctrine,
share with the seven planetary angels the government of
the divine creation. Against the angel of Saturn they set
the demon *Nabam;* against the angel of Jupiter the demon
Acham; against the angel of Mars the demon *Nambroth;*
against the angel of Venus the demon *Lilith* or *Naemah;*
against the angel of Mercury the demon *Astaroth* or *Thar-
thac;* and against the angel of the Moon the demon *Sathan,*

---

[27] See Judges xvii and xviii. The Teraphim appear to correspond to the serpent
images or Seraphim, which in turn are said to derive from the Kabeiri,
Assyrian divinities worshipped at Hebron [Beni Anak]. The Daimons or male
spirits of the planets are now given by esoteric students of the Qabala as:
Adonai=Sun, Evoe=Moon, Saba=Mars, Astaphoi=Mercury, Eloi=Jupiter,
Ouraios=Venus and Ilde-baoth, or according to the Orphites Jahweh=
Saturn. Christian's text is defective; he omits the Sun, and what follows
appears to derive from second-rate sources.—*Ed.*

in whom Christians recognise the Prince of Darkness, the perpetual enemy of God and man.[28]

Nabam is represented in the Rabbinic Qabala as a very old man standing on a Tau or inverted Hebrew cross [⊥]. Christian mystics counter this representation with the sign of Jesus, or an upright T, with the name *Oriphiel*, angel of Saturday.

Acham is representeed as a crowned king walking proudly along; a small demon carries the train of his cloak. Against him Christians set the image of a spirit-level and compass intersecting in a triangle with the name of *Zachariel*, angel of Thursday. Under the level is inscribed the word *Justitia*, and around the compasses: *Qui se exaltat humiliabitur.*

Nambroth, demon of Tuesday, is represented as a warrior wearing an iron crown. In his right hand he carries a sword; his left holds a buckler on which is depicted a tower being attacked by an enemy. Christians set against him a chalice surmounted by the peaceful Host, over which is inscribed *pax* with the name of the angel *Samaël*. Two serpents form the handles of the goblet, their fangs biting the rim.

Lilith, demon of Friday, is represented as a naked woman whose body terminates in a serpent's tail. Christians counter this with the sign of the double Lingam [see note,

---

[28] For these the proper range of usual names considered correct by modern occultists is:

Planet	Spirit	Intelligence	Princes of Qliphoth
♄	Zazel	Agiel	Isheth Zominim
♃	Chismael	Iophiel	Samael
♂	Bartyabel	Graphiel	Asthteroth
☀	Sorath	Nakhiel	Chivah
♀	Gedemel	Hagiel	Armodei
☿	Tophtharthareth	Tiriel	Belial
☾	Chasmodai	Malkah Be Tarshishim va A'ad Be Quah Shehalem	Lilith

p. 96], monogram of the Virgin Mother, with the name of the angel *Anaël*.

Astaroth, demon of Wednesday, is represented as a man with an ass's head, bearing a book which he holds upside down on which is written the word *Scientia*. Christians oppose this image with the seal of Solomon, two concentric triangles forming a six-pointed star, round which are written the names *Jehova* and *Raphaël*.

Satan or Lucifer, demon of Monday, is represented by an angel with plucked wings. He has a star on his forehead and the moon at his feet; in his hand he bears a flaming torch. Against him Christians set a five-pointed star, in the centre of which is written the name of the angel Gabriel, whose seven letters, linked in a monogram, read BRALGEI, meaning: *Bone Redemptor Athanatos, Lux Gloriae, Eleison Imas* [O blest eternal Redeemer, light of the glory, have pity on us.]

Belief in the efficacity of talismans has always existed. Adepts to-day are rare, but they are no less fervent than those of antiquity. They realise that this doctrine considers the talisman not as a superstitious object but as a visible sign having as its effect the constant recalling of the believer's spirit to confidence in God and to the sanctity of the will. The truth of this is so fundamental that, according to hermetic doctrine, the talisman was considered to have lost all its virtue as soon as its possessor gave way to a guilty thought or an impure desire. As for the actual value of this *supernatural virtue*, it should be believed in or doubted only with an extreme reserve; it is a problem which should be allowed to resolve itself in the liberal speculation of the individual conscience.

It is less permissible to hesitate in condemning all practices which have as their aim *the conjuring of the Devil* or the making of a pact with him. To believe in the Devil is to blaspheme against God. If we admit that there exists a being invested with the power of being the adversary of

God, the Creator of the Worlds, we deny the very existence of God Himself by setting a limit to His infinite perfection. Indeed, God would not be omnipotent if He had an equally powerful rival; He would not be the representative of sovereign good if He allowed some being, inferior to Himself but superior to Humanity, to drag the weak into so-called abysses of Hell and eternal damnation. 'Man,' says the religion of the Magi, 'is born free and eternally perfectible. Good and evil are the products of his liberty. Evil takes its part in the trials and the triumphs of the just. Goodness, in its own way, produces the redemption of sinners; and so is realised, in the course of time, the harmony of divine justice and pity.' There is no room in this doctrine for the fantastic idea of a Devil disputing the government of the universe with God.

Whatever its origins, the union of the Devil with Magic was to produce great perturbation in the human spirit. The ancient world had made everything divine, even its vices. Christianity divided this pantheon into two parts: one belonged to God and His angels, the other to Satan and his infernal legions. When the Roman Empire fell into the hands of the Barbarians, the profound ignorance of this new race was unable to explain the dreadful phenomena of life such as epidemics, epilepsy, madness, rage, hysteria; their causes were alleged by the priests to be the influences of evil spirits. Sick people who could not be cured by any known remedy were said to be possessed of the Devil. This so-called possession played a great part in the beliefs of the Middle Ages, and the Christian priesthood, imitating polytheistic priesthoods, invented rites in order to triumph over it by supernatural means. This was called exorcism.

'Exorcism,' says M. A. Maury, 'had a considerable place in the liturgy; it had a part in the most solemn ceremonies; it became a succession of rites whose complete performance was obligatory. The Christian was for a long time more occupied with the Devil than with God, and in this respect we are reminded of the inhabitants of Madagascar who, questioned on the motives which make them prefer to offer their gifts to evil gods, reply: "It is because we have nothing to fear from the good gods, whereas we must at all costs appease those who are evil." The Devil in Christian dogma is supposed to be abroad in all places, and each locality had to be previously exorcised before any religious ceremonies were performed there. Under the pontificate of Pope Sixtus V, when the Egyptian obelisk was brought to Rome it had to be exorcised before being erected in the square where it now stands. Exorcism was not carried out merely by the recitation of certain formulae, but also by the laying-on of hands, the sign of the cross. This sign put the Devil to flight. Apart from cases of ordinary possession, the pagan or heathen regarded as mentally possessed by the evil spirit had to submit to exorcism before entering a Christian community. Holy water was sprinkled over dead people to chase away the demons which might seize their spirits. Exorcism was carried out by water and by salt, as well as by prayer. This continual intervention of exorcism is proved to us by the large number of conjurations adopted in the Liturgy. These were veritable litanies of anathema against Satan.[29] He was qualified as a perfidious machinator, a thief, a suspicious character, a wild beast, an infernal dragon, a murderer, etc., and in order not to be obliged always to repeat a long list of accusations, they were engraved on pantacles, or mysterious metal figures which thus acquired the virtue of warding off evil spirts. Formerly the Neoplatonists and the Gnostics, in their formulae for exorcisms, accumulated an assembly of curious names and strange epithets, to which they attributed a much greater efficaciousness than the simple enunciation of God's name. The faith in these nomenclatures was so great that the Church was forced to preserve them, at the same time also introducing new names. And so a good number of exor-

[29] One of the most curious collections of exorcisms is one composed by Pope Honorius II in the VIIth century, with a title: *Conjurationes adversus Principem Tenebrarum et Angelos eius* [Rome, 1529]. The book is a rarity.

cisms begin with the name of God repeated in all its forms. Sometimes the invocation is addressed to the God of Abraham, of Isaac, of Jacob, of Moses and Aaron, of Tobias and Elias; sometimes to the God of the angels, of the archangels, of the prophets, of the apostles, of the martyrs, of the confessors, of the virgins, etc.

'Recourse to exorcisms was, in principle, a common right; but later the privilege was reserved for ministers of the temple. Sometimes these strange ceremonies were accompanied by a strident music. It is said in accounts of the life of St. Patrick that swarms of bats, which had been taken for hosts of demons and which the reverent apostle had not been able to drive away by his exorcisms, departed at the sound of a cymbal which he caused to be struck as he was invoking the name of God.'[30]

When the priests reserved for themselves the exclusive right of exorcism, the laity did not all by any means renounce their common right and some attempted to enter into communication with infernal spirits. These were the first sorcerers of the Christian era, who thus set up the altar of the Devil against the altar of God. Certain priests secretly supported them and they worked jointly: an accursed business whose adherents soon increased in numbers in all countries.[31] We find the Devil at the height of his powerful reign in the XVIth century, and, strange to relate, he roasted his followers to the profit of the Church. This was because the clergy in those days were as ignorant as they were vicious. They grew rich on the confiscated property of wretches who, at the clergy's request, were sent to the stake by the secular arm. The Inquisition, invented by Pope

---

[30] A. Maury *Magie et Astrologie* [Paris, 1860]: p. 318.

[31] Charles Williams' remarkable book on *Witchcraft* and Montague Summers' books *History of Witchcraft, Witchcraft and Black Magic, Geography of Witchcraft*, etc., are good and available recent treatments of the subject for the general reader. There are also Margaret Murray's *Cult of Witchcraft in Western Europe* and the more recent Trevor Davis' *History of Witchcraft in the XVIIth century.* See Eliphas Levi *Rituel de la Haute Magie*, recently republished in English translation, for the actual ceremonies.—*Ed.*

Innocent III, was the all-powerful instrument of this lucrative form of speculation. In Spain especially, during the
reign of Isabella the Catholic and under the direction of
Cardinal Ximenes, even women accused of sorcery were
sent to the stake [1506]. At Geneva, a city governed by a
bishop, more than five hundred were burned in the short
period of three months during the year 1515. The Bishop
of Bamberg burned six hundred people and the Bishop of
Wurzburg nine hundred. The mania for burning people
became so great that the Emperor Ferdinand II was forced
to intervene. In 1782, only seven years before the French
Revolution, Spain was still burning unfortunate women to
the greater glory of God and, if we are to believe
M. Michelet, 'Rome still burns heretics, secretly it is true,
in the furnaces and caves of the Inquisition. This detail,'
adds M. Michelet, 'is passed on to us by a Counsellor of
the Holy Office [Inquisition] who is still alive. I have before
me a vehement defence of torture written in 1780 by a
parliamentary *savant,* Muyart de Vouglans, later member
of the Great Council of France, which is dedicated to
Louis XVI and is adorned by the flattering approval of
His Holiness Pius VI.'[32]

If these words of M. Michelet are correct, we must
admit that in spite of the lessons of philosophy and the
progress of science human reason is still far from regaining
its primitive stature.

Witchcraft trials in France gave rise to tragedies in
which sin and horror were inextricably mixed. Dominicans,
Capuchins, Jesuits and Carmelites soiled the memory of
their worthy founders with ineffaceable blemishes.

There were Gaufridi, a priest, burned alive at Aix
30 April 1611 after his scandalous adventures among the
Ursulines; the curate Urbain Grandier, burned at the stake
18 August 1634 at Loudun for similar adventures with
another set of nuns; in 1730 the Jesuit priest Girard who

---

[32] J. Michelet *La Sorcière,* Book II, p. 194 [Bruxelles, 1863].

seduced his penitent Catherine Cadière, a girl of seventeen, and accused her of witchcraft so that he might escape punishment. Surrounding these criminal priests were monks who looked complacently on their odiously cynical dealings. These are the three principal dramas which represent France in the history of witchcraft. M. Michelet has examined carefully the archives concerning these trials and has set forth fearlessly his incredible revelations in his descriptions of witchcraft trials. Without wishing to criticise this fine historian, I cannot bring myself to embark upon the same road; I recommend the study of his work on witches to those whose curiosity has been aroused. Witchcraft moreover has nothing to do with Magic. The licentious biographies of Gaufridi, Grandier and Girard do not even hint at the slightest shadow of a supernatural event.

THE HISTORY AND
PRACTICE OF MAGIC
VOLUME II

BOOK FIVE

BOOK FIVE

SUPERNATURAL SCIENCES AND CURIOSITIES

I

IMAGINE yourself on a vast moor studded with clumps of wild trees, or in some great clearing in the depths of a forest. Suppose in the middle of this space a man-made mound or some ancient Celtic dolmen, altar of some vanished cult. Here and there bonfires of resinous wood cast their flickering lights on moving shadows, and dominating the scene a tall statue of the Devil in black wood with a he-goat's head carries in his outstretched arms blazing torches which make his terrifying figure stand out vividly against a starless sky.

This is the usual setting for a Witches' Sabbath.[1] Around the mound, or under the dolmen's rough stone table, a few old women with ghostly faces are crouched, burning aromatic concoctions made from poisonous plants and human remains stolen from graveyards. These are the priestesses of the Devil.

A strange gathering of men, women and even children collects in silence at nightfall, coming from all directions; newcomers keep joining the groups in this living chain which gradually surrounds the infernal effigy.—Do not

[1] Locations for these gatherings include by general belief not only the famous Bröcken, in the Hartz Mountains, but in Russia the Bald Mountain [Lyssaya Gora, near Kiev] and the unspecified Devil's Pond in the U.S.A., said merely to be 'in a large forest'. A good popular description of the assembly and its rites is given in Dennis Wheatley's *The Devil Rides Out;* for a more scholarly account, see Margaret Murray *The Witch Cult in Western Europe,* chap. 5. For the central figure at these obscene revels see the same author's *The God of the Witches.* Many works now exist on witchcraft generally, of which those by Charles Williams and Montague Summers may be held to be authoritative.—*Ed.*

think that this often very numerous assembly is composed only of lunatics, beggars and bandits. High-born ladies and gentlemen, masked and disguised, have paid costly sums for admission; the rich mingle with the poor, the nobility with the ne'er-do-wells, the lady of the castle with the kitchen maid. Nor are priests lacking: they are given the titles of Bishops of the Witches' Sabbath.

What happened on these much-frequented occasions? The Black Mass was celebrated—the Devil's Mass, a licentious parody of the Christian ceremony, the lewd details of which the pen of not even the most liberal-minded of thinkers could be brought to describe. After this blasphemous service a banquet was served in the open air, terminated by a wild dance through the almost extinguished embers of the fires; and when darkness had again fallen completely on the moor or the forest clearing, even the audacious pen of a Petronius or a Juvenal would not venture to describe what took place under the cover of night.[2]

What is the meaning of the word *Sabbath*? Scholars are not at all agreed on its correct etymology. As the Jews of the Middle Ages prided themselves on being the first to possess the secrets of the supernatural, and as they were the objects of general scorn and hatred, the victims of fanatical persecutions on the part of the Christians, they had had to seek out solitary places for their religious meetings called *Sabbaton*, the Sabbath, God's day of rest, the seventh day after the beginning of Creation. But these Jews, dispersed and scattered among all the nations of the earth, were a timid and unhappy race; they would not have dared, at peril of their lives, to hold open gatherings, which would always be exposed to the risk of being broken up by their enemies. The name Sabbath may have been given to assemblies of magicians and witches as a popular expression of

---

[2] See Del Rio *Disquisitiones Magicae*, 1599; De Lancre *Traité de l'Inconstance des Démons*, 1612; Wyerius *De Prestigiis Daemonum*, 1569; Scribonius *De Sagarum Natura et Potestate*, 1588 [Marburgi]; Remigius *Demonolatria*, 1596; and Boguet *Discours de Sorciers*, 1605. Also list in note in Book IV, p. 323.

the contempt which the Jews inspired; but obviously the meaning of the word must be sought elsewhere.

Actually, the Witches' Dance [Danse du Sabbat], followed by its mysterious vices, was the supreme moment of the infernal cult, and it recalls the frantic orgies at the ancient festivals of Bacchus, called *Sabazies*. Bacchus, the god of wine, drunkenness and its attendant debauches, had received the name *Sabazios* [Σαβάζιος], which is derived from the Greek verb Σαβάζω, meaning to shout, to throw oneself about, to abandon oneself to the furious convulsions produced by the abuse of the gifts of the god Bacchus-Sabazios. Another Greek word, Σαβοῖ, expressed the cries uttered by the priests and priestesses of Bacchus during the festivals of Sabazios: 'Ηυοῖ, Σαβοῖ—which the Romans translated as Evoë or Saboë when they imitated these festivals of the Hellenic cult. This very name, Saboï, referred not only to the initiates of the mystery of Bacchus and the rural places consecrated to the god but also to loose-living women; and this latter sense by extension fits in well with what occurred during the Witches' Sabbath, or rather the *Sabazie*, of the Middle Ages.[3]

Catholicism had appropriated to itself a large part of the ideas and ceremonies which constituted the ancient cults, and it was quite natural that everything it denounced became the province of all those who rejected its doctrines. It had scarcely come to power, after trials which have been much exaggerated by its first adepts, before it began very quickly to forget the laws of the Gospel and treated its former adversaries with the utmost cruelty, in its bloody deeds more odious and better substantiated than those committed by the objects of its vengeance. Christians were no longer disciples of Jesus, gentle and humble of heart like their master; they were now a triumphant sect, which throughout

---

[3] The modern English word Sabbath seems to be a mixture between the Latin *Sabbatum* [derived from the Greek σάββατον], in medieval Latin *Sabbat*, and the Hebrew *Shabbath*. See Skeat.—*Ed.*

the centuries has remained merciless to whoever would not bow the knee to its all-conquering egoism and its domination over anti-Christians. This Catholicism of the Middle Ages and the Renaissance, which ruled by torture and provided arms for religious civil wars, is therefore guilty of the superstitions propagated by the cult of the Devil under the name of Witchcraft; the Black Mass was a brutal protest against vices masked by hypocrisy and concealed under the cloak of the true faith.[4] How could sensible people respect the Catholicism of the XIVth century when in 1351 one could see the Pope, Clement VI, concede to the kings of France a Papal Bull authorising the royal confessor to absolve them and all their descendants from all perjuries, past, present and future, and from all oaths which they could not *conveniently* carry out?[5] How could one respect the Papacy when John XXII put a tax on the remission of sins and invented for his own profit a sliding scale of absolution which catalogued the most unbelievable horrors of which the human spirit can be conscious?

The depiction of such a deplorable epoch does not belong to my subject; I shall confine myself to one incident, to show to what depths of barbarity even the upper classes degraded themselves during those centuries.

'Gilles de Laval, Baron de Retz, had married while she was still a girl Catherine de Thouars, Dame de Tiffauges. Through his father he was the possessor of the most important seigniories of Brittany and through his mother, Marie de Craon, owned a large number of lands, estates and castles in Maine, Anjou and Poitou. His revenue was

---

[4] See notes pp. 298 and 420 for historical authorities for this period.—*Ed.*

[5] Here is the relevant passage from the Bull: 'In perpetuum indulgemus ut confessor juramenta per vos praestita et per successores vestros praestanda in posterum, quae vos et illi servare commode non possetis.' [*Epistolae Clementis Papae VI*, given in *Spicilegio Dachery* Book III, p. 724, 1723 Edition.]

[6] Numerous books exist on Gilles de Rais, of which Gaborry Emile *La Vie et la Mort de Gilles de Rais* and the *Procès Inquisitonel . . . avec un Essai de réhabilitation* edited by L. Hernandez may be mentioned. A recent English book is Francis Winwar *The Saint and the Devil* [a double biography].—*Ed.*

estimated at a million francs in present-day money [1870], and he also enjoyed a host of residuary rights which brought him in immense sums. He counted among his relations the royal family of France, the ducal family of Brittany and the majority of the princes and great lords of the two countries. Like all those of his birth and rank he entered the military profession, distinguished himself by his bravery, and rendered great services to Charles VII by putting himself at the head of numerous troops of soldiers levied at his own cost: a field-marshal's baton was his reward. An exaggerated opinion of his own position led him astray; he raised a personal army of two hundred horse-guards, who accompanied him everywhere; his prodigality became excessive, his revenues soon became insufficient to pay for his wild extravagance. He raised loans at an exorbitant rate of interest, then, at the end of his resources, unable to find any money-lender who would help him further, he felt he ought to address himself to God who, he thought [such was his extraordinary vanity], held the house of Rohan and Laval in too high esteem to let it fall into penurious decay.

He had built, in his manor at Tiffauges, a chapel in which officiated a dean, archdeacons, precentors, canons, choir-boys and musicians brought from Italy at great expense. One of his canons had the title of bishop and officiated with all the outward trappings of such a dignitary. The Marshal sent several times to Rome soliciting the Pope to accord the rank of archbishop to the head of his chapel; he also asked permission for his precentors to wear mitres the same as prelates, claiming that this would give them greater power in the eyes of God. When the Pope refused to allow such curious fantasies, Gilles de Laval compensated his clergy by giving them extra pay. Nevertheless, God seemed to turn a deaf ear to his chaplains' vows and prayers. So the Marshal resolved to try his fortune in other ways.

He had heard talk of certain men who, according to the beliefs held at the time, had lifted themselves through the medium of the occult sciences above this humdrum exist-

ence and had at their command the powers of darkness
which they called up in awful ceremonies.

He at once sent to Germany and Italy emissaries whose
task was to put him in touch with these people. Charlatans,
infidels and even criminals of the worst kind were soon
on the road to his manor in the hope of exploiting his passions. Gilles de Laval wanted above all to discover the
secret of making gold. He had had laboratories built and
stoked his furnaces with the proceeds from the sale of his
estates. The alchemist's search for gold was a ceaseless drain
on his money, which he spent on wild experiments; and he
was beginning to despair of success, when there arrived
at his court, under the auspices of a priest from St. Malo,
a person who claimed to have been born in the east and to
possess secret spells which could unfold all the mysteries
of nature.

He was of an imposing presence, with burning eyes, a
deep voice and the face of one of the Magi of old; all
these points seemed to recommend this mysterious stranger,
who spoke little but who really seemed to have been initiated into transcendental mysteries. Such a man could easily
exploit the anxieties and the greed of Gilles de Laval. Soon
the underground vaults of the Castle of Tiffauges resounded
with terrible shrieks and were drenched in tears of pain.
The Marshal wanted to call up the Devil, and the stranger
from the east had persuaded him that he would succeed
only if he offered to the prince of darkness the blood of
little children. Gilles de Laval had himself to plunge the
knife into the breasts of his victims; he had to count, according to certain magical rules, the number of convulsions
preceding death. He fearlessly consented to these monstrous
cruelties, and in this most hideous mixture of credulity,
doubt and superstition, whilst he carried out mercilessly
in his vaults the most dreadful immolations, his priests, com-
fortably ensconced in the stalls of his splendid chapel, offered
hymns to high heaven and prayed, at his orders, for the souls
of the innocent victims.

One day after numerous murders the man from the east set Gilles de Laval at the end of a gallery where soon, doubtless by some conjuring trick, he heard voices wailing all round him, whilst at the other extremity of the gallery the conjurer's face was illuminated by sinister and phosphorescent glimmers. But this phantasmagoria still did not result in any apparition, and what Gilles de Laval wanted was the presence of the Devil in person. His accomplice needed great skill to temper his impatience and restrain his violent outbursts of baffled rage. Pressed to put an end to what was becoming a perilous game, he finally hit upon the idea that, before he would show himself, Satan insisted on the Marshal's signing with his own blood a memorandum delivering up his soul to the Devil for eternity in exchange for the years of wealth and power that would be his on earth.

Gilles de Laval consented: but heaven, weary of his crimes, was about to put an end to them. More than two hundred children had disappeared, stolen here and there from all over the countryside by his henchmen. A reign of terror spread all round Tiffauges, and the public outcry accused the sinister overlord. The complaints reached the ear of John V, Duke of Brittany, who ordered an enquiry. The Bishop of Nantes, John de Malestroit, Chancellor of Brittany, Maître Jean Blouin, Inquisitor of the Faith, and Pierre de l'Hôpital, Seneschal of Rennes, were charged with the task of instituting proceedings. Gilles de Laval, arrested in his castle, was caught red-handed murdering five or six children who had only recently been seized at Nantes; he could not deny his misdeed and fell into a state of idiotic stupor. The vaults at Tiffauges revealed their mysteries, and the stranger from the east, the accomplice of Gilles de Laval, was found to be a Florentine priest named Prelati. This scandalous trial was held at Nantes on the 25 October 1440. Gilles de Laval was burned alive; but Prelati and the canons of the infernal chapel were saved by the Inquisition: their deaths would have discredited the clergy too much.

II

LET us return to the Witches' Sabbaths. These assemblies had no fixed date and were not always held in the same place, so as to escape the attentions of their enemies. For a long time adepts were rarely found in towns and cities and even fought shy of them; but in the country they could be found everywhere. Each little town, each village, had its magician or sorcerer, often both, presiding over a school and a shop for cures and curses, which were always there for the asking. They gained people's confidence through the helpful science of medicine. They made themselves feared through the use of secret poisons; they made themselves respected through their pretensions to knowledge of hidden things.

The witches were the midwives and the magicians the popular physicians of the Middle Ages. The little we know about their medical skill is revealed to us by Paracelsus, the greatest doctor of the XVIth century. The secret art, he tells us, owes its most miraculous cures to vegetable poisons.[7]

---

[7] *General note*: Herbalism to-day forms a strong movement, of which the British Herbalists' Union Ltd. [Secretary: J. Hewlett-Parsons, British Herbal Union Registered Office, 34 Sackville Road, Bexhill-on-Sea, Sussex] is one of the main bodies. Readers who contemplate the possible use of any of the following remedies are strongly advised to consult a Fellow of the Union [F.B.H.U. after the name indicates a Fellow]. Modern herbal practice differs from remedies such as those that follow here in that research is now able to measure accurately the mineral content, including trace elements, which exists in botanical drugs. This can be allied to modern biochemical therapeutics with more accurate results in the constructive treatment of disease than heretofore. These herbalist remedies, unlike the drugs of orthodox medicine, are non-suppressive in the body, and even when they do no good they can do no particular harm. In general, it may be said that herbalists hold that the crude herbal infusions indicated in the following are far more effective than the modern spirit infusions common in orthodox medical practice. In the text, the remedies as given by Christian are printed in *italics*, whilst modern herbal knowledge, comment and use of the ingredients, added by the editors, are given in roman type.—*Ed.*

Diseases of the breast, so painful for women, disappear as if by enchantment by the application of sedative cataplasms made of henbane. Henbane seed is still used for irritable conditions; it acts as a sedative in such complaints as asthma and whooping cough. For breast complaints generally however the modern herbalist has several other remedies, such as red clover.

The same for convulsions accompanying a difficult childbirth: a sachet of belladonna, applied to the stomach, soon brings relief and soothes away pain. Belladonna plasters are of course still a common if slightly old-fashioned alleviant. They are now used for febrile conditions, coughs, etc., and for the suppression of glandular secretions; and externally in applications for the relief of gout and rheumatism.

Bites by mad dogs or other venomous beasts are cured by drinking wine in which stalks of verbena have been boiled, or by applying to the wound leaves plucked from this plant. Verbena [vervain] is a well-known antiseptic, used as a nerve tonic and for feverish colds, fits, convulsions and similar complaints. Plantain might also well be used.

Myrtle berries, dried, pounded and preserved with white of egg, then applied in the form of a plaster to the mouth and the stomach, prevent vomiting. And an infusion of this plant's leaves, applied in compresses on the forehead, the temples and the feet, brings a calm and healing sleep to fever sufferers. Obdurate colds and violent pains in the head [neuralgia or migraine] can be cured by inhaling the warm vapours of the same infusion. The myrtle leaf is frequently used for chest complaints and night sweats, also for general pulmonary disorders.

Bean-flour, applied to the breast, cures abscesses which often prove mortal under the scalpel of surgery. The present-day herbalist would use ordinary white flour and honey. A number of other plants have been found sovereign for curing abscess—marshmallow, red clover, slippery elm and aconacia.

Leaves from a peach-tree, preserved in vinegar with mint

and alum, then applied to the navel, are a dependable dis-
peller of worms for children. The peach is now used for the
relief of gastric surfaces and in pulmonary complaints. For
expelling worms quassia chips are now the usual remedy;
coriander and wormwood have also been found useful.

If you chew burnet in times of plague, it will preserve
you from contagion. The greater burnet is now used as an
astringent and tonic, also for stopping haemorrhages.

The flower of the marshmallow, pounded with pork-fat
and turpentine, then applied to the stomach, cures inflam-
mations of the womb. The root of the same plant, infused
in wine, prevents retention of urine. Its seed, pounded and
kneaded in the form of an ointment which is rubbed lightly
over the face and hands, protects from wasp and bee stings,
etc. The marshmallow is a demulcent often now used to
remove inflammation both internal and external. In the
old herbal books it was known as the 'mortification root',
i.e. for the prevention of mortification.

A decoction of the kind of camomile which we call royal
comfrey brings still-born children from the womb. Used in
compresses on the eyes, the same decoction removes film
from the eye. Royal comfrey or 'knitbone' definitely helps
the growth of bones. It is used for duodenal ulcers, while
the leaf subdues inflammation. It is a demulcent and astringent used extensively in pulmonary complaints.

Stalks of anet, cooked in oil and applied to the head,
deliver patients from insomnia. Probably dill seed is meant.
This is a carminative and tonic. Dill water is used for children's complaints such at flatulence.

Leeks, ground up and mixed with barley flour and oil,
clear away herpes and other skin-eruptions. Leeks are freely
used now as a general purifier of the blood.

Plantain leaves, pounded and applied as poultices, cure
ulcers on legs and feet. The seed of the same plant, pul-
verised in wine, or its leaves preserved in vinegar, stop
attacks of dysentry. The same plant, eaten raw after dry
bread taken without drink, cures dropsy. The root of the

fresh-water plaintain infused in wine neutralises opium poisoning and the effects of other narcotic juices. These remedies are mainly correct as stated in modern practice; the plantain is a valuable diuretic. The late W. H. Box, a famous herbalist, said that plantain would cure nearly anything, from poisons and insect stings to piles.

Fumigations of boiled wormwood, taken in a hip-bath, deliver women in travail of their still-born children. The same plant, cooked in wine and taken in small doses, preserves women from the dangers of miscarriage. Wormwood has always been known not merely for its value in expelling worms [see above] but also for its semi-anaesthetic power in child-birth. It used to be known as 'old woman'.

Aniseed infused in wine with saffron cures inflammations of the eye. Pieces of the same plant, introduced into the nostrils after having been soaked in holy water, cure ulcers in the nose. Aniseed is a carminative and pectoral medicine, said to be excellent for coughs; but it is little used now except for certain complaints in horses.

Leaves and tendrils of the vine, pounded to make a poultice and applied to the stomach, bring relief to women who after giving birth may be tormented by an insatiable hunger. Grapestones roasted, pulverised and applied in poultices to the stomach, cure dysentery. The medicinal uses of the vine are little known now. The Oregon or mountain grape vine is used to improve digestion and for certain skin diseases. Modern practice would always tend to use the root of a plant and not the stone, wherever stones are prescribed throughout this and the other recipes.

A concoction of viburnum leaves in wine cures epilepsy. Viburnum or cramp bark is used in herbal treatment of convulsions and spasms.

Nettle seeds cooked in wine cure pleurisy and inflammations of the lungs. Nettle leaves, pounded and applied to sores and ulcers, prevent gangrene. A decoction of the seeds of the same plant cures mushroom poisoning. The same result is obtained by swallowing a little nitre mixed with oil. The use of nettle seeds is recognised for pleurisy. We should however now use water and not wine for the infusion. Mixed with honey and sucked, nettle seeds are excellent for goitre; they are also used in cases of consumption. Nettle seeds supply the chlorophyll commonly used in modern practice.

Here are some even more curious properties: he who holds in his hand a nettle-stalk and a milfoil stalk picked whilst the sun is passing through the sign of the Lion, 19 July—23 August, will be impervious to fear. The juice of the nettle, mixed with the juice of snake-root [serpentaria] is a wonderful bait for amateurs of rod and line; it is sufficient to anoint the hand with this liquid and to plunge it into a river or a lake to attract and capture whole schools of fishes. Nothing is known in modern practice of these surprising properties of the nettle.

The juice of purslain, mixed with sweet wine, cures henbane poisoning. Chewed raw, the same plant cures ulcers in the mouth. Its seeds, crushed and eaten with honey, cure asthma. According to Nicholas Culpeper, purslain is an all-embracing remedy for inflammatory conditions. It does not appear to have been used in very recent times. Several herbal remedies for mouth ulcers are current, including decoctions of raspberry leaves.

An infusion of thistles cures ulcers in the lungs. The application of its root, powdered fine, cures ulcers of the breast. Knapweed or ray-thistle is now often used as a tonic; its ulcer-curing properties however are unknown.

An infusion of angelica in wine cures interior ulcerations. A pinch of this plant reduced to fine powder and swallowed in winter with a little wine before breakfast every day preserves the taker from epidemics which break out in that season. During the summer, the same dose, taken with a little rosewater, produces the same effect. Its leaves, pulverised with rue and honey, then applied to a dog-bite, prevents rabies. Angelica is a well-known carminative, diuretic and diaphratic. Probably it is the root which is indicated here.

It might certainly be a very present aid in epidemics, though we know nothing of its uses to prevent rabies.

The juice of aloes, mixed with vinegar, prevents falling hair. Aloes are not today used in hair treatment, but mainly for intestinal complaints. In modern usage rosemary, southernwood or citric acid [vinegar] would be prescribed for falling hair.

A strong decoction of agnus castus [a disagreeable aromatic shrub, once supposed to be a preservative of chastity], smallage and sage in salt water, applied as a liniment to the back of the head, brings back to life sick people who fall into a coma. Modern herbalists attach no virtues to agnus castus, which is ignored by Culpeper.

If you wear a belt made from juniper, leeks or verbena stalks, you will be free from attacks by vipers or any other venomous reptiles. Is there someone sick who is very dear to you? Do you wish to find out how his sickness will end? Then take in your left hand a sprig of verbena and, approaching the sick-bed, ask the person how he feels. If he replies 'unwell' he will get better; if he replies 'well' he is in danger of death. The celandine possesses, they say, a similar virtue. Put a stalk of this plant on a sick person's head: if he is about to die, he will burst into song; if he is to recover, he will weep. These remedies appear to appertain rather to magic than to herbal remedies.

One of the most dangerous things that can happen to a woman's health is the accidental suppression of the menses. In order to re-establish the natural flow infusions of fresh parsley leaves should be taken in the form of tea: this is also an excellent remedy for pale complexions. In order to stimulate the appearance of the menses when they are overdue, take a very finely-chopped agrimony, feverfew and parsley, mix them with oatmeal grits and cook the whole with fresh pork. The liquid only must be drunk; the meat must be thrown away. The uses of parsley for menstrual trouble are well-known. So are the uses of agrimony, parsley and fever-

few to stimulate the menses; but we know nothing of its
mixture with fresh pork juice.

*Teeth will never decay if every morning you dissolve
in your mouth three grains of sea-salt, spread with the
tongue over the teeth and gums.* The use of salt as a stimulant and antiseptic has had an enormous extension in recent
orthodox medical practice. The use therefore of salt,
whether sea or otherwise, to preserve teeth seems by no
means a mere superstition.

*The root of the barberry, sorrel or plantain hung round
the neck cures scrofula or scrofulous tumours.* Barberry is
an antiseptic usually used for piles and liver complaints,
also in cases of jaundice. For plantain see above.

*To cure erysipelas, take two ounces of oil of roses, three
ounces of oil of nenuphars [water-lilies], five ounces of
warm goat's or cow's milk; mix together well, let them cool,
pass them through very fine linen and apply them in compresses to the affected part. Rye flour mixed with honey and
elder flowers produces, it is said, the same effect.* Erysipelas
would in modern herbal practice be treated internally; for
skin troubles and even gangrene echinacia is sovereign. The
elder plant is known as a remedy against inflammation.
Elder flowers are generally used for the reduction of inflammation in any part of the body.

*To cure haemorrhage of the uterus, take seven oranges,
stew their skins in three pints of water until one pint of
liquid is left. Throw in a few handfuls of sugar and make
the patient take twelve spoonfuls three or four times a day.*
For uterine complaints of this nature we should now probably use white pond lily. The great value of oranges, which
contain vitamin C in larger quantities than any other fruit,
now needs no emphasis.

*A decoction of tobacco leaves, boiled and applied as a
lotion, clears up pimples and blotches on the face.* We know
nothing of this remedy; we should now use any of several
plants such as echinacia.

The gall of a cow, mixed with eggshells dissolved in vine-

gar, *effaces freckles or patches of redness. Goose-droppings, soaked in wine, cure jaundice. However disagreeable it may seem, a dose of this substance [about the size of a walnut] must be taken every day for nine days.* Nothing can usefully be added on these topics, which the reader can adopt if he wishes. Cucumber rind is now held to be very effective for curing freckles.

To rid oneself of erotic dreams, which weaken the character, a sheet of lead, cut in the form of a cross, must be laid on the stomach. The advice is obviously symbolic, possibly valuable to a Christian believer.

If a fish-bone sticks in your throat, put your feet in a bowl of cold water. If a bread-crumb threatens to choke you, stuff your ears with the same bread. The uses of these quaint devices are problematical. Lemon juice is the usual recommendation for dissolving fish bones, and a hearty thump on the back would seem to be more efficacious if bread crumbs stick in your throat than stuffing the ears.

Eagles' droppings, dried and reduced to powder, then burnt over glowing embers, procures a fumigation which delivers women from the pains of childbirth. No-one in recent times appears to have used this distasteful remedy. Raspberry leaf tea [1 oz. steeped in a pint of water] taken in large quantities over the whole child-bearing period, has been found almost invariably to be of the very greatest assistance in achieving a painless delivery, especially after the first six months.

To make the hair grow, roast some bees; mix their ashes with mouse-droppings and infuse this mixture in oil of roses; add to this the ash of roasted chestnuts or beans, and hair will grow on whatever part of the body you choose to anoint with this preparation. Readers are invited to experiment with this; we can however take no responsibility for the result.

Goat's blood, heated and then drunk, cures dysentery and dropsy. The gall of the same animal, mixed with honey and applied as an ointment, cures jaundice. A goat's head roasted cures dysentery. Its gall, dried and placed on the stomach, prevents intestinal inflammation. You will invariably *cure a dropsical person if you make him swallow, over a period of nine days, in any sort of beverage, the droppings, dried and powdered, of a little unweaned dog; but the sick person must not know the nature of this remedy. An ointment made from the gall of a hare, with the juice of leeks and the fat of a he-goat, if applied to the stomach, will bring a dead child from the womb. A wolf's liver, dried, crushed to a powder in Madeira wine, cures diseases of the liver. Rub children's gums with hens' brains and they will cut their teeth painlessly.* All that can be said of these strange remedies is that some of these kinds of remedy are now used in minute quantities in homoeopathic practice.

Tie round children's wrists bracelets of raw silk and they will never suffer from convulsions. These bracelets must be left on always, except for being replaced by clean ones when they become dirty, until the child has passed the dangerous period of its first teething. Another process consists in steeping the seeds of a male peony [they are black] in white wine. Make a necklace of them with linen or a hempen thread; there should be an odd number of seeds. These remedies again appear to pertain to the realm of magic rather than medicine.

If you wish to enjoy constant good health and reach a ripe old age, take every day two or three spoonfuls of honey before dinner. Honey is generally recognised now as one of the very best forms of natural sugar. Sugar is, of course, together with fat, the chief easily assimilated energy and heat-providing substance in the human diet.

And if, to create a diversion from the monotony of flourishing health, you wish to give yourself the pleasure of a temporary feverishness, have a stag-beetle cooked in olive oil and rub your pulse with the oil. Again, the reader is invited to experiment. He will probably have the advantage, if it is one, of being the first in several centuries to do so.

These little recipes, which I could easily treble in number, though without any guarantee of their efficaciousness, by no means made the fortunes of the country witches, who were the *hoi polloi* of the magical fraternity. More fortunate were those who claimed they could foretell the future and who had enough business sense to make a certain reputation for themselves. The latter were also more learned than their colleagues; some of them had frequented schools opened in certain convents and had learned to read old manuscripts; often they were even monks who had grown weary of monastic seclusion and who were sufficiently crafty to make a profitable living by exploiting the credulity of their contemporaries. They worked according to the ancient superstitions of Hellenic mythology, and in the following chapter I shall give the principal means of divination which they practised in accordance with the documents handed down to us by the neoplatonist schools.

III

DIVINATION BY THE RING (Dactyloscopy) employed constellated rings, that is, rings composed of the metal and set with the precious stone sacred to each of the seven planetary Genii and with certain engraved images, as follows:

Planet	Metal	Stone	Engraved Image
Saturn	Lead	Onyx or Garnet	Serpent coiled round a stone
Jupiter	Tin	Topaz, Sapphire or Amethyst	Eagle holding in beak a five-pointed star
Mars	Iron	Ruby, Red Jasper or Haematite	Serpent biting the hilt of a sword
Sun	Gold	Jacinth or Chrysolite	Lion-headed Serpent wearing a crown
Venus	Copper	Emerald	Indian Lingam, emblem of sexual union
Mercury	Tin, lead and solid quicksilver	Cornelian or Alectorine	Caduceus or wand with two intertwined serpents
Moon	Silver	Crystal or Selenite	Sphere cut by two crescents

The priest or the pythia took the ring indicated by the day and the hour of the consultation. If, for example, the consultation took place on the day of Mars [Tuesday], it had to be in the 1st, 8th, 15th, or 22nd hour, all of which belong to the Genius of Mars. The consultant and the fortune-teller approached a round table on which were engraved the signs of the zodiac and the planets. On this table were scattered three alphabets cut out on little disks made from the metal sacred to the planetary genius of that day, and these were shuffled thoroughly. Then, on a linen thread, the ring appropriate to the day and the hour was suspended above the table. After a prayer addressed to the genius of the occasion, the priest or the pythia took a torch consecrated to Hecate, goddess of enchantments, and burnt the thread. The ring fell and rolled on the table and the letters over which it passed and on which it finally stopped had to be noted at once. This operation was performed seven times, and then a reply to the consultant's question was formed from the letters. If the letters formed words, divinatory inspiration provided links which made sentences; and if letters were left over, they were taken to be the initials of a sentence which was revealed after a short period of meditation.

DIVINATION BY WAND [Rhabdoscopy][1] had as its

---

[1] See W. H. Trinder *Dowsing*. Regular investigations into the subject began in 1910 with Prof. Mager; in 1930 a British Society of Dowsers was formed. Observations established by T. Bedford Franklin and J. Cecil Maby, published in *The Physics of the Divining Rod*, show that a measurable change of muscle tone measured in electromagnetic waves takes place in most people when walking over water or other substances beneath the ground if holding the divining rod, whether or not actual twitching of the rod by the muscles occurs. Mr. Trinder lists out types of instruments used, rods of whalebone, hazel, apple, privet and other woods or of brass, copper or steel wire: 'motorscopes' of cranked wire: pendulums of various kinds and 'angle rods'. Dowsing is regularly resorted to by modern firms of well-sinkers. Trinder gives lists of colour, sound and number reactions, their correspondencies with each other and affinities with various substances. He indicates the possibilities of divining rod indications for soil and seed affinities, medically for diagnosing suitable foods and the seat of trouble in the human body. Dowsing can be effected from photographs and maps. The first English references are XVth century, German dowsers being then employed to rediscover Cornish tin mines.—*Ed*.

object the finding of hidden treasure. At the time of the full moon, on a day and at an hour consecrated to the Genius of Mercury, a hazel wand had to be cut at a single stroke: it had to be as long as an ordinary walking-stick. It was carried parallel to the horizon, the two ends held in the hands, and slightly bent. At the moment when the magician passed over the place where the treasure was hidden, the wand twisted of its own accord, and the apex of the curve pointed to the earth; it only remained for the ground to be dug in order to discover either the buried treasure or a rich vein of precious metal.

I do not know whether such a wand has ever produced this admirable result, but it is certain that it turned the brains of many people, if it did not turn itself. The Jesuit Athanasius Kircher claims that the true divining rod should be cut in two equal pieces. The end of one piece must be cut to the shape of a cone, and the end of the other in the form of a pointed cup in which the cone is inserted. The wand is carried before one in this way, held lightly by the index fingers until the wand turns. The Abbé Valmont de Bomare has written no less than two large volumes in favour of the wand. He claims that it must be forked, that it should be six inches long and as thick as one's finger. 'It is held,' he says, 'in both hands, very lightly, with the back of the hand turned towards the ground, the point of the fork held parallel to the horizon, and away from the body. One must walk softly in the places where one thinks there may be water, mines or hidden silver. No rapid movements must be made, because in doing so one would disperse the vapours and effluvia which rise from the places where these things are, and which, impregnating the wand, make it bend towards the earth.'

The Abbé Bignon, contemporary and rival of the preceding diviner, says that one must take a wand forked at one end; it must be of hazel, alder, oak or apple, about a foot long and as thick as one's finger, and should be balanced

on the back of the hand, the ends of the fork being parallel
with the horizon.

Father Malebranche states that it is the Devil who
makes the wand turn, in order to enrich his slaves in this
world before roasting them in the next. I should not be
so foolish as to deny this, but I do not believe a word of
it. Repeated failures have disillusioned the seekers after
hidden treasure, but there are simple people who still
believe that the wand can discover water in regions where
it appears to be lacking, and there are others who, under
the name of water-diviners, exploit this innocent credulity.
Whenever you need to find a spring, look closely at the
ground, and if you see a fresh piece of grass in times of
drought, you can be sure that a watercourse exists not very
far down, whose vapours are feeding the grass.

DIVINATION BY WAX AND COFFEE-
GROUNDS. Cereoscopy requires very refined wax which
is melted in a brass bowl and stirred gently with a spatula
until it is entirely liquified. Next it must be poured very
slowly into another bowl filled with cold water, so that it
spreads in thin wafers on the surface of the water. The con-
gealed wax then presents an infinite variety of shapes of
which the ancients had made a descriptive catalogue, accompanied by mysterious explanations.[9] This kind of divination
has been replaced nowadays by the study of figures traced
in coffee grounds on a plate.[10] This is yet another of the
wretched subterfuges used in the business of cheap fortune-
telling.

If the fortune-teller sees in your plate the shape of a

[9]   Graham Dalyell in his *Darker Superstitions of Scotland* 1835, p. 512, says:
'Among the Samagitae were diviners called Burty, who, invoking Potrympus,
an aquatic divinity, determined futurity from the figures of melted wax
poured into water. Meletius says he knew a woman who consulted a diviner
on the return of her son, expected long from Prussia: when the melted
wax, assuming the form of a vessel with a man floating supine beside it,
indicated that he had perished by shipwreck.' See Meletius *De Diis Samagi-
tarum, circa ad anno* 1580; Gaguin *Rerum Polonicarum*, vol. 2, p. 241.—*Ed.*

[10]   This corresponds with fortune-telling by leaves left in a teacup in the tea-
drinking countries.—*Ed.*

spider, she will foretell misfortune. If she sees an altar, there will be consolation for your troubles. If she sees a column, you will obtain a large and lasting fortune. If she sees a cross, you are assured of a peaceful death. Three crosses predict employment in high positions. If the sorceress sees an elephant, a man who wishes you well will bring you your fortune. If she sees a house, however poor you are today, you will become its owner. If she sees a wheel, fortune will overwhelm you with her blessings.

But if you return a few days later to the same fortune-teller, or to another, she will tell you that pride comes before a fall, because there is a peacock in your plate. There may be a dagger, which threatens murderous vengeance; or a serpent, which warns that you will be the victim of frightful calumnies; or an iron grating, which shows that you will be going to prison. These examples are sufficient to prove the foolishness and the inanity of these contradictory predictions.

DIVINATION BY SIEVE [Coscinoscopy] is still practised in the villages of Brittany. There it is called turning the sieve [*tourner le sas*]. Whenever, for example, some object has been stolen or taken away, a sieve is suspended from the ceiling on a length of rope. The magician then offers up his prayer and slowly pronounces a list of the names of those on whom suspicion might fall. He pauses after each name, in order to give God, or the patron saint of the village, or the Devil, time to reflect and indicate the guilty person by making the sieve turn after his name has been uttered. If the sieve moves, woe to the neighbour whom this practice has singled out; the village is convinced and he is branded as a criminal.[11]

[11] See Dalyell *op. cit.* p. 521 [the allusions are to the superstition in England and given in the old English speech]: 'Sticke a pair of sheeres [scissors] into the rind of a siue, and let two persons set the top of each of their forefingers upon the upper part of the sheeres, as holding it with the siue up from the ground, stedelie, and ask Peter and Paul whether A, B or C hath stole the thing lost, and at the nomination of the guilty person the siue will turn round.' The practice was a common one in Scotland. See also Peucerus *Divinationum*, p. 321.—*Ed.*

DIVINATION BY KEY [kleidoscopy] is a variant of the preceding method and is practised in Russia. When it is desired to find out the author of a murder or a theft, the name of the suspected person is written on a slip of paper; then this slip is placed under a key which is attached to a Bible or a Testament and the whole is placed in the hands of a young girl. The magician then recites in a low voice a prayer in which the name in question is pronounced, and if the slip of paper moves, the guilty person is held to have been found. If it remains motionless, it is a proof of innocence.

Kleidoscopy is also employed in Russia to find hidden treasure. A key is placed on the first page of the Gospel according to St. John, care being taken to allow the ring of the key to pass beyond the edge of the book; then the volume is closed and tied with a piece of cord. The treasure-seeker passes the index finger of his left hand through the ring and pronounces the name of various places in which he asks if treasure is to be found. If the key moves on the supporting finger, the consultant is assured that the place where his fortune has been hidden has been indicated to him.

DIVINATION BY WATER [hydroscopy] consists in throwing over stagnant water or the calm water of a pond or a pool three stones, the first round, the second triangular and the third a cube. The undulations which they caused were observed and noted, and the magician explained them by referring to a black-book containing the presages indicated by each figure.[12]

The maritime peoples of antiquity also used to observe phenomena presented by the varying surfaces of the sea; calms, storms, the light ripples caused by a gentle wind and

[12] In England, girls at the well of St. Maddern, Cornwall who wanted to know when they would be married joined two straws in the form of a cross and dropped it into the water. The resulting bubbles which rose on the surface were as many in number as the years which must pass ere they achieved the matrimonial state. See R. Hunt *Popular Romances of the West of England*, pp. 285-300.—*Ed.*

the great waves raised by tempests, all furnished predictions whose significance seem to have been already understood.

DIVINATION BY SACRIFICE [hieroscopy] was perhaps the summit of human absurdity and madness. The innocent oblations of flowers and fruits of the earth instituted by patriarchal families were first succeeded by the sacrifice of domestic animals, but soon the increasing superstition of ignorant nations demanded the immolation of human victims. We feel sick when we read in the Bible of the God of Moses relishing the odours of burning fats on His altars and descending even to the formation of rules and recipes for this far-from-divine cookery. He took pleasure also in the steaming blood of men, since He ordered so many murders, all executed with impunity under His protection by Moses and his successors. The Hebrews therefore found themselves naturally disposed to imitate their neighbours, and like them to sacrifice children to the Phoenician Moloch in the valley of Tophet. These abominable holocausts spread in time across the entire world as it was then known. The historians of the east, of Greece and of Rome have handed down to us accounts of this tradition. There was a theory by which the convulsions of the dying were closely examined, and the future was also forecast from the state of the blood, the liver and the entrails.[13]

When these practices fell into disuse, fanatics replaced them by inventing the tribunal of the Holy Office, the tortures and the butcheries of the Inquisition instigated at the beginning of the XIIIth century by Pope Innocent III and

---

[13] Facts about divination from entrails are extraordinarily difficult to procure. Rich in his *Occult Sciences* says that the Roman Aruspices had four distinct duties: to examine the victims before they were opened, to examine the entrails, to observe the flame as the sacrifice was burned and also to examine the meat and drink offering which accompanied it. It was a fatal sign when the heart was wanting; this was said to have been the case with two oxen that were immolated on the day when Julius Caesar was killed. If the priest let the entrails fall, or there was more bloodiness in them than usual, or if they were livid in colour, it was understood to be a portent of instant disaster. For many out-of-the-way aspects of divination, see chapter 8 of Lewis Spence's *The Magic Arts in Celtic Britain.—Ed.*

by a Spanish priest named Dominic [1170—1221] whose memory another Pope, Gregory IX, was not ashamed to sanctify with the title of Founder of the Order of Preaching Friars, commonly called the Dominicans.[14]

DIVINATION BY FIRE [pyromancy] was practised by throwing resin on burning coals. If this substance took fire swiftly and brilliantly, the presage was favourable; it was the contrary if it was consumed slowly and with clouds of dense smoke.

The peoples of the north made prognostications by observing the combustion of wood in their chimney-hearths. Everyone has sometimes fancied on long winter evenings in the chimney-corners that he could see in the shifting shapes of the fire figures of men, women, animals . . . and a thousand other objects. There were black-books also for the interpretation of these capricious visions.

Another type of divination by fire bore the name of LYCHNOSCOPY. It was practised with three candles of very fine wax arranged in a triangle. If the flame wavered from left to right it presaged an early change of surroundings. If it turned in a spiral, it announced manoeuvres by secret enemies. If it alternately rose and fell, it signified perilous vicissitudes. If one of the three candles burned more brightly than the other two, it was a sign of unforeseen good fortune. If the flame threw out sparks, it was an appeal to prudence, and a warning of reverses or disappointments. If a very bright point formed at the end of the wick,

---

[14] The reference is to Dominic's mission to the Albigenses of Languedoc [1205—1215], the failure of which by 1208 was followed by a seven years' war of extermination after the Pope's appeal to the princes of Christendom. The most reliable authorities say nothing of Dominic's having acted as inquisitor; on the contrary it appears that he tried to continue his mission on peaceful lines. The Order grew out of the banding together of his followers in these activities. The Albigenses professed an extreme and anti-social form of Manichaeism, that is they believed that all matter was evil and lay in the dominion of a second god, equally powerful with the God of Christianity, whose son was Satan. The greatest of evils was sexual intercourse; evil too were all material possessions, flesh-eating and many other matters. Suicide was exalted as a merit. Even the Emperor Frederick II was moved to suppress similar sects, for the sake of civil order.—*Ed.*

this sign was held to mean that successes would come in increasing numbers. If the brilliance of this point died away, good luck would only be fleeting. If one or several of the candles suddenly went out, it was a very tragic augury, either for the consultant himself or for the objects of his consultation.

DIVINATION BY THE FOREHEAD [metoposcopy][15] observed the general shape and the wrinkles or lines marked on the forehead. By this process the character of the consultant could to a certain extent be divined, as well as his capabilities and his future life.

A very high forehead, but narrow and receding, with a long face and pointed chin, was considered to be the mark of a narrow mind. Broad and square, it signified wisdom and courage and inflexible will. If it was protuberant at the top, it showed a tendency to violence and a very mediocre intellect. Rounded, and vertical over the eyes, it signified, if it was also broader than it was high, an active mind, a good memory, sound judgment, but an absence of sensitivity. If it was irregular, bony, bumpy, it indicated a perfidious nature and evil tendencies. Two-thirds vertical and the rest gently rounded, it denoted noble and well-balanced faculties.

This doctrine also states that seven principal lines, approximately parallel, cross the forehead from one temple to the other. Saturn presides over the highest, Jupiter over the second, Mars over the third, the Sun over the fourth, Venus over the fifth, Mercury over the sixth, and the Moon over the last, at the base of the forehead.

If the *line of Saturn* is very faint, it presages misfortune resulting from imprudence. If broken in the middle

[15] Christian's text on this theme seems to be based on nebulous data, but it certainly reflects some elements from an Indian system. Metoposcopy is at present out of fashion and veracious material about it is not available. The greatest authority is a work by an Indian, Chattopadhya. A more recent work, but also unobtainable, is Holmes W. Merton's *Descriptive Mentality from the Head, Face and Hand* [1899].—*Ed.*

of the forehead, it means a life full of vicissitudes. If strongly marked, it indicates patience and perseverance.

If the *line of Jupiter* is strongly marked, it tells of good fortune in the future. If very faint, it indicates a weak, inconsequential mind, at the mercy of any chance event. If broken, it denotes a future compromised by a false appreciation of men and things.

If the *line of Mars* is well marked, it indicates a tendency to anger, audacity, temerity. If broken, an unequal character, if very faint, timidity.

If the *line of the Sun* is very pronounced, it speaks of kindness, generosity, and a love of luxury. If uneven and broken, then kindness and cruelty, liberality and avarice alternate in an unpredictable fashion. If very faint, it shows egoism and avarice.

If the *line of Venus* is clearly defined, it denotes ardent passion. If it is uneven and broken, it signifies struggles between reason and passion. If it is very faint, coldness and insensibility.

If the *line of Mercury* is very strongly marked, it tells of a noble, lively imagination, fluency in speech, an elegant and sympathetic conversationalist. If broken, it denotes a very ordinary mind. If very faint, a thoughtful but uncommunicative mind.

If the *line of the Moon* is clearly marked, it shows a cold nature, inclined to melancholy. If broken, then gaiety and sadness unaccountably follow one another. If very faint, it indicates indifference.

A *cross on the line of Mercury* foretells persecution for scholars, philosophers, writers; this persecution will be motivated by their works and their doctrines.

A figure shaped *rather like a C*, and placed on the *line of Saturn*, shows a good memory. A *letter C*, on the *line of Mars*, courage: on the *line of Venus*, dangers arising out of amorous adventures: on the *line of Mercury*, a mind that sees both sides of a question, and supports them: false judgment: on the *line of the*

Moon, between the brows, an irritable temperament, a vindictive spirit.

A *square* or a *triangle* in the middle of the *forehead,* on the *line of the Sun,* presages an easily-acquired fortune: if this sign is on the *right* on the same line, it prognosticates unforeseen bequests: if on the *left,* they will be acquired by foul means.

A *figure S,* placed on the right on the *line of Venus,* indicates a tendency towards adultery. If *three figures of an S shape* are found close together, on whatever line it may be, they are a warning of death by drowning.

Two lines, rising from the *top of the nose* and curving outwards *over the brows,* presage some accusation which will end in imprisonment. If these two lines cross the *line of the moon,* there is a threat of condemnation. If the lines are *double,* there will be captivity in a foreign land.

Two circles on the *line of the Moon,* on the *right-hand* side of the forehead, foretell future blindness or almost complete loss of sight: if they are in the *middle* of this line, danger of losing an eye: if on the *left,* blindness in old age.

A *figure like a Y* on the *line of Mars* on the *right* of the forehead, indicates rheumatism or paralysis: if in the *centre,* it means dangerous attacks of gout: if on the *left,* death from an attack of gout.

A *figure rather like a 3* on the *line of Saturn* warns of some future ambush: on the *line of Jupiter,* success in all enterprises: on the *line of Mars,* a fortunate future in the Army, but with a threat of captivity: on the *line of the Sun,* loss of fortune: on the *line of Venus,* unfortunate marriage through wife's infidelity: on the *line of Mercury,* a prosperous future in the priesthood or at the Bar: on the *line of the Moon,* menace of violent death.

A *figure shaped like a V* on the *line of Mars* indicates a possibility of a future spent in the Army: on the *line of*

Saturn or the Sun, a threat of political persecution, exile or banishment.

A *figure in the form of a P,* on any line whatsoever, denotes sensuality and love of good food.

A *figure shaped like an M* is the presage of a peaceful life spent in the sweet mediocrity praised by the ancient scholars.

Whenever an adult person has kept a child-like look, it is a sign of longevity. Eyes tinted with yellow signify depravity and violent instincts. Small eyes denote malice and pusillanimity. Large eyes with long lashes foretell an aptitude for the sciences, but a short life. Eyes which open and shut with great frequency and with a mechanical movement announce a perfidious nature capable of much evil. Eyes set deeply under the eyebrows presage malignity and an acute memory for past injuries.

IV

DIVINATION BY GENII [demonoscopy] was used to evoke supernatural beings who were inferior to the gods but whose pagan presence peopled air, fire, earth and water. Belief in them still persists among all the northern races. Official Christianity made repeated and vain efforts, especially in wooded and mountainous regions, to uproot these poetic superstitions. France has retained these creatures under the name of *fées* [fairies]; they still reign in England, Scotland and Ireland under the name of fairies or fays [the more correct generic name], as *sidhe* [pronounced shee] in Eire, as *Tylwyth-Teg* ['the fair family', Cymric] in Welsh areas; particular kinds being known as moorland elves [*aelf,* Saxon] or pixies—this perhaps being akin to the Scottish *pech,* a dwarf or goblin; and in Eire the *leprechaun.* In Germany and the Scandinavian countries these beings go under the names of *stille-volk, kobbolds, alfen, nokke* and others.

Documents of great antiquity on the origin of the fairies exist in Wales. Among the Armorican Bretons the same beliefs are linked with the very oldest traditions and we can find a first mention in the geography of Pomponius Mela. 'The Isle of Sena,' he says, 'is off the coast of the Osismiens. It is distinguished by the presence of the oracle of a Gallic divinity whose priestesses must take vows of perpetual virginity. They are nine in number. The Gauls call them *Saynètes;* they believe that these virgins can raise tempests, take on various shapes, cure sick people and foretell the future.'[16]

We know that the Druidical cult, proscribed in Gaul by Roman policy, took refuge in Great Britain, which was still unconquered, and that its original survivals were for a long time afterwards found among the descendants of the Cymric race.

The fairy beings of both countries had so much in common that for a long while they were considered to be the souls of the ancient Druids who, not having died in a state of sufficient purity to enable them to rise at once to an abode of perpetual bliss, had to remain between heaven and earth until the Judgment Day. These mysterious beings exercised a great hold over the imagination of the Middle Ages and their power was much feared.

In Scotland, Wales, England and France it was the custom to dedicate new-born children to them. When Ogier the Dane came into the world the tiring-ladies at the castle took him into a hall sacred to the fairies. Six of these marvellous creatures immediately appeared. The first, called Gloriande, took the child in her arms and said:

[16] The Isle of Sena is the modern Sein, off the Pont du Raz, W. Brittany. These priestesses were known as Gallicenae and were consulted as weather controllers by seamen. Another female community called Namnites is mentioned by Strabo as on an island near the mouth of the Loire. There are mentions in Norse literature of cults of the same kind in the Channel Islands. See Lewis Spence *History and Origins of Druidism*, pp. 62-63.—*Ed.*

'Lovely child, all your life you will be the bravest of knights.' Each of the others added her special gift, though Montguel, the last and the most powerful, added: 'Thou shalt never enjoy my sisters' gifts until thou has inhabited my castle at Avalon.' Now the castle of Avalon, in the west of England, was famous in the legends of the XIIIth century. Any wounded knight who touched one of its stones was cured immediately. These stones shone like fire. Each doorway was of the purest ivory; five hundred windows lit its golden tower, which was studded with precious stones. The roofs were of gold, and on the topmost point of the edifice gleamed an eagle made of gold and bearing in its beak an enormous diamond.

Whenever a rich lady was about to give birth to a child, a table laden with exquisite wines was placed in her room, with three goblets and three white loaves. The new-born babe was laid on this table; the fairies appeared and pronounced gifts for its future. Often, instead of waiting for them to arrive, the child was carried to certain well-known spots where they liked to manifest themselves. These were places of special reverence, in the ancient beliefs of our ancestors, and have often retained the names of fairy grottos or rocks.

In Wales the fairies wore green the better to hide themselves among the foliage. They loved to dance by moonlight, sometimes in the fields, sometimes on grassy mounds surrounded by shadowy trees. Sometimes a mortal has mingled with their dances, but the fairies would drag him into a supernatural ring and make him dance so fast that he could not catch his breath, and he would be found dead the next morning. The mountain called Cader Idris, in Merionethshire, was for a long time the principal theatre of these fantastic dances. The summit of this peak is crowned by a circle of stones which are said to be the tomb of Idris, a spirit celebrated in the history of that region. The common people still believe that one has only to fall asleep in this circle of stones to have supernatural visions and prophetic dreams.

The Tylwyth-Teg have their principal habitat at the foot of a mountain in Brecknock which is surrounded by a lonely lake. At one time a secret doorway in the rocks was said to open on the first of May. Those who had the curiosity and the courage to enter arrived by a subterranean passage on a tiny island in the middle of the lake. They then found themselves in a magnificent garden inhabited by the Tylwyth-Teg. These fairies offered the visitor flowers and fruit, charmed him with delightful music, unveiled the future to him, invited him to remain with them as long as he liked; they merely required that he should take nothing away with him when he left the island. It would come to pass that some careless individual took no heed of this warning and wanted to take away with him, as a souvenir of his adventure, some flower of miraculous beauty. But scarcely would he have crossed the enchanted threshold than he went raving mad.

The general idea we have of fairies resembles that which the Arabs and Persians had of the Peris. Peris are represented as having a vague outline, a fantastic softness and an aerial lightness which cannot be adequately rendered by any word in our language. The variability of their shape is the most remarkable thing about them; and, reading oriental descriptions, we seem to see apparitions evanescent yet distinct, intangible, which rise slowly, sometimes visible, sometimes half-hidden from sight, or which skim lightly over dewy lawns. They smile sweetly, beckon, weave flowers in their hair, and are so beautiful, so full of grace and celestial dignity, that imagination provides us with only a very incomplete idea of what they are like, for we know of nothing on earth with which they can be compared. They inhabit moonbeams and feed on ambrosia sipped from roses or orange blossom; they love to alight on a wispy cloud of perfume. They scent the air through which they fly, and the water in which they watch their reflections; their

essence is their utter charm.[17] Against these angelic creatures
Persian Mythology has set its *devis* and Arabian mythology
its *Djinns*, monstrous and evil spirits, of which the demons
of Christian superstition are copies.

It was not rare to find fairies marrying simple mortals if
the latter attracted their attention by some great deed or
by some extraordinary virtue. The Fairy Melusine is celebrated in French XIVth century legends. Raymond de
Lusignan, Lord of Poiteau, had met her in the forest beside
a fountain and had fallen madly in love with her. Melusine
agreed to become his wife, but on condition that he would
never go near her on a Saturday between sunset and the
following morning and that he would never try to find out
what she did on these nights.

Raymond having promised this, Melusine gave him as
a wedding present a castle which the genii of the forest, her
servants, had filled with marvellous treasures. The two
were happy for many years. Melusine kept for her own use
a high tower at the far end of the castle, to which she would
retire every Saturday night. Raymond had hoped that she
would one day tell him her secret; but as time passed and
he was still none the wiser, he became jealous and had unworthy suspicions concerning his wife's fidelity.

Advised by a friend to whom he had revealed his uneasiness, he resolved to investigate the mystery which
surrounded Melusine and at nightfall went and knocked
on the door of the room to which entrance was forbidden
him on pain of eternal separation. Not receiving any reply,
but thinking he had heard a strange voice muttering words

---

[17] Christian appears here to be influenced by the former etymological surmise
that 'fays' derive from the Persian 'peri', which is now known to be wrong.
'Fay' is more likely to derive from *fata*, a late Latin word for a concept fusing
the classical Fates [the *Morai* or *Parcae*, who span, wove and cut the thread
of life] and the *fatuae*, which in classical Latin would mean 'feminine jesters',
but also means nymphs or damsels who dwelt inaccessibly near lakes, mountains and woods, such as Egeria, the Roman King Numa Popilius' lover. See
Lewis Spence *Fairy Tradition in Britain*, pp. 114-115, which see also for the
nature of fairies and other spirits generally.—*Ed.*

which he could not make out, he thought he was betrayed and in a burst of violent rage smashed open the door with an axe. But he was stopped then by a terrifying spectacle. Melusine appeared as half-woman, half-serpent; so do the fables depict the sirens of antiquity. Instead of arms she had enormous bats' wings, and she flew out through the window crying: "Thou hast lost me forever!" In despair, Raymond left his native land, and, after a pilgrimage in the Holy Land, took up his abode in a hermitage near Rome where he died in the odour of sanctity.

According to Dutch traditions, the fairies inhabit beautiful castles built of gold and crystal, surrounded by magnificent gardens and limpid lakes. A music of exquisite loveliness is always to be heard; there winter is never felt, for a perpetual springtime reigns. But the curious thing is that to us these fairy castles appear to be dirty cottages, their gardens dung-heaps and their lakes muddy ditches. The enchanting music sounds to us like the croaking of frogs; snow seems to fall there as everywhere else and winter still lays bare the earth. In the same way the fairies live among us in the forms of poor old women; we meet them dressed in filthy rags, with reddened eyes in wrinkled flesh, grey hair, bare legs and thin, hunch-backed bodies. But if after having taken Communion we go on the Eve of St. John at midnight precisely, holding in the left hand a herb which the peasants call *Ren-vaen* [the common tansy or bachelor's button], to sit with crossed legs in front of a fairy's doorway, we shall see her as she really is—lovely, young, splendidly dressed, surrounded by maids of honour and seated on a crystal throne blazing with precious stones. We shall see the crystal palace, the fountains of rosewater, the cascades of milk, the translucent, scented flowers and the fairy's friends.

The White Ladies, known in Flanders since time immemorial, dwelt inside the great hills of that country. They were evil fairies who spent their time enticing unwary travellers into their subterranean domains. They also, but less frequently, stole young women and children from their homes. If one climbed one of these hills, one would hear such heart-rending shrieks that the hair turned white with terror.[18]

All fairies love to wander by night by bright moonlight, skimming over the earth with the swiftness of the wind. Often shepherds hear them pass quite close and are warned of their approach by a sharp whistling sound. It is dangerous to speak to them at this moment; if one does, one may be carried for a considerable distance and one's bones broken in a heavy fall. It is easy to recognise the traces left on the grass when fairies have been that way. Sometimes it appears to have been shaven smooth and is slightly browned; at other times it is parched yellow and one can see the imprint of tiny feet. At other times the grass has become a deeper green than the rest of the field; in the latter case, it is thought that the *Veld-Elven* or field-fairies have passed that way.[19]

In some countries, notably in England, Scotland and Saxony, the fairies have weapons which are called fairies' arrows or axes, tiny triangular pieces of worked flint which are found in rocky districts. In Flanders the fairies are less warlike and instead of arrows and axes they carry a light hazel-wand on whose bark they have traced magical characters that glitter bright as jewels. But these simple wands are far more powerful than any other weapon in

[18]   In this and the following passage balletomanes will recognise features in common with the *wilis* of Teutonic legend known best to us in the ballet Giselle. These White Ladies appear to have nothing in common with the widespread local traditions in England and elsewhere apparently derived from the late Roman *matri* or *matres*, spirits of river dedications; e.g. the White Ladies of Benwell, Cumberland.—*Ed.*

[19]   In Eire patches of long or rank grass which the cattle will not touch are said to belong to the *sidhe;* farmers will not plough them.—*Ed.*

the world. By waving them in a certain fashion it is said that Fays can stop rivers from flowing, halt and pile up clouds, change a man into stone, lead into gold, a dung-hill into a palace and the most frightful old man into a beautiful youth. With this wand they can raise up storms on land and at sea, shatter vessels like eggshells and rocks like rosebuds.

The *sidhe* and the glen spirits of Scotland inhabit lakes and mountains. One must take care not to annoy them, especially on a Friday, the day of their greatest influence, for these spirits can kill with a single breath.

Fays sometimes take up their abode underneath houses. Sir Walter Scott tells us how Sir Godfrey Mac-Culloch was taking the air outside his house when he was suddenly accosted by an old man dressed in green and riding a white horse. This old man complained to Sir Godfrey that his rain-water spout had just poured all over the old man's parlour. The Scots gentleman, who had neither tenant nor neighbour, realised that he was speaking to the genius of his dwelling-place and hastened to reply that he would give orders for the gutter to be removed to another side of the house. He kept his word, because he knew that it is dangerous to laugh at spirits. A few years later, having had the misfortune to kill a fellow-country-man in a quarrel, he was put in prison, tried and condemned to death. The scaffold on which he was to be beheaded had been set up on the hill where Edinburgh Castle now stands. He had just arrived at this fatal place when the old green man on his white horse rode through the crowd of onlookers with the speed of lightning. He snatched Sir Godfrey from the executioner's hands, laid him across his saddle and dashed off down the other side of the hill without anyone daring to stop or follow him. The knight escaped therefore with his head intact, and was never again seen in Scotland. Had the mysterious old

man taken him to live in some fairy palace? The Scots have
no doubt about it.[20]

V

In many parts of Wales it is the common belief that at
night, when everyone has gone to bed, if the hearth is
cleaned, the floor swept and the water drawn for the morning, the good fairies will come at midnight to the place
prepared for them; that they will continue their innocent
merrymakings until sunrise, when they will sing the well-
known air called 'Daybreak' and go away leaving a golden
coin on the hearth.

In the countryside, the English peasants believe in
supernatural beings called brownies [occasionally lubbers].
These brownies, who are rather like elves, come down the
house chimneys at night when there is no moon, sit down
quietly in front of the hearth and light the fire. Often, if
the busy housewife rises before daybreak, she will find that
the log which she left in a corner the night before is now
reduced to ashes; the strange thing is that these ashes give
off more heat than a whole Yule log would do. The housewife must be careful not to curse the lubber who has burned
her log or to make the sign of the cross if she is a Catholic,
for then the spell would be broken and she would find in the
hearth nothing but dead cinders.

Often people have drawn the wrath of these little creatures upon their heads by causing them some annoyance,
such as forcing them to go away or cursing them. One poor
peasant, whose wife was ill, had got up during the night
to churn the cream; on entering the dairy, where everything had been left ready the night before, he saw the fire
gently flickering, and, in front of the hearth, a little man
half-asleep. At the sound of his steps, the lubber [for that
was who it was] awoke, stood up and stared at him without

---

[20]   By the less fantastic accounts, the supernatural visitant was a brownie, not a
man in green, and he merely rescued Sir Godfrey.—*Ed.*

a word. The peasant did not say a word. He looked at the lubber out of the corner of his eye: the little man was all dressed in red, with green face and hands. Putting a fresh log on the floor beside him, the peasant went back to bed. The next morning, his cream was churned, the butter ready to be taken to market, and there was twice as much to sell. This lasted for seven years. The peasant's wife got well again; the house prospered, so much so that the peasant tripled his property and cattle, and managed to save much money, which he kept rolled up in an old stocking in a cupboard.

The lubber came regularly every night; sometimes he would make the butter, at other times he would work in the garden, and he did twice as much work as two labourers put together. This extraordinary being spoiled the peasant, who began to drink heavily at the local inn and would come home rolling drunk. The lubber would meet him with reproaches which were fairly well received; but it so happened that one night, the peasant, having drunk even more than usual, loaded insults and injuries upon his mysterious protector, seized the log that was burning in the fireplace, and threw it out of the window. In the morning, when he was sober again, he found his wife ailing, his old stocking full of cinders instead of savings, his cattle dead, and his crops destroyed: the brownie had had his revenge.[21]

In Germany there are the *Stille-Volk* who never speak. They are a race of familiar spirits who, according to popular belief, attach themselves to noble houses. Each member of a great house has his or her genius, who, as in classical beliefs, is born with him and accompanies him through life and all eternity. If danger threatens him or one of his family, this genius uses all means to warn and save him. If the misfortune is inevitable, the genius is heard weep-

[21] Lob Lie-by-the-Fire and Lubberkin are other names for this being. The best-known literary reference to this belief is in Milton's *L'Allegro*, where the 'lubber fiend' flails the corn. It is also recalled in one of Puck's songs in Shakespeare's *Midsummer Night's Dream.—Ed.*

ing and moaning all night round the castle and the fated family; his moaning resembles the howling of a dog. He sometimes takes on some fantastic form and comes into the room where the person he wishes to warn is sleeping. A German nobleman in this way saw a luminous spiral which alternately approached and withdrew from his bed. He roused himself and left post-haste, thinking that this sign was a warning to leave his home and thus avoid some unknown peril. A few hours later, armed forces came and ransacked his house in a fruitless effort to find him and drag him off to a State prison.

England, Scotland and Ireland possess another kind of supernatural beings, closely allied to the fairy; they are called spirit-rappers. Welsh miners affirm that they can be heard underground in the mines, and that, by their tappings, they generally draw the miners' attention to a rich vein of coal.[22]

In the county of Pembrokeshire, it is believed that a person's death is announced by the appearance of a light which passes from one place to another in the house of sickness. Sometimes it moves towards the cemetery, and frequently it seems to be carried by the figure of the man, the woman or the child who is about to die. Such an apparition is called *Canwyll Corph* [corpse candle, Welsh].[23] Another presage of death, often vouched for to the present day, is the vision of a coffin and a funeral procession leaving the house in the middle of the night and following the road to the cemetery.

As one goes further north,[24] the belief in elves and the

---

[22] This and a few similar allusions appear to be the sum of Christian's contribution to the literature of what are now called psychic phenomena. The subject is treated on a higher plane in a separate article attached to the end of this book, p. 452.—*Ed.*

[23] See Wirt Sykes *British Goblins*, p. 238 *seq.*—*Ed.*

[24] The accounts of Norse and Icelandic spirits in the following pages need supplementing considerably by modern standards. The reader is advised to consult Keightley *Fairy Mythology*, pp. 78-154; Grimm *Teutonic Mythology*, English translation by Stallybrass, generally; and W. A. Craigie *Scandinavian Folk-Lore.*—*Ed.*

like increases and spreads. The Norwegians imagine them as little naked men with blue skins who take up their abode underneath the hills, trees and houses. They sometimes attack a poor peasant and lead him miles out of his way, so far indeed that he never comes back. Nevertheless some of their victims have been seen again who, during their long absence, have lost their reason and cannot give any information about the mysterious creature who had led them astray. When an elf has taken possession of a tree or a house, woe betide anyone who would try to uproot or destroy it to plant or build something else in its place. They have been seen, it is said, to carry for considerable distances churches whose neighbourhood they felt to be unsuitable. Icelanders accuse them of sometimes stealing new-born children who have not yet been baptised and of putting one of their own in its place; but mothers and nurses take every precaution and these accidents are very rare. This type of elemental inhabits rocks, hills and often brooks, rivers and sea. It is said that their sisters and daughters who, in spite of their azure complexion, are of an enchanting loveliness, sometimes prefer the inhabitants of earth to their subterranean lovers. Tales are told of Icelandic families who owe their origin to this mysterious kind of union. They are believed to have no soul, or at least no immortal soul; but, as the children born of an elf and a man share the natures of both father and mother, they only have to be baptised by total immersion in holy water to obtain an immortal soul. Certain traditions speak of these marriages as examples of enduring affection; but it appears that however happy they may be at first these unions always have a tragic end.

Elves are invisible and only very rarely reveal themselves to the eye of man. Nevertheless, they can sometimes be seen gambolling in rays of sunshine, enjoying the gentle heat which they lack in their subterranean dwellings. They also like to walk the earth and especially to gather at crossroads [always much haunted places in early beliefs] during the first night of the New Year. At this period magicians walk abroad in the countryside, wait to see the genies go by and, by pronouncing certain magic words, compel them to reveal the future. Icelanders advise their children and their servants never to do anything which might offend these invisible hosts who might at any time visit their homes. Others, even more solicitous, open doors and windows, serve a meal of milk and fruit and leave a lamp lit on the table all night in order to show their sympathy towards any elves who may happen to pass that way.

In the Faroe Isles the elves, who otherwise resemble those of Iceland, wear a grey costume and a black hat. Their invisible herds pasture with those of the inhabitants; but sometimes the shepherds glimpse the shadowy image of a heifer or a dog that does not belong to our world and they consider this vision as a sign of the protection afforded them by the elves.

In Sweden these spirits are famed for their dancing and melodious singing. Often they gather in hollowed rocks, and, when the air is clear and the night still, they sing in soft and plaintive voices. If ever a traveller in the darkness accidentally breaks into one of the circles formed by these singers they disappear from sight, and his fate is then in their hands. But they never abuse their power when they have not been deliberately offended; at the very most they will play some harmless but mischievous trick on the innocent travellers.

The Island of Zeeland possesses elves who are much more formidable. They are the most mischievous and malicious sprites in all the north. The peasants have a magic tune which they call the Elf King's Air and which they are very careful never to play or sing. For scarcely have the first notes begun than all present, young or old, men, women and children and even inanimate objects, spring up and dance and dance without being able to stop, unless the imprudent musician is able to play the air backwards without a single false note, or unless a chance stranger comes in and cuts the violin strings.

The Scots see in their fairies, known by various names, dangerous enemies who poison the air of the place where they foregather to enjoy their nocturnal dances. The grass there withers at once and any imprudent passer-by who walks on this grass is seized by an irresistible drowsiness which ends in death. This grass is known as fairy or 'quaking' grass; in England it is 'briza' or 'dawdle' grass. It grows up when fragments have not been left after a meal for the fairies.[25] At the summit of Minchmuir passers-by must not fail to leave a 'wad' or gift of cheese, the favourite food of the elves. Elves are particularly fond of tormenting horses; often in the early morning when one enters the stable these animals are found exhausted and panting, with bloodshot eyes and bristling mane; obviously during the night they have been ridden almost to death by the elves of the neighborhood. In the cellars especially of rich people, bottles lie scattered, some empty, others filled with a liquid which is no longer wine. But the elves' chief passion is for hunting. One dark night a young sailor was journeying home in the Isle of Man. Suddenly he heard the sound of horses' hooves, voices, horns, barkings. Intrigued, he began to follow them in spite of himself. After running several leagues he at last leaped from the top of a high rock into a bog hidden in the darkness, in which he perished.

This supernatural luring to death is one of the commonest of themes in folk-tales everywhere in the west. The *Ellylldan,* or 'luring elf-fires', inhabit caves and precipices. They have the habit of seizing passers-by and forcing them to choose between a voyage above the air or one on earth. If the wretch's choice is the former, he is wafted up into the clouds, whence he is allowed to fall without warning and dash himself to pieces. If he choose the latter, he is at once dragged over stones, rocks, thorns, marshes and cliffs,

<hr>

[25] See Lewis Spence *Fairy Tradition,* p. 179.—*Ed.*

and perishes no less horribly. If his terror has prevented his making a choice and he remains silent, the *Ellylldan* merely spin him round and round until he is out of breath. Some of them live on farms. After having worked all day, when night falls and all is at rest they sit down by the fire, pull frogs out of their pockets, roast them and eat them. They look like old wrinkled men; they are never more than a foot tall and their garments are very poor. It is their nature to be helpful and not to do much harm; but sometimes they take pleasure in mischievous pranks. For example if a horseman loses his way in a mist, often an *Ellylldan* will climb up beside him on the saddle, seize the reins and lead the animal into a bog, then run away shrieking with merriment.[26]

Those spirits which are called in England elves are called *Duergar, Nokke, Droich, Kobbolds* and *Nixies* by the peoples of the extreme north of Europe. According to the customs of the country they inhabit, each species has different tastes, which nevertheless are very similiar when compared, and this seems to prove sufficiently their common origin. The spirits generally inhabit solitary places where men can rarely venture. In Denmark, where they are called *Nokke,* they live in the forests and the streams. They are great musicians, and are to be seen sitting in the middle of rivers playing on a golden harp which has the power to influence all nature. If one wishes to study music with them one must first of all seek an introduction to one of them with a black lamb and promise him that at the Last Judgment God will judge him like other men. It is said that once two children were playing in front of their father's house which stood besides a small stream, when a *Nokke* rose out of the water and began to play on his golden harp. 'Dear Nokke,' said one of the children to him, 'what is the good of your beautiful music? You will never go to heaven!' At these words the *Nokke* burst into tears.

[26] Compare however Wirt Sykes *British Goblins* p. 18 *seq.,* where the description differs from the foregoing considerably.—*Ed.*

The children went into the house and told their parents what they had seen. The father was angry at the children for having behaved so badly and told them to go back to the stream and comfort the *Nokke*. The children did as they were told, they found him sitting in the same place, still weeping. 'Dear *Nokke*,' they said to him, 'stop weeping, please, because our father has told us that you will have a place in heaven.' Immediately the *Nokke* took up his golden harp again and played wonderful music for the rest of the day.

VI

CHIROLOGY: THE SCIENCE OF THE HAND[27]

THE science of interpreting the symbols engraved in the palmar surface is as old as civilisation. The most ancient available written literature extant today comprises two treatises. One of these deals with woman's make-up or face paint, the other is concerned with hand symbols. These two books were excavated from Egyptian pyramids and belong to a period thousands of years B.C.

When Buddha was born, the story goes that the sages recognised him as the 'promised one'. This was accom-

---

[27] The text above is substituted for Christian's treatment, which by now seems so insufficient as to be incapable of amendment. That the reader may evaluate both accounts, Christian's text follows here.

DIVINATION BY THE STUDY OF THE PALM (chiroscopy), or the divination of the future through the lines of the hand, has had many followers in modern times. It has been the theme of numberless publications each no less absurd than the other, for they all contradict one another, and no ancient document has come down to us on the original rules governing this doctrine. All that it is possible to say is that the monks of the Middle Ages used the name Cheiromancy to extort money for the upkeep of their convents. Not only did they claim to read the future in the hands of their penitents [especially female penitents], but also, to lend a little more authority to the subject, they had printed and sold little popular books to which they affixed ecclesiastical appreciations. Here are a few examples.

"APPROVAL OF THE DOCTORS.—The *Natural Chiromancy* of Mr. Rampalle is very agreeable; it is a clear mirror in which everyone may find himself reflected and it can be read without scruple, for it contains nothing that may offend either against faith or modesty. Therefore we the undersigned,

plished by the study of specific symbols in his feet as well as particular markings in the palms of his hands. This examination of hand-symbols of newly born babes is quite in keeping with the hoary tradition of hand-reading in India. The Hindus have a system of reading human character and destiny from the markings in the hand which is nothing short of the miraculous. The Chinese as well as the Japanese claim to own their particular systems of hand-reading. The craft was known to the Romans, and the Greeks were reputed to be well versed in it. In point of fact, a peep into the history of different civilisations reveals that in the heyday of each culture kings, poets, philosophers, sages and politicians all seem to have patronised the art. Small wonder that some of the great personages in each successive civilisation not only took a keen interest in the study but seem to have taken pains to master its principles and to endeavour to make practical use of it. Julius Caesar and Aristotle could be cited as two outstanding examples.

Doctors in Theology, hereby append our unqualified approval of this work.—Lyons, 6 February 1653.—Fr. Nolin, Carmelite.—Fr. Nicard, Minorite."

"I, the undersigned, Doctor of the Sorbonne, Lecturer in Divinity at the Church of Lyons, certify that I have read the *New Chiromancy* of Mr. Adrian Sicler, physician, in the which I have discovered nothing contrary to the faith nor to the principles of the Church, nor to virtuous living.—Lyons, 31 March 1666.—Arroy, Doctor in Theology."

"I, the undersigned, Doctor in Theology at the University of Paris, hereby certify that the book entitled *Royal Chiromancy* is fully informed on its subject, being an abridgement of what all the best authors have written on the matter, and that it contains nothing offensive to the true faith.—Lyons, 12 April 1666.—Fr. Alexandre Richard, of the Order of St. Dominic."

"This work on Chiromancy is aptly named *Royal Chiromancy;* it is the result of such wide-spread, considered and well-applied research that it stands far above all others. In testimony whereof, etc., at Lyons, 23 April 1666.—Fr. Lombard, Carmelite."

In spite of these recommendations, Chiroscopy or Chiromancy includes no less than 433 different systems, each one claiming to be the authorised one: and the theological doctors who claimed, in the XVIIth century, that they had found nothing in these books which might be contrary to the principles of virtuous behaviour seem to me to have merely testified to their personal immorality. Moreover, it is well-known that lines imprinted on the human hand are infinite in their variety, differing not only according to persons, but also to age, and the nature of a person's manual occupations. Chiroscopy can therefore only be a chaotic jumble of chance observations,

For theoretical purposes, the study is divided into two component parts. One is known as Chirognomy, the other as Chirology. The former deals with the shape and formation of the palm, fingers and the fleshy elevations below the roots of the fingers, thumb, etc., generally known as the Mounts of the Palm. Chirognomy, in the main, deals with character study and health diagnosis.

Chirology covers the study of symbols and signs engraved in the hand. It aims at the understanding of character, health, destiny and other similar aspects of human life.

For practical purposes no distinct line of demarcation can de drawn between these two sections of hand-reading. A comprehensive knowledge of the study and a great deal of practical experience are essential for accurate interpretation of human hands. No single sign or isolated aspect of a given pair of hands can constitute a conclusive datum for pronouncing a judgment. For a coherent picture of characteristic trends of life and destiny a careful study and com-

to which every new author has added his own interpretations, according to his fancy or his interests. A few examples will suffice to prove the utter absurdity of these so-called oracles.

According to the books quoted above, a cross on the outside of the thumb gives promise of a rich marriage. A star in the same position signifies perpetual virginity. If you have a very well-developed index finger, misfortune will come to you during a long voyage. If there are several oblique lines on the top phalanx of this finger, you will be beaten with a stick. A line above the joint of the same finger's second phalanx is a warning that you will be hanged, and if this line is red, you will have your head cut off. If you have a circle on the second phalanx of the ring finger, you will die in the madhouse. If you have a cross above the first joint of the thumb, you will lose your right ear in an accident that will take place on a Saturday. If there is a half-circle above the last joint of the middle finger, it is a sign of shameful diseases brought on by loose living. If there are two crosses on the first phalanx of the little finger, they are a promise of great riches. If there are forked lines radiating from the base of the thumb, he or she who possesses these signs will be promiscuous and debauched. If you see three short lines at the base of the little finger, they denote a rogue; if these lines are fairly long, they reveal a practised thief; if they are very long, the rogue or thief will shrink from no crime, however terrible. I hardly think it is worth while to continue any further in our examination of this so-called science which does not even have any fixed principles, since its most highly-praised authors have to admit that out of a hundred thousand hands there are not two alike.

parative evaluation of both the aspects of two hands is essential.

The major lines which form the basis of judgment about character make-up and destiny among others include the Line of Life [A fig. 1], the Line of Mentality [B fig. 1], the Line of Heart [CC' fig. 1], the Line of Destiny [DD fig. 1], the Line of Sun [E fig. 2], the Line of Health [FF' fig. 1] and the Lines of Marriage [Gg fig. 3].

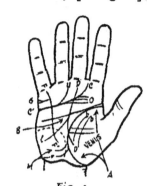

Fig. 1.

The Line of Life essentially denotes individual constitution, state of health and probable length of life. When it is long it promises long life; the contrary is the case when it is short.

When it sweeps distinctly through the palm thereby forming a large arch [A fig. 1], it denotes great constitutional strength. Such people have ingredients of great vitality and tend to be sympathetic and warm-hearted. They naturally respond to the healthy allure of sex life. Such a line is a good basis for matrimonial happiness.

When the line runs straight, as if drawn with a ruler [A fig. 3], it narrows down the scope of the Mount of Venus, the fleshy pad at the root of the thumb. This padded formation when full, round and large shows sympathy, affection, love of melody and of the opposite sex. When restricted and narrowed by a straight type of Life Line, it betrays lack of human warmth. Such people are cold by disposition. They are prone to be selfish. Their constitutional strength is by no means great. They are apt to prove poor marriage partners.

Lines running parallel to the Life Line, across the Mount of Venus, are said to denote good and helpful influences [b fig. 1]. Blades cutting across the Line of Life, on the contrary, are marks of obstructions and hindrances [b fig. 3].

When the Line of Life deviates from its normal track and proceeds towards the Mount of the Moon, the fleshy pad situated at the edge of the palm near the wrist [N fig. 2], it denotes an innate urge to go abroad. Such people feel a restless longing to travel and often manage to visit other lands. Marked offshoots of the Line of Life which make their way towards the Mount of the Moon show the times when a great urge for movement generally precedes a journey. The longer the offshoot the farther the destination of the travel [M fig. 1].

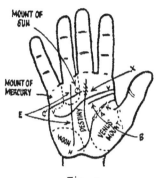

Fig. 2.

A long, distinct and well-marked line shows prospects of good health, smooth life and promise of long life [A fig. 1]. A chained line betrays poor health and changeable disposition [A fig. 2]. When numerous blades cut across the line [b fig. 3], they are marks of misfortune and worries repeatedly harassing the owner. A break [K fig. 2] or a cross [t fig. 3] indicates the sudden advent of danger to life or health; a star [y fig. 3] signifies the same. A square, however, is a symbol of protection from harm [S fig. 3].

The Line of Mentality [B fig. 1] is of great importance. It represents the main trends of human attitude towards life. It is in fact the symbol of all that appertains to the mental mechanism of the individual.

There are two important variations; the straight line and the one with a downward curve. When it proceeds in a straight direction [B fig. 1] it is the mark of a realist. When it gently slopes downwards, towards the area of the Mount of the Moon [B fig. 3], it speaks of a creative and imaginative trend of mind.

A deep line indicates depth of mind. It is a symbol of good memory. It implies power of concentration [B fig. 1].

A shallow line which seems to be floating across rather than imprinted in the palm surface betrays a shallow mind.

A long line when well marked is a sign of great intellectual potentialities [B fig. 1]. Foresight, power of analysis and depth of understanding are some of the attributes of such a line.

·A short line betrays paucity of insight and points to a restricted intellectual horizon. Such people seem to be unable to visualise anything beyond their immediate environment. Though practical they seem to be superstitious and tend to be somewhat primitive in their devotion to convention and tradition [B fig. 2].

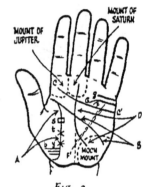

Fig. 3.

A long Line of Mentality, which towards its termination tends to curve upwards [VV fig. 2] indicates a tendency to accumulate and collect. Other aspects of the hand will probably provide clues as to the nature of collection, whether it be scarabs, scientific data, money or jewels.

The Line of Heart in the main represents emotional attitude. It also throws light on health and affairs of the heart [CC' fig. 1].

When it proceeds across the palm like a straight line [CC' fig. 3], it speaks of a nature that is apt to be fastidious and seeks intellectual stimulation in matters of emotional relationship. Such people need finesse in handling without which they obviously appear to be cold and selfish. When the line is long and well marked, such people could prove to be emotionally dynamic and extremely passionate.

When the Heart Line curves through the palm like a large arch, it reveals a nature that is warm, sympathetic and readily responsive. These people, as a rule, have ingredients of good comradeship and healthy sex responses which tend to cement ties of love and affection [CC' fig. 1].

When the Line of Heart is long, originating close to

the edge of the palm below the index finger, particularly on the fleshy pad called the Mount of Jupiter, it reveals a nature that seeks perfection in matters of love. Such people tend to place the object of their love on a pedestal. They endeavour to choose a partner of whom they can be proud. There is a streak of jealousy and possessiveness in their make-up [CC' fig. 3].

When the Line of Heart is short it betrays lack of aesthetic sense. When it begins below the base of the middle finger, especially in the area of the Mount of Saturn, it is a mark of selfish love. Such people seem to be devoid of delicate emotions. They are obviously sensuous and given to the pleasures of physical love. They are prone to be callous and prove to be sadistic if thwarted in their physical urges [CC' fig. 2].

Several downward offshoots of the Line of Heart are ill omens. They speak of repeated emotional frustrations. Such people tend to be perpetually on the rebound [O fig. 1]. Upward branches on the contrary are marks of affectional gains [U fig. 1]. Such people have the makings of good friends and often benefit by such contacts. They seem to have the delightful attributes of making and keeping friends.

The Line of Destiny begins near the wrist and crossing the palm vertically tends to terminate below the middle finger [DD fig. 1]. In the main, is stands for the mundane aspect of human personality. Vocational activities, changes of fortune and such matters are associated with this line.

When it reaches the area of the Mount of Saturn situated at the base of the middle finger, without any breaks or malformations [D' fig. 1], it reflects material security and a stable destiny. Such people as a rule take to callings which show definite prospects of future security.

When the Line of Destiny starts from the Mount of Venus, inside the Line of Life, it speaks of a person whose material life or career owes much to affectionate influences. Generally such people are helped by their parents to start off in life [D fig. 1]. When it begins from the Line of Life it denotes a self-made individual. These people are the architects of their own fortunes [see fig. 2].

When the Line of Destiny begins from the Mount of the Moon, it speaks of an extremely independent nature. Such individuals seem to have ingredients of personal charm and often become great public favourites. They tend to take to the stage, screen or such callings which require being perpetually in the public eye [D fig. 3].

When the Line of Destiny originates near the wrist but during its course gets tied to the Line of Life, it indicates that the owner will be called upon to sacrifice a great deal for his or her loved ones. Such people seem to be restricted in their life owing to emotional bondage.

A well-marked line which originates from the area of the Mount of the Moon in some hands seems to merge into the Line of Destiny [l fig. 1]. This is a sign of a romantic influence. Union, and in some cases marriage, is the outcome of such a romantic encounter.

A broken or an islanded Line of Destiny betrays a career full of ups and downs [X fig. 2]. An unbroken one denotes a smooth career [D fig. 3].

The Line of the Sun is otherwise known as the Line of Success. When normal it begins near the wrist and crossing the palm vertically tends to terminate at the base of the third finger. When thus marked it speaks of distinction and success [E fig. 2]. When it is absent it betrays lack of satisfaction with life and career. When marked in segments or broken at intervals it shows alternate periods of success and misfortune.

The Line of Health extends between the Mount of Mercury, situated at the base of the little finger, and the wrist. It runs in a slanting fashion [F' fig. 1]. When well-marked and clear it shows prospects of good health [F' fig. 1]. Broken, chained or malformed, it is indicative of periods of ill health [F' fig. 3].

The Line of Marriage seems to pierce from the outside edge of the palm below the little finger and above the Line of Heart. Generally one sees several such lines of varying depth and distinctness. Each line is a symbol of attachment. The strongest line shows the one that really matters [Gg fig. 3].

A large fork at the start denotes a period of long waiting before the actual union. Such people go through a period of long engagement [G fig. 1].

When the line ends in a large fork it is an ill omen. Such a union seems to contain seeds of discord and ultimate separation [G fig. 3].

A neatly engraved long Line of Marriage is the best to own. Such a line stands for deep attachment and a happy married life [g fig. 3].[28]

M.B.

DIVINATION BY DREAMS [oneiromancy]. This is another of those subjects on which even today innumerable books are published whose absurdity exceeds all bounds.[29] Nevertheless, there is a short study written in Greek and published in the IXth century by St. Nicephorus, the Patriarch of Constantinople, which contains short explanations of a certain number of dreams which, in his time, were considered as veritable prophecies whose authority had been proved by experience. Here, for the benefit of readers, is a translation of this curious relic of the Middle Ages.[30]

'Before you can even hope for the future to be revealed to you in dreams,' says Nicephorus, 'you must learn to

---

[28] Space limits do not permit further details here. Serious students are advised to refer to authentic literature of the subject amply available today.—*Ed.*

[29] This is doubtless still so; nevertheless, the study of dreams in a psychological sense has in the present century achieved the proportions of an autonomous science or craft. Of observed phenomena locally collected, Lewis Spence's new *Second Sight in Scotland* contains a good deal, with comments. Of interpretations in the psychoanalytical sense the reader will hardly need to be reminded of Freud's *Dreams* and of C. G. Jung's, Adler's and others' work, now fairly readily available.—*Ed.*

[30] Νικηφόρου Πατριαρχοῦ Κωνσταντίνου πόλεως Ὀνειροκριτικὸν : This is a supplement to a study *Artemidori Daldyani Oneirocritica*: library of St. Geneviève, Paris, no. 893.—R.

know yourself and to dominate your passions and carnal appetites. When you are master of yourself, if you go to sleep [first having prayed to God] you may see some symbolic images representing future events. But if your belly is loaded with meat, if you have drunk more wine than was fitting, you will be obsessed by trivial fantasies, and your spirit will be lost in the realms of darkness.' Nicephorus continues with the following list: [31]

If you see an eagle, it means that your dream, whether happy or tragic, is a warning come from God. An eagle is a creature that hovers for the purpose of preying only. Hence in dreams it signifies a warning of danger from above, from something unknown. Further, the eagle is itself a God symbol in mythology.

If you see a cock, your dream will soon be realised. The characteristic of a cock is that it crows at dawn; hence, is a symbol of coming light and the dawn of hope.

If you dream you are eating new-baked bread, it means imminent misfortune. Bread is the staff and stuff of life; but new bread signifies that the present life or its immediate future is being made anew; hence that it will be different, so that a transition is indicated. By the principle of contrast indications in dreams, a freshness indicates the advent of its opposite quality, decay; hence the transition bodes ill.

If you dream you are holding a bee, your hopes will be disappointed. A bee is a creature from which you hope for honey, but its characteristic is a sting if you hold it, so that when you are hoping for something sweet you receive in fact a shock or disappointment. This is a common love dream.

If you walk slowly, it means success won with difficulty. A walk is a common symbol for progress in life, so that to walk slowly means slow progress.

[31] After each item of St. Nicephorus' catalogue [printed in *italics*] has here been inserted a present-day interpretation drawn from modern psychoanalytical knowledge and also from traditional oriental lore. It will be seen that St. Nicephorus' brief statement is in every case justified in its general meaning by today's practice.—*Ed.*

To meet a person you love is a very hopeful augury. A loved one who is met in dreams is typically the *anima* of the psychological self [*animus* in the case of a woman], the idealistic and affectionate part of the mental characteristics. To meet your *anima* therefore means that the part of your mind which deals with love is ready for encounter.

To talk with a king means your plans will not mature. This everywhere, but more typically in the east, is the poor man's dream. It signifies speaking with someone unduly exalted; symbolically therefore planning too high or over-ambitiously—a symbol that you know your plans are not really practical.

If you see burning coals, there is a threat of some harm at the hands of your enemies. This is in all countries a symbol of the wastage of resources—that is, unless some reason or necessity for the fire appears in the dream. This means therefore a lowering of your psychic reserve and its con-sequent liability to be harmed externally.

If you dream you are flying, it means a journey in a foreign land. In flying the unconscious is indicating that it is reach-ing out for escape, for release from restrictive conditions, for travel in a new element or different place. Flying is *par excellence* the symbol of free movement, hence of travel, which implies an element of liberty.

If you are holding a book, it means you will rise in the world. A book is a general symbol of prestige, doubtless dating from the days when reading and the ownership of books was a rare and expensive privilege.

If you hear thunder, it means unexpected news. Thun-der is essentially that which suddenly startles—a very apt symbol for unexpected news, presumably of an unpleasant nature.

If you dream you are walking straight forward, you will triumph over difficulties, obstacles and enemies. Your path of life, says the unconscious, is clear, your inner self is prepared for success. Another way of putting it would be that the *anima* [or *animus*] knows of no obstacles.

If you dream you are eating grapes, it means rain, and by analogy success, realisation of your fondest hopes. This is an oriental dream, where rain is the great hope; upon it essentially grapes depend. Grapes supply a large part of daily needs—the characteristics of the vine have played an immense part in the build-up of civilisation, providing amongst other necessities drink, food and wood. Hence to eat grapes implies the coming of the rain which is necessary for grapes, a parable for the meeting of our needs and hopes.

If you are walking with back bent under a heavy burden, it foretells pain, oppression, humiliation. This indicates psychologically that the *anima* is unready for the burden placed upon it and is carrying too much.

If you walk on broken shells, it means that you will escape from the snares of your enemies. This dream has a variant of walking on broken skulls; both would mean the same thing, that is that your life is passing over something not substantial yet not dangerous—if you fall on either, you will not fall very dangerously; these empty shells or skulls will not harm you much, the plans of your enemies are therefore mere husks.

If you are shut in some underground place, it means great danger. What is underground is always hidden life, the unconscious, or an intrigue—that which is hidden. This dream probably shows in fact a love intrigue, which is that whence your consciousness apprehends most likelihood of danger.

If you are kissed by a king, it signifies that you will enjoy the benevolence, favour and support of powerful persons. A king is the common surrogate for the father image and for God. Hence a kiss from him means the support and approval of the father element in yourself.

If you see your own face in the features of an old man, it means you will be lucky in your enterprises. Seeing yourself in the guise of an old man means that you are assuming to yourself the qualities of age; that is, you are drawing upon the unconscious wisdom of the well-known Wise Old Man element, one of the dozen or so constantly repeating archetypes listed by C. G. Jüng. It signifies wise and ripe accomplishment.

If you see milk, it means that your enemies' plans for your downfall will not succeed. A common oriental saying is that milk is milk and water water. The common practice is to adulterate milk with water; but the dreamer in this dream is saying that his milk is not adulterated, that what he is doing—the substance of his life—is correct; therefore by implication any plans made against him will not succeed, his life is integral.

If you are eating something very sweet, it means an imminent setback, a bitter disappointment. Anything too much or excessive in a dream always means that the dreamer is stating that he has been overdoing things in some way, hence the anticipation of a bitterness or disappointment coming if he is eating something over-sweet.

If you laugh in a dream, you will cry when you awaken. The same interpretation applies to this as in the last example. Laughter in a dream is something excessive and implies that the contrary is to follow.

If you dream of a marriage contract, it means a change of abode. Woman is in oriental and in some western symbolism the dress and house of the man. Hence the contract of marriage which implies the addition of a mate implies also a change of dwelling.

If you receive a present, it means imminent success. This almost speaks for itself; something is due to be given to you, and success is the thing we all crave.

If you are bitten by a dog, it means injury, affront or harm from some enemy. An oriental but also a western dream. That is, taking the dog as the common scavenger of the east, to be bitten by it would imply harm from some low quarter; taking it in the western sense of the dog as the faithful friend, if this friend bites you, this implies harm from some unexpected quarter.

If you see your house fall down, it means the loss of your worldly goods. Another application of this dream is to see your house burning. Since the house stands for worldly possessions, the meaning of the dream is very simple.

If you dream you are breathing an unpleasant aroma it foretells sadness, affliction. Smell is something which is always close or imminent; hence it stands for something in the self and an unpleasant smell means discord in the unconscious, something imminent in the environment which is disharmonious.

If you eat the fruits of a foreign land, it means illness. In dreams aliens are always distrusted and bad, so that to eat alien fruits would imply something evil having been taken into the self, hence illness on the way.

If you receive letters written in purple ink, it means promotion for some, death for others. Purple is a double colour containing red and blue and the meaning of it accordingly mingles light and shadow, sadness and joy. If it is chiefly reddish it means royalty; but if considered as more mauve in shade it implies mourning, hence death. The royal element, by the reasoning indicated above, means advancement.

If you eat with an enemy, it means reconciliation. To eat with somebody means amity and that the *persona* is ready to meet the outside world, hence is in a psychological state for reconciliation.

If you walk in light-coloured mud, it signifies the vanity of all your plans. Mud can be of two colours: black or dark mud, which means deep and dangerous mire, or the light-colour mud of small puddles and sandy surfaces. Hence to walk in the lighter coloured mud means that you are walking in shallowness, hence the vainness of your projects.

If you see yourself standing up in some assembly, there is a threat of some accusations being brought against you. If an assembly of people indicates general concord, then if you stand up, it means that you are conscious of being prominent or aloof, that is, not in unison with your fellows; they are together, you apart. Hence they may accuse you.

If you meet an eunuch, it is an excellent augury for the

success of an enterprise or the realisation of a hope. This is an eastern dream. The eunuch being deprived of sex stands for the negation of both male and female elements. Hence if you meet your eunuch self it will signify that there is no struggle between the elements in you; that is, a unified self goes forward to meet some project.

If you are pursued by a viper or any venomous reptile, you must beware of very dangerous enemies. This scarcely needs interpretation. The snake or a similar reptile has throughout recorded time stood for all which is sinuous, subtle and lives in dark holes—the very image of an enemy.

If you dream you are burning incense, it foretells danger. See above, burning coals. Incense is that which is sacred, and to burn it unnecessarily in a dream is an extreme phenomenon, meaning that you are destroying the holy or protective element, which implies that you will be vulnerable to some attack.

If you eat pomegranates or oranges, it means illness. Both kinds of fruit contain pleasant and soothing juices such as are considered appropriate to convalescents after illness; hence by anticipation illness itself is predicted.

If you dream your eyes are bigger than they really are, it means you will enjoy some unexpected benefit. Large eyes are obvious symbols of surprise since you open them widely when astonished at something, hence you are ready for something unexpected.

If you dream you are holding nails, it means attacks by your enemies. Nails to the primitive mind signify weapons or means of defence; it was a nail that Jael drove through the head of Sisera to defend the Israelites. Hence the expectation of attack.

If you see your hair looking well-dressed, success and favour. This means that the self is preening itself on success, that the difficulties of life are, for the time being at least, laid to rest and there is a time of ease and favour coming. It may be worth recalling that the Spartans before battle invariably spent a long time combing and dressing their long hair, obviously an invocation of success by anticipation.

If you see yourself dead, your troubles will soon be ended. If the self seen in dreams indicates life, then to dream yourself dead means that the life is at rest, that is, its difficulties are ended.

If you see an ox, beware of an imprudence. An ox is a creature that advances impulsively forward without much judgment of what it tackles. Hence it is an emblem of tactlessness and imprudence.

A tranquil sea indicates success in your enterprises. This again scarcely needs interpretation. A tranquil sea means that it can be safely sailed upon, that the sea of life is now easy to navigate.

If you eat lettuces, it means you will be ill. Similar interpretation to the eating of pomegranates or oranges. Lettuces are something of a luxury and considered suitable to the weak and convalescent.

If you see or hold a broken stick or wand, it is a threat of failure. In the hand of the self is something that breaks; something therefore in you is weak and may fail, especially when you may want to use it, even as the stick has broken.

If the door of your house falls off, you will lose some property. This in dreams is similar to losing a tooth which, like your house door, is an intimate part of your life. To lose either is therefore a symbol of disgrace, and as the house symbol stands for personal possessions [see above], the direction of the loss is likely to be property.

If you eat fish in a dream, it is a bad sign for all your plans. The fish is the beautiful silvery thing which glints and is to be admired. Success is always the beautiful thing to be admired from a distance. To eat fish means that you are consuming that of which the essential quality is that it should be looked at rather than handled; thus a bad sign.

It is the same if you see black horses. This has a similar interpretation to the last dream. Like the fish, the horse has a beautiful shape to be admired; but if it is black, which is the colour of the dark side of the unconscious, the recessive element, it is a bad sign.

If you fall from a horse or a cart, it means a bodily or monetary collapse. A four-wheeled cart or four-legged horse usually stands in dreams for the 'vehicle' [*vahana*, Sanskrit] of the self, which is also four-limbed; either the body itself or the life erected about the self. Hence a fall from either may mean either bodily collapse or failure of the essential element of the machinery of life, i.e. money.

If you walk on slime or mud, it means an accident or misfortune. See above on light-coloured mud. If the mud is darker or more slippery, then the trouble is obviously deeper or more dangerous and something untoward will occur: you are, as the saying is, in deep water.

To see olives is a good sign in every way. See the above interpretation of grapes. The olive usually is an even stronger symbol than the grape, for if the grape fulfils certain needs the olive fulfils nearly every need—in Greece the olive was the tree of Athene herself, her gift to Athens; certainly it provided the Athenians, as indeed all Greece, not only with fruit which was also a food, but also with the oil which was alike cooking fat, soap and the oil burned for giving light. It also provided wood for fuel and furniture making. Hence to see olives means that material needs are going to be supplied in full measure.

If you dream you are holding keys, it means some obstacle in your way. A key indicates that there is a door. A lock is, to the primitive mind, a tricky thing. The appropriate place for the key is in the lock; but it is not there, you are holding it in your hand; therefore the solution of the obstacle ahead is in your own hand, but you do not use it. This is also a sexual dream, the key being a well-known symbol of the male organ.

If you hold a palm-branch, you will be accused of something. The common eastern palm is typically a fruitless tree; its branch waves easily but is not strong. In dreams it stands for a similar quality to the peacock's tail, that is, showiness or empty boastfulness; and if you boast, you are liable to be accused or attacked in retaliation.

If you hear a dog barking, beware attack by an enemy. In this dream the dog bears the western sense of a faithful friend; his bark gives a warning, therefore danger is imminent.

If you see yourself covered with dirt, it means material loss, humiliation. This is almost self-explanatory. That which should be underfoot and humiliated now covers you with humiliation. Things are upside down, hence loss.

If you see crows, it warns of dangerous advice or shameful action. Crows are typically mean and ill-omened birds, hence danger, shame or treachery are flying abroad.

To hold a wax candle is a fortunate sign. Everything in dreams is some element from your own life; hence a wax candle, if alight, means that the substance of your life is lit up, happy or glowing in some way.

To pour oil on one's head has the same meaning. Oil is a symbol of riches, and to put it on one's head means a vindication of the self, that the self approves of itself.

If you eat meat, it means you will enjoy a dubious reward. Meat is the substantial and enjoyable item of the meal of life, hence it signifies some kind of reward. But in this dream it is not a specific kind of meat, just meat of some kind—of any kind; hence the reward may be of dubious quality.

If you wear a necklace, it means imminent danger. In the east, prisoners normally wear chains round the necks, hence the necklace is a very general symbol of restriction; that is, the self feels itself trammelled in view of some contingency which is feared.

If you see trees felled, it is a threat of misfortune. This is a simple symbolism of strength falling—the tree [a father or mother emblem] commonly means established things or power.

If you hold or brandish an axe or a hatchet, it is a good sign for those who have enemies, or who are at grips with great obstacles. This again has a simple and obvious interpretation. The self is aware of being conscious of an attack pending and that it is ready to head it off with an offensive defence.

If you see a wolf yawning, it is a warning to beware of empty promises. When a wolf's jaws are open, it is normally either sleepy or hungry. Hunger however would be the normal identification; so that the wolf is waiting to swallow something or take something from you—its mouth is empty like the promises that may come.

If you see a naked woman with very fair skin, it is a good sign. This signifies that the *anima* [or *animus*] finds itself in a beautiful and clean form—a good psychological symptom.

If you see a lion, it means an attack by powerful enemies. The lion is the universal symbol of strength and commonly connected with attack.

If you see yourself with white hair, it is a fortunate sign. See the interpretation above of seeing yourself with an old man's features. This has a similar significance, i.e. that you see yourself dowered with the wisdom of age, in fact as the Wise Old Man of Jüng.

To embrace one's mother is also a very good sign. This indicates that the child is at one with its parent, that the father and mother principle are unified and that negative and positive are in collaboration in the ego.

To hold a sword in one's hand means fighting and great danger. The symbol here is very obvious—the sword is always a warning of danger.

To see or handle pearls means affliction, tears and mourning. In both east and west pearls are identified with tears, hence to handle them means that the reason for tears is on the way.

If you see a man or a woman with a black face, it means a long sorrow. Darkness is commonly identified with a prolonged [all night] sorrow, and a person with a black face means a personal sorrow.

To see a negro signifies illness. Similar to the above.

To hold fine fruits means luck in love. Love is the fine fruit of life, which you are holding in anticipation and expectation.

If you see dead strangers, it means loss of property, ruined hopes. To see a living stranger in a dream means strange hopes, personal property coming to you; but if the stranger or strangers is or are dead, then these hopes become estranged from you, or alien.

A tree without leaves means vain attempts to achieve success. If leaves signify the living results of life, i.e. success, a tree without them indicates a life barren of success. See palm leaves, above.

If you see an oak, it is a favourable presage for all enterprises. The oak tree is a universal symbol of strength, hence here an unconscious awareness of strength in oneself, resources ready to meet demands.

An olive tree means victory over one's enemies. This has a similar *motif* to the last dream. The olive is generally considered to give strength, which is needed to fight enemies; hence victory may be anticipated. The real classical symbol of victory was in fact an olive crown.

If you see a serpent in your bed, it is a good sign. The serpent is a symbol both of sex and of strength; seen in your own bed it means that these characteristics exist in your own constitution.

Climbing a mountain means strength and good luck. This is a very simple piece of symbolism. Climbing a mountain means going upwards, hence success; while the mountain itself as a father-symbol signifies strength—often, indeed, godhead itself.

Drinking wine foretells great obstacles and struggles. To drink wine signifies getting tipsy, hence losing balance; the result will be that struggles may be needed and that the self may be overwhelmed.

If you see a house burning, it is a good sign. Flame, as

distinct from smoke, indicates that strength and power, sometimes anger, is present in the self-awareness.

If you see a house enveloped in smoke, it is a bad sign. Smoke, on the other hand, means something cloudy, dubious or nebulous, hence bad.

If you dream of your teeth falling out, it is a bad sign. Teeth are an indication of looks as well as health and to lose them means loss of personal appearance, hence of prestige.

If you dream you lose a tooth and that it grows again, it means an unexpected piece of good fortune. If a tooth grows and replaces one which is lost, then good fortune results from an apparent loss.

If you see purple cloth, it means illness. Purple could be a symbol of the advent of dark things: cloth, the covering, is symbol of and similar to the body which is the covering of the spirit. Hence the combination may well signify illness.

If you see mists, it means be careful before you act. See smoke above: nebulousness and uncertainty, hence the objective is not clear.

If you dream your feet have been cut off, it means misfortune at the beginning of a voyage. Feet and heels are dream symbols of mobility, cp. the winged heels of Mercury, messenger of the gods. Mobility is what is needed essentially for a journey, so that a journey you are about to take is somehow limited at the beginning.

If you dream you have big feet, it means afflictions of all kinds. Big feet symbolise backwardness or inability to act in the right way—a foreboding of happenings with which you will not be able to deal.

To dream of a dove is a good sign. In both east and west the dove is a symbol of love, sweetness, peace and goodness, which are hereby announced as present in the self.

If you dream of a clear fountain, it means the end of your troubles or imminent happiness. A spring of water or fountain is always the symbol of happiness. Something new is welling out of the unknown which is pleasant to you.

If you are carrying sandals in your hands, it means unfore-seen perils. If you are walking bare-footed, which is the consequence of carrying your sandals, you are walking riskily and dangers may occur.

To be seated on a rock means your hopes will be realised. Rock is generally a sign of strength and stability or realisation, and to be seated on it can mean nothing but the realisation in fact of some such need in your life.

If you see a tower fall, it announces the death of high-placed persons. The tower, as the place whence news is announced and a look-out kept for the general good, also as a place of general defence, is a very general symbol of national life. Hence if it falls it means the fall of national figures.

If you see the skies or the stars falling, it means great danger. The sky or the stars in it are essentially the elements in experience which are always there and which do not fall; consequently if the sky falls it means some extraordinary catastrophe. The stars within it signify death or great danger to individuals.

If you imagine that you have wings and dream you are flying between heaven and earth, it means promotion to undreamed-of heights. To fly towards heaven or half-way to heaven means that you are well away from material troubles and on the way upward to great things.

If you hold a partridge, it signifies that you will possess the woman you desire. In the east it is common to recommend the eating of a partridge as a sexual stimulant; hence to hold this bird signifies possession first, by anticipation, of sexual stamina, and second of the 'bird', a common and vulgar expression for woman in both hemispheres.

To see or hold onions or leeks means sadness and mourn-ing. By similar anticipatory interpretation to that in several examples above, onions or leeks, the smell of which causes tears, mean that cause for tears will come.

To wear black clothes is a bad sign. See above on black faces. In dreams black is always a sign of ill-luck, death or illness.

To wear white clothes is a good sign. The meaning contrary to the above.

To wear purple clothes is a sign of sickness. Purple is an unusual colour for clothes, hence the self is seen by anticipation as not clothed in its usual colouring of health. Further, purple recalls shrouds and the colour of mourning.

If you dream you are holding sparrows and let them escape, it is a bad sign. If you allow sparrows to escape it means that you have not valued them enough to hold them properly. Hence something has not been valued sufficiently.

To embrace a column means divine support. A column, especially in Egyptian symbolism, means the divine support of the universe or a divine element in creativeness. If the pillar is God, to embrace it signifies prayer to Him and its consequent answer.

To break swords means triumph over enemies. If one breaks swords it obviously means that they are needed no more, hence that victory is complete.

To eat figs means deceit and disappointments. Figs are a juicy fruit, perhaps rather too pleasant; maybe you are being hoodwinked with pleasant words and suchlike. Further, a fig is often swallowed whole and the expression 'he swallowed it whole', i.e. was completely taken in, is probably drawn from this.

If you see wasps, it means danger and attacks by your enemies. Wasps are essentially creatures that have stings and obviously signify enemies.

If you see worms coming from a dead body, it means a host of annoyances. A dead body means that hope is dead in the self and is leaving something of a stink behind, from which worms of irritation and annoyance proceed.

If you eat a cuttlefish, it means sickness. A cuttlefish distributes a cloud of 'ink' in the water and disappears through it. Hence this dream means that the principle

of life is being disturbed by nebulousness and that strength
the fish, is being lost.

*To see or feel an earthquake, means danger for people
in high positions.* See above on the tower. An earthquake
essentially concerns a wide area, hence a national danger
or danger to those in authority over the nation. More
anthropomorphically the earthquake is the king's anger
when he stamps on the ground.

*If you dream you are rich, it is a threat of ruin or loss
or damage.* By the principle of boding anticipation, if
images in dreams mean the opposite of any excessive
quality that they show, riches are an anticipation of their
opposite.

*If you dream you are cutting your hair, it is a very bad
sign.* Hair in nearly all myth and legend signifies animal
and sexual strength. Hence if the self is frittering away
and getting rid of its own strength it cannot but be an
unfortunate symbol of loss.

*If you dream your hair is falling out, it is a sign of great
danger.* Similar to the above. In this case the *anima* [or
animus] knows that its strength is being lost.

*If you dream you are carrying a blind man on your
back, it is a very favourable augury.* To carry something
means a growing and worthy responsibility. By the principle of opposite meanings indicated above, a blind man
indicates that you are aware of the direction of your
success.

To hear singing means quarrels with your neighbours.
Singing is noise which comes from your immediate
neighbourhood. Since it is held to be a beautiful noise,
by the principle of opposites it will mean an unpleasant
noise, that is quarrels.

*If you see lights, it means a clarification of your prob-
lems.* See above interpretation of a lighted candle. Lights
naturally and inevitably mean increased visibility, hence
more intellectual clearness; you see your way clearly.

If you see a stormy sea, it means overthrow from your present position. The sea of life is going to be troubled; you are in for a rough time.

If you hear strange voices, it means the dream is a divine warning. Voices that are strange come from the unknown, hence from the divine; they are giving you information or guidance.

If you dream you are plunged into darkness, it means that people who hate you are plotting against you. Darkness essentially means evil or mystery; hence a scare or plots, for night is the womb of treachery.

If you dream you lift your hands to the heavens, it means an end of your troubles. You lift your hands to heaven in anticipation of your prayers being answered, that is, of your troubles being ended.

If you see yourself in torn clothes, it means the same thing. Clothes which are torn mean that material possessions or troubles are wearing out. Your body, or your true self, is perhaps already looking through them and some change is happening.

If you dream you are covered with lice, it means all sorts of troubles. See the interpretation of worms from the dead body above. Lice are also connected with the dirt which signifies humiliation [see being covered in mud above].

If you hold eggs or cook them, it means quarrels, sorrows, disgrace. Eggs mean potential energy or power; you are however holding this, retaining and not using it. Cooking eggs may mean killing potentiality, hence disgrace.

If you eat cooked eggs, it means gain and success. In this dream eggs have the reverse meaning; the potential is now being used rightly, and satisfactory results will follow.

If you dream you are sitting with no clothes on, it means privation. Nakedness in dreams usually means that the self is open to danger, or is deprived of some essential protection. You are separated from and to some extent ostracised by your fellows.

If you capture falcons, hawks or other birds of prey, it means success. These birds are essentially those which conquer other birds; hence to capture them signifies that victory is in your grasp—'the victor vanquished'.

.*If you dream you are weeping, it means happiness to come.* By the principle of opposites, the *anima* [*animus*] is hereby signifying that it is ready for the opposite excess, i.e. happiness.

If you fall down a precipice, it is a bad sign for everyone and especially for people in high positions. The interpretation here is obvious. To fall is a common sign of disgrace, and to be on a cliff signifies that the person is elevated in life.

To dive into a lake means danger. A lake here signifies the unknown, and to dive into it has the same significance as the expression 'putting your foot in it'; you are immersed in the proverbial sea of trouble.

If you see dead oxen, it is a threat of some misfortune. Oxen are creatures of great strength, used in the East for ploughing. Hence to see them dead means that the self is losing its creative strength.

If you dream you are swimming in the sea or in salt water, it means sickness. You are immersed in something which you cannot overcome or probably cross by that means of progress; it indicates therefore that you lack strength.

If you see spilt wine, it means an end to your troubles. If wine signifies lack of balance [see above], to spill wine means that you do not need such a stimulus and that your self is quite healthy. The interpretation is parallel with that of the broken swords [above] which are broken because they are no longer needed.

If you drink sour wine, it signifies trouble to come. To drink wine, again, signifies future lack of balance, and if it is sour also, that balance will be upset in a troublesome way.

If you walk on serpents, it means triumph over your enemies. Serpents are typically harmful creatures, so that if you walk upon them, you are trampling over those who wish to injure you.

If you dream you are washing your feet, it means the end of your troubles. You are cleansing from you the dust of your travels; you are therefore at home, at the end of your journey, and your troubles are at an end. Muslims wash their feet before they pray, and there may be a hint of this significance here.

If you dream you have burnt some part of your body, it is a warning of some scandal which will plunge you into ignominy. If you have been burnt you have obviously opened yourself to attack somewhere. Burning moreover is a peculiarly unpleasant experience and likely to signify a serious personal *exposé.*

If you dream you are seated on a wall, it is a fortunate sign. A wall is something which has been constructed, and is a solid achievement. You are therefore already resting on something which is strongly based.

To dream that one is running signifies strength and stability in one's enterprises. See above interpretation of feet being cut off. This dream means the opposite, that mobility is unimpeded, that strength is being used well and actively and that plans are going ahead fast.

To dream that one has a black skin means mortal sickness, especially if it is dreamed by a child. As above indicated, a black skin signifies death or serious illness. A child typically has a fair skin, hence for it to dream of a black one would be particularly significant.

To drink muddy water presages sickness. See above interpretation concerning cuttle-fish. Here again we have cloudy water, this time clouded with mud; hence nebulousness and uncertainty is being taken into the self, causing doubtful health.

To dream of a hare before setting out on a voyage presages an accident. A hare signifies something unexpected, which springs out suddenly and then either vanishes or stays unnaturally still; moreover it dies young.

The hare's speed here signifies the voyage and its common vanishing or death indicates some luckless happening.

To dream of washing one's hands means one's troubles are ending. See above on washing feet. To wash one's hands means the end of toil and the beginning of rest. Moreover food is eaten with the hands, and without washing there cannot be clean eating, so the dream anticipates eating, source of fresh strength.

To dream of holding or handling gold means failure of enterprises and disappointed hopes. See above on holding eggs. Again you are handling or retaining that whose value depends upon its being in use, so that what you possess is in fact being mis-handled.

If you dream of a river in full spate, it means triumph over obstacles and enemies. If in the river of life the stream is running fully, no obstacle can hold it; it is moreover going in the right direction, towards the sea of life.

We are indebted to the bibliophile Jacob [M. Paul Lacroix] for his learned study of Oneiromancy which he concludes with these words: 'There is in all things a golden mean which must be sought after continuously, and when it has been found, adhered to. Whenever we consider the art of dream-interpretation let us always remember this final axiom: that what it may be dangerous to admit blindly need not be systematically rejected. Eradicate errors and prejudices, but on condition that we do not offend reason by an excess of credulity; in the place of false gods let us not set up a complete void.'

What M. Paul Lacroix expresses here in such admirable terms corresponds to the general opinions of La Bruyère and Pierre Bayle and may be extended to all the occult arts. I may even add that at the present time many serious thinkers are applying themselves to research into the mystery of astral influences on character, inclinations and the destiny of man. Astrology, which comprises this special kind of study, is perhaps on the threshold of new qabalistic studies; and as astrology holds the keys to all occult science, its resurrection would perhaps revive the great truths of the past, hidden under centuries of error and abuse. But before embarking on this theory, let us conclude our review of the magical traditions of the Middle Ages and the Renaissance.

VII

In remote country districts the witch's remedies are still used. Families transmit them to one another; they are despised by doctors, but they are nevertheless effective, and they sometimes bring about surprising cures. The virtues of wild flowers, forest plants and mountain simples are better known to the peasants than to our professors of botany. This popular science of vegetable medicines, of which I have given a few examples [see Chap. II, p. 334], has its secrets classed nowadays under the uniform title of *good women's remedies* [remèdes de bonnes femmes][31] and this title explains its origin, for in days gone by witches were called *wise* or *good women,* an expression of gratitude or fear used by their clients[32].

That great and powerful physician of the Renaissance, Paracelsus [*circa* 1490—1541],[33] declares that all books of medicine should be burnt, whether they were in Latin, Greek, Hebrew or Arabic, and that all he had learnt about medicine had come from wise old women, shepherds and hangmen [the latter were often clever bone-setters and excellent veterinary surgeons]. His admirable and

[31]   More or less corresponding to our old wives' simples.—*Ed.*

[32]   A typical meiosis. Compare the Greek pseudonym for the Furies: 'Eumenides' or well-willers.—*Ed.*

[33]   A general treatment of Paracelsus which indicates the living value of his philosophy to the modern world is the *Life and Soul of Paracelsus* by John Hargrave [Gollancz, 1951]. See also the study by Van Helmont, a pupil of Paracelsus.—*Ed.*

genial treatise on women's illnesses, the first ever written on the subject, was drawn from the experiences of women themselves, from those to whom other women looked for help, since witches were also generally midwives.

But how did this humane and helpful art go hand in hand with sorcery and the art of black magic? Paracelsus, who knew so many things, does not answer this question. The fact exists and that is enough for him. He believes or pretends to believe in the intervention of the Devil, in the pacts which are able to draw us into his dangerous power, in the spells which can make the spirits of heaven and hell submit to our will. He made it the theme of ten books written under the generic name of *Archidoxy* or the arch-science. Taking popular medicine from the point where it begins to lack resources, in the case of every disease he substitutes a talisman of supernatural power whose picture he carefully reproduces with the imperturbable assurance of an initiate. Unfortunately for our curiosity, and perhaps also for science itself, many of his manuscripts have only come down to us in an incomplete state; whole chapters have disappeared, here and there, in the most interesting parts of his books. Maybe he destroyed them as being excessively indiscreet, or maybe their loss is due to simple accident.[34]

This wonderful man Paracelsus not merely claimed to cure the most stubborn and mortal diseases by magical means; he affirmed the possibility of controlling the laws of chance and of obtaining complete success in all things. The means he proposes to use are too curious to pass without mention. 'Concentrate,' says Paracelsus, 'for forty days in an alembic a sufficient quantity of *Sperma Viri* [human semen]. At the end of this period you will see

[34] The list of works attributed to Paracelsus runs into many hundreds, some being obviously more authentic than others. Students of this master aver that his style is distinctive and that much that is attributed to him has no resemblance to his writing. The chief trouble perhaps originated with Paracelsus' habit of dictating his books.—*Ed.*

moving in the receptacle a little human form, perfectly clear but almost non-existent. If you feed this embryo with a little human blood, being careful to keep it for four weeks in an even temperature equal to that in a horse's stomach, you can create a real child, but very, very small. It is what we call a Homunculus or little man. The art which gave him life, and which can perpetuate that life, makes him one of the most extraordinary productions of human science and the power of God. This little creature has intelligence, and its mysterious manner of birth gives it the ability to investigate and communicate to us the secret of the most inscrutable mysteries.'[35] But Paracelsus does not take us any further into his confidence, 'for fear of the serious and tragic consequences which might result from his indiscretion.' He only tells us that his contemporaries in the art of magic also knew how to make out of soil, wax or metal artificial homunculi, whose possession made their owner invulnerable, brought him great riches and honour, and could compel the most beautiful woman in the world to love a monster of ugliness. Paracelsus was a serious person, highly respected in his time, who would not have wished to compromise his good reputation by printing deliberate lies. It must however be regretted that he should have said too much, and yet too tantalisingly little, about the homunculus. Criticism must treat him lightly, until modern science has earned the right to prove him wrong beyond all doubt.[36]

But before and after this great doctor, as he is called by Michelet, there were recipes for compelling destiny even better known, more highly praised if not more suc-

[35] Christian's sources here are not perhaps first-rate in a field wherein much work has since been done. A more genuine version of this exists wherein the direction is that a certain mixture of chemicals or 'spyagyric substances' shall be placed in horse's dung, with the obvious object of keeping it at a certain temperature, for forty days. See John Hargrave's amusing fantasy *The Imitation Man* [Gollancz].—*Ed.*

[36] Theophrasti Paracelsi *De Natura Rerum* and *Archidoxorum Libri Decem* [2 vols. quarto, Geneva 1658]: St. Geneviève's Library R. 96.

cessful than the homunculus. Who has not heard of the mandragora [mandrake], a sort of man-root, whose happy possessor, it was said, could have success in everything, as long as he did not reveal to anyone the occult servant of his will? There are still people who look for the mandrake root, just as there are still people who believe in evil spells, or that somnambulists have second sight, or in the fortune-teller's power over the cards.

To satisfy this special public, more numerous than one might think, I have decided to quote from XVth and XVIth century manuscripts a few examples of sorcery. The Bibliothèque de l'Arsenal in Paris is fairly rich in this sort of fantastic curiosities; some of them once belonged to President de Thou, others to Cardinal de Rohan —these to the Prince de Soubise, those to the Marquis de Paulmy and so on. These illustrious personages were certainly not adepts in the art of magic, but innocent collectors of novelties.

It was also at the Arsenal that in the reign of Louis XIV the tribunal called the *Chambre Ardente* had its sittings when it passed judgment on accusations of magic and witchcraft. The black-books in this library may be pieces of evidence used in the trials.[37] We know from the letters of Bussi-Rabutin that the Duke of Montmorency-Luxembourg, Captain of the King's Guard, had a warrant issued against him for having tried to make a pact with the Devil by using as intermediary a priest called Le Sage. The Countess de Soissons, Superintendent of the Queen's Household, notorious for her moral depravity, was also accused of witchcraft and compelled to flee to Brussels,

---

[37] Here is a list of the principal Arsenal black-books [all quarto size] which I have been able to consult on these matters, from which the following chapter is drawn: *La Kabbale Intellective*, Sc. et A., no. 72; Pierre d'Abanne *Eléments de Magie*, Sc. et A., no. 81; *Livre de la sacrée Magie*, Sc. et A., no. 79; P. Mora, *Zekerboui*, Sc. et A., no. 46; *Traité des Opérations des sept Esprits*, Sc. et A., no. 70; *Le Grimoire d'Armadel*, Sc. et A., no. 88. *Grimorium, seu totius Kabalae secretarius*, Sc. et A., no. 46; *Les vrais Talismans*, Sc. et A., no. 91; *Secrets pour l'Amour*, Sc. et A., no. 92; *Traité des Esprits Célestes et Terrestres*, Sc. et A., no. 68-69, etc.

then to Spain and finally to Germany where she died. The Duchess de Bouillon, the Princess de Polignac, the Duchess de Foix, the Princess de Tingry, the Marshal de la Ferté and other women of quality were more or less compromised in affairs where love-philtres and poisons had been procured by supernatural and diabolical means.

Moreover these accusations spread to all classes of society. The Receiver-General of the Clergy, a certain Penautier, was himself accused and obliged to sacrifice half his worldly wealth to have the case suppressed.[38] The clergy of that time, utterly corrupt, saw in this belief in the Devil a useful prop to their prestige which was being destroyed by their own vices. The merciless persecutions of the Chambre Ardente raised such a scandal that Louis XIV was obliged to put a stop to it by his statute of July 1682. The great King had still not yet succumbed to the power of the Jesuits.

SPELLS FROM THE BLACK BOOKS[39]

Would you like *to make a Mandragora,* as powerful as the homunculus so highly praised by Paracelsus? Then find a root of the plant called bryony. Take it out of the ground on a Monday [the day of the Moon], a little time

---

[38] Voltaire *Le Siècle de Louis XIV* [ed. Plancher 1817] p. 370; and Dulaure *Histoire Physique Morale et Politique de Paris,* vol. IV: *Paris sous Louis XIV.*

[39] The apparently senseless and arbitrary nature of these following spells and the ingredients used conceals a good deal of genuine knowledge which the spell as written is designed to conceal. It must be understood that they are a system of allusive shorthand for the initiated, based on a system of correspondencies. For example, the bat is connected with all the powers of darkness. If you merely anoint your eyelids with a bat's blood before sleeping, nothing will happen; but if you concentrate on the powers of darkness, further concentrate upon them by sacrificing a captured bat with due ceremonial and evoke further demonic forces by eating frogs' legs—another demonic symbol—and drinking red wine, by the time you are ready for sleep and, last thing, dab bat's blood on your eyelids, you will certainly be very likely to experience the promised diabolical dream. Again, to discover a woman's deepest secret you are bidden to tear out the tongue of a

after the vernal equinox. Cut off the ends of the root and bury it at night in some country churchyard in a dead man's grave. For thirty days water it with cow's milk in which three bats have been drowned. When the thirty-first day arrives, take out the root in the middle of the night and dry it in an oven heated with branches of verbena; then wrap it up in a piece of a dead man's winding-sheet and carry it with you everywhere.

Another recipe for Mandragora. Take a black hen's egg, and extract as much of the white as would equal in volume a large bean. Replace this white of egg by *Sperma Viri* [human semen] and seal the egg with a piece of virgin parchment, slightly moistened. Then put your egg in a pile of dung on the first day of the March moon, which you will find in the table of Epacts. After allowing thirty days for incubation, a tiny monster resembling a human being will come out of the egg. You must keep it hidden in some secret place, feed it with lavender seeds and earth worms. You will have success in everything as long as it lives.

A third method, but one which is said to lose its beneficial effect after twenty years, consists in bleeding a black chicken during the night at a crossroad where four paths meet. As you cut its throat, say: *Berith, do my work for*

---

living toad and place it over her heart while she sleeps. But this toad is the 3rd of Beelzebub's 72 spirits, Bilifares, who appears as a great black-headed toad—he is the opposite of the good spirit Vassago. The spell means that Bilifares is to be compelled to make her talk in her sleep. One of the recipes following is to cause a sleepless night: pick a lily in June, moisten with laurel sap and bury in dung; the black worms so bred are dried and powdered and distributed upon the pillow of the victim. The lily in June under a waning moon means Lilith Queen of Night under the influence of the demon Shimri; the laurel is the Raven of Dispersion, Q'areb Zarag. If these three are conjured, their joint forces might certainly upset sleep. Again, there are names prescribed for inscription that combine the initial letters of certain forces. These are some of the kinds of interpretation necessary for the recipes. The rose and lily stand for and attract the power of a virgin goddess, the appropriate wood is laurel; for a war god a nettle is the correspondency and the oak is the tree. Such representative objects partake of and attract the power of the spirits with which they are in affinity.—*Ed.*

twenty years, and bury the chicken very deep, so that dogs and other wild animals will not be attracted to the place. The spirit thus invoked will follow you everywhere and will bring you success.

Or do your modest wishes extend merely to *the acquisition of enough money to last you until the end of the year?* Then make some pancakes with eggs, milk and flour while, in the church nearest to your house, the first mass of Candlemas is being said [on the day of the Purification of the Holy Virgin], and try to make a dozen pancakes before the mass is ended.

Here is an even more curious secret *for doubling one's wealth.* Seize a hair from a mare in heat: this hair must be taken from a place as near to the *vulva* as possible and must not have the root broken off. As you pull it out, say: *Drigne, Dragne.* Then go and buy an earthenware pot with a lid: you must take care not to haggle over the price. Fill it with drinking-water until the liquid is three finger-breadths from the rim; put in the mare's hair, cover the pot, and hide it away in some secret place. After nine full days, bring out the pot and you will find in it a sort of little serpent which will rear up quickly. When you see it rear up, say out loud: 'I accept the pact.' Then take this serpent with your right hand wrapped in kid skin and shut it in a box made of young pine, which you will have bought without haggling over the price. You will have put in it some wheat bran which is to feed the mysterious serpent and which you must renew each morning. Whenever you want silver or gold, put a little in the box, then lie down on your bed near the box and remain motionless for three hours. At the end of this time open the box and you will find in it twice as much as you put in. When you want to do this again, be careful to place inside the box silver or gold coins which have not already been used for this purpose. Note also that you must not put in more than a hundred coins, and make sure that in your horoscope for that day the Sun is in a favourable aspect with the

Moon, and free from the harmful influences of Saturn or Mars.

The black book goes on to say that the possession of this serpent is not without danger. When you want to get rid of it, you must write on a piece of virgin parchment the name and the sign of the spirit *Clamey*, put the writing in the box, and, instead of the wheat bran, put in a handful of the flour whence the host was prepared with which a priest said his first mass. The serpent then dies, and the pact is broken.

If *the existence of hidden treasure is revealed to you* in a dream, and if some local tradition authorises you to believe that you are not the victim of some illusion, here is a way to find it. Take a candle prepared with wax and human fat, and, for a candlestick, cut a piece of hazelnut wood in the shape of a horse-shoe. Go at midnight to the cellar or the field or whichever place has been dreamed of, and light your candle. If the flame sparkles, you are not far from the treasure; if it sparkles with increasing brightness, you are very close; if it suddenly goes out, you are at the place. You now merely have to dig. To light your digging, you should have three lanterns, each containing an altar candle. But if you are not firmly resolved to give to the poor a tithe of this fortune, you will never succeed in finding it.

If you wish *to live safe from lightning, epidemics and the effects of any poison whatsoever*, always carry a piece of serpentine in your left armpit. If you live in a snake-infested country, plant strawberries round your house and these dangerous reptiles will never come near you.

Take care never to quarrel with a man who has been eating lentils, for, if he were to bite you, the wound would never heal.

A lily, picked while the sun is passing through the sign of the Lion, and mixed with laurel-juice, then placed under a layer of dung, produces worms. Collect these worms, grind them to a powder, and if you put this powder in someone's clothes or in his bed, he *will not be able to sleep* until the powder is removed. If this powder is thrown in a jug full of milk, and this is then placed in a byre, being first covered with a piece of cowhide, all the cows in the byre whose colour is the same as that of the piece of hide will go dry.

Wrap stalks of henbane in the skin of a young hare, and bury the whole at a crossroads: *all the dogs of the neighbourhood* will collect there, and will not go away until the spell has been removed.

Would you like *to make a young girl, whom you love very much, dance against her will* and in your presence? Take wild marjoram, wild thyme, myrtle leaves, three walnut leaves and some sprigs of fennel. All these herbs must be picked on the Eve of St. John. Dry them in the shade; then grind them into a very fine powder which you will pass through a silken sieve. All you have to do is to blow a little of this powder into the air or get the girl to smell a pinch of it, and she will begin to dance like mad.

Would you like *to revenge yourself on someone who has offended you?* Go on a Saturday and cut, before sunrise, a branch of a year-old hazel which has never been touched by hand. At the same time say these words: 'I cut you, branch grown this summer, in the name of [here you name your enemy] whom I wish to punish.' When you are back at home, spread a new woollen cloth on a table which has never been used saying three times: *In nomine Patris* ✱ *et Filii* ✱ *et Spiritus* ✱ *sancti, et in cute Droch* ✱, *Mirroch* ✱, *Esenaroth* ✱, *Betu* ✱, *Baroch* ✱, *Maaroth* ✱. [You must make the sign of the cross at each ✱.] After the third invocation, say: *Holy Trinity, punish him* [or *her*] *who has done evil towards me, and deliver me from this evil by thy great justice:* ✱ *Elion* ✱, *Elion* ✱, *Esmaris. Amen.* On the final word, beat with your stick on the table and the person who has offended you will receive, invisibly, the number of blows you care to make on the table.

Yet another tradition gives you an even simpler method. On any Friday, obtain a hair belonging to the person who has harmed you and for a period of nine days make a knot each day in this hair. On the ninth day wrap it in virgin parchment and beat it; your enemy will feel each blow.

VIII

WOULD you like *to win at gambling*? You only have to choose between the following methods.—On the first Thursday of the new moon, at the hour of Jupiter, before the sun rises, write these words on virgin parchment: '*Non licet ponare in egarbona quia pretium sanguinis.*' Then take a viper's head, and put it in the middle of the writing; fold the four corners of the parchment over the head and, whenever you wish to gamble, attach the whole to your left arm with a red silk ribbon, and no one else but you will win.

Second method: on the day and at the hour of Mercury, before the sun rises, write on virgin parchment these words: * *Aba* * *athai* * *abatroy* * *agera* * *prosha* *. Write the crosses with blood drawn from the four fingers [not the thumb] of your left hand. Then scent the parchment with church incense, and carry it on you during the game.

Third method: write on virgin parchment the words: * *Lo* * *ma* * *na* * *pa* * *quoa* * *ra* * *sata* * *na* *. Wrap a silver coin in this piece of parchment. On a Sunday which is a day of the Sun, before midnight take this talisman to a crossing where four roads meet. After having buried the coin there, stamp on the ground three times with your left foot, pronouncing the words and making the nine signs of the cross as indicated. Then go away without looking back. The next day, at the same time, go and dig up the coin and go away without looking back. Whenever you carry this coin, you will have good luck.

Fourth method: on St. John the Baptists's Day, before the sun rises, go and gather some plantain seeds which you must powder and put in a tube made from a goose quill with three drops of holy water. Close the tube at each end with a little wax taken from the altar candles. Whoever carries this talisman will be beloved of everyone and will not fail to gamble successfully.

Fifth method: on the Eve of St. Peter look for the herb called *Morsus Diaboli* [St. Joseph's herb—a kind of scabious]. When you have found it mark on the ground in front of you a half-circle terminating in two crosses, and before picking the herb, pronounce the words: *Agla* ✱ *Adonay* ✱ *Jehova* ✱. Take this herb to the church, leave it for a whole day under the altar-cloth on the left-hand side of the altar and afterwards dry it and reduce it to a powder which should be carried in a little sachet suspended round the neck. Each time you carry this talisman, you will have good luck at the tables. The effect will be even more remarkable when the Eve of St. Peter coincides with a full moon.

Sixth method: on the first Tuesday of the new moon look for a four or five-leafed clover before sunrise and at the hour of Jupiter, saying as soon as you find it: *Christus factus est obediens usque ad mortem, mortem autem crucis. Propter quod Deus exaltavit Jeschue.* Carry this clover leaf with you everywhere and touch it before playing.

Seventh method: take three laurel leaves, which you must dedicate to the good genius *Balay*. Write on each leaf one of the names of the three angels Michael, Gabriel and Raphael, and carry them on you. On entering the place where you are to play pronounce the words: *'Balay dat ludenti victoriam.'* And you cannot fail to win.

Eighth method: this is especially suited to lotteries. Before going out to buy lottery-tickets recite backwards the words of the Creed, and add at the end these words: *'Lux lucidum lucidentes.'*

Ninth method: take the cast-off skin of an eel that has died of thirst and the gall of a bull killed by dogs. Put the gall into the eel-skin, after having sprinkled it with bull's blood. Tie this skin at both ends with a piece of hangmans's rope and hide it for twenty-one days in a heap of dung. Then take it out and dry it in an oven heated with fern picked on the Eve of St. John. The best way to use it is to make it into a bracelet on which you should write in blood and with a new pen the letters HVTV. Each time you wear it luck will be with you.

Whichever of these methods you choose, never forget to keep a tenth part of what you win for the poor. If you forget this precept, instead of winning you will lose.

If you meet an epileptic while he is having a fit, your charitable compassion must wish to find some means of helping him. In order *to stop the epileptic fit,* recite in a low voice over the sick man this prayer: *Praeceptis salutaribus moniti, et divina institutione formati, audemus dicere: Pater noster . . .* Before you reach the end of the Lord's Prayer, the fit will have stopped. But take care to step over the sick man if he rolls on the ground, for his illness would leave him only to enter your own body if you were to touch him. Another tradition says that to cure epilepsy you only need to whisper into the patient's right ear: *Gaspar fert mirrham, thus Melchior, Balthassar aurum,* and he will recover at once. If he can show you the place where he first fell to the ground during his fit, you must drive three iron nails into the ground pronouncing his name each time, and his cure will be complete.

Have you *any enemy whose attacks you fear?* Write your name on a verbena leaf with the blood of a crow or a white hen; carry this leaf everywhere you go, and your enemy will never be able to harm you. If you carry a wolf's eye encased in an iron ring, you will pass through every danger unharmed.

Do you want *to protect your garden against the invasion of caterpillars and may-bugs?* Write on a strip of virgin parchment in a single line the words: *Christus regnat ✻ Christus vincit ✻ Christus vobis imperat ✻ Ibi ceciderunt qui operantur iniquitatem, nec potuit stare adversus Dominum.* The strip of parchment must be long enough to go round a tree trunk, and every tree to which one of these talismans is tied will be protected or delivered from caterpillars, may-bugs or any other voracious insects.

Do you wish *to make a tree barren?* Take rose and mustard seeds and a polecat's foot. Reduce them to a fine powder with which you will sprinkle any tree when it is covered with blossom, and it will not bear a single fruit. If you put this powder in a lamp, the people who gather round it will see each other as negroes. If you mix it with olive oil and a little of the flowers of sulphur and anoint the walls of a room with it, they will seem to be on fire.

Take mistletoe from an oak, and suspend it with a swallow's wing on any tree, and *all the swallows of the neighbourhood will gather there.*

If you hang up in a house, by a piece of red string that has never been used before, the feathers from the right wing of a blackbird, *no one will be able to sleep in the room.* The same effect is produced by rubbing the sheets of the bed with very fine-powdered alum.

In times of plague, however violent it may be, write on a piece of virgin parchment the following letters and crosses: Z ✻ O A ✻ B I Z ✻ S A B ✻ Z H G F ✻ B F R S ✻. I have not been able to find the meaning of these mysterious letters; but tradition has it that any house under which this talisman is buried will never be visited by the plague.

To prevent a person from leaving his room, take the hearts of a wolf and of a horse, dry them and reduce them to powder. Spread this powder on the ground outside the room. As long as it remains there the person for whom this spell is intended will never leave the room.

Do you wish *to travel without encountering any dangers,* but rather many unexpected pleasures? Write on a piece of virgin parchment the names of the three Kings, Gaspar, Melchior, Balthazar, put them in your left shoe, and when you leave your house make the first step with your left foot, pronouncing the names.

Centaury, reduced to powder, with a peewit's blood and a little honey, mixed into the oil of a lamp exerts a spell on those who gather round the lamp; they imagine that *they have grown to gigantic proportions,* and that their heads are touching the sky. If this substance is kept in a phial and if it is shaken out under someone's nose, that person will be suddenly stricken with horror and will run away.

Sage receives the influences of Jupiter and Venus. Go and pick this plant, as much of it as possible, while the sun is passing through the sign of the Lion. Grind it to powder in an earthenware mortar that has never been used before. Then put it in a glass vessel or in a new earthenware pot, freshly glazed. Bury the matrass or the pot in a dung-hill and expose it to the sun for thirty days. At the end of this time you will find that the mixture has turned into worms. Take these and burn them between two red-hot bricks; reduce them to a fine powder which you must place in a well-corked phial. Expose this phial to the sun or put it in some warm place. If you scatter this powder on your feet, *you will obtain from princes and powerful men every favour you ask of them.* If you put some under your tongue *everyone you kiss will love you.* If you put a little of this powder in the oil of a lamp, those who sit in its light will *believe that the room is filled with serpents.*

If you throw into a pond some periwinkle stalks reduced to a powder and mixed with flowers of sulphur, *all the fish in the pond will die.* If you can make an ox swallow it, he will die.

Would you like, as a joke, *to stir up a quarrel* among all the guests seated round a table? Take the four feet of a mole and slip them under the tablecloth without being seen. The guests will not fail to come to blows.

If you place beneath a table, at the same time whispering the words *Coridal, Nerdac, Degon,* a needle which has been used to sew up a dead man's winding-sheet, an inexplicable and uncontrollable horror *will prevent anyone from eating* at that table.

If someone carries on his person a sunflower plucked while the sun is passing through the sign of the Lion, together with laurel leaves and a wolf's tooth, *no one will be able to speak to him except with the greatest courtesy.* If you have been robbed, put some of these flowers under your pillow and while you are sleeping *you will see the face of the thief in a dream.*

Do you want *to have the power to make anyone start dancing wildly,* even the good old solemn curate of your parish? Write with a bat's blood, on virgin parchment, the words: *Sator Arepo Tenet Opera Rotas.*[40] Put this parchment under the threshold of your house and you will have a good laugh.

Make with the purest wax two statuettes, one of a man, the other of a woman. Cover them with a thin sprinkling of human blood and stuff the heads with poppy seeds, then throw them on the ground. There will appear *as many little men and women as there are seeds in the heads.*

Would you like *to enjoy diabolical dreams?* Rub your eyelids with bat's blood before going to sleep and put laurel leaves under your pillow.

Or would you prefer *to dream of a woman* you have seen but whose love is more than you can hope for, *according you her favours?* and would you like to renew this

---

[40] These are the famous words of the best-known perfect square in Latin. It will be noted that whichever way it is read the words are correct. Their meaning, however, is negligible: Arepo the sower is holding back the work [lit. 'things being done'] with his wheels [lit. 'as to the wheels'].

<pre>
S A T O R
A R E P O
T E N E T
O P E R A
R O T A S
</pre>

—*Ed.*

illusion as often as you like? Here is how you can do it. Take two ounces of scammony [convolvulus] and Roman camomile, three ounces of cod bones and tortoiseshell, and heat them until they become powdery. Mix the whole with five ounces of male beaver fat and add two ounces of oil of flowers made from blue scammony picked in the early morning in the first days of spring; boil this composition with an ounce of honey and six drams of dew gathered from poppy flowers. You may add then a sixth part of opium and, after having put it all in a hermetically-sealed bottle, you must expose it to the sun for 72 days. At the end of this time, you must put the bottle in a cool cellar and leave it there all the winter buried in very fine river sand. Next spring break the bottle and extract the ointment, which you must pour into a stoneware jar that has never before been used. The way to use this ointment is to rub it before sleep on the pit of the stomach, the navel and the nape of the neck.

And now, since we are on the subject of love, let us pass from dreams to spells which promise *actual possession of the loved one.*

On a Friday, at the hour of Venus and before the sun rises, take from near a river or a pond a live frog which you will hang by its hind legs over a blazing fire. When it is burnt black, you will reduce it to a very fine powder in a stone mortar and wrap it in virgin parchment. This sachet must lie for three days under an altar where mass is said. After the three days you must uncover it at the hour of Venus. The way to use this powder is to sprinkle it on flowers; every girl or woman who smells them will then love you.

Second method: if you can stick on the head of a girl's or a woman's bed, as near as possible to the place where her head rests, a piece of virgin parchment on which you have written: *Michael, Gabriel, Raphael, make* [the name of the person] *feel a love for me equal to my own, that per-*

son will not be able to sleep without first thinking of you and very soon love will dawn in her heart.

Third method: while in conversation with the young lady whose heart you wish to win, pretend you want to cast her horoscope in order to find out, for example, if she will marry. During this conversation, which must have no witnesses, try to make her look you straight in the eyes and when she does, say in a compelling voice: *Kaphe, Kasita, non Kapheta et publica filii omnibus suis.* Do not be surprised at or ashamed of these enigmatical words whose occult meaning you do not know; for if you pronounce them with sufficient faith you will very soon possess her love.

Fourth method: on the Eve of St. John, before the rising of the sun, go and pick the plant called *Œnula campana*. Wrap it in fine linen and wear it on your heart for nine days; then grind it to powder and sprinkle it on a bouquet or on the food of the person you desire, and soon you will be overwhelmed with love.

Fifth method: take a pigeon's liver and a blackbird's brains, dry them and grind them to a very fine powder, which you must sprinkle on the loved one's food, and there will be a similar very sudden result.

Sixth method: periwinkle, reduced to a powder and employed as above, produces the same result.

Seventh method: take five of your hairs, plait them with three belonging to the person you love and cast them on the fire, saying: *Ure igne sancti Spiritus renes nostros et cor nostrum, Domine, Amen.* The same success will be yours.

Eighth method: to make the person you love remain faithful to you, take a lock of her hair, burn it and sprinkle the ashes on the wooden parts of her bed, after having rubbed them with honey. She will then dream only of you. It should be easy to repeat this simple little operation from time to time to keep her constant in her love.

Ninth method: take a dove's heart, a sparrow's liver, a swallow's womb and a hare's kidney, and after having dried them, reduce the whole to a very fine powder, to which you will add an equal quantity of your own blood and leave the mixture to dry. If you make the person you desire eat it, she will not be able to resist you for very long.

If you want to make certain *that a woman will not cease loving you,* take the marrow from the bones of a wolf's left foot, and make an ointment with it from some amber-gris and powdered cypress wood. After perfuming the mixture with some delightful scent, carry it on your person and make your beloved smell it sometimes. Her attachment will grow ever stronger.

Always when you are happy in love protect yourself against spells which may be cast on you by some wicked rival. It is a fact that if someone picks verbena while the sun is passing through the sign of the Ram, and if, after having pulverised this plant, he scatters the powder in the place where the most devoted couples or the happiest lovers live, *quarrels arising from sudden mutual aversion will not fail to break out.* If the spell is kept up it will *cause an irreparable rupture.*

Would you like *to find out if a girl is still a virgin?* Pulverise some lily-pollen, and find an opportunity of making her swallow it without knowing, for example at table in some dish. If she is no longer virgin she will be seized with an irresistible urge to urinate. If you give her a lettuce seed, and make her smell it, the effect will be the same.[41]

If a woman wishes *to prevent herself from conceiving,* let her drink the blood of a ram or a hare.

Would you like *to know a woman's most intimate secrets?* Take a live toad, pull out its tongue and throw the toad back into the water. Put this tongue on the woman's heart while she is asleep and she will talk and answer all your questions.

Second method: take a pigeon's heart and a toad's head; dry them and reduce them to a powder which you must

[41] Compare Webster *The Duchess of Malfi* where the two brothers give their sister apricots to eat. She is seized with faintness and this is taken as proof of her being *enceinte.*—Ed.

sprinkle lightly over the stomach of the sleeping woman. The effect will be the same.

If a man wishes *to see in a dream the image of the woman he will marry,* he must obtain powdered coral, a powder of magnetic iron and the blood of a white pigeon, and make a paste which must be stuffed into a large fig. It must then be wrapped in blue silk square and hung round the neck. He then puts a branch of myrtle under his pillow and says the following prayer: *Kyrie clementissime, qui Abrahae servo tuo dedisti uxorem, et filio ejus obedientissimo per admirabile signum indicasti Rebeccam uxorem, indica mihi servo tuo quam nupturus sim uxorem, per mysterium tuorum Spirituum Baalibeth Assaibi Abumastith. Amen.*

In the morning, he must try to remember what he has seen in his dream. If he has seen nothing, the magical operation must be performed on three successive Fridays; and if after the third attempt there is still no vision it can be assumed that he will never marry.

If a woman wishes *to see in a dream the man she will marry,* she must take a small branch of poplar, wrap it in her stockings and tie it all up with a white ribbon. After putting this under her pillow she must rub her temples with a pee-wit's blood before getting into bed, then recite the above prayer, replacing the formula: *Servo tuo quam nupturus sim uxorem* . . . by: *Ancillae tuae quem nuptura sim virum* . . .

IX

BLACK AGATE, veined with white, *protects whoever wears it from all danger,* and will give him *victory over his enemies.*

ALECTORINE is a white stone the size of a bean; it grows in the ventricle of cocks castrated at the age of three and which live for another seven years after the operation. It gives *possession of, or protects, all worldly goods;* to those in disgrace it accords the favours of princes, and maintains affectionate regard between husband and wife.

PINK AMETHYST *prevents drunkenness* if it is attached to the navel. It must be set in a silver plaque, and on i must be engraved a bear. The water in which it is dipped cures sterility.

CORNELIAN on which is engraved the image of a man holding a sceptre in his hand has the virtue of being able to *to stop haemorrhages* and *brings good luck* to whoever carries it on him always.

CHALCEDONY, a white stone resembling crystal, *protect. from quarrels and law-suits*, and it *protects the traveller*. On it should be engraved a man on horesback riding at full speed and brandishing a pike in his right hand.

RED CORAL on which is engraved a man bearing a sword can, like cornelian, *stop haemorrhages*. It also *protects the home from epidemics*. Crushed and sprinkled between fruit trees, *it guards against hail*.

CHRYSOLITE, a green stone with golden tints, on which the figure of an ass is engraved, *protects from attacks of gout.*

CRYSTAL, worn as a necklace, *increases the supply of milk in wet-nurses.*

DIAMOND, with green tints, worn as a necklace, *protects the fruit of a woman's womb* and ensures safe parturition.

EMERALD, on which should be engraved the image of a starling, *strengthens the eyes*. Whoever wears it in a gold setting will have *prophetic dreams*. This stone also *preserves chastity*.

TOPAZ, a golden-yellow stone, on which a falcon is engraved, both *preserves chastity* and helps *to gain everyone's sympathy.*

GARNET, a vermillion-coloured stone, on which a lion is engraved, *preserves good health*, *protects the traveller*, and *keeps epidemics at bay.*

JACINTH, with saffron-coloured veins, when set in gold *guards against conception* and *protects from or cures dropsy.*

BERYL, a sea-green stone, when set in gold and with a frog engraved upon it gains for the wearer *the affection of anyone who touches it or who is touched by it*. Water in which it is dipped procures *the friendship of all who drink it.*

ONYX, a black stone, on which a camel's head is engraved, gives the wearer *terrifying dreams.*

SARDONYX, a beautiful red stone, if set in gold and engraved with an eagle brings *good luck.*

JASPER, an opaque green stone, but sometimes red, protects the wearer from *snake bites.*

SAPPHIRE, a blue stone, on which a ram is engraved, cures *inflammations of the eyes, preserves chastity,* and *brings good luck.*

The PEARL when worn in a necklace makes its wearer *chaste.* Crushed to a fine powder and mixed with milk, it *sweetens irritable temperaments.* Crushed and mixed with sugar, it *cures pestilential fevers.*

SELENITE or moonstone is green, and should have engraved on it a swallow; it brings the wearer *the good-will and friendship of all.*

The LODESTONE, a well-known ferruginous stone, *denounces adulterous wives.* A fragment of this stone is hidden under the wife's pillow. If she remains faithful, she will turn in sleep and embrace her husband; but if she has violated conjugal faith, she will suddenly wake up overcome by some guilty dream, and will give her secret away in a shriek of terror.

If some powdered lodestone is sprinkled on chafing-dishes filled with blazing coals and placed at the four corners of a house, as soon as the vapour is given off the inhabitants of the house, seized with vertigo, imagine that the ground is shaking and that the house is about to fall down on their heads.[42]

Would you like your *love letters or your business let-*

---

[42] From *Traité des Secrets de Nature, touchant les Animaux, Plantes et les Pierres,* which King Alphonso X of Spain had translated from Greek into Latin: 1 vol., folio MS. in the Arsenal Library, Sc. et A., no. 101—C. Leonardi *Speculum Lapidum, cui accesserunt Metallorum Sympathiae* [Paris, 1590], Library of St. Geneviève, V, 694.

ters to obtain a success beyond your wildest dreams? Take a sheet of virgin parchment and cover it, on both sides, with the following invocation: ADAMA, EVAH, *even as the all-powerful Creator did unite you in the earthly Paradise with a holy, mutual and indissoluble link, so may the heart of those to whom I write be favourable to me, and be able to refuse me nothing*: ✶ ELY ✶ ELY ✶ ELY. This sheet of parchment must then be burnt and its ashes carefully collected. Then obtain some ink which has never been used before; pour it into a small new earthenware jar and mix in the ashes together with seven drops of milk from a woman who is giving suck to her firstborn, then add a pinch of powdered lodestone. Use a new pen, which you must trim with a new knife. Everyone to whom you write with ink prepared in this manner will be disposed when reading your letter to accord you everything in their power.

In order to practise the art of *envoûtement*, that is, the art of making *an enemy die by invisible means,* here are the two principal spells contained in the black-books.

After having procured a little of the urine of the person whom you have sworn to kill with an implacable hatred the sorcerer buys a hen's egg without haggling over the price and goes at night, on a Tuesday or a Saturday, to some field sufficiently far removed from human habitation to prevent his odious plan from being discovered or disturbed. If there is no moonlight he may carry a dark-lantern. When he has found a suitable place he makes a circular incision at the broad end of the egg, extracts the white but leaves the yolk. He then fills up the egg again with the urine, pronouncing the names of the condemned person, and closes the aperture with a piece of wet virgin parchment. When this is done he buries the egg in the field and goes away without looking behind him. As soon as the egg begins to rot, the person concerned is attacked by jaundice, and no remedy can cure him until the egg is withdrawn from the earth and burned by the same hands that buried it. If it is allowed to rot completely, the person on whom the spell has been cast dies within the year.[43]

The magicians of ancient Thessaly made images of wax which they pierced every day with needles, offering up homicidal incantations. But the witch of the Middle Ages and the Renaissance advised her clients to use more expeditious means. 'On a Saturday,' she said, 'buy an ox heart without haggling over the price. Then go to a field, a copse or a deserted cemetery. Dig a deep hole in the ground, put in it a layer of quicklime, and place the heart on the quicklime. Prick it as often as you like, pronouncing each time the name of the man or woman who is the object of your hatred, and conclude the operation by reciting over the hole the first chapter of the Gospel according to St. John. Then go away in silence, without speaking to anyone you meet. Each day following recite the same gospel before breakfast with the firm intention of being avenged. Soon the person whom you have laid under this spell will begin to feel internal pains which will become more and more agonising, especially at the moments when you are thinking of your revenge; and if you continue with this practice, the person will die of consumption.'[43]

X

SUCH were the works in which magicians gloried. I have had to quote rather a large number of them in order to make my readers appreciate the extent of this great sickness in the human mind. My readers will excuse me from adding to what has gone before the ritual of the Conjurations, by means of which the worst type of sorcerers claimed to conjure up Satan himself, or at any rate one of the princes of the infernal legions. The witchcraft of the Middle Ages

[43] Compare the west-country belief in England that warts can be cured by stealing a piece of meat and burying it. So long as the theft is unconfessed and the meat rotting, the warts will continue to disappear.—*Ed.* See also *Le Livre des Secrets de Magie*: MS of the Arsenal Library, Sc. et A; no. 84.

had substituted for the ceremonies and incantations used in the temples of Roman and Greek idolatry a blasphemous parody of the Christian rites. There were sacrilegious priests who transformed the intentions and the style of the Church's prayers, adapting them to the cult of the devil. It was in the Middle Ages that Satan became the *Prince of the World* and drew everything into his power. The Black Mass and the Witches' Bishops by setting one altar against the other for a long time threatened to drag Catholicism into irreparable ruin.[44]

A reliable authority, Cardinal Jacques de Vitry,[45] relates how during the XIIIth century 'in those days of ignorance, wickedness and danger, the cities of the west were rotten with crime, and the clergy were even more corrupt than the rest of the people. Like a mangy horse or a sick sheep, the clergy communicated everywhere and to everyone the contagion of their impious habits'. Prelates and the superiors of convents rivalled the feudal lord in debauchery, theft and violence. This scandalous tyranny went so far that the laity would say by way of imprecation: 'I'd rather be a priest than do such a thing.' The ecclesiastics, pursued by hatred and scorn, hardly dared to show themselves in public: if they did venture out, it was always in disguise.[46] Gaultier de Coinsy, in his poem *Sainte Leocade,* accuses them of a depravity which is beyond the descriptive powers of a respectable writer. We read in the criminal registers of the Parlement of Paris [1339—1341] that a witch named Marguerite de Belleville was visited by a hermit named Brother Regnaud, by a Jacobin monk from the convent at Troyes,

---

[44] Concerning the corruption and degradation of this period generally, a great deal of recent research has been done, and on church matters especially Dr. G. G. Coulton opened up whole new fields of knowledge by the careful examination of records of all kinds. The best general reference for this is therefore to his *Five Centuries of Religion* vol. 4. *The Last Days of Medieval Monachism* [C.U.P., 1950]. There are also more obscure works by Waller, Valois, Calmette, Colville and others.—*Ed.*

[45] J. de Vitriaco *Historia Occidentalis,* pp. 277 et seq.

[46] *Histoire Générale de Languedoc* par Un Benedictin Vol III, Bk. 21 p. 129.

named Jean Dufay, and by Perrotte La Baille, wife of the bailiff of Poissy. These persons were ordered by Guischard, Bishop of Troyes, to make a *Volt* for him, a spell which was to bring about the death of the Queen, Jeanne de Bourgogne, wife of Philippe le Long. The *Volt* was a waxen image which the Jacobin baptised under the name of Jeanne and whose godmother was Perrotte. The witch was later denounced and sent to the Châtelet prison in Paris.[47]

From 1494 to 1508, the celebrated and fiery preacher Maillard fulminated in his church of Saint-Jean-en-Grève, in Paris, against the avarice of priests who sold baptisms, confessions, communion, marriages and prayers for the dead; against prelates who ceaselessly robbed the poor and the poorhouses, refused alms and employed the revenues of the Church to pay for hunting dogs, concubines and panders. 'If the pillars of the churches had eyes,' cries Maillard, 'and if they could see what goes on; if they had ears, and if they could speak of what they hear, what would they say? . . . I do not know: but you, my fine fellow-priests, what do you think about it?'[48]

Gerson, the illustrious Canon and Chancellor of the Church of Paris, describing the vices of his period, says that the convents for girls and women are more like brothels.[49] Nicolas Clémangis, doctor of the Sorbonne and Rector of the University, confirms Gerson's words: 'I am prevented by modesty from making too detailed accusations; but in all truth can our monasteries, which I cannot call sanctuaries of God, at present be called anything else but the mere abodes of Venus? And nowadays is it not recognised that if a girl takes the veil she is going to perdition?'[50]

[47] For further information on this case see the *Chronicles* of William of Nangis [1308—1313].

[48] Maillard *Advent. Serm.* 28, 33—*Quadrag. Serm.* 17, 19, 20 etc.

[49] *Quasi Prostibula Meretricum* [Gersonii Declaratio defect. vicor. eccles., no. 65.]

[50] Nic. Clemangus *De Corrupto Ecclesiae Statu* [cap. de impudica vite].

When, in the XIVth century , we see Pope John XXII
drawing up a tariff for the absolution of the most abject
crimes, and in the XVth century Pope Alexander VI as an
incestuous father,[51] and in the XVIth Pope Julius II clad
in armour and cursing like a trooper, and after him Pope
Leo X, that loose-living atheist, surrounded by a completely
pagan court which set up statues of false gods around the
Cross, can we wonder that the populations of western
Christendom fell from one misery to another until they
reached the lowest depths of superstition?

In 1579 René Benoist, curate of the church of St.
Eustace in Paris, author of a treatise on witchcraft, sorcery
and spells, wrote in his third chapter: 'We are afflicted and
molested by evil spirits. The Devil, with his ministers of
impurity, error, heresy, magic, idolatry, sorcery and ignorance, sets himself up as God.' We read in the famous
Journal of Henri III, by Pierre de l'Estoile, that under
Charles IX there were more than thirty thousand sorcerers
in France.

Priestly authority, compelled to defend itself, was unable to imagine anything better than the Inquisition's
stakes and pyres: a remedy as frightful as the evil itself.
Theologians wrote huge and indigestible treatises in which
they depicted magic under the most sombre colourings.
Councils passed useless sentences of excommunication,
popes thundered in their papal bulls, parliaments and
courts of justice increased their hangmen and executioners.
Fanatical jurisconsults like Sprenger, Jean Bodin, Henri
Boguet, Wierus and de Lancre organised the prosecution
of witchcraft. 'Until the middle of the XVIIIth century,'
says M. Alfred Maury, 'the theory of communication with
the Devil and the efficaciousness of witchcraft was rigorously

---

[51] Modern research is inclined to be rather kinder to the Borgia Pope. That
he was over-indulgent to his family is certain, but in that he merely exaggerated a typical Italian trait. Two recent lives in English are those
by G. Portigliotti 1928 and O. Ferrara 1942.—*Ed.*

upheld, even though occult science was daily falling into greater disrepute in the face of the great advances made in the physical sciences, in chemistry, natural history and medicine. At the beginning of the XVIIth century a few rare, enlightened minds tried to combat the general prejudice and to defend the wretched madmen or imprudent seekers after occult truth from the wrath of the tribunals. It needed great courage to do this, for, in attempting to save the accused, there was a risk of being taken oneself for an advocate of the Devil, or, which was no better, for an unbeliever.[52]

While it struck against the witches, the Roman Church realised the great profit that could be derived from witchcraft. If, on the one hand, it tortured the adepts, on the other hand it broadcast innumerable legends about the deeds of Beelzebub, Lucifer, Baalberith, Asmodeus and all the infernal host. The monks were great fabricators of this fantastic literature cast to the hungry imaginations of an ignorant populace. Their imagination was never very fertile in varying the settings of these legends; the Devil is always a usurer who buys eternal possession of a soul in exchange for a few years of wealth and pleasure, and he always arrives at the time stated in the pact to carry off his victim. I shall quote two examples only of these strange legends: that of Faust and that of the monk, by Lewis.

Born at Weimar in Germany at the beginning of the XVth century, Johann Faust had manifested from his youth a powerful and audacious quality of mind. After having exhausted at an early age all the learning of his time, he took up witchcraft. His historian Widmann assures us that he finally discovered the formula by which the most powerful infernal Spirits are compelled to obey man. One of these appeared to him under the name of Mephistopheles in a forest near Wittenberg, and promised to serve him for 24 years in exchange for a pact by which Faust signed away

[52] A. Maury La Magie dans l'Antiquité et au Moyen Age [Paris, 1860].

his soul to hell. From that moment he thought he was the ruler of the earth. His familiar demon served him with the most complete obedience and satisfied all his desires. Having become possessed of inexhaustible wealth and using his knowledge of all the occult sciences in the furtherance of his passions, the supreme doctor, as Faust called himself, travelled the length and breadth of Germany, now in a princely procession, now transported in the twinkling of an eye by the invisible powers which were at his disposal. He appeared, it is said, at the court of the Emperor Charles V and conjured up for him Alexander the Great and Julius Caesar, then the lovely Helen of Troy, then Aspasia, Lucretia, Cleopatra and other famous personages of antiquity.

Faust did not disdain to mingle with ordinary people. One day he met in a tavern a crowd of students who had heard a great deal about him and who begged him to show them some example of his magic art. Faust pierced the table with his dagger and from the split poured a delicious wine with which he made them drunk. In their frenzied drunkenness they asked to see the vine that had produced this supernatural wine. The magician did not refuse, on condition that they would give their word not to move from their seats, and at once a magnificent vine, loaded with ripe red clusters of grapes, appeared before them. The temptation to taste them was so great that the students, forgetting their promise, seized their knives to cut off these most succulent grapes. Faust then broke the spell, and each of the drinkers, thinking he was holding his bunch of grapes, found himself holding his neighbour's nose; so that, if they had succeeded in cutting off what they thought were grapes, they would have cut off each other's noses.

After having exhausted every pleasure that the sensual mind can imagine, Doctor Faustus one day remembered the fatal pact. He found with horror that the 24 years were almost at an end. Nevertheless, he had hopes of defeating the powers of hell by taking refuge in a church, where he prayed for divine mercy. But the demon Mephistopheles could read his thoughts and would not let him escape. During the night which preceded the last day of the pact the demon appeared for the last time and ordered Faust to follow him. Faust was afraid, but he had to obey. Mephistopheles carried him up into the air to the top of the highest mountain in Saxony, from which he threw him down into a terrible abyss full of sharp rocks.

I relate this story of course for what it is worth. One of the biographers of Faust, Conrad Durius, identifies the famous sorcerer with the celebrated Fust who shares with Gutenberg and Scheffer the honour of having invented the printing machine; and he believes that German monks made up this legend to revenge themselves for the loss of money made by the writing of manuscripts. We know that when the first Bible appeared from Fust's press the populace was roused by the monks who claimed that the new ink was composed of human blood mixed with magical juices. Without the protection of Louis XI, Fust would have been burned as a sorcerer.[53]

NOTE ON THE FAUST AND MEPHISTOPHELES LEGENDS. The existence of an historical Faust has long been admitted: in fact, it has never been seriously denied. That there were actually two Fausts does not seem to have been hitherto realised, at least not generally; yet it can be clearly established.

Between 1507 and 1587, the year of publication of the first Faust Book, we meet with a number of historical records and references bearing the name of Faustus. These records have been generally considered to refer to one and the same person, although their subject is described, in some, as a charlatan and imposter, 'a mere braggart and fool', 'a man, indeed, entirely devoid of education',

[53] Palma Cayet, *Histoire du Docteur Faust et de sa Mort Epouvantable,* 12mo [Paris, 1598]. See also H. B. Cottrill, *The Faust Legend and Goethe's Faust,* 1912, and H. G. Meek, *Faust: the Man and the Myth,* 1930.—Ed.

obtaining money by fraudulently duping the credulous, and, in others, as a 'philosophus', a revered and feared Astrologer, Magician and Necromancer. What is more, two praenomens are given in these records. Sometimes we find Georgius Faustus, at others Johannes Faustus, and it is to be remarked that whenever these names appear, that of Georgius is associated with the impostor, that of Johannes with the Magician. Johann is invariably given as the wizard's Christian name in the Faust Books: it was 'Doctor John Faustus' whose 'Damnable Life and Deserved Death' grew with the rapidity of a Fakir's mango seed into the formidable fabric of the Faust Legend. The first extant record of Faustus the magician, not the impostor, is an entry in the account-book of the Bishop of Bamberg, 12 February 1520, by the bishop's chamberlain: 'Item, 10 gulden given and presented to Doctor Faustus philosophus in honour of his having cast for my gracious master a nativity or indicium, paid on Sunday after Scholastica by the order of Reverendissimus'. He reappears in the 'Sermones Convivales' of Johann Gast, 1548; and, with his full name of Johannes Faustus, in the 'Locorum Communium Collectanea' of Johannes Manlius [Johann Mennel], 1563. Manlius was councillor and historian to the Emperor Maximilian II, and his above-mentioned work consists chiefly of reported conversations with Melancthon, to whom the remarks on Faustus are attributed. The entry in the minutes of the Town Council of Ingolstadt 1528 refers to Georgius Faustus. He appears in his usual character: 'the fortune-teller shall be ordered to leave the town and spend his penny elsewhere,' and, in the record of expulsions from the city, we find that of Dr. Jorg Faustus of Heidelberg. The reference to Faustus by the physician Philipp Begardi of Worms in the 'Index Sanitatis,' 1539, as one of the 'wicked, cheating, useless and unlearned doctors', is clearly to the same person.

It is remarkable that neither Dr. William Rose nor

Prof. W. Alison Philipps in their learned writings on the
subject of Faust, should have perceived the fact of there
being two distinct historical personages of that name. Dr.
Rose indeed raises the question, but fails unaccountably
in the interpretation. 'The difficulty with regard to his
Christian name [he writes] has already been mentioned.
If his real name was Georg, it may have been forgotten
and replaced by the more common one of Johann, or
there may have been two magicians of the name of Faust,
the older one named Georg and the later one Johann,
who may have taken the name of Faust because it had
already been rendered famous by his predecessor. The
latter hypothesis is, however, extremely unlikely, and
there seems very little reason to doubt that all the references are to the same individual'. The hypothesis in
question is, however, not only likely but provable. There
were two magicians of the name of Faust, but their
chronological order and relationship were exactly the
reverse of those suggested by Dr. Rose. The key to the
mystery is to be found in the earliest of all the existing
records: a letter written in Latin by the Abbot Trithemius [Tritheim] of Wurzburg to the mathematician and
astrologer, Johann Virdung, on 20 August 1507. The
Abbot writes to warn Virdung against an imposter of the
name of 'Georgius Sabellicus, who has ventured to call
himself the prince of necromancers'. He goes on to say
that this man, who 'is a fool and no philosopher', has
'adopted the following title: *Magister Georgius Sabellicus, Faustus Junior,* Fountain of Necromancers, astrologer, *magus secundus,* chiromancer, aeromancer,
pyromancer, second in hydromancy'.

If, then, Georgius Sabellicus was, as he clearly styled
himself, the younger Faust and the second magician and
hydromancer, who was Faustus Senior, magus primus,
first in hydromancy? Who, in fact, was the magician of
whom Dr. Rose declares there is no trace? ['It cannot
be explained why Faust should have called himself junior,

for there is no trace of any earlier magician of the same name': *History of Dr. John Faustus*, edited by William Rose, M.A., Ph.D., introduction]. The answer is, that he was that Johannes Faustus whom the records describe as being not a charlatan but a philosopher, not a vagrant rogue but a dangerous sorcerer. Georgius Sabellicus, as his string of self-assumed titles demonstrates, was plainly an itinerant fortune-teller who had presumptuously taken to himself the name of Faust, rendered famous by his redoubtable predecessor Johannes Faustus. That this man [Johannes Faustus] actually taught magic publicly at the University of Cracow in Poland [see *De Praestigiis Daemonum* by Johannes Wierus 1568, etc.] proves the degree of respect in which his learning was held. That there should have anywhere existed a professorship of the occult arts is an example of the often fantastic extremes to which the individualism of the age of the Renaissance extended.

Before taking leave of the historical Faust, it is necessary to mention that the magician Johann Faust has by some been identified with the printer Johann Fust, the rival of Gutenberg. Fust was born at Mainz about 1400, printed his famous Psalter, 'remarkable for the beauty of the large initials printed each in two colours, red and blue, from types made in two pieces,' in 1457 and, after issuing many important publications, died of the plague in Paris in 1466. There is obviously no connection whatever between this celebrated man and the magician Faustus. Not until the seventeenth century was any suggested.

Research into the origins of the Faust Legend comprises of necessity inquiry into the origin of Mephistophiles, the familiar spirit to whom, or rather through whom, Faustus sells his soul. [The name has many forms: Marlowe writes Mephistophilis, Goethe Mephistopheles.] The popular notion that Mephistopheles personifies the Supreme Spirit of Evil, as does the Satan of Milton, is

erroneous and has risen from misunderstanding of the
Faust Legend and ignorance of its origins. [For this
Goethe himself is partly responsible]. In the first Faust
Book, published at Frankfort-on-Main 1587, in which
for the first time the name of Mephistophiles appears, we
read that when Doctor Faustus commenced his Incantation in the Spisser Waldt 'he began to call for Mephistophiles the Spirit, and to charge him in the name of
Beelzebub to appear there personally without any long
stay', and that he 'began again to conjure the Spirit
Mephistophiles in the name of the Prince of Devils to
appear in his likeness'. Later, when Faustus demands of
Mephistophiles his agreement to the articles drawn up
by the doctor, we read: 'Hereupon the Spirit answered
and laid his case forth that he had no such power of
himself until he had first given his Prince [that was ruler
over him] to understand thereof, and to know if he could
obtain so much of his Lord: therefore speak farther that
I may do thy whole desire to my Prince: for it is not in
my power to fulfil without his leave. Show me the cause
why [said Faustus]. The Spirit answered: Faustus, thou
shalt understand that with us it is even as well a kingdom,
as with you on earth: yea, we have our rulers and servants,
as I myself am one, and we name our whole number
the Legion: for although that Lucifer is thrust and fallen
out of heaven through his pride and high mind, yet he
hath notwithstanding a Legion of Devils at his command-
ment, that we call the Oriental Princes; for his power is
great and infinite. Also there is an host in Meridie, in
Septentrio, in Occidente: and for that Lucifer hath his
kingdom under heaven, we must change and give ourselves unto men to serve them at their pleasure. It is also
certain we have never as yet opened unto any man the
truth of our dwelling, neither of our ruling, neither what
our power is, neither have we given any man any gift, or
learned him anything, except he promise to be ours'.

From this it is plain that 'this swift flying Spirit' was

a familiar of the same nature as that Orton who served
the Lord of Corasse and of whom the Squire of Gascony
told Froissart in the chapel of the Count of Foix's Castle
at Orthez [see Froissart *Chroniques*, ed. Kervyn de
Lettenhove, vol. xi., pp. 189-201]; or as Redcap the
familiar of whom we read in the ballad of Lord Soulis of
Hermitage [see Scott's *Minstrelsy of the Scottish Border*:
Lord Soulis by John Leyden].

'The origin of the conception and name [of Mephis-
tophiles] has,' according to Prof. Philipps [*Encyclopædia
Britannica*, 14th Edition, article *Mephistopheles*], 'been
much debated. In Dr. Faust's *Höllenzwang* which pur-
ports to be one of the magical books, according to the
Zimmern chronicle left behind by Dr. Faustus which
came into the possession of the Lord of Staufen, "Mephistophiel" is one of the seven great princes of hell; "he
stands under the planet Jupiter, his regent is named
Zadkiel, an enthroned angel of the holy Jehovah". The
origin of the idea of Mephistophiles in Faust's mind is
thus clear. He was one of the evil demons of the seven
planets, the Maskim of the ancient Akkadian religion, a
conception transmitted through the Chaldeans, the
Babylonians and the Jewish Qabala to mediæval and
modern astrologers and magicians'. The most plausible
interpretation of the name Mephistophiel appears to be
that of Herr Schrör [*Faust*, ed. 1886, i.25], who derives
it from the Hebrew *mephiz* = destroyer, and *tophel* = liar,
'a derivation which is supported by the fact that nearly
all the names of devils in the sixteenth-century magic
books are derived from the Hebrew'. [See Prof. W.
Alison Philipps, *Encycl. Brit.*]. Other derivations: C
Kiesewetter [*Faust in der Geschichte und Tradition*,
p. 163].

Of the Maskim, of whose number Prof. Philipps
believes Mephistophiel [Mephistophiles] to be, Prof.
Zenaïde A. Ragozin writes: 'All the more terrible are

the seven spirits of the abyss, the Maskim, of whom it is said that, although their seat is in the depths of the earth, yet their voice resounds on the heights also: they reside at will in the immensity of space' [*Chaldea: Story of the Nations*, pp. 154-155: also F. Lenormant *Chaldean Magic* 1877, pp. 17-18, 25-32]. There is extant a Chaldean conjuration of these demons, a relic of great antiquity:

A charm of awful power . . .
A spell that's older than the walls, long buried,
Of Babylon; ere Nineveh was dreamed
'Twas old beyond the power of computation.
'They are Seven, they are Seven—Seven they are:
They sit by the way. They sleep in the deep:
                   down far—
             Seven they are!

They are Seven, they are Seven—Seven are they!
Out of the Abyss they rise, when day
Sinks into darkness.
                 Seven are they!

Born in the bowels o' the hills,
Evil ones, sowers of ills:
Setters of unseen snares,
Deaf to all pity, all prayers:
Male they are not,
Female they are not,
No wives have they known,
No children begot.
The Fiends, they are Seven:
Disturbers of Heaven
They are Seven, they are Seven—Seven they are!'

If such an one was the spirit conjured by him, Faustus would seem to have been a man aspiring and intrepid to no ordinary degree, a figure not unworthy to become the pivot of so sinister a legend.

                                C.R.C.

Another story of a pact with the Devil is borrowed
by Gregory Lewis from the annals of the Spanish Inquisi
tion. Don Ambrosio, Prior of the Dominicans of Madrid
and a famous preacher, having allowed himself to be
tempted by the demons of pride and luxury had been
arrested by order of the Holy Office and accused of rape
and black magic. He was in the throes of rather belated
remorse and terrified by the threat of torture. A nun, an
accomplice in his crimes, had been arrested at the same
time as himself. Tortured by the judges of the merciless
tribunal, Ambrosio had the strength of will to uphold
his innocence; but the nun under torture confessed that
she was a witch. She was condemned to the stake, whilst
Ambrosio was held for further questioning in the hope
that he would be forced to admit his guilt.

It appears, according to the story, that the nun was
a real witch, for she came to Ambrosio in his cell and gave
him a book of spells, advising him to read the first four
lines of the seventh page, so that he might make a pact
in exchange for which the infernal powers would deliver
him from death at the stake. 'Do as I have done,' she told
him. 'My sins are too great to be forgiven by God; I have
renounced Him and I belong to Satan. He offers me a
long life filled with every kind of delight which you may
be able to share with me.'

Ambrosio, in spite of his fears, could not bring himself to add apostacy to his crimes. The nun disappeared,
leaving him the magic book. During the night following
this apparition the officers of the Inquisition came to take
him once more before his judges. Faced once again by the
torture chamber he no longer had the courage to endure
further pain and continue the fight against the accusation.
His condemnation was pronounced and the execution
fixed for the next day.

Back in his cell, he was awaiting in a state of stupor
the arrival of the fateful moment when his gaze fell upon

the book of spells which now seemed to contain the secret of a possible salvation. He opened it automatically at the seventh page, and began reading in a trembling voice Suddenly the ground trembled; it opened, and a fiery demon was standing before him, holding in one hand a scroll of parchment and in the other an iron pen. 'Sign this pact,' he said to Ambrosio, 'and you shall be saved at once!'

The monk still hesitated, but the noise of weapons and keys was heard approaching the cell. It was the jailers and guards coming to take him to his death. 'Save me, save me!' cried the condemned man.

'Then sign!' replied the agent of the Devil. Ambrosio obeyed. At once the vault opened and he was free. His liberator seized him in his arms, and flying as swiftly as a lightning-flash carried him to the edge of a precipice on the Sierra Morena.

In the faint twilight that precedes the dawn Ambrosio gazed at this wild landscape. 'Where are you taking me?' he asked his guide. 'We have arrived!' replied the demon. 'I have saved you from the justice of man, but none can save you from the justice of God!' With these words, he dug his red-hot claws into the wretch's flesh, and, laughing at his agonised shrieks, flew with him to an immense height and let him fall.

Ambrosio fell to the bottom of a rocky ravine through which a wild torrent roared. Every bone in his body was broken, but there was still a faint breath of life left in him. Soon the sun rose and its rays lit up this horrible scene: thousands of insects, roused by the heat, lighted on the dying man; the mountain eagles came and tore at his quivering flesh and in his death-throes Ambrosio uttered irreparable blasphemies. Then the heavens burst open in a furious storm; the winds unleashed, shook the rocks to their foundations and uprooted the twisted trees hanging over the precipice. The rain fell in an unceasing deluge, the waters of the torrent gradually rose and dragged off in their muddy, foaming depths the remains of the damned towards some unknown shore . . .

XI

BEFORE leaving the subject of witchcraft, it might be useful here to rectify an error which has become all too common recently and which M. Alfred Maury has too readily approved. 'Pursued, hounded by the magistrates and anathematised by the Church,' says M. Maury, 'the magicians avenged themselves by placing the responsibility for their criminal activities on two of the most orthodox of the popes, Leo III and Honorius III. Under the cloak of these pontiffs' names, they forged two books of magic, the *Enchiridion* and the *Grimoire*, which have been several times reprinted and in which are collected all the ridiculous recipes for their imaginary art. The old rabbinical tradition which claimed that Solomon was a magician was revived in the composition of a book similar to these black-books called *Clavicula Salomonis*, of which three translations exist in French. Embedded in all the childish rubbish which packs these books can still be recognised the trace of the ancient beliefs from which they sprang more than twenty centuries ago; with them are mingled remains of neo-platonic evocations and the adoration of infernal spirits. The Devil makes his appearance in the company of ancient gods disguised as demons.'[54]

The learned academician who wrote the above in 1863 is completely mistaken, I regret to say, on the contents of the three works which he accuses of being black-books without having examined them.

Pope Leo III came to the throne of St. Peter on 20 December 795. He was a man of learning and great piety who wished to uphold the law and wipe out abuses.

[54] *La Magie et l'Astrologie dans l'Antiquité et au Moyen Age* part 1, ch. 4.

Two officers of his household, Dean Pascal and Sacellary Campule, nephews of Pope Adrian I, his predecessor, conspired against him. On the 23 April 799 during a procession in honour of the evangelist St. Mark they attacked the pontiff, and, with their accomplices, tried to tear out his tongue and eyes. Dragged through the streets by these wretches and overwhelmed by the violence of their attack, Leo III could only have escaped their fury by some sort of miracle. He managed to find refuge in the monastry of St. Silvester, from which a few faithful followers accompanied him secretly on the next night and took him far from Rome to Paderborn in Prussia, where was the court of the Emperor Charlemagne.

The great king welcomed the unfortunate pontiff and gave him a troop of picked men to escort him back to Italy with the announcement that a Frankish army would soon come to Rome and punish the guilty ones. The whole population of Rome ran to welcome Leo III and delivered Pascal and Campule into his hands; Charlemagne at once ordered them to be put to death with their accomplices. Armed with this right of reprisal, the Pope could have enjoyed the sweets of revenge; but, giving the world a sublime example of charity, he let them go unharmed.

The next year Charlemagne appeared in Rome preceded by his great fame and followed by his succession of victories. He came to seek a solemn consecration for the great mission of political and social reconstruction which he was carrying out in Europe. Leo gave him the imperial consecration and anointed him, conferring upon him the title of Protector of the Church.

A venerable tradition recounts that after this ceremony Charlemagne received from the Pope a precious memorial of his visit to Rome. It was a collection of prayers containing the most beautiful sacred texts of the Church's liturgy. These texts formed a breviary for every day of the week. The Pope, who had made the collection himself, declared that miraculous virtues which had been proved by a great number of authenticated experiences were attached to the possession and pious use of this little book. 'Whoever,' he said, 'carries it on him with the respect due to the Holy Scriptures and recites it each day to the glory of God will perish neither by fire, iron nor water, nor by sudden death; he will triumph over his foes, he will emerge safe and sound from the most dreadful perils, and divine protection will lead him happily to the termination of a glorious career.'

This book is the famous *Enchiridion* of Leo III. It was first printed in Rome in 1525. Another edition exists printed in Rome in 1606; four were printed in Lyons from 1584 to 1633 and one in Mainz in 1637. We look in vain in any one of them for adorations of infernal spirits, for the remains of neo-platonic doctrine and for the intervention of the Devil accompanied by the ancient gods. In Rome, the seat of Catholic orthodoxy, no pope, even in the worst days of the papacy, would have tolerated the printing of a book tainted with magic and imputed to one of his predecessors. The original edition of 1525 was made under the reign of Clement VII [Giulio de' Medici, 1523-1534]. This pope was a courageous defender of Christian morals and he was not afraid to excommunicate Henry VIII, that English monster who never spared a man's life if his death could assuage his anger nor spared the honour of a woman if she could satisfy his senses. How could Clement VII have allowed the memory of Leo III to be outraged by the publication of an absurd or damnable book? Simple common sense tells us how ridiculous is this suggestion.

Leo III's *Enchiridion* is full of crosses printed in red; these are an invitation to the reader to make the sign of the cross himself every time he comes across it in his prayers. We notice also, both in the printed and the manuscript copies, a few mysterious figures; but these are only mysterious at first glance: they are the monograms of Christ or Hebrew words whose meaning expresses the attributes of divine wisdom and power. There is nothing remotely approaching a diabolical invocation.

It was also in Rome that for the first time, in 1629 and not in 1525, as M. Maury states, the so-called *Black Book* of *Pope Honorius III* was printed. This pope's work is properly entitled: *Honorii Papæ adversus tenebrarum Principem et ejus Angelos Conjurationes, extractæ ex originali Romæ servato*—Conjurations of Pope Honorius against the Prince of Darkness and against his Angels. It is, therefore, a book of exorcisms, the exact opposite of a work dedicated to the invocation of infernal spirits.

As for the *Clavicula Salomonis*, it is more difficult to assign to this its true origin. The Jesuit Gretser, a *savant* of the XVIth century, assures us that no one had seen the Hebrew manuscript of this singular work, but that a Greek translation of it existed in the library of the Duke of Bavaria. The Abbé d'Artigny, an XVIIIth century bibliophile, cites several examples of it in the Latin tongue under the titles of *Clavicula Salomonis ad Filium Roboam* and *Liber Pentaculorum*. He says he possessed a copy of an edition printed in 1655, but he does not indicate in which country it was published.[55]

We know that rabbinical tradition attributes to King Solomon the divine privilege of perfect wisdom, the understanding of all secrets of the universe, the faculty of communication with the angels and the ability to operate, with their help, all kinds of miracles. Unfortunately this superabundance of good fortune made the son of David forget, towards the end of his life, the condition of saintly living imposed upon him in order to obtain it. Intoxicated by the admiration of the whole world, he cast away the majestic crown of the dignity of age and lighted in his palace the torch of lewd immorality. The servants of his decadence were employed solely in finding and buying for

[55] A facsimile of the *Clavicula* has since been printed.—*Ed.*

large sums of money the most beautiful girls of Sidon, Moab, Egypt and Idumea as ornaments for his royal couch.

The influence which these women exerted on the old king did not stop at the overthrow of his kingly intelligence. Jerusalem, which at first had beheld with terrified amazement the fall of this crowned genius, soon felt the contagion of his example and the city of the true God was peopled with impure idols whose mysteries had been introduced to the race of Abraham by foreign harlots. Astarte, the Phoenician Venus, and Moloch, the fiery Saturn of the Syrians, had sanctuaries on the Mount of Olives, opposite to the temple of Jehovah, whose majesty they seemed to defy. The new god of the prince who had raised the temple of the Eternal God was now a statue of a beautiful woman with a cow's head. Offerings were made to her of lotus and rose, dove, horse and lobster, emblems of the creatures of earth, air and water whose creation was attributed to her. But soon Solomon plunged into the horror of an even more sinister adoration. The cult of Moloch demanded human sacrifices. This god of murder consisted of a colossal hollow statue of bronze which was heated like a furnace and into which were cast little children whose shrieks were drowned by the beating of cymbals and drums.

This was the infernal madness which possessed the last years of Solomon. His wisdom, his knowledge, his power, all the gifts which he had received from heaven and which he had abused, were taken from him. But their tradition did not die. Whether Solomon himself wrote it down for the instruction of his son Rehoboam or whether he dictated it to the doctors of the tribe of Levi, it has passed from generation to generation down to our own times. The documents containing it are in two parts. The first is called *Secretum Secretorum;* this is a ritual of the ceremonies to be performed before entering into communication with the angels whom God puts in charge of the government of this world. The second part is called *Psalterium Mirabile*, a collection of the 150 Psalms of David, explaining the mysterious virtues which are attached to each and which can obtain for the faithful believer all the good things of this earth, victory over enemies and the safe conquest of every danger.

I am inclined to believe that this book, considered as a Latin translation of a Hebrew manuscript whose original can no longer be found, may be attributed to Popes Leo III and Honorius III, as well as the *Enchiridion* and the *Conjurationes*. We would have, in that case, not the rabbinical *Clavicula* but an imitation of that work adapted to the Christian habits of the Middle Ages by a theologian whose name we do not know. Moreover, to lend a mystical interpretation to the Psalms, to write them out in a certain manner, to recite them at certain hours, to carry them like talismans, is no stranger than to make a novena or any other exercise of Catholic piety in which the Virgin or some saint is invoked. It is an affair of conscience and faith which, by the essence of its mystery, escapes the narrow judgments of reason.

In order to give some idea of the *Psalterium Mirabile* I may cite the legend of St. Martha, one of the patron saints of Provence who, having inscribed the 31st Psalm on a kid-skin belt, made use of the belt to strangle the *Tarasque*, an amphibious monster whose voraciousness laid waste the banks of the Rhône in the first century A.D. But as such an example would hardly find occasion to be repeated in our own days, I propose this more interesting experiment with the 137th Psalm, which begins: *Confitebor tibi, Domine, quoniam audisti* . . .

This Psalm has, says tradition, *the power of exciting love* in the heart of the person who is the object of our desires. This is how we must use it. Pour oil from a white lily into a crystal goblet, recite the 137th Psalm over the cup and conclude it by pronouncing the name of the angel

Anael, the planetary spirit of Venus,[56] and the name of the person you love. Next write the name of the angel on a piece of cypress which you will dip into the oil; then lightly anoint your eyebrows with the oil and tie the piece of cypress to your right arm. Then wait for a propitious moment to touch the right hand of the person with whom you are in love, and love will be awakened in his or her heart. The operation will be more powerful in effect, the unknown author assures us, if you perform it at dawn on the Friday following the new moon.

EASTERN AND TIBETAN MAGIC.[57] Book V of this work deals mainly with the western magical tradition from Egypt onwards; it is impossible in a short supplementary section to do more than indicate some of the wealth of material that eastern traditions and practices yield in this field. The east and the west, in this as in other matters, have approaches which differ fundamentally. To quote a recent work[58] which posits this difference clearly: 'Western man is at last searching for syntheses, for the integration of various inter-related or conflicting portions of human knowledge, instead of denying the reality of what does not fit into his personal conception of the cosmos.' De Riencourt further proceeds to speculate upon Tibet as possibly yielding a resolution to the eastern and western differences of attitude. 'Can Tibet,' he says, 'by any chance contribute something to this task of providing a solution to the greatest problem man has ever had to face? For thousands of years the Orientals have taken the existence of psychic forces for granted, and it has never occurred to them to question their reality. By accepting as a fact what could not in those days be proved by scientific methods, and by applying to the study of

56 Also spelt Hamiel, Haniel and even Onoel.—*Ed.*
57 This and the following sections are additions to Christian's text.—*Ed.*
58 Amaury de Riencourt, *Lost World: Tibet, Key to Asia.*—*Ed.*

psychic forces a purely logical and experimental method, the easterners, and especially the Tibetans, were able to accumulate a vast occult knowledge, which is still largely unknown to the rest of the world. While Christianity gradually transformed itself into a group of powerful religious institutions, in which practical research into psychic matters was discouraged, in which metaphysical speculations were confined between the narrow limits set by dogmas, Buddhism and Hinduism encouraged individual or collective researches into the mysterious world of the psyche. While faith in the dogmas was the motto of the west, complete freedom of research was the motto of the east. When the Christian oecumenical councils crushed the Gnostic believers in reincarnation and devotees of esoteric knowledge [in the 5th century A.D.], blind faith became the supreme argument of religion in the Christian world. Slowly and gradually, the energies of the occident were diverted towards the physical world, and the same rational and experimental approach built up western science which had helped to build up psychic knowledge in the east. Yet a basic difference exists nowadays between those two knowledges, a difference which has to be taken into account when trying to apply scientific methods to psychic research. Knowledge in the east has one aim, the discovery of ultimate truth.'

Since this book is not dealing with mysticism or philosophy, only magic, the wider implications of this cannot be discussed. However, as regards psychic phenomena the frequency of these in Tibet, where thought-transference, mediumship, astral travelling and projected thought-forms, as well as complicated doctrines of reincarnation, are commonplaces, is such that nothing save considerable works are at all adequate.[59] The majority of these manifestations of the Tibetan mind would be most inadequately described as magic; they form part of a general system of beliefs and a way of life whose description

[59] See short book list at close of this section.—*Ed.*

is no necessary part of this work. We may however select
a few of the outstanding powers, claimed with apparent
truth to be part of the Tibetan heritage, as examples of
magic in the western sense.[60]

. Two that have struck the European imagination are
the ability to generate *tumo,* a kind of internal heat which
enables ascetics to live naked among snows at some 15,000
feet altitude; and the power of *lung-gom* or hypnotic
walking or bounding at great speed practised by the *lung-
gom-pa,* messengers specially trained who are sent on
errands across the barren flat table-land of Tibet.

[61]The training necessary to produce *tumo* or *tūmmo*
is long and severe. There are in fact three kinds of *tumo,*
of which the kind showing itself in physical manifestations
is that which is more generally known. A long period of
probation precedes a process of 'empowerment' called
angkur, a rite by which the master communicates peculiar
power to his disciple. After some closely supervised exercises, the novice retires, according to Alexandra David-
Neel, to some utterly solitary place, well over the 10,000
feet level; for *tumo* must never be practised near a house
or inhabited place, and once initiated into it, the initiate
must renounce woollen and fur clothing and never
approach a fire. At the most a single cotton garment is
allowed. Disciples must fast completely before practising
various breathing drills during which pride, anger, hatred,
covetousness, sloth and stupidity are rhythmically breathed
out, and blessings and the five wisdoms, goodness and
loftiness are breathed in. The disciple thus calmed,
imagines a golden lotus inside the body, level with the
navel. In it stands the symbol *raṁ,* shining sun-like, and
above it the symbol *ma.* Thence issues the feminine deity
called Dorjee Naljorma. These symbols are not mere

---

[60] Much of the following is from Alexandra David-Neel *With Mystics and
Magicians in Tibet,* the work of a trained and experienced observer, a member of the French Academy.—*Ed.*

[61] See W. T. Evans-Wentz *Tibetan Yoga and Secret Doctrines,* Book 3.—*Ed.*

words—*raṁ* is the seed [*bija mantra,* Sanskrit] of the fire itself. In pronouncing these sounds a power is created. The pupil identifies himself with Dorjee Naljorma; then he imagines the letter *A* in the navel and the letter *Ha* at the top of the head. Deep breaths then blow up the smouldering internal fire—a minute ball existing at *A*—as would bellows. Each inspiration is a wind penetrating the abdomen and increasing the flames.

The retention of the breath is gradually increased; thought follows the awakening of fire along the *sushumna* [Sanskrit] vein rising up the spine—this is one of three mystic *nadi* [imaginary channels] containing psychic energy. The exercise continues through ten stages with appropriate subjective visions; inhalations, retentions and expirations of breath rhythmically continue, mystic formulæ continually repeat, while the mind remains utterly 'one-pointed' on the vision of fire and the sense of warmth during the periods of breath retention.

The ten stages are : —

    [1]   The psychical *uma* is formed in the mind as the thinnest of hairs, but filled with rising flame and crossed by the wind of the breath.

    [2]   This increases to the thickness of the little finger :

    [3]   It increases to the size of an arm :

    [4]   It has become the body itself, now filled with blazing fire and air.

    [5]   Enlarged indefinitely, the artery envelops the world in an ocean of fire.

Now these visions reverse :

    [6]   The wind abates and the fire-waves sink and are absorbed into the body :

    [7]   The arm-sized artery returns :

    [8]   It is now the little finger size :

[9]   It becomes as thin as a hair:

[10]   It entirely disappears, and with it all forms and references whatever: 'the mind of the knower sinks and the object perceived dies into the great "Emptiness" where duality does not exist any longer.'

This is in fact a trance.

This exercise may be repeated whenever desired, although the training in it is always practised before dawn. Various other forms of practice besides the above also exist. The great Tibetan mystical teacher Milarepa resorted to the practice in his cave on Mount Everest and wrote a poem about it. Alexandra David-Neel herself testifies to the efficacity of the method in her own case. Tibetan *tumo* initiates prove their abilities by drying off wet sheets in remarkable numbers on their bodies while sitting naked in the snow, sometimes forty sheets in a night.

One afternoon in her Tibetan travels Alexandra David-Neel saw a strange traveller proceeding with an unnatural gait and at an extraordinary speed, which her attendants informed her was a *lama lung-gom-pa*. They indicated that she must not interfere with or deflect his journey, or fatal results might follow should he be awakened from his trance condition. 'I could,' she says, 'clearly see his perfectly calm impassive face and wide-open eyes with their gaze fixed on some invisible, far-distant object situated somewhere high up in space. The man did not run. He seemed to lift himself from the ground, proceeding by leaps. It looked as if he had been endowed with the elasticity of a ball, and rebounded each time his feet touched the ground. His steps had the regularity of a pendulum. He wore a short monastic robe and toga, both rather ragged. His left hand grasped a fold of the toga and was half hidden under the cloth. The right held a *phurba* [magic dagger]; his right arm moved slightly at each step as if leaning on a stick, just as though the *phurba,* whose pointed extremity was far above the ground, had touched it and were actually a support . . . He went his way, perfectly unaware of our presence.' She concluded that, in order to reach the place where he was later reported to her, the *lung-gom-pa* must have travelled in this fashion not merely during most of the day on which she saw him, but also the whole night and the next day without stopping and at a similar speed.

It appears that originally this power was developed as part of a ceremonial originating in the XIIIth century which required the gathering of demons from various parts by a runner messenger. Preliminary training includes, after due breathing practices, jumping up with legs crossed to a considerable height; and eventually at a more advanced stage the aspirants are immured in darkness for three years. The essential concentration during the *lung-gom* is upon a certain mental recitation timed with in and out breathing; and the retention of breath. 'The walker must neither speak nor look from side to side : he must keep his eyes fixed upon a single distant object and never allow his attention to be attracted by anything else.' Alexandra David-Neel concluded from her observations that uniformity in landscape as in a wide plain or a forest of regular trees without undergrowth was conducive to this practice.

Telepathy, or the 'message sent on the wind', has been more scientifically studied in Tibet than in the west; that is, over a far longer period and more methodically. It depends, say Tibetans, on 'one-pointedness' of thought, and the receiver's part is as difficult as the sender's. Since 'one-pointedness' or intense concentration is in any case the basis of Tibetan psycho-spiritual training, telepathy forms a natural by-product of it. There exist, however, more specialised practices to cultivate the power. Various sensations and memories are discriminated between and the communication of simple mental images between *guru* and teacher is practised. Mental orders and messages are then transmitted until they are perceptible even when the receiver's mind appears to be completely occupied with other matters.

Tibetan séances do not need darkness and resemble shamanist dances. 'The *pawo* begins chanting, accompanying himself on a little drum and a bell. He dances, first slowly then faster and faster, and, finally, trembles convulsively. A being of another world, god, demon or spirit of a dead person, has taken possession of him. In a kind of frenzy he utters broken sentences which are supposed to convey that which the invisible being wishes to communicate to the assistants . . . the most intelligent men of the village are called upon to listen attentively. It sometimes happens that different gods or spirits take possession of the medium one after another.' Incidentally, it may be remarked that the spiritual world in Tibet would appear to the western imagination to be somewhat over-populated. There are demons of all varieties, including creations of concentrated thought known as *tolpas* and *tulkus,* semi-divine beings and human spirits on a high plane, demi-gods or genii called *mi ma yin,* also beings of enormous size called *yidags,* who are perpetually tortured by thirst and hunger—lamas offer them water daily; not to speak of *yidams* or tutelary deities who may be given substance by the devotion of a worshipper. An advanced spiritual exercise, for instance, is the making real of a *yidam* by a disciple at the instance of his *guru,* and the eventual discovery by the disciple that he does not really believe in it: which is part of the advanced teaching that the whole phenomenal world, natural and spiritual, is in fact illusion. Negotiations with demons are usually carried out through *böns* [sorcerers]. Besides the *pawo, buntings* and *yawa* are names for other varieties of medium.

Lamaist teaching in Tibet emphasises the importance of a detailed knowledge of the region beyond death, in order to better one's lot there. Those who have been properly instructed should be able to maintain their consciousness and direction during the passage from life. However, those who have not learned it—and indeed also those who have—are assisted in dying by lamas who instruct or remind them, one of the objects being to induce the spirit to leave the body through the top of the head.

Most of the dealings with the dead and their effects are designed to prevent the return of the spirit to earth and stop its connections, so as not to hinder its progress elsewhere. The detailed ceremonies, instructions and ritual for the dying and dead are given in full in the *Tibetan Book of the Dead*, or *After-Death Experiences of the Bardo Plane*, by W. Y. Evans-Wentz, which was taken down from the translation by the lama Kazi Dawa-Samdup. It embodies much of the teachings of the northern Greater Vehicle or Mahayana school of Buddhism; this originates from the Yoga science of the northern Indian Buddhist university of Nālanda, the text being attributed to Padma Sambhava, the *guru* who introduced Tantric Buddhism or 'lamaism' into Tibet [VIIIth century A.D.]. Briefly, the teaching is that all the various figures seen during the 49 days of the *bardo* or planes of consciousness beyond death are illusion and the object is to induce the spirit to awaken into a *nirvana* state beyond the whole cycle of *sangsāra* or phenomenal existence with its *karma* of rebirth—to bring the spirit where it may join Maitreya, the spirit of the next Buddha who is to come. On the *bardo* plane the deceased is tested by being introduced to the five various divine-human attributes. Then deepening hallucinations intervene. The whole judgment process is so akin to the Egyptian Book of the Dead that some derivative link seems certain. The bardo judge Dharma-Rāja or Yama-Rāja is an Osiris; black and white pebbles are placed in opposite scales of a balance; the heart is addressed, as in Egypt; the supervisor of the weighing is the monkey-headed Shinji, replacing the Egyptian dog-headed ape Anubis, companion of Thoth, and a posse of devils wait for the evil-doer, as does the monster Amam or Ammit in Egypt. Something very similar to all this is given by Plato in an account of other world adventures in the *Republic*, Book X.

The separation of the *bardo* body and the earthly one takes $3\frac{1}{2}$ to four days, whether or not a priest called a *hpho-bo* or 'extractor of consciousness' assists it. Normally he chants for about an hour directions for the spirit to find —if the *karma* of its earthly days permit—the western paradise, Amitābha. He looks at the crown of the skull to see if the spirit has escaped properly through the sagittal suture, the 'aperture of Brahma'. The corpse is tied in a birth-posture, symbolising the beginning of its new life, and details of the funerary rites are decided by an astrologer who casts a chart of the moment of death. The chanting of the ritual to assist the dead goes on at intervals for the 49 days of the *bardo* period. The corpse may be disposed of eventually in various ways—there is here no general pre-occupation as in Egypt over its preservation. It may be given any of four burials according to which of the four elements has it, earth, air, fire or water; more commonly it receives air burial, when it is cut into pieces for birds and beasts, this method being particularly efficacious in preventing the return of the spirit and hence stopping possible vampirism. Only the very great or holy are embalmed in marsh salt.

In the *bardo thödol*, or 'liberation by hearing on the after-death plane', the spirit is instructed in how to choose a rebirth, for if the prime object of avoiding the need for it is rare of attainment, then the 'art of choosing a womb' is naturally of great importance.

Rebirth is a debatable doctrine in the east, though the fact is on the whole accepted. Western biologists in recent times have found it not contrary to modern scientific obser-vations; T. H. Huxley in *Evolution and Ethics* and Dr. E. B. Tylor in *Primitive Culture* have found *karma* and its corollary of re-incarnation essentially reasonable. Huxley emphasises that 'the sum of tendencies that we call charac-ter' traces through a long line of predecessors. A germ develops according to a certain specific type', resultant from inherited conditions.

Instructions are given in the *Tibetan Book of the Dead* for 'closing the door of the womb', i.e. avoiding rebirth, and also where to choose amongst the preliminary visions showing possible birth-places if and when the rebirth has become inevitable. Of the four continents, only the southern one is recommended; of classes of beings, the heavenly *devas* are the best. If however these are unobtainable, by concentrating the mind on being a Brahmin or an adept, a priest or a humble but faithful believer, entry is obtained into a womb that will make these things possible, providing always that there is impartiality of mind, the quality with which Aldous Huxley has familiarised us as 'non-attachment', that is, being non-attached to the results of actions.

Liberation from fear and the inducing of the realisation that the whole phenomenal world is subjective, and the very self a nothingness, are the aims of many spiritual exercises, the most striking being the performance of *Chöd*,[62] which is described as a mystic play by one actor. An awe-inspiring spot such as a demon-haunted cemetery is often chosen. All passions are first ritually 'trampled down', then the *kangling* or trumpet made of a human femur calls the hungry demons to the mystic feast on the body of the celebrant. He imagines a female form emerging from his head who cuts it off, then his limbs; she skins and disembowels him. The celebrant, in an ecstacy of self-abnegation, urges on the hungry ghouls to eat himself: 'I have borrowed,' he says, 'from countless living beings food, clothing, and all kinds of services ... To-day I pay my debt ... I give my flesh to the hungry, my blood to the thirsty, my skin to clothe those who are naked, my bones as fuel to those who suffer from cold. I give my happiness to the unhappy ones. I give my breath to bring back the dying to life. Shame on me if I shrink from giving myself! Shame

[62] See Evans-Wentz. *Tibetan Yoga*, Book 5.—*Ed*.

on you, wretched and demoniac beings, if you do not dare to prey upon it!'

This 'red meal' is followed by a 'black meal'. The celebrant is now but a few charred bones amongst the black mud of misery and degradation. Now he cannot sacrifice, for he has nothing, is nothing; sacrifice itself has become illusion. The ascetic rite closes with this last renunciation.

For the novices for whom the demons are still real *Chöd* is sometimes dangerous and even fatal, for it is necessary for them first to credit the phenomena of life's illusions before they can effectively learn to discredit them.

The *Yoga* upon the practices of which so much of the Tibetan ascetic trainings depend came originally from India, probably in fact with Padma Sambhava. However for the study of this, which is basic to both Tibetan and Indian religions, the reader must be referred elsewhere.[63]

R.N.

WERE ANIMALS AND BELIEFS CONCERNING CORPSES. Little can be reliably written on Voodoo, the African magic, and the reader must be referred to the few works that exist.[64] One aspect of it however links with similar phenomena reported elsewhere and is worth a note. West Africa has a number of animals said in different districts

---

[63] On Yoga practices, *Heaven Lies Within Us* by Theos Bernard gives in intelligible form for the west his personal experiences of practices up to a high degree of initiation. W. Y. Evans-Wentz' *Tibetan Yoga and Secret Doctrines* quoted above gives the substance of the Seven Books of Wisdom of the *Mahayana* school. The same author's *Milarepa, the Jetsum Kahbum* is the autobiography of that great 11th-12th century teacher; his indispensable *Tibetan Book of the Dead* is mentioned in the text. Another invaluable source is the Buddhist tantra *Shrichakrasambhara Tantra*, edited by Kazi Dawasamdup [Tantrik Texts, vol 7]. Of general books on Tibet probably Theos Bernard *Land of a Thousand Buddhas* is the best for a general account, also Ekai Kawaguchi *Three Years in Tibet.—Ed.*

[64] See W. B. Seabrook, *The Magic Island* and M. D. Cassecanarie *Obeah Simplified, The True Wanga,* the author of the last being himself a Voodoo priest; also Montague Summers *The Vampire.—Ed.*

to be *were* or *wir*, that is to be demon or human elementary transformations: there are the were-tiger, the were-jaguar and the were-alligator. Now India also has a were-tiger, and in Australia amongst certain tribes is the were-dingo. In America there is a were-coyote, and in Europe the evidence for the were-wolf, as lately as 1935 in Bavaria, is strong. Ancient Egypt is said to have had a were-jackal, and nearer home the were-cat is reported from Scotland.

In Tibet the object in reviving the corpse in a rite called *rolang* is to bite off its tongue whilst it is leaping in a violent dance. If this is not done the corpse kills the sorcerer who has revived it. This process must be distinguished from the animation of a corpse by a wandering spirit seeking embodiment, a process said to be accomplished by the *trong jug* rite in Tibet. The *jibbuk* of Hebrew folk-belief is such a reinhabited corpse; in this case it usually seems to be acting as a kind of medium for the re-establishment of communications with this world by a departed human spirit. More horribly, West Africa, together with the other Voodoo regions of Haiti, Jamaica, British Guiana, Cuba and parts of South America, has its *zombies*, revived corpses acting as servants and slaves of the living.

The above must be distinguished again from the vampire or *voordalak* [Slavonic], which is defined as the human personality devoid of the ego, seeking continued life by blood-drinking at night from the living. The evidence from the Carpathian and neighbouring areas of Europe appears to be strong; the general beliefs there do not differ widely from the popular 'horror' treatment given to it in the well-known *Dracula* of Bram Stoker. Vampirism is or has been alleged to occur amongst most of the Romanian, Moldavian, Serbian and the other Slavonic races, and also amongst the Czechs; precautions against it are taken in Greek burial customs.

R.N.

PSYCHIC RESEARCH.[65] Spiritualism is a word that
all serious students of psychic science heartily dislike
with its flavour of dark stuffy rooms, floating tam
bourines, neurotic women, and scheming mediums. Yet it
must perforce be used, as it is the accepted modern word
for the study of those mysterious laws that govern what I
must call 'the Other Side of things': the Other Side as
opposed to the normal side, the everyday world in which
we live. That Other Side that can be reached and studied,
given patience or persistence; that Other Side that has been
the goal of all wise men and women, all advanced thinkers,
philosophers, scientists, metaphysicians all down the ages,
ever since man evolved from the primeval stage that he
shared with his distant cousins the apes.

The word Spiritualism is new—but not the study!
The fact that a world of spirits existed, a world that could
be 'tapped' and with which communication could be held,
given the right conditions, has been known to mankind all
down those same ages. The conditions necessary to the
modern seance room—darkness, silence, concentration—
have been and are still being fulfilled amongst countless
savage tribes, from the Eskimos to the Andaman Islanders,
from Zulus and from voodoo-worshippers of Haiti, to those
last remnants of a great race, the Red Indians—[what better
'cabinet' could there be than a wigwam?]

The secret of communication with the spirit-world,
the understanding and use of mediumship in all its
branches, has never been forgotten amongst these simpler
folk of the eastern races. It was left to us, in the western
world, to commit one of the greatest crimes and follies in
history—when in the XVIth and XVIIth centuries we killed
off, in the mighty witch-hunting mania that swept western

[65] This book would be seriously defective for the modern reader did it not
contain at least some reference to the psychic studies which indeed were
already in Christian's time known in an unsystematic way in France, and
which have since developed into the great movement of spiritualism, with
its own institutions and churches. The following, therefore, has been added
as an authoritative general statement to round off this part of Christian's
magnum opus.—Ed.

Europe, England and even America, countless thousands of mediums and of potential mediums.

All that time, in that insensate mass-murder, the light of knowledge of the Other Side all but faded out here in the west. Our modern revival of this knowledge only began a hundred years ago, when the famous Fox Sisters in their simple rustic home in the Middle West of America developed mediumship—and suffered for it, as so many mediums suffer. But though they were persecuted, reviled, vilified right and left—sometimes with some little justification, more often with none—they left their mark on the world. Interest was aroused, other mediums came forward, and from that day onwards psychic investigation [now called Spiritualism] has gone steadily forward, till today the number of people seriously interested in this vital matter, the study of what man is, whence he came and where he is going, runs into many millions, and is growing by leaps and bounds.

Thousands are not merely sketchily interested but are deeply convinced that their experiences *viâ* Spiritualism are true and vital; are convinced that they have talked with those whom the world calls 'dead'—in some cases, where the medium possesses the rare gift of materialisation, they have seen and touched them. They know, with a profound certainty that nothing in the world can shake, that there is no death—regarding death as we once did, as separation between those who live here on this earth and those who have left it. There is only change—a very different thing!

If one reads the classics seriously one cannot escape the conviction that many of these writers of a long-past age knew what we Spiritualists know today—that we are closely and often consciously in touch with the unseen world. These old sages knew that each man has a Guide attached to him, and that at times this Guide can show himself to his charge. If not, what can Socrates have meant when he spoke of his 'daimonion' [a Greek word that does *not* mean what our word 'demon' does] without whom he never took a decision?

Stories of ghosts and apparitions—of warnings given from beyond the grave, of predictions, curses, blessings—are rife in these old writings—and we have still a long way to go before we recover their ancient wisdom.

In the Bible the accounts of the miracles—not only those performed by Christ but by his disciples and many others—can only be explained by a sound knowledge of what Spiritualism teaches concerning psychic laws that on these occasions supersede the ordinary laws by which we live. The account of the escape of the disciples from prison is plainly dematerialisation: the Voice from the Burning Bush, a Spirit voice speaking from a Spirit light; the angel that appeared to Hagar was her Guide, seen by clairvoyance, like that other Guide who appeared to Abraham to prevent the sacrifice of Isaac; the walking on the water is levitation; the changing of water into wine, the Miracles of the Fishes, materialisations . . . Those [and they are many] who fear that the study of Spiritualism may upset sincere religious belief, should realise that Spiritualism dots the i's and crosses the t's of true religious teaching! Without the practical scientific knowledge that Spiritualism gives, these Bible stories are fairy tales:—with that knowledge they become profoundly interesting facts.

A wise priest would know this and realise that the Church can only live by truth—and by denying the truths proved and taught by Spiritualistic experience and experiment, it is depriving itself of its very lifeblood. Many priests know this, but they dare not run counter to the conventional viewpoint of their church; and so the two that should be mated, Spiritualism and Religion, march still apart, kept away from each other by man's fear, ignorance and suspicion.

Ultimately of course they will be mated—they will come together. Solid practical proof, viâ the study of Spiritualism, of what the Church teaches, is available for all who seriously and patiently seek for it; Spiritualism can give not only communication with those we love who have gone before us, but countless other deeper forms of knowledge, dealing with life on the Other Side, the sciences, arts, interests, life on other planets—all these and countless other matters are taught to seekers by the advanced Guides viâ their 'telephones', their mediums.

The majority of men and women still scoff at those of us who *know* that this is true because we have proved it for ourselves. But the numbers of those who 'come to scoff and remain to pray' is increasing daily. Put sensitiveness behind you, you who long to learn the inner truths of life, of man, his past and his future—and set forth humbly on the upwards path of knowledge that awaits you.

The facts are there. It is up to you to learn them.[66]

M.L.

THE SAVAGE BACKGROUND OF WITCH BELIEFS.

Of the extensive literature of the modern anthropological approach to such beliefs as witchcraft, one illustrative extract must suffice from a recent autobiographical work [1948] by an observer who spent most of his life amongst the savage races of the southern Andes. It shows how living myths even today shape complex rituals and life-patterns of the same type as those we meet in the past amongst other peoples. Of extant tribes, the inhabitants of Tierra del Fuego have been held to be the nearest to the palaeolithic (old stone-age) peoples in their ways, which are therefore of peculiar importance. From such half-fantasy beliefs—real enough in their compulsion upon those they are intended to

[66] The following list of authoritative works on the subject may be useful to readers not in touch with spiritualism. W. H. Myers *Human Personality and its Survival after Death* is the basic and classical work for English readers. J. W. Dunne *Nothing Dies* is a semi-mathematical essay. A. Conan Doyle *The New Revelation* and *The Vital Message* are the work of the ardent proselyte. Orthodox and recent spiritualist expositors are Rev. C. Drayton Thomas *Life Beyond Death with Evidence* and *Precognition and Human Survival*, also Arthur Findlay *On the Edge of the Etheric*. Spirit teachings are given in Palmstierna *Horizons of Immortality* and *Widening Horizons*, Rev. Stainton Moses *Spirit Teachings* and Harry Boddington *The University of Spiritualism.—Ed.*

impress—which can be paralleled in hundreds of cases amongst tribes in Africa, Australia and elsewhere, there evidently developed along its own lines the mass of European folk beliefs which were the background for the later witch cults generalised in Christian's account [pp. 327 *et seq*].

' ' . . . From a jumble of fable and ancient tales—told to me piecemeal, with no cohesion and much repetition—emerges the story of the *Hain'* [lodge of the initiated males] 'of the Ona' [a tribe in the most southerly part of Tierra del Fuego]. 'In the days when all the forest was evergreen, before *Kerrhprrh* the parakeet painted the autumn leaves red with the colour from his breast, before the giants *Kwonyipe* and *Chashkilchesh* wandered through the woods with their heads above the tree-tops, in the days when *Krren* [the sun] and *Kreeh* [the moon] walked the earth as man and wife, and many of the great sleeping mountains were human beings: in those far-off days witchcraft was known only by the women of Ona-land. They kept their own particular Lodge, which no man dared approach. The girls, as they neared womanhood, were instructed in the magic arts, learning how to bring sickness and even death to all those who displeased them.

'The men lived in abject fear and subjection. Certainly they had bows and arrows with which to supply the camp with meat, yet, they asked, what use were such weapons against witchcraft and sickness? This tyranny of the women grew from bad to worse until it occurred to the men that a dead witch was less dangerous than a live one. They conspired together to kill off all the women; and there ensued a great massacre, from which not one woman escaped in human form.

'Even the young girls only just beginning their studies in witchcraft were killed with the rest, so the men now found themselves without wives. For these they must wait until the little girls grew into women. Meanwhile the great question arose: How could men keep the upper hand now they had got it? One day, when these girl children reached maturity, they might band together and regain their old ascendency. To forestall this, the men inaugurated a secret society of their own and banished for ever the women's lodge in which so many wicked plots had been hatched against them. No woman was allowed to come near the *Hain*, under penalty of death. To make quite certain that this new decree was respected by their womenfolk, the men invented a new branch of Ona demonology: a collection of strange beings—drawn partly from their own imaginations and partly from folk-lore and ancient legends—who would take visible shape by being impersonated by members of the Lodge and thus scare the women away from the secret councils of the *Hain*. It was given out that these creatures hated women but were well-disposed towards men, even supplying them with mysterious food during the often protracted proceedings of the Lodge. Sometimes, however, these beings were short-tempered and hasty. Their irritability was manifested to the women of the encampment by the shouts and uncanny cries arising from the *Hain*, and, it might be, the scratched faces and bleeding noses with which the men returned home when some especially exciting session was over.

'Most direful of the supernatural visitors to the *Hain* were the horned man and two fierce sisters . . . The name of the horned man was *Halahachish* or, more usually, *Hachai*. He came out of the litchen-covered rocks and was as grey in appearance as his lurking-place. The white sister was *Halpen*. She came from the white cumulus clouds and shared a terrible reputation for cruelty with her sister *Tanu*, who came from the red clay.

'A fourth monster of the *Hain* was *Short*. He was a much more frequent participator in Lodge proceedings than the other three. Like *Hachai*, he came from the grey rocks. His only garment was a whitish piece of parchment-like skin over his face and head . . .

'Certain explorers have noticed these wigwams' [containing the Hain] 'and have concluded that they were places of worship. It was not, however, any idea of religion or the cult of the rising sun that made them place the Lodge in that position, but merely because the prevailing winds came from the west. With the *Hain's* entrance facing east, there was more shelter from the weather. Another reason for having the meeting-place to the leeward of the village was the mystical nourishment with which the men were supposed to be supplied. The scent of roasting meat borne on the breeze to the village might have cast doubts on that story."[67]

R.N.

[67] From E. Lucas Bridges *Uttermost Part of the Earth* [1948].—*Ed.*

BOOK SIX

BOOK SIX

GENERAL THEORY OF THE HOROSCOPE[1]

I

THE art of casting and explaining a horoscope comprises several operations, all linked together and needing some preliminary instruction which I shall here briefly undertake.

The reader already knows how to draw this astrological figure which is divided into twelve solar houses fixed in an unchangeable order; he knows too the symbols that the Magi attached to each house [Book I, p. 59].

On this frame are imposed the twelve signs of the zodiac. The sign of the zodiac under which the child is born whose horoscope is to be cast will always be placed in the first house. The other eleven signs fall into the successive houses. For example, if Taurus presides over the birth, it occupies House I; Gemini is placed in House II and so on, until in the XIIth House we find the final sign, that of Aries. The sign which is to be received by the first house is indicated by the date of birth; and so first of all we must draw up a calendar, as follows.

THE ASTROLOGICAL CALENDAR[2]

The civil year of the Egyptian Magi was composed of twelve months, each having thirty days, the total sum of the latter corresponding to the three hundred and sixty degrees of the zodiac. But as the annual evolution of the sun takes 365 days and some hours, the Magi added, at the end of the 12th month, five days called epacts [complementary days].

The year began on the 1st day of the month of *Thoth*, and this month, corresponding to the 30 degrees of Virgo, began on 23 August in the Christian calendar.

[1] Books VI and VII will be of interest to practising astrologers from the historical point of view. They are not recommended for beginners who should study from modern text-books or, if in London, attend the meetings and classes of the Astrological Lodge at 6 Queen Square, W.C.1. With regard to the general contents of this Book, see also Book I, p. 59 *et seq.*—*Ed.*

[2] The following are drawn from W. Marsham Adams *The Book of the Master*, p. 195, and Sir E. Wallis Budge *The Rosetta Stone*, p. 244. The former transposes the months Phamenoth and Pharmuthi (making them the seventh and eighth months respectively).—*Ed.*

Paophi, the 2nd month, similarly corresponding to Libra, began on 22 September.

Hathor or *Hathyr*, 3rd month [Scorpion], on 22 October.

Choiak or *Choiakh*, 4th month [Sagittarius], on 21 November.

Tybi, 5th month [Capricorn], on 21 December.

Mechi or *Mechir*, 6th month [Aquarius], on 20 January.

·*Phamenoth*, 7th month [Pisces], on 19 February.

Pharmuthi or *Pharmuti*, 8th month [Aries], on 21 March: [vernal equinox].

Pachon or *Pachons*, 9th month [Taurus], on 20 April.

Payni, 10th month [Gemini], on 20 May.

Epiphi, 11th month [Cancer], on 19 June.

Mesori or *Mesore*, 12th month [Leo], on 19 July, and was followed by the 5 Epacts or unallotted days.

Besides this division of the year into months the Magi observed, in their secret temple traditions, another division of the year which was called the fatidic or sacred year. This began at the vernal equinox. The adoption of the Roman year, following the tradition of the Calendar of Julian, has not altered the correspondence of the first degree of Aries with the vernal equinox and with the ancient order of the 12 signs. But astrologers differ over the placing of the epacts. Some maintain that these five days should follow the 30 degrees of Leo, that is to say, 18—22 August. Others arrange them under Cancer in the following order:

19 June	*Cancer* 1°		25 June	*Cancer* 4°
20	„	unallotted	26	„	unallotted
21	„	*Cancer* 2°	27	„	*Cancer* 5°
22	„	unallotted	28	„	unallotted
23	„	*Cancer* 3°	29	„	*Cancer* 6°
24	„	unallotted	30	„	*Cancer* 7°

Those who support this variation claim that the beginning of Cancer marks the summer solstice, that is, the longest day, when the sun seems to stand still in the heavens before descending towards Capricorn or the winter solstice. We shall adopt this method because its application does not in any way alter the general laws of the horoscope. So we must draw up an ordinary calendar in which all the signs and all their degrees are placed under months and days according to the following rules:

TABLE OF SIGNS AND DATES

1 Jan.: Capricorn 12	20 Jan.: Aquarius 1	31 Jan.: Aquarius 12
1 Feb.: Aquarius 13	19 Feb.: Pisces 1	28 Feb.: Pisces 10
1 Mar.: Pisces 11	21 Mar.: Aries 1	31 Mar.: Aries 11
1 Apr.: Aries 12	20 Apr.: Taurus 1	30 Apr.: Taurus 11
1 May: Taurus 12	20 May: Gemini 1	31 May: Gemini 12
1 June: Gemini 13	19 June: Cancer 1	30 June: Cancer 7
1 July: Cancer 8	24 July: Leo 1	31 July: Leo 8

1 Aug.: Leo 9	23 Aug.: Virgo 1	31 Aug.: Virgo 9
1 Sept.: Virgo 10	22 Sept.: Libra 1	30 Sept.: Libra 9
1 Oct.: Libra 10	22 Oct.: Scorpio 1	31 Oct.: Scorpio 10
1 Nov.: Scorpio 11	21 Nov.: Sagittarius 1	30 Nov.: Sagittarius 10
1 Dec.: Sagittarius 11	21 Dec.: Capricorn 1	31 Dec.: Capricorn 11

20 June: 1st Epact; 22 June: 2nd Epact; 24 June: 3rd Epact;
26 June: 4th Epact; 28 June: 5th Epact.

Note: A modern astrologer would, of course, consult an ephemeris for the appropriate year. The dates in the above Table are only approximate.—Ed.

Next we must study the astrological hierarchy of the years in the cycles of time.

CYCLIC TABLES OF THE YEARS.

Periods of time are divided into cycles of 36 years. Each of the seven planetary Geniuses comes, in turn, to open and to close one of the cycles, that is to say, to rule the 1st and the 36th year of each cycle.

SATURN opens and closes the cycles figured by the years 1 to 36 inclusive. 253 to 288; 505 to 540; 757 to 792; 1009 to 1044; 1261 to 1296; 1513 to 1548; 1765 to 1800.

VENUS opens and closes the cycles figured by the years 37 to 72 inclusive. 289 to 324; 541 to 576; 793 to 828; 1045 to 1080; 1297 to 1332; 1549 to 1584; 1801 to 1836.

JUPITER opens and closes the cycles figured by the years 73 to 108 inclusive. 325 to 360; 577 to 612; 829 to 864; 1081 to 1116; 1333 to 1368; 1585 to 1620; 1837 to 1872.

MERCURY opens and closes the cycles figured by the years 109 to 144 inclusive. 361 to 396; 613 to 648; 865 to 900; 1117 to 1152; 1369 to 1404; 1621 to 1656; 1873 to 1908.

MARS opens and closes the cycles figured by the years 145 to 180 inclusive. 397 to 432; 649 to 684; 901 to 936; 1153 to 1188; 1405 to 1440; 1657 to 1692; 1909 to 1944.

The MOON opens and closes the cycles figured by the years 181 to 216 inclusive. 433 to 468; 685 to 720; 937 to 972; 1189 to 1224; 1441 to 1476; 1693 to 1728; 1945 to 1980.

The SUN opens and closes the cycles figured by the years 217 to 252 inclusive. 469 to 504; 721 to 756; 973 to 1008; 1225 to 1260; 1477 to 1512; 1727 to 1764; 1981 to 2016.

This table, applied to the Christian era, takes us to the 16th year of the 21st century. There is no point in taking it any further.

In order to find out the planet governing the year, the Magi used a seven-pointed golden star, on which were engraved the signs of the seven planets. Given for example the cyclic number 1808, they would have discovered, from the preceding table, that this number belongs to one of the cycles of Venus, beginning in 1801 and ending in 1836. Then, taking the seven-pointed star, they would count 1801 at the sign of Venus, and, following the order of the planets, 1802 on Mercury, 1803 on the Moon, and so on.

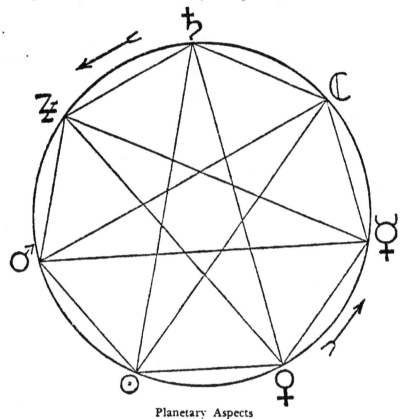

Planetary Aspects

II

After inscribing the twelve signs of the zodiac in the houses of the horoscope, it is ready for the fatidic signs, that is, the signs of the seven planets and those of the symbolic arcana. Knowing the planet governing the year, we must take this planet's fatidic circle, and use it according to the method explained later in the examples. Here are the seven invariable circles from which As-trology draws its endless variations, using the Keys of the Tarot.

CIRCLE OF FATE: SATURN

1. The Magus [Arcanum 1].
2. The Moon [Arcanum 2 Door of the Sanctuary].
3. Venus [Arcanum 3 Isis Urania].
4. Jupiter [Arcanum 4 The Cubic Stone].

5.   The Master of Mysteries [Arcanum 5 Aries].
6.   The Two Paths [Arcanum 6 Taurus].
7.   The Chariot of Osiris [Arcanum 7 Gemini].
8.   The Scales and the Sword [Arcanum 8 Cancer].
9.   The Veiled Lamp [Arcanum 9 Leo].
10.   The Sphinx [Arcanum 10 Virgo].
20.   Mars [Arcanum 11 The Tamed Lion].
30.   The Sacrifice [Arcanum 12 Libra].
40.   The Reaper [Arcanum 13].
50.   The Solar Angel [Arcanum 14 Scorpio].
60.   Typhon [Arcanum 15 Sagittarius].
70.   The Lightning-struck Tower [Arcanum 16 Capricorn].
80.   Mercury [Arcanum 17 The Star of the Magi].
90.   Twilight [Arcanum 18 Aquarius].
100. The Resplendent Light [Arcanum 19 Pisces].
200. Saturn [Arcanum 20 The Last Judgment].
300. The Crocodile [Arcanum 0].
400. The Sun [Arcanum 21 The Crown of the Magi].
9.   The Royal Star of Leo [King of Wands].
5.   Aries [1st decanate] Saturn [Queen of Wands].
6.   Taurus [2nd decanate] Venus [Knight of Wands].
7.   Gemini [3rd decanate] Jupiter [Page of Wands].
1.   Ace of Wands.
2.   The Moon [2 of Wands].
3.   Venus [3 of Wands].
4.   Jupiter [4 of Wands].
5.   Aries [2nd decanate] Jupiter [5 of Wands].
6.   Taurus [3rd decanate] Mercury [6 of Wands].
7.   Gemini [1st decanate] The Moon [7 of Wands].
8.   Cancer [1st decanate] Mars [8 of Wands].
9.   Leo [2nd decanate] The Moon [9 of Wands].
10.   Virgo [3rd decanate] The Sun [10 of Wands].
6.   The Royal Star of Taurus [King of Cups].
8.   Cancer [2nd decanate] The Sun [Queen of Cups].
9.   Leo [3rd decanate] Saturn [Knight of Cups].
10.   Virgo [1st decanate] Jupiter [Page of Cups].
20 and 1.   Mars: Ace of Cups.
30 and 2.   Libra [1st decanate] Venus [2 of Cups].
40 and 3.   The Reaper [3 of Cups].
50 and 4.   Scorpio [2nd decanate] Jupiter [4 of Cups].
60 and 5.   Sagittarius [3rd decanate] Mercury [5 of Cups].
70 and 6.   Capricorn [1st decanate] The Moon [6 of Cups].
80 and 7.   Mercury [7 of Cups].
90 and 8.   Aquarius [2nd decanate] The Sun [8 of Cups].
100 and 9. Pisces [3rd decanate] Saturn [9 of Cups].
200 and 10. Saturn [10 of Cups].
90.   The Royal Star of Aquarius [King of Swords].
30.   Libra [2nd decanate] Mercury [Queen of Swords].
50.   Scorpio [3rd decanate] Mars [Knight of Swords].
60.   Sagittarius [1st decanate] The Sun [Page of Swords].

Footnote: The first 22 Arcana of the Circle of Saturn are to be used as the first 22 Arcana of the other six Circles which follow.

1.   The Ace of Swords.
2.   The Moon [2 of Swords].
3.   Venus [3 of Swords].
4.   Jupiter [4 of Swords].
5.   Aries [3rd decanate] Mars [5 of Swords].
6.   Taurus [1st decanate] The Sun [6 of Swords].
7.   Gemini [2nd decanate] Saturn [7 of Swords].
8.· Cancer [3rd decanate] Venus [8 of Swords].
9.   Leo [1st decanate] Mercury [9 of Swords].
10. Virgo [2nd decanate] Mars [10 of Swords].
50. The Royal Star of Scorpio [King of Pentacles].
70. Capricorn [2nd decanate] Saturn [Queen of Pentacles].
90. Aquarius [3rd decanate] Venus [Knight of Pentacles].
100. Pisces [1st decanate] Mercury [Page of Pentacles].
20 and 1.   Mars. The crowned Pentacle [The Ace of Pentacles].
30 and 2.   Libra [3rd decanate] The Moon [2 of Pentacles].
40 and 3.   The Reaper [3 of Pentacles].
50 and 4.   Scorpio [1st decanate] Saturn [4 of Pentacles].
60 and 5.   Sagittarius [2nd decanate] Venus [5 of Pentacles].
70 and 6.   Capricorn [3rd decanate] Jupiter [6 of Pentacles].
80 and 7.   Mercury [7 of Pentacles].
90 and 8.   Aquarius [1st decanate] Mars [8 of Pentacles].
100 and 9. Pisces [2nd decanate] The Moon [9 of Pentacles].
200 and 10. Saturn [10 of Cups].

CIRCLE OF FATE: JUPITER.

This Table begins with the 22 Arcana of the Circle of Saturn.

9.   The Royal Star of Leo [King of Wands].
5.   Aries [1st decanate] Jupiter [Queen of Wands].
6.   Taurus [2nd decanate] Mercury [Knight of Wands].
7.   Gemini [3rd decanate] Mars [Page of Wands].
1.   Ace of Wands.
2.   The Moon [2 of Wands].
3.   Venus [3 of Wands].
4.   Jupiter [4 of Wands].
5.   Aries [2nd decanate] Mars [5 of Wands].
6.   Taurus [3rd decanate] The Moon [6 of Wands].
7.   Gemini [1st decanate] Saturn [7 of Wands].
8.   Cancer [1st decanate] The Sun [8 of Wands].
9.   Leo [2nd decanate] Saturn [9 of Wands].
10. Virgo [3rd decanate] Venus [10 of Wands].
6.   The Royal Star of Taurus [King of Cups].
8.· Cancer [2nd decanate] Venus [Queen of Cups].
9.   Leo [3rd decanate] Jupiter [Knight of Cups].
20 and 1.   Ace of Cups.
30 and 2.   Libra [1st decanate] Mercury [2 of Cups].
40 and 3.   The Reaper [3 of Cups].
50 and 4.   Scorpio [2nd decanate] Mars [4 of Cups].
60 and 5.   Sagittarius [3rd decanate] The Moon [5 of Cups].
70 and 6.   Capricorn [1st decanate] Saturn [6 of Cups].
80 and 7.   Mercury [7 of Cups].
90 and 8.   Aquarius [2nd decanate] Venus [8 of Cups].

100 and 9. Pisces [3rd decanate] Jupiter [9 of Cups].
200 and 10. Saturn [10 of Cups].
90. The Royal Star of Aquarius [King of Swords].
30. Libra [2nd decanate] The Moon [Queen of Swords].
50. Scorpio [3rd decanate] The Sun [Knight of Swords].
60. Sagittarius [1st decanate] Venus [Page of Swords].
 1. Ace of Swords.
 2. The Moon [2 of Swords].
 3. Venus [3 of Swords].
 4. Jupiter [4 of Swords].
 5. Aries [3rd decanate] The Sun [5 of Swords].
 6. Taurus [1st decanate] Venus [6 of Swords].
 7. Gemini [2nd decanate] Jupiter [7 of Swords].
 8. Cancer [3rd decanate] Mercury [8 of Swords].
 9. Leo [1st decanate] The Moon [9 of Swords].
10. Virgo [2nd decanate] The Sun [10 of Swords].
50. The Royal Star of Scorpio [King of Pentacles].
70. Capricorn [2nd decanate] Jupiter [Queen of Pentacles].
90. Aquarius [3rd decanate] Mercury [Knight of Pentacles].
100. Pisces [1st decanate] The Moon [Page of Pentacles].
20 and 1. Mars: The Crowned Pentacle [Ace of Pentacles].
30 and 2. Libra [3rd decanate] Saturn [2 of Pentacles].
40 and 3. The Reaper [3 of Pentacles].
50 and 4. Scorpio [1st decanate] Jupiter [4 of Pentacles].
60 and 5. Sagittarius [2nd decanate] Mercury [5 of Pentacles].
70 and 6. Capricorn [3rd decanate] Mars [6 of Pentacles].
80 and 7. Mercury [7 of Pentacles].
90 and 8. Aquarius [1st decanate] The Sun [8 of Pentacles].
100 and 9. Pisces [2nd decanate] Saturn [9 of Pentacles].
200 and 10. Saturn [10 of Pentacles].

CIRCLE OF FATE: MARS.

This Table begins with the 22 Arcana of the Circle of Saturn.

 9. The Royal Star of Leo [King of Wands].
 5. Aries [1st decanate] Mars [Queen of Wands].
 6. Taurus [2nd decanate] The Moon [Knight of Wands].
 7. Gemini [3rd decanate] The Sun [Page of Wands].
 1. Ace of Wands.
 2. The Moon [2 of Wands].
 3. Venus [3 of Wands].
 4. Jupiter [4 of Wands].
 5. Aries [2nd decanate] The Sun [5 of Wands].
 6. Taurus [3rd decanate] Saturn [6 of Wands].
 7. Gemini [1st decanate] Jupiter [7 of Wands].
 8. Cancer [1st decanate] Venus [8 of Wands].
 9. Leo [2nd decanate] Jupiter [9 of Wands].
10. Virgo [3rd decanate] Mercury [10 of Wands].
 6. The Royal Star of Taurus [King of Cups].
 8. Cancer [2nd decanate] Mercury [Queen of Cups].
 9. Leo [3rd decanate] Mars [Knight of Cups].
10. Virgo [1st decanate] The Sun [Page of Cups].
20 and 1. Mars: Ace of Cups.

30 and 2.   Libra [1st decanate] The Moon [2 of Cups].
40 and 3.   The Reaper [3 of Cups].
50 and 4.   Scorpio [2nd decanate] The Sun [4 of Cups].
60 and 5.   Sagittarius [3rd decanate] Saturn [5 of Cups].
70 and 6.   Capricorn [1st decanate] Jupiter [6 of Cups].
80 and 7.   Mercury [7 of Cups].
90 and 8.   Aquarius [2nd decanate] Mercury [8 of Cups].
100 and 9.   Pisces [3rd decanate] Mars [9 of Cups].
200 and 10. Saturn [10 of Cups].
  90.   Royal Star of Aquarius [King of Swords].
  30.   Libra [2nd decanate] Saturn [Queen of Swords].
  50.   Scorpio [3rd decanate] Venus [Knight of Swords].
  60.   Sagittarius [1st decanate] Mercury [Page of Swords].
   1.   Ace of Swords.
   2.   The Moon [2 of Swords].
   3.   Venus [3 of Swords].
   4.   Jupiter [4 of Swords].
   5.   Aries [3rd decanate] Venus [5 of Swords].
   6.   Taurus [1st decanate] Mercury [6 of Swords].
   7.   Gemini [2nd decanate] Mars [7 of Swords].
   8.   Cancer [3rd decanate] The Moon [8 of Swords].
   9.   Leo [1st decanate] Saturn [9 of Swords].
  10.   Virgo [2nd decanate] Venus [10 of Swords].
  50.   The Royal Star of Scorpio [King of Pentacles].
  70.   Capricorn [2nd decanate] Mars [Queen of Pentacles].
  90.   Aquarius [3rd decanate] The Moon [Knight of Pentacles].
 100.   Pisces [1st decanate] Saturn [Page of Pentacles].
 20 and 1.   Mars: The Crowned Pentacle [Ace of Pentacles].
 30 and 2.   Libra [3rd decanate] Jupiter [2 of Pentacles].
 40 and 3.   The Reaper [3 of Pentacles].
 50 and 4.   Scorpio [1st decanate] Mars [4 of Pentacles].
 60 and 5.   Sagittarius [2nd decanate] The Moon [5 of Pentacles].
 70 and 6.   Capricorn [3rd decanate] The Sun [6 of Pentacles].
 80 and 7.   Mercury [7 of Pentacles].
 90 and 8.   Aquarius [1st decanate] Venus [8 of Pentacles].
100 and 9.   Pisces [2nd decanate] Jupiter [9 of Pentacles].
200 and 10.   Saturn [10 of Pentacles].

CIRCLE OF FATE: THE SUN.

This Table begins with the 22 Arcana of the Circle of Saturn.

   9.   The Royal Star of Leo [King of Wands].
   5.   Aries [1st decanate] The Sun [Queen of Wands].
   6.   Taurus [2nd decanate] Saturn [Knight of Wands].
   7.   Gemini [3rd decanate] Venus [Page of Wands].
   1.   Ace of Wands.
   2.   The Moon [2 of Wands].
   3.   Venus [3 of Wands].
   4.   Jupiter [4 of Wands].
   5.   Aries [2nd decanate] Venus [5 of Wands].
   6.   Taurus [3rd decanate] Jupiter [6 of Wands].
   7.   Gemini [1st decanate] Mars [7 of Wands].
   8.   Cancer [1st decanate] Mercury [8 of Wands].

9. Leo [2nd decanate] Mars [9 of Wands].
10. Virgo [3rd decanate] The Moon [10 of Wands].
6. The Royal Star of Taurus [King of Cups].
8. Cancer [2nd decanate] The Moon [Queen of Cups].
9. Leo [3rd decanate] The Sun [Knight of Cups].
10. Virgo [1st decanate] Venus [Page of Cups].
20 and 1. Mars: Ace of Cups.
30 and 2. Libra [1st decanate] Saturn [2 of Cups].
40 and 3. The Reaper [3 of Cups].
50 and 4. Scorpio [2nd decanate] Venus [4 of Cups].
60 and 5. Sagittarius [3rd decanate] Jupiter [5 of Cups].
70 and 6. Capricorn [1st decanate] Mars [6 of Cups].
80 and 7. Mercury [7 of Cups].
90 and 8. Aquarius [2nd decanate] The Moon [8 of Cups].
100 and 9. Pisces [3rd decanate] The Sun [9 of Cups].
200 and 10. Saturn [10 of Cups].
90. The Royal Star of Aquarius [King of Swords].
30. Libra [2nd decanate] Jupiter [Queen of Swords].
50. Scorpio [3rd decanate] Mercury [Knight of Swords].
60. Sagittarius [1st decanate] The Moon [Page of Swords].
1. Ace of Swords.
2. The Moon [2 of Swords].
3. Venus [3 of Swords].
4. Jupiter [4 of Swords].
5. Aries [3rd decanate] Mercury [5 of Swords].
6. Taurus [1st decanate] The Moon [6 of Swords].
7. Gemini [2nd decanate] The Sun [7 of Swords].
8. Cancer [3rd decanate] Saturn [8 of Swords].
9. Leo [1st decanate] Jupiter [9 of Swords].
10. Virgo [2nd decanate] Mercury [10 of Swords].
50. The Royal Star of Scorpio [King of Pentacles].
70. Capricorn [2nd decanate] The Sun [Queen of Pentacles].
90. Aquarius [3rd decanate] Saturn [King of Pentacles].
100. Pisces [1st decanate] Jupiter [Page of Pentacles].
20 and 1. Mars: The Crowned Pentacle [Ace of Pentacles].
30 and 2. Libra [3rd decanate] Mars [2 of Pentacles].
40 and 3. The Reaper [3 of Pentacles].
50 and 4. Scorpio [1st decanate] The Sun [4 of Pentacles].
60 and 5. Sagittarius [2nd decanate] Saturn [5 of Pentacles].
70 and 6. Capricorn [3rd decanate] Venus [6 of Pentacles].
80 and 7. Mercury [7 of Pentacles].
90 and 8. Aquarius [1st decanate] Mercury [8 of Pentacles].
100 and 9. Pisces [2nd decanate] Mars [9 of Pentacles].
200 and 10. Saturn [10 of Pentacles].

CIRCLE OF FATE: VENUS.

This Table begins with the 22 Arcana of the Circle of Saturn.

9. The Royal Star of Leo [King of Wands].
5. Aries [1st decanate] Venus [Queen of Wands].
6. Taurus [2nd decanate] Jupiter [Knight of Wands].
7. Gemini [3rd decanate] Mercury [Page of Wands].
1. Ace of Wands.

  2. The Moon [2 of Wands].
  3. Venus [3 of Wands].
  4. Jupiter [4 of Wands].
  5. Aries [2nd decanate] Mercury [5 of Wands].
  6. Taurus [3rd decanate] Mars [6 of Wands].
  7. Gemini [1st decanate] The Sun [7 of Wands].
  8. Cancer [1st decanate] The Moon [8 of Wands].
  9. Leo [2nd decanate] The Sun [9 of Wands].
 10. Virgo [3rd decanate] Saturn [10 of Wands].
  6. The Royal Star of Taurus [King of Cups].
  8. Cancer [2nd decanate] Saturn [Queen of Cups].
  9. Leo [3rd decanate] Venus [Knight of Cups].
 10. Virgo [1st decanate] Mercury [Page of Cups].
 20 and 1. Mars: Ace of Cups.
 30 and 2. Libra [1st decanate] Jupiter [2 of Cups].
 40 and 3. The Reaper [3 of Cups].
 50 and 4. Scorpio [2nd decanate] Mercury [4 of Cups].
 60 and 5. Sagittarius [3rd decanate] Mars [5 of Cups].
 70 and 6. Capricorn [1st decanate] Sun [6 of Cups].
 80 and 7. Mercury [7 of Cups].
 90 and 8. Aquarius [2nd decanate] Saturn [8 of Cups].
100 and 9. Pisces [3rd decanate] Venus [9 of Cups].
200 and 10. Saturn [10 of Cups].
 90. The Royal Star of Aquarius [King of Swords].
 30. Libra [2nd decanate] Mars [Queen of Swords].
 50. Scorpio [3rd decanate] The Moon [Knight of Swords].
 60. Sagittarius [1st decanate] Saturn [Page of Swords].
  1. Ace of Swords.
  2. The Moon [2 of Swords].
  3. Venus [3 of Swords].
  4. Jupiter [4 of Swords].
  5. Aries [3rd decanate] The Moon [5 of Swords].
  6. Taurus [1st decanate] Saturn [6 of Swords].
  7. Gemini [2nd decanate] Venus [7 of Swords].
  8. Cancer [3rd decanate] Jupiter [8 of Swords].
  9. Leo [1st decanate] Mars [9 of Swords].
 10. Virgo [2nd decanate] The Moon [10 of Swords].
 50. The Royal Star of Scorpio [King of Pentacles].
 70. Capricorn [2nd decanate] Venus [Queen of Pentacles].
 90. Aquarius [3rd decanate] Jupiter [Knight of Pentacles].
100. Pisces [1st decanate] Mars [Page of Pentacles].
 20 and 1. Mars: The Crowned Pentacle [Ace of Pentacles].
 30 and 2. Libra [3rd decanate] The Sun [2 of Pentacles].
 40 and 3. The Reaper [3 of Pentacles].
 50 and 4. Scorpio [1st decanate] Venus [4 of Pentacles].
 60 and 5. Sagittarius [2nd decanate] Jupiter [5 of Pentacles].
 70 and 6. Capricorn [3rd decanate] Mercury [6 of Pentacles].
 80 and 7. Mercury [7 of Pentacles].
 90 and 8. Aquarius [1st decanate] The Moon [8 of Pentacles].
100 and 9. Pisces [2nd decanate] The Sun [9 of Pentacles].
200 and 10. Saturn [10 of Pentacles].

CIRCLE OF FATE: MERCURY.

This Table begins with the 22 Arcana of the Circle of Saturn.

9. The Royal Star of Leo [King of Wands].
5. Aries [1st decanate] Mercury [Queen of Wands].
6. Taurus [2nd decanate] Mars [Knight of Wands].
7. Gemini [3rd decanate] The Moon [Page of Wands].
1. Ace of Wands.
2. The Moon [2 of Wands].
3. Venus [3 of Wands].
4. Jupiter [4 of Wands].
5. Aries [2nd decanate] The Moon [5 of Wands].
6. Taurus [3rd decanate] The Sun [6 of Wands].
7. Gemini [1st decanate] Venus [7 of Wands].
8. Cancer [1st decanate] Saturn [8 of Wands].
9. Leo [2nd decanate] Venus [9 of Wands].
10. Virgo [3rd decanate] Jupiter [10 of Wands].
6. The Royal Star of Taurus [King of Cups].
8. Cancer [2nd decanate] Jupiter [Queen of Cups].
9. Leo [3rd decanate] Mercury [Knight of Cups].
10. Virgo [1st decanate] The Moon [Page of Cups].
20 and 1. Mars: Ace of Cups.
30 and 2. Libra [1st decanate] Mars [2 of Cups].
40 and 3. The Reaper [3 of Cups].
50 and 4. Scorpio [2nd decanate] Mercury [4 of Cups].
60 and 5. Sagittarius [3rd decanate] The Sun [5 of Cups].
70 and 6. Capricorn [1st decanate] Venus [6 of Cups].
80 and 7. Mercury [7 of Cups].
90 and 8. Aquarius [2nd decanate] Jupiter [8 of Cups].
100 and 9. Pisces [3rd decanate] Mercury [9 of Cups].
200. Saturn [10 of Cups].
90.   The Royal Star of Aquarius [King of Swords].
30.   Libra [2nd decanate] The Sun [Queen of Swords].
50.   Scorpio [3rd decanate] Saturn [Knight of Swords].
60.   Sagittarius [1st decanate] Jupiter [Page of Swords].
1. Ace of Swords.
2. The Moon [2 of Swords].
3. Venus [3 of Swords].
4. Jupiter [4 of Swords].
5. Aries [3rd decanate] Saturn [5 of Swords].
6. Taurus [1st decanate] Jupiter [6 of Swords].
7. Gemini [2nd decanate] Mercury [7 of Swords].
8. Cancer [3rd decanate] Mars [8 of Swords].
9. Leo [1st decanate] The Sun [9 of Swords].
10. Virgo [2nd decanate] Saturn [10 of Swords].
50.   The Royal Star of Scorpio [King of Pentacles].
70.   Capricorn [2nd decanate] Mercury [Queen of Pentacles].
90.   Aquarius [3rd decanate] Mars [Knight of Pentacles].
100. Pisces [1st decanate] The Sun [Page of Pentacles].
20 and 1. Mars: The Crowned Pentacle [Ace of Pentacles].
30 and 2. Libra [3rd decanate] Venus [2 of Pentacles].
40 and 3. The Reaper [3 of Pentacles].
50 and 4. Scorpio [1st decanate] Mercury [4 of Pentacles].

60 and 5. Sagittarius [2nd decanate] Mars [5 of Pentacles].
70 and 6. Capricorn [3rd decanate] The Moon [6 of Pentacles].
80 and 7. Mercury [7 of Pentacles].
90 and 8. Aquarius [1st decanate] Saturn [8 of Pentacles].
100 and 9. Pisces [2nd decanate] Venus [9 of Pentacles].
200 and 10. Saturn [10 of Pentacles].

CIRCLE OF FATE: THE MOON.

This Table begins with the 22 Arcana of the Circle of Saturn.

9. The Royal Star of Leo [King of Wands].
5. Aries [1st decanate] The Moon [Queen of Wands].
6. Taurus [2nd decanate] The Sun [Knight of Wands].
7. Gemini [3rd decanate] Saturn [Page of Wands].
1. Ace of Wands.
2. The Moon [2 of Wands].
3. Venus [3 of Wands].
4. Jupiter [4 of Wands].
5. Aries [2nd decanate] Saturn [5 of Wands].
6. Taurus [3rd decanate] Venus [6 of Wands].
7. Gemini [1st decanate] Mercury [7 of Wands].
8. Cancer [1st decanate] Jupiter [8 of Wands].
9. Leo [2nd decanate] Mercury [9 of Wands].
10. Virgo [3rd decanate] Mars [10 of Wands].
6. The Royal Star of Taurus [King of Cups].
8. Cancer [2nd decanate] Mars [Queen of Cups].
9. Leo [3rd decanate] The Moon [Knight of Cups].
10. Virgo [1st decanate] Saturn [Page of Cups].
20 and 1. Mars: Ace of Cups.
30 and 2. Libra [1st decanate] The Sun [2 of Cups].
40 and 3. The Reaper [3 of Cups].
50 and 4. Scorpio [2nd decanate] Saturn [4 of Cups].
60 and 5. Sagittarius [3rd decanate] Venus [5 of Cups].
70 and 6. Capricorn [1st decanate] Mercury [6 of Cups].
80 and 7. Mercury [7 of Cups].
90 and 8. Aquarius [2nd decanate] Mars [8 of Cups].
100 and 9. Pisces [3rd decanate] The Moon [9 of Cups].
200 and 10. Saturn [10 of Cups].
90. The Royal Star of Aquarius [King of Swords].
30. Libra [2nd decanate] Venus [Queen of Swords].
50. Scorpio [3rd decanate] Jupiter [Knight of Swords].
60. Sagittarius [1st decanate] Mars [Page of Swords].
1. Ace of Swords.
2. The Moon [2 of Swords].
3. Venus [3 of Swords].
4. Jupiter [4 of Swords].
5. Aries [3rd decanate] Jupiter [5 of Swords].
6. Taurus [1st decanate] Mars [6 of Swords].
7. Gemini [2nd decanate] The Moon [7 of Swords].
8. Cancer [3rd decanate] The Sun [8 of Swords].
9. Leo [1st decanate] Venus [9 of Swords].
10. Virgo [2nd decanate] Jupiter [10 of Swords].
50. The Royal Star of Scorpio [King of Pentacles].

  70. Capricorn [2nd decanate] The Moon [Queen of Pentacles].
  90. Aquarius [3rd decanate] The Sun [Knight of Pentacles].
 100. Pisces [1st decanate] Venus [Page of Pentacles].
  20 and 1. Mars: The Crowned Pentacle [Ace of Pentacles].
  30 and 2. Libra [3rd decanate] Mercury [2 of Pentacles].
  40 and 3. The Reaper [3 of Pentacles].
  50 and 4. Scorpio [1st decanate] The Moon [4 of Pentacles].
  60 and 5. Sagittarius [2nd decanate] The Sun [5 of Pentacles].
  70 and 6. Capricorn [3rd decanate] Saturn [6 of Pentacles].
  80 and 7. Mercury [7 of Pentacles].
  90 and 8. Aquarius [1st decanate] Jupiter [8 of Pentacles].
 100 and 9. Pisces [2nd decanate] Mercury [9 of Pentacles].
 200 and 10. Saturn [10 of Pentacles].

III

The seven circles we have just examined each contain 78 symbols, corresponding to a sequence of numbers which remains in a stationary position around the circle. These 78 symbols are divided into five series:

1. The 22 Major Arcana, meaning submission to the invariable laws of divine wisdom.
2. The 14 Arcana of Wands, meaning man's active intelligence in the face of life's trials.
3. The 14 Arcana of Cups, the desires, passions, joys, and hopes which are the mainsprings of humanity.
4. The 14 Arcana of Swords, labour, obstacles, fights, disappointments, perils, afflictions and pains.
5. The 14 Arcana of Pentacles, which symbolise material fortune.

The mysterious influence of the occult powers governing all lives is marked on each circle:

1. By the greater Genii, or archangels of the seven planets, with Arcana II, III, IV, XI, XVII, XX and XXI in the first series.
2. By the Masters of the Royal Stars, each of them opening their consequent series.
3. By the 36 planetary Genii or Decans, each presiding over 10 degrees of the fatidic zodiac (10 days in the year), an arrangement which assigns three Decans to each of the twelve signs.

The mystical theory of these occult powers would take too long to explain, so I shall confine myself here to a practical demonstration.

Let us remind ourselves once more that Hermetic doctrine, rejecting the idea of an implacable fate, considers all the chances of good or evil fortune as tests in the education of our intelligence and will. They are not blind and irresponsible forces. The fifth aphorism in the *Centiloquium* of Ptolemy runs: 'The mind trained in occult knowledge can deflect many presages and prepare itself to sustain the shock of future events.'[3]

Man cannot fail to die, because death, or rather transformation, is a universal law; but he can, if he has warning, protect himself from violent death, because such a death is not a law of nature. Let us suppose that Louis XVI is warned of the catastrophe hanging over his head and refuses to go on reigning in such perilous circumstances: his abdication, or timely escape, would have preserved him from the scaffold without putting obstacles in the way of the moral conquests of the 1789 Revolution. From the point of view of destiny, the Revolution did not require his head. The same thing can be said of Maximilian of Austria, the short-lived Emperor of Mexico who was killed in 1867. It is no less reasonable to believe that Napoleon had sufficient genius to avoid the storm which overwhelmed him. He only needed to appreciate the value of a few men who were not blinded by the splendour of his great successes. His fall was merely a personal accident, which neither hindered nor advanced the general forward march of humanity.

THE MYSTERY OF THE TWELVE SIGNS OF THE ZODIAC.

1. Amûn, Genius of Aries: the head and its disorders.
2. Apis, Genius of Taurus: the neck, shoulders, and their disorders.
3. Herakles Apollo, Genius of Gemini: the arms, hands, and their disorders.
4. Hermanubis, Genius of Cancer: the chest, lungs, ribs, spleen and their disorders.
5. Momphtha, Genius of Leo: the stomach, the heart, the liver and their disorders.
6. Isis, Genius of Virgo: the spleen, the belly, the intestines and their disorders.
7. Omphtha, Genius of Libra: the spine, the kidneys and their disorders.
8. Typhon, Genius of Scorpio. the hips, the sexual organs and their disorders.
9. Nephthys, Genius of Sagittarius: the thighs and their disorders.
10. Anubis, Genius of Capricorn: the knees and their disorders.
11. Canopus, Genius of Aquarius: the legs and their disorders.
12. Ichthon, Genius of Pisces: the feet and their disorders.

[3] Potest qui sciens est multos stellarum effectus avertere, quando ea noverit, ac seipsum ante illorum eventum praeparare [Ptolemaei Centiloquium, amph. V —Basiliae 1551].

The seven great planetary genii govern the head, seat of the intellect and the will. Rempha, Genius of Saturn, governs the left eye: Pi-Zeus, Genius of Jupiter, the right eye: Ertosi, Genius of Mars, the right nostril: Pi-Ré, Genius of the Sun, the forehead: Suroth, Genius of Venus. the left nostril: Pi-Hermes, Genius of Mercury, the tongue: Pi-Joh, Genius of the Moon, the brain.

In Greco-Roman polytheism, the twelve great gods correspond to the twelve signs of the Zodiac in the following order: Minerva = Aries; Venus = Taurus; Apollo = Gemini; Mercury = Cancer; Jupiter and Cybele = Leo; Ceres = Virgo; Vulcan = Libra; Mars = Scorpio; Diana = Sagittarius; Vesta = Capricorn; Juno = Aquarius; Neptune = Pisces.

In the Hebrew Qabala, the twelve tribes of Israel, and the twelve precious stones which decorate the breast of the High Priest, used to correspond to the signs of the Zodiac, in the following order: —the tribe of Gad and the amethyst = Aries; Ephraim and the jacinth = Taurus; Manasseh and the chrysoprase = Gemini; Issachar and the topaz = Cancer; Judah and the beryl = Leo; Naphtali and the chrysolite = Virgo; Asher and the sard = Libra; Dan and the sardonyx = Scorpio; Benjamin and the emerald = Sagittarius; Zabulon and chalcedony = Capricorn; Reuben and the sapphire = Aquarius; Simeon and jasper = Pisces.

The genii of the Egyptian Zodiac also take on, in Hermetic language, divers *qualifications* which are frequently quoted in the aphorisms. Here is a list (their influences are notified later, in Book VII).

AIR. Gemini, Libra, Aquarius. The triangle marked on the horoscope by joining these signs forms a triplicity governed, in diurnal nativity, by Saturn and in nocturnal nativity by Mercury.

ANIMALS: Aries, Taurus, Leo, and the last fifteen degrees of Sagittarius and Capricorn.

AUTUMN: Libra, Scorpio, Sagittarius.

DANGER: Gemini, Libra, Aquarius, especially when Gemini is angular.

DOUBLE SIGNS: Otherwise termed bi-corporal or common: Gemini, Virgo, Sagittarius, Pisces.

WATER: Cancer, Scorpio, Pisces. These three signs form a triplicity governed by Mars in diurnal or nocturnal nativity.

EQUINOCTIAL SIGNS: Aries, Libra.

SUPERIOR SPIRIT: Capricorn and Aquarius, especially in House X.

SUMMER: Cancer, Leo, Virgo.

FEMININE SIGNS: Taurus, Cancer, Virgo, Scorpio, Capricorn, Pisces.

FIRE: Aries, Leo, Sagittarius. These three signs form a triplicity governed by the Sun in a diurnal nativity, by Jupiter in a nocturnal nativity.

FIXED SIGNS: Taurus, Leo, Scorpio, Aquarius.

WINTER: Capricorn, Aquarius, Pisces.

HUMAN SIGNS: Gemini, Virgo, Libra, first half of Sagittarius and Aquarius.

MASCULINE SIGNS: Aries, Gemini, Leo, Libra, Sagittarius, Aquarius.
SOUTH SIGNS: Libra, Scorpio, Sagittarius, Capricorn, Aquarius, Pisces.
MOBILE SIGNS: Aries, Cancer, Libra, Capricorn.
OBSTINACY: Taurus.
PASSIONS: Aries, Taurus, Leo, Scorpio, Capricorn.
SPRING: Aries, Taurus, Gemini.
QUADRUPEDS: Aries, Taurus, Leo, Sagittarius, Capricorn.
RELIGION: Taurus, Libra, Pisces, especially when they occupy the XIth
house in diurnal or nocturnal nativity.
REPTILES: Cancer, Scorpio, Pisces.
ROYAL SIGNS: Aries, Leo, Sagittarius.
NORTHERN SIGNS: Aries, Taurus, Gemini, Cancer, Leo, Virgo.
SOLSTITIAL SIGNS: Cancer, Capricorn.
EARTH: Taurus, Virgo, Capricorn. These three signs form a triplicity
governed in diurnal nativity by Venus, and in nocturnal nativity by the Moon.
VIOLENT SIGNS: Aries, Libra, Scorpio, Capricorn, Aquarius.

THE THIRTY-SIX DECANS

	DECAN	ARCHANGEL	DEGREES GOVERNED	DATES COVERED	CHARACTER INDICATIONS
1	Asiccan	Mars	Aries 1-10	21-30 March	reliability, fearlessness pride and obstinacy.
2	Senacher	Sun	Aries 11-20	31 March —9 April	nobility of mind generosity, and ability to command.
3	Acentacer	Venus	Aries 21-30	10-19 April	quick brain, kindliness and love of pleasure.
4	Asicath	Mercury	Taurus 1-10	20-29 April	highest intellectual powers, aptitude for difficult mathematics legislation: love of achievements in arts especially architecture
5	Viroaso	Moon	Taurus 11-20 .	30 April —9 May	easy ascent to highest spheres of fortune.
6	Aharph	Saturn	Taurus 21-30	10-19 May	obstacles to enterprise dependance, threats of disaster.
7	Thesogar	Jupiter	Gemini 1-10	20-29 May	aptness for unprofitable abstract sciences
8	Verasua	Mars	Gemini 11-20	30 May —8 June	proneness to anxiety to destruction by striving against the difficulties of life.

DECAN	ARCHANGEL	DEGREES GOVERNED	DATES COVERED	CHARACTER INDICATIONS
9 *Thepisatosoa*	Sun	Gemini 21-30	9-18 June	carelessness, neglect of own interests, empty-headedness, vanity, enjoyment of mere talk.
10 *Sothis*	Venus	Cancer 1-10	19 June —3 July	vivacious mind, sociable nature, desire for sympathy.
11 *Sith*	Mercury	Cancer 11-20	4-13 July	leaning to spiteful gossip, love of gain, likelihood of acquiring wealth.
12 *Thuimis*	Moon	Cancer 21-30	14-23 July	a nature relying on force.
13 *Aphruimis*	Saturn	Leo 1-10	24 July —2 Aug.	a violent nature with evil passions.
14 *Sithacer*	Jupiter	Leo 11-20	3-12 August	a provocative nature with a tyrannical will.
15 *Phuonisi*	Mars	Leo 21-30	13-22 August	love for alliances, inflexible obstinacy in adventure even to loss of life.
16 *Thumis*	Sun	Virgo 1-10	23 August —1 Sept.	timidity, liking for the sedentary; aptitude for mechanical pursuits.
17 *Thopithus*	Venus	Virgo 11-20	2-11 Sept.	love of money, avarice.
18 *Aphuth*	Mercury	Virgo 21-30	12-21 Sept.	indolence of mind, weakness, non - productiveness, joy in destruction.
19 *Serneuth*	Moon	Libra 1-10	22 Sept. —1 Oct.	a spirit of justice and truth, protection of weak against strong.
20 *Aterechinis*	Saturn	Libra 11-20	2-11 October	peaceful life, no ambitions or desire for wealth.
21 *Arpien*	Jupiter	Libra 21-30	12-21 October	mainly sensuality.
22 *Senthacer*	Mars	Scorpio 1-10	22-31 October	disappointments, plots, hidden and dangerous enemies.

	DECAN	ARCHANGEL	DEGREES GOVERNED	DATES COVERED	CHARACTER INDICATIONS
23	*Thepiseuth*	Sun	Scorpio 11-20	1-10 November	disappointments, antipathies, revivals of forgotten enmity, onslaught of fresh foes.
24	*Senciner*	Venus	Scorpio 21-30	11-20 November	a sensual nature, tending to violence.
25	*Eregbuo*	Mercury	Sagittarius 1-10	21-30 November	love of independence; possible career in armed forces or allied professions.
26	*Sagen*	Moon	Sagittarius 11-20	1-10 December	dangers and sorrows.
27	*Chenen*	Saturn	Sagittarius 21-30	11-20 December	obstinacy, violence, evil and dangerous tendencies.
28	*Themeso*	Jupiter	Capricorn 1-10	21-30 December	travel, good fortune and bad alternate.
29	*Epima*	Mars	Capricorn 11-20	31 Dec. —9 Jan.	intelligence given to useless research in vain enterprises.
30	*Homoth*	Sun	Capricorn 21-30	10-19 January	suspicious, irritable, weak nature.
31	*Oroasoer*	Venus	Aquarius 1-10	20-29 January	anxiety from actual livelihood; deferred hopes.
32	*Astiro*	Mercury	Aquarius 11-20	30 Jan. —8 Feb.	intelligence, gentleness, manners, personal virtue.
33	*Thepisathras*	Moon	Aquarius 21-30	9-18 February	disappointments in all directions.
34	*Archathapias*	Saturn	Pisces 1-10	19-28 and 29 Feb.	restlessness, confused ideas, instability and changeableness, pursuit of elusive fortune.
35	*Thopibui*	Jupiter	Pisces 11-20	1-10 March	ambition, desire for fame, boldness in enterprise.
36	*Athembui*	Mars	Pisces 21-30	11-20 March	indolence, love of pleasure, narrow mind.

These 36 Decans exert over every horoscope influences emanating from superior Genii or archangels whose interpreters they are. For example, when drawing up a horoscope by means of the fatidic

circle of Mars, if we encounter the number 9 attached to Decan II
in the sign of Leo, thus

9 Leo [Decan II].—Jupiter [The 9 of Wands]

this line indicates that we must mark the sign of Jupiter in the
house of the horoscope where the sign of Leo is found, since
Decan II of Leo is governed by the archangel of Jupiter.

ASTROLOGICAL NOTES ON THE PLANETS

This is how the occult powers are distributed among the Twelve
Signs of the Zodiac.

SATURN [meaning this planet's archangel] is in a diurnal house
[or on his throne] in Aquarius. In a nocturnal house in Capricorn.
In exaltation in Libra. In detriment in Cancer and Leo. In fall in
Aries.

JUPITER is in a diurnal house [on his throne] in Sagittarius. In

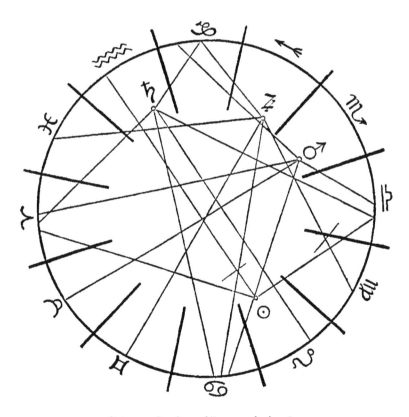

Saturn, Jupiter, Mars and the Sun

a nocturnal house in Pisces. In exaltation in Cancer. In detriment in Gemini and Virgo. In fall in Capricorn.

MARS is in a diurnal house in Scorpio. In a nocturnal house in Aries. In exaltation in Capricorn. In detriment in Taurus and Libra. In fall in Cancer.

· THE SUN is in a diurnal and a nocturnal house in Leo. In exaltation in Aries. In detriment in Aquarius. In fall in Libra.

VENUS is in a diurnal house in Taurus. In a nocturnal house in Libra. In exaltation in Pisces. In detriment in Aries and Scorpio. In fall in Virgo.

MERCURY is in a diurnal house in Virgo. In a nocturnal house in Gemini. In exaltation in Virgo. In detriment in Sagittarius and Pisces. In fall in Pisces.

THE MOON is in a diurnal and nocturnal house in Cancer. In exaltation in Taurus. In detriment in Capricorn. In fall in Scorpio.

The signs of the zodiac opposite the signs where the planets are in a diurnal or nocturnal house are these planets' signs of detriment. The sign of their fall is the sign opposite the place of

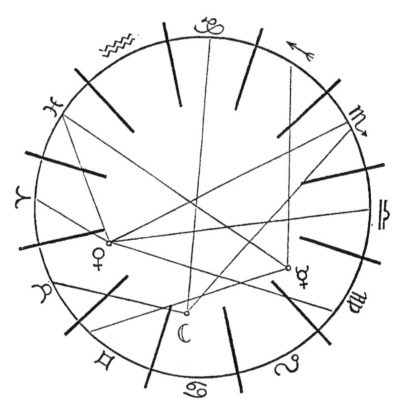

Venus, Mercury and the Moon

exaltation. Detriment and fall are more or less dangerous aspects; they diminish or efface the influence of beneficent planets and increase that of the maleficent ones.

The benefics are Jupiter, the Sun, Venus and the Moon.

The malefics are Saturn and Mars.

Mercury has a mixture of good and evil influences which are determined by his relationships with the other planets.

Certain regions in the zodiacal circle in which the favourable influences of the planetary signs suffer heavy reverses and evil influences become more dangerous are said to be combust. This stretches from Gemini 18° to Cancer 2°, and from Sagittarius 24° to Capricorn 2°.

There are two other signs called the Dragon's Head and Tail whose aspects are favourable or dangerous according to the position of the planets.[4]

We give the name of triplicity to the triangle formed on the zodiacal circle by the signs of Air, Water, Fire or Earth, that is, the signs whose Genii govern these four elements.

The word nativity signifies day of birth. It is diurnal, if the child is born between midday and midnight: nocturnal, if between midnight and midday.

If the terms Nativity and Progression are encountered in an astrological aphorism, the first signifies the general horoscope which is drawn up at the moment of birth. The second indicates a particular horoscope in which are sought presages relative to a certain year of the subject's life. The horoscope which would be drawn up nowadays for someone born in 1769 would be called a general horoscope or a Nativity. The one drawn up in order to find, for example, events in which the same person took part in, say, 1815, would be called a Progression of the horoscope. This new operation would consist in comparing the two diagrams in order to observe the differences of aspects produced by the movement of the fatidic circles. We shall see a practical demonstration of this later.

PLANETARY ASPECTS.

The term Aspect signifies the number of houses separating two or more planets on the horoscope. The aspect is called a conjunction when two or more planets are joined in the same house. The aspect is called Sextile when only one house separates two or several planets.[5]

---

[4] Dragon's Head and Tail = The Nodes of the Moon. The Head is regarded as a benefic, resembling Jupiter and Venus. The influence of the Tail resembles that of Saturn and Mars.—*Ed.*

[5] It would be more accurate to say that planets in sextile are 60 degrees apart; in square 90 degrees; trine, 120 degrees; in opposition, 180 degrees.—*Ed.*

It is called Quadrature when two houses separate them. It is called
Trine when the interval consists of three houses. Finally they are
said to be in Opposition when two or more planets are separated by
five houses.

We call Houses I, IV, VII, X the cardinal points of the horoscope. Houses II, V, VIII, XI are called succedent houses. Houses
III, VI, IX, XII are cadent houses.

We term *Ruler of the Year* that planet which governs any year
in a cycle. Thus, for example, the year 1808 belongs to the cycle of
Venus, and has for its ruler the planet Venus which governs the
years 1801, 1807, 1815, 1822, 1829, and 1836 of this cycle.

The term *Ruler of the House* is given to the planet which has
as its throne a zodiacal sign placed in any house whatsoever of the
horoscope; the said planet may be found in the same house as the
sign, or it may occupy quite a different place in the diagram. For
example, if the Sun is in House X, and if Leo, which is its throne,
occupies House V, we say that the Sun is ruler of House V, but
occupies House X. The abbreviated term Ruler of I, of II, of III,

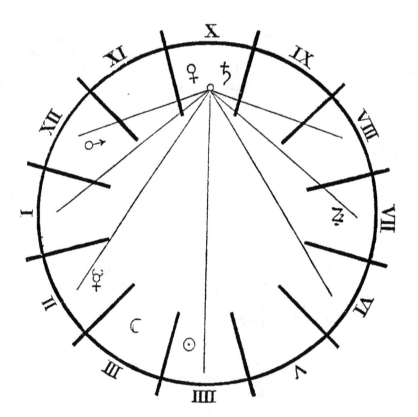

Planetary Aspects

etc., which will be found frequently repeated further on, signifies therefore Ruler of House I, etc.

In aphorisms, a planet is often said to be *Oriental* or *Occidental* in its relation to the Sun. Occidental includes the region between the degree of the zodiacal sign in which the Sun is placed and the degree diametrically opposite, following the order of the sequence of the signs. For example: if the Sun is in a degree of Aquarius, its diametrically opposite point will be in Leo; and if Saturn is encountered between these two points, following the order of the signs [Aquarius, Pisces, Aries, Taurus, Gemini, Cancer], it is said to be Occidental. Oriental is *vice versa,* proceeding contrary to the order of the sequence. Consequently, if Saturn were encountered proceeding from Aquarius to Leo *via* Capricorn, Sagittarius, Scorpio, Libra, Virgo, it would be called Oriental.

The Moon is termed *waxing* from the new moon on the first day of its monthly course to the full moon, on the 15th day. It is said to be *waning* from the full moon until the next new moon. In order to find out these two aspects, both very important in astrology, the two following tables must be employed.

TABLE OF LUNARY EPACTS

6	1754	1773	1792	1811	1830	1849	1868
17	1755	1774	1793	1812	1831	1850	1869
28	1756	1775	1794	1813	1832	1851	1870
9	1757	1776	1795	1814	1833	1852	1871
20	1758	1777	1796	1815	1834	1853	1872
1	1759	1778	1797	1816	1835	1854	1873
12	1760	1779	1798	1817	1836	1855	1874
23	1761	1780	1799	1818	1837	1856	1875
4	1762	1781	1800	1819	1838	1857	1876
15	1763	1782	1801	1820	1839	1858	1877
26	1764	1783	1802	1821	1840	1859	1878
7	1765	1784	1803	1822	1841	1860	1879
18	1766	1785	1804	1823	1842	1861	1880
30	1767	1786	1805	1824	1843	1862	1881
11	1768	1787	1806	1825	1814	1863	1882
22	1769	1788	1807	1826	1845	1864	1883
3	1770	1789	1808	1827	1846	1865	1884
14	1771	1790	1809	1828	1847	1866	1885
25	1772	1791	1810	1829	1848	1867	1886

TABLE OF MONTHLY PHASES OF THE MOON

Days	1	2	3	4	5	6	7	8	9	10	11	12
1	0	29	0	29	28	27	26	24	23	22	21	20
2	29	28	29	28	27	26	25	23	22	21	20	19
3	28	27	28	27	26	24	24	22	21	20	19	18
4	27	26	27	26	25	23	23	21	20	19	18	17
5	26	24	26	24	24	22	22	20	19	18	17	16
6	25	23	25	23	23	21	21	19	18	17	16	15
7	24	22	24	22	22	20	20	18	17	16	15	14
8	23	21	23	21	21	19	19	17	16	15	14	13
9	22	20	22	20	20	18	18	16	15	14	13	12
10	21	19	21	19	19	17	17	15	14	13	12	11
11	20	18	20	18	18	16	16	14	13	12	11	10
12	19	17	19	17	17	15	15	13	12	11	10	9
13	18	16	18	16	16	14	14	12	11	10	9	8
14	17	15	17	15	15	13	13	11	10	9	8	7
15	16	14	16	14	14	12	12	10	9	8	7	6
16	15	13	15	13	13	11	11	9	8	7	6	5
17	14	12	14	12	12	10	10	8	7	6	5	4
18	13	11	13	11	11	9	9	7	6	5	4	3
19	12	10	12	10	10	8	8	6	5	4	3	2
20	11	9	11	9	9	7	7	5	4	3	2	1
21	10	8	10	8	8	6	6	4	3	2	1	0
22	9	7	9	7	7	5	5	3	2	1	0	29
23	8	6	8	6	6	4	4	2	1	0	29	28
24	7	5	7	5	5	3	3	1	0	29	28	27
25	6	4	6	4	4	2	2	0	29	28	27	26
26	5	3	5	3	3	1	1	29	28	27	26	25
27	4	2	4	2	2	0	0	28	27	26	24	24
28	3	1	3	1	1	29	29	27	26	25	23	23
29	2	,,	2	0	0	28	28	26	24	24	22	22
30	1	,,	1	29	29	27	27	25	23	23	21	21
31	0	,;	0	,,	28	,,	26	24	,,	22	,,	20

The use of the lunary tables does not offer any difficulty. On the first the numbers on the left are those of the Epacts which coincide with the first day of the new moon for the seven years printed horizontally after each numeral. The second table is a perpetual calendar of lunar days divided into thirteen columns, the first of which, headed 'days', gives the days of a 31-day month, the others containing the lunar numbers for the twelve months January—December [shown by numbers].

Let us now suppose that a horoscope whose nativity is the 15 August 1868 is being consulted to find out the chances of a long life for the child born on that date. We need to know the age of the moon at the time of his birth. The column of Epacts gives us the number 6. August being the 8th month, let us pass to the second table, and look for the number [Epact] in column 8. We find it on a level with the 17 August, which would be the period of the new moon. But the real new moon arrived one day before the one indicated by the vulgar Epact. So we must fix it on the 16 August; then, counting 30 on the 17th and 29 on the 16th day, we find that on the 15th the moon was in its 28th day, entering the sign of Pisces. The full moon, that is, the opposition of the Sun and the Moon taking place on the 15th day of each lunation, the moon is therefore on the wane in this example.

We give the term *ill-aspected* to planets which are found on the horoscope in aspects of quadrature or opposition with Saturn or Mars, both malefic planets.

We say that there is a *Mutual Reception* of signs when two planets have changed their diurnal and nocturnal houses, or their place of exaltation. As for example when Saturn is in Sagittarius, the diurnal house of Jupiter, and Jupiter in Aquarius, diurnal house of Saturn; or when the Sun is in Taurus, place of exaltation of the Moon, and the Moon in Aries, place of exaltation of the Sun.

A planet is said to be in *Reception* when, finding itself in a zodiacal sign which is its sign of detriment, it is in an aspect of conjunction, sextile, trine, quadrature or opposition with another planet of which the zodiacal sign is the diurnal or nocturnal house or the place of exaltation. If, for example, Jupiter is in Virgo [its sign of detriment], and if he receives from Mercury one of the five above-mentioned aspects, he is in reception, because the sign of Virgo is the diurnal house of Mercury.

A planet is said to be *superior* to another when [taking House 10 as the culminating point of the horoscope], that planet is above one or several other planets. If two planets are at an equal height, that is, in Houses 11 and 9, 12 and 8, 1 and 7, 2 and 6, 3 and 5, the most dignified is superior to the other.

The *hebdomadal years* occur on every seventh year after the nativity: 7, 14, 21, 28, 35, etc.

The *enneatic years* occur on every ninth year after the nativity: 9, 18, 27, 36, 45, etc.

The *Sign of Chance* is a small circle divided by a cross which is put in the place assigned to it by certain calculations, with a number which records its key, according to the kind of chance which is sought for in the table of Aphorisms: chance of long life, of good luck, fortune or death, etc. [See Book VII.]

The name *Master of Chance* is given to the planet which has the dignity of diurnal or nocturnal house in the sign in which is placed the indication of a chance, even though this planet may actually be elsewhere in the horoscope.

TABLE OF PLANETARY DIGNITIES

Every planet not combust[6] receives 5 degrees of dignity.

If Saturn, Jupiter and Mars are oriental in their relation to the Sun, they receive 2 degrees of dignity.

If Venus and Mercury are occidental in their relation to the Sun, they receive 2 degrees of dignity.

The waxing Moon [from 1st to 15th day] receives 2 degrees of dignity.

Every planet in a nocturnal or diurnal House or in mutual reception with another receives 5 degrees of dignity.

Every planet in its place of exaltation receives 4 degrees of dignity.

Every planet in trine aspect receives 3 degrees of dignity.

Every planet in Houses 1 or 10 receives 5 degrees of dignity.

Every planet in Houses 4, 7, or 11 receives 4 degrees of dignity.

Every planet in Houses 2 or 5 receives 3 degrees of dignity.

Every planet in House 9 receives 2 degrees of dignity.

Every planet in House 3 receives 1 degree of dignity.

Every planet in conjunction with Jupiter or Venus receives 5 degrees of dignity.

Every planet in trine with Jupiter or Venus receives 4 degrees of dignity.

Every planet sextile to Jupiter or Venus receives 3 degrees of dignity.

Every planet sextile or trine with one of the four Royal Stars receives 6 degrees of dignity.

TABLE OF PLANETARY DEBILITIES

Every planet in the *Via Combusta*[7] suffers 5 degrees of debility.

Every planet under the influence of the Sun, that is, in the sign which the Sun enters, suffers 4 degrees.

---

[6] A planet is said to be combust when too close to the Sun to manifest its own power. Some writers say that combustion occurs when the planet is within 3°; others say, within 8° 30′ of the Sun. [Mercury is excepted in traditional horary practice.] If, however, the planet be within less than 17′ of exact conjunction, or 'within the heart of the sun', it is highly strengthened. —*Ed.*

[7] *Via Combusta*: placed in the zodiac at any point from Libra 15° to Scorpio 15°.—*Ed.*

If Saturn, Jupiter and Mars are occidental in relation to the Sun, they suffer 2 degrees of debility.

If Venus and Mercury are oriental in relation to the Sun, they suffer 2 degrees.

The waning Moon [from its 15th day to the next new moon] suffers 2 degrees.

Every planet in its sign of detriment suffers 5 degrees.

Every planet in its sign of fall suffers 4 degrees.

Every planet found in a place where it receives no dignity is said to be peregrine, and suffers 5 degrees of debility.

Every planet in House 12 suffers 5 degrees of debility.

Every planet in House 6 or 8 suffers 4 degrees of debility.

Every planet in conjunction with Saturn or Mars suffers 5 degrees of debility.

Every planet in quadrature to Saturn or Mars suffers 3 degrees of debility.

Every planet in an aspect of opposition to Saturn and Mars suffers 4 degrees of debility.

GENERAL INDICATIONS

The name of *Ruler of the Horoscope* is given to the most dignified of the seven planets. In order to find out which this is, first of all 5 degrees are attributed to the planet which enjoys the dignity of a diurnal or nocturnal house in House 1, even if it does not actually occupy that house. A planet in its sign of exaltation receives 4 degrees of dignity. A planet in trine aspect, 3 degrees of dignity. A planet occupying its Decan, 1 degree of dignity. A planet in conjunction with the Ruler of the Year in House 1, 12 degrees of dignity. Each planet in House 10, 11 degrees of dignity. In House 7, 10 degrees. In House 4, 9 degrees. In House 11, 8 degrees. In House 5, 7 degrees. In House 2, 6 degrees. In House 8, 5 degrees. In House 9, 4 degrees. In House 3, 3 degrees. In House 6, 2 degrees. In House 12, 1 degree. The planet which governs the hour of the nativity receives 6 degrees. The planet which has the greatest number of degrees of dignity receives the title of Ruler of the Horoscope.

Certain degrees in each zodiacal sign increase the chances of good fortune for children born in the period corresponding to these degrees.—Aries, 19. Taurus, 3, 15, 27.—Gemini, 3, 10, 11, 12, 15.—Cancer, 1, 2, 3, 4, 8, 19.—Leo, 2, 5, 7, 19; 22; 23.—Virgo, 3, 4, 14, 16, 20.—Libra, 3, 16, 17, 21, 28, 29.—Scorpio, 5, 7, 12, 15, 18, 20.—Sagittarius, 3, 13, 15, 18, 20.—Capricorn, 8, 12, 13, 14, 20, 24.—Aquarius, 7, 15, 16, 17, 20, 29.—Pisces, 13, 17, 19 and 20.

The *Major Fortune* confirms and increases favourable influences, or lessens contrary ones; but, except for very serious exceptions, its effects are increased or limited according to the use man makes of his will. If will is lacking or weak, or if it ceases to be balanced by intelligence and a sense of proportion, this talisman loses its value and allows man to fall back under fatal influences. This is the reason for the fate of so many great destinies which have flashed like meteors through the skies of history.

This chance of good fortune manifests itself whenever the epoch of the nativity and the names and titles which define the individual form a series of numbers whose total is 21; this is written in House 10 in Roman numerals [XXI].

Let us take as an example 1848, the number which, on the 20 April 1808, constituted the astrological personality of Napoleon III, and the figures of this number, 1, 8, 4, 8, added together, give us Arcanum 21, sign of the greatest good fortune.

It is more powerful, and has for its symbol, in House 10, the astrological sign of the Sun surmounted by a crown, when, arranging these figures on the points of a star composed of two concentric and antipodal triangles, the number can be formed by reading from the top to the right and then to the left, and when the six figures add up to 21. Let us take as an example 1804, the number which, on the 15 August 1769, constituted the astrological personality of Napoleon Bonaparte. We make a star with six points:

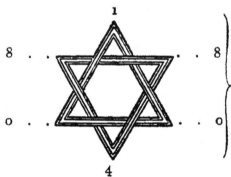

This star is composed of two triangles: one ascending: 1+0+0; the other reversed: 4+8+8. Each figure, starting at the top, stands at one of the six corners of the interlaced triangles.

Reading from the top downwards, to either left or right, we get 1804, and the 6 figures 1+8+0+4+0+8 give us Arcanum 21, sign of supreme good fortune and the wealth gained by that famous man who let himself be ruined by his faults.

The *Minor Fortune* is symbolised by a small circle quartered by a cross and surmounted by a crown. It is placed in the sign or the house attributed to it by the fatidic circle. It serves as a help in times of danger, provided that it is in a sextile or trine aspect with Jupiter or Venus. If it is in quadrature or in opposition with Saturn or Mars, its benevolent influence is lessened.

If Major or Minor Fortunes are found in conjunction, sextile or trine, with a planet that augurs violent death or future misfor-tune, the peril has a chance of being avoided, if the subject refuses to abandon himself to the fatal trend of the powers of destiny.

Whenever the epoch of the nativity and the names and titles which define the subject's personality form a number whose figures total 9, 11, 14, 17 or 19, the number obtained is written in Roman numerals at the top of the 10th House. These numbers belong to the series of the 21 Major Arcana. IX tells us that prudence can lessen the influence of dangerous presages. XI signifies that the strength of a well-directed will may triumph over difficulties. XIV symbolises the force of enlightened initiative and its ability to produce good and overcome evil. XVII means that hope should never be lost, even in the most critical times. XIX reveals that faith in God and in oneself are instruments of incalculable power. Horo-scopes which include these arcana leave a great deal to the exercise of individual free-will.

IV

MORIN DE VILLEFRANCHE, Cardinal Richelieu's astrologer, declares in his *Astrologia Gallica* that no child's horoscope should be cast without knowing what country it was born in and the condition of its parents.

Let us suppose that several children, all born on the same day of the same year, each have identical horoscopes; let us say that one is the son of a prince, the second the son of a well-to-do merchant and the third the son of an obscure labourer, and that outstanding good fortune is predicted for them all. According to his country and his high place in society, the prince's son may become king; the merchant's son may attain to high political rank, or make a name for himself in the Church, at the Bar or in the Army; the labourer's son may acquire great wealth through the exercise of an art, a craft, or a strong business sense. There are, I know, examples in history of extraordinary good fortune falling to the lot of men born in conditions which would never lead one to expect such results. But these cases are very rare. If therefore such an eventuality is predicted in the horoscope of a child of humble birth, it must be stated with many reservations that if certain conditions which are in the hand of God come to fulfil-ment, the subject of the horoscope may see himself drawn almost effortlessly along on a rising current of events towards unforesee-able destinies. The astrological arcana are brief and can only

indicate wide generalities; human intelligence must therefore take
some part in guiding their interpretation according to the era,
the locality, the social milieu and the family.

NUMBERS AND NAMES

On his entry into the world, the prince's, like the shepherd's
son, is no more than a piece of organised matter. He receives
individuality and is distinguished from other human beings when he
receives the name imposed upon him by parental authority. In
modern society, this may include several Christian names, a patro-
nymic and sometimes an appellation or a title.

All these must be arranged in the order in which they have
been conferred upon the newborn child. Next they must be translated into Latin. If there are Christian names of Greek origin, they
must be translated into their original language. Those which come
from a doubtful source should be written in the sacred language
of the Christian era, Latin. For example, the names Achilles, Alexander, Basil, Eugene and Nicolas should be written in their
original Greek form: Achilleus, Alexander, Basileus, Eugenes,
Nikolaos. Names like Auguste, Benedict, Napoléon, Maximilian,
Peter, Vincent, become in Latin: Augustus, Benedictus, Napoleo,
Maximilianus, Petrus and Vincens. The titles of Emperor, King,
Duke, Prince, Count, Dauphin, are really derived from imperator,
rex, dux, princeps, comes and delphinus. In Germanic tongues
there is often great difficulty in obtaining the original form of the
name. Thus Khlodowigh, Klowigh, Ludwig, Luduwig, are all vari-
ants of the modern Louis, and are all vague and variable forms
from the Middle Ages. In order to obtain stable forms, the Masters
of the Qabala tell us that we must look for it in Latin, the one
language we know which has kept the traditions of the sacred
tongues of the ancient east. Thus Ludovicus, Carolus, Franciscus
were ecclesiastical forms of barbarian names which became Loys or
Ludovic, Karl or Charlen and Frantz, Francis or François. We
must therefore delve into the hagiographical monuments of Christianity to discover the precise forms of names derived neither from
Latin nor Greek. As for the family name, it should be retained in
its national form with full spelling.

Let us now refer back to the Alphabet of the Magi [p. 143],
which consists of 22 letters, each of which has a number. In astrology
we must reduce to a single figure all numbers higher than 9, by
eliminating 0 [Y becomes 1, C becomes 2, etc]. Diphthongs [PH,
TH, TS] are suppressed so that each letter of the name has a
separate value. Here is a practical example.

Louis XVI was born during the night of 23 August 1754, and
was given the names and title of Louis-Auguste, Duc de Berri. This
becames Ludovicus Augustus Dux de Berri. Next we arrange in two

vertical columns the names Ludovicus and Augustus, placing beside each letter its corresponding number. Then, beginning with the final letter, we inscribe the numbers of the solar houses, separated by a multiplication sign from the alphabetical numbers. After making the multiplications, we add up the columns, obtaining 200 for Ludovicus, 137 for Augustus.

L	3	×	IX	=	27	A	1	×	VIII	=	8
U	6	×	VIII	=	48	U	6	×	VII	=	42
D	4	×	VII	=	28	G	3	×	VI	=	18
O	7	×	VI	=	42	U	6	×	V	=	30
V	6	×	V	=	30	S	3	×	IV	=	12
I	1	×	IV	=	4	T	4	×	III	=	12
C	2	×	III	=	6	U	6	×	II	=	12
U	6	×	II	=	12	S	3	×	I	=	3
S	3	×	I	=	3						
					200						137

Operating in the same way on the word Dux, we get 30; De gives us 13, and Berri 41.

On the astrological calendar at the beginning of this Book [p. 462], we find that 23 August corresponds to the first degree of Virgo. Consequently we place this zodiacal sign in House 1 of the genethliac figure. Libra will occupy House 2, Scorpio House 3, etc., until we arrive at House 12, which will have Leo. The Zodiac has now been completed and it is a question of placing in position the signs of the seven planetary Genii.

The cyclic table of years [p. 463] shows us that the year 1754 is part of a planetary cycle of 36 years beginning with 1729, ending with 1764 and governed by the Sun. When we consult the cycle of the Sun, we discover that 1754 is dominated by the Genius of Saturn. Consequently, it is the fatidic circle of Saturn which we must consult to find out the future of Louis Auguste, Duc de Berri.

How to Use a Fatidic Circle.

Write the date 1754 in a horizontal line. Underneath, write in a vertical column the number 6, which represents Virgo, 6th sign of the zodiac; degree 1, which corresponds to the 23 August; 200, the hermetic total derived from Ludovicus; 137, derived from Augustus; 30, from Dux; 13, from de; and 41, from Berri. The total, 32, added to 1754, gives us 1786.

Proceeding now by an inverse operation, we compose with all these numbers a scale of fatidic signs of which 1754 will form the

base, and 1786 the top. The culminating point of the horoscope is
House 10, in which we write 1786. Then following the order of the
houses, we put 41 in House 11; 13 in House 12; 30 in House 1;
137 in House 2; 200 in House 3; 1 in House 4; 6 in House 5; and
1754 in House 6.

Next, the numbers must be broken up in order to make them
correspond, where necessary, with the numbers marked beside
each of the 78 arcana in the circle. 1786 is broken up into 1,000,
700, 80, 6. But 1,000 and 700, which do not appear in the fatidic
circle, are reduced to 10 and 7. Numbers 80 and 6 are in order. 41
does not exist in the circle, so is reduced to 40 and 1. 13 is reduced
to 10 and 3. 137 is reduced to 100, 30, and 7. The number 200,
which does not appear in the circle, remains as it stands, as do
1 and 6. 1754 is reduced to 10, 7, 50 and 4; this method is used
with all horoscopes.

Here now is the appearance presented by the fatidic scale,
with the planetary signs and other arcana from the circle of
Saturn:

House 10	10	=	Jupiter in Virgo.
	7	=	The Seven Cups.
	80	=	Mercury.
	6	=	Arcanum VI [The Two Paths].
House 11	40	=	Arcanum XIII [The Reaper].
	1	=	The Sceptre.
House 12	10	=	The Sun in Virgo.
	3	=	The Three Cups.
House 1	30	=	Mercury in Libra.
House 2	100	=	Mercury in Pisces.
	30	=	The Moon in Libra.
	7	=	The Seven Pentacles.
House 3	200	=	Saturn.
House 4	1	=	Arcanum I [The Magus].
House 5	6	=	Arcanum VI [The Two Paths].
House 6	10	=	Arcanum X [The Sphinx or Wheel of Fortune].
	7	=	Jupiter in Gemini.
	50	=	Jupiter in Scorpio.
	4	=	Jupiter.

As the prince's nativity corresponds to the 1st degree of Virgo,
and therefore to the 1st Decan of this sign, we next look for this
Decan on the circle, and we find it with number 10, at Jupiter.
We then write Jupiter on the horoscope, in House 10.

Next, looking on the circle for 7 we find that the symbol of
the 7 cups corresponds to it. This we write in House 10, since
no zodiacal sign in particular is ascribed to it.

We find 80 with Mercury, which we write in House 10, as no other zodiacal sign is ascribed to it.

In looking for number 6, we reach the end of the symbols, and must begin again at the beginning, with Arcanum I; following the order of the symbols, we find 6 with Arcanum VI, the Two Paths. We inscribe this arcanum in House 10, to which no other zodiacal sign is ascribed.

40 is found with the Reaper in Arcanum XIII. It is written in House 11. Number 1 is found with the symbol of the Sceptre, which we place in House 11.

We find 10 with Virgo and under the Sun. We write the Sun under the sign of Virgo, after Jupiter, which is already there.

Number 3 is found with the symbol of the 3 Cups, which we inscribe in House 12, since no other sign is attributed to it.

30 is found under the sign of Libra with Mercury. As this planet is already placed in House 10, we draw a line from Mercury to the sign of Libra in House 2. This line signifies that, from the culminating point of the horoscope, Mercury sheds its influence over House 1 and over the sign which occupies it.

100 is found with Pisces and Mercury. We draw another line from Mercury to Pisces in House 2.

Number 30 is found with Libra and the Moon. We inscribe the Moon under Libra in House 2.

Number 7 is found with the symbol of the 7 Pentacles, which we place in House 2, as it has no other zodiacal sign.

We find 200 with Saturn, which we inscribe in House 3, as no other zodiacal sign is ascribed to it.

Number 1 is with Arcanum I [the Magus] which we place in House 2, as no other zodiacal sign is attributed to it.

6 is found with Arcanum VI, the Two Paths. This symbol is placed in House 5. Number 7 is found with Gemini and Jupiter. As this planet is already actually in House 1, we draw a line from Jupiter to Gemini in House 10.

We find number 50 with Scorpio and Jupiter, and draw a line from Jupiter to Scorpio in House 6.

Finally, number 4 is found with Jupiter, but with no Zodiacal sign attached; and as the planet is already placed in House 6, we have only to keep this fact in our memory.

Mars and Venus, not having been encountered by any of the numbers on the fatidic scale, are placed in their nocturnal houses, as the birth took place during the night. We write Mars in Aries, House 8, and Venus in Libra, House 2, after the Moon which is already there.

The signs from the fatidic circle having thus already been disposed on the horoscope, it only remains for them to be translated into predictions. In order to avoid confusion, we must follow the usual order of the seven planets, Saturn, Jupiter, Mars, the

Sun, Venus, Mercury and the Moon. Let us consider these planets: firstly, in relation to the 12 houses; secondly, in relation to the 12 signs; thirdly, in relation to themselves, in what are called their aspects. Then we shall proceed to predictions of enemies and dangers, and finally to chances of good or evil fortune. All these divisions are contained further on [Book VII], under the title General Keys to Astrology.

Take some slips of paper, and on each one write the prediction given by each key, with the key's number, to facilitate verification if needed. These slips should be classified in groups showing the influences which the various fatidic signs may indicate concerning each fact. It then only remains to combine the different texts, in order to define firstly the child's character and chances of a long life; secondly, his chances of good fortune or otherwise; thirdly, the affections and friendships, or the obstacles, dangers and enemies, which he will meet with in life, and fourthly, his manner of death, whether peaceful or tragic. These four general themes may be subdivided into endless special points, all of which, with their solutions, may be found in Junctin's *Speculum Astrologiae*. Limits of space do not allow of all the details: but if this work has any success with the public, I shall follow it with a translation of Junctin's complete works.[8]

How To Study the Horoscope of Louis XVI

Could Louis XVI when born be assured of a long life?

This question is answered by key 399. Let us look at the Table of Lunary Epacts [*page* 483] and that of the monthly phases of the Moon [*page* 484]. The year 1754 has number 6 of the Epacts. The month of August being the 8th in the year, we must look in column VIII of the monthly phases for this number. We find it placed beside August 19, on the left of the table in the column of days. The new moon of August 1754 therefore corresponds to the 19th of that month; but as in reality it appeared one day earlier, we say that it started on the 18th. We next count 1 on 18, 2 on 19, 3 on 20, 4 on 21, 5 on 22, and 6 on 23, the date of birth. It is therefore preceded by a conjunction of the Moon with the Sun. The conjunction having taken place in Aries, we count 1 on this sign, 2 on Taurus, 3 on Gemini, 4 on Cancer, 5 on Leo, 6 on Virgo, and 7 on Libra, where we find the Moon. Then count 1 on House I, and so on, to 7 on House VII, where we place the sign of the Chance of Long Life—a small circle divided by a

---

[8]   There is no record of Christian's having published this.—*Ed.*

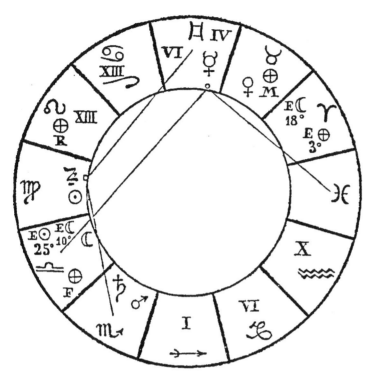

Horoscope of Louis XVI: nativity [daytime] 1754

cross, and write beside it the number 399, which is the number of the key.

Pisces occupies House VII; it is a feminine sign, and the chance of long life is not under the Sun's rays, as it is diametrically opposite. The chance, at first sight, is therefore in favour of longevity [key 399]. But the Sun is in opposition, always a malignant aspect, and Jupiter, Master of the Chance, is also in opposition, and most unfortunately so, in the sign of Virgo, which is his sign of detriment.

Moreover, Saturn, linked with Scorpio, announces troubles in this life—dangers whose baleful influence will extend to the 42nd year of his existence, and whose cause will be thoughtless enthusiasms and resolutions which will make him fall into the hands of his enemies. Saturn is sextile Jupiter, and this aspect would seem to favour deliverance from danger; but as Jupiter is in detriment in Virgo, this position neutralises his protector influence [key 20].

At the very outset, therefore, we are confronted with very doubtful chances of long life; existence may, indeed, be violently interrupted between the 1st and 42nd year by falling into dangers whose nature we do not know.

What sort of intellectual faculties will this new-born prince have?

The Sun in Virgo indicates marked intellectual gifts [key 150]. Mercury, trine Moon = outstanding intellectual ability, an aptitude for letters and arts [key 226]. Mercury in Gemini = a resourceful mind [key 215]. The ray cast by Mercury on Libra = aptitude for mathematics, a taste for higher studies, tendency to favour new inventions and discoveries [key 219]. The influence of Mercury on Pisces = excellent faculties, a lively and delicate wit, aptitude for legal studies [key 224]. Venus in House 2 = an inventive mind devoted to the arts [key 170]. Venus trine mercury gives the same presages as Jupiter with Mercury, that is, aptitude in science and art [keys 195 and 81]. The Moon in House 2 = superiority in the domains of culture and the arts [key 230].

Now for character. Jupiter in Virgo indicates an upright mind and heart, affectionate fidelity [key 66]. Venus in Libra = a spirit of justice [key 187]. Mercury in House 10 = gravity of demeanour and a serious mind; but as Jupiter is in an aspect of quadrature, this gravity and high seriousness will profit him little [key 208] and Saturn, occupying House 3, presages indifference to the things of ordinary life [key 3].

As nothing must be concealed, we must add that Mars in Aries presaged in Louis XVI, besides an irritable temperament, a physical predisposition to youthful excesses [key 105]. Mars opposition Venus announced a few sensual vices, either apparent or hidden [key 130]. Venus conjunction Moon could incline him towards conjugal infidelity and adultery [key 194]. But these inclinations might be, and were, overcome by education.

The *General Chance for Mind and Character* is indicated by key 411. In a nocturnal nativity, it is counted from Mars to Mercury, and then from House 1 to House 3, in which the sign is placed. This sign, being in an aspect of conjunction with Saturn, a malefic planet, indicates a mind generally unskilled in the conduct of life. Moreover, Mars, Master of this chance, as he has the dignity of a house in Aries, is found in House 8, where he gives baleful warnings as we shall see.

What the horoscope has revealed to us concerning the intellectual faculties and character of Louis XVI is verified by the history of the French Revolution.

The *Chance of Fortune* is indicated by key 410. It is counted, in a nocturnal nativity, from the Sun to the Moon, if the Moon is placed below the horoscope's horizontal equator. This is the case on our figure where the Moon is in House 2. We therefore place the sign of chance in that house to which belongs an increase in material gains. Venus, which has the dignity of a nocturnal house in Libra, adds to it the dignity of Master of the Chance of Fortune and promises elevation, but followed by great dangers, because Venus is opposition Mars, an essentially malefic planet.

Saturn, in conjunction with the ray cast by Jupiter on Scorpio, again announces elevation [key 25]. Saturn, sextile Jupiter, and the waxing Moon [in its 9th day], announce a fresh increase of fortune and elevation in dignity [key 31].

The ray cast by Jupiter on Gemini in House 10, where Mercury is found, announces a great elevation [key 76]. The Sun in House 1 [Jupiter] also being on a cardinal point, and the Moon occupying House 2, again presages an advance towards higher elevation. But this will prove precarious, because Jupiter is in detriment in Virgo, Virgo is a feminine sign, and the Moon is opposition Mars [key 133]. Jupiter in quadrature with Mercury announces an increase in fortune because Mercury has the dignity of a throne in Virgo, sign occupied by Jupiter [key 86]. Mars in a sextile aspect with the ray cast by Jupiter over Gemini foretells elevation, self-confidence, and triumph over enemies; but this good luck will be temporary, because Mars is in 8, an unfortunate house, and Jupiter is in detriment in Virgo and Gemini [key 78]. Mars, sextile Mercury, again presages a short-lived good fortune [key 124].

This good fortune which cannot last can only be the accession to the throne. But we must remember the oracle composed by Cagliostro: 'Let Louis XVI, a sham king, cast down from the ruined throne of his ancestors, let him beware of dying on the scaffold towards the 39th year of his life.'

The *Royal Chance* is indicated by key 404. It is counted from the Moon to Mars, and is placed in House 7. It is without aspect in Mars, and trine Saturn: its master is Jupiter who is allied to the Sun in House 1. These dispositions are fortunate; but there is a quadrature between the sign of chance, its master, and House 10, the place in which ascent of Fortune takes place. This is an indication of danger after the first favourable presage has been accomplished, and a gradual collapse in this prince's position will be worked out in the following presages.

Saturn, sextile Sun, announces loss of material wealth, but this might be followed by a return of good luck [key 33]. Jupiter in Virgo = instability of fortune [key 66]. Jupiter in oriental conjunction with the Sun = chances of good fortune which only last a short while, because Virgo is Jupiter's sign of detriment [key 74]. Jupiter in House 1, but in a sign of detriment = loss of position [key 49]. The Dragon's Tail, which influences the 30 degrees of Virgo = tribulations [key 389]. Venus in Libra = threats of adversity, all the more redoubtable as she is in opposition to Mars [key 187]. Mars in opposition to the influence cast by Mercury on Libra = great misfortune [key 328]. Mercury in Gemini = danger of a disastrous fall [key 215]. The Moon in House 2 and in opposition to Mars = afflictions and loss of property [key 384].

The affections of domestic life and outside friendships are the consolation and support of man against the onslaughts of adversity. Could Louis XVI hope for such protection?

The *Chance of Marriage* is indicated by key 406. It is counted, in a nocturnal nativity and in a masculine horoscope, from the Sun to Venus, and is placed here in House 2, in the sign of Libra. It is opposition Mars, and Venus, which has the dignity of a nocturnal house in Libra is in a masculine sign. Consequently, the marriage will be an unfortunate one, and the pair are both under the malevolent influence of Mars, of which we shall later on see sinister signs. The Moon in Libra [key 247], announces that the increase of Fortune will be compromised by his being dominated by a woman.

Discords in the royal family were all predicted in the horoscope. Jupiter, in opposition to the ray cast by Mercury on House 7 [the house of marriage], announces domestic discords [key 90]. The sun, placed in a similar aspect, repeats and reinforces the same presage. Jupiter, square Mercury [key 86] adds discord with near relations, and the Sun, in the same quadrature, reiterates this.

The *Chance of Friendship* is indicated by key 407. It is counted from the Moon to Mercury, and is placed in House 9, under the sign of Taurus. Venus, having the dignity of a throne in Taurus, is mistress of this chance, and, finding herself in House 2, and opposition Mars, reveals that the king's friends will be unfaithful, and moreover quite powerless to stop the downward course of his fortunes. In 1789, they responded to the king's appeal in his hour of trial by a general emigration. Those whom the Crown had most loaded with honours were the first deserters.

What is Louis XVI's *Chance of Enemies?* It is indicated by key 408, and is counted, in a nocturnal nativity, from House 12 to the master of that house, and is placed in House 2, under the influence of Venus who has the dignity of a nocturnal throne in Libra. Venus, mistress of the chance of enemies. opposition Mars, announces numerous enemies, all powerful. Jupiter, ruler of House 7, and angular [House 1], presages victory to the king's enemies [key 258]. The Sun, ruler of 12, fortunate in 1, conjunction Jupiter, and sextile Saturn, confirms the eventual triumph of the enemies [key 259]. Mercury, ruler of 1, and occupying House 10 [a cardinal point], announces that the strength of the enemy cannot be overcome except by the presence of Saturn, Jupiter or Mars in House 1. Now, Jupiter is there, but he is in his sign of detriment in Virgo, and so loses his tutelary influence [key 261].

The *Chance of Victory* indicated by key 405 is counted from Saturn to the Sun, and is placed in House 11 [place of support]. But the sign of Cancer occupies this place; the Moon, mistress of the chance as this sign is her throne, occupies House 2, opposition Mars; this malefic position again assures the victory of his enemies. Thus on all sides the supports of the throne collapse or disappear.

Now, what character does Astrology give to this hostility? The only planet that can explain it clearly and completely. Jupiter, in quadrature with Mercury, announces dangerous popular uprisings [key 86]. The same planet, in opposition with the ray cast by Mercury on House 7, announces a rising fraught with danger, and an explosion of hatred on the part of the people [key 91]. The Sun, square Mercury, and in opposition to the ray cast by Mercury on House 7, reiterates the presages enunciated by the aspects of Jupiter [keys 164, and 86, 167 and 91].

What will be the consequences of these uprisings? The captivity and death of Louis XVI.

The *Chance of Captivity*, indicated by key 402, is calculated, in a nocturnal nativity, from the Chance of Fortune to Saturn, and is placed in House 2, where its ruler is Venus who has her throne in Libra opposition Mars. This malefic position announces imprisonment [key 285]. Mercury being ruler of House 1, and occupying House 10, trine Venus, might be thought to offer some hope of deliverance [key 286], but Venus, made malefic by the aspect of Mars, has lost her power of protection.

Here is the decisive indication of catastrophe. Mercury in House 10, being square Jupiter, and the Moon being found at the same time opposition Mars announces a violent death [key 208].

Moreover, as Mars is alone in House 8, it recalls the popular rising which will be the cause of that death. The Moon being at the same time in House 2, with no aspect from Jupiter, and opposition Mars, reiterates the menace of violent death. The Moon being in a human sign [Libra], signifies that this violent death will be caused by a murderer's weapon, or following a sentence of death [key 90].

Finally, the Moon being waxing [the sixth day], and being opposition Mars, dispels all preceding uncertainty by revealing that the violent death shall be inflicted in public as the result of a sentence of death [key 329].

In this manner the whole catastrophe, from 23 August 1754, could have been predicted according to the hermetic treatises of Ptolemy, Julius Firmicus, and Junctin of Florence.

Here we must remark that if Louis XVI had been born during the day, Mars would have occupied Scorpio [diurnal throne] in House 3, and Venus would have occupied Taurus [diurnal throne] in House 9. In this case, the malefic influence of Saturn and Mars in conjunction in House 3 under Scorpio, would have been lessened by the sextile aspect of Jupiter found in House 1, and these chances of the King's future safety would have equilibrated the dangers [see figure].

But let us go even further, and try to find out if the same doctrine ccould have revealed, on the nocturnal horoscope, the time when Louis XVI's fatal destiny would be accomplished. Let us look at the instrument which the Magi called the Table of Life.

This Table is divided into 14 columns each containing 7 years. Above these columns are arranged the 7 planets in their proper order, dominating 7 septenaries from 1 to 49. The same system embraces the years 50 to 98. If one needed to extend this table, Saturn would govern years 99 to 105, Jupiter 106 to 112, etc.

On the left of this table, we read the word Day, signifying that the planetary order beginning with the Sun and finishing with Mars is employed for diurnal nativities. On the right, we read the word Night, signifying that the planetary order beginning with the Moon and finishing with Mercury is employed for nocturnal nativities.

On Louis XVI's horoscope Mercury is placed at the cardinal point, House 10, the culmination of the horoscope. Mars, occupying House 8, is, after Mercury, the highest-placed planet; next come Jupiter and the Sun [House 1], the Moon and Venus [House 2] and Saturn [House 3].

We must remember that the presence of Saturn in Scorpio has foretold that the life of the new-born child will be in danger towards his 42nd year [key 20]. Beginning therefore with the first year, let us look for Mercury, the highest planet in the horoscope. It is found, in the Table, above the vertical column which contains the years 36 to 42. As the child was born at night, let us look, on the extreme right of the Table, for the column of Night, and descending to Mars, the highest-placed planet after Mercury, we find the age 39 inscribed at the top of the right angle formed by the conjunction of Mercury's vertical line with Mars' horizontal line. We may deduce, from the presages given by Mars, that the catastrophe will take place in the King's 39th year.

A similar operation on the relationship of Mercury with the other planets gives us the years just before and after the catastrophe. Thus Mercury dominating Jupiter = 38; Mercury dominat-

ASTROLOGICAL TABLE OF THE YEARS OF LIFE FOR DAY AND NIGHT NATIVITIES

DAY	SATURN	JUPITER	MARS	SUN	VENUS	MERCURY	MOON	SATURN	JUPITER	MARS	SUN	VENUS	MERCURY	MOON	NIGHT
Sun	1	8	15	22	29	36	43	50	57	64	71	78	85	92	Moon
Venus	2	9	16	23	30	37	44	51	58	65	72	79	86	93	Saturn
Mercury	3	10	17	24	31	38	45	52	59	66	73	80	87	94	Jupiter
Moon	4	11	18	25	32	39	46	53	60	67	74	81	88	95	Mars
Saturn	5	12	19	26	33	40	47	54	61	68	75	82	89	96	Sun
Jupiter	6	13	20	27	34	41	48	55	62	69	76	83	90	97	Venus
Mars	7	14	21	28	35	42	49	56	63	70	77	84	91	98	Mercury

ing the Sun=40; Mercury dominating the Moon=36; Mercury dominating Venus=41; Mercury dominating Saturn=37 years of age. We see that the 39th year which is governed by Mars, signifying death in public after sentence, begins on the 23 August 1792, and ends in 1793.

The first year of danger, the 36th, begins on 23 August 1789; it began between the Assembly at the Jeu de Paume [20 June], and the taking of the Bastille [14 July]. This later date was a mere skirmish; the real declaration of war against the throne dates from the Jeu de Paume.

Let us take simply the first manifesto passed by majority vote on the motion put forward by Sylvain Bailly: 'The Deputies of the Tiers-Etat [the people], assembled in the Hall of the Jeu de Paume, Versailles, on the 20 June 1789, swear that before rising they will have established and confirmed the Constitution of the kingdom of France.' *Les Députés du Tiers-Etat, réunis dans la salle du Jeu de Paume, à Versailles, le vingt juin mil huit cent quatre-vingt-neuf, jurent de ne point se séparer avant d'avoir établi et affermi la Constitution du royaume de France.*

Peaceful and straightforward, Bailly did not suspect that the oracles of regicide and of the Terror period were contained in this innocent announcement. Nevertheless, here it is:

'This oath, taken at the Jeu de Paume, is a plaything of deceitful destiny, becomes the foundation, and gives the sign of bloody revolution, in which the King and Queen will die here in Paris, slain at the hands of the executioner, and their son will be put in prison.' *Ce serment, fait au Jeu de Paume, est un jeu des destins si décevants, et devient fondement, et vaut signal d'une sanglante révolution, laquelle fera mourir dans Paris le Roi et la Reine, tués par les mains du bourreau, et leur fils captif en prison.*

There remain seven mute letters D S T J V D D, signifying: *Dùm Salutis Testamentum Jurant, Vitae Damno Devoventur.* 'While they vow to support the public good, they delived themselves to death.' And in actual fact, Bailly and the majority of his courageous colleagues died in an unforeseen cataclysm; it is in this sense that their devotion to the cause was a mere plaything, a bait set by deceiving destiny.

Was Louis XVI ever warned of the misfortunes which lay in store for him? Did Cagliostro or Pierre Le Clerc have sufficient intelligence or power to accomplish such a delicate task? We shall never know. In any case, the horoscope's fatality enclosed his free will in an inescapable circle, and, when he wanted to escape, fate lay in wait for him, and he was recaptured at Varennes. Here again, the secret is hidden like a light under a bushel in the plain statement of his intended escape: *Le vingt-un juin mil sept cent nonante-un, Louis Seize, roi de France et de Navarre, veut tenter de s'échapper de Paris, avec sa famille, sous un déguisement . . .*

'On the 21 June 1791, Louis XVI, King of France and Navarre, will try to escape from Paris with his family in disguise.'

We know that he tried to reach the frontier, disguised as a valet, with a passport in the name of a Baroness de Korf, whom the Queen tried to impersonate. But this is what the oracle says: *Cet infortuné, vite capturé à Varennes, et humilié sous ce déguisement de l'épée, sera, dans un an, réduit avec sa famille en plus étroite prison.* 'This wretched man, promptly recaptured at Varennes and, in this disguise, humiliated by the sword, will, within a year, be reduced, with his family, to an even more confined prison.'

There remain 8 mute letters Z D G J N N U N, signifying: *Zonatim Detentus, Gemens, Jactatus, Negare Nomen Ultra Nequit* 'Enclosed in a hostile circle, groaning, mocked at, he can no longer pass himself off as someone else.' A king who exchanges the consecrated sword for the livery of a servant, degrades himself. The executioner's hand, seizing him from the throne, may make him a martyr; but the hand of a postillion stopping him on the highway, caught redhanded in his undignified behaviour, seizes more than his life.

The 39th year on the Table of Life will be revealed to us again if we add to the number 1786, which recapitulates the astrological numbers of the horoscope, the dynastic number XVI. This number is connected by the great Arcana [*page* 95] and on the fatidic circle with the Lightning-struck Tower.

Total [horoscope]	1786	
Dynastic number...	1	
	6	$XVI = 16 = 1 + 6$
39th year	1793	

This Arcanum XVI, whose occult influence Louis was to encounter on his accession, seems to indicate perhaps that this prince of misfortune already bore, in the celestial spheres, the name of Louis the Beheaded.

How To Cast the Annual Horoscope

The yearly horoscope is cast in the same manner as the Nativity. The correct year is chosen also the Circle of Fate. Thus, for 1793, we must take the Circle of Saturn, and adding to the 1st degree of Virgo, the 6th sign, the numbers 200, 137, 30, 13, 41, plus the number 16 [mark of the dynasty], we find the result is 1831, that is to say $1 + 8 + 3 + 1 = XIII$, the Arcanum of The Reaper, significator of Death.

From 1793 we must subtract 1754, the year of birth. 39 results and after dividing it by 12, the number of the Houses, there remains 3. Add to 3 the number 6 representing Virgo, the zodiacal sign of the nativity, and the product 9 signifies that for the horoscope for 1793, Sagittarius rules the 1st House and Scorpio the 12th.

Let us now take the Circle of SATURN and construct the table of the horoscope in the following manner:

10th House	10	Jupiter in Virgo
	8	The Sun in Aquarius
	30	Mercury in Libra
	1	Venus
11th House	10	Mars in Virgo
	6	Jupiter in Capricorn
12th House	40	Arcanum XIII The Reaper
	1	The Sceptre
1st House	10	The Sun in Virgo
	3	The three Cups
2nd House	30	Mercury in Libra
3rd House	100	Mercury in Pisces
	30	The Moon in Libra
	7	Mercury
4th House	200	Saturn
5th House	1	Arcanum I The Magician
6th House	6	Arcanum VI The Two Paths [The Lovers]
7th House	10	Arcanum X The Sphinx [The Wheel of Fortune]
	7	Jupiter in Gemini
	90	The Sun in Aquarius
	3	Venus

These are the signs taken from the Circle of SATURN. Let us now explain our second operation using this Circle. This second example will suffice to make the reader familiar with the method.

Let us take as starting-point the Decan of the Nativity, that is to say, 1st Virgo. We find it with the number 10 and Jupiter. We place Jupiter in Virgo in the 10th House.

For number 8, we find the Sun and Aquarius. We put the Sun in the 3rd House.

For number 30, we find Mercury and Libra. We put Mercury in the 11th House.

For number 1, we find Venus with no sign indicated. We put it in the 10th House.

For number 10 we find Mars and Virgo. We place Mars in the 10th House to the left of Jupiter.

For number 6, we find Jupiter and Capricorn. As it is actually in the 10th House we draw a line from Jupiter to Capricorn in the 2nd House.

For number 40, we find the Arcanum XIII with no sign indicated. We put it in the 12th House.

For number 1, we find the symbol of The Sceptre with no sign indicated. We put it in the 12th House.

For number 10, we find the Sun and Virgo. As it is actually in the 3rd House, we draw a line from the Sun to Virgo in the 10th House.

For number 3, we find the symbol of the three Cups with no sign indicated. We put it in the 1st House.

For number 30, we find Mercury and Virgo, and as it is already in the horoscope, we do not need to draw it twice.

For number 100, we find Mercury and Pisces. As it is actually in the 11th House, we draw a line from Mercury to Pisces in the 4th House.

For number 30, we find the Moon and Libra. We put it in the 11th House, after Mercury.

For number 7, we find Mercury, with no sign indicated and as it is actually in Libra, we do not need to draw it twice.

For number 200, we find Saturn with no sign indicated. We put it in the 4th House.

For number 1, we find it with the symbol of The Magician. Arcanum I. We put this symbol in the 5th House.

For number 6, we find it with the symbol of The Two Paths. Arcanum VI. We put this symbol in the 6th House.

For number 10, we find it with the symbol of The Sphinx. Arcanum X. We put this symbol in the 7th House.

For number 7, we find Jupiter and Gemini and as it is actually in the 10th House, we draw a line from Jupiter to Gemini in the 7th House.

For number 90, we find the Sun and Aquarius and as it is already shown in this sign in the 3rd House, we do not need to draw it twice.

For number 3, we find Venus with no indication of sign and, as it is already shown in the 10th House, we do not need to draw it twice.

The Annual Horoscope's value is only to help us to foretell the approach of events signified in the Nativity. Now, 1793 being marked as the time of the tragic end of Louis XVI, let us look for the indications and the keys. The two charts being studied together, let us compare their aspects and we find the following:

SATURN in the 4th House holds Louis XVI in captivity. Mercury in the 11th House badly aspected by Arcanum XIII, symbol of the

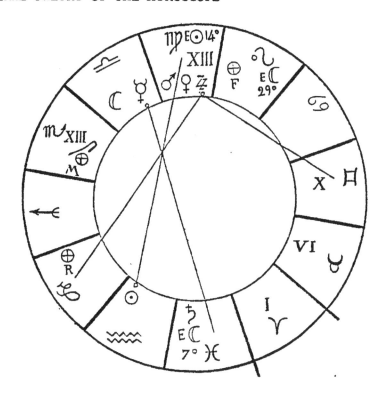

Horoscope of the Death of Louis XVI, 1793

Reaper, sign of Death, produces the same effect. The Moon in the 11th House badly aspected by the same Arcanum shows that imprisonment will end in death [key 402].

JUPITER in the Annual Horoscope in Virgo—its natal sign— and badly aspected by opposition to Saturn, foretells a disastrous year [key 426].

MARS passing into the sign occupied by Jupiter and the Sun in the Nativity and badly aspected by Saturn confirms the above forecast [keys 433 and 435].

VENUS passing into the sign occupied by Jupiter and the Sun in the Nativity and badly aspected by Saturn strengthens the above forecast [keys 440 and 449].

MERCURY, passing into Libra which has Venus and the Moon in the Natal map, is badly aspected by Arcanum XIII which foretells danger of treason and death [keys 457 and 459].

The MOON returning to Libra, her natal sign, shows that the year will be dangerous for princes and for highly placed persons [key 468].

Nothing ameliorates the threat of disaster from the seven

planets; fatality broods over the whole chart. But we may be even more exact.

VIRGO, sign of the 1st House in the natal chart passing into the 10th House, occupied by Mercury in the natal chart, forecasts a dangerous year, for Mercury is badly aspected in the 11th House by Arcanum XIII, symbol of Death [key 416].

The 1st House, in opposition aspect to Saturn and Mars; then Jupiter, lord of the 1st, for he rules Sagittarius, but badly aspected by opposition with Saturn; then the Moon, badly aspected in the 11th House by Arcanum XIII, clearly shows by this configuration the imminence of a catastrophe [key 569].

JUPITER, lord of the House, in the 10th, ill aspected by Saturn, foretells rebellion by subjects against their princes [key 555], signifying a mortal blow by iron [key 562].

We need not look further for if Saturn has revealed the instrument of death, Jupiter dominates the catastrophe, the outrage on the royal person.

Let us now make a Table for the days of 1793.

This operation for every annual horoscope is used to find the period of the year when a grave prophecy is about to be fulfilled.

In every year, Saturn governs 85 days; Jupiter 30 days; Mars 36 days; the Sun 53 days; Venus 33 days; Mercury 57 days; and the Moon 71 days. We take as ruler of the first days the planet which has the dignity of diurnal or nocturnal throne in the sign on the Ascendant, even when this planet is found in another sign, in another House. Then we divide the remaining days between the six other planets, according to the order in which they appear in the map. The examples we are studying will show how to proceed in every annual horoscope.

The Ascendant is occupied by Sagittarius, ruled by Jupiter; Jupiter therefore rules the first thirty days of the year 1793 [1 to 30 January].

Next, the Sun follows in the order of the houses and signs. It rules then 53 days [from the 31 January to the 24 March].

Saturn succeeds the Sun for 85 days [from the 25 March to the 17 June, then we come to Jupiter in the 10th House; but as Jupiter, lord of the Ascendant has already opened the cycle of days, we do not count it a second time and we pass to Venus which rules 33 days from the 18 June to the 20 July].

Mars, after Venus, rules for 36 days [from the 21 July to the 25 August].

Next Mercury governs 57 days [from the 26 August to the 21 October]; and the remaining days of the year are ruled by the Moon [from the 22 October to the end of December].

If now we note that Jupiter, lord of the Ascendant, and ruling the first thirty days of 1783 is badly aspected by Saturn, showing the attack by the subjects upon the person of the prince [key 552], we are in a position to foresee that this attack will take place between the 1 and the 30 January of this year. We remember that sentence of death was passed on Louis XVI on the 17 January, a Thursday, the day ruled by Jupiter, and that he was executed on the following Monday, the day ruled by the Moon. The Moon showed in the natal chart a public death, following condemnation [keys 100 and 329].

Let us recall that Saturn, showing a mortal blow by iron [Key 562] is the ruler of Aquarius, the first degree of which corresponds to the 20 January in the Egyptian Calendar. This coincidence of Saturnian presage with that of Jupiter made it possible to foretell that his tragic death would take place in the last ten days governed by Jupiter in 1793, that is to say between the 1st degree of Aquarius [20 January] and the 11th degree of the same sign [30th day of the month].

This example of the inner illumination which Astrology may give is of grave importance. The Hermetic horoscope and the Sibylline Oracles are in agreement and if space permitted me to translate the voluminous collection of Keys made by Junctin de Florence, the biography of Louis XVI could be revealed in its entirety.

I recalled, in the Fourth Book, the Oracles composed by the Benedictine Pierre le Clerc on the destiny of Napoleon Bonaparte and of some other contemporary personages. In order to refresh ourselves for a moment after the monotonous study of the planetary circles, let us examine the influence of predestination in the lives of some historical figures nearer our own time.

One of the most interesting is assuredly that of the Prince called to power in 1848, made Emperor in 1852, by the will of France. Napoleon-Louis-Charles-Bonaparte, born on the 20 April 1808, had disappeared while yet a child in the stormy times of 1815. The death of the Duke of Reichstadt left him, in 1832, the heritage of the imperial traditions. A secret instinct may, perhaps, have given him a presentiment of his future high rank but not clearly enough to give him the strength to await his destiny which twice checked his impatience: at Strasbourg in 1836 and at Boulogne in 1840. Although well educated, he had never encountered Astrology which would have given support to his great moral strength; or, perhaps he considered it useless to study the old books of an art so much decried. However, nothing would have been easier than to examine, in secret, every imprudence, before taking a risk.

Let us suppose that we are taken back to the 29 October 1836, and informed of the adventurous project of the next day. We should have written, on the spot, and without commentary[9]: *30 October, 1836, at Strasbourg, the Prince Napoleon-Louis-Charles Bonaparte attempts a revolt against Louis-Philippe the 1st, King of France.* The oracle would be set out in these terms, without any ambiguity, from the 141 letters of which the preceding announcement is composed: —

Useless attempt against King Louis-Philippe. It soon miscarries Prince Napoleon-Louis imprisoned and disillusioned goes free and will be sent to the United States.

Six mute letters remain B R B O R T, signifying: *Bis redux, Bis Oblitus, Reditum Timeat;* that is to say, he will come back twice, and will twice see his name forgotten; let him not return.

Thus the failure of the movement attempted at Strasbourg contained for the future a hidden threat which prefigured the renewed failure at Boulogne. Later, Prince Louis Napoleon would not have stopped because of so puerile an exhibition of divination; his inflexible will would have scorned the sibylline twaddle. But oracles also have their inflexibility. In 1836 Louis-Philippe was as firm as a rock; the memory of the outrage of Fieschi rallied the populace about the throne. Prince Napoleon went free after his short adventure and was sent to the United States by order of the King without other distress than that of not knowing the fate of his companions; they were handed over to a jury which did not treat them as enemies.

The Prince saw the future more and more clearly but always with too much impatience, since in 1840 he believed that his hour had come. Let us reconstruct the preceding announcement by simply changing the date and the place: *6 August 1840 at Boulogne-sur-mer, Prince Napoleon-Louis-Charles-Bonaparte revolts against Louis Philippe the First, King of the French.*

Here is the response of the oracle: *Oh, unfortunate Prince, ill-advised attempt . . . Legal action by the citizen-King. Sentenced to perpetual imprisonment: escape in 1846.*

Three mute letters remain B L L, signifying *Bis Libertas Luet,* that is to say: twice captive, twice free. The use of the expression 'citizen-King' marks the peaceful character of Louis-Philippe who was given that title.

---

[9]   For the rest of this Book, to save space the translation only of these statements and answers, 'Sibylline oracles' or Prenestine fates are given, since a number in both languages are already printed in Book III. Those following are entirely similar; they have been checked in French and in all cases are genuinely resolvable into their answers or 'oracles'.—In these examples as elsewhere the somewhat flowery translations of the Latin are Christian's, not the present translator's.—*Ed.*

The oracle predicted an escape. Let us state by itself the announcement of the sentence and the detention of Prince Louis Napoleon in the fort of Ham. *Prince Napoleon Louis Charles Bonaparte, sentenced at Paris, on 6 October 1840 to perpetual imprisonment by the judgment of the Court of Peers of France and confined in the fortress of Ham.*

That is the situation. Any political bias is excluded from the statement. Neither flatterers nor detractors are permitted by Magic; it only sees men and events under the hand of God. The oracle predicts two future events. Suppose that the Pythian Oracle came back to life and that, prophesying in our language, she stretched her right hand towards one vision and her left hand towards another—this is what the oracle would read under the veil of the preceding statement.

There—the Prince who has been sentenced will break free from the fortress by his skill in his flight. And there!—Supported by the wisdom and the strength of God, Napoleon will ascend the throne of the restored Empire in 1852.

Six mute letters remain L S B O E P, signifying:—*Libero suffragio Bis Ovans, Electus Populi*, that is to say 'Elected by the escape [from Ham, of which we already knew the date], and on the other hand by the prevision of the double vote [which led the Prince to the throne].

But in order to realise this supreme good fortune, he had first to escape from the well-guarded fortress of Ham. Everyone knows with what coolness Dr. Henri Conneau drew the governor of the State Prison away from his duties. M. Conneau gave an example of signal devotion in this crisis, acting with wisdom as well as resolution. It is important to note that his conduct in this matter was perhaps an effect of predestination and the result of old links with the Bonaparte family, for he had been secretary to Louis, King of Holland, father of the captive prince. Let us place before us the statement of this fact: *Henri Conneau, doctor of medicine, formerly the secretary of Louis Bonaparte, King of Holland.*

From these 71 letters flashes out the oracle of devotion, seeming to be the simple continuation of the preceding statement:—*will aid Louis Napoleon, encircled but determined, to escape from Ham and to be crowned.*

Five mute letters remain: H C N C L, signifying *Horae Cavens Nexum Carcare Liberat;* that is to say: 'Awaiting the critical hour, he assures the deliverance of the captive.'

The word 'encircled' expresses well the position of the Prince surrounded by guardians whose vigilance he found it difficult to evade. The escape must have taken place on 25 May 1846 at the first hour which seemed favourable. What would have been the joy of the captive if, instead of the feverish insomnia of the night before his flight, he had been able with his trusted friend to read, as we shall do, the simple history of the plan they had conceived! To taste this joy and this encouragement, all that would have been necessary would be to write the sibylline anagram of this simple question: *Prince Napoleon Louis Charles Bonaparte, aided in his flight by Dr. Henri Conneau, can he escape from the Fortress of Ham on 26 May 1846?*

Here is the reply: *Let the Prince be confident, bold and go out! He will escape as a workman carrying a board, while the wily Conneau will distract the vigilance of the Governor.*

Three mute letters remain P X R, signifying: *Per Xylum Robur,* that is to say: 'wood makes him strong'—he owes his strength [his success] to the board which he carried to disguise his appearance when passing his jailers.

This escape was only one step towards the predicted future. Between the exile of the fugitive and the throne which awaited him, a revolution was needed, for experience forbade fresh risks. Time brought the political upheaval. At the first shot on 22 February 1848, one could have written on the walls of Paris: *Revolution on 22 February 1848 by the Republicans of Paris against Louis-Philippe the 1st, King of the French.*

From the statement of this event we may draw in these words the predestination of the Prince: *Prince Louis Napoleon, led by his slow destiny, Emperor by universal suffrage, will replace this wretched Republic.*

Sixteen mute letters remain T I I I X V T H I T T H I I I R, signifying: *Tacens, Ignotus, Inops, Inter Xenia Vagatur, Tempestatis Hospes; Imperii Tandem Tardus Hoeres, Inter Ignes Incedit Radians;* that is to say: 'Silent, unknown, poor, he wanders like one who, tossed by tempest, accepts the hospitality of strangers; then, belated heir of the Empire, he advances radiant among the fires [of Revolution].' Silence was, in fact the characteristic of his thoughtful nature at that time. Taken while still a child far from France after the disaster of 1815, he was for a long time unknown; poor because of the despoiling of his family, wandering on foreign soil, asking in turn from Switzerland, Italy, America and England a precarious hospitality: that is the first phase of his story. At last, the heir of the Empire, after false hopes and vain efforts, he retrieved his fortunes, was crowned in the greatest name of modern times, in the midst of a new Revolution the flames of which Providence wished him to put out.

A transition regime called the Presidency was introduced before the Republic became the Empire. Public opinion chose Louis Napoleon for this honour and the Radical Party put up an opposition candidate, M. Cavaignac: *Eugene Cavaignac, general, candidate for the Presidency of the French Republic.*

The oracle which is drawn from this statement is ironical: *What does this general with the Republican cloak want, this son of a bloodstained regicide?*

Eight mute letters remain A A N D A A A D, signifying: *Aerumnatis Aerae Nomen Deterius Adscribens, Armiferum Ambitio Dementat;* that is to say: 'In displaying one of the most sinister names of a deplorable age ambition has struck this man-of-arms with madness.'

The 'Republican cloak' was the rôle of the conventional Cavaignac who did not fear to wear it when shouting one day from the Tribune: 'My father, a virtuous citizen and martyr for liberty, was a member of the Convention. I am proud to be the son of such a father.' To appreciate this touching declaration, it is only necessary to read in the *Moniteur Universel* the following dispatch with the signature of Cavaignac senior: 'A new guillotine has been set up in the Square Saint Sever. Well-known aristocrats are guillotined and their goods confiscated. You may see their heads rolling from the scaffolding every day.' France refused the President's Chair to the man proud of such a heritage and the meaning of the oracle was fulfilled.

The Prince-President, elected in 1848, was not to reach the throne until 1852. His coup d'Etat of 2 December 1851 was but a call to Destiny. Here is the question which he might have put to himself at the time of carrying out so grave an act: *What will happen to Napoleon Louis Charles Bonaparte, President of the French Republic, as the result of the coup d'Etat risked by him in Paris, on 2 December 1851?*

The word 'risked' is not too strong, for unforseen obstacles might have led to disaster. But the reply of the Oracle would have been decisive. Here it is: *Triumph won by the support of the soldier. The Republic broken by the dictatorship of the army. Silence of the people. Ascent to the throne certain, in a year's time. God wishes it.*

Seven mute letters remain Q U Q Q X R H, signifying *Quietem Urbis Quotidiè Quassantes Xystici Rapiuntur Hiantes;* that is to say: 'The Xystici who every day disturbed the calm of the city are carried off with gaping mouths.' The Xystici were athletes of antiquity who exercised under porticoes or other covered places, sheltering from bad weather. It is the only Latin word (and it is adopted from the Greek) that we can find to give a meaning for X; but by analogy it gives a clear sibylline signification. For the Xystici among the Greeks like the circus drivers in Rome often formed rowdy cliques. We may compare them in our times to some political agitators who are very courageous in defying danger when they know they are safe themselves. Some of these worthies were carried off in such a ludicrously easy manner that one could apply to them the expression *rapiuntur hiantes,* for they were actually taken with mouths agape in a trap of which they had not the slightest suspicion. A year later, according to the oracle, the provisional authority granted in 1848 assumed the imperial form and the occult power which announced this conclusion signed the statement by this formula: 'God wishes it.'

Both friends and enemies of the Napoleonic Restoration have sometimes asked if Napoleon III was protected against an attack on his life. Several plots vigorously denounced by public opinion broke out from time to time. The most dangerous was engineered by the Italian Orsini. Let us suppose that before acting on 14 January 1858 Orsini had been in a position to consult Fate, he might have put the following question: *The Italian Orsini will attempt to kill Napoleon III on 4 January 1858 at Paris, near the Opera-house, by the use of bombs.*

The assassin might well have recoiled before this warning:

Let Orsini abstain, or not far from here he himself will lose his life. The Emperor of the French Napoleon III is protected from every vile attack which may threaten him.

Six mute letters remain P Z R H R H, signifying *Perfidiae Zonam Rumpit Hecate, Refringit Hostem,* that is to say: 'Hecate, goddess of the night breaks the circle of treachery and the weapon of the enemy.' I do not think that any attempted murder worse than Orsini's could be imagined but the Oracle affirms in unequivocal terms that the life of Napoleon III will be preserved.

6 June 1867 gives us a memorable proof of this preservation. Napoleon was not aimed at, but he could have been hit by the careless shot of the Pole Berezowski. Let us state the situation thus: *6 June 1867, Napoleon III and Alexander II, Emperors of France and of Russia, are going to a Military Review, outside Paris.*

The curious who crowded to stare at the autocrat of the North could not have stated the case more simply, less occultly. But from these 123 letters which tell of a peaceful walk there lie hidden the threat of danger, even the echo of gunfire.

The Russian will be in peril of death by shooting while driving, the assailant being a Pole. A plot by his enemies in exile, inspired by hatred but without result.

Six mute letters remain X J H I X E, signifying: *Xenia Juratus Hospis Incendit: Xenia Evadit;* that is to say: 'A conspirator will set fire to his hosts, but the foreigner will escape the peril.' This image expresses the fire flashing from the murderer against the prince who was the guest of France.

The perils of death by violence, whatever may be the result, are generally strongly accented in the oracles which reveal them.

While considering the crime of Orsini, let us recall the infernal machine which in 1800 threatened the life of Bonaparte as First Consul.

24 December 1800 George Cadoudal, Saint-Regent, Limoëlant and Carbon, four accomplices, will attempt to kill the First Consul, Napoleon Bonaparte, at Paris, by the explosion of a barrel of gunpowder and by shooting.

From these 190 letters the following oracle is drawn:

A futile plot by a corrupt Government aided by English money. The explosion will take place, blood will flow, but the First Consul Bonaparte will certainly escape the hard lot by which he was threatened.

Nine mute letters remain C D Q B T D D N D, signifying: *Criminis Diri Quaesitores Britannia Tegit; Domos Delent, Non Ducem;* that is to say: *England supports these seekers after [wishers for] a barbarous crime; they destroy people's houses and not the leader.* History relates that the infernal machine, ambushed in the Rue Saint-Nicaise, should have struck Bonaparte at the time he passed by going to the Opera. The explosion shook the whole neighbourhood, demolished several houses and killed or wounded 52 persons. The inquest revealed that the guilty men were Royalist agents in the pay of the British Government. Georges Cadoudal, who had taken flight, was arrested in February 1804 as leader or accomplice in a new conspiracy and confessed that he acted under the auspices of a prince of the House of Bourbon with subsidies furnished by England. Furiously Bonaparte learned at the same time from police reports that the Duc d'Enghien was at Baden on the borders of the Rhine and that he had several times secretly entered Strasbourg. This young Prince had served in Condé's army but he had withdrawn from the emigration camp and lived at Ettenheim with his mistress, Mademoiselle de Rohan. He was dragged from his retreat by French dragoons on the night of 16 March 1804, taken to Strasbourg, then transferred to Vincennes near Paris where he was handed to a Military Commission and shot during the night of 21 March. Bonaparte was bitterly reproached by historians for this cruelty. He justified himself at St. Helena saying: 'The death of the Duc d'Enghien should be eternally laid at the door of those who, led away by a criminal zeal, did not await the orders of their sovereign before carrying out the sentence of the Military Commission.' Yes, certainly, there was a criminal zeal; but there was also in this case the hand of Fate. Let us first put a question, very vaguely: *Louis-Antoine-Henri de Bourbon Condé, Duc d'Enghien, will he be fortunate until the end of his life?*

The oracle replies by a sinister warning: *Oh! he will seldom be fortunate. His end will be violent and at night—at Vincennes.*

This end, violent and at night, can it be death? What event is hidden in this veiled prediction? There remain 13 mute letters I D B B O O D D D H I I D in the midst of which the Latin word *Ibo* is formed twice. Is this a mysterious echo of a warning whispered in the ear of the Duc d'Enghien: 'Take care! *I shall come . . .* I shall come to take you at an hour when you least expect me.' Did the Prince never have one of those presentiments which sometimes save those who listen to them?

Subtracting the twice-repeated word *Ibo* there remain 8 mute letters D D D D H I I D, signifying: *De Domo Demum Direptus, Horrendo Interitu Innocens Deletur;* that is to say: 'Dragged from his hearth, he perished although innocent, struck by a violent death.'

But this is only partly clear; Fate will show itself more definitely. Let us consider his arrest. *Louis-Antoine-Henri de Bourbon Condé, Duc d'Enghien, is carried off at night, from Ettenheim, on 16 March in the year 1804, by the order of Napoleon Bonaparte, First Consul of the French Republic.*

This statement, like an item in a calendar, only seems to state an arrest; yet for those who know how to read it contains the account of the final catastrophe: *Oh, this Duc de Bourbon will perish very miserably at night, on 21 March . . . 4, shot by order of Fate in the region of Vincennes, a lantern attached to his breast.*

Six mute letters remain E E Q H O O, signifying: *Extinguit Ejus Querelas Homicidium: Oppressus Obruitur;* that is to say: 'Murder stifles his cries; the unfortunate man is smothered.' He was killed at night by the haste of secret malefactors. This order of Fate ended his tragic destiny. While soldier-executioners established his identity, others dug his grave. The lantern on his breast is a savage detail, worthy of this hideous scene.

It is not long since violent death struck two great blows on the heights of the political world. A man of obscure origin, a courageous worker, intelligent and upright, was raised by the acclaim of a great nation to the highest dignity in his country. You have already guessed who; he is *Abraham Lincoln, President of the Republic of the United States of America.*

In the simple statement of these two names and of this high estate, read the Arcanum of another tragedy: *He will be brought low, killed in the evening by a wicked enemy.*

Eight mute letters remain H I D D A Q D D, signifying: *Histrionis Ictu, Decretoria Die, Æternae Quietis Dormitorium Datur;* that is to say: 'On the day appointed by Destiny, the dastardly attack of an actor opens to him the place of eternal rest.' In fact Booth, the murderer of Lincoln, was a comedian in a stage act.

Let us replace the statement by the following question which will elucidate the matter further: *Abraham Lincoln, elected President of the Republic of the United States of America, will he be fortunate to the end of his life and will he be re-elected?* This question could have been put on the very day of his election, and here is the reply which is hidden within it. Read: *Not re-elected. He will be killed, while holding office, by a wicked scoundrel. Let him beware of being publicly assassinated, in a theatre.*

Another man, a young prince, hitherto fortunate, suddenly sacrificed in 1864 the love of his country to the dreams of ambition. He set out full of illusions and three years later, on 19 June 1867, there only remained a miserable corpse. This page, recently added to the history of Fate, demands a moment's notice.

The crown of Mexico after long hesitation was accepted on 10 April 1864 by the Archduke Maximilian of Austria. He was to enter under the auspices of French victories the dream of Empire from which short-sighted politicians hoped to reap a wonderful reward. About that time, I framed this question, more grave in its humble simplicity than the frivolous eloquence of our parliamentary speeches. *Ferdinand-Maximilian-Joseph Archduke of Austria, will he be fortunate as Emperor of Mexico, to the end of his life and will he leave the throne to his son?* There was no son, it is true; but the Empress Charlotte, born in 1840, was in the full bloom of youth and hope. The sibylline reply seemed to me to be strange. Here it is: *He accepts the crown, unfortunately. Mexican blood will be fatal for him. He will perish, shot in Quérétaro, but will later be exhumed and brought back.* Eight mute letters remain I J I H D H J D, signifying: *Insidiis Jactatus, Inermis, Homicida Die, Hostium Jure Deletur;* that is to say: 'Passing without arms from ambush to ambush, he is crushed on a fatal day by his enemies, now become judges.' Turning away from this sinister text which seemed to me to be fantastic, I tried a counter check, in questioning the future of the Empress in the following terms: *Marie-Charlotte-Amelie-Auguste-Victoire-Clementine de Saxe-Cobourg Gotha, daughter of the King of Belgium, married to Ferdinand-Maximilian-Joseph, Archduke of Austria, Emperor of Mexico, will she be fortunate on the throne?* Here is the reply given to me by Fate: *Abandoned to catastrophes, she will go from storm to storm. She will return from Mexico to Austria before Maximilian perishes, unhappy—so fit to be pitied—overcome by the madness of despair—her heart broken.* Five mute letters remain H C F G H signifying: *Heu! Corona Fracta, Gemens Hebescit;* that is to say: 'Alas! moaning and leaning on her broken crown, her reason clouded.' The unfortunate Princess did, indeed, return before the murder of her husband on the walls of Quérétaro. A biography published in 1867 declares that unknown hands gave her a tropical poison having the effect of clouding the mind to any degree required; a dastardly crime, if it is true that it was committed.[10]

Be that as it may, nothing pointed in that direction in April 1864, and the occult arts lost much of their prestige in my eyes when news came to Paris that Maximilian had disembarked at the port of Vera-Cruz on 28 May. I do not know what instinct led me to question the statement of a fact so simple in appearance: *Ferdinand-Maximilian-Joseph, Archduke of Austria, Emperor of Mexico, enters his Empiire on 28 May 1864, at the port of Vera-Cruz.*

Fate replied again, as if it addressed the unfortunate Prince directly: *Learn, Maximilian, that you will perish, betrayed, humiliated, judged, condemned and executed in mid-June, 1867, at Quérétaro, by order of the leader ['chef'] Juarez.* Thirteen mute letters remain R N D D D P D R L N M P R, signifying: *Regnum Neptunus Die Dira Dedit: Periculosum Declina Regnum. Luctuosa Nex Mox Patriam Redit;* that is to say: 'It was an unlucky day for you when Neptune gave you the kingdom; refuse this perilous gift. A deplorable death will bring you back to your own country.'

The whole drama is in these words—even to the nearly exact date of the fatal event—even to the name of the enemy who precipitated it—even to the name of the place which appears here for the second time. The story of this venture is well known. Let us only recall here that on 3 October 1865, when his mind was torn between generous emotions and lively fears, Maximilian signed a decree which committed him to implacable vengeance. Martial law was proclaimed, not only against the declared adversaries of his frail power but also against suspects. The right of killing prisoners was entrusted to quite junior officers and, as the last straw, article 5 of the imperial decree stated: 'Appeal for pardon is forbidden.' In thus abdicating the highest privilege of the Crown, Maximilian signed his own doom. Fate entered the lists. Executions multiplied and hatred with them. The oracle which had announced that Mexican blood would be fatal for Maximilian, that is to say would be a reproach to him, began to be fulfilled. Betrayal did the rest.

Let us transport ourselves in thought to Quérétaro, on 13 June 1867, at the hour when the captive Prince had to appear before a council of war. His judges are seven in number and their names are posted on the walls of the town before being transmitted to Europe with the death bulletin. Let us link their obscure names to that of the royal captive and ask the following question: *What judgment will be returned on 13 June 1867, for or against Maxi-*

---

[10] *Maximilien Ier, Sa Vie et Sa Mort,* 1 vol., 16mo., without author's name. [Paris, Lebigre-Duquesne, 1867.]

milian I [*Ferdinand Joseph, Archduke of Austria*] *Emperor of Mexico, by Platon Sanchez, President José Ramirez, Miguel Lojéro, Juan Quéda y Ansa, José Versategin, Lucas Villagran, judges, and Manuel Aspiroz prosecuting counsel?* The names are taken from the biography I have already mentioned. Fate mixes them, transposes their letters and produces immediately this revelation which confirms the preceding ones: *The evil Fate acts; Juarez controls it. What prince lies here crushed? Maximilian, unhappy Archduke of Austria, prisoner through the vile conspiracy of Miguel Lopez, will be judged on 13 June and put to death without the right of appeal by the decision of a council of war held at Quérétaro, in Mexico.* Thirteen mute letters remain Z H P P N H J D Y A A Z A, signifying: *Zonatim Hostes Procedunt. Princeps, Necis Hostia, Judicio Damnatus, Infaustam Accedens Aream, Zonatim Atteritur;* that is to say: 'The enemies advance in a circle. The condemned Prince is slaughtered as he enters the circle formed on the fatal ground.' That statement tells of the execution. The remains of Maximilian were exhumed later and were interred in the royal crypt where his ancestors rested. A sad witness to the ill-luck from which princes themselves are not always preserved, and of that Fate whose unseen presence follows those great ones who believe they are invincible!

Let us end these examples with the oracle which announced in 1833, 35 years in advance, the fall of the throne of Isabella II. We know that this Princess became Queen of Spain on 29 September 1833, succeeding her father Ferdinand VII, under the Regency of her mother Maria-Christina. Let us ask Fate if this child-Queen will be fortunate in the future and if, in accordance with the hopes of her friends, she will later give Spain an heir to the throne. *Isabella II* [*Marie-Louise de Bourbon*], *born on 10 October 1830, Queen of Spain on 29 September 1833, will she be fortunate to the end of her life and will she leave the throne to her son?* From these 172 letters is revealed the prophecy of the fall of Isabella in these words: *She will be rejected from the throne of the Bourbons and exiled in September 1868 by the rebel soldier of a fatal military revolution. Sebastian will be a dangerous place for her. Let her take refuge in France.* Three mute letters remain O G Q, signifying: *Omnia Gementem Quatiunt;* that is to say: 'She will succumb, mourning under the presages of her destiny.' The prophecy was fulfilled with a remarkable exactness. Let us give the rebel soldier the name of Prim, of Serrano or of Topete, each of these persons was a link in the chain of betrayals, an element of the military revolution. St. Sebastian only offered to Isabella a precarious haven where she ran the risk of being seized at any moment, if France had not opened to her a supreme refuge.

These rapid studies, which I could have extended considerably,
prove sufficiently that the individuality of a person or the statement of a fact carries always in its simple definition some revealing
sign of good or evil fortune. The more one studies this singular
subject, the more serious it appears; and without offering to the
oracles a blind faith, for one must always make allowance for the
part played by freewill in the handling of events, serious students
will agree that between the names, the happenings and the word
which expresses them there obtains a secret, inexplicable but real
affinity.

The operation has been sufficiently clearly shown in the
example of Louis XVI to make it superfluous to analyse any further
subjects. I shall therefore indicate briefly, as astrological exercises,
the charts of Napoleon I and of the Archduke of Austria, the
Emperor Maximilian of Mexico.

Napoléon Bonaparte was born on 15 August 1769.[11] The year
belongs to the cycle of Venus; the month and the day corresponding
to the 23rd degree of Leo, consequently Leo occupies the 1st House
and Cancer is found in the 12th House. The signs of Fate are
extracted from the circle of Venus, taking for point of departure
the third decanate of Leo. Napoleon gives the number 135 and
Bonaparte 178. The sum of the numbers produces 1804, the year
of his ascent to the throne. The nativity is diurnal.

Could Napoleon Bonaparte according to the order of nature
count on a long life?

This problem is resolved, as in the horoscope of Louis XVI,
by the key 399. The year 1769 has for epact the number XXII.
In working by the method already demonstrated, we see that the
Moon has reached by 15 August the 14th day from the Lunation.
Therefore a conjunction of Sun and Moon preceded the birth.
The sign of *Chance of Long Life* is placed in the 11th House in
the sign Gemini, a masculine and dangerous sign. Mercury, Lord
of luck, is ill-aspected by the opposition of Mars in the 8th House,
the House of death. There is not therefore outstanding longevity,
for there is danger from heart disease or from parts of the body
near the heart by the opposition of Mercury and of the Sun which
is conjunct with Mars in the 8th House [Key 140].

On comparing the planets in the horoscope, we find that
Saturn is the second-last planet and Mercury the last. The nativity
being diurnal, if we descend on the Table of Life the length of
the vertical column dominated by Saturn starting from the 50th
year and go on to the level of the horizontal line which shows
Mercury [at the extreme left of the table, on the side of the diurnal
horoscopes], then we shall stop at the 52nd year at the top of the

11   See note 14 Book III, p. 231.—*Ed.*

right-angle formed by the junction of two signs. It is not therefore likely, according to Astrology, that his life will extend for more than 52 years. This calculation is not far from the historic fact.

What will be the intellectual faculties and the character of Napoleon Bonaparte?

The aspect from Mars to Sagittarius in the 5th House, shows a somewhat weak and inactive childhood [Key 113]. But soon Jupiter in the 10th House strengthens this frail nature and by its sextile to Mars, gives him confidence in himself and audacity [Key 78]. Jupiter in Taurus gives him strength of mind, a spirit of justice and boldness to sport with danger [Key 62]. Jupiter, trine Mercury develops his aptitude for science [Key 81]. Mars in Pisces prepares for him the goodwill of powerful men [Key 116]. Mercury in Virgo predicts energy of mind, sagacity, a special aptitude for military science [Key 218]. Mercury in the 2nd House adds to these faculties pride and the spirit of domination [Key 202]. The Sun lends its light to an arrogant and tyrannical will whose pleasure it will be to rule and who will stop at nothing to attain his ends [Key 156].

With this character and these faculties, will Napoleon Bonaparte attain to outstanding success?

Saturn in Aquarius predicts that he will know how to make friends and to acquire powerful support [Key 23]. Jupiter in Taurus presages difficult and even dangerous beginnings, but these dangers will be overcome thanks to the support of friends and they will be succeeded by good fortune [Key 62]. Venus in the 9th House, free from dangerous aspects from Saturn and Mars, shows that the love of a woman will contribute to his fortune [Key 177]. Saturn in conjunction with the waxing Moon promises fortune [Key 77]. Saturn sextile Venus and with the ray Mars throws to Sagittarius announces prosperity and elevation [Key 32]. Jupiter in the 10th House presages elevation into public life, ascent to high dignities, popularity [Key 58]. Jupiter trine Mercury promises good luck in enterprises, assured by great strength of mind and of heart [Key 81]. The ray which Jupiter throws to Sagittarius announces elevation and success [Key 69]. Jupiter sextile Mars confirms this testimony and, granted that Bonaparte's special aptitude is applied to military science [Key 218], and that the Genius of Mars rules his warlike activities, elevation and good fortune in enterprises will probably be realised in the profession of arms; Jupiter and Mars show here victory over his enemies [Key 78]. The influence of Mars uniting in the 5th House with the influence of Jupiter on Sagittarius shows again elevation and success [Key 73]. Jupiter sextile Sun promises constant fortune, but the conjunction of Mars with the Sun in the 8th House throws a shadow over the future [Key 79].

Prediction does not go much further. History tells us that Bonaparte was born in somewhat humble circumstances, that he was educated at the military school, that his oustanding ability guaranteed from the first success and advancement; that this increasing fortune was threatened by poverty, but that the interest of Madame de Beauharnais obtained for him the protection of Barras, member of the Directoire, and by this favour the restoration of his fortunes. We know that starting from this time Bonaparte mounted steadily the ladder of fame and glory, of popularity and of power. But where is the astrological sign for this predestination?

Let us draw two interlaced equilateral triangles, one with the apex reversed, the figure called by Qabalists the Seal of Solomon. Let us draw on the six points the culminating number of the horoscope, 1804, in such a way that one may read it to the right or to the left of the seal. The sum obtained by adding the numbers $1+8+0+4+0+8$ is 21, that is to say the great solar Arcanum XXI which has for symbol the *Crown of the Magi*, talisman of the human beings predestined to illumine or to burn the path they follow here below [*page* 111].

This supreme sign in Astrology is always placed in the 10th House, the culminating point of the horoscope. The human being on whom it is conferred at birth might take for his device: *Quo non ascendam?* 'To what height may I not attain?'

At the time when Bonaparte was born the *Crown of the Magi* dominating his horoscope confirmed the sibylline prediction of Cagliostro on the French Revolution: *An elected Corsican will finish it*. The sum obtained as shown from 1804 corresponds to Bonaparte's 35th year marked on the horoscope and on the Table of Life by the sign of Venus dominating the sign of Mars, symbol of armed force.

Above Venus is the comet which appeared in 1769, nine years before the birth of Bonaparte in the last degrees of Aries, and which disappeared under Sagittarius to mark, without doubt, the sinking of the Napoleonic sun, for in the progressed horoscope for 1815 Sagittarius is in the 7th House, a cardinal position in western astrology. Comets in the Egyptian teaching are always precursors of the birth or the fall of a great man. That which appeared in 1811 presaged the fatality of 1812 which opened a period of irreparable reverses with the disaster in Russia.

The fall of Napoleon I was precipitated by his unbridled will and the abuse of his power when he saw Europe at his feet. In turning to the Table of Decanates we see that Phuonisi, the Genius governed by the archangel of Mars, governs the degrees 21—30 of Leo, showing an inflexible character, opinionated in adventurous plans even at the risk of ruining himself. Phuonisi is the 15th decan of the Solar circle, and the number XV contains a warning of Typhon, genius of unforeseen affairs which seems to say to Fortune's favourite: 'Beware of the future! If you do not know how to equilibrate your will, your sun will not shine. The *Crown of the Magi* will break in your hand; the unforeseen will one day show your self-confidence to be misplaced and Fate will overrule the decrees of your pride. Time-honoured oak trees are not protected from lightning; you are but a reed in the hands of God.'

The Sun shows that as a result of the excesses of his unbridled will Bonaparte prepared a future of unlucky struggles and adversity [Key 156], and the conjunction of Sun with Mars strengthens the situation that the genius of war will be the animating source of these struggles. Saturn in the 7th House presages misfortune in the west, that is to say, towards the end of the career [Key 303]. Jupiter trine Mercury shows elevation which does not last long [Key 202]. Mercury in opposition Mars shows that adversity is almost inevitable [Keys 218 and 131]. Jupiter in the 10th House with Saturn in square aspect and Venus not being placed in the 7th House, presages reverse of fortune [Key 58]. The ray thrown by Jupiter to Sagittarius in the 5th House [where the good genius is found], Mars being actually in square, shows the chance of ruin [Key 69]. The Moon in Aquarius foretells instability of fortune, agitation of mind with changes of plan and a wandering life [Key 251]. This wandering life is shown in the retreat from Russia in 1812, the fruitless campaign of 1813—1814, during which Napoleon, at grips with invasion, made prodigious efforts to bolster up his failing power. Mars in the 8th House shows loss of goods, that is to say, loss of the throne [Key 100]. Mars in conjunction with the sun shows a vacillating mind, under the blows of ill-fortune, hard and painful work, afflictions [Key 117]. Venus in Aries in the 9th House, anxiety, troubles, sadness while travelling [Key 181].

During the hazards of his military career, Napoleon faced many physical dangers. Saturn in Aquarius presaged danger of wounds by iron or fire [Key 23]; Saturn in quadrature with Jupiter, peril of death [Key 307]; Mars conjunct Sun, danger of perishing in a fire [Key 323]. The First Consul was in fact endangered by the explosion of the infernal machine [December 1800], and the Emperor by the burning of the Kremlin at Moscow [October 1812]. 'Napoleon,' General de Segur writes, 'did not wish to leave. To persuade him, he had to be told that the palace had probably been mined by the Russians and that he had not the right to expose himself when the safety of the army depended upon his life. When he yielded to the entreaties of his staff he found his way barred by flames. All the doors of the palace seemed like entrances to infernal vaults. After many vain efforts a postern gate was discovered which gave on to the Moskowa. It was by this narrow passage that Napoleon and his guards managed to escape. At every moment the roaring of the flames increased. A single tortuous and burning alley looked more like the entrance to, than the exit from, this inferno. The Emperor rushed without hesitation into this dangerous passage. He advanced through the flames to the sound of cracking roofs and floors with the fall of beams and molten metal impeding his path. It was a case of walking on a fiery ground, under a curtain of fire and between two walls of fire. Penetrating heat burned the eyes which had to be kept open, concentrated on the danger ahead. There the career of the adventurous captain might have been terminated if some wandering soldiers had not recognised him and hastened to his aid; they guided him to a neighbouring place which had been burned to the ground that morning.'

Fate did not intend that Napoleon should die at Moscow; his tomb awaited him under another burning sky. He still had some stages of his journey to make. *Danger from enemies* is found in the 6th House of the horoscope; the ruler, Saturn, whose nocturnal throne is Capricorn, is in the 7th House, a House which shows declared enemies, powerful, redoubtable [Key 408]. Saturn is also lord of the 7th House where Aquarius, his diurnal throne, is found and his position on the western angle shows that good fortune has vanished and that triumph belongs to the enemies of this illustrious soldier [Key 258]. Jupiter in Taurus shows that his friends on whom he showered favours and gifts proved to be ungrateful, with neither fidelity nor devotion [Key 62]. To cite but two historical examples of this ingratitude, everyone knows that at the news of the return from Elba, Marshal Ney said to Louis XVIII: 'I shall bring him to you in an iron cage', and Marshal Soult cried: 'It is a matter for the police!'

What light does astrology throw upon the last consequences of this fall?

Saturn in the 7th House reveals the danger of captivity [Key 23]. The Moon, ruler of the 12th [for her sign of exaltation Cancer is found there], is herself in the 7th House in conjunction with Saturn showing again danger of captivity [Key 278].

The *Chance of Captivity* is counted from Saturn to the *Chance of Fortune* and is found in the 6th House. Saturn is its ruler and we see that captivity is twice shown: by its own significator and by its conjunction with the Moon [Keys 23 and 278].

The *Chance of Fortune* is counted from the Sun to the Moon and is found in the 12th House where it signifies eclipse of the power of warriors [Key 410]. In the case of Cancer, a watery sign, it further signifies that this eclipse will have to do with water or on land surrounded by water. The Moon, ruler of Cancer and of the *Chance of Fortune,* confirms the forecast of captivity by its conjunction with Saturn in the 7th House [Key 278].

Finally, that nothing may be lacking from the profound misery following so high a destiny, the Sun opposition Mercury foretells an explosion of hatred on the part of the populace against this 19th century giant who, after having crushed millions of men in the mortar of war and bought his sterile triumphs at the price of so much blood, would possess here below six foot of earth in a hollow of a rock in St. Helena [Keys 167 and 91]. The heavy suffering of France, held to ransom by enemy armies, caused fresh insults to his memory and mothers whose sons had been slaughtered on all the battlefields of Europe bestowed upon the vanquished one the name of the Ogre of Corsica.

In the horoscope, the Moon is between Mars and Saturn, the two malefic planets. This position, described as 'besieged' in astrological language, is considered as an almost inevitable and fatal confirmation of the evils it foretells, according to the points of the circle where any planet so afflicted is to be found. On the *Table of life,* the 46th year belongs to the Moon alone, that is to say, isolated by Saturn and Mars from moderating influences from Jupiter and Venus, the two benefic planets. Now this 46th year corresponds to 1815, the year of disaster.

From 1815 let us subtract 1769; the result is 46 which, divided by 12, the sum of the Houses, gives a remainder of 10. Add to 10 the number 5, representing Leo, the zodiacal sign of the nativity, and from 15 subtract 12, sum of the signs of the zodiac; the number 3 remains, signifying that for the progressed horoscope for the year 1815 Gemini, the 3rd sign, should be in the 1st House and Taurus in the 12th. The year 1815 belongs to the cycle of Venus and should be studied on its circle of Fate. Let us examine briefly if the evils shown by the natal horoscope will be manifested in the year under consideration.

Mercury, lord of the year, because Gemini in the 1st House is his throne, rules the first 57 days of 1815, that is to say, from 1 January to 26 February.

Jupiter follows ruling the next 30 days, that is to say, from 27 February to 28 March.

We shall pass over Mercury who is already lord of the year and we come to the Moon which governs 71 days, that is to say, the last three days of March, the whole of April and May and the first 7 days of June.

Saturn comes next, governing 85 days, that is to say the 23 last days of June and the whole of July and August.

Mars rules the whole of September and the first 6 days of October, 36 days in all.

The Sun rules 53 days, that is to say the remaining 25 days of October and the first 28 days of November.

Lastly, Venus rules the remaining 33 days of the year.

Now let us compare the two horoscopes. The fulfilment of the predictions will be evident.

· Jupiter, occupying the 2nd House under Cancer its sign of exaltation and sextile Mercury, foretells prosperity, increase of worldly goods [Key 50]. In Cancer it promises powerful friends, strong support, though not lasting, rather alternation of good and bad [Key 64]. The trine with Mars promises boldness, confidence in himself, victory over obstacles and enemies [Key 78]. The trine with the Sun presages constant good fortune, provided such an influence is not negatived by evil aspects [Key 79]. The trine with the waxing Moon in its 12th day adds again rise of fortune [Key 82].

Here history has verified the findings of astrology. In fact it was at the beginning of 1815 that Napoleon, reduced to the little sovereignty of the Isle of Elba, resolved to seize power again. He landed on 1 March on the coast of France. From 27 February, the benefic influence of Jupiter prevailed and protected his adventurous journey. He entered Paris on 20 March, after a triumphal progress and might have believed his fortune secure [Key 79], if Mercury, lord of the year, had not been gravely afflicted. Now Mercury, in sextile to Jupiter but in opposition to Mars, foretells vicissitudes, alternations of good and ill [Key 50]. Mercury in Virgo, afflicted by Mars, brought adversity after the burst of good fortune from Jupiter [Key 570]. Being in opposition to Mars in the horoscope of birth, we have confirmation of the presages of adversity and captivity predestined from the start [Key 554]. As *lord of the year*, it is in quadrature with the 1st House, an unfortunate aspect [Key 548]. The 1st House is itself in square with Mars, and the Moon is square Saturn; here is a threat of ruin for even the highest fortune [Key 487].

Mars passing into the sign Pisces, and elevated in the 10th House, announces war [Key 435]. Here it foretells bad luck and misfortune if the subject of the horoscope was a warrior [Key 433]. Dominating Mercury, *lord of the year*, it announces great peril and profound distress [Key 546].

Saturn in Aquarius announces dangerous enemies, instability of fortune, obstacles and failure, annoyances, chagrins [Key 570].

The 1st House, being in quadrature with Mars, the *lord of the year*, Mercury, being in opposition to Mars, and the Moon square Saturn, the armed force will remain in the hands of the enemy [Key 496].

Leo, sign of the 1st House replacing in progression the sign which was in the 3rd House of the nativity, and being in opposition to Saturn in the 9th House, announces great adversity, over-throw by enemies, captivity [Key 471].

Chance of Fortune, which is counted, in a diurnal nativity, from the Sun to the Moon and is found in 1815 in the 9th House, is ill-aspected by conjunction with Saturn; this shows that the misfortunes presaged will be fulfilled on a course of action when Saturn, lord of this *Chance* and the most formidable of the malefic forces, will destroy the last hopes of the Emperor Napoleon I.

Now the influence of Saturn on the horoscope begins on 8 June 1815, only finishing on 31 August.

18 June marks the overthrow of Napoleon by his enemies at Waterloo. On 15 July, the Emperor was a captive on board the Bellerophon. The Moon, afflicted by its square with Saturn, is in Scorpio, a watery sign, showing that captivity would be on a river, on the sea or in a place surrounded by water.

Let us glance at the *Chance of Captivity* to see if deliverance is possible. In a diurnal nativity this hazard is counted from Saturn to the *Chance of Fortune* which are together in the 9th House so that it is in the 1st House, in square to Mars, the Sun and Mercury.

Now Mercury is ruler of the 1st House; it is in the 4th House, in opposition to Mars and it is said [Key 402 of the Arcana]: 'If the ruler of the 1st House is afflicted in the 4th, 6th, 8th or 11th House, it is a sign of death in a state of captivity.' No human power, therefore could release from the rock of St. Helena this new Prometheus. Fate to which he bound himself by his own actions held in one hand the key of his prison and with the other hollowed out his sepulchre.

Ferdinand-Maximilian-Joseph, Archduke of Austria, was born on 6 July 1832. Let us translate these names as *Ferdinandus-Maximilianus Archidux de Ostreich,* reserving for the German language the name of nationality. The Qabalistic calculation of these definitions of individuality give us the following: for *Ferdinandus*—277; for *Maximilianus*—224; for *Joseph*—92; for *Archidux*—108; for *de* —13; and for *Ostreich*—146. The year 1832 belongs to a cycle of Venus and is ruled by Saturn. 6 July corresponds to the 13th degree of Cancer and consequently it is the 2nd decanate of this sign which marks the beginning of research into the Arcana. The epact of the year 1832 is marked by the number XXVIII; and birth having taken place on 6 July, the Moon is waxing and in its 9th day. The nativity is nocturnal.

Now that we are acquainted with the method of casting a horoscope, let us discover by what principal signs the catastrophe of Maximilian could have been foretold.

First, does astrology promise a long life to this prince?

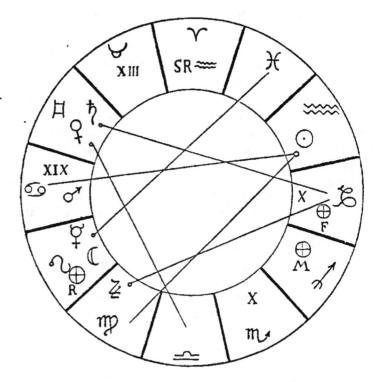

Horoscope of Maximilian of Mexico: night nativity 1832

The Moon being in its 9th day at the time of birth, a lunation preceded that event. In using the rule, already applied, the *Chance of long life,* we count from Aries to the Moon and find it in the 5th House in Scorpio, a feminine sign. It is found in opposition to the Arcanum XIII, symbol of the Reaper, in the 11th House; this symbol veils a danger, the birth being at night, Jupiter being the planet in the lowest place and the Moon soaring above. The Table of Life seems to limit the duration of existence to the 45th year which is found at the point of junction of the vertical column of Moon and the horizontal line of Jupiter [p. 500].

Mars, lord of the *Chance of Long Life,* being in the 1st House and in opposition to the ray projected by Saturn to Capricorn, presages by this evil aspect that if the life reaches the indicated limit, it is unlikely to extend beyond.

Suppose that we are at the cradle of the archduke, let us see what his intellectual faculties will be, of what nature will be his character.

Mercury in the 2nd House foretells aptitude for science and for literature; a proud and dominating character [Key 201]. Venus sextile Mercury shows strength of mind and of heart, strong liking for science and art [Key 81]. Jupiter in Virgo shows upright mind and heart, fidelity in the affections [Key 66]. Mercury in Leo shows a good memory, rectitude of judgment, taste for arms and warlike adventures, a spirit wishing to dominate at all costs [Key 217]. Mercury in conjunction with the Moon promises success in the study of science [Key 225]. The Moon in the 2nd House confirms this prediction [Key 230]. Venus in Gemini, sextile Mercury, shows an ingenious mind, goodness, wisdom and refinement [Key 183]; but Saturn conjunct Venus diminishes the expression of these happy qualities, making inconstancy of will in the conduct of the affairs of life predominate.

Rise of fortune for a man born a prince is manifested by attainment of political power. Was the archduke predestined to such power?

Royal Chance in a nocturnal nativity is counted from the Moon to Mars and is found in the 12th House, in sextile to the 10th House. The ruler of this *Chance* is Mercury, placed in the 2nd House, in trine aspect to the 10th House. Here is a double presage of elevation but, the 12th House being unfortunate, this rise of fortune will not be without peril [Key 404] . . .

Saturn trine Mercury and the Moon shows elevation of fortune proportionate to the condition of the person who is the subject of the horoscope [Keys 136 and 137]. The same Saturn in the 12th House and in trine to the Sun in the 8th, shows again rise of fortune; but the 8th and 12th Houses are unfortunate: here we have a threat of misfortune after elevation [Key 33].

Jupiter in the 3rd House, sextile Mars, shows elevation of fortune, boldness, self-confidence [Key 78]. But the sign Virgo is Jupiter's place of detriment and Mars is in its fall in Cancer; these unfortunate positions presage future perils. Jupiter in Virgo foretells instability of fortune [Key 66]; and Mars in Cancer inspires temerity which will increase the inconstancy of will [Key 108]. The ray which Jupiter projects to Capricorn in opposition to Mars shows misfortunes and the hate of powerful men [Key 70]; alliances and friendships which change to hostility; great perils, resulting from dangerous connections or from reckless actions [Key 88].

The royal star of Aquarius is of the nature of Saturn; it culminates in the horoscope in square to Mars signifying the same as a square from Saturn to Mars, namely loss of goods [Key 38].

The ray thrown by the Sun on the 1st House, in conjunction with Mars, shows miscarriage of enterprises [Key 133]. The Sun in opposition to the Moon shows alternation of good and evil fortune, a wavering and irresolute character, a troubled mind in difficult times [Key 168].

Mercury in conjunction with the Moon shows unstable and precarious fortune [Key 225]. Saturn in Gemini presages many obstacles and hindrances in the affairs of life and the square from

Jupiter adds perils thereto [Key 15], after arrangements and calculations which only bring barren results [Key 37]. The ray thrown by Saturn to Capricorn announces tribulations, hopes followed by deception, slight success followed by failure; the trials of an ambition which does not perceive the dangers [Key 22]. Mars in the 1st House shows great perils brought about by great faults [Keys 314, 356, 357].

The ray thrown by Saturn to the 7th House foretells powerful enemies who will fight in the open [Key 7]. *The Chance of Enmity,* which is counted in a nocturnal nativity from the 12th House to the lord of this House is found in the 3rd House and, in square aspect to Saturn, in Gemini, it shows secret enemies or traitors [Key 408]. Venus, being in the 12th and Mercury, lord of the 12th, being in opposition to the Sun, announce that the enemies will triumph over all resistance [Key 269].

What will be the consequence of the superiority of the enemies?

Saturn, in the 12th House, being neither in dignity nor in his own sign forecasts captivity or exile [Key 368], and as neither Jupiter nor Venus is at one of the cardinal points, this danger could entail a miserable death [Key 12]. Venus in the 12th also threatens captivity [Key 380].

The *Chance of Fortune* which is counted from the Sun to the Moon is placed in the 7th House where it suffers from the malefic opposition of Mars, also the conjunction of a ray from Saturn to Capricorn. This *Chance* is therefore in great peril [Key 410].

The *Chance of Captivity,* which is counted from the *Chance of Fortune* to Saturn, is found in the 6th House. It is in opposition to Saturn and its ruler Jupiter is square Saturn. Captivity is, therefore, imminent and strongly confirmed [Key 285] . . .

The ray which Mercury throws to the 1st House, Saturn being square Mercury, threatens condemnation for acts regarded as culpable in the foreign country where they were perpetrated. The only chance of salvation would be in flight [Key 209].

But this flight is impossible, for the *Chance of Death* is as ill-aspected as the *Chance of Captivity.* It is counted, in a nocturnal nativity, from the Moon to the 8th House and is found in the 6th House, opposition Saturn. Its ruler Jupiter is square Saturn ruler of the 8th House and this aspect shows death by murder [Key 394].

When does astrology show that death will take place?

Saturn and Venus, significators of captivity in the 12th House, which holds the bitterest trials of existence, seem by that very fact to be the nearest to the dénouement. The natural end of Maximilian's life would be about the 45th year by ordinary calculations of longevity. In view of the forecast of death by murder which will only take place after great vicissitudes of fortune, Saturn does not answer the question for it appears, on the Table of Life, from 1—7 years or from 50—56 years, that is to say, too early or too late, relative to the calculation of longevity, in a general sense.

Venus, on the other hand, appears from 29—35 years. Let us take 35, the latest of these years which finishes on 6 July 1867; since Maximilian was born in 1832, he would reach this phase of his destiny.

From 1867 let us subtract 1832, the year of birth; the result is 35 which, divided by 12, sum of the Houses, leaves a remainder of 11. Let us add 4, number of the sign Cancer, zodiacal sign of his birth, to 11 and from the product let us subtract 12, sum of the signs of the zodiac; the number 3 remaining signifies that for the progressed horoscope of 1867 Gemini, the 3rd sign, should be in the 1st House and Taurus in the 12th. The year 1867 belongs to one of the cycles of Saturn and should be studied on the *Circle of Fate of Mars*. Let us look there for the last act of the Mexican tragedy, the murder in a foreign land.

The epact of 1867 is marked by the number XXV. Birth having taken place on the 6 July 1832, the table of lunar months for 1867 places the Moon in its 6th day of waxing.

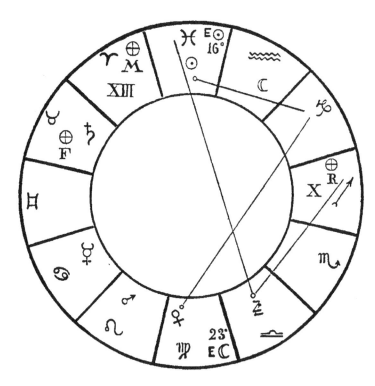

Horoscope of Maximilian of Mexico, death in 1867

The auguries of death are striking in the progressed horoscope for this year.

Mercury, lord of the year, in opposition to the ray cast by the Sun to Capricorn, shows first, for 1867, loss of position [Keys 167 and 90].

The *Chance of Fortune,* which is counted in a nocturnal nativity, from the Moon to the Sun is found in the 2nd House. The Moon, ruler of this Chance, since Cancer is her throne, being opposition Mars, square Saturn, shows complete ruin [Key 410].

Saturn, in the 12th House, both of the nativity and the progressed horoscope, foretells very great misfortune [Key 521].

The Moon in Aquarius, a masculine sign, square Mars, opposition Saturn, and the 9th House having Saturn as ruler which has Aquarius as its throne, this configuration reveals an enemy to be greatly feared [Key 505].

Gemini, in the 12th House at birth, passing into the 1st House, gives evidence of a friend becoming an enemy [Key 512].

The Moon, more elevated than Saturn and in square aspect, shows secret or open treachery, the consequences of which will consign Maximilian to the violent death shown in his natal horoscope [Key 42].

Mars having passed into Leo, the Moon in its waxing phase and Mars afflicted by the square from Saturn—this configuration shows risings against princes, also traps and ambushes [Key 438].

Chance of Captivity, which is counted in a nocturnal nativity from the *Chance of Fortune* to Saturn, is found in the 11th House, under the symbol of the Reaper, Arcanum XIII. Mars is ruler and is square Saturn [Key 402]. These malefic aspects render captivity inevitable.

The waxing Moon opposition Mars, foretells a miserable death [Key 132].

The waxing Moon square Saturn foretells a violent death [Key 38].

The *Chance of Death,* which is found in a nocturnal nativity from the Moon to the 8th House, is found in the 9th House where Saturn is ruler, Saturn having its throne in Aquarius. Afflicted by its ruler, in square aspect, and by the opposition of Mars, it renders almost inevitable the murder of Maximilian and impresses on all the earlier presages the seal of an ominous Fate.

The treachery of Colonel Lopez at Quérétaro is apparent to us under the veil of the Arcana.

Aspects of the Moon have clearly revealed to us the violent death.

Let us try to establish the fatal day.

Mercury, lord of the year, rules the first 57 days of 1867, that is to say, from 1 January to 26 February.

Mars rules the following 36 days, from 27 February to 3 April.
Venus governs the next 33 days, from 4 April to 6 May.
Jupiter rules the next 30 days, from 7 May to 5 June.
Then begins on 6 June the fatal influence of the Moon, in force for 71 days, and, on 19 of the same month, the ephemeral Empire of Mexico crumbled under the corpse of Maximilian.

The three horoscopes in this book are examples of what is called in ordinary language the decrees of Fate. The art of casting horoscopes and of using the Keys for judging them have been, I hope, sufficiently elucidated to permit the reader to practise in his turn. I beg him in conclusion never to lose sight of the fundamental principle of horoscopic divination.

'All the events which in their totality make up life on earth are only tests, designed by Divine Wisdom for the education of our intelligence and our will. Fate,' said the Magi, 'is the natural order of events, from effects and causes, in the system established by absolute Reason. But the Will is the director of the powers of Intelligence to reconcile the liberty of individuals with the necessity of things. A wise use of Will produces an incalculable power and makes Fate itself serve for the fulfilment of the plans of the man who takes Eternal Truth and Immortal Justice as guides for all his actions.'

In consequence, whatever may be the signs and the aspects, remembering always the factor of human will, which God has created free, surmise with great reserve but never affirm. See in every horoscope a warning and a counsel; but beware of reading into it an inflexible decree of Destiny.

N O T E

It will be obvious to students that much of Book VI is not devoted to Astrology at all but to fortune-telling by means of questions, in which the author finds the answer. 'The more one studies this singular subject,' he writes, 'the more serious it appears; and without offering to the oracles a blind faith, for one must always make allowance for the part played by free-will in the handling of events, serious students will agree that between the names, the happenings and the word which expresses them, there obtains a secret, inexplicable but real affinity.' Psycho-analysis would be in agreement with him for, once a problem has been *correctly* stated, free from shifts and evasions, the solution, however much disguised, is to be looked for in the form of the statement itself.

At the close of the 19th century astrologers set out, as a well-known exponent put it, 'thoroughly to purify and re-establish the ancient science'. Not for the first time, rejected material has later proved to be valuable.

J.S.

BOOK SEVEN

BOOK SEVEN

THE GENERAL KEYS OF ASTROLOGY

THESE keys are drawn from *Occult Mathematics* by Julius Firmicus Maternus, and the *Commentaries* of Junctin of Florence on the *Apotelesmatic Doctrine* of Ptolemy of Pelusium (Péluse).

Of these three volumes sacred to the memory of Magism, Ptolemy's work should be consulted first; Firmicus Maternus clarifies the obscurities of the Ptolemaic revelation and Junctin's *Speculum* then becomes a complete manual, theoretical and practical, in which, converging towards a systematic unity, may be seen the medieval works of Qabalists, Arabs and Hebrews, the last masters of the science of which Morin de Villefranche under Louis XIII, Cagliostro under Louis XVI, and the Benedictine Pierre le Clerc under Bonaparte as First Consul, were the last disciples.

I borrow first from Julius Firmicus the explanation of the influences of the seven planets: *first* in the 12 *Houses; second* in the 12 *zodiacal signs; third* according to the *aspects* formed between them in the horoscope. That is the basis of astrology.

Next, I borrow from Junctin the explanation of the *planetary aspects* from which are forecast the principal misfortunes and perils which can menace existence. I extract from the same author the art of studying the *fortunate* or *unfortunate chances* which favour, thwart or destroy our plans.

These studies, presented under the title KEYS OF THE NATAL HOROSCOPE, may be used for the examination of the horoscope in general, the object being to give as possibilities [never definite assertions] the good and bad of which our destiny as a whole is composed.

Passing then to KEYS OF THE ANNUAL HOROSCOPE, again I extract from Junctin's work the method of comparing the aspects of the natal horoscope with those of a particular year.

PART I

KEYS OF THE NATAL HOROSCOPE

SATURN IN THE 12 HOUSES

1 *Saturn in the 1st House:* pride. If the nativity be diurnal, and if Mars be on one of the other cardinal points, or in a succedent house, great perils, many difficulties. If without good aspects from

the benefics, and if the waxing Moon be in aspect to Mars, danger of violent death.

If the nativity be nocturnal, without good aspects from the benefics, weariness of mind or body; the dangers shown by the horoscope increased.

Good aspects from the benefics diminish the risk of danger.

2 *In the 2nd House:* weakness of will. Diurnal: slow and tardy fortune. If Cancer, Scorpio or Pisces be in 2nd, lucky for business on the sea or waterways or for any industry using water. Nocturnal: illnesses, loss of goods, reverses. Mars angular, Moon [waxing] or the Sun square or opposition Saturn, danger of great trouble, especially if the Moon be in 8th and opposition Saturn. Mars in 7th, the native will be in danger from the spouse. If the waxing Moon be in 5th square Saturn and if Mars be in 4th, the partner may plot to kill the child.

3 *In the 3rd House:* Nocturnal: neglect of the true interests of life; conjunction Mercury and the Moon: character inclined to evil; sterile projects [or projects which rarely succeed]; danger in travel; discord with near relatives. Saturn square or opposition Mars, peril of unhappy death, brought on by evil actions. Saturn in 3rd or 9th, square Mars and the Moon conjunction square or opposition either, danger of homicidal action, bringing the penalty.

4 *In the 4th House:* nocturnal: weakness of stomach or chest; loss of goods or position. Moon conjunction, square or opposition Saturn, loss of children. Diurnal: love of gold, crude desire for gain, avarice.

5 *In the 5th House:* diurnal: good fortune. The Sun in the 1st, the waxing Moon in 5th with Saturn, chance to rise in the world, great elevation. Jupiter instead of Sun in 1st, less chance of elevation but favourable for worldly goods. Without the help of Jupiter or the Sun, but with the waxing Moon conjunction Saturn, chance of wealth mediocre but sufficient, according to the sphere in which the native is born. Nocturnal: changeable fortunes in youth, elevation at maturity; with waning Moon conjunction Saturn, loss of goods or of position in distant future; marriage probably childless or with loss of children. If Mars be in the 12th and Saturn in 5th and if the Moon be square or opposition either, danger of violent death.

6 *In the 6th House:* loss of goods, position, revolt of subjects against princes, clients against patrons, servants against masters. Waning Moon in conjunction, square or opposition, danger of serious illness; loss of reputation, wandering life, without support or rest. Mars in conjunction, square or opposition, danger of phthisis or fatal dysentery, above all, if the Moon be in 7th and if neither Jupiter nor Venus ameliorate the case by sextile or trine.

7 *In the 7th House:* sextile or trine Jupiter or Venus: long life, good fortune, avaricious character. Without good aspects from

benefics, trials in marriage, powerful enemies, nervous illnesses, dangerous haemorrhoids. Mercury in conjunction, Moon in 1st, Mars angular, danger of violent death.

8 *In the 8th House*: diurnal: augmentation or acquisition of means at maturity. Mars in conjunction: prospect of inheritance or of good legacy under a will. Nocturnal: Moon square or opposition, loss of goods, deception in enterprises, especially if the Moon be in Aquarius or Capricorn. Mars square or opposition [the Moon being as aforementioned], peril of violent death. If Saturn and the Moon, although in square or opposition, receive good aspects from Jupiter and Mars, material good fortune but inconstancy of conjugal affections.

9 *In the 9th House*: diurnal. Elevation in religious Hierarchy; great aptitude for studies in transcendental philosophy. Nocturnal: brain trouble; enmity of powerful persons, especially if the waning Moon approaches Saturn direct. More formidable enmities if Saturn be conjunct Moon and square or opposition Mars. Perils in journeys. If Saturn be in Sagittarius, Pisces, Leo or Libra, the dangerous forecasts are diminished.

10 *In the 10th House*: diurnal and in Aquarius or Libra: elevation of fortune; conjunct Sun without aspect from Mars: riches, glory, dignities; with sextile or trine from Mars, the presage is lessened; with Mars in square or opposition, the presage lessens still more. Nocturnal: little happiness, dispersion of property, cares in marriage, few or no children, especially if Saturn be in Aries, Cancer or Leo. Good aspects from Jupiter or Venus will weaken the effect of the bad aspects. If Saturn be angular, some misfortune may be forecast especially in connection with marriage or children. Conjunct Moon [waning] and in a feminine sign, danger of fall into great distress. In aspect with the waxing Moon: vicissitude, alternation of good and ill, success followed by downfall: if, in addition, Mercury be in good aspect, strength of mind and heart, especially if Saturn be ruler of the nativity. If Mercury be in bad aspect, danger of early death. Mars conjunct Moon a languishing, melancholic mind; restless, unsound character. If the Moon be at the end of her waning period, danger of phthisis. This danger will be greater if Saturn be ruler of the nativity and square or opposition Mars. If Saturn be in Leo, with Sun and Moon in conjunction, danger of death in captivity. If the 10th be occupied by Sagittarius or Pisces and if Saturn be conjunct Jupiter, danger of violent death. Saturn and Mars in Aries or Scorpio, rash crime followed by a terrible expiation. Mercury conjunct Saturn in Virgo or Gemini, danger of condemnation through false witness.

11 *In the 11th House*: small misfortunes followed by better times. Good aspects from Jupiter and Venus kindness and protection from powerful persons and the aged. If they be in square or opposition, deadly consequences of dangerous liaisons.

12 *In the 12th House:* sickness, misfortunes, disappointments, especially if square or opposition Moon, unless Jupiter or
Venus be angular. This presage is lessened in a diurnal nativity.
If the nativity be nocturnal, great danger of captivity or exile, and
even of a miserable death.

SATURN IN THE 12 SIGNS

13   In *Aries:* diurnal, signifies obstacles to fortune. In seven
and nine-year cycles, dangers escaped with difficulty unless the benefics be in good aspect. If Saturn be ruler of the nativity, disappointment in marriage. The Moon in square or opposition or if, in
Leo or Sagittarius it be in sextile or trine, marriage to a widow
or to a girl who is not a virgin. If, in the progressed horoscope,
Saturn be in Aries in the 6th or 8th House, danger of downfall in
such a year. In the 9th, grave dangers in travelling.

14   In *Taurus:* good inclinations but uncertain and precarious
fortunes, for the first half of life. Without help from the benefics,
unless the Moon be in good aspect to Venus, risk of loss of property,
distress, illnesses, perils in journeys, especially during the 9th, 14th,
25th and 32nd years, but if, during these periods, Jupiter or Venus
be in conjunction with Saturn, these threatened disasters disappear
or are greatly lessened. If a man born with Saturn in Taurus
marries before his 32nd year, he will rarely marry a virgin unless
in his 30th year Saturn was in Cancer, Scorpio or Capricorn.

15   In *Gemini:* signifies perils and illnesses until the 23rd year,
especially every 7th and 9th year. An ingenious and positive mind,
active but many obstacles in life. The man born in this sign will
gain when Saturn transits through Virgo; but let him not marry
during that time or the woman will not be virgin. If Jupiter
be in good aspect, marriage with a virgin but few or no children,
and separation. If Jupiter be in square or opposition frequent
dangers during life.

16   In *Cancer:* signifies intelligence and will; obstacles of fortune; loss of goods but this will be made up. Illnesses, attacks of
human malevolence, every 7th and 9th year, unless in those years
Jupiter, Venus or the Moon be in good aspect to Saturn. If
Saturn be in 8th or 12th House, or in the opposite houses, illnesses
or perils according to the nature of the house. The Moon in bad
aspect shows few or no children, open or secret inclinations towards
depraved beings. Saturn in the 3rd or 9th, dangerous journeys.

17   In *Leo:* signifies an envious nature. Unless it be in the 1st
decan, alternation of success and failure. If the Moon be not in
conjunction, two marriages, loss of children. If Saturn be in the
1st decan and in good aspect to the benefics, strength to surmount
the trials of life; good faith, good judgment, many friends.

18   In *Virgo:* signifies hindrances or illnesses in the 1st half
of life; inventive mind; aptitude for science; strength of mind

against obstacles and dangers; taste for public life. If, in transit, Saturn be in Taurus, Gemini, Sagittarius or Pisces, anxiety of mind, bodily sufferings, sudden or unforeseen dangers. Transitting Virgo, instability of fortune, alternation of good and ill fortune. Those who are born with Saturn in Virgo are rarely happy in marriage and give themselves up to passions full of dangers. If Saturn be ruler of the nativity, tardy and precarious fortune, dangerous journeys, menace of fall or drowning.

19 In *Libra:* with good aspects to the benefics signifies good fortune; without these aspects, the fortune is lessened; if the aspects be evil, the promise is negated. Mars in bad aspect signifies great perils every 7th and 9th year; in angular houses or by transit, danger of all kinds of misfortune and, in particular, a serious accusation and imprisonment. In a fortunate house, love of science but with a contradictory character and nervous susceptibility; kindness of elderly people, favour of highly placed personages; sentimental attachments bring him under the yoke of women.

20 In *Scorpio:* signifies troubles and dangers, especially every 7th and 9th year until the 42nd year. In good aspect to the benefics, these dangers will be removed. Disposition to rash and ill-considered resolutions which will make him fall into the snares of his enemies.

21 In *Sagittarius:* signifies torment of mind, bodily suffering, imprudent acts which will entail dangers especially every 7th or 9th year. If, in transit, Saturn and Sagittarius be in the 10th or 4th, popular risings, domestic discords and sometimes sentence and imprisonment. If Saturn be in Pisces by transit, the dangers disappear and good fortune comes according to the state of life of the native. Unless Jupiter be in good aspect, troubles in marriage caused by the spouse. Perils also on water or near water.

22 In *Capricorn:* signifies troubles, hope followed by deception, success followed by failure, miseries of an ambition which does not see the abysses. In the 5th, 7th, 9th, 15th, 21st and 27th years, great misfortune, according to the state of life of the native; but with good aspects from the benefics, a serious and prudent mind, a little melancholy, inclined to be proud, but attracting benefit and favour from powerful persons, especially if Saturn be in the 10th House.

23 In *Aquarius:* signifies friends, supporters and benefactors amongst the aged and powerful; but the first part of life will be only moderately lucky. Perils in journeys, sicknesses, danger of captivity will be manifest every seven and nine years. But if Jupiter and Mercury be in good aspect, better fortune. If Saturn transit Leo at the time, the dangers vanish . . . In bad aspect to Mars, danger of imprisonment but if at the same time, there be a good aspect to Jupiter, the danger is avoided. In favourable years, with good aspects, fortune will come easily according to the state of life of

the native. Priests, in particular, will be raised in the hierarchy. Constant danger of injury by iron or fire.

24 In *Pisces:* signifies loss of position and goods followed by restoration by the efforts of a persevering will. Sickness and dangers every 7th and 9th year; misfortune in marriage, danger of drowning. Better fortune when Saturn transits Cancer. Good fortune in the 1st decan of Leo. . . In good aspect to the benefics, bad aspects are ameliorated and dangers disappear.

SATURN AND ITS ASPECTS

25 Conjunction JUPITER: especially in a diurnal nativity, good fortune, elevation. If Mars, better placed, be in square or opposition, this prediction becomes a threat of misfortune.

26 Conjunction MARS: signifies powerless ambition; if in an unfortunate house, it signifies biliousness. This prediction is accentuated if they are angular, unless Jupiter be in Sagittarius or in Pisces in 1st or 10th.

27 Conjunction SUN: especially in an unfortunate house, nocturnal, danger of a miserable death. Placed in Leo, Capricorn or Aquarius, without good aspect to the benefics, carried away by parricidal hatred.

28 Conjunction VENUS: inconstancy of will and of conduct; poor choice of partner in marriage. If the conjunction be in Aquarius or Pisces, without good aspect to Jupiter, this prediction is strengthened.

29 Conjunction MERCURY: some infirmity of the voice or of hearing. Inclined to be unreliable, obstinate, given to dissimulation. Aptitude for science. Instability of fortune. Powerlessness before the trials of life.

30 Conjunction MOON: secret fear of death which discourages the will and destroys the creative activity of the mind. Diurnal, waxing Moon, without good aspects to the benefics, this prediction is ameliorated. Nocturnal, adversity and often an unfortunate end. If the benefics be in bad aspect, the bad augury is accentuated. Conjunction in the 8th, unless one of the benefics be angular, danger of death by the carelessness of a doctor.

31 Trine JUPITER: in a fortunate house, or if either be in its own house, signifies rise of fortune, gains, especially if the waxing Moon be also in good aspect. This aspect favours priests and if Mercury be also concerned, it signifies elevation to religious dignities. Mars in bad aspect destroys these promises. Unexpected gains, sometimes the discovery of hidden treasure.

32 Trine MARS: if the benefics be also in trine, signifies prosperity and elevation, according to the status of the native.

33 Trine SUN: in a fortunate house, diurnal, signifies eleva-

tion, especially if the two planets be in masculine signs. Nocturnal, loss of goods, deceptions followed by a return of good fortune.

34 Trine VENUS: in fortunate houses and without bad aspects, signifies a peaceable uneventful life, marriage often late in life, few or no children. Perils resulting from harmful liaisons.

35 Trine MERCURY: aptitude for science, serious and penetrating mind. Elevation according to position in life.

36 Trine waxing MOON: elevation according to position in life. If the Moon be waning, good fortune is lessened or comes late.

37 SATURN elevated square Jupiter: loss of goods and dangers; obstacles in enterprises and calculations which only produce poor results. Jupiter elevated, this prediction is ameliorated and the aspect may even bring good fortune.

38 SATURN elevated square Mars: impotent activity, illnesses, loss of goods. Mars elevated, short life, domestic unhappiness, loss of reputation, obstacle in enterprises, failure, deceptions. If both are square or opposition Moon, danger of violent death.

39 SATURN elevated, square Sun: loss of goods or position; misfortunes resulting from dangerous liaisons; loss of reputation. Sun elevated, domestic strife, obstacles in enterprises; nervous illnesses.

40 SATURN elevated square Venus: misfortunes occasioned by women; hopes disappointed. Venus elevated, happy marriage but the husband will be under the domination of the wife.

41 SATURN elevated square Mercury: weakness of mind, lack of resolution, inert before the trials of life, troubled by envy, enslaved under the will of another. Mercury elevated, the ill effects are lessened.

42 SATURN elevated square Moon: temperament weakened by bad moods. Discord between mother and child and sometimes the impulse towards parricide. Moon elevated: many dangers, sometimes terminated by a miserable death. Disappointment in marriage, loss of reputation; domestic strife, deserted by friends, public or secret betrayals.

43 SATURN opposition JUPITER: loss of children, misfortunes, dangers. If Saturn be in 1st and Jupiter be in 7th, a little happiness will succeed long and cruel trials.

44 SATURN opposition MARS: contradictions, obstacles, failure, dangers, unsatisfied envy, danger of great distress, serious illnesses, frequent fear of death, domestic strife. In the horoscopes of princes, danger of terrible seditions. These presages may be still more formidable if this opposition be not tempered by a good aspect from Jupiter. If the Moon, angular, form also a square or opposition aspect, very grave perils, captivity, exile and sometimes violent death in public. Saturn or Mars in 5th or 10th, great misfortune, loss of position. Middle age is the worst time. Saturn or Mars in 3rd, 6th, 9th or 12th, these presages will be less formidable. Every

opposition of Saturn to Mars, without good aspect from Jupiter or Venus, danger of violent death.

45 SATURN opposition SUN: [without Jupiter in good aspect to Sun] signifies collapse of fortune, downfall in great distress, peril of unhappy death. This augury is stronger, if the opposition be in feminine signs.

46 SATURN opposition VENUS: luxury, unhappy marriage, choice of a bad partner, separation.

47 SATURN opposition MERCURY: haughty spirit creating enemies and serious embarrassment of position. Aptitude for science, penetration, sagacity, which however bring no financial gains.

48 SATURN opposition MOON: many perils. In bestial signs, danger of injury by an animal. In human signs, danger of a trap. In water signs, danger of drowning or of death by inflammation. This aspect also signifies the necessity to flee the country.

JUPITER IN THE 12 HOUSES

49 *In the 1st House:* diurnal, if without bad aspects, signifies elevation. With bad aspect from Saturn or Mars, eclipse. Nocturnal and Jupiter unfortunate, loss of goods and of position. If the waxing Moon be in good aspect, powerful friendships, considerable elevation according to the status of the native.

50 *In the 2nd House:* inheritance, or adoption by foreigners. Mercury in conjunction, sextile or trine, riches likely. If these aspects be diminished by square or opposition from Saturn or Mars, vicissitudes of fortune and alternation of good and ill.

51 *In the 3rd House:* balance of gains and losses in life. It inspires prudence, moderation of wishes and favours modest enterprises and short journeys.

52 *In the 4th House:* diurnal, signifies elevation, gives the esteem of princes and the great. It creates legislators, judges, royal envoys, sacerdotal dignitaries. It discovers hidden treasure and promises stable fortune. If the Sun be in opposition, loss of goods or of position, followed by a return of fortune; discord in the family. Nocturnal, mediocre fortune which time will improve.

53 *In the 5th House:* diurnal, dignity of judges, especially if in one of its own signs, or sign of exaltation, or in the sign of the Sun. Good aspect from Mars signifies good fortune in the profession of arms. Mercury and Moon in good aspect, without aspect from Mars, fortune with princes and the great. If Venus only be in aspect with Jupiter, good fortune, Nocturnal, if Mars, Venus or Moon be in bad aspect with Jupiter, many vices. Mars, in opposition, dangerous quarrels with subjects, clients or other inferiors. Jupiter in 5th favours priests and those who seek their aid.

54 *In the 6th House:* nocturnal, opposition Saturn, Mars or Sun, signifies many ills, especially if it rules the sign on the 1st or 10th. This presage is further accentuated if the waning Moon

be in conjunction or square. The waxing Moon in sextile or trine without bad aspect, diminishes the evils.

55 *In the 7th House*: diurnal, signifies riches, happy old age, if without bad aspect; helps to overcome obstacles and conquer enemies. Nocturnal, disappointments in marriage, early loss of wife or son, if with bad aspects. However, age will bring some increase of fortune.

56 *In the 8th House:* loss of goods, powerful enemies, formidable sedition against princes, peril of violent death. Saturn or Mars in opposition, irascible character with transports of rage approaching dementia. Mercury and the waxing Moon in good aspect, fortune in association with princes. Danger of early death, unless elsewhere longevity be clearly indicated.

57 *In the 9th House:* diurnal, good fortune in the priesthood. Some suffering of mind or body. In a favourable sign and in good aspect, fortune met with in travelling. In bad aspect, the reverse happens.

58 *In the 10th House:* diurnal, signifies elevation, popularity in public life; high dignity in the priesthood; luxury in private life. High rank which does not diminish if without bad aspects. If there be a bad aspect, unless Venus be in the 7th, the prediction given will be reversed. Nocturnal: weak character, easily deceived, loss of goods.

59 *In the 11th House:* diurnal, great fortune if in conjunction with the waxing Moon and if the Sun and Venus be in good aspect. Nocturnal: this presage is weakened. With Mars in 8th, fortune followed by downfall.

60 *In the 12th House:* victory over the most powerful enemies, especially if Saturn or Mars be in 1st. Mars in 8th, peril of violent death. Saturn and the Sun in opposition, threat of great calamity. Waning Moon in opposition, downfall in profound distress. Waxing Moon, and without bad aspect from Saturn, Mars, in favourable signs and houses, and if Venus be in good aspect, the favourable presages are strengthened. If Jupiter be very badly aspected, distress, captivity, exile, proscription.

JUPITER IN THE 12 SIGNS

61 In *Aries:* especially if angular and in good aspect with Saturn, Mars, Sun, Venus, Mercury or Moon, signifies happiness in enterprises, friendship and favour of powerful persons.

62 In *Taurus:* difficult beginnings and perils succeeded by powerful friendships, fortunate enterprises. Favour of distinguished women but dangerous liaisons with male perverts. Strength of mind, spirit of justice, devoted heart, boldness. Ingratitude of friends. Favours the fortune of priests.

63 In *Gemini:* powerful friendships and good fortune but exposed to vicissitudes and sudden reverses until the 45th year.

After that age, peaceful life. Aptitude for science and gain through negotiations.

64   In *Cancer:* powerful friendships which do not last. When Saturn transits Aquarius or Pisces, dangers, troubles, sickness, discord with important persons, quarrels with near relatives, false accusations, malicious prosecution. These presages will be changed when Saturn transits Cancer or, better still, Leo for then the enemies will be vanquished. In Cancer, Jupiter always brings alternations of good and ill.

65   In *Leo:* wisdom, strength of mind, sympathy and favour of important persons. Saturn in trine from Aries brings thwarting of fortune but in trine from Sagittarius, enterprises will succeed. However, there will be a bad choice of spouse and little happiness in marriage.

66   In *Virgo:* honesty, fidelity in affections, but instability of fortune, and unfavourable opportunities when Saturn transits its place in the nativity. When Saturn is in Pisces torments of mind, loss of property, illnesses followed by better conditions. Jupiter in Virgo favours negotiations.

67   In *Libra:* difficult beginnings especially if Saturn or Moon oppose; but when this unfortunate experience is over, opportunities improve. Favours fortune for priests, gives the goodwill of the great and promises inheritance or legacies.

68   In *Scorpio:* religious spirit, good opportunities for the future, especially when Saturn transits Cancer. Saturn in Pisces, in good aspect to Mars, powerful friends; journeys by water which will bring great profit. However, Jupiter in Scorpio signifies alternation of good and ill.

69   In *Sagittarius:* elevation; success in all interests unless ill-aspected. Saturn in square or opposition, misfortune in marriage, hardship or loss of children.

70   In *Capricorn:* goodwill of the great; fortunate enterprises according to status, provided there be no bad aspects. Particularly favourable for the fortune of priests.

71   In *Aquarius:* in 1st or 2nd: great fortune, if it receive trine aspect from any planet well-placed. At the same time, it shows carelessness about the interests of life, softness, love of repose, mental laziness. Does not augur well for the fortune of priests.

72   In *Pisces:* aptitude for science, wisdom, remarkable faculties, but danger of adversity, sudden and overwhelming. However the end of life will have its consolations.

JUPITER IN ITS ASPECTS

73   Conjunction MARS: elevation, success in enterprises, especially if angular and if in a sign ruled by Jupiter or Mars.

74   Conjunction SUN: good opportunities if Oriental: danger of adversity and distress if Occidental.

75 Conjunction VENUS: sympathy and support from important persons. Danger of seduction for young girls. With Mars also in conjunction, great dangers. If Mars, Jupiter and Venus be in Libra, Capricorn or Aquarius and if Saturn be in the next house, and if the Moon be in aspect with Mars with no planet between them, and if the Sun be in 10th, and if the Moon be in Cancer in 1st, danger of incest between the son and the mother or the step-mother. In a female horoscope, the girl will love her father or her step-father.

76 Conjunction MERCURY: great elevation in the priesthood or in law; great aptitude for mathematics; good fortune with princes or powerful persons.

77 Conjunction MOON [waxing]: fortunate; [waning] unfortunate.

78 Trine MARS: elevation, happiness in enterprises; fortune with princes or the great; boldness, self-confidence, triumph over enemies.

79 Trine SUN: constant good fortune except when badly aspected.

80 Trine VENUS: happiness in marriage, increase of wealth, favour of the great especially of women in high place.

81 Trine MERCURY: strength of mind and heart; fortunate opportunities in enterprises; aptitude for science and art; fortune with princes and the great.

82 Trine FULL MOON: elevation, celebrity, high office; rise of fortune according to status.

83 JUPITER elevated, square Mars: powerful protection of the great, rise of fortune. Mars elevated leads to mistakes which will compromise future chances and create frequent dangers.

84 JUPITER elevated square Sun: rise of fortune. Sun elevated: good fortune, followed by the attacks of enemies which may cause the native to flee the country.

85 JUPITER elevated square Venus: many friends; favour and support of women. Venus elevated promises the joys of love followed by disappointment, broken promises, or separation unless Venus have four dignities in the same sign as Jupiter.

86 Square MERCURY: formidable uprisings and public anger against princes. Discord between relatives, sometimes mortal hate. Elevation of fortune and riches if Mercury have four dignities in the same sign as Jupiter.

87 Square WAXING MOON: elevation of fortune and protection against enemies. WANING MOON: great misfortune especially if nocturnal.

88 Opposition MARS: vicissitudes of fortune, loss of goods; alliances and friendships which change to hostility; great perils resulting from dangerous liaisons or rash actions.

89 Opposition SUN: loss of goods, especially if nocturnal.

90   Opposition VENUS: impotence, failure in enterprises; infidelity; deceptions, perfidies, ingratitude on the part of friends; misfortune in marriage.

91   Opposition MERCURY: serious uprisings against princes, explosions of popular hatred. Domestic discord.

92   Opposition FULL MOON: fortunate enterprises, strength of mind in the trials of life. WANING MOON: danger of great misfortune, especially if nocturnal.

MARS IN THE 12 HOUSES

93   *In the 1st House:* in masculine sign, nocturnal, without good aspect to Jupiter, ruinous extravagance. If in Aries or Scorpio and in good aspect to Jupiter, chance of fortune in the army. Diurnal, bold cunning but inconstant; inability to carry out plans, precarious fortune. If Jupiter be in his own sign, or in exaltation and trine Mars, chances improve. Mars in 1st, danger of exile, especially for princes and the great.

94   *In the 2nd House:* if in conjunction or opposition Moon [waxing], danger of wounds, perhaps captivity. Danger removed if Jupiter be in good aspect. Nocturnal, danger for warriors; loss of goods for all others if Jupiter be not in good aspect.

95   *In the 3rd House:* elevation but at the cost of great effort. Inquisitive character, usurps the property of others and capable of a secret crime. Jupiter in 7th or 11th, great fortune laboriously acquired. In bad aspect with Jupiter, Venus or Saturn, dangerous journeys, ambush or some great unforeseen misfortune.

96   *In the 4th House:* nocturnal, good opportunities for army men, in the employment of princes or great men, but little gain. Diurnal, danger of wounds by iron. Sun in conjunction, square or opposition, frequent dangers. If a sign ruled by Mars be in 1st, and if Mars itself be in 4th or if the *Chance of fortune* be in a sign ruled by Mars, perils more certain.

97   *In the 5th House:* nocturnal and in sign or exaltation of Jupiter, or in trine, elevation of fortune and prosperity in all enterprises. The same applies also to Venus. Diurnal, loss of goods or of position, unsettled place of abode, emigration to distant lands, frequent dangers. But if Jupiter or Venus be in sextile or trine to Mars, fortune acquired in distant journeys and happy return home. Waxing Moon opposition Mars, great vicissitudes, menace of captivity, unless Mars be in a sign of Jupiter or in good aspect.

98   *In the 6th House:* many evils, life full of vicissitudes, illnesses. Favourable for the study and practice of medicine. Menace of revolt of subjects against princes and of criminal attempts of servants against their masters.

99   *In the 7th House:* great misfortunes and perils. It excites to crimes, to homicide and to treason. With Aries or Scorpio in ascendant, it does not signify violent death but it shortens the

ordinary length of life, especially if Jupiter be not in good aspect with the 1st and the Moon. If a sign of Mars be not in 1st and if Mars be opposition or square the waxing Moon, menace of premature death. Any sign other than Aries or Scorpio in 7th with Mars therein brings peril of violent death. If Jupiter be not in sextile or trine, menace of death by fall or from the sufferings of captivity. Nocturnal, danger of wounds by iron. If Mars be ruler of the year, it inflicts great bodily sufferings. The same applies to the Moon. If Saturn be in 1st or 10th and if the waxing Moon be neighbour to Mars or if, waning, she be next to Saturn, presage of many ills; danger of accusations, of captivity, sometimes even of capital sentences. Peril of fatal falls, of death by ambush or by drowning. Mars in a human sign, peril of death by sword. Sun opposition or angular, danger of perishing in flames. Mars in 7th menaces some wound by iron or fire, either by accident or by the hand of a murderer. Disappointment in marriage and death of children.

100   *In the 8th House:* loss of goods. Sun and Moon in opposition, danger of blindness. If Mars be alone, menace for princes of serious popular risings; for others, adversities. Moon in 2nd, Jupiter without aspect to Moon or Mars, danger of violent death. Moon in 2nd and in human sign, peril of death by iron, by a murderer or by capital punishment. Moon in an earth sign, peril of violent death in a lonely place or in the desert. Moon in a water sign, danger of drowning. Moon in an air sign, danger of death by fall. Nocturnal, Mars inspires cunning, disregard for danger; at the same time, it threatens violent death or sudden death. Jupiter in aspect with Mars lessens the dangers. Jupiter in 1st, in Taurus, Libra, Sagittarius or Pisces with Venus opposition Mars the unfortunate presages are lessened in effect still more.

101   *In the 9th House:* diurnal, favourable, if in one of its own signs or in its sign of exaltation. If Jupiter be in 1st, fortunate opportunities. Nocturnal, with Jupiter in 1st, a sign of elevation but with the danger of perils in travelling. If Gemini or Virgo be in the 9th, or Taurus or Libra, prospect of aptitude for science, eloquence and the renown associated therewith. In Aries, Scorpio, Sagittarius or Pisces, or in its sign of exaltation, with Jupiter in 1st, a malicious mind, little frankness, tendency to perjury. Mars in 9th, favourable for the priesthood, signifying elevation in office.

102   *In the 10th House:* nocturnal, in a masculine sign or in Sagittarius or Pisces, or in its sign of exaltation, signifies perils and deceptions but nevertheless favourable for fortune; civil and military dignities. If the Moon be near Mars and if Jupiter in one of its signs or in its sign of exaltation be angular, one may predict power, command, authority; with Jupiter less favourably placed, the prediction is weakened. If Saturn occupies another angle, with Mars in 10th and Jupiter in 1st, the native may be raised to the highest fortune but death will be early; some of those who will be

elevated under these aspects will lose power and life together or they will fall into the power of their enemies. Nocturnal and feminine signs, sterile marriage, or few children, or children who will have a short life. Diurnal, little success in enterprises, loss of goods, proscriptions, condemnations, necessity to leave the country, exile, death in distant land.

·103 *In the 11th House:* much good signified; popular sympathy for princes and other important personages, ability to reach high positions if the Moon be waning and if Jupiter be in good aspect; for example, it is particularly fortunate for those who become judges or for professions connected with tribunals. Mars in its sign of detriment or fall, or if afflicted, signifies the ruin of enterprises, treason of friends, and similar troubles. Mars conjunction Saturn or if one of them be in this house and the other conjunction or square Moon and if Mars and Mercury be in any aspect, signifies dementia, epilepsy or violent death as the result of an accident.

104 *In the 12th House:* diurnal. Great illness. Princes menaced by popular risings. Frequent perils if Jupiter be not in good aspect. Nocturnal, these presages are lessened. Diurnal, Jupiter conjunction Mars, angular, with Saturn on another angle, portent of violent death by external cause or by suicide. Mars angular with Venus on another angle, draws to thoughts about murder or suicide in marriage. If, instead of Venus, Mercury be angular, danger of heart disease, and sometimes of capital punishment. The Sun in the same position, danger of death by fire. If the waxing Moon be in conjunction with one of the planets so placed, danger of violent death may be imminent.

MARS IN THE 12 SIGNS

105 In *Aries:* irritable character, quarrelsome, litigious, always ready to attack by word or action. Predisposition to licentiousness in youth.

106 In *Taurus:* boldness, temerity, ready to do anything to succeed. The young come under the yoke of women and fall into misfortunes resulting from this weakness. Knavish and perfidious character. Tendency to abduction, rape, adultery and therefore liable to the dangerous consequences of these acts.

107 In *Gemini:* love of arms and warlike strategy. Prudence with cunning. Acute mind in judges and officers of justice, facilitating inquiry and enabling them to discover hidden crimes.

108 In *Cancer:* favourable for those who choose a military career; also for the arts of medicine and surgery. It inspires boldness but with it, inconstancy of will. Menace of blindness.

109 In *Leo:* force of character, boldness but with a tendency to sadness. Serious illnesses threatened especially of the breast and stomach. Danger of blindness and sometimes of violent death.

110 In *Virgo:* predisposition to anger but this is held in leash

until a suitable occasion comes to take vengeance; sometimes homicide is contemplated. Danger of wounds and of blindness and sometimes a condition of distress.

111   In *Libra:* love of arms but exposes to great adversities. Danger of wounds by iron or fire but promises rest towards the end of the career unless other indications limit it too much.

112   In *Scorpio:* in a fortunate house, inspires strength of mind, boldness and predisposes to triumph over enemies. It signifies wisdom, good reputation, sometimes celebrity. However, it inclines to excess in the matter of love of women and leads to commit acts of violence in order to possess them. Fortunate sign for those who choose an army career, except in 1st or 12th.

113   In *Sagittarius:* effeminate, inactive at the beginning of life. It presages however, sympathy and favour of the great. Mars square Sun in 12th and in a human sign, especially if Mars be square Moon presages death by murder.

114   In *Capricorn:* gives courage and prepares sympathy and favour of powerful men.

115   In *Aquarius:* inclines to evil, to perfidy, to crime, to violent quarrels. Menace of blindness.

116   In *Pisces:* inclines to licentiousness. Favour of princes and the great.

MARS AND ITS ASPECTS

117   Conjunction SUN: loss of goods, afflictions, hard work. Danger of wounds by iron or fire. Weak and unstable in resolution. These predictions are strengthened if Mars and Sun be in angular or succedent house.

118   Conjunction VENUS: discords, embarrassments, law-suits occasioned by women. If the nativity be feminine, the woman will be bold and free in her manners. Dangerous adultery with men or women of inferior station, according to the sex of the subject of the horoscope.

119   Conjunction MERCURY: good judgment, an intelligence which seizes the interests of life but inclines to lying, unless Saturn be in good aspect. Mercury angular and the Moon in bad aspect, signifies evil thoughts, inclination to cheating and to theft.

120   Conjunction MOON: danger of wounds by iron and violent death. Angular: skill in the arts but with little profit and loss of goods.

121   Trine SUN: in fortunate house, rise of fortune especially if nocturnal and the Sun be elevated. This prediction is strengthened if Jupiter and the Moon be in good aspect; still more so, if Mars, Sun and Jupiter be in masculine signs.

122   Trine VENUS: gain, fruit of constant activity; happy marriage if Saturn be not in evil aspect. Inclination to pride and licentiousness and gains through the favour of women.

123   Trine MERCURY: in fortunate houses and favourable

signs, presages wisdom and success in enterprises; intelligence which knows how to turn aside threatened danger or to repair misfortunes. A shrewd mind and aptitude for sciences needing calculations.

124   Trine MOON: both well-placed and especially if the moon be waning, nativity nocturnal, forecasts good luck in enterprises. Elevation of fortune if Jupiter, at the same time, be sextile. If the Moon be full, this prosperity will be troubled by illness or vicissitudes.

125   MARS elevated square SUN: danger of a great adversity, upsetting all enterprises and all chances or occasions to succeed. Sun elevated, unfortunate, unhappy end. Rising of subjects against princes, bloodshed, popular hatred. Presages more accentuated if diurnal, especially if 1st be involved, or if Mars in 7th or 10th and if the Moon be waxing; then public administration would be shaken by irremediable excesses. Nocturnal, the same.

126   MARS elevated square VENUS: every kind of affliction occasioned by women. Venus elevated: secret licentiousness if Jupiter be conjunction Venus or trine Mars or Venus.

127   MARS elevated square MERCURY: all kinds of ills, all kinds of obstacles and lack of success and dangerous accusations. Nocturnal, less menacing. Mercury elevated: malice, dishonesty, cupidity, rapacity and wish to usurp. Peril of accusation and of captivity.

128   Square MOON: early death or many perils to menace life. Sometimes also public animosity, crushing accusations, danger of a miserable death, especially if the Moon be full. Bad choice of partner and unhappy marriage.

129   Opposition SUN: diurnal, future blindness and, if other aspects of the horoscope be dangerous, atrocious death. In every case, unexpected perils, menace of a terrible downfall. Nocturnal, serious illnesses, distress.

130   Opposition VENUS especially diurnal: vices, open or concealed; frequent illnesses especially if the opposition be in Cancer/Capricorn and if Jupiter does not temper it by a good aspect.

131   Opposition MERCURY: great adversity. Mercury in Capricorn or Aquarius shows exile.

132   Opposition MOON: early death after many afflictions. Blindness. Moon waxing, angular, menace of miserable death; disappointment in marriage.

THE SUN IN THE 12 HOUSES

133   *In the 1st House:* in Leo or Aries with good aspects, elevation. This prediction is lessened or negatived if there be bad aspects. Mars aspecting favourably, elevation exposed to the assaults of envy, to struggle, to ruin. Jupiter angular, in masculine sign with full Moon angular or succedent: can lead to the highest

elevation. Mars in 10th or 7th, Jupiter and Sun as before and Moon conjunction Mars: presage of violent death, or fall from power. Moon in 4th, Sun in 1st: fortune terminated by captivity or violent death, or at least by a humiliating and irreparable downfall. Sun in 1st, Saturn in 10th, full Moon in 4th or 7th, or in 2nd or 8th conjunction Mars; captivity, exile or violent death. Mars in succedent house, Moon angular or in another succedent house: presage of violent death and of downfall for princes. Moon in 10th, 7th or 4th with no aspect to Mars; Jupiter conjunction Sun, on another angle or in a succedent house: very high elevation. If, in addition, Saturn and Mars be in any aspect: elevation followed by downfall, exile or violent death. Nocturnal, in bad aspect to Saturn or Mars: miscarriage of enterprises. Saturn conjunction Mars in 12th, Moon in 6th, violent death, especially for those who live under the dominion of others. Sun and Moon angular, Saturn and Mars in Cancer or Leo or angular: presage of violent death.

134   *In the 2nd House:* grace and goodness but a languishing nature, exposed without defence to the shocks of life. Jupiter or Venus in good aspect, increase of wealth. Sometimes natives rise from obscurity to a great fortune but at the cost of long and painful effort.

135   *In the 3rd House:* wisdom and good judgment in the affairs of life, especially if Jupiter and Mercury be in good aspect. The Sun in Leo, Sagittarius, Pisces, Taurus, Libra, Gemini or Virgo inclines to religion and favours those who consecrate their lives to the priesthood. Saturn and Jupiter conjunction Sun predisposes to perjury, to perfidy and mental troubles. Fortune increased in a foreign country.

136   *In the 4th House:* in aspect with Saturn or Mars presages loss of means or difficulty of acquiring means. Inconstancy of domestic affections. Mediocre but adequate fortune in old age if the horoscope show longevity.

137   *In the 5th House:* in a favourable sign and receiving good aspects, signifies goodness and favours the success of enter· prises. Venus in good aspect sometimes raises to a very high fortune. Even if a malefic be conjunction Sun, this favourable prediction will not be cancelled for the 5th is the house of good fortune. If the Sun be alone in 5th, danger of loss of children.

138   *In the 6th House:* many ills. Mars in 1st, danger of iron. If there be no benefic in 10th, loss of means. Jupiter and Venus conjunction Sun cancel these misfortunes. Sun alone in 6th, heart trouble. Discord and struggle between the prince and his subjects. Sun in 6th or 12th with the Moon, opposition Saturn, danger of violent death. Sun and Moon with Mars in Cancer, Scorpio or Pisces strengthens this presage death being caused by shipwreck or drowning.

139   *In the 7th House:* illnesses especially if with Saturn or Mars in conjunction, square or opposition. Moon conjunction Sun or in 10th, Jupiter being in its own sign or in sign of exaltation presage of elevation which may be confirmed by the *Chance of Fortune* angular. If, in addition Jupiter be in good aspect to the Sun, likelihood of the highest elevation. But if Saturn or Mars be in 2nd or 8th, this hope will be disappointed, or if the elevation be attained, it will be followed by downfall, exile or captivity, and sometimes suicide. Mercury conjunction or trine Sun gives aptitude for letters or science. Saturn conjunction Sun and Mercury inspires malice, ill-will, and refuses means by which intelligence could triumph. Sun in 7th signifies numerous and very powerful enemies.

140   *In the 8th House:* in bad aspect to Saturn or Mars predisposes to disease of the heart and of neighbouring organs. Moon in opposition, with Saturn and Mars [or one of them] in square, many illnesses, especially of the head, but these illnesses will be followed by healing if Jupiter and Venus be linked to the above aspects by good aspects. Mercury conjunction Moon: the illnesses will not be healed nor relieved except by supernatural means. The Sun in 8th, the Moon in 10th and Leo or Cancer in 1st is a presage of an access of madness which will be the cause of violent death.

141   *In the 9th House:* conjunction Jupiter or Venus presages happiness and increase of wealth. If, instead, Saturn or Mars be found with the Sun there will be danger in travelling and even of a miserable death in a foreign land. Sun in 9th signifies elevation of fortune for priests especially if in a masculine sign.

142   *In the 10th House:* diurnal and in Leo, Sagittarius or Pisces or in its sign of exaltation signifies high fortune. Mars in 1st, 4th or 7th signifies the same fortune but with great perils and pursued by envy and hatred. Mars in 7th and the full Moon in 1st or 10th, presages captivity or exile. Mars in 1st or 9th with Moon in bad aspect presages violent death. Sun in 10th favoured by good aspects gives the opportunity to the most obscure man to raise himself to a great fortune. If in a sign of fire, Aries, Leo or Sagittarius, the good auguries will be more strongly confirmed.

143   *In the 11th House:* elevation, especially if Jupiter or Venus be in good aspect. This elevation will be due to the good offices and devotion of friends. If a malefic be with the Sun or in bad aspect, it signifies misfortune, not for the native but for the children who may one day be his. The Sun in 11th or in 6th with the Moon and with Saturn in opposition is a menace of violent death. If Sun and Moon be in a water sign and if Mars be in conjunction, the presage will be stronger. Sun in 11th with Saturn, Mars and Mercury, with Moon in 3rd without good aspect to Jupiter presages violent death in expiation of a crime.

144   *In the 12th House:* loss of means, captivity, sad life, grave and dangerous illnesses. This presage will be stronger if a malefic be with the Sun; even if a benefic be with the Sun, the misfortune follows for 12th is the house of the evil Genius. Treason of subjects against their princes and oppression by powerful enemies of every kind.

THE SUN IN THE 12 SIGNS

145   In *Aries:* variable fortune; alternation of elevation and fall. But Sun angular, without bad aspect from Saturn, or succedent, there will be some fortune. The Sun badly aspected, the evil will dominate; menace of burning fever. Sun in Aries, Moon in Libra: danger of violent death.

146   In *Taurus:* contests, law-suits, dissipation of means by licentiousness. If bad aspects threaten, much adversity.

147   In *Gemini:* mediocre fortune, limited mind, loss of means unless a favourable planet aspects. This sign is however favourable for the study of science and especially mathematics; but little profit will be drawn therefrom.

148   In *Cancer:* many enemies, many tribulations but this presage is lessened by the presence of good aspects. Frequent journeys. If the Dragon's Tail be conjunction Sun, Saturn or Mars, menace of drowning or blindness.

149   In *Leo:* great elevation and proud self-confidence especially if in a fortunate house and with good aspects. Life will however be troubled by some illnesses. Less favourable if nocturnal. Diurnal, if the Sun be angular or succedent, the outlook is excellent.

150   In *Virgo:* a high degree of intelligence. If badly aspected, a sign of weakness or of great difficulty in enterprises.

151   In *Libra:* sign of the Sun's fall, some great adversity likely. It is especially fatal for princes and without special succour from the Almighty, the great ones of the world will be overthrown and sometimes reduced, in their fall and terror, to find not a single man to whom they could look for help. This presage will be the more grave if the Sun be in an unfortunate house and square or opposition Saturn or Mars.

152   In *Scorpio:* reputation and sometimes celebrity; sympathy and favour of princes and the powerful. This presage will not hold if the Sun be badly aspected by a malefic.

153   In *Sagittarius:* elevation but abuse of fortune which will lead to punishment. Danger of losing children especially if the Sun be badly aspected. This sign favours the elevation of priests to high rank in their profession. It inclines to licentiousness.

154   In *Capricorn:* reputation and sometimes celebrity. If badly aspected this presage will be lessened and honour will be degraded by frequenting low society. Nocturnal: vicissitudes. Diurnal: success in enterprises.

155   In *Aquarius:* elevation, but princes and great men, born under this sign will seldom find faithful subjects or obedient servants. Vacillating grandeur, changing fortune, dangerous enmities, menace of downfall and despoiling especially if nocturnal. Diurnal, less danger.

. 156   In *Pisces:* arrogance, tyrannical will which desires to subdue everyone and will stop at nothing to accomplish its designs; consequently a painful struggle with resistance and adversity especially if the Sun be badly aspected. The sign is nevertheless favourable for priests and promises elevation in the Hierarchy. Leaning to licentiousness.

THE SUN AND ITS ASPECTS

157   Conjunction VENUS and in 7th: diurnal, reputation and sometimes celebrity, great fortune, especially if Venus and Sun be in 1st or 10th and without bad aspect to Saturn or Mars. Fortune favoured by the protection of highly-placed women.

158   Conjunction MERCURY: rich faculties of mind which will lead to fortune: wisdom, eloquence, imagination.

159   Conjunction MOON: some adversity and diminishes good fortune. In 7th, presages misfortune in marriage and illness, especially blindness. However, there will be useful friendships although they will not last.

160   Trine VENUS: the same as Jupiter trine Venus.

161   Trine MERCURY: the same as Jupiter trine Mercury.

162—Trine MOON: friendly nature, lover of peace, receiving the fruits of such a character especially if the Moon be waxing; if waning, the prospect is not so good. If they are not in fortunate houses or if one of them receive bad aspects, the good presage does not hold.

163   Square VENUS: the same as Jupiter square Venus.

164   Square MERCURY: the same as Jupiter square Mercury.

165   Square MOON: changing fortune; alternation of good and ill; nervous illnesses; many ill-wishers and enemies.

166   Opposition VENUS: the same as Jupiter opposition Venus.

167   Opposition MERCURY: the same as Jupiter opposition Mercury.

168   Opposition MOON: changing fortune, alternation of good and ill, irresolute character, troubled spirit in difficult time.

VENUS IN THE 12 HOUSES

169   *In the 1st House:* nocturnal, riches of the mind, friendship of princes and of the great if Venus be in Gemini or Virgo. If it be in a human sign, it predicts for priests dignities in their Hierarchy. With good aspects, it presages riches. In conjunction with Mercury in the aforementioned signs, it promises to priests the highest rank. Favourable for those who wish to become musicians. In fixed sign, favour of princes. Diurnal, if Jupiter be

not in conjunction or trine, licentiousness and the shame attaching to it.

170   *In the 2nd House:* nocturnal, inventive spirit applied to the arts. Diurnal, great hindrances in enterprises. Saturn or Sun square or opposition, secret and infamous vices especially if Venus be in Capricorn or Aquarius, Aries or Scorpio, Gemini or Virgo. Elevation of priests to sacred dignities. Good fortune aided by the protection of highly-placed women.

171   *In the 3rd House:* in good aspect to Jupiter, good fortune. Conjunction Mercury or Moon, priests raised to high dignity. Gain through travel.

172   *In the 4th House:* diurnal, loss of means and great difficulty in obtaining more. Mercury in conjunction, perils incurred by adultery or abuse of confidence. Nocturnal, powerful friendships about the middle of life. Venus in Cancer or Capricorn, embarrassment, quarrels, law-suits, occasioned by women. In Aquarius, conjunction, square or opposition Moon, infamous vices. See also the presages for Jupiter in 4th.

173   *In the 5th House:* inspires goodness and presages good fortune. With good aspects from Jupiter, priests are raised to high dignities; success over the envious and over enemies and obstacles. Powerful friendships and fortune come through marriage. Aspected by the waxing Moon, high elevation but exposure to envy and strong hatred; suspicion and quarrels between husband and wife.

174   *In the 6th House:* without a benefic in 10th, unfortunate marriage. In a woman's horoscope, peril in childbirth; abortion or fatal operation. Nocturnal, if a benefic be in 10th, happiness in marriage and success in enterprises. If not cardinal and if the Moon, cardinal, receives a bad aspect from a malefic, menace of great misfortune and of being abandoned by relatives. In a man's nativity, love for servants or other women of low condition. In every nativity, kidney trouble, weakness of genital organs.

175   *In the 7th House:* nocturnal, in one of its own signs, nearly always longevity, unless very much afflicted. Mars in conjunction, leaning to licentiousness; if Saturn be in bad aspect to both from Cancer or Capricorn women will be very amorous. With Saturn in Capricorn and Mars in Aries, this presage will be stronger.

176   *In the 8th House:* diurnal, late marriage or with a sterile woman. Mercury conjunction Venus, with Saturn or Mars in bad aspect, loss of means, adversity, menace of death by spasms, convulsions, apoplexy. Nocturnal, legacy from a woman. Prompt death, without suffering, sometimes from a weapon of war.

177   *In the 9th House:* diurnal, favourable for priests and presages elevation in dignity, especially if Saturn be sextile or trine; nocturnal, this elevation will be even greater. Nocturnal and with Saturn and Mars conjunction or square Venus, misfortune occasioned by women, especially if malefics be in Cancer or Capricorn.

Jupiter in good aspect and Saturn and Mars not adverse: love of women of high rank who will help to bring fortune. Mars angular and square or opposition, many enemies and perils. Journeys and the interests attaching to them.

178 *In the 10th House:* in good aspect, presages elevation of fortune. Mercury in conjunction and Saturn in bad aspect, distinguished reputation followed by disparagement. Mars in aspect, has the same effect. Venus in a favourable sign and well-aspected; favour of princes and of the great.

179 *In the 11th House:* afflicted by bad aspects from Saturn and Mars, infamous vices and leanings against nature; but if Saturn and Mars be in good aspect, powerful friends who will help to bring fortune. Aspected by the Moon; riches and lucrative employment. Mercury in good aspect to Venus and the Moon: powerful friendships, fidelity in affection, success in enterprises.

180 *In the 12th House:* unhappiness caused by women. Mars and Mercury in bad aspect: traps laid by servants or other women of low condition. Licentious instinct. Diurnal, danger of a frightful death occasioned by the intrigues of women. Saturn aspecting Venus, a mind incapable of doing any good, especially in nocturnal nativity. Venus in Virgo, Capricorn or Aquarius conjunction Saturn, Sun or Mars: peril of violent death occasioned by women.

VENUS IN THE 12 SIGNS

181 In *Aries:* vices of mind or body, anxiety, cares, sadness, weariness of life, impure love especially if Mars aspects Venus. If there be a good aspect from Jupiter the outlook is better. Moon conjunction Venus and the Sun in a masculine sign, unbridled licentiousness.

182 In *Taurus:* rise of fortune especially if Jupiter be in good aspect. Dangerous passions for women in low estate.

183 In *Gemini:* goodness, wisdom, refinement, ingenious mind especially if Mercury be in good aspect. Saturn, in transit, in conjunction, square or opposition: great embarrassment of position. Licentious passions. Venus in 9th and in good aspect: elevation in dignity for priests.

184 In *Cancer:* greed, abandonment to gross voluptuousness especially if Jupiter be sextile or trine.

185 In *Leo:* vices, leaning to evil, precarious fortune, frequent straits but Jupiter in good aspect brings amelioration and hope for favours of the great; good reputation, modest fortune. Without good aspect to Jupiter, dissolute manners.

186 In *Virgo:* dangerous relations with people in low condition, cares, disappointments, especially if Venus or Mercury be badly aspected by malefics. Jupiter in good aspect to Venus or Mercury gives hope of some favours from fortune. Venus in 9th: kindness and support from priests and religious persons.

187   In *Libra:* spirit of justice but danger of adversity. Dangerous passions for women of low degree.

188   In *Scorpio:* violent character, quarrelsome, proud, stops at nothing to satisfy his lusts. Shameful passions and such as are against nature, especially if the Moon be in Aries and the Sun in a masculine sign.

189   In *Sagittarius:* aptitude for an army career and goodwill of powerful men. In bad aspect with a malefic: loss of goods or of position. Discord with near relations and, for princes, enmity and revolt of subjects. For priests, elevation; for others, goodwill and support from women of high rank.

190   In *Capricorn:* gentleness, love of the table, instincts of luxury and of refinement in pleasure. In cadent house and with bad aspect from Saturn, perverse and dangerous associations. Danger of perilous adulteries.

191   In *Aquarius:* effeminate type, inertia, fornication, adultery.

192   In *Pisces:* knowledge and wisdom, aptitude for the study of law, good reasoning power, ingenious mind; favour of princes and of the great, especially if Jupiter be in good aspect. This benefit will however be mixed with some unhappiness. For priests, elevation; for others, favour and support from women of high rank. In bad aspect, discord with near relatives, neighbours, subordinates of all kinds; for princes, danger of popular risings.

Venus and its Aspects

193   Conjunction MERCURY: diminishes the mental faculties and disturbs judgment. Jupiter in good aspect: protection from women of high rank. In 1st, opportunities for elevation. Conjunction with Mercury and Dragon's Tail in 7th, danger of a horrible death.

194   Conjunction MOON: infidelity in marriage, leaning to adultery and danger of being drawn into crimes provoked by sensual passions. This presage will be stronger if Mars aspects Venus and if there be no favourable aspect from Jupiter.

195   Trine MERCURY: the same as Jupiter trine Mercury.

196   Trine waning MOON, nocturnal: elevation. Dangerous tendency to adultery, menace of its gravest consequences.

197   Square MERCURY: good reasoning power and discernment of true future interests; science, outstanding achievement in the arts. Dangers which result from imprudent love-affairs.

198   Square MOON elevated: acquisition of means. Menace of scandal and of graver perils as result of imprudent love-affairs. Venus elevated, great chance of prosperity. For women, fidelity in affections. For men, danger of being drawn into passing love-affairs.

199   Opposition MERCURY: weakening of intellectual and moral faculties by the abuse of sensual pleasure.

200 Opposition MOON: disappointments in marriage, unless the opposition be tempered by a good aspect from Jupiter. There is danger that the native will marry a proud, arrogant, imperious woman from whom he will suffer much.

MERCURY IN THE 12 HOUSES

201 *In the 1st House*: great aptitude for science and art. With Saturn, Jupiter or Sun in good aspect, favour of princes and the great. Mars square or opposition Mercury, danger of much adversity. Mars trine, success in enterprises or, at least, less adversity. Excellent augury if Sun and Moon be in good aspect. Nocturnal, Mercury favours development of intellectual faculties.

202 *In the 2nd House*: diurnal, aptitude for science and letters, pride, dominating spirit. Jupiter and Moon is good aspect, elevation but for a short time only.

203 *In the 3rd House*: chance of high elevation for priests. For others strength of mind, invention; favours enterprises. Jupiter in good aspect, eminent faculties; with good aspect from Moon, elevation of fortune by the favour of princes and the great; a character superior to the caprices of fortune. Mercury and Venus conjunction, sextile or trine in Gemini or Libra, chance of renown in the fine-arts and especially in music.

204 *In the 4th House*: science and refinement of mind. Saturn and Mars on other angles, an accusing mind, inquisitor, always ready to condemn. Aptitude for mathematics.

205 *In the 5th House*: avarice. Badly aspected, difficulty in obtaining or retaining money; danger of being robbed, by theft or by any other method. Waxing Moon in aspect, illness, ill-humour. Waning Moon, obscure illness and danger of madness; favours particularly the talents of writing and painting; elevation of fortune by intellectual work; strengthens the mind against the shocks of fortune.

206 *In the 6th House*: fluency, eloquence if well aspected by benefic, elevated. Nocturnal, sculptors and polyglot scholars. Without a benefic in 10th, malignity, perverse mind, envy of others and happiness in their misfortune; instinct to spy and to be an informer; greed which sacrifices all morals to its satisfaction. Moon conjunction Mercury, chance of elevation, especially if a benefic be in 10th. This aspect also inclines to licentiousness. Saturn or Mars conjunction Mercury, danger of poison given by subjects, or by servants, or by enemies and peril of a violent death.

207 *In the 7th House*: diurnal, many vices; with Venus in bad aspect, infamous tendencies, against nature. In Aries, Scorpio, Capricorn or Aquarius, unbridled immodesty. Mars in opposition or in 10th or in 7th, danger of phthisis. Nocturnal, fortune aided by the protection of women, either rich or of high rank. Aptitude for literature, mathematics and music. In every nativity, conjugal

discords; one of the partners will be tempted to kill the other especially if Mars be in opposition.

208   *In the 8th House:* diurnal, timidity, laziness of mind and activity; discords with near relatives or neighbours. In Capricorn or Aquarius, danger of deafness. Nocturnal, inheritance or legacy and sometimes the discovery of hidden treasure. Good opportunities spoilt by vices; sufferings of mind and body.

209   *In the 9th House:* malice, bad instincts which are rarely satisfied. Malefic in square or opposition, danger of sentence for culpable acts, or necessity to flee to escape punishment. With good aspects profitable happy journeys. For priests, chance of elevation to high dignities.

210   *In the 10th House:* diurnal and nocturnal with good aspect from Jupiter or Venus, wisdom, seriousness, chance of elevation. Mars square or opposition, wasted fortune, adversity, danger of sentence and of exile; if, in addition, the Moon be in bad aspect to both, danger of violent death. Saturn in good aspect, chance of a fortune by business concerned with the seas or rivers or employing the forces of water.

211   *In the 11th House:* inventive mind, clever calculation of interests: kindness and support from powerful people.

212   *In the 12th House:* inventive mind, aptitude for mathematics, eloquence of orator or writer. Jupiter in good aspect, with no malefic aspect, ability to direct great enterprises and to make them prosper. Without a strong aspect from a benefic, fortune will be in danger. Mars square or opposition, peril of conviction. For princes, danger of great losses. If the waxing Moon, in addition, be in conjunction, danger of violent death. If the Sun be also involved, danger of death by fire, especially in a nocturnal nativity. Diurnal, with Sun, Jupiter and Mercury in good aspect, chance of great prosperity, but Mars conjunction Mercury, danger of great misfortune.

MERCURY IN THE 12 SIGNS.

213   In *Aries:* quarrelsome, contentious spirit, sometimes urge to homicide, downfall in extreme calamity; gift of speech, cunning in enterprises, desire to usurp power. If Saturn does not aspect, and if a benefic be in trine or sextile, perils will be lessened or averted by devoted friends.

214   In *Taurus:* happy character, love of the table, of games, of repose. Ingenious mind, sagacious, clever in planning. Saturn or Mars, square or opposition: anxiety, obstacles, hindrances, injuries. With favourable aspects, numerous and faithful friends. Success in the fine arts and particularly in music.

215   In *Gemini:* clever and sagacious mind; menaced by adversity, especially every seventh and ninth year. Peril of downfall in great distress.

216   In *Cancer:* restless suspicious crafty mind, cunning for

bad ends; menace of great adversity. A better outlook if Saturn be in good aspect.

217   In *Leo:* a taste for arms and opportunity to succeed in the army. Wishes to dominate at all costs. Danger of difficulties if Mercury be badly aspected. Aptitude for literature, science; good memory and soundness of judgment.

218   In *Virgo:* strength of mind, sagacity, aptitude for sciences concerned with war. With good aspects, outstanding ability. With bad aspects, danger of adversity almost inevitable.

219.   In *Libra:* aptitude for mathematics, love of serious study, inventions, discoveries. Chance of celebrity and fortune; faithful friends.

220   In *Scorpio:* bad instincts, tendency to violent homicides. Scorn of justice and law especially if Saturn and Mars be in bad aspect. Inclination to lying, trickery in business, covetousness of the possessions of others.

221.   In *Sagittarius:* goodness, honesty, liberality; kindness and support of powerful men. But fortune will be moderate, hampered by various hindrances and by ingratitude of those aided or served.

222   In *Capricorn:* without good aspects from the benefics, danger of illness, or failure, of downfall in distress. When Jupiter in transit comes to the conjunction, sextile or trine, these ills will be lessened. Aptitude for science and for acquaintance with learned men but without material profit.

223   In *Aquarius:* aptitude for the study of astronomy, for occult sciences; chance of renown and for making money. When Saturn, in transit, is in bad aspect, bad actions committed in secret will provoke dangers.

224   In *Pisces:* excellent faculties, refinement of mind, special aptitude for legal studies and jurisprudence; gains, especially if Jupiter be in good aspect. Powerful and devoted friends aid fortune.

MERCURY AND ITS ASPECTS.

225   Conjunction MOON and in good aspect to JUPITER: strength of mind strong spirit but tendency to lying; precarious and shifting fortune. Success in the study of science.

226   Trine MOON: excellent intellectual faculties, aptitude for literature, oratory, painting, music; success in enterprises.

227   MERCURY elevated, square MOON: wisdom, eloquence, but danger of being caught up in public disturbances. In bad aspect with a malefic, danger of captivity following an accusation of forgery.

227A MOON elevated: versatile character, vacillating will, uncertainty and difficulty at the moment of taking action. Danger of being the victim of serious accusations and of being exiled; in some cases danger even of capital punishment.

228 Opposition MOON: perfidy, dangerous betrayal. For

princes: rising of an unrestrained horde with clamours of public hate and sanguinary struggles.

THE MOON IN THE 12 HOUSES

229 *In the 1st House:* every opportunity for good fortune, if nocturnal and with good aspects. Gains in any enterprise using water or on rivers or the high seas. Diurnal, with Saturn and Mars in 4th, 7th or 10th: indication of piracy and the accompanying dangers. Without benefic aspects to temper the influence of the malefics, life may be short, probably terminated by some fatality.

230 *In the 2nd House:* nocturnal, superiority in the arts, gains, leaning to licentiousness. Diurnal, loss of property, hopes prove unreliable. In all cases, journeys. Waning Moon conjunction Saturn or if Saturn be in 1st, danger of blindness or of great weakness of sight. Mars in 1st, pains in joints, dangerous haemorrhoids.

231 *In the 3rd House:* conjunction Jupiter, acquisitions. Mercury in good aspect, elevation for priests. Venus in conjunction, chance of fortune in the commerce of wines or perfumes. Nocturnal, with Saturn in conjunction, few lucky chances. Diurnal, if Mars and Mercury be conjunction Moon, they inspire evil and sometimes homicidal instincts.

232 *In the 4th House:* waxing and nocturnal, inheritance or legacy. Sun in 1st, chance of elevation for priests. Diurnal, perilous journeys, especially if the Moon be badly aspected.

233 *In the 5th House:* nocturnal, happiness in marriage if without bad aspects. Love of good cheer, sensuality.

234 *In the 6th House:* waxing and in good aspect indicates gain. With bad aspects, danger of humiliations and of downfall in distress. Danger of blindness or of weakness of sight. Dangers resulting from bad associations.

235 *In the 7th House:* waxing, diurnal, with good aspect from Jupiter or Venus, longevity. If there be no threat of violent death in the horoscope, happiness in marriage. If the moon be ill-aspected, especially if diurnal, and if it be waning, then late or unhappy marriage. Mars and Mercury, conjunction in 10th, tendency to homicide or even to parricide, committed in a moment of madness. Moon in a violent sign, with Saturn or Mars in 8th, danger of violent death.

236 *In the 8th House:* early death unless the Chance of longevity be strongly signified. Saturn or Mars in square or opposition, loss of position and danger of death in indigence. Madness. Moon conjunction Saturn with no benefic angular, danger of death by bloodshed; but if there be a benefic aspect, the peril will be averted. Moon conjunction Mercury with Saturn opposition Mars in 7th or 12th, violent death. Mars conjunction Moon, Sun in 7th and Saturn in 10th or another cardinal point, danger of violent death. Waning Moon in this house is generally a warning of a sad end.

Waxing Moon, in a favourable sign, with Jupiter in 11th, nocturnal, signifies success in enterprises. Moon alone in 8th especially if nocturnal, indicates success.

237 *In the 9th House:* diurnal, aptitude for advanced studies and intuition about the future. Nocturnal, elevation to dignities for priests. Journeys.

238 *In the 10th House:* diurnal, waxing, in its sign of exaltation, and in good aspect to Jupiter, rise of fortune, according to the status of the native. Saturn angular, danger of adversity. Nocturnal, shattering of hopes. Diurnal, with the Sun in 1st, in its own sign or sign of exaltation, or if it be in Sagittarius or Pisces, rise of fortune. With Jupiter in good aspect, chance of elevation will be greater. If Saturn be in a succedent house (not the 8th) and Mars in 1st, danger of violent death. If a malefic be angular and if another malefic be opposition Moon or be in 5th or 11th, danger of violent death.

239 *In the 11th House:* the same as in the 5th.

240 *In the 12th House:* a short life unless the Chance of longevity strongly affirms the reverse. If Jupiter and Venus, or either of them, be in 1st, a weak chance of happiness. Diurnal, loss of goods, shattering of hopes, dangerous journeys. If Saturn and Mars, or either of them be in 1st, much adversity, danger of downfall, illness. Nocturnal, the Moon being alone, deceptions, perils in travel; danger of captivity and of a sad end, especially if the Moon be badly aspected. Saturn and Sun in 2nd, danger of violent death.

THE MOON IN THE 12 SIGNS

241 In *Aries:* rise of fortune but danger of drowning.

242 In *Taurus:* wisdom, rectitude of judgment, gentleness, vivacity, sympathetic character, prosperity in the conduct of business, especially if Jupiter or Venus be in good aspect. The Moon badly aspected indicates the reverse. Every seventh and ninth year, great danger of misfortune. In prosperous years, fortune aided by women.

243 In *Gemini:* excellent mental faculties, but little prudence and enthusiasms which may lead to grave embarrassment. A keen mind with aptitude for science and art. Amorous pursuit of very young girls.

244 In *Cancer:* rise of fortune, irascible character, bitter and likely to make dangerous enemies. Saturn in good aspect, the character will be restored to calm and to a sense of equity. Danger of death by drowning during a voyage. Illnesses; danger of blindness.

245 In *Leo:* elevation but dangerous pride, especially in princes causing the people to rise against them. With Saturn in good aspect, the princes, recalled by prudence to better sentiments, will extricate themselves from danger.

246 In *Virgo:* the ills which come from lack of experience and of reflection in the business of life. With Saturn in good aspect, experience will come later and the dangers will be averted. Danger of great affliction every 7th and 9th year.

247 In *Libra:* rise of fortune which will be compromised by acting on impulse under the domination of women. Saturn in bad aspect: great adversity and fall from position or loss of means.

248 In *Scorpio:* harsh character, a mind limited by material considerations; careless in regard to good and evil. Attraction to bad company. Danger of drowning. Afflictions every 7th and 9th year.

249 In *Sagittarius:* rise of fortune; a well-dowered mind, rectitude of judgment, love of equity, aptitude for literature and science; but not much activity, little care for the interests of life and, in consequence, danger of great losses. Saturn in bad aspect, great and unexpected dangers; tendency to luxurious living which will make the native commit great faults. Angular, always threatens violent death.

250. In *Capricorn:* rise of fortune, especially if Jupiter be in good aspect and without a bad aspect from Saturn. Saturn in bad aspect, fall into adversity; danger of blindness.

251 In *Aquarius:* instability, vacillating fortune, continual agitation of mind through changing plans. Every 7th and 9th year, menace of adversity and of a wandering life. Saturn in good aspect lessens this danger. Danger of blindness or of great weakness of sight.

252 In *Pisces:* without good and strong aspects from benefics, weakness, inertia, feebleness of character, destruction of faculties in the pursuit of infamous pleasure.

ENEMIES AND PERILS.

253 If the ruler of 7th be in 10th, or the ruler of 10th be in 7th: triumph over enemies.

254 If the ruler of 12th be in 10th, or the ruler of 10th be in 12th: triumph over enemies.

255 If the ruler of 12th be in its sign of detriment or fall, and in 6th: triumph over enemies.

256 If the *Sun,* diurnal, or *Moon* nocturnal be in a sign of Mars, or in Mars' sign of exaltation and if there be mutual reception, otherwise than in the 8th, great triumph over enemies.

257 If *Venus, Mercury* or *Moon* be ruler of 7th, and if the ruler of 1st be not ill-aspected by Saturn or Mars, nor in a cadent house; triumph over enemies.

258 If *Saturn, Jupiter* or *Mars,* be ruler of 7th, not in a cadent house: the enemies will triumph.

259 If the ruler of 12th be in 1st, with good aspects: enemies triumph.

260   If the ruler of 1st be in 12th: enemies will triumph and will do much harm.

261   If *Venus, Mercury* or *Moon* be ruler of 1st, in its own sign or in its sign of exaltation, or angular; the superiority of the enemies will not be overcome except by the presence of Saturn, Jupiter or Mars in 1st.

262   If the ruler of 1st be in aspect with a planet in 12th: reconciliation with secret enemies.

263   If the ruler of 12th be unfortunate in aspect, triumph over enemies.

264   If the ruler of the *Chance of enemies* be in 1st; reconciliation with secret enemies.

265   If the sign of *Chance of enemies* or the ruler of this *Chance* be in *via combusta*, secret enemies will do much harm. Danger of accusation, peril of death by poisoning.

266   If the sign of *Chance of enemies* or its ruler be in the 12th: triumph over enemies.

267   If a malefic be in 12th: triumph over enemies.

268   If a malefic be in 12th, in bad aspect to another malefic: triumph over enemies.

269   If a benefic be in 12th, and if the ruler of the house be in aspect with another benefic: triumph over enemies.

270   If one malefic be in 12th and the other in 6th: danger of death at the hands of enemies.

271   *Saturn* in *Cancer:* discord and struggles on all sides.

272   *Saturn* and *Mars* in conjunction in 11th: the native is in danger of killing one of his friends.

273   If the *Sun* or *Moon* be in bad aspect with a malefic, angular, one or other being in Aries, Taurus, Gemini, Cancer, Libra, Scorpio, Sagittarius, Capricorn or Aquarius, and if the malefic be in Cancer or Leo: danger of captivity. However, this presage will not be realised if the Sun, Moon or malefic be in its own sign or in its sign of exaltation.

274   The *Sun* or *Moon* in 12th in conjunction with a malefic, with little or no dignity: captivity.

275   *Saturn* or *Mars* in 7th or 12th in Aries, Scorpio, Taurus, Capricorn, Leo, Cancer and square or opposition Sun or Moon: presage of captivity.

276   *Saturn* and *Mars* in bad aspect, not in their own sign or signs of exaltation: presage of captivity.

277   *Sun* and *Moon* on the cusp of 7th or 12th: presage of captivity. The same presage if Saturn and Mars or Sun and Moon be in opposition, the one in 1st, 7th or 8th, the other ruling the sign on cusp of 12th.

278   *Ruler of 12th* being in 7th in a sign of Mars and in bad aspect to Saturn or Mars: presage of captivity.

279 *Ruler of 12th* in its sign of detriment or fall and badly aspected by aspect from Saturn or Mars: presage of captivity.

280 *Sun* and *Moon* in conjunction in 8th, in any other sign than either of their own and without good aspect from Jupiter or Venus: presage of captivity. If they be in either of their own signs but badly aspected: same presage.

281 *Saturn* or *Mercury* in 6th, 7th or 8th, badly aspected: presage of captivity.

282 *Saturn* in 10th, badly aspected: captivity.

283 *Mars* in 7th or 12th, in Aries, Taurus, Scorpio, Capricorn, Aquarius, Leo or Cancer, or if the Sun or Moon be in bad aspect with Mars or Saturn: presage of captivity.

284 *Sun* or *Moon* badly aspected, angular, and in Aries, Scorpio, Libra, Capricorn or Aquarius and if Saturn or Mars be in Cancer or Leo: presage of captivity.

285 If the sign of the *Chance of captivity* be free from bad aspect and its ruler also, the danger of captivity is lessened; but it is strengthened if the Chance and its ruler be badly aspected.

286 *Ruler of 1st,* angular, in bad aspect with the ruler of 12th: presage of captivity, but if a benefic be in good aspect with the ruler of 1st, the peril will be avoided or he will be delivered.

287 If the *Ruler of 1st* be in 4th, in a human sign and in square or opposition to the ruler of 12th: captivity. The same presage if the ruler of first be in 6th, in the same condition. If a sign of Saturn be in the house: danger of long captivity.

288 If the *Ruler of 1st* be conjunction Sun and if Mars be in 1st: captivity.

289 If the *Ruler of 12th* be in conjunction with the ruler of 1st and if both be in 5th, 6th or 12th and if the ruler of 1st be badly aspected: presage of captivity.

290 *Saturn* in 10th in bad aspect to Sun or Moon and having some dignity in 1st or 8th presages a fall.

291 If the *Ruler of 10th* be a malefic in its sign of detriment or fall and badly aspecting Sun or Moon and if Saturn or Mars have some dignity in 1st or 8th: danger of a fall.

292 *Saturn* angular, Mars succedent, with Moon in opposition and if Saturn be in the 8th place counting from Saturn to the Moon: danger of fall. The same presage if, counting from Moon to Saturn, it be in the 6th place. If Mars be opposition Saturn and if the Moon be in the 6th place counting from Mars to the Moon, or in the 8th place, counting from the Moon to Mars: danger of mortal peril by a wall collapsing, a vehicle overturning or fall from a horse while travelling.

293 *Saturn* and *Mars* in 7th, in a bicorporal sign, especially if the Moon be opposition 1st: danger of fall.

294 *Saturn, Mars* and *Head of Dragon* in 6th: peril of fall.

295 *Saturn,* angular, Mars succedent and Moon opposition

either *Saturn* or *Mars*: presage of fall or of injury by a quadruped.

296 *Saturn* and *Mars* in *Taurus*, in 4th: fall.

297 *Head of Dragon* in 6th, in a fixed sign without good aspect from Jupiter or Venus, diurnal: danger of fall.

298 *Head of Dragon* in 6th with Saturn or Mars, or in bad aspect with them: danger of fall. With a good aspect from a benefic, this danger will be avoided. The peril will be greatest from the 26th to the 35th year.

299 If *Saturn, Sun* and *Mercury* are in 10th and in conjunction, square or opposition Mars: danger of proscription and exile.

300 *Saturn* in 9th or 3rd, in a water sign: danger of shipwreck or of drowning in sea, river, lake, pond or well.

301 *Mars* in 9th or 3rd: great dangers on land, especially if the ruler of 9th be badly aspected.

302 If the Ruler of the *Chance of fortune* be in 6th, 8th or 12th and if it be in aspect with the sign of this Chance and above all, if it receives a bad aspect from a malefic: indication of many ills.

303 *Saturn* or *Mars* in 7th: misfortunes.

304 *Saturn* or *Mars* conjunction *Sun* or *Moon* in 7th: presage of misfortune to people who seem to be protected from all dangers.

305 *Saturn* and *Mars* in a fiery sign: danger of peril by fire. In an airy sign: danger from wounds and loss of blood.

306 *Saturn,* in nocturnal nativity, in Leo: loss of reputation; fall from position.

307 *Saturn* elevated, square Jupiter: danger to life. Jupiter elevated and square Saturn: the presage is lessened.

308 *Saturn* and *Mars* in opposition: to princes, great dangers, rebellions, unhappy death; domestic strife, serious illnesses. If either be in a water sign, danger of drowning, of death in an epidemic or by inflammation. The danger will be greater if Jupiter be not in good aspect. If the Moon, angular, be square Saturn or Mars: proscription, exile, and sometimes even violent death by torture.

309 *Saturn* opposition *Sun,* without good aspect from Jupiter: misfortune, miserable end.

310 *Saturn* opposition *Moon:* anxious life, fall into distress. If Moon be in a water sign: danger of drowning or of death caused by malignant tumours. In a human sign: danger of death by the hand of man.

311 *Jupiter,* ill-aspected in 6th: misfortune and perils.

312 *Jupiter* opposition *Mars:* great perils resulting from foolhardy actions.

313 *Jupiter* opposition *Mercury:* danger for princes of serious popular sedition. Hatred between brothers or near relatives.

314   *Jupiter* opposition *Moon:* misfortune especially if nocturnal nativity. Sad end.

315   *Mars* in 1st: danger of proscription, exile or disgrace for men in public appointments.

316   *Mars* in 2nd, diurnal nativity: many misfortunes. Conjunction, square, or opposition waxing Moon: danger of captivity, of wounds by iron. Jupiter in good aspect: danger lessened.

317   *Mars* in 4th, diurnal nativity: wounds by iron; misfortunes caused by women. Square or opposition Sun: great perils.

318   *Mars* in 5th, diurnal nativity: great perils. Moon in opposition: accusations, serious sedition against princes, unexpected perils. Jupiter in good aspect Mars or Moon: danger lessened.

319   *Mars* in 7th, not in Aries or Scorpio: danger of captivity and of murder by the hand of enemies, especially if nocturnal.

320   *Mars* in 10th, nocturnal: unhappy end. Loss of throne and sometimes of life for princes. Menace of death in captivity. Diurnal: painful and dangerous journeys; flight necessitated by proscription, miserable end.

321   *Mars* ill-aspected by Saturn in 11th, diurnal nativity: assault by subjects against princes, by servants against masters.

322   *Mars* in *Libra:* peril by iron or fire.

323   *Mars* conjunction *Sun:* peril of death in flames.

324   *Mars* conjunction *Venus:* lawsuit and losses occasioned by women.

325   *Mars* square *Sun,* if the Sun be elevated: misfortune. Mars in 7th or 10th, in aspect with the waxing Moon: princes are threatened by public criticism.

326   *Mars* elevated square *Mercury:* all kinds of misfortunes, especially in diurnal nativity. Nocturnal: less danger. Mercury elevated: danger of captivity.

327   *Mars* opposition *Sun:* diurnal nativity: danger of fall

328   *Mars* opposition *Mercury:* great misfortune, especially if Mercury be in Capricorn or Aquarius, without good aspect from Jupiter.

329   *Mars* opposition *Moon:* great perils, danger of public death following sentence, especially if the Moon be waxing and the nativity nocturnal.

330   *Sun* conjunction *Mars* in 1st or badly aspected by Mars: elevation of fortune, followed by great perils.

331   *Sun* in 2nd: obstacles to enterprises; hindrances to fortune, troubles, anxieties.

332   *Sun* in 4th: great obstacles, great afflictions.

333   *Sun* in 6th: if Mars be in 1st: danger of wounds by iron.

334   *Sun* in 10th, in Leo, Sagittarius or Pisces, if Mars be in 2nd or 9th, and if the Full Moon be conjunction or opposition Mars: danger of proscription, exile and even sometimes of violent death.

335   *Sun* in 12th: danger of captivity; conjunction Saturn or Mars: danger of captivity for life.

336   *Sun* square or opposition *Moon,* badly aspected by Saturn or Mars: great adversity.

337   *Venus* in 6th, in a woman's nativity: dangerous childbirths, abortions, fatal operations.

338   *Venus* in 12th: embarrassments and afflictions occasioned by women. If Mars and Mercury be in aspect: amorous inclinations for servants and danger of the life which will result therefrom. Diurnal, with Mars aspecting Venus: danger of some great misfortune.

339   *Venus* in *Leo:* peril of death occasioned by some relation with women.

340   *Venus* conjunction *Mercury:* loss of goods or of reputation on account of women.

341   *Mercury* in 1st, square or opposition *Mars:* danger of many misfortunes.

342   *Mercury* in 7th, conjunction or opposition *Mars:* sentence, exile or necessity to flee.

343   *Mercury* in *Aries* or *Scorpio,* in cadent house, square *Mars* [elevated]: necessity to flee to avoid a proscription or sentence. Besieged by Saturn and Mars: same presage.

344   *Mercury* elevated square *Moon:* danger to princes of formidable popular movements. If, at the same time, the Moon be square or opposition Mars: dangerous accusations.

345   *Mercury* opposition *Moon:* danger to princes of the rising of a frenzied and furious multitude.

346   *Moon* in 10th, nocturnal, square or opposition Saturn: prosecution through envy; adversity.

347   *Moon* in 12th, nocturnal, if Saturn or Mars be in 1st: many ills, peril of fall, dangerous illnesses.

348   *Moon* in *Cancer,* diurnal: obstacles, painful work, dangerous journeys.

349   *Moon* [waning], conjunction *Mercury* in Gemini or Virgo: danger of a formidable prosecution and of captivity.

350   *Saturn, Sun* and *Mercury* in conjunction in 10th: prosecution and danger of sentence for actions believed to be perfectly hidden.

351   *Saturn* and *Mars* in 9th, not having any dignity of sign or exaltation; danger of frequent prosecution, with or without evidence.

352   *Moon* and *Mars* in conjunction or opposition, angular, and if one or the other be in an airy sign, especially Gemini or Libra: danger of wounds. If they be in the signs or signs of exaltation of Saturn or Mars risk of being drawn into homicide.

353   *Jupiter* in *Aries* or *Scorpio:* wounding by soldiers.

354   If *Jupiter* be with *Mars,* or *Saturn* with *Venus,* or *Sun*

with Moon, or if Saturn or Mars be in conjunction with Sun or Moon: always a presage of great adversity.

355 If *Mars* be angular and if Scorpio be in 1st, it is the presage, almost always inevitable, of a great misfortune.

356 *Mars* in 1st always presages dangers.

357 *Mars* angular, especially in 1st or 10th, diurnal: danger of a great peril brought about by the fault of the native.

358 *Mars* in 10th in *Aries*, square Jupiter in Capricorn: wounds. The same presage if Mars be in Scorpio and if Aquarius be in 1st and if Mars ill-aspect the Sun in Leo.

359 *Mars* in 12th, diurnal: danger of wounds by iron.

360 Waning *Moon,* opposition Mars oriental, and if Mars be not tempered by a good aspect from Jupiter or Venus: danger of a mortal wound.

361 Waning *Moon* in 8th and the ruler of 12th in its sign of detriment and Saturn or Mars ill-aspecting the Moon: danger of wounds.

362 *Moon* conjunction *Mars* in an airy sign, especially in Gemini: danger of wounding by the hand of man.

363 The sign of the *Chance of infirmity* placed with the Moon in 9th or with Mars in 8th: danger of the loss of a limb.

364 The *Ruler of 1st,* ill-aspected in 9th: peril of attack by thieves.

365 The *Ruler of 1st,* ill-aspected in 11th: danger of harm done by friends by betrayal or otherwise.

366 The *Ruler of 2nd,* ill-aspected in 3rd: danger of harm by brothers or near relatives.

367 *Saturn* in 10th, being neither in its own sign nor in its sign of exaltation: danger of captivity.

368 *Saturn* in 12th, being neither in its own sign nor in its sign of exaltation. danger of captivity or exile.

369 *Jupiter* in 4th, especially in its own sign or sign of exaltation: preserves from perils.

370 *Jupiter* in 12th, being neither in its own sign nor in its sign of exaltation: danger of captivity.

371 The *Sun* in 12th: presage of captivity for a homicidal act or for an act of hatred against princes and the great.

372 The *Sun* in *Cancer* with the Tail of the Dragon or with Saturn or Mars: peril on water.

373 *Mars* in 1st, being neither in its own sign nor in its sign of exaltation: head wounds.

374 *Mars* in 4th: wounds, unhappy end.

375 *Mars* in 7th, being neither in its own sign nor in its sign of exaltation: lack of success in everything followed by an unhappy end: danger of loss of a limb.

376 *Mars* in 10th, neither in its own sign nor in its sign of exaltation: frequent perils, unhappy end.

377   *Mars* in 12th: many afflictions, wounds, captivity.

378   *Mars* in its own sign or sign of exaltation: danger of fall or of acute illnesses.

379   *Venus* in 6th: in a woman's nativity: danger to life during childbirth.

380   *Venus* in 12th: enmities, captivity, proscription or exile. Conjunction Saturn, Mars or Sun, in Virgo, Capricorn or Aquarius: danger to life occasioned by an amorous intrigue.

381   *Mercury* in 1st, conjunction Mars in Aries or Scorpio: head wounds.

382   *Mercury* in 6th, conjunction Saturn or Mars: danger of death ocasioned by a man-servant or maid-servant, either by accident or by poisoning. Danger of captivity.

383   *Mercury* in 12th: danger of captivity.

384   *Moon* in 2nd, badly aspected by Saturn or Mars: afflictions, robbery of goods.

385   *Moon* in 8th, badly aspected by Saturn or Mars: quarrels, violent enmity, captivity.

386   *Moon* in 12th, badly aspected by Saturn or Mars: hindrances in enterprises, captivity, persecutions, exile. If it be in *Via Combusta*, much adversity.

387   *Moon* in *Aries* or *Scorpio:* danger of drowning.

388   *Moon*, badly aspected in its own sign: danger of shipwreck or drowning.

389   *Tail of the Dragon* in 1st: tribulations, menace of blindness, or of great infirmity of sight.

390   *Tail of the Dragon* in 2nd: danger of fall.

391   *Tail of the Dragon* in 10th: danger of fall.

392   *Head of the Dragon* in 5th: preserves from great dangers threatened by the horoscope.

393   Ruler of 4th in 7th and in a Fiery sign [*Aries, Leo, Sagittarius*]: danger of death by fire.

394   If the ruler of the *Chance of Death* be opposition or square the ruler of 8th: danger of death by murder. If it be sextile or trine the ruler of 8th: preservation from murder especially if Jupiter be ruler of 8th.

395   If the sign of the *Chance of Death* and its ruler and the ruler of 7th be in 1st, or in a sign in which the ruler of 1st have dignity of sign, exaltation or triplicity: death takes place far from the land of birth.

396   If the *Sun*, ruler of the nativity be badly aspected: violent death far from the land of birth.

397   If *Mars* be in *Leo:* danger of sudden death by iron or fire, far from the land of birth.

398   If *Mercury* be in 7th, with Saturn or Mars: violent death by capital punishment.

Fortunate or Unfortunate Chances

399   *Chance of Longevity*. It is calculated, in either diurnal or nocturnal nativity, from the Soli-Lunar conjunction or opposition preceding the birth. The conjunction is always placed in Aries and the opposition in Libra. The manner of finding this point by the Table of epacts and that of the lunar phases has been indicated in the horoscope of Louis XVI. When this point is fixed, we count 1 from Aries or Libra as the case may be, then 2, 3, 4, etc., for each following sign until we come to the Moon in the horoscope. Then we go to the 1st House and if, for example, we have counted 7 to the Moon's place, starting from 1 [Aries or Libra] we shall count 7 houses as we had counted 7 signs and we shall mark the sign of the Chance in the 7th House. The Chance will have as ruler the planet possessing the dignity of diurnal or nocturnal throne in the 7th House even when the planet itself be in another house. If the Chance of Longevity be in a masculine sign and within orbs of the Sun, it is generally a presage of a short life, unless other presages, strongly accentuated, promise long life.

400   The sign of the *Chance of Infirmities* is found, in diurnal nativities, counting from Jupiter to Saturn. In nocturnal nativity, we count from Saturn to Jupiter. We start from the 1st House and counting the same number of houses, we place the Chance. If the sign and its ruler are fortunate, it is a general sign of health. If the contrary: danger of serious illnesses.

401   The sign of the *Chance of Death* is found in diurnal or nocturnal nativities starting from the Moon to the 8th House. Then we start from Saturn and count the same number of houses; there we place the sign of the Chance. If this sign and its ruler be badly aspected and without aspect from a benefic: danger of violent death. If Saturn or Mars be in the 8th House; if the ruler of this house be badly aspected or if it be itself of a malefic nature and in a violent sign; if the Sun or the Moon or either of them be ill-aspected or in a violent sign: a strong indication of violent death. If the ruler of the 1st House be in a violent sign or ill-aspected and if the Sun or the Moon be in like case: indication of the same danger. If the ruler of the 1st House be in 8th if it be a malefic or, if it be a benefic but ill-aspected or in a violent sign: danger of violent death.

Conjunction of *Saturn* and *Mars* angular, especially in the 10th House and in a violent sign or if the conjunction be square or opposition Sun or Moon: danger of violent death. The square or opposition of Saturn and Mars, angular, is another indication of violent death if either be ruler of the 8th House. If a human sign be in the 12th House and if the horoscope give signs of a violent death, death will come by means of an ambush.

The principal significators of *Violent Death* are the Sun in Aries and the Moon in Libra. If Saturn and Mars be in Aries,

Libra, Scorpio, Capricorn, Aquarius and ill-aspect Jupiter or Venus angular, it is equally a menace of violent death. The same presage if the rulers of the 1st and 10th Houses are respectively: one a malefic, the other in its sign of fall.

402   The sign of the *Chance of Captivity* is found, in diurnal nativity, by counting from Saturn to the sign of the Chance of Fortune. In nocturnal nativity, we count from the Chance of Fortune to Saturn. Starting from the 1st House and counting the same number of houses, we place the Chance. If this Chance and its ruler be ill-aspected, captivity is likely. If well-aspected, the danger is averted or deliverance comes. Saturn or Mars in 1st, 4th, 7th or 10th Houses always presage some captivity but Saturn's influence is more menacing. Mercury in the same houses and ill-aspected gives the same presage. If the ruler of 9th be angular, it signifies danger of arrest on a journey and of captivity. If the ruler of the 1st House, or the Sun or the Moon be ill-aspected in cadent houses: sign of death in a state of captivity, especially if they be neither in Aries nor in Leo or if they be ill-aspected by Saturn or Mars as ruler of the cadent house concerned. If the ruler of the 1st be in 12th, in a human sign, without an aspect from the Sun or Moon: peril of captivity during the early years of life. The principal significators of captivity are the Sun and the Moon badly aspected and the conjunction of Saturn and Mars in the 12th House.

403   The sign of *Military Chance* is found in diurnal nativity, counting from the Sun to Saturn. Nocturnal, we count from Saturn to the Sun. Then we start from the 1st House. If this Chance does not fall in Aries, Scorpio or Capricorn, it presages little courage and little fortune in a military career. It is very lucky if it be conjunction Mars and if Jupiter, in good aspect be ruler of the Chance. If it be conjunction Mars in a water sign [Cancer, Scorpio or Pisces]: natural timidity which suddenly changes to extreme boldness. Mars in Cancer may indicate cruelty. If Mercury be in a sign ruled by Mars, especially if angular, it indicates intrepidity born of reflection. The position of the ruler of the Chance should also be considered.

404   The sign of the *Royal Chance* and its ruler, favoured by good aspects and in good aspect with the 1st House and especially of the 10th indicate an exalted position. In diurnal nativity, this Chance is counted from Mars to the Moon; nocturnal, from Moon to Mars. Starting then from the 1st House we place the Chance by counting the same number of houses. If this Chance be well-aspected, it indicates, for princes, accession to the throne or to the exercise of considerable power at Court.

405   The sign of the *Chance of Victory* is counted from the Sun to Saturn in diurnal nativity; nocturnal, from Saturn to the Sun. Starting from the 1st House, we place the Chance by counting the same number of houses. If the sign of this Chance, or its ruler be conjunction the ruler or 1st or 10th, it indicates elevation.

If one or the other be in the sign, or sign of exaltation of the ruler of 1st: indication of triumph over enemies.

406   The sign of *Chance of Marriage,* in a masculine horoscope is found by counting from the Sun to Venus. Starting from the 1st House we place the Chance by counting the same number of houses. If Venus be in a masculine sign or in the 12th House, and if the Chance and its ruler be badly aspected, little happiness in marriage. In a feminine horoscope, we count from Venus to Saturn and then start from the 1st House as before. If Saturn or Venus be ill-aspected little or no happiness in marriage.

The significators of marriage, in a masculine horoscope, are the Moon, Venus, the 7th House, planets therein and the ruler of the house. In a feminine horoscope the Sun and Mars are considered instead of the Moon and Venus. If the Sun and Moon be inimical in the horoscopes of a man and a woman, they should not marry. If the Sun, in the horoscope of the man be in Aries and if the Sun in the horoscope of the woman be in Taurus; if the Moon in both horoscopes be in Scorpio, or if the Sun and the Moon of the one have no aspect to the Sun and the Moon of the other, their marriage will be troubled by great afflictions.

If the sign on the cusp of the 1st House, in the horoscope of a man, be the same as that on the cusp of the 7th House of a woman, their marriage will bring bitterness. The union will be constant and faithful if the Sun and Moon in the man's horoscope favourably aspect the Sun and Moon in the woman's horoscope. The two horoscopes should be considered together.

407   The sign of the *Chance of Friendship* is found by counting from the Moon to Mercury. Count the same number of houses and place the Chance. If this Chance and its ruler be well placed, it indicates devoted and faithful friendships. If they be in cadent houses and in mutable signs: fickle and sterile friendships. Saturn and Mars well-placed: many friends and alliances which one should distrust. Badly placed: few ties and they will not last. The Sun, Moon and Mercury, well-placed, indicate many friends, moderately useful; badly placed, few friends and they cannot be trusted. If these three significators be in debility, there will be a mixture of good and bad connections. The significators of alliances and friendships are especially the planets in the 11th House or which aspect that house; and the ruler of that house, with any planet in aspect.

408   The sign of the *Chance of Enemies* is counted, in diurnal nativity, from the ruler of the 12th House to the cusp of the 12th. In nocturnal nativity, it is counted from the cusp of the 12th to the ruler of the house. Starting from the 1st House, as before, we count the same number of houses. If this Chance and its ruler be angular or in succedent houses, it indicates numerous and powerful enemies. In cadent houses, the enemies will be less numerous and less to be feared. The 7th is the house of open enemies;

the 12th, of secret enemies. Planets in opposition to the Sun and the Moon indicate declared and formidable enemies; Saturn and Mercury, occult enemies; Saturn in 12th, envious and vile enemies; Jupiter in 12th, enemies of high rank; Mars in 12th, armed enemies; Venus in 12th, enmity of women; Sun in 12th, princes as enemies; the Moon in 12th, low enemies. Benefics in 12th signify powerful enemies; malefics, occult enemies. If the planets in 12th be in their own signs or signs of exaltation, they will be very formidable. If they be in signs of the same triplicity, the enmity will be less dangerous. If they be in their signs of detriment, the enemies will be of low condition. If Gemini be in 12th, it indicates secret enemies or traitors. The principal significators of enmity are the planets in 7th and 12th, the rulers of these houses and the planets in opposition to the Sun and the Moon.

409 The sign of the *Chance of land journeys* is found by counting from the ruler of the 9th House to the cusp of the 9th. The *Chance of journeys by water* is found by counting from Saturn to Cancer, in diurnal nativity; in nocturnal, from Cancer to Saturn. These journeys will be fortunate or unfortunate according to the aspects of the Chances and their rulers.

410 The sign of the *Chance of general fortune* is found by counting from the Sun to the Moon, in diurnal nativity. In nocturnal nativity, we count from the Moon to the Sun if the Moon be 'above the earth'. If the Moon be below, count as in diurnal nativity. Proceed as in the other Chances. The Chance of Fortune is of value according to its aspects. If the Chance of Fortune or its ruler be in the 6th House, it indicates a struggle with men or against crushing infirmities, according to the general character of the horoscope. If in the 7th, in Leo, it indicates danger of death in battle. If in the 12th, it indicates ruin for military men.

411 The sign of the *Chance of Mind* is counted in diurnal nativity, from Mercury to Mars. In nocturnal, from Mars to Mercury. Then proceed as before. If this Chance and its ruler be conjunction the ruler of the 1st House, or if the ruler of the Chance have some dignity in this house, and if it be sextile or trine Mercury, it indicates an excellent mind, gifted with faculties which are able to lead a powerful and persevering will to all success.

PART II

KEYS OF THE ANNUAL HOROSCOPE[1]

412 The sign of the 1st House and a malefic: a bad year, especially if it be Saturn in a nocturnal or Mars in a diurnal horoscope. Danger to life, illnesses, accusations, troubles.

413 The sign of the 1st House and JUPITER: a favourable year,

dangers escaped, justice obtained, favour of princes and powerful persons. Return for exiles, deliverance for captives.

414 The sign of the 1st House and the SUN: a happy year.

415 The sign of the 1st House and VENUS: a good year.

416 The sign of the 1st House and MERCURY: a good year for enterprises. But if Mercury be ill-aspected, the opposite will apply.

417 The sign of the 1st House and the MOON: alternation of good and ill; profitable journeys if the Moon be in good aspect.

418 SATURN passing in transit into the sign it already occupied in the natal horoscope indicates annoyances, disappointments, dangerous enmities, obstacles in enterprises, instability of fortune. If square Mars or Mercury, calumny, loss of means.

419 SATURN and JUPITER: a good year, inheritance or legacy, presents, unlooked for gains. If Mercury be in bad aspect, adversity, lawsuit, sudden quarrels.

420 SATURN and MARS: a bad year, illnesses, prosecutions by envy or hatred; troubles, discords with near relatives; domestic quarrels, accusations, enmity of important and powerful persons. If the sign be water, danger of drowning.

421 SATURN and the SUN: disputes, enmities, rupture of affections, betrayal by friends. Diurnal, gain painfully acquired, legacies or presents.

422 SATURN and VENUS: conjugal quarrels, separation; obstacles in enterprises, adversities, disputes, and law-suits; sometimes danger of poisoning. In a feminine horoscope, danger of abortion.

423 SATURN and MERCURY: obstacles in enterprises, deception of hopes, enmities.

424 SATURN and the MOON: disappointment in marriage, separation; rupture with friends, slanders, obstacles in enterprises, nervous illnesses, sudden fall.

425 JUPITER and SATURN: dangers in travelling, revolt of subjects against princes, servants against masters, subordinates against chiefs; rupture of societies, alliances, friendships.

426 JUPITER transitting its own place indicates good or evil according to sign and the aspects it receives.

427 JUPITER and MARS: enmity of powerful persons, slanders, attack on reputation, treachery, dangerous journeys, illnesses. If the horoscope be that of a powerful individuality and if the aspects be favourable, the year will be generally prosperous.

---

1 The author describes the annual horoscope as 'Revolution of the signs'. it would make for confusion to use the generally accepted terms progressed horoscope, directions, etc., for it must be borne in mind that the system expounded earlier in the work makes use of *Circles of Fate*, instead of 'a day for a year'. The 'Revolution' planet, sign or House is the first named in these keys. The second is drawn from the nativity.—*Translator's note.*

428 JUPITER and the SUN: for persons of high birth, rise of fortune. For those born in a more humble condition: freedom from troubles and cares, obliging friends, beginning or increase of fortune, especially if the horoscope be diurnal.

429 JUPITER and VENUS: if without bad aspect, a good year according to the status of the native.

430 JUPITER and MERCURY: a prosperous and profitable year. If Mercury be ill-aspected: trouble connected with personal interests, prosecutions, loss.

431 JUPITER and the MOON: a favourable year, dangers escaped, legacies from influential women or from persons of rank. If ill-aspected, the opposite will apply.

432 MARS and SATURN: difficult year, law-suit, disappointed hopes, illnesses, sudden dangers, loss of means, revolt against princes, attacks of hate. If Mars be in Aries or Scorpio, these presages are lessened.

433 MARS and JUPITER: prosperous year for military men or for persons in public office. If ill-aspected: difficulties in enterprises, adversity. If in good aspect, a prosperous and lucrative year.

434 MARS transitting its own place, in a diurnal horoscope: unsettled year, enmities, loss of means. Unfavourable for soldiers. Nocturnal, prosperous year if Mars be in Aries or Capricorn.

435 MARS and the SUN: dangerous illness, intestinal trouble; danger resulting from an outbreak of fire; danger of fall or of some other sudden injury. Accidents on a journey; quarrel with soldiers and risk of death if Mars or the Sun be ruler of the year. Well-aspected: a good year in spite of some traps laid by enemies.

436 MARS and VENUS: enmities of women, conjugal quarrels, separations, illnesses, dangerous adultery; rupture of friendship, loss of reputation. Great peril of death for pregnant women.

437 MARS and MERCURY: a year tormented by discords, lawsuits, perils, bodily sufferings and particularly cerebral trouble, especially if Mars be in a bicorporal sign. If the 1st House, the Sun and the Moon are free from bad aspects, these presages will be lessened. Ill-aspected, adversity and, in particular, losses in business.

438 MARS and the MOON: bad year, revolt against princes, attacks against the great, lawsuits, prosecutions, traps, ambush. Disappointments in marriage, separations; rupture of friendship; popular risings. Acute illnesses; weakness of memory or of sight; danger of injury by iron or fire; peril of drowning. If the Moon be waxing and ill-aspected, these presages are more formidable. With only favourable aspects, these presages will be lessened. In a woman's horoscope, great danger for pregnant women; danger of a fatal operation.

439 The SUN and SATURN: difficult year; constitutional disorder, many enemies; in disgrace with superiors; obstacles in enterprises; illnesses of the head, stomach, or the heart. Rising of sub-

jects against princes, servants against masters; traps, ambush. Dangerous prosecutions, thefts. If Mars and Saturn be in mutual reception, these fatal auguries will be lessened.

440 The SUN and JUPITER: a good year and success in hopes or in enterprises, in course of execution.

441 The SUN and MARS: a dangerous year, illnesses, danger to life; danger of injury to the head by fall or by a quadruped, trouble in personal matters, loss of means, enmity of subjects or of underlings; popular risings; danger of death by iron or fire.

442 The SUN transitting its own place: rise of fortune if signified by aspects . . .

443 The SUN and VENUS: prosperous year; kindness and favour of powerful persons; success and gains in enterprises.

444 The SUN and MERCURY: favourable year for enterprises. If Mercury be ill-aspected, discords, disputes, law-suits, loss in business.

445 The SUN and the MOON: useful relations with the great and with influential women; good outlook for enterprises.

446 VENUS and SATURN: difficult year. Conjugal discords, separations, loss of reputation, enmities, scandalous passions inflicting public dishonour. Obstacles in enterprises. Intestinal trouble, secret and shameful illnesses. Danger of poisoning especially if Mars and Mercury be square or opposition Venus.

447 VENUS and JUPITER: fortunate year.

448 VENUS and MARS: troubled year, discords, lawsuits, disappointments in the household, separations. Danger of seduction for girls. Dangerous adulteries, perfidy of false friends.

449 VENUS and the SUN: a good year.

450 VENUS transitting its own place, especially if it be ruler of the year: prosperous year; but if there be square or opposition from Saturn or from Mars, or if it be without dignity, or if it be in 12th or in 6th: jealousy, injustice, danger to life. Danger of rising against princes.

451 VENUS and MERCURY: favourable for the success of enterprise; gifts and legacies; business profits if the aspects be good. Otherwise, difficulties.

452 VENUS and the MOON: favourable for the success of enterprises but troubled by prosecutions and by enmities which, however, will slacken or be overcome.

453 MERCURY and SATURN: perilous year; obstacles in enterprises, lawsuits, loss of goods; illness, phthisis, black bile, danger of poisoning. If Mars be in bad aspect: danger of drowning.

454 MERCURY and JUPITER: prosperity, especially in business enterprises.

455 MERCURY and MARS: enmities, law-suits, loss of goods, perfidy. Disloyal inclinations, malicious instincts of which one will be the victim and which will endanger life.

456 MERCURY and the SUN: a good outlook.

457 MERCURY and VENUS: a good outlook.

458 MERCURY and MERCURY: good augury unless there be bad aspects [see Key 570].

459 MERCURY and the MOON: if ill-aspected, personal troubles, enmities, treasons, peril of death.

460 The MOON and SATURN: vicissitudes, many enemies; obstacles in enterprises, instability of position. Illness affecting the head or intestines will endanger life especially if the Moon be occidental. Oriental, less danger.

461 The MOON and JUPITER: rise of fortune, obliging friends, happy marriage, realisation of hopes, unless there be bad aspects.

462 The MOON and MARS: difficulties, danger of bloodshed, of fall or of injuries by fire. Domestic discords, disappointment in marriage, separation. Popular rising against princes.

463 The MOON and SUN: obstacles in enterprises, deception of hopes, domestic discords, little happiness in marriage.

464 The MOON and VENUS: good augury but if ill-aspected, disappointments, illnesses, loss of means or of position, cruel jealousy in marriage, family quarrels especially in women's horoscopes.

465 The MOON and MERCURY: good for enterprises; ill-aspected, discords, law-suits, trouble in enterprises, loss of means. If Mercury be in Gemini or Virgo: fortune in business. In any other sign, danger of death.

466 The MOON and the MOON: difficulties in enterprises, powerful enmities especially from women and the common people. In bad aspect, sudden perils, especially if the Moon be ruler of the year. In good aspect, the dangers are lessened.

467 1st House and MOON: honour and profit. 2nd House and Moon: financial interests but some danger of theft. 3rd House and Moon: danger of lasting hatred and of obscure illness. 4th House and Moon: inheritance or legacies; danger of fall or of drowning; perils on ice or on a journey. A bad time for asking a favour from princes or great men. 5th House and Moon: perfidy, treachery. 6th House and Moon: lasting and dangerous enmities, serious illness. 7th House and Moon: danger of theft and of fire. A good time for marriage. A bad time for undertaking a war, especially if the 1st House, the Sun, the Moon and the Chance of Fortune be ill-aspected. 8th House and Moon: illness, treachery, danger of death. A bad time for making war or for beginning a lawsuit. 9th House and Moon: good for journeys, if the nativity promises them; favourable for new ties of love or friendship and for seeking the goodwill of princes or of priests. 10th House and Moon: good for every enterprise which could create or augment fortune, for sea-voyages, for attacking and conquering enemies. 11th House and Moon: the same presages. 12th House and Moon: hatred, difficult to appease; obstacles in everything. Obscure illness. A bad time for

undertaking a long journey, for beginning a business or for engaging in a struggle against enemies. Danger of captivity.

468 *1st House* and MARS: conjunction, square or opposition indicates injury by iron or fire, captivity, exile.

469 *1st House* and SATURN or MARS, either of them progressing to the 1st House: great peril.

470 *1st House* and *2nd*: If Venus be ruler of the year, Saturn in the 4th House: captivity.

471 *1st House* and *3rd* or *9th:* Saturn or Mars in the sign or in bad aspect: great adversity, captivity or overthrow by enemies.

472 *1st House* and *4th* or *7th;* Saturn or Mars in the sign or in bad aspect: many evils, sedition against princes, captivity, exile.

473 *1st House* and *12th:* with a sign ruled by Jupiter on the cusp, Saturn therein and Mars in 4th: deadly perils.

474 *1st House* and *1st, 2nd, 4th, 5th, 7th, 9th, 10th* or *11th* and the ruler of the year being in 3rd, 6th, 8th or 12th; or 1st House and 3rd, 6th, 8th or 12th and the ruler of the year being in 1st, 2nd, 4th, 5th, 7th, 9th, 10th or 11th: balance of good and ill and the chance of triumphing over bad luck by a heroic effort of intelligence and will.

475 MARS or MOON in *11th:* friends on whom one can rely.

476 *12th* and ruler of *11th:* treachery of friends.

477 SATURN ruler of *11th* or *12th:* unfaithful or inconstant friends.

478 The SUN square JUPITER ruling *10th*: position and honour will be endangered.

479 The *ruler of the year* ill-aspected and unfortunate: hindrance in enterprises.

480 The *ruler of the year* unfortunate also in the nativity: restlessness, obstacles, deceptions.

481 *7th, 8th* or *12th* and the *ruler of 10th:* disgrace in the service of princes or other persons of high rank.

482 The *ruler of the year* in *6th* or *7th* and if the ruler be Saturn or square or opposition Saturn: collapse of fortune, loss of dignity or of employment, if the ruler be cadent in the nativity.

483 If SATURN or MARS be in *10th;* if they be not rulers of the year; nor in good aspect with the other planets: a collapse is threatened.

484 *2nd House* and *ruler of 1st,* if it be Saturn or Mars: danger of loss of means.

485 If the *ruler of the year* be angular, square or opposition Saturn or Mars; if, in nativity, it was in conjunction with the same malefic: menace of great loss, distress, catastrophe.

486 If the *ruler of the year* be in 7th or 12th in bad aspect to Saturn or Mars; unless Jupiter be in good aspect to the Moon and to the ruler of the year: loss of means.

487   If the *ruler of the year,* the 1st House and the Moon be in bad aspect to a malefic: danger of ruin for great fortunes. If Jupiter or Venus be in aspect instead, the danger will not eventuate.

488   *1st House, ruler* and the Moon in bad aspect to Saturn or Mars: danger of ruin and great distress.

489   JUPITER in 6*th* or 12*th:* powerful enemies, prosecution through envy or hatred but they will not succeed.

490   MERCURY opposition 7*th:* paralyses the manoeuvres of enemies.

491   MERCURY in 12*th:* uncovers the manoeuvres and snares of enemies.

492   MARS in 1*st,* in bad aspect to the Moon and ruler of the year, strengthens enemies. If in a sign of Jupiter, it gives strength against enemies.

493   Malefics in 12*th* paralyse manoeuvres of enemies unless they be ill-aspected.

494   If the *ruler of* 12*th* [nativity] pass to the 1st House: numerous and formidable enemies. If it pass to the 8th, danger of murder by enemies. If it pass to 11th, few friends and many enemies.

495   If the *ruler of* 1*st* [nativity] pass to the 12th, well-aspected: defeat of enemies. Ill-aspected: enemies triumph.

496   The 1*st House,* its ruler and the Moon in bad aspect to Saturn and Mars: power is in the hands of the enemies.

497   *A solar or lunar eclipse* in 1st or 10th: enemies triumph if the ruler be also in the same sign.

498   If *Capricorn* be in 12*th* and Aquarius in 1st: hidden enemies will cease to do harm. If Capricorn or Aquarius be in 12th and Saturn in 7th, secret enemies will become declared enemies.

499   SATURN in 1*st,* 6th, 7th or 8th: relentless enmities.

500   JUPITER and SATURN: instability of alliances, rupture of friendship.

501   MARS in 1*st:* dangerous enemies. In 7th: quarrels, law-suits.

502   SUN in 7*th:* support of friends. Ill-aspected in 12th: hidden enemies who can do much harm.

503   VENUS, JUPITER or another favourable planet in 12th: superiority of enemies.

504   MERCURY in 7th: much harm from crafty and perfidious enemies.

505   The MOON in a masculine sign, square or opposition Saturn or Mars; the ruler of its sign being malefic: powerful enemies from whom everything is to be feared.

506   The *ruler of the year* in 7th or 12th; in bad aspect to Saturn or Mars; Jupiter being without aspect to the Moon or the ruler of the year: loss of means or of position by the manoeuvres of powerful and relentless enemies.

507   The *ruler of the year* within orbs of the Sun: dangerous activity of enemies.

508   The *ruler of the year* opposition Mars and square Moon or Sun; if it be a benefic and without aspect to its own sign: great perils which enemies create.

509   The *ruler of* 11*th* passing to 12th: friends become enemies.

510   The *ruler of* 1*st* in 12th: numerous enemies, great tribulations, captivity.

511   The *Tail of the Dragon* in 1st House: danger of falling into the power of enemies and the need to flee.

512   1*st House* and 6*th* or 12*th* [nativity]: friends change to enemies.

513   If 4*th and* 7*th* and their rulers be ill-aspected, many evils will be inflicted by enemies.

514   JUPITER and VENUS conjunction MOON or the ruler of the year: deliverance from the power of enemies.

515   JUPITER in 3*rd:* lessens perils, weakens enemies and procures peace.

516   The *Head of the Dragon* in 5*th* preserves from every mortal peril.

517   The *ruler of the year* in good aspect: extricates from perils.

518   SATURN in 1*st:* danger of captivity, of grave injury and even of death.

519   If SATURN, ruler of the year be under the horizon, conjunction Mars, or if Mars be in Saturn's natal sign; if the ruler of 1st be in 7th and if Jupiter and Venus be cadent: imminent danger of captivity.

520   SATURN ruler of the year in its natal sign with the SUN in opposition: danger of adversity or of divers ills, according to the sign.

521   SATURN in 12*th:* threat of very great misfortune or of dangerous injuries.

522   SATURN, ruler of 1*st,* in 12*th:* danger of captivity if without an aspect from the Sun.

523   SATURN in 6*th:* perils and captivity.

524   JUPITER in *Capricorn,* ill-aspected by Saturn and the Sun, at the same time ill-aspected by Mars: great misfortune.

525   JUPITER, ruler of the year in the sign which the Sun has just left: humiliations and distress.

526   If MARS be ruler of the year and if Saturn be in the sign of Mars (nativity); if Mars be angular or succedent and above Venus and if benefics be cadent: menace of captivity.

527   MARS, ruler of the year in 1st, in a sign where it possesses no dignity, especially if it were in 1st [Nativity] or in square aspect, or opposition: danger of captivity.

528   MARS in 4*th:* danger of dementia.

529   MARS in 12*th:* danger of captivity, loss of reputation, perils. Mars in 12th but in another house in nativity: danger of a sinister and unforeseen accident.

530   MARS in the Sun's natal sign: danger of violent death if such be presaged in the nativity; or danger of an illness which might prove fatal.

531   MARS in 10*th:* danger of a fall or of an injury by a quadruped.

532   MARS in Saturn's natal sign: unforeseen perils.

533   SUN square or opposition Mars: danger of fall.

534   SUN in 12*th:* danger of captivity.

535   VENUS, ruler of the year in *via combusta:* humiliations occasioned by women.

536   MERCURY, ruler of the year in *via combusta:* anxieties, tribulations, adversity, losses in business.

537   The MOON in *Cancer* and the SUN in *Aries,* both ill-aspected by Saturn or Mars: misfortune and ruin. The Moon, square or opposition Mars: danger of blindness, of fall, or of injury by a quadruped.

538   The MOON in Mars' natal sign: many perils; danger of injury by fall or by iron. Formidable seditions for princes, insurrections. Domestic strife, accusations.

539   The MOON in a masculine sign, in bad aspect to Saturn and Mars and if Saturn or Mars rule the Moon's sign: great adversity, great perils.

540   The MOON in 7*th:* adversity, enmities, perils.

541   The *ruler of the year* being a malefic, while the ruler of the year in the nativity was a benefic; if the Moon be ill-aspected: danger of mortal blow or of very grave injury by enemies. Danger of amputation.

542   The *ruler of the year* in 6*th,* ill aspected: great misfortune.

543   The *ruler of the year,* angular and square or opposition Saturn or Mars: great adversity.

544   The *ruler of the year* in 2nd, 6th, 8th or 12th: danger of some calamity which no one will foresee.

545   The *ruler of the year* in 7th, ill-aspected: menace of dangerous fall; peril which will make it necessary to leave the country.

546   The *ruler of the year,* ill-aspected by an angular planet [square or opposition]: danger of great adversity, great distress, great perils. If the hostile planet be cadent, the presage is lessened.

547   If the *ruler of the year* be without any dignity, the ruler of 1st [nativity] combust, and the Sun and Moon also ill-aspected: danger of suicide or danger of committing an action which will be

expiated by death. But if the benefics be in favourable aspect with the ruler of the year, these dangers will not be realised.

548 The *ruler of the year* square or opposition 1st house: bad year. If sextile or trine: favourable year.

549 If the *ruler of the year* be a malefic and was in 7th in natal chart; if it ill-aspects the Moon, if it be in 1st House or if another malefic be in 1st: a sign of very great perils.

550 If the *ruler of the year* be a benefic and if a malefic be in 1st, and another in 7th and if one or other afflicts the Moon: presage of very grave perils created by enemies, especially if the 1st House have no favourable aspect.

551 The *ruler of the year*, in a cadent house in the natal chart and near the Sun; if it be again near the Sun and in 6th, 9th or 12th and conjunction Saturn: menace of extreme calamities.

552 If the *ruler of the year* be a benefic but if it be in 6th, 8th or 12th and if Saturn or Mars be in 1st or 10th: superiority of enemies, wounds by iron or fall.

553 If the *ruler of the year* be a malefic: if it be in *via combusta* or in an unfortunate house; if the Moon be in bad aspect to Saturn or Mars; if the ruler of the year be in 6th or 12th: danger of captivity.

554 If the *ruler of the year* be benefic but afflicted: danger of adversity and captivity.

555 If the *ruler of 1st* be in 4th, 7th or 10th and afflicted: danger of attack by subjects against the person of their prince or of servants against their masters.

556 The *ruler of 1st* in 8th: life is endangered.

557 The *ruler of 1st* conjunction the *Tail of the Dragon:* danger of poisoning from which one will escape.

558 SATURN or MARS in 1st: a bad year, especially if in bad aspect to the ruler of the year or the Moon.

559 *Two malefics,* one in 1st and the other in 1st in the natal chart: presage of a very difficult year.

560 If *a malefic be in 1st:* and another afflict the *Moon* or a cardinal point of the natal chart: a very troublesome year.

561 If *a malefic be square* 1st House but if the ruler of the house be in good aspect to a benefic and also to the house: the influence of the malefic will be decreased.

562 If *a malefic be conjunction,* square or opposition a benefic and if it were in aspect to the same planet in the natal chart: danger of a mortal blow by iron.

563 A *malefic in 4th:* obstacles in enterprises and perils.

564 If a sign in the 1st House were linked to a malefic in the natal chart: danger of overthrow of fortune and of exile.

565 If the *1st House* be the same as in the natal chart, if the Sun be eclipsed or the Moon waning and if one or other be in bad aspect to Saturn: danger of insurrection against princes.

566   If *a malefic be in 1st House* with the ruler of the year and afflict the Moon: indication of great perils during the year.

567   The sign of the *cusp of the 1st House* being that on the Midheaven in the natal chart: a fortunate year for enterprises. Badly aspected: the contrary . . .

568   The sign of the *Chance of Fortune* passing into the 1st House is favourable for enterprises; in 2nd, a good and profitable year. A happy sign for going into business; in 3rd, profit coming from brothers or near relations; in 4th, a good time for material interests; in 5th, a good time for love, mental work, the practice of medicine; in 6th, chance of gain; in 7th, gains from lawsuits, triumph over enemies; in 8th, danger of some loss, by theft or otherwise. A bad year for lending money with safety; in 9th, profitable journeys if they are promised in the natal chart. Fortune acquired abroad. Sign of elevation in dignity for priests; in 10th, favour of princes and the great, profit in enterprises, realisation of hopes; in 11th, gain or elevation by the aid of friends, supporters or benefactors. Success in enterprises, a good year for receiving money which was lent or for soliciting a favour from princes and the great; in 12th, a favourable year for illicit gains or for drawing profit from secret bad actions.

569   The 1st *House*, its *ruler* and the MOON all afflicted: a catastrophe.

570   When *a planet returns* to the sign in which it is found in the natal chart, it takes again the same significance with, in addition, the effects of any new aspects which it forms.

EPILOGUE

I HAVE kept for these last pages information about a theurgic experience; to experiment with it is not without danger for nervous people. This ritual[2] aims at evoking the spirits of those dear to us who are dead. I borrow the formulae from a very ancient, secret teaching. The supernatural results have been attested for me, many times, by people not easily deceived and whose quite disinterested testimony seemed to me unimpeachable. I do not cite any names, because this revelation of one of the greatest mysteries of occult science is linked with communications of a private nature imposing upon me a scrupulous reserve. Some personal reasons incline me also to believe that manifestations from the Beyond can be obtained if the evocation is made, in a place suitably prepared at a specified time, and with the aid of certain rites whose efficacy will be realised more or less keenly according to the degree of development of the religious sentiment which animates us.

By a vow of ineffable tenderness, some people consecrate to perpetual mourning the room where a loved one died. Their touching distress refuses to allow outsiders to remove traces of the disorder which precedes and follows the supreme moment. The deserted couch still holds the imprint left by the dead. The pieces of furniture—cold witnesses of the agony—are enveloped in a shroud of dust, image of the ashes of the tomb. The clock is stopped when the heart ceases to beat. The candles burned during the vigil go out one after the other like the failing of the breath, at the foot of the pale crucifix which watches over the last sigh. All that recalls a last thought, a last movement, a last look, will henceforth signify only the immobility of sorrow. The room is closed as a holy place which will be re-visited in tears on anniversaries of happiness which will not revive and of a separation that is without hope of a reunion here below.

However, the soul which has disappeared is sometimes brought back by the worship of the heart. It is present, invisible, at the mourning; and then, if it be night and if an exalted act of faith and pure love evokes it in the name of the Almighty, it can for a moment show the radiance of its immortal essence across the darkness where nature sleeps after sunset.

---

[2] A modified form of this ritual appears to have been used by Eliphas Levi when he evoked the shade of Apollonius of Tyana before Sir Edward Bulwer-Lytton in London.—*Ed.*

These consoling apparitions are rare, for the necessary solitude, self-recollection and ardent faith which may draw them are conditions which are difficult to assemble. But it is only necessary for the experiment to succeed occasionally to impose some reserve on too hasty negations born of a sterile scepticism. Be that as it may, here, according to the Theurgic tradition, are the dispositions of mind and the external acts which are necessary to obtain the manifestation of the beloved dead.

.   .   .

The affection which unites us, beyond the tomb, to the person mourned must be entirely pure. The father, the mother, the child, the brother, the sister, the husband, the wife—near relations and intimate friends are particularly prone to the desire to see these again, if one considers them simply as transfigured beings in a higher sphere who, in this new life, pray to the Almighty to make us worthy to come to the same happiness.

Another provision, not less necessary, is the examination of conscience. If one has caused injury to a neighbour, one must repair it; if one has unjust enemies, one must grant them in one's heart unreserved pardon; if one has neglected towards God the duties of adoration and prayer, it is necessary to return to the practice of worship, according to the form of religion in which one was instructed. These preliminaries prove sufficiently that there is in the evocation of the dead neither sorcery nor the slightest appearance of an impious pact; and it is only after being thus prepared that we can endure, without peril to life or reason, the approach of the invisible world.

The place chosen for the evocation is important. The most propitious assuredly will be the room where the loved one left the last traces of his presence. When this condition cannot be realised, we should obtain, in some solitary spot, a place of which the proportions and the orientation recall exactly the death-chamber.

The window should be covered up by boards of olive wood so that it is hermetically sealed allowing no outside light to penetrate. The ceiling, the four walls and the floor should be covered by hangings of emerald green silk which the one who is performing the evocation will adjust himself with copper nails, without calling in the aid of any outsider because, from this moment, he alone should enter this reserved place, now called the Oratory.

Next, the pieces of furniture which the loved one used, the objects cherished and on which the last gaze rested, should be collected. They should be arranged as they were at the moment of death. If these objects are not available, a full-length portrait of the person should be procured or painted, with the most faithful resemblance possible, in the dress and in the colours worn during the last days of life. This portrait should be placed on the eastern wall held in place by copper clips and covered by a veil of white silk. It should be given a crown of flowers of the kind that the person represented liked best.

Before this portrait should be erected an altar of white marble with four columns, with bulls' feet at the base. On the altar a five-pointed star should be inlaid, made of sheets of very pure copper and drawn according to the talisman of Anael, the planetary Genius of Venus. The centre of this star should be large enough to surround the base of a copper brazier in the form of a cup containing dried fragments of alder and of laurel wood. Near the brazier should be placed an incense burner, ready-filled. Another five-pointed star should be prepared in sky blue, gold, emerald green and red-purple on the skin of a male white lamb without spot, stretched before the altar.

In the middle of the oratory a copper tripod of triangular shape should be placed, carrying a brazier similar to the one already mentioned and containing very dry fragments of olive wood.

Near the wall on the south side should be placed a tall copper candelabra for the reception of a candle of very pure white wax which should be the only illumination for the mystery of the evocation.

The white colour of the altar, the lamb-skin and the veil are consecrated to Gabriel, planetary archangel of the Moon and Genius of the mysteries. The green colour of the hangings and the copper belong to the Genius of Venus.

The altar and the tripod should each be surrounded by a chain of magnetised iron and by three garlands composed of flowers and leaves of myrtle, olive and rose.

Lastly on the west side, facing the portrait, a canopy should be set also draped with emerald green and resting on two triangular columns, made of olive wood and faced with very pure copper. Between the wall and each column on both north and south sides the hangings should fall in long folds to the ground, in such a manner as to form a sort of tabernacle open on the eastern side. At the foot of each column should be placed a sphinx sculptured in marble like the altar. The head of each sphinx should be hollowed out to hold a brazier to burn perfumes. Under this canopy the apparition will be manifested and we should remember that the evoker should turn towards the east to pray and to the west to evoke.

Before entering this little sanctuary, consecrated to the religion of remembrance, the seeker puts on an azure-blue silk robe, fastened by copper hooks in each of which an emerald is mounted. On his head he wears a tiara surrounded by a circle embellished by twelve emeralds and a crown of violets. On his breast he wears the talisman of Venus [*page* 313], suspended by a ribbon of azure-blue silk. On the ring finger of the left hand he puts on a copper ring in which a turquoise is mounted. On his feet are shoes of azure-blue silk and he holds a fan of swan's feathers to ward off, at need, the smoke from the incense.

The oratory and all that it contains should be consecrated on a Friday during one of the hours of the Genius of Venus. This consecration is made by burning violets and roses in a fire of olive-wood. In some part of the oratory a ventilator should be prepared which will draw off the fumes without allowing light to filter in from outside.

When these preparations are finished, the seeker undertakes a retreat of 21 days beginning on the anniversary of the birth or death of the loved one. During this time he will refrain from giving to anyone even the smallest of the tokens of affection which the deceased received from him; he will maintain an absolute chastity in both acts and thoughts; he will only have one meal a day, composed of bread, wine, roots and fruit. These three conditions are indispensable to the success of the evocation and their accomplishment demands the most complete solitude.

Every day, a few minutes before midnight, the seeker will put on the consecrated clothes. When midnight sounds, he will enter the oratory holding in his right hand a lighted candle and in his left an hour-glass. The candle will be placed in the candelabra and the hour-glass on the altar will mark the hour. He will next proceed to renew the crown of flowers and the garlands. Then he will uncover the portrait and, motionless before the altar, that is to say, facing the east, he will re-live in his heart all the remembrances he has preserved of the loved one.

When the sand has fallen from the upper part of the hour-glass, the meditation hour will be over. The seeker will light, from the flame in the candelabra, the little pieces of alder and laurel wood contained in the brazier on the altar; then, taking from the incense box a small quantity of incense, he throws it three times on the fire, pronouncing these words: *Glory to the Father of universal life, in the splendour of the infinite heights, and peace, in the profound and endless dusk, to the Spirits of good will.*

He will next veil the portrait again and, taking his candle in his hand, he will leave the oratory, going backwards slowly to the threshold. The same ceremonial will be used every night at the same hour of midnight for the first twenty days of the retreat. The crown suspended on the portrait as well as the garlands surrounding the altar and the tripod will be renewed at each visit. Withered flowers and leaves will be burned in an adjoining room and the evoker will keep the ashes and add to them the ashes gathered after each visit.

The twenty-first day having arrived, the seeker will do his best to have no communication with anyone whatever. If he cannot absolutely dispense with an interview, he will not be the first to speak and he will defer any business till the following day. At the stroke of noon, he will set up a small round table in the oratory covered with a linen napkin, perfectly white, which has never been used. He will place there two copper chalices, a whole loaf of bread and a crystal flask containing very pure wine. The bread will be broken, not cut; the wine will be poured equally into the two chalices. The evoker will offer to the dead person half of this mysterious communion, which will be, for that day, his sole food. He will consume the other half standing and in silence before the veiled portrait with only a candle for light. Then he will retire as usual, going backwards to the threshold. The bread and the chalice which were offered should be left on the table.

In the evening, at the solemn hour the seeker will take into the oratory some very dry cypress wood which he will set alight on the altar and on the tripod. He will throw on the flame of the altar three pinches of incense in honour of the *Supreme Power* which manifests itself by *Intelligence perpetually active* and by *absolute Wisdom*. When the wood of the two offerings has been reduced to charcoal, he will again make the triple offering of incense on the altar and will throw it seven times on the tripod, in honour of the seven mediating Genii which accomplish the Divine will. During each exhalation of the sacred perfume, he will repeat the Doxology: *Glory to the Father of the universal life.* Then, turning to the east, he will invoke God by prayers of the cult which the person evoked professed when alive.

After these prayers, turning towards the west he will light the braziers placed on the head of each sphinx, and when the cypress wood is burning he will cover it with perfectly dry violets and roses. Then he will extinguish the candle which lights the oratory and kneeling before the dais, between the two columns, he will speak mentally to the loved one with affection, with faith. He will supplicate her to show herself and will renew seven times this mental adjuration, under the auspices of the seven good Genii, while endeavouring to raise his spirit above the weaknesses of human nature.

Then the postulant, his eyes closed and his face covered by his two hands, will call, aloud but gently, the person evoked, pronouncing three times all her names.

Some moments after the third call, he will stretch out his arms in the form of a cross and, opening his eyes, he will see the beloved perfectly recognisable, that is to say, her ethereal substance which is separated from the terrestrial and mortal body and which the Qabalists called *périsprit*, the fluidic envelope of the soul,[2] which conserves the human form freed from its infirmities and with the distinctive features by which the imperishable individuality of our essence shows itself.

The soul so evoked gives counsel; sometimes she reveals secrets, knowledge of which might be useful for the happiness of people loved during terrestrial life. But she will reply to no question having for object the satisfaction of greed or sensual passion; she will not reveal the hiding-place of hidden treasure, nor the secrets of others; she is silent about the mysteries of the new existence into which she has entered. It may happen, however, that she describes herself as happy or punished, and in the latter case she will ask for prayers or religious observances which must be faithfully carried out. She will also indicate when the evocation may be made again.

When she has disappeared the evoker must return to the eastern side, relight the fire of the altar and make a last offering of incense. Then he detaches the crown and the garlands, takes his candle and retires, facing the west until he is outside the oratory. His last duty is to burn what remains of the foliage and flowers. Their ash placed with the ash already collected during the twenty preceding days will be mixed with myrtle seed and buried secretly in a field at a depth which the plough-share will not reach.

The ceremonial conditions of evocation are, as you see, perfectly simple; those of moral aptitude are more difficult to realise but they do not go beyond human power. Theurgic doctrine has foreseen the possibility of failure; it advises to experiment again on the date of the second anniversary, bringing to the work greater care and self-recollection, and it affirms that a third attempt is never without results unless the evoker be under the influence of an inveterate vice which has become as second nature to him.

In this matter, I have received many serious confirmations; but I leave the field open to objectors, only observing to them: 'Before making a categorical denial, make the experiment. Miracles are promised to faith. Faith is the boldness of a will which does not hesitate in the shadows and which advances towards the light through all trials and surmounting all obstacles. The will is the supreme arcanum of high Magic.'

·   ·   ·

[2] 'The Astral Light or *Anima Mundi* is dual and bisexual. The [ideal] male part of it is purely divine and spiritual, it is the Wisdom, it is Spirit or *Purusha;* while the female portion [the *Spiritus* of the Nazarenes] is tainted, in one sense, with matter, *is* indeed matter, and therefore is evil already. It is the life-principle of every living creature, and furnishes the astral soul, the fluidic *périsprit* to men, animals, fowls of the air, and everything living . . . '—H. P. Blavatsky, *Secret Doctrine*, Vol. 1.—*Ed.*

To believe nothing or to believe everything: these attitudes are both indications of a feeble intellect or of a dulled consciousness. In taking this opinion, pronounced by Bayle in the 18th century, in his *Replies to the questions of a Provincial,* I hope not to hurt anyone's feelings and to keep the sympathy of the serious public which for thirty years has taken an interest in my writings.

Its esteem is precious to me and this new work would lose all value if critics accused it of being simply a blind apology for occult arts.

As a lonely worker, accustomed to fix my gaze beyond time, I have let myself be carried along by my pen, under the charm of the pursuit of the unknown and of mysteries which proudly disdain the progress of enlightenment. Attracted by false fires into the ruins of antiquity, could I have taken their deceptive light for the dawn of a new day, and should I destroy, before the bar of reason, the pages where I forgot to be sceptical?

My studies of Magic date far back. I have already told how they began.

The further I advanced in this labyrinth peopled by revelations or by dreams, the more I felt the peril of straying there, in dazzled comtemplation, without hope of return.

Urgent to attain some height where my thought could orientate itself and find its way, how many times have I experienced the anguish of discouragement at the edge of the abysses which opened before me!

Dupe of my aspirations and suspected, at the very lowest, of madness by our scoffing and blasé age, might I not be a ridiculous Tantalus, a counterfeit Prometheus?

Let me dare to say that I do not condemn myself to such a level and that I expect more justice.

Magic, a philosophic doctrine which must never be confused with sorcery, is the most ancient stratum of human knowledge; all scholars are agreed in this respect.[4]

Tradition, handed on at first by word alone in the secret teachings of the primitive priesthood—entrusted later to the symbolic writing to be found on the ruins of India, Persia, Chaldea and Egypt—delivered to the disputes of the Greek, Roman, Hebrew and Arab schools by writings in the common tongue and also by conquest: Magic has suffered down the centuries the corroding influence of time and has only descended to us in fragments.

From these fragments, some enquiring, patient and learned men—cardinals, bishops, doctors of Theology—have tried to shape a body of knowledge which would epitomise what has been lost.

---

[4] Still more so today, when paintings on palaeolithic cave walls are generally held to have been magical in intention. The recently revealed Lascaux Caves seem particularly eloquent in this.—*Ed.*

A strange work for churchmen, but protected precisely because of the character of such notable workers, this restoration of Magic has not been completed nor can it be.

We halt with regret, sometimes before an irreparable breach, sometimes before a door without a key, or to speak more simply, learned commentaries have not been able to fill in the gaps nor to penetrate all the obscurities of the old Magi.

The shadows of the Pyramids seem to reach the books of the Middle Ages and of the Renaissance, to be revealed by means of modern exegesis.

Motionless and mute, the Sphinx of ancient days has not yielded up all its enigmas.

Is it possible, nevertheless, still to catch a glimpse and to grasp some useful truths under the veils with which the sciences called occult remain enveloped?

Is initiation into this branch of study worthy or unworthy to occupy vigorous minds for a moment?

Let us pause before replying; let us not hasten to protest.

Nature is always full of unfathomable mysteries, and the more we augment the store of our discoveries, the more the horizon of the unknown increases beyond our pride of knowledge.

After so many false steps on the path of wisdom, perhaps the time has come not to despise too much certain experiences which have many times given the lie to our most superb negations.

Two questions have above all preoccupied me in these discourses on Magic: first, the *spells* and *oracles* such as were consulted by the Greek and Roman world; second, the *horoscopes* as cast by the priests of Egypt.

To admit as scientifically true either of these means of questioning the future would invite derisive laughter from the newspapers.

Do not let us risk such an insult; but without drawing any imprudent conclusion from the examples I have presented in my book, let us welcome spells and horoscopes as divinatory playthings which have at least the merit, if it is one, of amusing children.

Study the scheme of the Oracles like a game of patience, the aphorisms of astrology as the shapes in a kaleidoscope; I am quite of this opinion; but do not throw a stone at inoffensive people who still persist in seeing in these shreds some imprint of the hand of God; for, after all, who knows that they are wrong?

Whether a sublime emanation from unseen worlds or seductive superstition, prescience of the future can neither be denied nor proved by ordinary reasoning.

We admit it when it flatters us and we accord it the honour of representing Providence; we reject it when it shocks us, and then it justifies itself by blows of Fate.

Blows of Fate: I uphold the word, audacious and impertinent as it seems in the middle of the XIXth century.

The examples I have given are my authority and I could have multiplied them by linking an oracle to every event in our history.

It has, however, seemed to me to be more becoming to halt at the limit of accomplished fact, while making it clear that in any case I shall not lend myself to fortune-telling.

Being attentive to the general current of events, I sometimes study from the shore the rising tide or the lightning which illumines a chasm; I see the dark spot in the depths of a sky which still seems cloudless; but it is not my mission to teach the pilots.

This book was written for myself alone long before I thought of addressing the public and perhaps it should never have left my retreat.

To brave criticism with six hundred pages[5] on Magic as my only defence requires more heroism than my age and sober habits could sustain.

On the one hand I saw M. Alfred Maury, of the Institute, tilting against the great queen of the sciences of the past much as Don Quixote tilted at windmills; and on the other side M. Michelet reducing all to the rags of sorcerers and to the witch's broom.

I was not able to resist the desire to make an appeal to the tribunal of history.

I may have been inexpert in pleading the cause, but I have always wished to anchor myself to the truth while avoiding absolute judgments.

It is a matter of good taste not to decide one way or the other, even when we have, or believe we have, our hands full of proofs.

To await public opinion, to give way, instead of striding ahead, is frequently the way to obtain better results and for a longer time.

An interesting page is missing from my book: I know it.

The curiosity of the reader would like to find there predictions for the near future on the eventualities which remain at the moment in the Divine counsels.

To examine these problems in silence and solitude is the right of everyone; but it would be difficult to publish the solution.

If my reserve in this matter does not give satisfaction to people who are too impatient, it will at least be understood and appreciated.

For the rest, everyone can, like myself, read in the *Tetrabiblion* of Ptolemy and in the *Speculum Astrologiae* of Junctin de Florence the response to all the questions it is possible to imagine on the subject.

Let us hope that these two treatises will, one day, be exhumed by some intelligent and bold translator: I recommend them to the leisure hours of the Benedictines of Solesmes. There, since the

---

[5] The 1870 French edition has 666 pages, to be quite accurate.—*Ed.*

advent of Christianity, are to be found the two poles of the sciences called occult, and, in particular, that which claims to open the apocalyptic book, sealed with seven seals, in which our destinies are written.[6]

Is divination a universal but sterile error, or a powerful and fruitful truth? Will it disappear before human logic, or will it one day take its honoured place amongst serious studies?

That is a decision on which it is hardly likely that an understanding will be arrived at.

In some respects the opposing sides seem to be equally matched, in an uncertain light; from other points of view chaos returns, obscure, heavy, impenetrable.

Divination is a star shining and dimming like the beam from a lighthouse; it lends us and it refuses us, in its own time, its capricious intuitions.

Is it diabolical or celestial? Where does it come from? Who shall say what it is or what it is not?

Seen close at hand, it is a card-reader, the last incarnation of a contagious stupidity; seen at a distance, it is a manifestation of the Divine Mind in a Hermes or a Zoroaster, in an Elijah or a Daniel; it is the majesty of the Magi and the prophets; it is the mystery of the Sibyls and the Vestals; it is the poetry of the Druidic virgins and the nymphs of Hercynos; it is the eternal Tomorrow which passes in the vibration of an electric current.

Ah, I repeat, let us beware of premature negations.

Let us walk softly on the path between abysses, the path which separates error and truth.

If our lofty self-sufficiency denies what it cannot touch, do not let us believe that we are infallible: it does not demonstrate strength of mind to defy the future.

Diminished but not destroyed, the traditions of high Magic may suddenly regain their immense prestige.

A belief cannot perish when it has had the privilege of enthralling a world, and the day when Magic was proscribed, the Caesars condemned themselves to fatality.

---

[6] This is still true. Claudius Ptolemy or Ptolemy 'de Péluse' [second century A.D.: named from his alleged birthplace, Ptolemais Hermii, a Greek city of the Thebaid: 'observing' between 127 and 141 or 151 A.D.] collected the physical knowledge of his day into the 13 books of the first general account of the phenomenal world which he called *The Great Construction*, commonly known to us as the Ptolemaic System; it was chiefly geographical and astronomic, and astrological lore was gathered separately into four books, *Tetrabibloi or Tetrabiblion*, on the influence of the stars. See Dane Rudhyar *The Astrology of Personality* and Temple Hungad *Brief History of Astrology*. Junctin or Junctinus of Florence [16th century], more properly Francesco Giuntini, D.D., besides the *Speculum* [1573] mentioned by Christian wrote treatises *On the Judgment of Nativities* [1570] and *On Divination* [1580]. He began the modern ephemeris with his *Ephimerides* 1583—1606 [1585].—Ed.

The eclipse of the occult arts does not at all entail their downfall; it adds but a shadow the more to their mystery.

In the distance or close at hand, in spite of the efforts of philosophy, the world of the marvellous will never cease to attract the human spirit in its real sphere or in phantasmagoria.

Overwhelmed by so much misery during the whole of his short life, the one who is downtrodden needs someone in whom he can confide, who will give him consolation; he is the client of the fortune-tellers. And however birth and fortune may have placed a member of the privileged class, he likes to think that a Guardian Spirit smiles on him from heaven.

To believe in Destiny in the truest sense of the word is to catch a glimpse of the plan of God. For great minds, this faith is the magnet which attracts great things; its loss is the augury of spectacular downfalls.

The *Fatum* of antique theology to which it is said that the gods themselves [i.e. the occult forces of nature] were obedient in company with man, personified absolute wisdom.

The eternal Eve, true mother of all living, supreme reason having spoken [*fata*], the future, in union with universal life at all times and in all modes, is the manifestation of *fatum*, of the spoken word, if I dare to express myself thus.

In attempting to compose the Oracles, we may seek again a remote echo of this divine word; and I have shown that this research is not undertaken in vain. Those who are interested may go further.

To prolong these considerations would, I feel, be a digression.

To win proselytes for the old faith of the Magi is not at all my design, and perhaps I should lose something more than time wasted.

Let us stop, then, at an equal distance from baseless credulity and unwise scepticism.

The true, said a poet, may sometimes not be credible.

Let us avail ourselves of this warning; but do not let us exaggerate its significance.

Isis is dead, truly dead, with her sphinxes, her rites and her learned priests; no hand of man will ever raise again her fallen temple.

Sacred fictions of the olden times, resplendent symbolism to the eyes of initiates, grandiose myths which stretched a ladder of marvels from man to God, all have disappeared like a dream.

The Orient is empty like the rifled Pyramids.

But let us stop short of complete negation; for whatever has existed never perishes entirely.

Across the clouds of dust shaken by the passing of the centuries, some fragments of papyrus have survived, poor epitaphs of that which is no more.

As an antiquary without an axe to grind, I bend over these stray relics of a lost story.

Dream or reality, I bring my offering to the curious without expecting any gratitude.

As a worker, I have performed my task without ambition for success but not without the desire to be useful. Why should not this book be worthy of producing some good results, even if only to help some discouraged people to enjoy the fortifying hope of better days to come?

In the hard struggle of life, the greater our chances the more are we at the mercy of the unexpected.

In spite of our wisdom, which always falls short in some respects, as Bossuet said, everywhere the spectre of Fate goes before us or follows us.

To enquire of its mystery by the feeble methods remaining to us is to avoid a surprise; to ignore it is dangerous, to brave it is folly, for too many examples warn us.

Preneste, Antium, Delphi, Eleusis, Babylon, Memphis—these sacred tombs of a science formerly colossal are no more than mythological memories; the learned men of today hardly mention the names in their books.

Deadly scorn is perhaps as much to be condemned as the silly credulity which accepts everything without thinking.

For my part, I am a zealous admirer of the progress of enlightenment; but it seems to me that true progress should not make a *tabula rasa* of these traditions under the somewhat threadbare pretext of enfranchising the human spirit.

Prudence is worth more than pride in the conduct of life, and one need not be a hundred years old to see that this most obvious truth is a law outside which there is salvation neither for nations nor for individuals.

The Collège de France and the Sorbonne, the University and the Church, platform and pulpit with their divergent theories, have torn these matters from their contexts and have given no answers.

After so many words and so much writing, the eloquent seduction of which I do not fail to recognise, what certainty have we gained?

Carried away by the winds of doctrines, towards what shore do we hope to arrive?

The port is behind us: it is the Past, whose tranquil depths are sheltered under an immutable rock, crowned by an eternal dawn.

Beyond, there is only an eternal tempest, each wave of which breaks from century to century on the reefs of the Future in an eternal twilight!

THE first thing that strikes a reader of Paul Christian's astrology is that he lived before Freud. He takes historical characters, studies the known facts of their lives, consults Junctinus and fits the jigsaw puzzle neatly together; then, tiring of the routine, he turns to his beloved game of Oracles which gave more scope to his imagination. Yet he was always searching for the psychological key. In the closing pages of his Epilogue he weighs Fate and Free-will in finer and ever finer scales until, at last, he calls it a day; more precisely, 'twilight'. What could be fairer than that!

He is so dazzled by the light of the past that he can only see the present in terms of sceptics or the superstitious; those who believe too little and those who believe too much. His spirit seems to droop under the weight of the innumerable catastrophes and fatalities remorselessly collected by his authorities who followed the old map-makers' practice: 'Where unknown, place terrors.' But if he had taken his favourite Egyptian studies a little further, not as history but as experience, he would have said, like the postulant gazing on the dark passage which points onwards to the pole-star: 'I proceed to heaven; I kneel among the stars.' Then the terrors and the twilight would have been forgotten.

Astrologers no longer use rays from Circles of Fate; yet there is little doubt that ultimately these circles, related to the whole ancient philosophy of the seven spheres, will be re-stated in modern terms. They seem mere relics because they are presented as 'keys'. Now keys, offered as short cuts, add nothing to our knowledge; but these same keys, examined in the light of modern psychological methods, may lead us back to the reason why they were forged; as one writer has put it, 'We, together with the earth, are within mutually intersecting spheres. Seven spheres are thrust into one another, and we grow into this thrusting together in the course of our life'.

In this century, with its rapidly shifting viewpoints, astrology has not remained where Junctinus—or Alan Leo—left it; indeed the possibilities are now seen to be so vast that only the co-operation of many trained scientists in different fields of research will make it possible to bring it into its true place as the link between Science and Religion, between Art and Healing, between Psychology and Education. The individual astrologer, however able, needs the assistance of statistical experts on a world scale.

'Judgment', which seeks to describe the native and his possibilities, is not a XXth century word; 'assessment' is better. The astrologer's work is first to analyse the chart and then to synthesise: to take the watch to pieces to understand its mechanism and then to put it together again so that it works. Nothing is more dangerous in astrology than to fail in synthesis. To extol a good aspect regardless of qualification, or to regard a bad aspect as an omen of disaster, is to meddle with the very mainspring of man's actions. Clients go to an astrologer believing that he knows all the facts and taking his judgment as gospel; this negative attitude sometimes seems to give the astrologer a power-complex. When we add to the situation the fact that many people turn to astrology when they are in a difficulty, have lost their way or are afraid of the future, the danger of advice from well-meaning practitioners is very great. 'A little astrological knowledge is one of the worst things that can happen to one who is not altogether solidly established in his own selfhood', writes Dane Rudhyar and goes on: 'he is handling, promiscuously, psychological acids and explosives'.

The average client who has perhaps read a popular book on astrology believes that he can be shown how to escape the ministrations of Saturn and bask always in the radiance of Jupiter. 'Can you tell me if there is some Saturn about?' wrote one such person anxiously. The true answer of course is that there is always some Saturn about. In fine, we may ask: does not the astrologer very often open up more problems than he solves?

As astrology increases in importance it is likely that the true practitioners will be trained psychologists who will use dates to confirm their independent findings but who will treat their clients by psychological methods. Jung has stated that he uses astrology in difficult cases and other psychologists may follow his example.

The psycho-analyst does not predict the goal for his patient beyond integration. The patient's own dreams, his own creations, point the way and once he sees the way himself, he is cured and departs needing nothing more. It is tempting for the astrologer to predict from the evidence in the chart; but the maxim in *The Secret of the Golden Flower* is timely: 'one must not wish to leave out the steps between and penetrate directly'.

Horoscopes of countries are interesting if correct maps can be drawn, but frequently they seem to depend upon earlier maps for which data is not available or reliable. The horoscope of the United Nations Organisation which we reproduce is an example of the difficulty of deciding upon the time and place of birth. The first session of U.N.O. which opened in London on 10 January 1946 was used for the chart by some astrologers, but C. E. O. Carter points out that two earlier dates must be considered: first, the date of the decision to found U.N.O. which was taken at a meeting in the Albert Hall on 10 October 1945 at about 7 p.m., and second, 24 October 1945 at 4.45 p.m. E.S.T. at Washington D.C. when Secretary Byrnes announced that the required 29 nations had ratified the Charter. Mr. Carter considers the second to be the true figure.

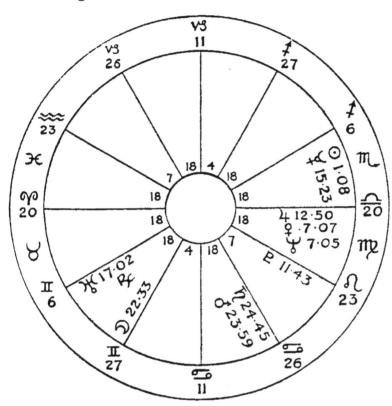

U.N.O. Map for 4.45 p.m. E.S.T. 24 October 1945 at Washington, D.C.
[The figure is erected according to the method of Campanus.]

It is interesting to note the distribution of the bodies: 4 in Water, 5 in Air, 1 in Fire—and Earth unrepresented. While a date which offered a more balanced map might have resulted in ability to move more directly to practical work, it is likely that thereby a 'circle premature' might have been created. Because of the extreme danger of the world situation as a whole and the vast possibilities of the future, fluidity may prove to be a saving grace. True, Air-Water, as Mr. Carter points out, is 'the neurotic combination *par excellence*'; but when two things are happening at the same time, the death of the old and the birth of the new, what seems, close at hand, to be retreat to the edge of the abyss may prove to the historians of the future to be a necessary, even if an insecure, stage. It looks like the alchemical

formula Solvé et Coagula, and the Solvé process is certainly function-
ing. In an earlier world crisis the Hebrew prophets used the symbol
of the winepress.

A horoscope which may well be compared with U.N.O.'s is
that of Albert Einstein.

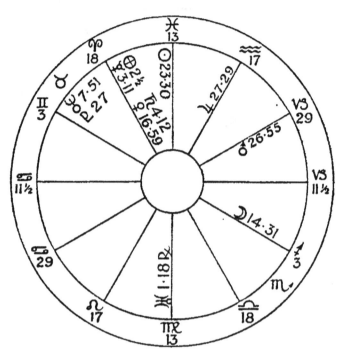

Albert Einstein, born at Ulm 14 March 1879 11.30 a.m. [Placidus Houses.]

It is interesting that the Sun is in Pisces, for this Water sign
gives the imagination needed by the creative as opposed to the
academic scientist. Uranus in Virgo shows the mind lively in devis-
ing techniques, and Mars is strong in Capricorn, its sign of exaltation. He has four bodies in Fire, four in Earth, one apiece in Air
and Water.

While Pisces has sometimes been called, by older astrologers, the
sign of self-undoing on account of its association with the 12th
House, it frequently figures prominently in the horoscopes of great
men and seems to impart a mystical quality which, rightly handled,
makes its natives highly magnetic. This magnetic quality is best
seen in cases where personal interests are entirely subordinated to
the task undertaken. The present Pope, Pius XII, with Sun in
Pisces, may be cited as an example. Ramakrishna had Sun, Moon

and Mercury in Pisces, Sun and Moon in the 12th House and Pisces rising. Rudolf Steiner, founder of the Anthroposophical Society, had Sun in Pisces and H. P. Blavatsky had the sign in Midheaven.

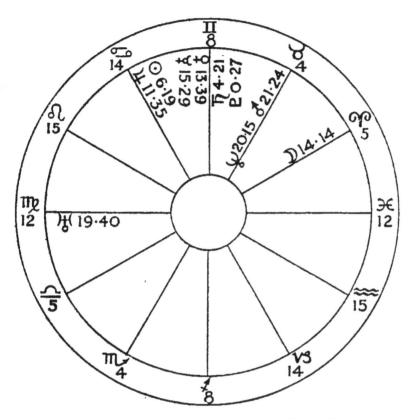

Pierre Laval, born at Chateldon in Auvergne 28 June 1883. 10 a.m.
[Placidus Houses.]

The above horoscope of Laval shows Sun and Jupiter in the Cardinal sign of Water. The chart is impressive because of the concentration of planets in houses 9 and 10. The trine in Earth signs from Mars and Neptune to Uranus rising gave him a practical grasp of affairs; his castles were built on the ground. In fact, he bought a castle in his native Chateldon when he became Prime Minister and it is said that he had decided when still a child that one day he would possess it. The group of planets in Gemini may be regarded as indicative of his mental agility.

Laval has been the subject of much condemnation, but the astrologer should not be led into partisanship and should see him rather as part of the total situation. In an article which recently appeared in France the writer recalled a conversation he had with de Gaulle in which the General said that Gaullism and Vichyism were, historically, part of the same thing. 'If Resistance was the sword,' he is quoted as saying, 'Vichy was the shield of France.'

Many thoughtful people who consult astrologers are less perplexed about their personal affairs than about the scheme of things and the problem of Fate and Freewill. A very interesting instruction is given in *Letters from a Sufi Teacher* concerning those who declare that everything is according to the Divine Will. 'When the Prophet spoke of the Divine Will his companions said, "We shall depend upon it and refrain from exertion." The Prophet replied: *"Ye shall exert* and [then] what has been ordained will be given." ' There are many astrology-addicts who become too negative and wait to be told what to do with their lives. If the analysis of the chart does not aid a man to obey the Delphic instruction 'Know Thyself', it is worse than useless. For the horoscope is nothing new. Like M. Jourdain's prose, we have expressed it all our lives from our first cry. It reveals itself in our walk, our speech, our silences; in our work, our methods of approaching work, our evasions; our likes and dislikes; the contractual obligations we accept, the gifts that come to us from outside. If the astrologer faithfully and without any moral emphasis reveals the pattern in a general sense, we should be able to realise the command 'Know Thyself' in its more extended sense, 'Become what thou art'. And that is the exciting adventure of living.

Our plans for the future are dreams and if they are not realised, or, more often, if they are realised and we look with dismay at the mess we are making of things, it is simply a sign that we are not acting from the centre. Horoscopic progressions if translated into detailed predictions may lead to unbalanced activity like walking on—or avoiding—the cracks on the pavement.

The astrologer must of course scale his discourse to the stature of his client. To the more enlightened, he may quote Sir James Jeans as saying 'Time and Space begin to appear as fictions created by our own minds'. Within that framework, events promised by progressions may arise naturally, like features in a landscape when mist has cleared away. They will be recognised and accepted in terms of our own values and way of life.

J.S.

BOOKS FOR REFERENCE

BOOKS FOR REFERENCE

Containing all works mentioned in either text or footnotes in the foregoing pages, together with some few additions. In some cases fuller bibliographical particulars will be found in the text and notes.

WORKS OF GENERAL REFERENCE
> La Grande Larousse
> The Encyclopaedia Britannica

PHILOSOPHY AND ESOTERIC WORKS

C. E. M. Joad
> Outline of Philosophy

Bertrand Russell
> History of Philosophy

G. H. Lewes
> Biographical History of Philosophy

Shaikh Sharfuddin Maneri
> Letters from a Sufi Teacher

H. P. Blavatsky
> The Secret Doctrine

Bayle
> Replies to the Questions of a Provincial

C. G. Jung
> The Secret of the Golden Flower

ANCIENT RELIGIONS
> The Sanskrit Vedas
> The Zend Avesta
> The Shastabad

N.B.—For parallels between Indian and Christian religions, see p. 31 of this present work.

COSMOLOGY AND GENERAL

H. S. Bellamy
> *Built Before the Flood*

I. Velikovsky
> *Worlds in Collision*

Camille Flammarion
> *Les Mondes Imaginaires et les Mondes Réels*

Athanasius Kircher
> *Voyage Ecstatique*
> *China Illustrata*
> *Mundus Subterraneus*

Honoré de Balzac
> *Etudes Philosophiques* (Serafita)

Court de Gebelin
> *Plan Général du Monde Primitif*

Claudius Ptolemy 'de Péluse'
> *The Great Construction*

GENERAL AUTHORITATIVE TEXTS FOR MAGIC

Eliphas Levi
> *History of Magic*
> *Transcendental Magic*
> *Histoire de la Kabbale*
> *Dogme et Rituel de la Haute Magie*
> *Clefs de la Magie*

Alfred Maury
> *Magie et Astrologie*
> *La Magie dans l'Antiquité et au Moyen Age*

Pierre d'Abanne
> *Elements de Magie*
> *Livre de la Sacrée Magie*

Francis Barratt
> *Abramelin the Magus*

M. A. Attwood
> *A Suggestive Inquiry into the Hermetic Mystery*

S. Liddell May [editor]
> *Clacivula Salmonis*
> [also in English: *The Keys of Solomon the King*]

By the Head or Forehead

Chattopadhya

Holmes W. Merton
Descriptive Mentality from the Head, Face and Hands

DOWSING

W. H. Trinder
Dowsing

T. Bedford Franklin and J. Cecil Mayby
The Physics of the Divining Rod

Other authorities include: the Abbé Bignon, the Abbé Valmont de Bomare, Athanasius Kircher, S. J., and Fr. Malebranche.

GENII OR FAIRY LORE

Pomponius Mela
Geography

Lewis Spence
History and Origins of Druidism
The Fairy Tradition in Britain
and other works *passim*

Wirt Sykes
British Goblins

Keightley
Fairy Mythology

Grimm [trans. by Stallybrass]
Teutonic Mythology

W. A. Craigie
Scandinavian Folklore

James Macpherson
Fingal, an Ancient Epic, composed by Ossian

Paul Christian
[*Translation of the above, Paris* 1858]

Milton
L'Allegro

Shakespeare
> *Midsummer Night's Dream*

HERBALISM

Chief authorities are Nicholas Culpeper, W. H. Box and C. F. Leyel

CURATIVE AND OTHER PROPERTIES OF STONES, ETC.

Anonymous
> *Traité des Secrets de Nature, Touchant les Animaux Plantes et les Pierres*

C. Leonardi
> *Speculum Lapidum, Cui Accesserunt Metallorum Sympathiae*

CHIROLOGY (Cheiromancy)

> Works quoted for disparagement by Christian:

Rampalle
> *Natural Chiromancy*

Adrian Sicler
> *New Chiromancy*

> Sound Modern Works:

Catherine St. Hill
> *The Book of the Hand*

St. Germain
> *The Study of Palmistry for Professional Purposes*

Cheiro
> *The Language of the Hand*
> *You and Your Hand*

Benham
> *The Laws of Scientific Hand Reading*

DREAM INTERPRETATION

S. Freud
> *Dreams*

C. G. Jung and Alfred Adler
> *Works* [*passim*]

Lewis Spence
> *Second Sight in Scotland*

St. Nicephorus of Constantinople
> *Oneirokritikon*

THE FAUST LEGEND

H. G. Meek
> *Faust: the Man and the Myth,* [1930]

H. B. Cottrill
> *The Faust Legend and Goethe's Faust*

Palma Cayet
> *Histoire du Docteur Faust et de sa Mort Epouvantable*

William Rose, M.A., Ph.D.
> *History of Dr. John Faustus*

Professor Philipps
> article on Mephistopheles in the
> *Encyclopaedia Britannica*

Bishop of Bamberg
> *Account Book of* 1520

Johann Gast
> *Sermones Convivales* [1548]

Johannes Manlius [Johann Memmel]
> *Locorum Communium Collectanea*
> *Minutes of the Town Council of Ingolstadt* [1528]

Philippe Bergardi of Worms
> *Index Sanitatis* [1539]

Abbot Trithemius [Triethim] of Wurtzburg
> *Letter to Johann Virdung, August* 1507

Johannes Wierus
> *De Praestigiis Demonum* [1568]

Froissart
> *Chroniques* [edition by Kervuin de Lettemhove)

C. Kiesewetter
>   *Faust in der Geschichte und Tradition*

Prof. Zenaide A. Ragozin
>   *Chaldea: Story of the Nations*

Sir Walter Scott
>   *Ballad of Lord Soulis of Hermitage* [in *Minstrelsy*
>   *of the Scottish Border*]

John Leyden
>   *Lord Soulis*

ASTROLOGY

>   Introductory and General Modern:

Temple Hungad
>   *A brief History of Astrology*

Alice A. Bailey
>   *Esoteric Astrology*

Manly P. Hall
>   *Astrological Keywords*

Francis Rolt-Wheeler
>   *Summa Astrologicae* [and other works *passim*]

Dane Rudhyar
>   *The Astrology of Personality*
>   *New Mansions for New Men*

Also to be consulted: books by Alan Leo, Sepharial and C. E. O.
Carter [editor of *Astrology*]

>   The Egyptian Calendar:

Sir E. Wallis Budge
>   *The Rosetta Stone*

W. Marsham Adams
>   *The Book of the Master*

>   Hermetic Doctrines:

The teachings of Thoth-Hermes recorded in
>   the *Pymander* and in
>   *Concerning Thrice-Greatest Hermes*

The Asclepios

Patricius
> *Nova de Universis Philosophia*

The Hundred Aphorisms of Thoth-Hermes

G. R. S. Mead
> *Thrice Greatest Hermes*

Source Books:

Claudius Ptolemy 'de Péluse'
> *Tetrabiblion, Tetrabibloi* or *Tetrabiblos*
> *Centiloquium* [concerning chances of fortune]
> *Apotelesmatique* or *Apotelesmatic Doctrine*
> [revised by Junctinus or Junctin de Florence]

F. Junctin [de Florence] or Junctinus, i.e. Francesco Giuntini, D.D.
> *Speculum Astrologiae*
> *On the Judgment of Nativities*
> *On Divination*
> *Ephimerides* 1583-1606
> *Commentaries* [upon Ptolemy *Apotelesmatique*]

Julius Firmicus Maternus
> *Traicté des Mathematiques Celestes* or *Occult*
> *Mathematics*

J. Baptiste Morin de Villefranche
> *Astrolgica Gallica*

Auger Ferrier
> *Iugements Astrologiques sur les Nativités*

ORIENTAL AND TIBETAN MAGIC

Theos Bernard
> *Land of a Thousand Buddhas*
> *Heaven Lies Within Us*

Ekai Kawaguchi
> *Three Years in Tibet*

W. Y. Evans-Wentz
> *Tibetan Yoga and Secret Doctrines*

W. Y. Evans-Wentz and the Lama Kazi Dawa-Samdup
>   *Tibetan Book of the Dead, or After-Death Experiences*
>   *on the Bardo Plane*
>   *Milarepa, the Jetsum Kahbum*

The Lama Kazi Dawa-Samdup
>   *Shrichaterasambhara Tantra*

The Egyptian Book of the Dead [for general comparison]

Amaury de Riencourt
>   *Lost World: Tibet, Key to Asia*

Alexandra David-Neel
>   *With Mystics and Magicians in Tibet*

WESTERN REACTIONS TO THE DOCTRINE OF RE-BIRTH

T. H. Huxley
>   *Evolution and Ethics*

Dr. E. B. Taylor
>   *Primitive Culture*

VOODOO AND VAMPIRES

W. B. Seabrook
>   *The Magic Island*

M. D. Cassecanarie
>   *Obeah Simplified, The True Wanga*

Montague Summers
>   *The Vampire*

Bram Stoker
>   *Dracula*

PSYCHIC RESEARCH

W. H. Myers
>   *Human Personality and its Survival after Death*

J. W. Dunne
>   *Nothing Dies*

A. Conan Doyle
>*The New Revelation*
>*The Vital Message*

Rev. C. Drayton Thomas
>*Life Beyond Death with Evidence*
>*Precognition and Human Survival*

Arthur Findlay
>*On the Edge of the Etheric*

Palmstierna
>*Horizons of Immortality*
>*Widening Horizons*

Rev. Stainton Moses
>*Spirit Teachings*

Harry Boddington
>*The University of Spiritualism*

CPSIA information can be obtained
at www.ICGtesting.com
Printed in the USA
BVHW012305280522
638401BV00004B/38